Fountain-Source
of Occultism

Fundamentals of the Esoteric Philosophy
The Esoteric Tradition
Occult Glossary
Man in Evolution
Questions We All Ask
Golden Precepts
Messages to Conventions
Wind of the Spirit
Studies in Occult Philosophy
The Dialogues of G. de P.

Fountain-Source of Occultism

A modern presentation of the ancient universal wisdom based on THE SECRET DOCTRINE *by* H. P. Blavatsky

G. de PURUCKER

Edited by
GRACE F. KNOCHE

THEOSOPHICAL UNIVERSITY PRESS
PASADENA, CALIFORNIA

THEOSOPHICAL UNIVERSITY PRESS
PASADENA, CALIFORNIA
1974

Manufactured in the United States of America

Foreword

A WORK OF ART stands or falls by its power to inspire. With a book such as FOUNTAIN-SOURCE OF OCCULTISM, which treats of cosmic truths and man's timeless search for answers, all the more must its message stand or fall on worth alone. Of this G. de Purucker is pre-eminently aware; he does not profess to provide the definitive statement, the final word of truth. What he does offer is an illumined interpretation of the universal wisdom on which the Secret Doctrine of the ages — and of H. P. Blavatsky's masterpiece of that name — is founded.

Born on January 15, 1874 in Suffern, Rockland County, New York, de Purucker lived in the United States until the late '80's when the family moved to Geneva, Switzerland. His father, an Episcopal minister, had been appointed chaplain of the American Church there; a learned man and utterly committed, his inmost wish was to have his son ordained in the Anglican Communion. So he personally taught the boy Latin, Greek and Hebrew, had him tutored in modern European languages, as well as in the history and literature of Biblical peoples and of ancient Greece and Rome.

The youth applied himself with assiduity, but his was a profoundly inquiring mind, with a natural intuitive sense of what was spiritually true and what was counterfeit. Before he reached eighteen, he knew with certainty that he could not enter the church; that, in fact, no formal religion could ever bind him. The quest for the gnosis, the living wisdom behind the externals of rite and dogma, had taken powerful hold.

The shock to the parents was grievous: here was their son, destined from childhood for the ministry, able to read the Holy Scriptures in their original tongues, and trained in the functions and responsibilities of a pastor — turned agnostic.

Deeply troubled, the young man left his home and studies in Geneva, sailed for America and, after spending a few months in New York, came to California where he worked on various ranches in San Diego County. All the while he continued his search, "looking around me, right and left, trying to find the clue to the mysteries of life and death which were

v

bothering me so badly." He bought books on the Tarot as well as on mind-healing, to find they did not satisfy. When he came across a translation of one of the Upanishads, he set to work to master Sanskrit, just as he had earlier perfected himself in Anglo-Saxon, believing with Heine, the poet, that "with every new language, one wins a new soul."

Then one day, he tells us, a small book on Theosophy fell into his hands, and "it startled me":

I saw high thinking! I felt that there was more in this book than what an agnostic had seen. My years of study and reading of the literatures of the world — ancient literatures especially — had taught me to recognize ancient truth when I saw it. I was fascinated with something that I had always known in my heart; and it was this, that there has always existed, and that there exists today, a band, a company, a society, an association, of noble Sages, great Seers, "Wise Men of the East," as this book called them.

We do not know the name of the book, but we do know that on August 16, 1893, Hobart Lorenz Gottfried de Purucker (later known as G. de P. to his associates) joined the Theosophical Society then headed in America by William Q. Judge, co-founder in 1875 with H.P.Blavatsky and H.S.Olcott of the modern theosophical movement. As a member of the San Diego Lodge and a regular user of their library, de Purucker helped organize a *Secret Doctrine* Class, and though only nineteen soon was appointed "permanent reader," moderating and guiding the studies of the members, most of whom were considerably older than he. For the next 49 years, to the day of his death on September 27, 1942, G. de P. gave of the fullness of himself in the service of his fellow men — a service which was to find magnificent expression in his elucidation of the spiritual principles of theosophy.

Everything he said, in private or in public print, was an amplification of his youthful vision of the Oneness of the divine impress, and of the experiencibility of that Oneness by every human being. FOUNTAIN-SOURCE OF OCCULTISM is no exception.

In July 1929, when Gottfried de Purucker succeeded Katherine Tingley to the leadership of the Theosophical Society with international headquarters then at Point Loma, California, he initiated a series of esoteric studies for the purpose of stimulating the seeds of altruism as well as of giving instruction in the deeper aspects of theosophy. No question was too simple, none too complex, for careful examination. He insisted, however, that always the 'scientific-philosophical' points of doctrine be infused with the 'ethical-mystical': only as one lived the teaching he learned about would it yield its esoteric content.

The present volume derives from twelve booklets of instruction privately printed in 1936. These had been compiled by a small committee under Dr. de Purucker's general supervision from the stenographic reports of esoteric meetings held by him from 1929 to 1933, to which he added certain relevant passages from his published works, as well as a copious amount of fresh material on a wide variety of subjects.

Of particular interest is the order of presentation, as he had himself arranged this with exceeding care. His primary concern, he explained, was to allow the student at the outset — before he might be caught up by the fascination of the highly philosophical teachings later developed — full opportunity to absorb the ideal of unselfish service, which marks the path of compassion chosen by mankind's spiritual Mentors. Moreover, when asked why he had started off the strictly doctrinal portion of the series with an abstruse treatise on Space and Māyā, instead of with the practical themes of karma and rebirth which are easily grasped, he countered that those ideas were already dealt with abundantly in the published literature of the Society. His whole endeavor was to raise the student's consciousness out of the narrow confines of the purely personal into cosmic reaches where even the knottiest of human problems could be seen in truer proportion.

Obviously, then, the book presupposes some knowledge of basic theosophical thought. But does this mean it has little to offer those to whom these ideas may be new? Quite the contrary, for here is food for reflection for all seekers, whatever their spiritual or religious leanings; and equally for those who have broken away from their credal moorings and are seeking a philosophy of meaning to which they can anchor. In brief, it addresses itself to all who recognize the interrelatedness of human destiny to the cosmic design; who intuitively sense that the pilgrimage of man spans a multiplicity of lives on earth so that the soul in the course of ages can bring forth its latent godhood. Above all, it speaks to those who in their most private moments feel the call of the inward way, to find the still, small path and take the ancient vow of self-dedication to the service of mankind.

There may be some, perhaps, who might wish that Dr. de Purucker had limited his use of foreign terms to the minimum, and presented the theosophical viewpoint simply, with a clear-cut exposition of theme. For in FOUNTAIN-SOURCE, in tracing the descent of spirit into matter and its reascent to its pristine source, we read of lokas and talas, of planes and dhātus, of monads and sheaths.

There is sound reason for the use of so rich a terminology, drawn from the religious and philosophic treasuries of Orient and Occident. The root ideas are identic, but each lightbringer transmits his vision of Reality through the lens of his own initiatory experience. Consequently, every spiritual seer gives what appears to be a unique presentation, when actually he is simply clothing in different outer form the same occult verity. It was not only to enrich the understanding of those attached to a particular faith, but likewise to aid students of comparative religion, philosophy and mythology that Dr. de Purucker exhaustively demonstrates that the many and various names in the ancient literatures for God and the gods and their manifold functions are but variant manners of describing the *one* evolutionary process.

But the book is more than an orderly treatment of doctrine; rather is it a quickener of the intuition. If the reader can follow the author's sometimes tenuous yet always unbreakable sequence of thought, he may discover, in a sudden flash of insight, what H.P.B. was actually saying in this or that "difficult" passage. What was formerly baffling even to the very astute, may become, often without his brain-mind being aware of it, luminous with practical wisdom.

However, just because the volume before us consistently delineates this and that teaching in *The Secret Doctrine* or *The Mahatma Letters*, let it not be thought that the author regards the writings of H.P.B. or her teachers as "a final test of infallible authority, the way the Christians have set up their Bible and then worshiped it" — to quote from a letter G. de P. wrote on June 14, 1932 to A. Trevor Barker. "If that were the case, we would never evolve. H.P.B.'s books would be sacrosanct. . . . We must stand for the principles of things. It is very important."

Time and again the author reminds us that the only authority, the only real initiator, for each individual is his own higher self. The paradox is that Dr. de Purucker does speak "as one with authority," the authority of profound spiritual experience. Because of this many, many doors are opened wide, although as many remain closed or only slightly ajar, awaiting the moment when the reader himself will give the knock that will open for him the doorway to the light of his own inner god. To place reliance solely on head learning, the eye doctrine, is to gain but little of permanent worth. It is the heart doctrine that should claim our allegiance, the heart wisdom that makes the impress on the soul.

Significantly, G. de Purucker, as early as 1935, publicly expressed the hope, if he could find "the time and strength so to do, to publish another volume or two containing Theosophical teaching" which up to then had been privately circulated. What had formerly been held as esoteric, he believed would even then be understood in greater measure, due to the "more awakened intelligence of modern men," as well as to the increased "receptivity to new ideas [which] has created an entirely different and indeed fallow field of consciousness" (*The Esoteric Tradition*, p. x). While he himself was unable to accomplish this, one of these projected works, *The Dialogues of G. de Purucker*, representing the meetings of the Katherine Tingley Memorial Group, was issued in 1948 by Arthur L. Conger. Now with the publication of FOUNTAIN-SOURCE OF OCCULTISM, both of these hoped-for volumes of hitherto esoteric material are available for students everywhere.

It is our deep regret that James A. Long, leader of the Theosophical Society from 1951 to 1971, did not live to see this work in finished form. But the guidelines he laid down in 1966 for the editing and preparation of the manuscript have been faithfully followed: to preserve the integrity of the teaching, both in atmosphere and content; to eliminate unnecessary repetitions; delete any purely organizational matters relating to the Theosophical Society or Esoteric Section; anglicize the spelling of those Sanskrit and other foreign terms now in current usage, such as karma, mahatma, etc.; and, where advisable, lift the presentation out of its private esoteric setting into a form suitable to public print. In brief, to condense and distill from the twelve booklets the marvelous treasury of wisdom contained therein so that the world may benefit.

As Mr. Long conceived Dr. de Purucker's intent:

All of this doctrinal esotericism is for one purpose, and one purpose only — not merely to satisfy the intellect of the reader, but to lay the groundwork for the development of the compassionate side of our nature in order that we may better serve our fellow men.

That is the basic value of the book: to see beyond the spacial and cosmic presentation to the wellspring of compassion flowing from the heart of cosmos, to the galaxy, the solar system, our globe earth, to man. It is all a manifestation of a compassion beyond our ken.

Mention must here be made of the tireless and painstaking efforts of every member of the editorial and printing staff: Kirby Van Mater, archivist; John P. Van Mater, who checked the manuscript prior to typesetting and prepared the Index; to Dorothy LeGros and Eloise Hart for the several typings required; to Madeline Clark, Manuel Oderberg, Ingrid Van Mater, Elsa-Brita Titchenell, Sarah B. Van Mater, and Lawrence Merkel, for the arduous task of proofreading; and not least, to the editorial committee, A. Studley Hart, the late Willy Ph. Felthuis, and Ida Postma, all of whom worked with me long and diligently to make this book a reality.

On this Centenary of Gottfried de Purucker's birth, we gratefully acknowledge our spiritual indebtedness to one who kindled anew the fires of aspiration, believing that FOUNTAIN-SOURCE OF OCCULTISM has power to inspire every earnest seeker for ages to come.

GRACE F. KNOCHE

January 15, 1974
Pasadena, California

Contents

IV — *Galaxies and Solar Systems:*
    their Genesis, Structure, and Destiny

V — *Hierarchies and the Doctrine of Emanations*

VI — *Invisible Worlds and their Inhabitants*

CONTENTS

I

The Primeval Wisdom-Teaching

The Primeval Wisdom-Teaching

PASSING ON THE LIGHT

THERE IS BUT ONE occultism, one truth. The fountain of wisdom on this earth is the Brotherhood of adepts, the spiritual heart of the world, from which streams unceasingly a flow of inspiration and enlightenment. It is the one supreme source from which have derived all the facets of truth that the religious and philosophical systems of the world contain. From there come forth not only the great sages and teachers from time to time as the guides and instructors of men, but also envoys or messengers, whether known or unknown, who work in the world for the benefit of mankind.

This fountain-source of wisdom is formed of the noblest spiritual and intellectual giants that humanity has ever produced — men who have become at one with the god within. Knowing each other they band together and thus form the great school of light and truth, the great Brotherhood. Called by various names in different ages, the higher ones are known in Buddhist countries as Dhyāni-chohans; the ancient Persians referred to the members of this solar hierarchy as Amshaspends. Jewish mystics and Qabbalists spoke of them as Bnēi 'Elohīm, Sons of the Gods; and in other countries they were called Sons of Light, or Sons of the Sun as in ancient Egypt.

Innumerable schools of occultism, all derivative from the mother-school, have existed in the past, exist presently, and will exist in the future. The Mysteries of the Greeks were one such school, as were those of the Persians and the Egyptians; the Mysteries practiced in the ancient Americas, such as among the Peruvians and the Mayas, were schools in the same sacred tradition. Both the Lamaism of Tibet and the Vedānta of Hindustan are essentially schools of occultism, although they are also systems of exoteric philosophy. The Rosicrucians of the mediaeval ages were originally a mystic theosophic and quasi-esoteric body; and the Martinists of France, existing even today, form one of the 'occultistic' schools. Then there are the so-called alchemical bodies, whether in India, Asia Minor, or in Europe, whose adherents, while possessing a modicum of spiritual aspiration, nevertheless yearn even more for powers or phenomena.

There are, moreover, in the Orient a number of quasi-occult groups,

3

some larger, some smaller, which study in their own way the different remnants of mystical literature which past ages have brought into being in those countries. In Persia, Egypt, Syria and in parts of Turkey, similar bodies exist, often very exclusive, and usually nothing is heard of them.

All such associations, in every country and every age, do a certain good work in their way in proportion to the amount of the ancient wisdom that they teach. But such truth as they do impart is too often seen through the distorting mental prisms of those who have wandered from the fountain-source. Only as they pass on faithfully the splendor originally received from the mother-school can they rightly be called schools of occultism. It may be added that there are in the world at the present time, in every one of the great continental masses, a few — a very few — genuinely esoteric schools connected with the Brotherhood.

A few intuitive scholars have suspected the existence of esoteric teachings in the archaic Mystery schools, but these have never yet been found in a coherent body. In the different literatures of antiquity we find an allusion here, a reference there, but a reasoned and explicit series of such teachings exists only in places to which no uninitiated student has hitherto consciously penetrated.

In recording the deeper truths for later generations, the ancient sages and seers adopted the use of metaphor or figures of speech, often in fantastic and curious tales: legends, fairy stories, mythological romances. Plato, for instance, through the use of myth gave out many guarded hints regarding matters taught in the Mysteries; but because he himself knew what he was about and had received permission to do this, and did it under the cloak of metaphor, it was not a violation either of the letter or of the spirit of his oath.

It is actually by so using esoteric terms that the great teachers of past ages wrote letters to each other, and composed their books, passing them from hand to hand. Those who were initiated could understand what they read; to them it was intelligible and clear; but to the man who had not been received within the 'temple walls,' the teachings were merely speculative philosophy, or perhaps meaningless jargon.

These wisdom-teachings have come down in direct succession from sage to sage, ever since the Mysteries were first instituted among men in late Lemurian and Atlantean times — a step which became essential because mankind had lost the power of direct and conscious communion with their divine ancestors. Men were thus taught to raise the soul by an effort of the will combined with intense aspiration so that they might be brought into direct intercourse, spiritually and intellectually, with their own inner god — or with some other divinity. It was in this way that the noblest truths about man and the universe were originally perceived, and thereafter 'sung' — to use the word of the Veda — i.e. formulated into human speech.

Why is it that in practically all the ancient literatures spiritual teaching was given in the vernacular of the battlefield? The *Bhagavad-Gītā*, for instance, tells of the conflict between the opposing armies of the Kurus and the Pāndavas. In the Germanic and Scandinavian mythologies there is the constant battling between the gods and the heroes; so also in the Greek, Egyptian, Persian, and Babylonian mythologies — all are alike in this respect.

The question is easily answered: to little children we give storybooks; to those who cannot understand the meaning of peace and quiet and the enormous strength that lies in these, we talk of battle and of fighting, because there is always a victor and a vanquished. Thus in the literatures of the world secrets of mystic truths were written in the epic vein in order to meet the mental characteristics of those ages. But behind all this there were the esoteric schools° which taught truth and compassion more directly, such as did Lao-tse of China: "The way of Tao is not to strive." This is the contrary of quietism, for quietism is usually spiritual stupefaction, whereas the whole effort should be to imbody in one's life and in every fiber of one's being an active spirit of compassion for all mankind.

Just as the original esoteric bodies became the great religious and philosophical schools of the past, just so the present theosophical movement was intended to be the spiritual-intellectual nursery from which will be born the great philosophical and religious and scientific systems of future ages — indeed, the heart of the civilizations of the coming cycles.

°Every system of religio-philosophical thought has had its own term for this universal esoteric doctrine. In the Hindu scriptures of the pre-Buddhist era it is referred to as brahma-vidyā, ātma-vidyā, and gupta-vidyā, meaning, respectively, knowledge of the supreme, knowledge of self, and secret knowledge: also as rahasya, a word signifying mystery and bearing the same connotation as the mysterion of the Greeks, and the gnosis of Neoplatonism and the Gnostic schools. In Buddhism, it was and still is known under such terms as āryajñāna, noble or exalted knowledge, and bodhidharma, wisdom-law or path.

In every important age, theosophical movements in various parts of the globe have been founded. A few succeeded; most of them lived for a while, did some good, achieved a certain amount of the work that was to be done, and then failed, becoming a church, a sect, a dogmatic set of beliefs. Such periodic efforts to instill into men's hearts the ageless verities will continue throughout future time, until human beings shall have so evolved that they will welcome light when it comes, and will honor it as the most precious gift that they have.

Thus it was that in 1875 two men of buddha-like soul took upon their shoulders the challenge of making themselves karmically responsible in a sense for the sending out of a new message which, by the force of its innate vigor and the persuasive power of its truths, would induce men to think. From then on science began to have stirrings of new ideas; fresh impulses were injected into the thought-atmosphere of the world and, not least, the ideal of working toward an eventual universal brotherhood among all peoples took firm hold. The chief objective was to have these ancient spiritual principles work as a leaven in human thought, in the religious and philosophical strata and, ultimately, in the social structure itself. H.P.Blavatsky was inspired to write her masterworks, *Isis Unveiled* and *The Secret Doctrine* — not for the purpose of founding another religion, but to restate once again and in fuller measure the archaic wisdom-tradition of mankind in its more esoteric aspects. As such, she was one of the links in the serial line of teachers who come at certain stated periods for the passing on of esoteric light and truth. She came at the beginning of a new Messianic cycle and the ending of an old one, and thus was the messenger for the age to come.

This succession of teachers, the one following the other, has continued through countless centuries. There is nothing amazing about it; it is simply an illustration of one of nature's laws, that just as generation succeeds generation, and one genus in evolutionary time comes after some other genus, so is there a chain of wise men continuing the flow of truth down the ages. In Sanskrit writings this is called the guruparamparā, of which there are two kinds: first, those sages who rise one above the other, as it were, in progressively greater wisdom and spiritual dignity; and second, those who follow each other in time, and in one line of succession in the outer world of men.

The same pattern was known to the Greek poets and philosophers, Homer and Hesiod both speaking of the Golden Chain connecting Olympus

6

and earth, and later Greek mystical writers referred to it as the Hermetic Chain. This passing on of the torch of light from hand to hand has always been, and always will be — as long as the call comes from the hearts of men. When that call dies, the chain of succession remains intact, but the teachers no longer work openly.

The guardians of mankind — name them as you will, masters, mahatmas, adepts or elder brothers of the race — work wherever they see the slightest chance to do good, to cultivate the spiritual nature of their fellow human beings. Obviously, any society or group of people, or any individual, who tries to follow a noble pathway in life will receive their help, if worthy of it. Worthiness is the test, the sole test. Whenever the right call is made, it will be answered. But any call merely for self-benefit most emphatically is not the 'right call.' The only call they recognize is that given by those whose hearts yearn for light, and whose minds seek wisdom and whose souls are swayed by compassion. And further, the call must be made solely in order to lay such wisdom and light as may be received on the altar of service to humanity. There is not a single earnest heartbeat that remains unanswered, not a single soul-aspiration to help that is not faithfully registered.

Thus is the Brotherhood of adepts the guardian and custodian of the primeval wisdom, whose members are sworn to preserve it in secrecy and in silence until someone knocks at the portals with the right knock. They in turn receive light from others higher than they; and so on forever is this theosophia — the wisdom of the gods — transmitted to men along the Golden Chain of Mercury, the interpreter.

SPIRITUAL ILLUMINATION vs. PSYCHIC ILLUSIONS

SPIRITUAL AND ASTRAL forces are at work continuously, and have been so from the very earliest ages of the earth. But there come certain times in human history when the doors between our physical world and the inner realms are partly open so that men become more receptive to these subtle influences. We are leaving an era of materialistic life and thought and are entering a more spiritual one. At the same time, the world is full of evidences of an outbreak of psychical influences, and these are always deceptive, always dangerous, because the astral realms belong to a lower range of material existence, filled with evil emanations, human and other.

Such indeed is the present period, one wherein not so much the spiritual and astral energies are quickened as that we are at the junction of two great cycles, the ending of one and the beginning of another; and, concordantly with this transition of cyclic periods, the minds of men are rapidly changing, becoming more psychically sensitive. There is great danger in this, but there is also a larger chance more quickly to progress, if man's consciousness is turned towards higher things, for this accelerated movement of change is especially potent in so far as spiritual forces are concerned.

There is nothing unique about this; it has taken place in the past. An immense effort was made at the time of the downfall of the Atlantean race — an effort which culminated in the establishment of the Mystery schools which long ages afterwards found expression in the various mystical, religious and philosophical centers of the ancient world. When we examine the world's sacred literatures, we find the oldest of them containing the fullest measure of the archaic esoteric teachings. The reason for this is that from about the time of the submersion of the last island of the Atlantean continental system — recorded by Plato as having occurred some 9000 years before his day — there has been a steady increase of materiality in the world, and a consequent and equal recession of spiritual impulses. But this cycle, as indicated, has recently come to an end. The one we are entering is a very unusual one, in that it does not belong to the so-called Messianic era which is 2,160 years long, but covers a time span of some ten to twelve thousand years.

Great events are in the making, for the entire civilized world is approaching a critical point in its history. There is literally a battle proceeding between the forces of light and the forces of darkness, and it is a matter of very delicate balance as to which side of the dividing line between spiritual safety and spiritual retrogression the scales of destiny will fall.

In a letter written shortly before her death, H. P. Blavatsky warned:

Psychism, with all its allurements and all its dangers, is necessarily developing among you, and you must beware lest the Psychic outruns the Manasic and Spiritual development. Psychic capacities held perfectly under control, checked and directed by the Manasic principle, are valuable aids in development. But these capacities running riot, controlling instead of controlled, using instead of being used, lead the Student into the most dangerous delusions and the certainty of moral destruction. Watch therefore carefully this development, inevitable in your race and evolution-period, so that it may finally work for good and not for evil.°

Unfortunately, as is always the case in an age which has lost touch with spirituality, people today yearn for powers, for the development of suspected but scarcely accepted higher faculties; and in their blindness they search outside of themselves. Their hearts are hungry for answers to the enigmas of life, and so they take what they can from self-advertised teachers about how to gain and use psychical powers, and such 'teachings' are always baited with personal benefit. It is difficult to speak of these things without hurting many trusting souls who, not knowing the truth, follow what seem to them to be glimpses of a greater life than that which they have; and this accounts for the many so-called psychical and quasi-mystical movements† presently existing which, in many cases, are leading

---

°From a letter dated London, April 15, 1891 to the Fifth Annual Convention of the Theosophical Society, American Section, held at Boston, Mass., on April 26–27.

†With a three times 'very' few exceptions, all these bodies more or less hunger after the lower siddhis which H.P.B., using the Pali term iddhis, speaks of in *The Voice of the Silence* (p. 73). In India they are represented by the different schools of yoga practice.

Siddhi, from the Sanskrit verbal root *sidh*, to be fulfilled, to attain an object, means 'perfect attainment.' There are two classes of siddhis: those pertaining to the lower psychic and mental energies, and those pertaining to the intellectual, spiritual, and divine powers, both types of which are possessed by the spiritual initiate, who uses them only for the benefit of mankind and never for self. The personal name of Gautama the Buddha, Siddhārtha, means 'one who has achieved his objective.'

people away instead of toward the light emanating from their own inner god. We have to be ever watchful in these matters. The waves of the astral light are exceedingly unreliable, and thousands and thousands follow the will-o'-the-wisps of psychic light instead of the steady burning splendor of the divinity within.

The plain fact is that the West is being misled by psychical teachings which in themselves have nothing permanent in them. And those who follow these practices are, ninety-nine times out of a hundred, people of untrained spiritual and psychical fabric of character who are thus easily caught by the māyā of psychism. This does not mean that such faculties and powers are evil or are not natural parts of the human constitution; nor that they are useless. The meaning is that they are very hazardous to one without spiritual vision and the power of intellect and spiritual will to guide and control the psychical nature in which these faculties inhere.

Dangerous also are the hatha-yoga practices of a psycho-astral type, usually connected with physical posturing, etc., to which certain individuals are addicted in their attempt to gain for themselves powers of a lower kind. These practices not only can affect the mind and even dislodge it from its normal seat, thus producing insanity, but also can interfere with the proper prānic circulations of the body. Religious fanatics often go insane; and in certain sensitive instances become the so-called ecstatics, believed by the ignorant to be exemplars of a holy life merely because their skin may bleed, and their hands or feet show wounds supposed to represent the nails of the Cross. The same may be said of the fakirs and lower type of yogis of the Orient. Results can be produced which endanger both the mind and the health, as well as the life itself. In all these practices there is not a breath of spirituality.

He who enters the path with the hope of gaining powers of any kind, regarding them as something of paramount importance, is destined to failure. Indeed, he is embarking upon a very hazardous and questionable road, which at worst could lead to sorcery and black magic, and at best will bring to him only the Dead Sea fruit of disappointment. Powers as such, whether spiritual, intellectual, or psychic, will develop in due course and in a perfectly natural way as we progress, provided that we have the unflinching determination to achieve, and, above all, that our heart is forever brightened and filled with compassionate love, a love that is even now a distinguishing characteristic of the spiritual soul within.

There is immense hope and spiritual beauty in the teachings of the esoteric tradition. In them is the path along which we may evolve, but it depends upon the individual whether or not he ascends along the ray which is living and working within him. While it is true that fully to understand the deeper reaches of the philosophy requires high intellectual power and a spiritual vision, it is often very simple natures who see a great light. Light passes everywhere. We have but to open the closed doors of our personality and the light of itself will come in, and we shall then understand instinctively the most recondite secrets of nature.

Jesus the avatāra, so ill understood in the Occident, taught the same truths. Seek first the treasures of the spirit, of the kingdom of heaven, and all other things will be added — all the psychical powers and energies and faculties will fall into place naturally and safely, enlightened and guided by the spiritual sun within.

Now what are these treasures of the spirit? None other than those spiritual and intellectual faculties and energies which make us godlike in thought and deed: will power, vision, intuition, instant sympathy with all that lives. There is no reason why we human beings should not begin to use our heritage. All powers and qualities and attributes are in us, even now, but they are latent for the most part, because we have not yet learned to bring them forth. In reality, it is we ourselves in our ordinary lower mind and feelings who are 'sleeping,' whereas our higher nature is not dormant at all, but intensely active.

For instance, when the spiritual will is evoked and active in a man, he becomes supreme over himself so that he has absolute self-command, and not even the denizens of the astral world can in any wise control him. Will in action is a current of energy, which means a current of substance, precisely as electricity is both force and matter. Back of will lies desire. If the desire be pure, the will is pure. If the desire be evil, the will is evil. Back of desire lies consciousness. Therefore will originates in consciousness through desire. We desire, and instantly will awakens intelligence which directs this will, and we act — or refrain from acting, which sometimes is nobler still.

There is divine desire° which in men is called aspiration, and also

---

°The saying in the old Veda: "Desire (kāma) first arose in It" and then the world sprang into being means that Brahman, sleeping in its aeon-long pralaya, first felt stirring within, the seeds of divine desire to become. Consciousness was behind the desire; desire arose in it and brought will into being, and will acted on the sleeping atoms and produced the worlds.

its material reflection. How many of us allow our will to be directed by the egoistic and selfish impulses of the lower aspect of our desire-nature, the kāma principle! Consequently, as the human will is rooted in buddhi-manas, it is the intuition and the higher mānasic principle which should guide our human will to the nobler acts which it is in our province to do: deeds of brotherhood and of impersonal service; and this is the very nature and characteristic of the spiritual ego, the buddhi-mānasic principle in man.

Intuition expresses itself as instant vision, instant knowledge. But there is a great difference between wisdom and knowledge. Wisdom may be called the knowledge of the higher ego, the spiritual soul, and knowledge the wisdom of the personality. In each case it is a storing up in the treasury of experience of what has been learned and unlearned — a treasury that is not a chamber, small or vast, but ourself. Each experience is a modification of the understanding self; and the repository of memory is filled with the record of the ages, precisely as the personality is stamped and impressed with the karmic record of all the personalities preceding it which made it.

Wisdom, knowledge, inner power, all are faculties of the spirit, signifying the fruits of evolutionary unfolding of the inherent power of the spirit-soul. Intuition per se is spiritual wisdom and garnered knowledge, gathered in the treasure house of the spirit-soul in past lives. Instinct, on the other hand, may be called the passive side of intuition, which is the energic, the will-side, the alert and active aspect. Instinct expresses itself all through natural being: the atoms move and sing by instinct, even as man using his consciousness and will, may do likewise; but the song and movement of intuition are incomparably loftier than the song and movement of instinct. Both are functions of the consciousness, the one vegetative, automatic; the other, energic, awake.

The spirit is all-permeant, living and moving everywhere for it is universal. Spiritual clairvoyance, of which the psychical clairvoyance is but a dancing shadow, enables one to see behind all veils of illusion, to see what is transpiring on some distant star in the fields of space. It is the power to perceive the truth of things at a glance, and to know the hearts of men and understand their minds. It is the faculty of visioning with the inner eye, not so much a seeing of forms as a getting of knowledge, and because this acquiring of knowledge comes in a way that closely parallels the way of seeing with the physical eye, it is called direct vision.[1]

So it is with spiritual clairaudience, which is not the power of hearing with the physical ear (or of seeing, for sometimes sounds are seen and colors heard, there being an interrelation between sense and sense), but of listening with the ear of the spirit. The sounds that are heard with the ear of the spirit are heard in the silence and with the repose of all the senses. Such spiritual clairaudience will enable one to hear the movements of the atoms as they sing their individual hymns; to hear the growing of the grass, the unfolding of the rose — to hear it all as a symphony.

Socrates used to say to those around him that his daimon, his inner monitor, never told him what to do, but always what not to do.° This daimon was the 'voice' of the higher ego, which in great men is often very strong in its energy; and in some hypersensitive constitutions may be heard as a 'voice.' It is not really a voice (although that is its effect at times on the physical brain), but rather is an urge from within, manifesting also, perhaps, as flashes of light and inner vision.

We cannot understand ourselves and others unless we have evolved the understanding heart. The key is sympathy, and the method is to look to the divine being within. As we aspire to become more like it in every moment of our lives, light will come and we shall know truth when we find it. We shall become compassionate and strong — qualities that are the true insignia of the self-illumined man. The first lesson, then, is to seek the light of our own inner god, and trust it alone. When we follow this light and are warmed by its sublime and life-giving rays, then we shall see the same god-light in others.

By going to the fountainhead we find the clearest water, so why drink from the muddy waters hundreds of miles from the spring? If a man would know himself and the wondrous powers and faculties that are his, let him see himself in the universe around him, and study that universe as being himself. An epigram, possibly, but a true master key to wisdom, and containing the essence not only of all initiation, but of all future growth.

°There is an interesting reason why these intimations rarely are of a positive type, being almost invariably urgings to pause, to reflect, or to *not* do thus and so. When a man is in a state of indecision, his mind makes pictures which are transmitted by sympathetic vibration into the inner consciousness; and because the inner consciousness has this contact with the brain-mind, if the pictured action be wrong, the answer comes back, No.

THE STILL, SMALL PATH

ALL ESOTERIC SCHOOLS have taught as the very foundation of their being: "Man, know thyself!" It has ever been thus, and the key to this lies in many things. It lies in the study of the suffering that the knot of personality experiences before its intricate labyrinth of selfishness is overpassed; it lies also, on a more exoteric plane, in the perusal of the majestic literatures of past ages: the brain work, the heart work, the work of the soul, of the seers and sages of every era. Greatest of all, it lies in the study of love for others and utter forgetfulness of self. Therein rests the mystery of Buddhahood, of Christhood: forgetfulness of self, absorption in love all-encompassing, unbounded, frontierless, of all that is.

Some people imagine that the path of spiritual attainment is far away over the mountains of the future, almost unreachable, when in reality there is a relatively narrow frontier between ordinary life and that followed by the neophyte or chela. Essentially the difference is one of outlook, and not of metaphysical distance. It is the same difference that exists between the one who falls under the sway of temptation and thereafter becomes its bondslave, and the other who successfully resists the temptation and thereafter becomes its master.

Anyone can enter upon the path, if his will, his devotion and yearnings are directed toward being of greater service to others. The only thing that prevents him from taking that most beautiful step is his convictions, his psychological and mental prejudices which distort his perspective. We are all learners, all of us have illusions. Even the mahatmas and adepts have illusions, albeit of an extremely subtle and lofty character, which prevent them from going still higher — and this is one of the reasons they are so compassionate towards those who are seeking to tread the very path along which they have successfully advanced in former days.

The quickest way to overcome these illusions is to cut the root of them, and that root is selfishness in its multimyriad forms. Even the yearning for advancement when it is for self alone is based on selfishness which in turn produces its own subtle and powerful māyās. Therefore every ambition to succeed, unless it be washed clean of all personality, will inevitably defeat itself, for the way of inner growth is self-forgetfulness, a giving up of personal ambitions and longings of any and every kind, and a becoming an impersonal servitor of all that lives.

It should be stated, however, that the purpose of genuine occultism is not to 'produce disciples' or to turn refractory human material into individuals striving for mere self-advancement. Rather is it to regenerate our imperfect human nature into becoming at first nobly human, and finally godlike — and this along the archaic and traditional lines of teaching and discipline which have been recognized and followed for ages past.

Chelaship is a vision, out of which arise conviction and definite action. All the rules of moral conduct that one may read about in the great literatures of the ancient philosophies as well as in theosophical writings, are simply powerful aids to help the aspirant cleanse himself of selfishness. The real code of ethics is an unwritten one, and therefore not subject to dogmatisms, not easily enslaved to conventional notions or misconstruction by minds debating and quarreling about mere words. In essence it is of the extremest simplicity, for the most beautiful and the most comprehensive truths are always the simplest. There are times when I throw my pen aside and say to myself: let us have just the simple truths that the little ones with their unspoiled natures and their direct and quick perception can grasp. It is difficult permanently to deceive a child. But when it is said that the neophyte must regain the child state, this does not mean childishness or stupidity! It is the child's heart that we need — trusting, intuitive, and alert.

Intellectual training is very valuable and a great help, but to become as a 'little one' is the most difficult lesson for human beings to learn. The brain-mind is a good instrument when guided and trained, but is a tyrant when left to its own devices and impulses, for it is always selfish; its vision is necessarily limited to the swirl of the lower and restricted field of consciousness of the mānasic knot of personality. In the higher nature lies the higher understanding, and it alone can arrive at the inner meaning of the teachings. The lower mind can achieve some success in the brain-mind comprehension of them, but only when helped from the inner understanding. An individual may be quite sincere, quite willing to know, quite ready to experiment and to investigate, but the buddhic splendor may be completely absent. The only test of fitness is that which is given by the individual himself. If the light of buddhi be shining even

15

by so much as a fugitive glimmer, that is enough. There is then in that individual the esoteric right to know.

Self-conquest is the path of growth. The whole truth is contained in these few simple words. It is a slow growth as with all great things; and if it is to be attained, it must be an unfolding of the man himself. There is no other path than that of inner development, no easy way: the one who cannot control himself in the affairs of daily life and does not know who or what he is, cannot control the events and experiences that inevitably arise around anyone who succeeds, even in small degree, in approaching that "straitest of all gates."

Here is a strange paradox: if one would be master of himself he must be utterly *selfless,* and yet he must be *himself* utterly. The lower self must be wiped out — not killed, but wiped out, which means withdrawn inwards and absorbed by the higher self. For the higher self is our essential or real being, and the lower is but a ray therefrom — soiled, rendered unclean, so to say, because it becomes attached to this world of multimyriad illusions.

The man most easily deceived is the man most infolded in māyā; and such are often the so-called worldly-wise. You cannot deceive an adept, as he would instantly see the attempt at deception; and the reason is that you cannot, as it were, throw hooks of personal attachment into his being. Nothing one can do or say will affect him or attract him to your thought if it is in the slightest degree selfish, nonuniversal. He is above those illusions, has fought through them, found them out and rejected them. Yet the masters feel, even before we ourselves would realize it, the slightest moving of the true chela spirit. The call upon them is tremendous, and a quick magnetic sympathy is thereupon established.

Taking the thought a step further: when a neophyte makes a deliberate and actual choice with all the strength of his being, he kindles a light within, and this is the buddhic splendor; and, as said, it is sensed understandingly and watched and cared for by the teachers, and thus he is an 'accepted chela.' How long will he remain such? None is picked out by perambulating magicians wandering the world, selecting whom they may think to be proper material — not at all. The choice is in the individual: he chooses his path; he makes his resolve; and if the buddhic light is seen, be it only a spark, he is accepted, although that fact may be unknown to himself for the time being. Thereafter all depends upon him, whether he succeed or fall by the wayside.

It is a matter of the rarest occurrence for one immediately to know that he has been accepted, for the usual rule is that he is tested in a hundred thousand different ways, these tests arising out of the ordinary events of life and the aspirant's reactions to them. Once, however, that he becomes cognizant of his teacher, the path becomes both easier and more difficult — easier because there is the new conviction that at least a certain success has been attained, and also because of the courage and self-confidence that arise out of this fact; vastly more difficult because from now on he is under more direct training and guidance, and small lapses and little backslidings, for which large indulgence is allowed in the beginning, have henceforth very serious consequences.

Moreover, no teacher makes himself known to his disciple without the latter's having previously received many instructive premonitions from his own inner being. The reason is clear: no one ever becomes accepted, until he has actually been accepted by his own inner divinity, i.e. until he has become more or less aware of the stirring within him of a wondrous mystery.

A certain stage of progress is of course necessary before such a choice can be made; but every normal being can make such a choice, because in him spirit and matter have attained a more or less stable equilibrium. In other words, chelaship may be undertaken at any stage by anyone who can arouse the Christ-light in his mind and heart. His resignation of the lower selfhood on the altar is what counts; and no human cry for help ever passes unheard, if that cry for more light be impersonal. *The test is impersonality.*

Let us not imagine, however, that, because the words renunciation and sacrifice are often used, these imply the loss of anything of value. On the contrary, instead of a loss, it is an indescribable gain. To give up the things that belittle, that make one small, petty, and mean, is to cast away our fetters and take on freedom, the richness of the inner life and, above everything else, self-conscious recognition of one's essential unity with the All.

It should be clearly understood that this training, which is one of study and of discipline arising in the spiritual and intellectual movements of the student's own soul, has never included and never will include any interference with or encroachments upon his family rights or duties. Chelaship is nothing weird, nothing queer or erratic. If it were, it would not be chelaship. It is the most natural path for us to strive to follow, for by allying ourselves with the noblest within we are allying ourselves with the spiritual forces which control and govern the universe. There is inspiration in the thought.

The neophyte's life is a very beautiful one, and grows steadily more and more so as self-forgetfulness comes into the life in ever-larger degree. It is also a very sad one at times, and the sadness arises out of his inability to forget himself. He realizes that he is very, very lonely; that his heart is yearning for companionship. In other words, the human part of him longs to lean. But it is just the absence of these weaknesses that makes the master of life: the ability to stand alone, erect and strong in all circumstances. But never think that the mahatmas are dried-up specimens of humanity, without human feelings or human sympathy. The contrary is the case. There is a far quicker life in them than in us, a far stronger and more pulsing vital flow; their sympathies are enlarged so greatly that we could not even understand them, although some day we shall. Their love encompasses all; they are impersonal and therefore are they becoming universal.

Chelaship means trying to bring out the master living in our own being, for he is there now.

There will come a time, however, if one progress far enough, when even the family duty will have to be dropped, but the circumstances then will be such that the dropping will actually be a benediction to the individual as well as to the one towards whom the duty formerly lay. Yet let no one be deceived by the dangerous doctrine that the higher a man goes, the less is he bound by the moral law. The direct converse of this is the truth; the doing of wrong to another is never right.

At no step along this sublime path is there ever exterior compulsion of any kind; only such lofty compulsion as springs forth from the aspirant's own yearning soul to advance ever farther and farther inwards and upwards forever. Each step is marked, during its earlier course, by dropping something of the personal shackles and imperfections which keep us enchained in these realms of matter. We are told with reiterated insistence that the grandest rule of life is to foster within one's own being undying compassion for all that is, thus bringing about the winning of selflessness, which in its turn enables the peregrinating monad ultimately to become the Self of the cosmic spirit without loss to the monad of its individuality.

In the above lies the secret of progress: to *be* greater one must *become* greater, to become greater one must abandon the less; to encompass a solar system in one's understanding and life one must give up, which means outgrow and surpass, the limits of the personality, of the mere human. By abandoning the lower selfhoods we pass into the larger selfhoods of selflessness. No one will progress a single step to the more expanded selfhood which already is his own higher nature, until he learns that 'living for self' means descending into still more compacted and restricted spheres, and that 'living for all that is' means an expansion of his own soul into becoming the larger life. All the mysteries of the universe lie latent within us, all its secrets are there, and all progress in esoteric knowledge and wisdom is but an unfolding of what is already within.

How little our human troubles which plague us so greatly — such a burden of sorrow — seem when we allow our minds to dwell upon these infinitely comforting realities. No wonder the Christian writer declared that not even a sparrow falleth from heaven without its being known to the divine; not even a hair of our heads but is counted and cared for. How much more so then we ourselves. Even this world of phantasmagoria and shadows is an intrinsic and inseparable part of the Boundless from which we sprang, and towards the divine heart of which we shall one day return on the wings of the experiences that we have been through, wings that will carry us over the valleys to the distant mountain peaks of the spirit.

PLEDGE-FEVER AND THE SPIRITUAL WILL

IT SOMETIMES HAPPENS that very sensitive natures when first coming in touch with the chela-path are shaken to the very core, and there is often real suffering of heart and of mind. This is all very natural. It is really the voice of the soul within that has caught a glimpse of the spiritual light, but because the brain can neither contain nor understand it, the resultant manifestation is an agony of soul. But there comes at times also, as twin sister of this interior suffering and pain, an agony of joy, an exultation so keen, that it may be even more difficult to bear.

Most of the cases where the aspirant finds himself involved in emotional or mental trials and stresses are typical of what H. P. Blavatsky has called pledge-fever. Unfortunately, few understand exactly what this is, even though many people experience it, unconsciously or only half-consciously. It can best be described as a fevered state of mind and feeling, often acting adversely on the body, and this arises out of a stirring up of the inner part of one's being, usually of the kāma-mānasic portion of the constitution.

Pledge-fever can have a noble side as well as an ignoble one. As pointed out by H.P.B.,° as soon as anyone pledges himself to give his life in service to others, "certain occult effects ensue. Of these the first is the *throwing outward* of everything latent in the nature of the man: his faults, habits, qualities, or subdued desires, whether good, bad, or indifferent. . . . You all know your earthly pedigree, but who of you has ever traced all the links of heredity, astral, psychic, and spiritual, which go to make you what you are?"

Commenting upon H.P.B.'s statement and the effect that pledge-fever has upon the earnest student, William Q. Judge wrote:†

. . . it is a sort of heat in the whole nature which, acting like the air in a hothouse, makes all seeds, whether of good or evil sort, suddenly sprout and show themselves to the person . . .

The field in which it works is that offered by the entire being, and therefore

---

°E.S. *Instructions,* I.   †"Suggestions and Aids."

will include the hidden, unknown part of us which in all ordinary cases lies back awaiting other incarnations and circumstances to arise in new centuries and civilizations.

And in a further Circular issued in 1890, he added these remarks:

Nor must it be forgotten that the taking of the pledge° brings into the field forces that help as well as forces that oppose. The appeal to the Higher Self, honestly and earnestly made, opens up a channel by which flow in all gracious influences from higher planes. New strength rewards each new effort; new courage comes with each new step forward. . . .

So take courage, disciple, and hold on your way through the discouragements and the successes that beset your earliest steps on the path of probation. Do not stop to mourn over your faults; recognize them and seek to learn from each its lesson. Do not become vain of your success. So shall you gradually attain self-knowledge, and self-knowledge shall develop self-mastery.

There are many kinds of pledge-fever, but most of them are rooted in the same cause. For instance, an excessive and unwise enthusiasm without proper mental and emotional balance is a distinct kind of psycho-mental fever. Outbursts of energy, followed by severe reaction; states of mind in which the student desires to abandon everything except the one objective, to cast aside as worth nothing at all even those things which he should value as a man; the unfounded conviction that everyone else other than oneself is to blame when difficulties arise — all these are conditions of pledge-fever, a fever arising out of an over-enthusiasm with which the heart is filled and a lively sense of the responsibility that one has sincerely undertaken.

Pledge-fever is a sign of honesty; it is also a sign that the heart has been deeply touched, and the mind profoundly impressed. It means actually that the disciple is beginning to view the circumstances of his life, whatever they may be, from a radically different aspect; and further, that he is striving to burst the old bonds of selfhood. Thus it is a good sign in one way, because it shows that the nature is being stirred, that the

---

°Any vow, any pledge, it should be remembered, is taken to one's higher self, the spiritual master within, and admonitions from this source take precedence over everything. However, let us also remember that very, very few of us can claim to be in hourly communication with the god within, much less under its sublime inspiration for lengthy intervals of time.

aspirant is progressing; and anything is better than coldhearted, dead indifference, which is a spiritual and intellectual sleep.

The blank, hopeless chill and 'dead' feeling that sometimes is experienced is simply a reaction, a part of the pledge-fever cycle; precisely as a fever in the body leaves the patient for the time feeble, exhausted and cold. But pledge-fever is dangerous too, even as are the fevers which arise from nature's effort to throw out poisons from the body in order to cleanse and purify it. Far better is it if the student is able to bring back by aspiration and inflexible will the true poise and the calm confidence of invincible strength that are imperatively required. One thinks of Horace's words in one of his *Odes* (Bk. Third, III): *Justum et tenacem propositi virum* . . . , "an upright man, tenacious of his purpose" — one whose steady mind is shaken neither by the threats of tyrants, nor the thunderbolts of Jove, the clamor of mobs, nor the movements of the great sea in storm. None of these can shake him of steady and upright mind.

In dealing with these situations, one must find the division line of safety and hold to it between cultivating unwholesome emotionalisms on the one hand, and, on the other hand, turning the cold shoulder and being unsympathetic to those undergoing the fevered trials of aspiring souls who are seeking light but who, nevertheless, are still involved in the blinding veils of emotions and therefore may at any moment be in real danger of wandering from the path.

Once our feet are set upon the path, we can never go back. That is impossible; the doors have shut behind us. We can fail and either fall asleep or die, but thereafter forward we must go. When inner disturbance comes, and the fevered condition is intense, the student should use his spiritual will and draw upon the divine wisdom in the higher parts of his being. For will is an energy, and functions, as do all energies, both actively and passively. The active will is the will consciously set in motion by the directing intelligence and the innate life. The passive will is the vegetative will, those aspects which govern the automatisms of the body or mind.° Anyone can develop the spiritual will. As W. Q. Judge wrote:

°Sleep is due to the automatic action of the will, in degree at least. The circulation of the blood, the beating of the heart, and the winking of the eyelids, in fact, growth — these are ultimately derived from the automatic or vegetative part of the will, the passive side; and this acts not only in man, but in all lower things. Likewise it is the will which has been taught, through repetition after repetition, to work in grooves, properly, easily — usually unconsciously to the perceiving mind.

It is developed by true unselfishness, a sincere and full desire to be guided, ruled, and assisted by the Higher Self and to do that which, and suffer or enjoy whatever, the Higher Self has in store for one by way of discipline and experience; by sinking as much as possible, day by day, little by little, the mere personal self.°

In one sense the great teacher is life itself, and the learner is he who lives each day with its varied experiences, temptations, attractions, and ups and downs of mental activity and emotional feeling. The way of meeting these tests is by equanimity, a steadiness of both mind and soul that nothing can shake; also by magnanimity, unfaltering courage, and a positive refusal to be discouraged by failure.

Whenever there is any feeling of ungoverned vaulting enthusiasm, or again of blank despair, the student should simply wait and do his utmost to regain the calm consciousness that he is a spiritual being in his inmost. For all anyone may know, his past karma may have been so noble that, like a burst of sun from behind black clouds, he may suddenly one day be illuminated, and realize that his feet are on the path.

It is a curious paradox that the outer teacher works with entire harmony and in rigid accord with the intimations arising in the neophyte's own consciousness of the presence of the inner teacher — the greatest one of all so far as he himself is concerned. Sometimes these intimations are like flashes of dazzling light breaking into his consciousness, illuminating what seems to be the dark, gloomy night of his being; and at such moments he has a realization of being on the path that is almost painful in the intensity and reality that accompany it. But these flashes of inner recognition of one's steady advance should not and, indeed, can never be mistaken for the flickerings of the brain-mind which to the unwary or unprepared are often mistaken, because of an overweening confidence and personal egoism, for signs that he already has set his feet on the path. In truth, such would-be chela is very far from it, for he has not yet attained that development of his inner nature which can withstand the temptations of daily life.

One may think perhaps that because the operations of the universe move in the silences and make no immediate and visible impression that nature may be played with. She may not be played with. Whereas a large degree of toleration — and this is the precisely exact word — is allowed

---

° "Subsidiary Papers," September 1894.

23

in the beginning for human failings, the rules become stricter and more rigidly enforced the farther one goes, for the aspirant has taken a holy vow of obedience to his higher self. In the more progressed stages, there is the obedience of the willing heart and of the understanding mind, for the neophyte soon comes to feel that as he becomes like unto the gods, the more necessary is it to work in harmony with nature's laws, which means obedience not to one's own conceptions but *to things as they are.* And this is the meaning of the expression that the mahatmas never will nor do they dare interfere with karma. They are the servants of the law, the obedient instruments of the supreme spiritual teacher of our globe — the Silent Watcher of humanity — and the higher the mahatma is, the more willingly and joyfully obedient he is.

It is false pity as well as an esoteric crime for any so-called teacher to mislead aspiring students by promising them anything that is not the truth of the ages: *there is no short path, no easy way;* for inner growth, inner unfolding, inner evolution, is a matter of time and, above all, of self-effort. There are moments when the truth may seem to be cold and unacceptable, but this is the fault of the neophyte and not the fault of the teacher, and only proves that the student is not yet sufficiently awakened to recognize the true from the false, the right way from the left.

It should be obvious that no master living could make a chela out of unchela-like material, for that would be like saying it is possible to set something on fire with an element that is not fire. Even were it possible to transform, by some feat of magic, an average man into a successful chela, it would be a work of the worst kind of black magic, because it would in no wise help the man, but merely make of him a created mechanism without interior strength, without interior light, without interior ability to go farther on the path. There is no attainment unless the individual makes the progress himself. Hence it is that the mahatmas will not interfere in the slow unfolding of the inner faculties of the chela's constitution; if they did, it would be an interference with growth and would lead to a crippling and a weakening of the chela, which is exactly the opposite of what is needed.°

°Everything is karmic. Whatever happens is the resultant of the many karmic energies working to find expression in a life, the strongest of these coming into manifestation first, while the less strong are not turned aside but are dammed back, to await their turn. In certain very unusual circumstances it is possible for an adept or teacher with the full consent of his pupil to prevent the appearance of the strongest

The treading of the path leads to those higher spiritual and intellectual levels of consciousness whereon the masters live and have their being, but it is utterly impossible to approach them unless indeed one does just that, and breathes the rare spiritual and bracing intellectual atmosphere that they breathe. Those who would lead others should continuously remember this, for an injury is worked upon their souls if at any time they are misled by false hopes on the one hand, or, on the other hand, by the siren songs of personal ambition or the erroneous notion that the path can be followed by *leaning*. If anyone believes he can shoulder off responsibility for his thoughts and acts upon another, whether that other be a hypothetical god or demon, a human or an angel, from that moment he begins to follow the downward path. He gives up his own will to salvation, his will to achieve, his will to conquer.

How did the masters become the great and noble men they are? Through many ages by self-directed evolution. No one can succeed, can follow the path, unless his own strength is developed, unless his own inner powers and faculties are evolved, unless his own vision breaks through the veils of illusion which surround his consciousness. It is a long process, but a glorious one.

Some students have puzzled over a statement made by W. Q. Judge regarding an age limit of forty-four years beyond which "it is hard to enter through the gate"° of the inner world, and impossible for those who have only recently given thought to these matters. This is because around middle age the veils of selfhood so enshroud the inner being that the light from within cannot easily penetrate the brain-mind; and one beginning the study of esotericism at this stage finds it more difficult than if he had started thinking along these lines in youth, or better still in childhood. But exceptions to this are very numerous.

Actually there is no need for anyone to think that because he enters upon the path late in life, no progress is possible for him in the future.

---

karmic energy first, or so to smooth its action that other karmic energies or elements can appear almost simultaneously. These rare instances are always for the benefit either of the pupil or for some great and impersonal work for humanity, and can take place only in circumstances or conditions which are actually within what may be called a higher karma of the one so submitting himself to the destiny thus modified. But even here the karma so affected will find its expression just the same, and with its precisely normal condition of power and with precisely normal results.

°"Subsidiary Papers," October 1895.

Nothing can stay the imperious energy of the spiritual will, and the very fact that an individual in middle or even in advanced life is desirous of entering upon the pathway of splendor is in itself evidence that there are working through his being a will and a determination, an enthusiasm and an intuition, which themselves are proofs of the possibility, almost certainty, of the receiving of light. Coming events cast their shadows before, and so it is here, because the light is breaking through, is behind the future events, and heralds their coming.

Chelaship is exchanging the darkness of personality for the glorious sunlight of impersonality. It is a passing out of the mire of material existence, with its phantasms of thought and emotions, into the clear splendor of the inner spiritual sun, leading ultimately to a becoming-at-one with the soul of the universe. It is the age-old path that will lead the aspirant to become at one with his own spiritual essence, which means the attaining of an enormously increased range of consciousness and life. As our spiritual nature in a sense is universal, it is at once seen that chelaship is a continuous growth towards universality in thought and in feeling, a pressing forward along that wonderful path to the outermost veil of the inner confines of the universe.

Marvelous thought: we travel without advancing, we progress without any movement. We reach the heart of the universe by losing ourself in order to gain the cosmic Self seated in our inmost essence. The pathway that we travel is long and may be arduous, but it is also bright with joy, and lighted with the fires of the spirit. The 'travel' is really a changing of consciousness, a spiritual alchemy. The heart of the universe is at an infinite distance and yet is nearer than our own soul, for it is our Self.

II

Discipline precedes the Mysteries

Discipline precedes the Mysteries

ESOTERIC DISCIPLINE

COMING NOW DIRECTLY to the matter of actual discipline in esoteric training, every neophyte is taught at the outset that the first step is "to live to benefit mankind," and the second is to practice in his daily life the "six glorious virtues" or pāramitās. Until he has absolutely abandoned any desire for personal profit or gain, he is unfit even to attempt to tread the path. He must begin to live for the world; and when his soul is inflamed with this desire impersonally, he at least is ready to begin to try.

Perhaps the most important thing for the would-be aspirant to understand is that although the chela path is almost constantly represented as one of gloom, sorrow, and endless self-sacrifice, this is but a manner of phrasing the truth. Actually, it is the most joyous course of life and guide of conduct that it is possible for human beings to imagine. Still, I have often thought that the difficulties have been somewhat over-emphasized for a very good reason: to prevent personally ambitious individuals from rushing in where angels fear to tread. It is well that this is so, because the dangers of all kinds which beset the untrained and half-hearted postulant for occult progress are exceedingly real, and the chances of his making a mis-step, or of having his feet befouled in the mire of his own lower nature, are so certain that the warnings given are not only humane and dictated by the highest compassion, but are likewise nicely calculated to point out the need of discipline preceding any introduction to the Mysteries.

To restate the matter more succinctly, the path of chelaship is one of ineffable happiness for those who are fit to tread it. It means a constant living in the higher part of one's nature, where not only wisdom and knowledge abide, but where there is the continuous expanding of the heart in compassion and love to include the entire universe in its enfolding comprehension. Indeed, its beauties are so sublime that a veil is almost always deliberately drawn over these so that the unwary shall not be tempted to trespass into regions whose thin and life-giving aether their lungs cannot as yet in any wise breathe. Our West has forgotten for too long a time, despite the fine ethical teachings of its accepted religion,

29

that the life of the spirit while in the body is the only life worth while, and actually is a preparation for living self-consciously and without diminution of faculty or power beyond the portals of death.

Chelaship, therefore, is the learning to be 'at home' in realms other than the physical sphere; and it should be apparent that the untrained individual would be as helpless as a newborn babe were he to be faced with the extraordinarily changed conditions which would confront him at every turn if he were suddenly cast into these other worlds.

Esoteric training is the result of almost innumerable ages of the most careful study by the greatest sages and noblest intellects that the human race has produced. It is no arbitrary study of rules which the student is supposed to follow, although indeed he *is* both supposed and expected to follow certain rules; but it is likewise the making over — or conversion in the original sense of this Latin word — of the personal into the spiritual, and the casting aside of all limitations belonging to ordinary life, for the faculties and powers and the wider fields of action which belong to the initiate or adept in accordance with his degree of growth.

There is nothing so deceptive as the false lights of māyā. Often fine-looking flowers contain deadly poison, either in bud or in thorn; the honey thereof brings death to the soul. No chela is ever permitted to cultivate any psychical powers at any time, until the great foundation has been laid in the evocation of the spiritual and intellectual energies and faculties: vision, will power, utter self-control, and a heart filled with love for all. Such is the law. Therefore not only is it forbidden for the beginner to win and use powers now latent, and to awaken faculties not yet in function within him, but those who may through past karma happen to be born with such awakening inner faculties have to abandon their use when starting their training. And this for the reason that such training is all-round, i.e. every part of the nature must be brought into harmonious and symmetrical relation with every other part before one can tread the path safely.

There comes a time, however, when a pupil is taken individually in hand and instructed how to free the soul so that the body cripples it less, how to become nobler in every way, and this by certain rules of practice and of conduct and thought. First: philosophy, knowing something about the life in the universe; second, discipline; and third, the Mysteries. There is the order; to a certain extent they run concurrently, although each is emphasized in especial when its period arrives.

To elaborate: the first, philosophy, comprises teaching, with a certain amount of discipline, and an intuition, an intimation, given as to what the Mysteries are. Next, the discipline, with which likewise there are teachings, but, above everything, the neophyte is taught how to control himself, how to be and to do, with a larger intimation of the Mysteries to come. Then, third, the Mysteries, what is called practical occultism, when the individual is worked upon and taught how to release the spirit within him and also his faculties, the while experiencing a still loftier discipline and a loftier philosophy.

Seven are the degrees of initiation. The first three are schools of discipline and learning. The fourth is similar, but greater by far, for in it begins the nobler cycle of initiatory training. It depends upon the individual alone what progress he will make. The disciple is a free man, with free will, and it is his destiny to become a god taking a self-conscious part in the government of the universe. He must therefore choose his own pathway, but beware lest, in exercising the divine faculty of free will his egoism, his selfish propensities, if he have any left, run away with him into the left-hand path. Danger lurks at every step, a danger which is not outside, but in himself.°

Hence discipline is essential all along the line, differing from that which prevails in all stages of human relationships only in this, that it is the origin of those spiritual and ethical principles which have guided the civilizations of the past and the peoples who built them. The basis of this discipline is self-forgetfulness, which is the same as impersonality; and in order to achieve this, other minor rules have been introduced by

---

°It is often asked what guarantee can be proffered by an aspirant against the teachings being wrongfully and perhaps indiscriminately given out by him. There is no absolute guarantee. This is one reason the lines are always so tightly drawn, and why the knock given must be the right knock.

One of the protections against betrayal of the teachings of the higher degrees is the fact that the world would not understand them, and would think the man thus betraying the most sacred truth on earth is a lunatic. People always consider the things which they do not understand as foolishness — how many geniuses in the beginning of their careers have not been thought at least partly mad!

Another protection is that every individual belonging to one of the higher degrees knows perfectly well that a single betrayal means the cessation for him of all teaching for the future, and that every new degree explains the teachings given in the previous one. Consequently a betrayal in the third degree, for example, would mean betraying a 'veil' which itself has to be explained or gone behind in the fourth degree, and so forth through all further degrees.

the sages and seers who were the founders of the mystical schools of former eras.

The rules are simple in themselves, so simple that the novice, unversed in the occult code, is often disappointed at not finding something more difficult to achieve, forgetting that the grandest truths are always the simplest. One such rule is never to strike back, never to retaliate; better to suffer injustice in silence. Another is never to justify oneself, to have patience, and leave the karma to the higher law to adjust. And still another, and perhaps the greatest rule of this discipline, is to learn to forgive and to love. Then all else will come naturally, stealing into the consciousness silently, and one will know the rules intuitively, will be long suffering in patience, compassionate, and great of heart.

Can't we see the beauty of no retaliation, no attempt at self-justification, of forgiveness of injuries, of silence? One cannot take these rules too much to heart; but even so they should be followed impersonally in order that there be no possibility of brooding over real or imaginary hurts. Any rankling sense of injustice would be fatal and would in itself be a doing the very thing, in a passive way, that should be avoided — either passively or actively.

The reason for the prohibition of any effort at self-defense in cases of attack or accusation is training: training in self-control, training in love. For there is no discipline so effective as self-initiated effort. Moreover, the attitude of defense not only hardens the periphery of the auric egg, but also coarsens it throughout; it emphasizes the lower personal self every time, which is a training in the inverse direction, tending toward disintegration, unrest and hatred. Let the karmic law pursue its course. One exercises judgment and discrimination of an exceedingly high type when the consciousness of the effectiveness of this practice is gained. The more a man feels that he, in the light of his conscience, has acted well, the sense of injury, the wish to retaliate, the feverish need of self-justification, become small and unnecessary. Consciousness of right brings forgiveness, and the desire to live in compassion and understanding.

But let us not confuse the rule regarding self-justification with those responsibilities that as honest men and women we may be called upon to fulfill. It may be a clear duty actively to stand up for a principle that is at stake, or to spring to the side of one unjustly attacked. There is a kindness in being rigidly firm, in refusing to participate in evil doing. The sentimental crime of allowing evil to take place before our eyes, and thus participating in it for fear of hurting someone's feelings, is a moral weakness which leads to spiritual degradation. However, when we ourselves are attacked, preferable it is to suffer in silence. Only rarely do we need to justify our own acts.

Overcoming the eager itch of the lower part to prove that 'we are right' may seem a negative exercise, but we shall find that it requires very positive inner action. It is a definite spiritual and intellectual exercise that teaches self-control and brings equanimity. By practicing it, little by little, instinctively one begins to see the viewpoint of the other. Yet here again, there is a subtle danger, for this very practice may become so attractive after one has followed it faithfully for some time, that there is an actual risk of generating and cultivating a spiritual pride in the success thus far achieved. This is something that one must watch for and wrench out of one's soul.

I have known men who struggled and fought so hard to be good that they left a trail of broken hearts behind them, shattered hopes of other human souls — misery brought to others by their frenzied desire to be good. They wanted to advance so greatly that they forgot to be human. Is it wrong to read a good book, to take healthful exercise, or enjoy the food that we eat? Of course not. But if one is strongly attached to something which gives extraordinary pleasure and a duty is neglected, then one should conquer that attachment, for it is doing harm; it is no longer an innocent pleasure, but has become a vice. The simple answer is to forget ourselves and do what we can to benefit others, and we shall be happy, spiritually and intellectually natural and strong, and be respected; and, above everything else, we shall respect ourselves.

This leads on to another thought: it is rare that we make our worst mistakes through our vices; and the reason is that once vices are recognized as such we are seldom swayed by them, but become disgusted and cast them off. In fact, our most serious errors both of feeling and of judgment usually arise out of our virtues — a paradox, the psychological force of which grows upon us as we ponder it.

This can be illustrated by looking at the history of medieval Europe. I believe it is erroneous to suppose that the fanatic monks or ecclesiastical governors who incited those shocking religious persecutions were human devils deliberately excogitating ways of torturing the minds and bodies of their unfortunate fellow men who fell into their power. What they did was diabolic, sheer unconscious devilry, but it arose in their virtues which, because they were so grossly abused, became despicable vices. The most cruel persons usually are not they who are indifferent, but they who are driven by a mistaken ideal, behind which there is a misused moral force. Their virtues, now become unrecognized vices, make them seem for the time completely heartless.

Great thinkers like Lao-tse have pointed out to the confusion of the unthinking that the aggressively virtuous man is the vicious man — an extravagant paradox, and yet one which contains a profound statement of psychological fact. The really dangerous man is not the evil man, for he offends by his intellectual and moral deformity. It is beauty misunderstood and misused that seduces — not physical beauty alone, but beauty in a virtue which has become distorted and misapplied. Virtue itself raises us to the gods; and yet it is our virtues when selfishly applied which so often bring us to do our worst deeds.

There is a deep esoteric meaning in the old injunction: "love all things, both great and small." Hate is constrictive; it builds veils around the individual, whereas love rends those veils, dissolving them and giving us freedom, insight and compassion. It is like the cosmic harmony which manifests in the Music of the Spheres as the stars and planets sing in their courses. Love, impersonal love, harmonizes us with the universe, and this becoming at one with the universe is the last and greatest objective of all phases of the initiatory cycle.

Personal love, on the other hand, is uncharitable and often unlovely, for it is concentrated on one object; it thinks of self rather than of the other; whereas impersonal love gives itself fully, is the very soul of self-sacrifice. Personal love is self-remembrance; impersonal love is self-forgetfulness — there is the distinguishing test. Sentimentality has nothing to do with it; in fact, it is a detriment, for it is an accentuation of the personality. The emotion of love is not love; that belongs to the psycho-mental and animal side of our being. When we place no frontiers or limits to the current flowing forth from our heart, when we make no conditions as to whether we shall extend our protecting and helpful hand, we shall be as the sun, shedding light and warmth on all. And when love is wholly selfless, it is spiritually clairvoyant, for its vision penetrates to the very essence of the universe.

Among other good and simple rules is to *think* impersonally all the time; in our daily acts to try to detach our interest from them so far as any benefit to our own person is concerned. If we can do them as a work of love, whatever they are, we shall be impersonal naturally, for we shall have lost our self-absorption in the service of others. This is the royal road to self-knowledge, for we cannot become the self universal as long as our attention and thought are concentrated on the limited point of egoity.

Another splendid rule is one that the Lord Buddha gave as a favorite teaching of his to his disciples:

> When evil and unworthy thoughts arise in the mind, images of lust, hatred, and infatuation, the disciple must win from these thoughts other and worthy images. When he thus induces other and worthy images in his mind, the unworthy thoughts, the images of lust, hatred, and infatuation cease; and because he has overcome them his inner heart is made firm, tranquil, unified, and strong.°

All of which means that when we are bothered, tormented perhaps, with selfish and personal impulses and thoughts, we should immediately think of their opposites, holding them steadily in our mind's eye. If we have a thought of hate, we should conjure up a picture of affection and kindness; if of evil-doing, vision a magnanimous and splendid act; if a selfish thought, then imagine ourselves as doing some deed of benevolence, and at all times doing this impersonally. I am inclined to view this as the very best rule of all. It is a fascinating study outside of the benefit that comes: the strengthening of the will, the clearing of vision, the refining of the emotions, the stimulating of the heart-forces and the general growth in strength and nobility of character.

Nevertheless, when a thought has once left the mind, it is impossible to withdraw the energy with which we have charged it; for then it is already an elemental being, beginning its upward journey.† Still, if 'neutralizing' thoughts of an opposite character are immediately sent forth — thoughts of beauty, of compassion, of forgiveness, of a desire to help, of aspiration — the two then coalesce, and the effects of the evil ones are made 'harmless' in the sense that H.P.B. speaks of in *The Voice of the Silence* (p. 55).

°*Majjhima Nikāya*, I, 288.

†Do we realize that every human being is the thought of his own inner god — an imperfect reflection of that inner splendor, nevertheless a child of the thoughts of the divinity within — even as the thoughts of evolving human beings are living entities, embryo-souls developing and moving forward on the pathway of evolutionary growth?

However, I repeat: *a thought can never be recalled.* It is like an action, which once done, is done forever, but is not forever done with. By thinking a noble thought or doing a good deed, following upon an evil impulse, although we cannot recall the evil thought or action and undo it, we can, to a certain extent, render at least less harmful the evil that our wrong thought or act brought about.

We humans are personal precisely in proportion as the spiritual individuality is frittered away in the rays of the lower part of our constitution. When we lose personality, we release the hold which these unprogressed elements have upon our real being. This means a gathering together of the rays hitherto dissipated into the various atomic entities of our lower principles — gathering them into the sheaf of selfhood and thus rebecoming our essential Self. "He that findeth his life shall lose it: and he that loseth his life for my sake shall find it" *(Matthew,* x, 39).

If we can try at every moment to be selfless, we shall forget our personal wants. Our needs it is a duty to attend to, but these usually are not crippling to the spirit. As we strive to become impersonal, we shall in time enter into the universal consciousness — in these few sentences we have the secret and essence of esoteric training. But let us not kill our personality; instead let us use it, thereby changing the direction of its evolutionary tendencies so that the currents of its vitality may flow into the higher consciousness of our individuality. It is a marvelous thought that just to the degree that our individuality increases and our personality decreases, do we rise on the ladder of life towards a more intimate individual union with the cosmic divinity at the center of our solar system. This applies to the vast multitude of the human host, as well as to any other entity of equivalent evolutionary advancement possessing self-consciousness and the other attributes that make man man.

Impersonality, altruism and selflessness: these are magical in their effect upon our fellow men. When we can learn truly to forgive, and to love, the longing of our soul will be self-forgetful service for mankind. No one is too humble to practice it, and no one is so exalted that he can ignore it. The more exalted the position, the more imperative is the call to duty. Singlehanded we may have the world to battle; but even though we go down again and again, we can stand up and remember that the forces of the universe are back of us and on our side. The very heart of Being is with us and we shall win, ultimately, for nothing can withstand the subtle and all-penetrating fire of impersonal love.

36

In man lies the pathway to wisdom: one who knows himself, whose spiritual nature is brought forth in fuller degree, can comprehend the movements of the planets. One whose inner self is yet more evolved can confabulate with the beings who rule and guide our solar system; one whose entire being is still more unfolded can penetrate into some at least of the arcana of the macrocosm; and so on indefinitely. The higher the development, the larger the vision and the deeper the understanding. The pathway to the universal Self is the path that each individual must himself tread if he wishes to grow, to evolve. No one else can grow for us, and we can grow only along the lines that nature has laid down — the structure of our own being.

Man is indeed a mystery: under the surface and behind the veil there is the mystery of selfhood, of individuality, a career stretching into distant eternities. Man essentially is a godlike energy enshrouded by veils.

MEDITATION AND YOGA

IT IS IN THE SILENCE that the soul grows strong. For then it is thrown back upon its own energies and powers, and learns to know itself. One of the finest ways of getting light on a problem quickly and certainly, of cultivating intuition, is by not passing the trouble of solving it on to someone who you believe can help you. Seeing solutions and solving problems are a matter of training, of inner growth. One of the first rules that a neophyte is taught is never to ask a question until he has tried earnestly and repeatedly to answer it. Because the attempt to do so is an appeal to the intuition. It is also an exercise. It strengthens one's inner powers. Asking questions before we have ourselves tried to resolve them simply shows that we are leaning, and this is not good. To exercise our own faculties means growth, the gaining of strength and ability.

Certain questions, however, come with a force that compels an answer. They are like the mystic knocking on the door of the temple; they demand the giving of more light, for they come not from the brain-mind, but from the soul striving to understand the light flowing into it from the perennial fountains of divinity. Ask and ye shall receive; knock — and knock aright — and it shall be opened unto you. If the appeal is strong and impersonal enough, the very gods in heaven will respond. If the individual is very much in earnest, the answer will come to him from within, from the only initiator that any neophyte ever has.

Meditation is a positive attitude of mind, a state of consciousness rather than a system or a time period of intensive brain-mind thinking. One should be positive in attitude, but quietly so; positive as the mountain of granite, and as serene and peaceful, avoiding the disturbing influences of the ever-active and feverish mentality. And, above everything else, impersonal. Meditation in the better sense is the bending of the consciousness, and the raising of the mind to the plane where intuition guides, and where some noble idea or aspiration is native, and the holding of the consciousness in thought there. But one can meditate also on evil things and, alas, many do just this.

38

It is possible so to meditate before falling asleep that one's soul ascends to the gods, and is refreshed and strengthened by its confabulations with those divine beings. But it is likewise possible to brood before sleep comes so that when the bonds of wakefulness are broken, and the brain-mind is silenced, the soul is dragged downwards, and is thus degraded and weakened. One should never sleep until one has sincerely forgiven all injuries done unto him. This is very important not only as an ennobling practice, but as a much needed protection. Fill the heart with thoughts of love and compassion for all, and the mind with some lofty idea and dwell on it calmly, with the higher, impersonal brooding that is effortless and still, and then there will be a rest of all the senses, and quiet in the mind.

One reason for the need of strict impersonality, without the slightest thought of any destructive or morally offensive element intruding into the heart, such as hate, anger, fear or revenge, or any other of the horrid progeny of the lower self, is that when sleep steals over the body and the ordinary brain-mind consciousness drops away, the soul now released automatically follows the direction last given to it. Thus the practice of calming the mind before retiring can elevate the soul.

Meditate all the time — nothing is so easy and so helpful. Far better is this for most students than to have a set period: quiet, unremitting thought on the questions you have, continuing even when the hands are busy with the tasks of the day, and the mind itself quite absorbed by other duties. In the back of the consciousness there can still be this steady undercurrent of thought. It is likewise a protecting shield in all one's affairs, for it surrounds the body with an aura drawn forth from the deeper recesses of the auric egg, which is ākāśic, and through which, when condensed by the will of one who knows how to do it, nothing material can pass.

Yet even in the profoundest meditation, when one has lost all sense of surrounding circumstances, the trained chela is never in the condition of having lost his spiritual and intellectual grip. He is always alert, always aware that he is in control of the situation, even while the consciousness is passing in review the myriad phases of the subject under contemplation. It is highly inadvisable, as a general rule, to allow oneself to be on another plane in thought so greatly that one becomes a psychic or physical automaton.

There are two kinds of meditation: first, the keeping of some beautiful

39

idea clearly in the mind as a picture, and letting one's consciousness enter into that picture; and second, the casting of the consciousness into higher spheres or planes, and taking in and absorbing the experiences that flow into the consciousness by doing so. But if we set our teeth and grip our hands and mentally hammer this or that point of thought, we are not meditating at all. If we do this, we won't succeed, because such exercise is merely brain-mind cogitation, which is often exhausting, uninspiring and uninspired. There is a difference between just thinking concentratedly on a subject, especially if it means using the brain-mind, and a concentration or absorption of the consciousness in following the ennobling direction along which the spiritual will is guiding.

Meditation, then, is the holding of a thought steady in the mind, and allowing the consciousness to work interiorly upon this thought, easily and with delight. Let it dwell there; let the spirit brood over it. There is no need to put the physical or psychical will on to it. This is true meditation and is really the fundamental secret of yoga, meaning 'union' of the mind with the ineffable peace, wisdom and love of the god within. If one practices this simple rule of jñāna-yoga, after a while it will become natural, a part of the daily consciousness. Concentration or one-pointedness of mind is merely taking this thought into our consciousness more clearly, and centering all our attention upon it — not with the will, but with ease.

All other forms of yoga which depend more or less upon exterior aids, such as posturings, breathings, positions of hands and fingers and feet, etc., belong to the lower parts of hatha-yoga and are little more than crutches, because distracting the mind to these exterior methods and away from the main objective of true yoga itself, which is a reversal of the mind from exterior to inner and spiritual things. Thus all forms of the lower yoga, now become so popular in the West through the 'teachings' of itinerant and wandering 'yogis,' usually do more harm than good.

The hatha-yoga system is a fivefold method of attaining control of the lower psychic faculties through various forms of ascetic practices, requiring a scientific paralyzing of the physical and psychic parts by violent methods. The yogi effects this complete self-absorption by suspending his vital processes and causing a short-circuiting of certain prānic energies of his astro-physical body. As should be obvious, this practice is mentally and physically perilous as well as spiritually restricting, and hence is unequivocally discouraged by all genuinely occult schools. Certain powers can indeed be acquired by these means, but, I repeat, they are powers of the lowest kind, and have no lasting benefit, and, moreover, will greatly hinder one's spiritual progress.

In this connection, William Q. Judge wrote:[*]

. . . progress will be made. Not by trying to cultivate psychic powers that at best can be but dimly realized, nor by submitting to any control by another, but by educating and strengthening the soul. If all the virtues are not tried for, if the mind is not well based in philosophy, if the spiritual needs are not recognized as quite apart from the realm of psychism, there will be but a temporary dissipation in the astral realms, ending at last in disappointment as sure as the shining of the sun.

On the other hand, the rāja-yoga and jñāna-yoga systems, embracing spiritual and intellectual discipline combined with love for all beings, have to do with the higher portions of the inner constitution — the control of the physical and psychic following as a natural consequence of an understanding of the entire sevenfold man. True yoga controls and raises the mind, thus effecting the communion of the human with the spiritual consciousness, which is relative universal consciousness. The attaining of this union or at-oneness with one's divine-spiritual essence brings illumination.

In certain very exceptional circumstances where a chela has advanced relatively far, mentally and spiritually speaking, but has still a very unfortunate and heavy physical karma not yet worked out, it is proper to use the hatha-yoga methods to a limited degree, but only under the master's own eye. I may add that the *Yoga Aphorisms* (or *Sūtras*) of Patañjali is a hatha-yoga scripture, but one of the highest type. The terse instructions contained in this small work are well known to Western students, largely through the interpretation of W. Q. Judge and later writers.

Real yoga is meditation, as said, and this obviously includes the centering and holding of the mind with fixity on a point of noble thought, and a brooding upon it, pondering upon it. Patañjali in his *Sūtras* (i, 2) wrote: *Yogas' chitta-vritti-nirodhah* — "yoga is the preventing of the whirlings of thought." This is very clear: when the ever-active brain-mind, with its butterfly-like wandering from thought to thought, and its fevered emotions, can be controlled into one-pointed aspiration and intellectual vision upwards, then these 'whirlings' of thinking vanish, and the aspiring organ of thought becomes intensely active, manifests intuition, sees truth,

---

[*]"Answers to Correspondence," December 1893.

41

and in fact makes the man whose organ of self-conscious thought is so occupied, an imbodiment of wisdom and love — and this is the true yoga. It is the manas, the mind-principle, which is thus active and is, so to speak, turned upon itself upwards instead of downwards, becoming the buddhi-manas instead of the kāma-manas. The *chitta* of the Sanskrit phrase, i.e. the 'thinking,' becomes filled with wisdom and intuition, and the man becomes virtually, when expert in this sublime spiritual exercise, one with the divinity within.

In the next śloka Patañjali goes on to state: "then the Seer abides in himself," the meaning being that the man then becomes a seer, and abides in his spiritual self, the god within him.

Contrariwise, when the mind is not so restrained and directed upwards, then the "whirlings (activity) become assimilated mutually," as the 4th śloka has it — a very concise statement meaning that when the mind is fastened in lower things, its feverish activities enchain the higher manas, which thus becomes temporarily 'assimilated' with its lowest elements, and the man is in consequence no more than the ordinary human being.

An occult secret in connection with the mind is that it takes the form of the object contemplated or perceived, and so molds itself into the objects of thought, whatever their quality. If the mental picture is divine, the mind becomes similar to it because it flows into the divine and molds itself accordingly; and likewise, when the mind is held in the lower things it becomes assimilated to them, because flowing into their form and appearance.°

It is precisely the desire to know, not for oneself, not even for the mere sake of knowing in an abstract sense, but for the purpose of laying knowledge on the altar of service, which leads to esoteric advancement. It is this desire, this will for impersonal service, which purifies the heart, clarifies the mind and impersonalizes the knots of the lower selfhood, so that they open and thereby become capable of receiving wisdom. It is this desire which is the impelling force, the driving engine, carrying the aspirant forward, ever higher and higher.

°This great fact of occultism has therefore a high as well as a low aspect; and this faculty of the mind it is which is used by the adept of either the white or the black class in order to produce, when required, magical effects. Indeed, it is not too much to say that the powers of āveśa, the entering into and using the body of another, as well as the Hpho-wa, or the power of projecting the will and intelligence to other parts, sometimes to incredible distances, depend largely upon this attribute or characteristic of the fluid mind.

THE PĀRAMITĀS AND THE EXALTED EIGHTFOLD PATH

IN BUDDHIST as well as in modern theosophical literature a great deal has been written about the 'glorious virtues' or pāramitās, but unfortunately they have been too often looked upon as being merely a noble but relatively unattainable code of conduct, which indeed they are; but they are more than this. They are actually the rules of thought and action which the would-be chela *must* follow, in the beginning as best he can, but later in completeness, so that his entire life becomes governed and enlightened by them. It is only thus that the disciple can reach what the Lord Buddha called the 'other shore'° — the spiritual realms which have to be reached by crossing the stormy ocean of human existence, and doing so under one's own spiritual and intellectual and psychical power, with only such help as can be given him in view of his own past karma.

The idea of going to the other shore is commonly supposed to be typically Oriental, but this seems unjustified, as many Christian hymns speak of the mystical Jordan and of reaching the 'shore beyond,' a conception which appears to be more or less identic with that of Buddhism. 'This side' is the life of the world, the usual or common pursuits of men. The 'other shore' is simply the life spiritual, involving the expansion in relatively full power and function of the entire range of man's nature. In other words, to reach the 'other shore' means living at one with the

---

°Pāramita and pāragata (or its equivalent pāragāmin) are Sanskrit compounds denoting 'one who has reached the other shore'; pāramitā (the feminine form) is used for the transcendental virtues or attributes which one must cultivate in order to reach that shore. There is a shade of difference in meaning to be noted here: pāramita carries the idea of having 'crossed over' and therefore 'arrived,' while pāragata (or pāragāmin) implies 'departure' from this end and thus 'gone' in order safely to reach the other shore.

Another word of frequent use in Buddhist writings which also imbodies both subtle distinctions of the above term is Tathāgata, a title given to Gautama Buddha. This is a Sanskrit compound that can be divided in two fashions: *tathā-gata*, 'thus gone,' that is, departed for and reached the other shore; and *tathā-āgata*, 'thus arrived or come,' the significance of the term Tathāgata being one who has both 'departed' for and 'arrived' at the other shore, as his predecessor-Buddhas have done.

divinity within, and hence partaking of the universal life in relatively full self-consciousness. The teaching of all the great religious and philosophical systems has been to urge upon their followers the fact that our real goal is to learn the lessons of manifested existence and to graduate from this experience into the cosmic life.

As the *Dhammapada* (verse 85) has it:

There are few people who reach the other shore;
The others run wild on this shore.

A short Buddhist writing called the *Prajñā-Pāramitā-Hridaya Sūtra* or "The Heart or Essence of the Wisdom of the Passing-Over," closes with a beautiful mantra which runs as follows in the original Sanskrit:

Gate, gate, pāragate, pārasamgate, bodhi, svāhā!

O Wisdom! Gone, gone, gone to the other shore,
landed on the other shore, Hail!

Wisdom in this context may be taken as referring to the cosmic buddhi, otherwise called Ādi-buddhi or 'primeval wisdom,' and also in an individualized sense to the supreme Silent Watcher of our planetary chain, Ādi-buddha. The one addressed is he who has arrived at the other shore, the triumphant pilgrim who has become self-consciously at one with the god within him and thus has successfully perceived through the māyā or illusions of the phenomenal worlds. The highest ones who have attained this are jīvanmuktas, 'freed monads'; those less high belong to the different grades in the several hierarchies of the Hierarchy of Compassion.

The discipline of the pāramitās as H.P.B. gave them in *The Voice of the Silence* (pp. 47–8) is as follows:

DĀNA, the key of charity and love immortal.

ŚĪLA, the key of Harmony in word and act, the key that counterbalances the cause and the effect, and leaves no further room for Karmic action.

KSHĀNTI, patience sweet, that nought can ruffle.

VIRĀGA, indifference to pleasure and to pain, illusion conquered, truth alone perceived.

VĪRYA, the dauntless energy that fights its way to the supernal TRUTH, out of the mire of lies terrestrial.

DHYĀNA, whose golden gate once opened leads the Narjol [Naljor] toward the realm of Sat eternal and its ceaseless contemplation.

PRAJÑĀ, the key to which makes of a man a god, creating him a Bodhisattva, son of the Dhyānis.

THE PÄRAMITÄS AND THE EXALTED EIGHTFOLD PATH

The manner in which these pāramitās are to be practiced is well illustrated by the following extract from the *Mahāyāna Śrāddhotpāda Śāstra*°
which, however, mentions only six, although they are given elsewhere
as seven and, when more fully enumerated, as ten:

How should one practise charity (*Dāna*)?

If someone comes and asks for anything, disciples, as far as they are able,
should grant the request ungrudgingly and in a way to benefit them. If disciples
see anyone in danger, they should try every means they have to rescue him
and impart to him a feeling of safety. If any one comes to disciples desiring
instruction in the Dharma, they should as far as they are able and according
to their best judgment, try to enlighten him. And when they are doing these
acts of charity, they should not cherish any desire for recompense, or gratitude,
or merit or advantage, nor any worldly reward. They should seek to concentrate
the mind on those universal benefits and blessings that are for all alike and,
by so doing, will realise within themselves highest perfect Wisdom.

How should one practise virtuous precepts (*Śīla*)?

Lay disciples, having families, should abstain from killing, stealing, adultery,
lying, duplicity, slander, frivolous talk, covetousness, malice, currying favor, and
false doctrines. Unmarried disciples should, in order to avoid hindrances, retire
from the turmoil of worldly life and, abiding in solitude, should practise those
ways which lead to quietness and moderation and contentment. . . . They should
endeavor by their conduct to avoid all disapproval and blame, and by their
example incite others to forsake evil and practise the good.

How should one practise patient forbearance (*Kshānti*)?

As one meets with the ills of life he should not shun them nor feel aggrieved.
Patiently bearing evils inflicted by others, he should cherish no resentment.
He should neither be elated because of prosperity, praise, or agreeable circumstances; nor depressed because of poverty, insult, or hardship. Keeping his mind

---

°Often translated as "The Awakening of Faith in the Mahāyāna," but this very
inadequately conveys the significance of the original Sanskrit. *Śrāddha* means certainty
or confidence based on an unfoldment of inner experiences, the proof of which lies
both within and without the self, and implying here a continued process of inner
unfoldment, a connotation which is utterly lacking in the word 'faith.' As to *utpāda*,
this carries the same idea of continuance and progressive unfoldment, an awakening
or rising towards an awareness or realization of wisdom, culminating in the mystic
renunciation of the fruits of emancipation and the attainment of buddhahood. This
scripture belongs to the *Prajñā-Pāramitā* family of writings, and is usually credited
to Aśvaghosha, a notable Buddhist scholar who lived during the latter half of the first
century A.D., and whose outstanding work is the *Mahālamkara* or "Book of Great
Glory."

concentrated on the deep significance of the Dharma, he should under all circumstances maintain a quiet and equitable mind.

How should one practise courageous vigor (*Vīrya*)?

In the practice of good deeds one should never become indolent. He should look upon any mental or physical suffering as the natural following of unworthy deeds done in previous incarnations, and should firmly resolve that henceforth he would only do those things which are in keeping with a spiritual life. Cherishing compassion for all beings, he should never let the thought of indolence arise, but should ever be indefatigably zealous to benefit all beings. . . .

How should one practise meditation (*Dhyāna*)?

Intellectual insight is gained by truthfully understanding that all things follow the law of causation, but in themselves are transitory and empty of any self-substance. There are two aspects of *Dhyāna:* the first aspect is an effort to suppress idle thinking; the second, is a mental concentration in an effort to realise this emptiness (*śūnyatā*) of Mind-essence. At first a beginner will have to practise these separately but as he gains mind control the two will merge into one. . . .

He should contemplate the fact, that although all things are transitory and empty yet, nevertheless, on the physical plane they have a relative value to those who are cherishing false imagination; to these ignorant ones, suffering is very real — it always has been and it always will be — immeasurable and innumerable sufferings. . . .

Because of all this, there is awakened in the mind of every earnest disciple a deep compassion for the suffering of all beings that prompts him to dauntless, earnest zeal and the making of great vows. He resolves to give all he has and all he is to the emancipation of all beings. . . . After these vows, the sincere disciple should at all times and as far as his strength and mind permit, practise those deeds which are beneficial alike to others and to himself. Whether moving, standing, sitting or lying, he should assiduously concentrate his mind on what should be wisely done and wisely left undone. This is the active aspect of *Dhyāna.*

How can one practise Intuitive Wisdom (*Prajñā*)?

When one by the faithful practice of *Dhyāna* attains to *Samādhi*, he has passed beyond discrimination and knowledge, he has realised the perfect oneness of Mind-essence. With this realisation comes an intuitive understanding of the nature of the universe. . . . he now realises the perfect Oneness of Essence, Potentiality, and Activity in Tathāgatahood. . . .

Prajñā-Pāramitā is highest, perfect Wisdom; its fruitage comes unseen, without effort, spontaneously; it merges all seeming differences whether they be evil or good into one perfect Whole. . . .

Therefore let all disciples who aspire after highest, perfect Wisdom, which is *Prajñā-Pāramitā*, assiduously apply themselves to the discipline of the Noble Path for that alone will lead them to perfect realisation of Buddhahood.

46

In order to understand and spiritually to *feel* the true nature of prajñā, it is necessary to abandon the 'this side' view, and in spiritual comprehension to go over to the 'other shore' (pāra), or other manner of looking at things. On 'this side' we are involved in a sphere of consciousness of brain-mind analyses and particulars, which becomes a world of attachments and lower-plane distinctions. When we achieve this inner 'reversal,' this shifting of our consciousness upwards to the mystic 'other shore' of being, we then enter more or less successfully into a world of transcendent realities, from which we can view things in their original and spiritual oneness, beyond the māyā of the deceptive veils of multiplicity; penetrate into the essential nature of these realities and cognize them as they truly are.

This condition of inner clarity and of accurate spiritual and intellectual apperception is so different from the familiar operations of our 'this-side' consciousness in our everyday world of transitory appearances, that untrained minds associate it with the conception of emptiness, vacuity. Emptiness (śūnyatā, to use the Buddhist term), in its true metaphysical meaning, however, should not be confounded with 'nothingness,' implying an absolute negation of real being and thus annihilation. Nor is it to be understood through the ratiocinative faculties of the brain-mind, but rather by the direct or immediate perception belonging to the high spiritual-intellectual state called prajñā, which is above the māyāvi distinctions of being and non-being, of particular and universal, of the many and the one.

Indeed, this high state is the intuitive knowledge and penetrating insight of the spirit-mind in man, his buddhi-manas, which is immeasurably more powerful and penetrating than is mere intellection. Such intuitive knowledge and insight lie ever active in the loftiest and most universal recesses of our consciousness. It is through the gradual awakening of the lower man into self-conscious realization of this spiritual-intellectual consciousness — which in its active manifestations is identic with prajñā — that we arise from the lower realms of our consciousness and escape from the bondage of ignorance and nescience (avidyā), and thus become liberated from the various kinds of both inner and outer pain. This release is the attainment of supreme enlightenment and of emancipation (mukti). In brief, prajñā may perhaps best be translated as intuition, signifying that instant illumination or full knowledge which verily is godlike.

In the *Prajñā-Pāramitā* group of Buddhist scriptures, prajñā is regarded as the directing principle of the other pāramitās, pointing to them as being the method of reaching reality. It is compared to the perceiving and understanding eye that surveys with perfect clearness of vision the horizons of life and designates the path to be followed by the aspirant. Without prajñā, the other pāramitās would be devoid of one of their highest elements; it guides their progressive development, somewhat as the earth provides the fields of sustenance for the growth of vegetation.

All beings in the universe possess prajñā, although it is not functioning self-consciously except when the evolving entities in the course of their evolutionary pilgrimage have become at one with it. The animals have prajñā, including bees and ants, as instances, but any self-conscious awareness thereof is lacking, because such self-realization of union with prajñā begins only with man — at least on this earth. In its first feeble workings prajñā in the human being manifests as aspiration towards illumination, love and wisdom; blossoms in the bodhisattva, and is in full bloom in the Buddhas and Christs, which is the state of perfect enlightenment.

The high chela or initiate who has successfully reached the stage where he has *become* the pāramitās, with his consciousness crystal clear and relatively boundless, his whole being attuned to the spiritual soul of humanity, having given up his self to the selfless glory of living for all that is, is technically called a bodhisattva — 'one whose essence (sattva) is of the very nature of wisdom (bodhi).' The motive which prompts the true disciple to realize within himself supreme enlightenment is never personal gain, however exalted and spiritualized, but the urge to benefit the whole world, to raise all beings from the chains of ignorance and pain, to arouse within himself a compassionate heart for all that lives, so that every sentient being may in time attain to perfect emancipation.°

In the *Mahāprajñāpāramitā* the question is asked of Śāriputra whether the bodhisattva should pay respect only to other bodhisattvas, and not "to all beings generally." To which the sage answers that he should in fact "revere them with the same feeling of self-abnegation as he does the Tathāgatas." He then goes on to say:†

The Bodhisattva should thus awaken a great compassionate feeling towards all beings and keep his mind completely free from arrogance and self-conceit, and let him feel in this wise: I will practise all the skillful means in order to

---

°Cf. Fo-Mu *Prajñāpāramitā*, Fas. 14, Chapter "On Wise Men."
†Hsüan-chuang, Fas. 387, Chapter xii, "On Morality."

make all sentient beings realize that which is the foremost in themselves, i.e., their Buddha-nature (buddhatā). By realizing this they all become Buddhas, . . .

Prajñā in the individual entity, such as a human being, holds pretty much the same position that Ādi-buddhi or mahābuddhi does in the universe. One of the axioms of the esoteric wisdom is that our universe is an entity; hence we can figurate its individual universal mind or consciousness as a vast ocean of self-conscious buddhi-mānasic energy points. From this standpoint, prajñā may be described as the spiritual individual consciousness of every member of the hosts of dhyāni-chohans or cosmic spirits. Thus when one has attained prajñā-awareness, he is in self-conscious communion with the buddhi-mānasic mind of the Wondrous Being of our hierarchy.

From the foregoing it should be clear that there are numerous differences in grandeur of accomplishment as among the members of a hierarchy, for there are differences in grades of attainment between the chela beginning the path and a mahatma, followed by still higher beings having an even larger realization of prajñā on the ladder of achievement that extends steadily upwards until the Wondrous Being is reached. The prajñā is the same in all; the differences among individuals lie in their respective manifestation of it.

There are also differences of another kind, such as that between one who has attained a relative realization of prajñā and who enters nirvana, and another of similar attainment but who renounces nirvana. Here we have an important distinction based on cosmic ethics: the one who has won nirvana yet renounces it in order to turn back and help the world stands far higher ethically than does the one who enters nirvana for his own bliss. Each has reached a sufficiency of at-onement with prajñā to have gained the nirvanic state, but the one who renounces it has achieved a self-conscious realization of prajñā on a higher buddhic plane than the one who won nirvana and enters into it.

The key to this mystery lies in the fact that every one of the seven principles in the human constitution is septenary, and hence buddhi, which is the seat of prajñā, is sevenfold. We thus see that the one entering nirvana has reached what we may define as kāma-buddhi, but has gone no higher in the quality of his realization of prajñā; whereas the other one who renounced nirvana has attained that condition of buddhic prajñā which we may describe as either buddhi-buddhi or manas-buddhi. The buddhas and mahābuddhas are those who hold what we may call the ātmic state of buddhi — and thus feel themselves absolutely and unqualifiedly self-identified with the universe.

The seven pāramitās as given contain the gist of the code of conduct imbodied in the fuller enumeration of ten pāramitās, or the complete ethical decalog of occultism. The three additional pāramitās are: adhishthāna, upekshā, and prabodha or sambuddhi. Of these adhishthāna, meaning 'inflexible courage,' not merely awaits danger or difficulty, but when enlightened by intuition or prajñā 'goes forwards' and 'stands up' to it. Its natural place follows vīrya or 'fortitude.' The next, upekshā or 'discrimination,' searches for and finds the right method of applying the pāramitās, and appropriately comes after dhyāna. Two terms are given for the tenth pāramitā: prabodha, meaning 'awakenment of inner consciousness,' bringing knowledge and foreknowledge, thus opening up glorious visions on the pathway; and sambuddhi, 'complete or perfect illumination or vision' or self-consciousness of one's identity with the spiritual, the culmination or crown of all. Otherwise phrased, it is 'union with buddhi.'

Other 'virtues' are occasionally included by other schools of esoteric or quasi-occult training in the Orient. As examples, satya or truth, and maitra or universal friendliness or benevolence; but when analyzed these are seen to be already imbodied in the ten pāramitās. Also it may be mentioned here that in many parts of the world there are various systems of training, most of them futile, for on careful examination they will be found to be more or less modifications of hatha-yoga, and, as pointed out, these are extremely dangerous even at the best, and at the worst will produce insanity or loss of the soul.

Strength is born from exercise, and it is the exercising of our strength in the tests and experiences of daily life that in time leads to the treading of the path. Unless the student follow the inner discipline, which is the continuous and never-failing practice of the spirit of these ten glorious virtues or pāramitās as his inflexible rule of thought and of action from day to day, he will never succeed in his endeavors. It is just this discipline, this exercising of his will power and of his intelligence and of the love which should fill his heart, which eventually bring the neophyte to the new or 'second' birth, which produce the dvija, the 'twice-born,' the initiate, finally to become the master of life and of death.

THE PĀRAMITĀS AND THE EXALTED EIGHTFOLD PATH

The reader may be wondering just what connection the pāramitās have with the much more familiar teachings of Buddhism, known respectively as the Four Noble Truths and their logical corollary the Eightfold Path. The connection is both historical and intimate, for both contain the same root-ideas, only in the more popular teaching so phrased as to furnish a code of conduct which the average worldly man is capable of following, if he desire to avoid the harassing mistakes attendant upon human life, and to attain the peace and intellectual detachment which accompany a life well and nobly lived.

Briefly, the Four High Truths are: first, that the cause of the suffering and heartache in our lives arises from attachment or 'thirst' — trishnā; second, that this cause can be made to cease; third, that the cessation of the causes productive of human sorrow is brought about by living the life which will free the soul from its attachment to existence; and the fourth truth, leading to the extinction of the causes of suffering, is verily the Exalted Eightfold Path, to wit: "right belief, right resolve, right speech, right behavior, right occupation, right effort, right contemplation, right concentration."

Now this course of endeavor was called by the Buddha the Middle Way, because it involved no useless or fanatical asceticism on the one hand, and no laxity of principle and of thought and consequent behavior on the other hand. It is a code, as said, that is within the reach of every man or woman, calling for no special conditions or circumstances, but able to be practiced by anyone who yearns to better his life, and to do his part in helping to bring about the surcease of the world-misery surrounding us, and of which sensitive human hearts everywhere are conscious.

It must not be supposed, however, that the chela neglects the ethical injunctions of the Eightfold Path, for this would be a misapprehension of their import. In fact, he not only practices them, but does so with far greater concentration of mind and heart than the average man, because at the same time he is striving with all his soul to raise himself to the sublime altitude of the pāramitās by which he should live.

It is perhaps necessary to weigh somewhat strongly upon this point, because there is a totally erroneous idea current among some half-baked mystics that it is a part of the chela's life to ignore normal human relations, to take small account of them, and to imagine that he is freed from his duties, even of a worldly kind, towards his fellow men. This last supposition runs directly counter to all the teaching of occultism.

The principle behind the Four High Truths and their eight corollaries is this: if the root of attachment — desire — can be cut, the soul thereupon becomes freed, and in thus liberating itself from the chains of desire which bring about attachment, the cause of sorrow is made to cease; and the way of cutting the root of attachment is by so living that gradually the thirst of the soul for the things of matter dies. When this happens, the individual is 'free' — he has become a relatively perfected jīvanmukta, a master of life. Once he has reached this stage of utter detachment, he is a bodhisattva, and thereafter devotes himself completely to all beings and things, his heart filled with infinite compassion and his mind illuminated with the light of eternity. Thus it is that as a bodhisattva he appears again and again on earth, either as a buddha or as a bodhisattva, or indeed remains in the invisible worlds as a nirmānakāya.

The common idea regarding the bodhisattva, that he has only one more incarnation to undergo before he becomes a buddha, is correct as far as it goes, but as thus expressed is inadequate. As a matter of fact, the ideal both of esoteric theosophy and esoteric Buddhism is the bodhisattva, even more, perhaps, than the buddha, for the reason that the bodhisattva is one whose whole being and objective, whose whole work, is the doing of good unto all beings, and the bringing of them safely to the 'other shore'; whereas the buddha, while the same thing in an extended degree, nevertheless, by the very fact of his buddhahood in the present stage of spiritual unfoldment of the human race, is on the threshold of nirvana, and usually enters therein. It is, of course, quite possible for a buddha to refuse the nirvana and to remain on earth as a bodhisattva or a nirmānakāya; and in this last case, as a Buddha of Compassion he is at once a buddha by right and a bodhisattva by choice.

Too much stress cannot be laid upon the great need of understanding the inner significance of the bodhisattva doctrine, imbodying as it does the spirit of occult teaching running throughout the cycle of initiatory training as well as in the nobler schools of the Mahāyāna. It is at once seen why in northern Buddhism the bodhisattva is so greatly honored and occupies so lofty a position in the reverence of human hearts. For the Buddhas of Compassion are such because they themselves imbody this ideal when they renounce the spiritually selfish bliss of nirvanic buddhahood in order to remain in the world to work for it. Even the humblest and least educated can aspire towards this ideal.

In future aeons one must choose whether he will become one of the

Buddhas of Compassion or one of the Pratyeka-Buddhas. When the choice comes, it will come as the karmic resultant of lives previously lived, for it results from the bent of one's character, the spiritual faculties aroused, the will made to be alert, responsive to command: all these will govern and in fact make the choice when the time for choosing arrives. Therefore the training starts now: becoming great in small things, one learns to become great in great things.

As a final thought, one must not be heavy in living the life which the High Eightfold Path, or indeed the pāramitās, enjoin. He should joy in so doing. For I sincerely believe that everyone who practices these noble rules to some extent at least will be enormously bettered by them. Nor can we be oblivious of how greatly such consistent practice will increase the will power, strengthen the mind, enlarge the sympathies of the heart, and bring about a glorious illumination of soul, all of which in their final stages produce the mahatma — the true bodhisattva.

THE INITIATORY CYCLE

THE CORE OF OUR being is pure consciousness, and in proportion as we ally ourselves with our inner god, with that pure monadic consciousness, shall knowledge come to us naturally. Our understanding will expand, and finally become cosmic, and we shall then realize that there is another cosmos still grander of which our cosmos is but an atom. This is the path of evolution, of growth, inner and outer; it is the pathway of initiation, the pathway to almighty love and compassion.

The word initiation comes from a Latin root meaning to begin, and esoterically it connotes a new becoming, an entering upon a course of life and study which eventually will bring out all of the spiritual and intellectual grandeur that the individual has within him. It is in fact a hastening of the evolutionary process: not in the sense of omitting any stage, but in condensing within a short period what in the natural course would take aeons of striving to attain.

Esoteric training, therefore, is often painful, for it means accelerated growth, doing rapidly and vigorously what in nature's ordinary procedures would take many, many tens of thousands of years, millions perhaps. It is painful at times because, instead of slowly growing to see the beauty and harmony of life everywhere, one must learn to master oneself with an iron will; to forget oneself utterly, to serve all: to give up one's self for the universal self, to die daily so that one can live the cosmic life.

I suppose that every human being takes it for granted that from the time he first issued forth from the bosom of the Infinite as an unself-conscious god-spark until he reattains divinity as a self-conscious god, he will fail, and fail many times, but that ultimately he will achieve — if he rises and presses forwards. The failure is not so much. It is the going backwards, the stopping and allowing the evolutionary current to sweep by, leaving one in the rear: this is morally wrong. It is our duty to go forwards; to become impersonal, self-forgetful. Obviously, the expression 'going backwards' does not imply an actual retrograde motion of a body. The idea is adapted from human experience. We may set out with high courage and leaping ambition to do something, and then discouragement overtakes

54

us and we turn back, leaving the deed undone. Strictly speaking, going backwards is impossible, for nature closes the door behind us at every instant; nor does it mean undoing what evolution has brought to pass. Rather it denotes plunging farther into matter instead of rising more fully into spirit; in other words, changing the direction of our evolutionary journey.

Never was there a mahatma who had not failed and failed many, many times. Failure is unfortunate, but it can be remedied; and by the will of the strong turned into victory. To quote the words of W. Q. Judge:°

We may "fail" in specific acts or endeavor, but so long as we continue to persevere such are not "failures" but lessons necessary in themselves. Through resistance and effort we acquire fresh strength; we gather to ourselves — and by occult laws — all the strength we have gained by overcoming. Entire "success" is not for us now, but continuous, persistent effort is, and *that* is success and not the mere carrying out of all our plans or attempts. Moreover no matter how high we go in Nature, there are always new rungs of the ladder to mount — that ladder whose rungs are all mounted in labor and in pain, but also in the great joy of conscious strength and will. Even the Adept sees fresh trials before him. Remember also when we say "I have failed" it shows that we have had and still have aspiration. And while this is so, while we have before us loftier heights of perfection to scale, Nature will never desert us. We are mounting, and aspiring, and the sense of failure is the surest proof of this. But Nature has no use for anyone who has reached the limits of, or outlived, his aspirations. So that every "failure *is* a success." At the outset the greater your aspirations the greater the difficulties you will encounter. Forget not then that to continue to try even when one constantly fails is the only way to come to *real* success.

The aim of initiation is to ally the human being with the gods, which is begun by making the neophyte at one with his own inner god. It means not only an alliance with the divinities, but also that the initiant, the learner, if he succeed, will pass behind veil after veil: first of the material universe, and then of the other universes within the physical-material one, each new passing behind a veil being the entering into a grander mystery. Briefly, it is the self-conscious becoming-at-one with the spiritual-divine universe; enlarging the consciousness, so that from being merely human it takes unto itself cosmic reaches. The man in his thought and con- sciousness thus is at home in every part of universal Being — as much at

---

°*Answers to Correspondence*, September 1892.

home on Sirius or on the Polar Star as he is on Canopus or on earth, and even more so as regards the invisible worlds.

Initiation is a quickening of the process of evolution, an enlivening of the inner man as contrasted with the outer physical person. In its higher stages, it brings with it powers and an unfolding of the consciousness which are verily godlike; but also does it imply the taking over unto oneself of godlike responsibilities. No one becomes an esotericist merely by signing a slip of paper; he cannot become such unless some gleam of buddhic light shines in his heart and illumines his mind. A natural esotericist is one who is born with at least a glimmer of the Christ-light shining within. Such a one sooner or later, as surely as the working of karma pursues its invariable course, is attracted to the path, for it is the working out of his destiny, trained and shaped in the past, into his character as it now is, and in its fruition blossoming forth into an instinctual recognition of truth.°

The least and virtually negligible part of initiation is the ritual. No initiation can be conferred upon another. All growth, all spiritual illumination, takes place *within oneself.* There is no other way. Symbolic rites and outer paraphernalia are but aids to the learner, aids to the developing of the power of the inner vision, the inner eye. Therefore any initiatory trial, no matter where had or what the arrangements may be, is in essence an individual inner opening. Were it not so, there could be no initiation

---

°There are occasional cases of individuals who have been chelas in past lives, but who have stumbled on the path and broken the link in some very unfortunate way for themselves with their teacher. Yet because of past excellencies, when the next or possibly a second incarnation occurs, they come into life endowed with unusual powers or faculties; they enter with a reservoir of garnered inner spiritual, intellectual and psychical experiences which give them light, and help them to keep touch with the god within.

H.P.B. has called these the nurslings of the nirmānakāyas, and points to Jacob Boehme as an instance. There was an individual who through some willfulness of a serious character had broken the link, yet had advanced sufficiently far so that he did not lose the spiritual attainments he had made. Although no longer a direct chela, he was nevertheless watched over, aided, and his future progress gently stimulated, so that in the next life (or even at the end of the life he last lived as Jacob Boehme), he may again make or have made the conscious link. In other words, Boehme had spiritual experiences; he initiated himself from the fountain of light within himself, gained in former days when he was an accepted chela. In reality, as said, all initiation is self-initiation, self-awakening. A teacher merely guides, helps, comforts, stimulates and supports. Cf. *The Secret Doctrine,* I, 494.

except as a hollow ritual, much as are the sacraments of the churches today for the most part; even so, they are reflections, however faint, of once living experiences of chelas undergoing initiation.

The ancient Mysteries of Greece, for example, those conducted by the State at Eleusis and Samothrace, or at Delphi, or again those which took place at the Oracle of Trophonius, were largely ceremonial. Yet in all of them, even in the degenerate days, there was also a certain amount of actual spiritual experience. I might add that the hints found in literature of the ordeals to be faced and overcome should not be construed too literally; they are not imaginary exactly, but are symbolic representations of what the initiant has to meet in himself. For thoughts are mental entities and therefore have form and power of their own, and the individual must win over his lower nature, or fail.

There are actually ten degrees in the initiatory cycle, but only the seven that pertain to the seven manifested planes of the solar system need concern us — the three highest being utterly beyond present human understanding; and they will remain so until our consciousness will have become virtually universal, ultrahuman. These seven degrees are the seven great portals through which the pilgrim must pass before he attains quasi-divinity. Between each of these portals there are seven smaller doors through which one must pass, each being a step in training, in schooling, so that all in all there are forty-nine stages, just as there are forty-nine planes in our solar system: seven great planes and seven subplanes or minor spheres or kingdoms in each of the primal seven.

The first three grades or degrees are concerned with study, with unceasing aspiration to grow spiritually and intellectually, to evolve and become greater; and also with living the life. These are symbolic, i.e. dramatic in form so far as the rites go. There is likewise teaching (which is the main part of these rites) about recondite secrets of nature, teaching which is rarely given in a reasoned and consecutive form because that is the brain-mind way, but suggested by a hint here, an allusion there. The method is not to fill the mind of the learner full of other men's thoughts, but to arouse the spiritual fire in himself which brings about an awakening of the understanding, so that in very truth the neophyte becomes his own initiator.

What one receives from outside in the way of ideas, of thoughts, are merely the outward stimuli, arousing the inner vibration preparing for the reception of the light within. Transference of ideas is but a method of speaking. Impressions are made, which set up the corresponding vibratory chord in the recipient's psychological apparatus, and instantly the corresponding knowledge flashes from the recipient's own mind above. Devotion to truth, to the point of utterly forgetting oneself, opens the channel of reception. Light and knowledge then enter the mind and heart — from oneself, from one's inner god, which thus is awakened or, more correctly, begins to function, temporarily though it be; and it is in this wise that the man initiates himself. The whole process is based on nature's laws, on the natural growth of understanding, of interior vision.

With the fourth initiation begins a new series of inner unfoldings — that is to say, not only are the study, the aspiration, and the living of the life, continued in the future stages, but with this degree something new occurs. From that moment the initiant starts to lose his personal humanity and to merge into divinity, i.e. there ensues the beginning of the loss of the merely human and the commencing of the entering into the divine state. He is taught how to leave his physical body, how to leave his physical mind, and to advance into the great spaces not alone of the physical universe, but more especially of the invisible realms as well. He then learns to become, to be, to enter into the intimate consciousness of the entities and spheres he contacts.

The reason for this is that in order fully to know anything, one must *be* it; temporarily, at least, one must *become* it, if he would understand precisely what it is in all its reaches. His consciousness must merge with the consciousness of the entity or thing which he is at that instant learning to know the meaning of. Hence the quasi-mystical stories of the 'descent' of the initiant into 'hell' in order to learn what the life of the hellions is, and what their sufferings are; and also partly in order to bring out the compassion of the one experiencing what these entities go through as the karmic result of their own misdeeds. And equally, in the other direction, the initiant must learn how to become at one with the gods and to confer with them. To understand their nature and their life, he must for the time being himself become a god; in other words, enter into his own highest being.

Thus beginning with this fourth initiation the neophyte slips into new realms of consciousness; the spiritual fires of the inner constitution are most potent both in character and in functioning; the spiritual electricity, so to speak, flows with far more powerful current. One cannot really put these mystical things into everyday words. In addition to the teachings and the symbolic or dramatic ritual, the neophyte — and he is always such, no matter how high the degree may be — learns how to control nature's forces and become able to accomplish such wonders as consciously leaving the body, leaving our planet in order to pass to other centers of the solar system.

The fifth degree is along the same pathways of experience, when the man becomes a master of wisdom and compassion. In this degree there comes the final choice: whether, like the great Buddhas of Compassion, one will return to help the world, to live for it and not for self; or whether, like the Pratyeka-Buddhas, one will go forwards on the pathway of self — merely self-development.

The sixth initiation runs to still loftier realms of consciousness and experience; and then comes the last and supreme initiation, the seventh, which comprises the meeting face to face with one's divine self, and the becoming-at-one with it. When this occurs, he needs no other teacher. It also includes individual communication with the supreme Mahāchohan, who is practically identical with what has been called the Silent Watcher of the human race.

Each degree stands on its own basis of rule and training. Nevertheless, the one rule runs through all, to wit, that the supreme guide for the neophyte is the god within himself, which is his final spiritual and intellectual tribunal, and in second order only comes his teacher. To such the disciple gives glad allegiance — but in no case blind obedience — for he knows by this time that his own inner god and the inner god of the teacher are both sparks of Alaya's self.

I might add that the higher the degree, the more informal and less ritualistic become the relations between teacher and pupil, and the more is the pupil expected to strive to live in and to be at one with his inner divine monitor. Further, in the more advanced stages no record of any kind is made. It is solely the memory of the auditors which is trained to receive and to retain what has been impressed upon it, a training which a dependence upon written notes could never bring about. Neither in writing, in paint, in cipher nor in engraving, are the teachings committed to visible record; they are carried in the mind and in the heart alone.

The whole endeavor is to arouse the will power, the individuality, and the native faculties of the inner god. The transmission of intelligence, therefore, passes at low breath and with mouth to ear, to use the old saying. In the highest degrees not even this is permitted, for the neophyte, the recipient of esoteric knowledge and wisdom, has become so trained that he can receive by thought-transference, as it were, and need not even be in the presence of his teacher. More and more the teacher communicates through the soundless sound, the voice of the silence, the voice in which the teachings 'uttered' opens the spiritual vistas within the disciple.

Every step forwards is a going into a greater light, in comparison with which the light just left is shadow. No matter how high one stands on the ladder of evolution, even as high as the gods, there is always one other just ahead, one who knows more than he; and ahead of him there is a constantly ascending range of entities of progressively vaster cosmic consciousness. The hierarchical stream is nature's basic framework; hence, none of us is without a teacher, for there is the infinite universe above us — hierarchies of life and of evolutionary experience far superior to ours.

Consequently, when the monadic essence of a man, after leaving our own hierarchy, advances into the sublimer realms of cosmic Being, he does so as an embryo-entity, therein beginning his next upward climb on the first round of that new ladder of life, when perforce he will need someone to guide his steps. And that need for guides and teachers will remain until, in the course of the cycling ages, he will have climbed higher and higher to the topmost rung of *that* ladder of life, when again he shall become at one with that still sublimer mystery of the inmost of the inmost of his being. And to this sublimer mystery what name can we give? Human language fails, and only the spiritual imagination can soar into the spheres of the divine. Thus the evolving entity passes continually from one to another range of life, from one to another hierarchy of ineffable experience — and thus forwards forever. Is it not self-evident that one is always a learner in the school of life, for there are veils upon veils covering the face of eternal Reality?

When once the spiritual understanding has come, forgetfulness can never thereafter ensue. It is precisely in the inability to wipe out from the memory the glory seen and almost touched that lies the wretchedness of failure undergone by the unsuccessful aspirant. He who has never experienced heaven, yearns toward it, and with hope of success; whereas he who has skirted its boundaries and had a glimpse of the supernal through its portals, and then fails to pass within, will remember enough to fill his soul with agony and even despair at the remembrance of the vision seen and lost.

When it comes to the severe tests, terrific as they are in the more advanced degrees, the mentality must be such that it will repel outside influences of the most persuasive character. Such influences arise in impressionability, at once a great virtue, but in many respects a fatal weakness; and another psychological factor to be carefully watched is the too strong and too quick logical faculty of the brain-mind. The mentality must be rigidly subordinated to the nobler attributes and not usurp the place of mastery; if it is made subservient, then it is of genuine value. The higher mind rooted in the buddhi principle has an infallible logic as well as an infallible intuition of its own, of which the brain-mind procedures are pale and usually distorted reflections, and because of this are often most dangerous enemies.

One cannot trifle with occultism with impunity. The entire nature is aroused, and the battle with the lower self at times may take on the character of desperation, for the neophyte instinctively feels that he must conquer or fail. But if he perform faithfully the first duty that comes to hand, no matter how humble and simple, that is his path. In conquering our own weaknesses, we help not only our own nature, but all mankind; more, we help every sentient, living thing, for we are at one with the very forces which are the circulations of the universe.

To achieve the bond of union with one's essential Self is the supreme aim of initiation.° It is the pathway to the gods, which means making of each one of us an individual divinity. The following of this pathway is a most serious, a most sacred undertaking. It will call forth every particle

---

°For some reason there has been a singular misapprehension among a few to the effect that the highest initiations are denied to women. This is not the case. There is nothing in the world that prevents a woman from reaching the noblest pinnacle of attainment, from passing successfully the most severe tests of initiation. However, those who take the highest initiations usually do so in a man's body, simply because it is easier, the psychological and physiological apparatuses being better prepared for passing those initiations. But it is downright foolish to suppose that initiation in any age past or present has been or is the prerogative or especial privilege of men.

One has but to recall the long and uninterrupted line of prophetesses, even in the anthropomorphic and materialistic civilizations of historic Greece and Rome, to realize that women had their place in the temple schools and achieved high and outstanding honors in the esoteric training. The Oracle at Delphi is perhaps the most widely known; other examples are the Celtic Druids and the Germanic peoples who were famous in antiquity for their women leaders, their seeresses and prophetesses. However much women initiates may have kept behind the veil of seclusion, their inner capacity and power to achieve were universally recognized.

of strength, of will power, that one's nature contains, if one wishes to go forward to the sublime ultimate. How to achieve this is by totally ignoring the knot of personality, thus passing into the smooth, orbital movement of consciousness existing around the central core of one's being, and then finally to blend and become at one with the sublime wonder, the divinity within.

Behind every veil there is another, but through them all shines the light of truth, the light that liveth forever within every one of us, for it is our inmost self. Every human being in the core of the core of his essence is a sun, destined to become one of the starry hosts in the spaces of Space, so that even from the very first instant when the divine-spiritual part of us begins its peregrinations throughout universal Being, it is already a sun in embryo, a child of some other sun that then existed in space. Initiation brings forth this inner, latent, stellar energy in the heart of the neophyte.

Aham asmi Parabrahman, I am the boundless All — beyond both space and time. This idea is the very keystone of the temple of ancient truth. It is mother nature in her divine, spiritual, psychological, ethereal, and physical reaches that is our universal home — a home having no specific location because it is everywhere.

Here, then, is the pathway by which any son of man may ascend, if he have the inflexible will to do so and the yearning for a greater light. He may rise along the different stages of the hierarchy, taking each step upwards through an initiation until his being finally becomes at one with the Silent Watcher of our globe. Then, at a period still more distant, his monad will become at one with the Silent Watcher of our planetary chain and, at a period still more remote in cosmic time, he will become identified as an individual monadic life-center with the hierarch of our solar universe.

The inmost of us *is* the inmost of the universe: every essence, every energy, every power, every faculty, that is in the boundless All is in each one of us, active or latent. All the great sages have taught the same verity: "Man, know thyself," which means going inwards in thought and feeling, in ever-greater measure allying ourselves self-consciously with the divinity at the core of our being — the divinity which also is the very heart of the universe. There, indeed, is our home: boundless, frontierless Space.

Space and the Doctrine of Māyā

Space and the Doctrine of Māyā

THE VOID AND THE FULLNESS

"What is it that ever is?" "Space, the eternal Anupadaka." "What is it that ever was?" "The Germ in the Root." "What is it that is ever coming and going?" "The Great Breath." "Then, there are three Eternals?" "No, the three are one. That which ever is is one, that which ever was is one, that which is ever being and becoming is also one: and this is Space."
— The Secret Doctrine, I, 11

OF ALL THE truly wondrous teachings of the ancient wisdom, otherwise called the esoteric philosophy or theosophy, there is perhaps none so replete with suggestive thought as the doctrine concerning Space. In one of its aspects it is called Śūnyatā, a profoundly significant word found in the more mystical doctrines of Gautama the Buddha, meaning emptiness or the void; and in another aspect it is Pleroma, a Greek word frequently used by the Gnostics signifying fullness.

Modern astronomers often speak of empty space, and while this seems at first glance to be pretty much the same thing as Śūnyatā, we reject the idea if by empty space they mean absolute vacuity — something which is nonexistent. The extraordinary thing is that even the scientists, if driven into a corner by probing questions, would themselves acknowledge that this phrase merely signifies portions of space or cosmical fields which contain no 'matter,' i.e. no physical matter which they with their instruments can cognize or see.

When we examine the limitless expanse of boundless Space around us, as far as our vision and our imagination can carry us, we see fields of apparent cosmic emptiness sprinkled throughout with glittering stars, and with millions upon millions of wisps of light that are nebulae which, under the resolving power of the telescope, are seen to be universes themselves of other stars and star clusters — or again, vast bodies of cosmic gas. However, they are not gas in any single instance; but this need not concern us here except to remark that many, if not all, of these irresolvable nebulae belong to ranges of matter superior to the physical, which as yet have never been studied in the laboratory. In other words, they are composed of ethereal matter of a higher plane than our physical plane.

Wherever we look, we are cognizant that the universe is an immense fullness. When we add to this our knowledge of the structure of matter, composed as it is of molecules, atoms, and these again of electronic and protonic and other bodies, we realize that what seems to us to be empty space must actually be fields of cosmic ether which, because of its ethereality, neither our organ of vision, nor our sense of touch, nor our most delicate instruments, can subject to experimentation. Yet all these vast fields of glittering orbs are contained in the low cosmic plane which we know as the physical or material universe. We realize further that the physical sphere is but the outer garment hiding incomprehensibly immense inner or invisible worlds, ranging from the physical upwards into the ever-receding vistas of cosmic spirit which last, because it is to us formless, we call the spiritual Void or Emptiness, Śūnyatā. Not only does Śūnyatā signify the highest and most universal ranges of the boundless Infinite, but so does Pleroma. It all depends upon which angle of vision we take.

The doctrine of the Void, then, is identic in fundamental conception with the doctrine of the Fullness. There is a distinction, however, in that the doctrine of the Void is the more spiritual of the two, as it treats chiefly of the superior element-principles of the kosmos,° of the inwards and the yet more inwards of the spaces of Space; whereas the doctrine of the Fullness treats of the kosmoi or worlds as they are in manifestation. We can more easily comprehend the fullness of things than we can the profoundly mystical thought that out of the illimitable Void spring into life all the innumerable manifestations of kosmic Being; and that back into the same Void they disappear when their life cycle has run.

In other words, the Void has reference to the divine-spiritual side of Being; whereas the Fullness, the Pleroma,† refers to the prakriti or matter

---

°Throughout our literature there has been a consistent vagueness with regard to the difference, if any, between kosmos and cosmos. This is a Greek word, and if we desire to be strictly etymological, it should be spelled with a 'k' in all cases. Yet there is a certain advantage in adopting both terms: using kosmos to signify the greater universe, which almost invariably would mean the galaxy or a collection of galaxies, and cosmos to signify our solar system. It is somewhat of a pity that this usage has not been systematically followed by theosophical authors, including the present writer.

†There is in Sanskrit a term that is the precise philosophic and scientific equivalent of the Pleroma of the Greeks: Brahmānda-pūrna. Brahmānda or Egg of Brahmā applies not to any one particular solar system, planetary chain or galaxy, but to any or all, depending upon the scale used at the time. By adding the adjective pūrna, which means full, the idea of the World Egg as being filled with manifested entities is strengthened and better defined.

side, the side of manifestation, which vanishes away like a dream when the great manvantara or period of world activity is finished.

Another important point is that every *manifested* being or thing, precisely because of its temporal existence as a phenomenon, is noneternal. It is in consequence māyā or illusion; and therefore it would be foolish to search for the cosmic Real in such phenomena. Whatever makes an appearance in the fields of the Boundless, whether a collection of galaxies or an atom, whatever it be which is thus an object or a form, and no matter how short or how long its life term, is nevertheless an appearance, a phenomenon, and therefore is *de facto* empty in the sense of nonreal — which is an exactly opposite use of the term empty or void employed before. However, this opposite sense is strictly legitimate in metaphysical philosophy; and we see therefore why esoteric Buddhism constantly speaks of all the manifested universe as Śūnyatā, because nonreal, nonenduring, therefore temporary and transitory.

In the *Śūrangama-Sūtra*° (iv, 65) we find:

In this investigation, therefore, you must clearly understand that all mundane forms which enter into the composition of the phenomenal world are transitory and perishable. Ananda! of all these forms which you see, of the fictile nature alluded to, what one is there not destructible? They are all destined to be burned up; but after their destruction there is one thing that can never perish, and that is the void of space.

Nevertheless, it is these vast aggregates of worlds which form the Pleroma or Fullness of manifested space. The difficulty lies in the double usage of these two words, Śūnyatā and Pleroma; and yet this is easily understood when the root-thoughts are grasped. As H. P. Blavatsky expressed it:

Space is neither a "limitless void," nor a "conditioned fulness," but both: being, on the plane of absolute abstraction, the ever-incognisable Deity, which is void only to finite minds, and on that of *mayavic* perception, the Plenum, the absolute Container of all that is, whether manifested or unmanifested: it is, therefore, that ABSOLUTE ALL. — *The Secret Doctrine*, I, 8

Śūnyatā, as a word, can thus be taken with two different yet co-related meanings. When considered as a positive term, it stands for the boundless All, Space in its highest and most abstract sense, implying endless and

---

°Cf. Samuel Beal's *A Catena of Buddhist Scriptures from the Chinese* (1871).

limitless infinitude with no qualifications whatsoever, as well as the all-encompassing, endless, Fullness of the All. It is the universe with everything that is in it seen from the standpoint of the spiritual-divine realms, which to intelligences living in lower spheres seems to be the Great Void — Mahāśūnya.*

When Śūnyatā is considered negatively, it stands for the idea of kosmic illusion, the mahāmāyā. From the viewpoint of the divine-spiritual consciousness, the entire objective universe, visible or invisible, is unreal and illusive because it is so impermanent. It is empty in the sense of being evanescent. Not that the manifested universe does not exist; it does, or it could not provide an illusion, but it is not that which it *seems* to be. Thus both the positive and negative meanings of Śūnyatā are founded upon the same basic idea, namely, the reality of the divine-spiritual, and the relative unreality of all that is objective. The manifested kosmos, being relatively false and deceptive, is empty of essential significance when compared with the Real which it hides as if with a veil. It possesses only a relative reality derivative from the noumenal Root of which this objective universe is the phenomenal aspect.

To turn again to the *Śūrangama-Sūtra* (v, 8):

> The Pure Nature, as to its substantial Being, is empty; the influences, therefore, that produce birth are as a magical delusion. The absence of action, and the absence of beginning and end — these also are false ideas, like a sky-flower. The word 'false' does but originate (manifest) that which is true — false and true are together equally false; . . . Are not all things around us but as a bubble?

The Boundless, the infinitude of encompassing Space, is obviously beyond reach of any human conception, because it is both formless and without confining frontiers, and yet is the cosmic womb of all the universes which appear from it like "sparks of Eternity." Therefore have mystics of various ages and of all countries called it the Void.

This in fact was the original and truly sublime idea which the earliest Christian theological speculators seized upon and called 'Nothing,' thus not merely distorting but positively nullifying the conception as it was in its primeval grandeur. From that day to this, orthodox theology has

---

*The terms Śūnya, Śūnyatā, Mahāśūnya and Mahāśūnyatā, are not radically different from each other, the sole distinction being that the terms beginning with mahā — meaning great — apply to a scale of far vaster magnitude both in space and in duration.

made God Almighty create the world out of nothing, which is absurd. Had they conceived of this precosmic Utterness as No-Thing, then they would have preserved the correct idea. But they reduced it to nothingness. Preserving the verbal form, they lost the spirit.

Through the ages man in his uninitiated mind has degraded the intuitions of his spirit, confounding the objective and the illusory with the Real and, what is still more serious for his moral and spiritual well-being, ungearing the aspiring intellect from its root in the Boundless.

Let us not forget that we ourselves are offsprings of the Boundless, and urged by the impelling energy of our spirit are advancing through inner struggles and trials — always advancing to that ultimate consummation of our spiritual self with that limitless Wonder which is our inmost. Yet, most marvelous of paradoxes, this Wonder is throughout eternity unattainable, for it is limitless Space and frontierless Duration.

THE BOUNDLESS IN ANCIENT COSMOGONIES

Nowhere and by no people was speculation allowed to range *beyond* those *manifested* gods. The boundless and infinite UNITY remained with every nation a virgin forbidden soil, untrodden by man's thought, untouched by fruitless speculation. The only reference made to it was the brief conception of its diastolic and systolic property, of its periodical expansion or dilatation, and contraction. In the Universe with all its incalculable myriads of systems and worlds disappearing and re-appearing in eternity, the anthropomorphised powers, or gods, their Souls, had to disappear from view with their bodies: — "The breath returning to the eternal bosom which exhales and inhales them," says our Catechism. . . .

In every Cosmogony, behind and higher than the *creative* deity, there is a superior deity, a planner, an Architect, *of whom* the Creator is but the executive agent. And still higher, *over* and *around, within* and *without,* there is the UNKNOWABLE and the *unknown,* the Source and Cause of all these Emanations. — *The Secret Doctrine,* II, 42–3

MANY ARE THE names in the ancient literatures which have been given to the Womb of Being from which all issues, in which all forever is, and into the spiritual and divine reaches of which all ultimately returns, whether infinitesimal entity or macrocosmic spacial unit.

The Tibetans called this ineffable mystery *Tong-pa-ñid,* the unfathomable Abyss of the spiritual realms. The Buddhists of the Mahāyāna school describe it as Śūnyatā or the Emptiness, simply because no human imagination can figurate to itself the incomprehensible Fullness which it is. In the *Eddas* of ancient Scandinavia the Boundless was called by the suggestive term *Ginnungagap* — a word meaning yawning or uncircumscribed void. The Hebrew Bible states that the earth was formless and void, and darkness was upon the face of *Tehōm,* the Deep, the Abyss of Waters, and therefore the great Deep of kosmic Space. It has the identical significance of the Womb of Space as envisioned by other peoples. In the Chaldaeo-Jewish Qabbālāh the same idea is conveyed by the term *'Eyn* (or *Ain*) *Sōph,* without bounds. In the Babylonian accounts of Genesis, it is *Mummu Tiamatu* which stands for the Great Sea or Deep. The archaic Chaldaean cosmology speaks of the Abyss under the name of *Ab Soo,* the Father or source of knowledge, and in primitive Magianism it was *Zervan Akarana* — in its original meaning of Boundless Spirit instead of the later connotation of Boundless Time.

In the Chinese cosmogony, *Tsi-tsai*, the Self-Existent, is the Unknown Darkness, the root of the *Wuliang-sheu*, Boundless Age. The *wu wei* of Lao-tse, often mistranslated as passivity and nonaction, imbodies a similar conception. In the sacred scriptures of the Quichés of Guatemala, the *Popol Vuh* or "Book of the Azure Veil," reference is made to the "void which was the immensity of the Heavens," and to the "Great Sea of Space." The ancient Egyptians spoke of the Endless Deep; the same idea also is imbodied in the *Celi-Cēd* of archaic Druidism, Cēd being spoken of as the "Black Virgin" — Chaos — a state of matter prior to manvantaric differentiation.

The Orphic Mysteries taught of the Thrice-Unknown Darkness or *Chronos,* about which nothing could be predicated except its timeless Duration. With the Gnostic schools, as for instance with Valentinus, it was *Bythos*, the Deep. In Greece, the school of Democritus and Epicurus postulated *To Kenon*, the Void; the same idea was later voiced by Leucippus and Diagoras. But the two most common terms in Greek philosophy for the Boundless were *Apeiron*, as used by Plato, Anaximander and Anaximenes, and *Apeiria*, as used by Anaxagoras and Aristotle. Both words had the significance of frontierless expansion, that which has no circumscribing bounds.

Chaos° was another word used for Space in ancient Greek writings, and as originally employed, for instance by Hesiod in his *Theogony* (116) — "Truly, indeed, was Chaos first of all" — it had the meaning of the Void. Even the somewhat orthodox poet Milton grasped this idea in his "Void and formless Infinite" (*Paradise Lost*, Bk. III). As time passed, however, Chaos to most literate Greek thinkers came to mean a later stage in the evolution of any particular kosmos, and this would correspond to another phrase used by Milton, "Matter unformed and void" (Bk. VII); for here we have matter already existing through emanational unfoldment in its primordial or elemental stages. It would therefore be analogous to the Second Cosmic Logos of the theosophical philosophy.

Yet the earliest conception of Chaos was that almost unthinkable

---

°Chaos (χάος) comes from an ancient Greek root *cha* (χα) that has the twofold meaning of holding and releasing; hence chaos is the 'holder' and 'releaser' of all things.

condition of kosmic space or kosmic expanse, which to human minds is infinite and vacant extension of primordial Aether, a stage *before* the formation of manifested worlds, and out of which everything that later existed was born, including gods and men and all the celestial hosts. We see here a faithful echo of the archaic esoteric philosophy, because among the Greeks Chaos was the kosmic mother of Erebos and Nyx, Darkness and Night — two aspects of the same primordial kosmic stage. Erebos was the spiritual or active side corresponding to Brahman in Hindu philosophy, and Nyx the passive side corresponding to pradhāna or mūlaprakriti, both meaning root-nature. Then from Erebos and Nyx as dual were born Aether and Hemera, Spirit and Day — Spirit being here again in this succeeding stage the active side, and Day the passive aspect, the substantial or vehicular side. The idea was that just as in the Day of Brahmā of Hindu cosmogony things spring into active manifested existence, so in the kosmic Day of the Greeks things spring from elemental substance into manifested light and activity, because of the indwelling urge of the kosmic Spirit.

The early philosopher-initiates were extremely reticent, because of their oath of secrecy, in speaking of the kosmic (or cosmic) beginnings; and hence while archaic Greek literature, exactly as the literatures of all other ancient peoples, is replete with references to primordial cosmic beginnings, these are cloaked in carefully guarded language. There was the constant fear that teachings so abstract and difficult would be distorted and degraded if too openly enounced, becoming the common property of minds untrained by the discipline and teachings of the Mysteries. The common misunderstanding of Chaos as signifying merely confusion, or an unregulated vast aggregate of atoms in kosmic space, is simply a degradation of the original philosophical meaning.

We have then, first, Chaos as originally meaning the Boundless; and, as a later development, the conception of Chaos as the mighty womb of nature evolving from itself the germs and seeds in order to form and bring into being manifested worlds. These seeds were the sleeping monads of spiritual and divine characteristics coming over from the preceding kosmic period of manvantaric manifestation, and existing in their nirvana or paranirvana.

Chaos, therefore, may be looked upon as an expanse of spirit-substance, every point of which is a consciousness center or monad. This expanse is enwrapped in the paranirvanic rest and bliss, awaiting the time for awaking into a period of manifested kosmic life. The human monad resting in its devachanic bliss is an exact analogy on its own lower plane.

From the foregoing we see that Chaos was the same as Brahman-pradhāna in its condition of kosmic pralaya, and hence is identic with Space in its primordial state of abstract spirit-substance.

Thus it is that many peoples looked upon the Divine not only as being in itself utter Fullness, but likewise as the infinite Abyss, the boundless Void, the endless Deep, or the ocean of the kosmic Waters of Life. Water was so favorite a symbol of Space because of its suggestiveness: it is at one and the same time translucent, and yet solid; it is crystalline and yet dense, making it an excellent symbol of kosmic Aether. This sublime concept has been universal since the beginning of conscious thinking man on our earth in this round, and whether the adept was Lemurian, Atlantean, Turanian, or Aryan, the same intuitive conception guided the thoughts of all.

SPACES OF SPACE

SPACE, which, in their ignorance and iconoclastic tendency to destroy every philosophic idea of old, the modern wiseacres have proclaimed "an abstract idea" and a *void*, is, in reality, the container and *the body of the Universe* with its seven principles. It is a body of limitless extent, whose PRINCIPLES, in Occult phraseology — each being in its turn a septenary — manifest in our phenomenal world only the grossest fabric of *their sub-divisions.*   — *The Secret Doctrine*, I, 342

IN THE VISION of the ancient wisdom, Space is vastly more than a mere container, for it is fundamental essence, all-being, and not only the field of boundless life and frontierless mind, but actually the very stuff of mind and consciousness and life.

Further, Space is seven-, ten- or twelvefold, according to the manner of viewing it; and just because Space is the great web of the infinite number of hierarchies, *is* it these hierarchies themselves from the super-divine to the submaterial.° Space thus being manifold, there are what we may call the spaces of Space: not only the boundless fields of physical space, but, of incomparably greater importance, the limitless fields of inward Space — Space within, and still more withinwards. Space, in short, is everything, when considered abstractly; and, just because it is everything that is, it contains all minor beings and entities and things within its own encompassing infinitude, and indeed in this sense it is a container.

To illustrate: our galaxy in all its reaches not only is contained within its own space, but *is* that space itself; and, being an aggregate entity, it has its own swabhāva or essential characteristic or individuality, or what might be called kosmic soul. Our galaxy is contained within a kosmic unit of still vaster magnitude, which in its turn has its own swabhāva. In the other direction every galaxy contains many solar systems, each

---

°Cf. *The Mahatma Letters to A. P. Sinnett*, p. 404:

"The book of *Khiu-te* teaches us that space is infinity itself. It is formless, immutable and absolute. Like the human mind, which is the exhaustless generator of ideas, the Universal Mind or Space has its ideation which is projected into objectivity at the appointed time; but space itself is not affected thereby."

74

one of which is a spacial unit within its own spacial boundaries, i.e. it actually is the space it occupies within the greater space of the galaxy. Similarly so with a planet, such as our earth. It occupies space within the larger space of its solar system, yet is itself the space which it thus makes or forms within that solar system.

From the human standpoint, Space may be considered as being the higher principle-elements of a cosmos in the Boundless. Here we see another reason why Space is much more than a mere container of things. It has, it is true, the ordinary meaning of distance between objects; but, more importantly, Space is distance or extension inwards and upwards towards spirit and beyond into the abysmal deeps of the Divine. As H.P.B. has written: ". . . it is in space that dwell the intelligent Powers which *invisibly* rule the Universe."[°]

Any universe, or any smaller entity within it, such as a sun or a planet or a man, is a god imbodied. Consider man: a physical body in his lowest part, in his highest part a divine monad, a god; and in between there are all the intermediate and invisible ranges of his constitution. Just so is it with any universe, or sun, or planet. Going a step farther, we see that the space of any one universe is the visible-invisible 'body' of such universe. Its essence is divine, just as man in his essence is divine, although a physical human being when in incarnation upon earth, or when in a comparable imbodiment on any other globe of our planetary chain.

It is because Space, that is any spacial unit, is both conscious and substantial, that we can view the space of any one universe as an entity — a god. Essentially it is a divine entity of which we see only the material and energic aspect, behind which is the causal life and intelligence. There are innumerable such 'spaces' in the frontierless fields of the Boundless, and every such unit is a larger or smaller Egg of Brahmā or a cosmos, all existing within and forming part of the structure of an incomprehensibly vaster Space inclosing all.

Every spacial unit or celestial entity, like our solar system or our galaxy or some still greater kosmic unit, is a being, alive, infilled with mind, having its own karmic destiny and thus repeating on the grand scale what we and all other smaller units enact in our own microcosmic spheres.

Space, therefore, is at once consciousness throughout and substance throughout. It is, indeed, Consciousness-Mind-Substance. For all space

---

[°]*The Secret Doctrine,* II, 502.

is alive,° quivering with incessant activity; indeed, every point of infinite space can truly be looked upon as a consciousness center or monad, whether these monads be actively engaged in manvantaric operations and experience, or whether crystallized in passivity awaiting the coming of the magic touch from the spirit within. Moreover, every organic part of space, that is, every spacial unit or cosmic entity, as an aggregate, differs from all others because of its indwelling swabhāva or characteristic individuality.

From the time when H.P.B. began to write more or less openly about the esoteric aspect of the theosophical teachings, there have been in use certain terms, mostly taken from the Sanskrit language, to describe Space, Aether, Ether, Pleroma, etc. Among them, ākāśa — from the verbal root ākāś, signifying to shine, to be bright, like light — has been the most frequently employed.† It is essentially the spiritual and ethereal 'body' of manifested cosmic space, the subtle and ethereal cosmic 'fluid' pervading every manifested universe. It is the invisible cosmic field in and from which all the celestial bodies are born, in which they exist during their respective manvantaras, and into which they are again gathered at the manvantaric end.

Now because ākāśa is of such extremely tenuous or immaterial character, it is often rather loosely spoken of as being the emptiness of space,

---

°Professor John Elof Boodin, in his article "The Universe a Living Whole," *The Hibbert Journal*, July, 1930, has written:

"What we ordinarily think of as space is a mere negation. It is no thing in the sense of not matter. If we think of the cosmos as a living whole, what we call empty space may be the soul of the whole — all-pervasive spirit in which the transmitted patterns of energy are immanent and directed to their proper target. At any rate, to one who conceives the cosmos as a living whole space has lost its terror."

†Two other words for space, the spacial ether, etc., are *bhūman* and *kha*. Bhūman, from *bhū*, to become, conveys the fundamental idea of becoming, of growth and progress by serial steps. It is that portion of the universal ākāśa comprised within any single Brahmānda or cosmic hierarchy, and therefore on this smaller scale applies to the aggregate of all beings and things within that hierarchy. As such, it can carry the meaning of Pleroma or Fullness.

The word *kha* likewise has the sense of space and also ether because its original meaning is a hollow, a spacial cavity, popularly rendered by ether, sky, heaven, even air. Its usage is usually restricted to our atmosphere alone: as in *kha-ga* and *khe-chara*, both meaning going in the air, like a bird. H.P.B. in *The Voice of the Silence* uses khe-chara as a title for those adepts who have evolved the faculty of moving in and through the air — more truly, the invisible spaces — in their māyāvi-rūpa or illusory body, exercising the power which in Tibet is called Hpho-wa.

i.e. free of matter; yet, in truth, ākāśa is really the spacial body of the universe, and hence is *manifested* space itself. As the aggregated fields of the spaces of any Egg of Brahmā, whether a galaxy or a solar system, ākāśa is the field of action of cosmic fohat — the vital force of the universe — guided as it always is by cosmic mind. Like all other things in nature, ākāśa is divisible into different planes or degrees, increasing in ethereality until it merges into pure kosmic spirit. Its higher portions are called anima mundi, the soul of our universe, just as its lowest ranges comprise the astral light. Like the Latin word *spatium*, ākāśa conveys the idea of extension or spacial deeps, but from a somewhat different viewpoint the term also is used for both aether and ether. In the enumeration of the seven cosmic principles or tattwas, ākāśa is reckoned as the fifth highest which, in mediaeval European mystic thought, was called the *quinta essentia* — the 'fifth essence' — our word quintessence.

I have used this term spaces of Space under the happy illusion that it would help others to gain still another magnificent conception of nature: that there is in both concrete and abstract space not a needle's point which lacks life, substance, being and consciousness. To phrase it otherwise: within our physical space there is a space more ethereal, with its worlds, its suns and planets, its comets and nebulae; celestial globes with their mountains and lakes, their forests and fields and their inhabitants. Within this second space, there is a still finer, a more ethereal and a more spiritual space, the cause of the two former, each inner space being a mother or producer of the outer space; and thus we carry these spaces within space onwards and upwards and inwards indefinitely. This is what I mean by the phrase the spaces of Space.

We now see why all space — infinite space, complex space, spaces within space — is fullness, and there is not a point, inner or outer, which is empty. Empty space is but a figment of ignorance; it does not exist. We forget that these higher or inner spaces, far from being nonexisting, are the cosmic roots of things. We speak of them as empty because we cannot sense them. And yet actually we hear them, see them, taste, smell, and touch them all the time, for the space around us is infilled with these inner spaces, is given substance, life, vitality, movement, death, everything by these inner spaces. They are the causes, the noumena; the outer are the phenomena, the consequences.

Indeed, in one sense, the spaces of Space are its seven, ten or twelve principles. This is one reason why H.P.B. speaks of Space as being the utmost divinity, and yet Space is all that is. It does not mean that the divinity is a stock or stone, and yet that stock or stone is not outside of divinity. We see that there are spaces within spaces, and that the stock or the stone is infilled with repetitions of itself in inner and higher planes. Yet it is not divinity because it is not the all. It is a portion, a part, and these things are illusions. Cut such a portion or part into ever finer and finer pieces, and we shall come to the molecule, to the atom, to the electron, and in theory to still finer bodies. But some time in this process we shall reach what is for us homogeneity, and that is the spirit of that space.

We may use the words cosmic planes for these cosmic spaces. The cosmic space we live in is the cosmic plane prithivī. It is a plane; it is a space. On the next plane above us, the celestial bodies and our earth are invisible, and where they exist the entities there will see what to them is unfilled space, empty space. The inhabitants of each space or plane see what their sense-apparatus has been evolved to seize and bring to their percipient mind.

This is what we mean by the spaces of Space, the fullness of Space, or the emptiness of Space, all different ways of expressing the same wonder. Just here we recall the teaching of the Lord Buddha to the effect that the essence of Being is Śūnyatā, a word meaning emptiness, vacuity, but never intended to mean absolute nothingness in the physical sense. Actually it is the most complete fullness; however, because our sense-apparatus is utterly unable to understand it, it therefore denies the existence of a cosmic All. But then our mind, which is of a much more spiritual character than the gross matter of our physical senses, enters the picture several planes higher than the physical plane and it begins to understand; and then, if we can take one more step by rising from the mind to our intuition, our intuition will tell us clearly that this so-called Śūnyatā is only emptiness to the sense, but a fullness to the spirit — for Śūnyatā actually is cosmic Spirit.

SPACE, TIME AND DURATION

It is worth while to point out the real significance of the sound but incomplete intuition that has prompted . . . the use of the modern expression, "the fourth dimension of Space." . . . The familiar phrase can only be an abbreviation of the fuller form — the *"Fourth dimension of* MATTER *in Space."* But it is an unhappy phrase even thus expanded, because while it is perfectly true that the progress of evolution may be destined to introduce us to new characteristics of matter, those with which we are already familiar are really more numerous than the three dimensions. The faculties, or what is perhaps the best available term, the characteristics of matter, must clearly bear a direct relation always to the senses of man. Matter has extension, colour, motion (molecular motion), taste, and smell, corresponding to the existing senses of man, and by the time that it fully develops the next charac- teristic — let us call it for the moment PERMEABILITY — this will correspond to the next sense of man — let us call it "NORMAL CLAIRVOYANCE"; thus, when some bold thinkers have been thirsting for a fourth dimension to explain the passage of matter through matter, and the production of knots upon an endless cord, what they were really in want of, was a *sixth characteristic of matter.* The three dimensions belong really but to one attribute or charac- teristic of matter — extension; and popular common sense justly rebels against the idea that under any condition of things there can be more than three of such dimensions as length, breadth, and thickness. These terms, and the term "dimension" itself, all belong to one plane of thought, to one stage of evolution, to one characteristic of matter. So long as there are foot-rules within the resources of Kosmos, to apply to matter, so long will they be able to measure it three ways and no more; . . . But these considerations do not militate in any way against the certainty that in the progress of time — as the faculties of humanity are multiplied — so will the characteristics of matter be multiplied also.   — *The Secret Doctrine*, I, 251-2

FROM THE VIEWPOINT of the esoteric philosophy it is never proper to speak of abstract Space as having length, breadth and thickness, for these dimensions apply only to manifested space. For convenience Space may be described as existing in two forms: abstract Space or the Boundless, and manifested space, which is equivalent to saying limited space — in other words, manifested entities, whether such be compounded like a solar

79

system, or smaller entities like a human body or an atom. It is only among such manifested spacial bodies, whether great or small, that we can truthfully speak of dimensions, because these signify distance and direction as well as position and volume. Thus our own solar system is a portion of manifested space existing in the abstract Space of the Boundless.

To speak of more than three dimensions of space is simply a misuse of terms, for dimension means mensuration, and it is only concrete things which can be measured. The Infinite, for instance, has no dimensions because it is not subject to measuring. Nevertheless, the idea of a fourth, fifth or sixth dimension is an intuition of inner and superior worlds, i.e. directions and distance inwards, so to speak, into the invisible spheres. If the word dimension be restricted to this meaning alone, then there would be no especial objection; but unfortunately modern science and philosophy have not as yet clearly envisaged the reality of worlds and spheres within and invisible to the outer worlds and spheres. On the other hand, scientific theory and speculation in certain respects are becoming so highly metaphysical that they not only are beginning to merge at certain points with the teachings of the esoteric philosophy, but in some instances are actually crossing these teachings and going off at a tangent.

For example, the idea that the universe is expanding, and that all the different celestial bodies are rushing away from each other with a velocity which increases directly in proportion to the distance from us, is due largely to Abbé Lemaître, and the theory seems to have been adopted in its totality by the often intuitive Eddington, as well as by other scientific thinkers. However, there are several reasons why this notion of an expanding universe is unacceptable.°

Sometimes in both science and philosophy it seems to be forgotten that the mathematical mill produces only what is put into it: that whatever comes out of the chopper at one end was put into it at the other. Mathematics is an instrument of human thought, an intellectual tool of immense value, but obviously it cannot manufacture truth, nor of itself produce verities.

Occultism affirms that in all things both great and small, whether a universe, a sun, a human being, or any other entity, there is a constant secular cyclical diastole and systole, similar to that of the human heart. These cyclical expansions and contractions are manifestations of the cosmic

---

°Cf. *The Esoteric Tradition,* pages 435–8.

poles or what we may perhaps call the universal heartbeat; and the Dutch astronomer and mathematical physicist Willem de Sitter seems to have grasped some intuition of this fact. But the idea of an expanding universe, which according to Lemaître is simply the vast cosmic expansion of an original titanic atom, is all wrong.

Such cosmic diastole and systole is nothing at all like the expanding universe. The framework or corpus of the universe, whether we mean by this term the galaxy or an aggregate of galaxies, is stable both in relative structure and form for the period of its manvantara — precisely as the human heart is, once it has attained its full growth and function.

These scientists apparently ignore the fact that space is boundless and that consequently, if a universe is expanding continuously according to their theory, the nebulae and other celestial bodies rushing away from us will finally attain a speed incomparably greater than light. Yet, according to modern scientific theory itself, and Einstein's general relativity speculations, this is impossible!

It requires but a little reflection to realize that it is an utter impossibility to think of space apart from time, or of time or rather duration as existent apart from space, because if there were no time connected with space, space could not exist for two consecutive instants; and similarly time exists only because of the continuing space which brings time into birth; and, similarly again, kosmic mind not only infills space but is space and time; and because kosmic mind *is*, and *is* continuously throughout endless duration, therefore it exists in endless duration, which duration is itself.

Following along this line of thought, we realize also that abstract mind or consciousness, or what is sometimes called spirit or divinity, must have time or duration in order for it to continue, and it must have space in which to be. As we cannot have three infinites, to wit, kosmic mind, kosmic space, and unending duration, because this would be a logical monstrosity, therefore these are not three distinct and separate things in their essence, but are merely three aspects of the one underlying and ever-perduring Reality.

We see, then, that mind or consciousness, duration or abstract time, and space, are fundamentally one; but due to the limitations brought about by the evolving forth of beings and entities which are all limited during manifestation, we have the *appearances* or māyā — or rather mahāmāyā — of duration broken up into time periods; abstract space divided into spacial units; and similarly kosmic mind or consciousness expressing itself in rivers of minor minds or conscious beings, ranging from the divinest of the divine to the most material of entities in the matter-worlds. It is these illusory divisions or manifesting rivers of lives which bring about the differences and wonderful variety that surround us, and which consequently produce in us the māyā or the illusion that flowing time is one thing, space is something quite different and consciousness is again essentially different.

Thus it is that duration is identical with both space and kosmic mind. Yet even this mystery of mysteries, Space-Mind-Duration, is the production or appearance to our highest intellect of that ineffable Mystery which is called the Nameless or THAT. We see likewise that past and future, when properly understood, melt together into "the eternal Now."

H.P.B. in her *Secret Doctrine* (I, 37) has the following remarkable statement about time:

> Time is only an illusion produced by the succession of our states of con-sciousness as we travel through eternal duration, and it does not exist where no consciousness exists in which the illusion can be produced; but "lies asleep." The present is only a mathematical line which divides that part of eternal duration which we call the future, from that part which we call the past. Nothing on earth has real duration, for nothing remains without change — or the same — for the billionth part of a second; and the sensation we have of the actuality of the division of "time" known as the present, comes from the blurring of that momentary glimpse, or succession of glimpses, of things that our senses give us, as those things pass from the region of ideals which we call the future, to the region of memories that we name the past. In the same way we experience a sensation of duration in the case of the instantaneous electric spark, by reason of the blurred and continuing impression on the retina. The real person or thing does not consist solely of what is seen at any particular moment, but is composed of the sum of all its various and changing conditions from its appearance in the material form to its disappearance from the earth. It is these "sum-totals" that exist from eternity in the "future," and pass by degrees through matter, to exist for eternity in the "past."

She says further (I, 62) that the archaic wisdom "divides boundless duration into unconditionally eternal and universal Time and a conditioned one (*Khandakâla*). One is the abstraction or noumenon of infinite time (Kâla); the other its phenomenon appearing periodically, as the effect of *Mahat* (the Universal Intelligence limited by Manvantaric duration)."

It may be helpful to realize that khandakāla is a Sanskrit compound term which means broken time, signifying that duration in the manifested universe has the appearance of being broken up into time periods, whether long or short. Thus a year is a 'breaking' of abstract time into a limited time period of some 365 days. As the years follow one after the other, they produce the māyāvi effect of an entity which we call time flowing continuously; yet, because of their cyclical nature they give us the impression that time manifests in a divided or broken fashion, but nevertheless in itself is undivided. The only wrong aspect of this conception is that time is viewed as a thing-in-itself, and different from the space and the mind in which these time periods appear.

Space-time continuum is a phrase originally due to the mathematical and philosophical genius of Einstein. While it is not always easy to ascertain just exactly what is meant by it, because opinions of the mathematicians themselves seem to vary greatly, the general idea is clear: that space and time are not two separate and distinct absolutes, but are two aspects of one and the same fundamental entity. What is lacking, however, is the far grander conception that both space and time as coordinate factors in manifestation are but the resultant of cosmic spirit-substance; yet certain scientific philosophers, such as Sir James Jeans, do have an intuition that the space-time continuum is in some mysterious way involved with cosmic mind.

Although cosmic mind, time and space are all one, they appear to be three different entities during kosmic manvantara, and this apparent division of the One into the three is what archaic philosophy calls mahā-māyā. As just said, what the scientific space-time continuum needs is the recognition that space-time is identic with kosmic consciousness or kosmic mind, and equally so with kosmic substance. Blend these into a single unified and fundamental Reality, and we have the idea in a thumbnail picture.

The space-time continuum is but a first hesitant step towards truth, an intuition as it were of the archaic teaching that, when all the manifested universes are resolved back into their primordial superspiritual condition, the many re-enter the One. Manifestation dissolves into primordial spiritual homogeneity, so that not only does manifested space disappear and time likewise end with space its alter ego, but also kosmic mind re-enters kosmic spirit and therefore vanishes away.

In the words of the *Chhāndogya-Upanishad* (I, 9, 1):

"To what does this world go back?"
"To space (ākāśa)," said he. "Verily, all things here arise out of space. They

disappear back into space, for space alone is greater than these; space is the final goal."

When Brahman breathes forth the universe, it is the outflowing of the Great Breath which thereupon instantly becomes Brahmā; the kosmic (or cosmic) manvantara is the life term of Brahmā. When this life term ends, then Brahmā re-enters its own spiritual essence or Brahman, and all manifested space vanishes into abstract or potential Space, and this is the indrawing of the Great Breath, or the beginning of kosmic pralaya.

COSMIC REALITY AND MAHĀMĀYĀ

> The Universe is called, with everything in it, MAYA, because all is tempo-
> rary therein, from the ephemeral life of a fire-fly to that of the Sun. Com-
> pared to the eternal immutability of the ONE, and the changelessness of
> that Principle, the Universe, with its evanescent ever-changing forms, must
> be necessarily, in the mind of a philosopher, no better than a will-o'-the-wisp.
> Yet, the Universe is real enough to the conscious beings in it, which are
> as unreal as it is itself.   — *The Secret Doctrine*, I, 274

A DIFFICULT THOUGHT to grasp is the relation of māyā or, cosmically
speaking, mahāmāyā, with Space and that Reality often referred to as
Parabrahman. The word Parabrahman is employed in two senses: first
as signifying beyond Brahman, implying whatever in boundless Space is
beyond the Brahman or loftiest hierarch of our galaxy or universe; and
the other sense, much less frequent because really less accurate, is a
considering of Parabrahman to be the nameless and invisible beginning
or summit of that which men in their strivings to understand the incomprehensible speak of as the Divinity.

Parabrahman is therefore no entity. An entity, no matter how vast,
implies limitation. Boundless Parabrahman is beginningless, endless, timeless, deathless Space — interior space as well as exterior. It is, in short,
the endless continuation of the cosmic life, the cosmic *Tat* — THAT.

For example, an entity inhabiting an electron of one atom of my body
may look upon the passage of time comprised by one human second as
an eternity, and all that is outside of that second would be Parabrahman
to this atomic inhabitant. The point of consciousness to which that entity
may have evolved would be such that to it the atom would be its universe.
But think of the multitudes of atoms contained within the portion of space
that could be covered by the point of a pin! The physical existence of
the tiny area of matter covered by the pinpoint would be boundless space
to such an inhabitant of an electron. We are just such electron-inhabitants
of a vaster world, and hence we call Parabrahman — both in the spacial
and in the qualitative sense — all that is beyond the reach of our highest
spiritual consciousness. That to us is Parabrahman.

In a very true sense Parabrahman can be considered identical with abstract Space. This Parabrahman-space is not only the aggregate of hierarchies of intelligences and consciousnesses throughout the Boundless, but is likewise all their fields of activity in frontierless Being. By contrast the mūlaprakritic side of the Boundless, which is the divine-spiritual substantiality of limitless being, provides the vehicles of the hierarchies of divine intelligences, and hence is called mahāmāyā or great illusion because all these vehicles are composite and transitory.

It is obvious that the māyā of the vast aggregate of galactic universes scattered over the fields of the Boundless does not mean utter illusoriness in the sense of something that has no real existence. It does signify, however, anything, great or small, long-lived or short-lived, which by comparison with eternity is transient, limited in duration, changeable, and therefore presenting all the aspects and attributes of shifting and unstable existence — although of course there are māyās which last for periods of time so long that to us they are like a quasi-eternity.

Parabrahman is the only Reality, the great fundamental; but although all the rest, all beneath, is māyā, still that māyā is the universe in which our constitution exists — just as much so as we are linked by our inmost with Parabrahman; and as Parabrahman is the All, therefore even māyā is its garment or manifestation. Mūlaprakriti, root-nature, surrounds Parabrahman, so to speak, just as the human consciousness surrounds man's spiritual consciousness. In man's own constitution the monadic essence is his only real part, nevertheless his consciousness at the present time is centered in his human part, and it is his duty to raise this part of himself up to becoming one in self-conscious union with the Parabrahman or monadic essence within.

In the ancient literatures figures of speech were used which, unless we search out their inner meaning, are apt to distract the attention away from essentials. For instance, it has been said of the Boundless that it "brings forth the Universe in sport, as at play"; it moves, and the universe thereupon appears. These phrases are but metaphors, suggestive and beautiful when we understand the essential verity behind them. The expression that Brahman evolves forth the universe as if at play, is meant to convey the truth that Brahman is the essential Reality, and that all the rest of the universe evolving through the cosmic ages is like a phantasmagoria flitting before the eye of the Divine.

Māyā therefore does not mean that the exterior world, as viewed by the central consciousness within, is nonexistent, because the exterior world itself is included within the all-inclusive Reality of Parabrahman. If this were not the case, we should have Parabrahman on one side, and māyā on the other, forming two opposite or conflicting energies or essences, and this is impossible because Parabrahman is the All.

Māyā indeed exists; but as Parabrahman is everything, is essential Being or Be-ness, therefore even māyā is included within its essence. This is the very heart of the teaching of Adwaita-Vedānta, as Śankarāchārya taught it. We as beings are māyāvi, but the heart of the heart of us is Parabrahman; and therefore each atom of these māyāvi garments that we wear contains its own fundamental element or essence, which also is the Parabrahman.

So we see that the real teaching concerning māyā does not mean that the universe is illusory in the sense of being nonexistent, but merely that for us, as for other entities in other universes, the Reality is the Parabrahman within the temple of the boundless Self, our inmost essence.

The universe, both visible and invisible, is built up of hierarchies, interlinking groups of entities living and working together, following a karmic destiny more or less the same for all. This rule of hierarchical structures extends throughout cosmic infinitude. While one hierarchy of the Boundless may have evolved into divinity, almost ready to pass out into the Great Beyond — Parabrahman — in order to begin a new course of evolution on a higher plane at some future cosmic date, in some other part of the Boundless a new hierarchy is coming into being. And this applies not only to planets but to suns, solar systems, to galaxies or universes. Nature repeats herself everywhere, although ringing the changes in a perfectly bewildering way as regards details. It is these changes and details which make the māyā of the universe. The essence of everything is boundless love, harmony, wisdom and limitless consciousness: *this* is the heart of every individual entity — no matter where, no matter when — the summit of his hierarchy which is for him his Brahman.

These Brahmans are simply infinite in number and all-varying in characteristics, and in shade of consciousness or individuality. It is these infinite variations which produce the cosmic māyā; yet, all together, considered as the All, and especially in their highest portion, they are technically grouped together as THAT. You cannot describe this mystery in human words. To call it God is absurd, for the universe is filled full with gods. Every man in his inmost is a god. Every atom in its heart of hearts is a god. Every sun in space is but the physical manifestation

87

of a god; and each one of us, in far distant aeons, will grow to be such a sun. This is achieved, not by our accreting unto ourselves bits of experience, bits of consciousness or of intelligence, after the mistaken Darwinian idea, but by evolving forth what already is the Parabrahman within. This is what Jesus meant when he spoke of himself and his Father in Heaven as being one.

PARABRAHMAN-MŪLAPRAKRITI

There are, assuredly, two forms of Brahma: the formed and the formless.
Now, that which is the formed is unreal; that which is the formless is real,
is Brahma, is light.
That light is the same as the sun. — *Maitrī-Upanishad,* VI, 3

IN THEOSOPHY as well as in the Adwaita-Vedānta, Parabrahman and its
cosmic veil mūlaprakriti — two sides or elements of the one fundamental
conception — often signify the boundless expanse of both space and time
beyond the Brahman and its veil pradhāna of our own universe. Now
it is erroneous to consider Parabrahman as an entity, however vast or
sublime, for an entity of any magnitude is *de facto* limited, and Parabrahman means 'beyond' Brahman, and Brahman is the Absolute, the hierarch
of a universe, in other words, the highest divine-spiritual entity of a universe
or cosmos. Thus, Parabrahman is no entity; it is Infinitude, THAT, the
incomprehensible All, which with its shoreless fields is beyond the reach
of either human or divine consciousness.

Absolute is a relative term. It is the philosophic One, the cosmic
Originant: from the One come the Two; from the Two the Triad; from
the Triad the cosmic Quaternary, which again through emanational evolution breaks up into the manifested multiplicity of differentiation. The
philosophic One, therefore, is the cosmic Absolute; but it is not the mystic
Zero, representing Infinitude. Consequently the Zero contains, because
it is Infinitude, an infinite number of cosmic Ones, otherwise cosmic
monads, and the multitudes of minor monads which are derivatives of
any such cosmic One. There are no Absolutes in the sense of Infinitudes.

Every being or thing, no matter how vast, is relative — related to
something else and to all else. Every Absolute is the hierarch of its own
hierarchy, the One from which all subsequent differentiations thereafter
emanate to the limit of that hierarchy. Each such Absolute is a cosmic
jīvanmukta, signifying an entity which has reached a condition of relatively
perfect liberation — the moksha or mukti of Brahmanism and the Latin
word absolutum, both meaning set free, free from servitude to all the
lower planes because master or originant thereof. Thus the Absolute is

the highest divinity or Silent Watcher of the Hierarchy of Compassion which forms the light side of a universe or cosmic hierarchy.

There is an enormous difference between the cosmic jīvanmukta, which is an Absolute, a cosmic 'freed one' — and THAT. If we miscall Infinity the Absolute, we immediately create a mental picture of a finite Being, however high. It is impossible philosophically to predicate absoluteness of Infinity. Infinity is neither absolute nor nonabsolute; absolute is an adjective, connoting certain logical attributes, and therefore implying limitation. Of Infinitude no such attributes can be predicated; it is neither conscious nor unconscious, because these and all other similar human attributes belong to manifested and therefore noninfinite beings and things.

The misuse of the word Absolute arose out of the Christian psychology of a personal God, an infinite Person, which European philosophers could not shake off. They pursued a logical train of thinking arising in a proper conception; but the term they used is wrong. A person cannot be infinite: this is a contradiction in terms. Although there can be an absolute person, the summit of a hierarchy, this hierarch is only one of an infinite number of other hierarchs; but the Infinite, without number, attribute, qualification or form, is nonabsolute. This strikes at the roots of old theological and philosophical superstitions. Although H.P.B. frequently employed the word Absolute in its ordinary and mistaken significance, she was keenly aware of its proper grammatical and logical use. In her *Theosophical Glossary*, under the term 'Absoluteness' she writes:

When predicated of the UNIVERSAL PRINCIPLE, it denotes an abstract noun, which is more correct and logical than to apply the adjective "absolute" to that which has neither attributes nor limitations, nor can IT have any.

As to mūlaprakriti: this is a Sanskrit compound containing mūla, root, and prakriti, nature; therefore signifying elemental or originant nature. It is the other side of Parabrahman, but more particularly the root-matter of every hierarchical system.

A universe is both; in its essence it is mūlaprakriti as well as Parabrahman because it is formed of hosts of individual monads. The heart of a monad is boundless Space; and boundless Space has two aspects, life or energy, and substance or form. You cannot separate the one from the other.

Life or energy is what we may call Parabrahman; the substance side or vehicular side is mūlaprakriti. Wipe out mūlaprakriti, if it were possible, which it is not, and you would have pure consciousness, pure energy; and that again is not possible, because energy and matter are two sides of the same thing as are force and substance. Electricity, for example, is both energic and substantial; consciousness is both energy and substance.

Our body is fundamentally mūlaprakriti, root-substance, fundamental essence, manifesting in form. So is everything else — a star, a bit of wood, a stone, a beast, a bit of thistledown floating in the air. Its essence is mūlaprakriti; and out in the abysmal spaces is mūlaprakriti, but also Parabrahman.

In these two words, Parabrahman and mūlaprakriti, we get a conception entirely different from the Occidental vague mental abstraction of an Infinite signifying but a negation — nonfinite. All that the *human* consciousness is able to postulate is that Parabrahman is exactly what we see around us — as far as our physical senses can translate it to us — but limitlessly so. Parabrahman, therefore, is not an entity; as a term it is a descriptive adjective turned into a noun, and means simply beyond Brahman. "As above, so below" — and there is no essential difference between the above and the below. Every atom has its home in a molecule; every molecule has its home in a cell; every cell in a body; every body in a greater body; the greater body, in this case our earth, has its habitat in the solar ether; the solar system has its home in the galaxy; the galaxy in the universe; the universe has its home in a vaster universe; and so on, ad infinitum. And that ad infinitum is our way of saying Parabrahman — with this profound and radical difference, however, that the root-idea is the inner, invisible, spiritual worlds, which Western thought almost universally ignores.

Everything exists in something else greater than itself, and contains hosts of beings inferior to itself. When H. P. Blavatsky called Parabrahman Space, she did not mean emptiness, but used it in much the same way as she used Duration. Just as Duration is filled with time, moments, time-instants, so Space is filled with manifested monads, and with Absolutes which are monads of a far advanced type containing armies and hosts of evolving inferior monads.

This is all that Parabrahman means, and mūlaprakriti is but its other side — the side of expansion and change. We can say that Parabrahman is the consciousness side and mūlaprakriti the space side. Parabrahman is not a kind of god. It is simply Space. Like the word infinite, it is a purely generalizing term, a confession that here the human consciousness stops. The term Boundless is likewise a verbal counter. This very Boundless is filled full of finite, bounded beings and things. We use these terms which are pure abstractions as if they were concrete realities, and create thoughts about them, and thereby cheat ourselves.

Everything — even what we call THAT — is contained in something greater. But the word THAT is nevertheless sufficient to include the entire range of this conception. A galaxy is a cosmic cell; and what are called island universes are other cosmic cells; and these cosmic cells are bathed in the intergalactic ether and are united into some ultracosmic, incomprehensible Being. So too the cells of a human body, although under the microscope appearing separate from each other, are united to form that body which in turn lives in a world.

As an interesting scientific expression of the same thought, I quote two passages from *Consider the Heavens* (1935), by the well-known American astronomer, Dr. Forest Ray Moulton:

> The essential units of which we are composed are molecules and chains of molecules. Our life processes are expressed in terms of their properties, our thoughts are conditioned by their interactions. But perhaps in the infinite series of cosmic units there are others which play the rôle of molecules in living organisms. Sub-electrons of the hundredth order may be the molecules, so to speak, of conscious beings which live through a million generations in what to us is a second of time. And super-galaxies of the hundredth order may similarly be the molecules of conscious beings whose life cycles consume unimaginable intervals of time. At any rate, it would be unjustifiable for us in our ignorance to assume that only on our level out of the infinite possibilities is there life.
>
> — p. 300

> Let us, therefore, once more assume the existence of intelligent beings whose constituent elements — whose atoms, so to speak — are galaxies or super-galaxies of stars. Their life cycles are measured in millions of billions of years, for such periods of time are required for important transformations of super-galaxies of the higher orders, which are for these beings only the cells in their bodies or the corpuscles of the blood which circulates in their veins. When they breathe there are exhaled from their nostrils torrents of super-galaxies; when their heart beats, the galaxies of a billion light-years are in convulsions. For these beings the galaxies which we know are only electrons or photons whose gravitational expansions and contractions and whose oscillations in form are expressed vaguely in wave packets. To their gross sense organs such minute physical units as galaxies have no accurately definable locations or motions, though these entities persist and possess a quantitative property. For them the galaxies are the primary

elementary units in a chaos out of which by statistical averages a considerable degree of order emerges in the super-galaxies. — p. 330

Summarizing then, Parabrahman and mūlaprakriti simply mean boundless Space with all its indwelling hosts of beings. At any one particular point of it a logos may be springing into manifestation from its pralaya, here, there, or anywhere: millions of these logoi may contemporaneously be bursting forth into new manvantaras, and other millions may be passing into their respective pralayas.

Cosmic evolution and its beginning has been generally described in ancient cosmogonies as: "In the beginning was THAT"; and this beginning did not mean an absolute commencement of all Infinitude, which is absurd, but one of any beginnings of a system in boundless Duration. At its commencement of time the logos springs forth, the logos meaning one of these innumerable monadic points in THAT; and from this one logos is evolved forth a hierarchy — whether it be a cosmic hierarchy or a solar system, a human being or an atom. And these logoic points are numberless, every mathematical point in space being a potential logos.

Within and surrounding all such manifestations of cosmic logoi or universes, there is that mystery of mysteries which in their reverence the archaic sages rarely ever spoke of otherwise than by allusion, and which the Vedic rishis in ancient India called TAT. This is the Nameless, as much beyond the intuition of the highest gods in all manifested universes, as it is beyond the understanding of man. It is frontierless Infinitude, beginningless and endless Duration, and the utterly incomprehensible boundless Life which for ever is.

MANVANTARA: A DREAM, A MĀYĀ

O Brāhman, this earth and other things of the universe have for their substratum the mind, and do not exist at any period apart from the mind. Almost all persons in this world, walking in the path of this universe of dreams, delusion and egoism, look upon it as real and enjoy it. It is only in Chitta (the flitting mind) that the universe rests. . . . Truly marvelous are the effects or manifestations of the mind, like the analogy of a crow and the palmyra fruits. Thus do diverse persons view the one dream (of the universe) in various ways. With one sport, many boys divert themselves in different ways. — *Laghu-Yoga-Vāsishtha*, V, 5

MĀYĀ OR ILLUSION is not delusion in the popular use of the word, as signifying something which does not exist. The illusion around and within us is 'real' in the sense that it actually exists; our māyā or illusion arising from the fact that we do not see, and often willfully refuse to see, things as they are and thus fall under the deluding play of our own bewildered inner faculties. For example, the extremist of any kind, however sincere he may be, is entangled in the webwork of his own misunderstandings.

This fact alone has immense moral import, for it teaches us to be kindly towards others, recognizing our own weaknesses of understanding, and also our strong biases and tendencies to see things as through a glass darkly. The scientist of one hundred years ago who had what are now proved to be wrong ideas about the physical universe, and who was quite fanatical in thinking that he had attained truth, was under the māyā of his time as well as a māyā brought about by his own imperfect vision. Just so the religionist, who held the theological teachings which the greater knowledge of our day has shown to be false or only partially true, was laboring under a similar māyā. The materialist who said that there was naught of man but an animate mechanism was as much under the sway of illusion as was the religionist who thought that at the Day of Judgment "rattling bones together fly from every quarter of the sky," as the once highly respected Dr. Watts sang.

We weave, perhaps with utmost mental and emotional conviction,

94

many kinds of illusory webs of thought and feeling, and for a while we are convinced that we are right, only to learn later, when experience has taught us more, that we were but slaves of the māyā of our own false imaginings. Some of the scientific theories propagated so earnestly today are as māyāvi as anything that could be adduced from the annals of history; but as long as these illusions last, whether they be scientific, philosophical or theological, or of any other kind, they are relatively real for those who hold them.

The doctrine of māyā is taught in one or another form by virtually every one of the great religious and philosophical schools of ancient and modern Hindustan, and it is especially noticeable in the Adwaita-Vedānta. It is likewise a characteristic of Buddhism — more marked today in the Northern Schools of the Mahāyāna than in the Southern Buddhism of the Hīnayāna.[2]

The word māyā is derived from the verbal root *mā*, to measure out, to set metes and bounds to; and by extension signifies limitation, transient character, and whatever is nonenduring. Thus we see here pretty much the same distinction which is often drawn in certain European philosophical schools between that which *is*, otherwise the Real, and that which merely *ex-ists*, or that which presents a phenomenal appearance. It is a short step from these general ideas to a realization that whatever is phenomenal and hence transitory is deceptive, and as such has no ever-enduring reality. From this thought has grown the common idea in Hindu philosophical systems, inclusive of Buddhism, that whatever is illusory is in some strange manner magical, because presenting a false appearance which deceives both sense and mind.

Consider man himself: he is essentially a divine-spiritual monad peregrinating through all the phenomenal and therefore illusory worlds and spheres of manifested existence; this divine-spiritual monad is itself everlasting because it is a droplet of the cosmic logos, of the cosmic spirit, the Reality for all within our universe. Yet all the different parts of the human constitution in which this monad clothes itself are, because of their more or less impermanent nature, illusions by comparison with the divine monad itself. It would be ludicrous to speak of man as having no real being and no actual existence, for he most emphatically has; but it is only his different monads which are the droplets of eternity, and all the rest of him is the 'magic' wrought in time and space by karma combining to produce all the phenomenal aspects of his constitution.

While the māyā of the lower portion of any being or thing, whether we speak of a galaxy or of man, definitely exists and produces whatever is, it is clear that all the multifarious varieties which surround us are not absolutely nonexistent, nor are they in an absolute sense different and separate from the Reality behind. If this were so, we should be at once inventing an inexplicable duality between the fundamental Reality and the manifested illusion, and there would be no possibility of explaining how the phenomenal flows forth from the noumenal or the Real. According to this wrong theory the two would be utterly disjunct, and the phenomenal without links of origin in the Reality. Thus, philosophically speaking, even māyā or mahāmāyā is a function of Reality — its veil — emanating forth from Reality itself and ultimately destined to rejoin the Real.

Now let us touch upon an aspect of the doctrine of māyā which is usually slurred over in the exoteric philosophical systems. All manifested entities, worlds and planes, may in a profoundly true sense be considered as the visions or dreams produced in and by the cosmic mind or cosmic spirit, when the periods of universal manvantara begin.

In the case of man, the incarnation of the spiritual ego is a relative 'death' for that ego; and similarly the ending of the imbodiment in the worlds of matter is a reawakening of the spiritual ego to a wider range of self-consciousness in and on its own planes and worlds. In identical fashion, and following always the master key of analogy, what we call manvantara is a death of the cosmic spirit — is, in a paradoxical sense, a sort of devachan or even a kāma-loka of the cosmic spirit or mind; and it is only when manvantara ends and pralaya begins that these dreams and visions of the cosmic spirit fade away, and its vast consciousness awakens once more to the full reality of its own sublime Selfhood.

From this we may draw two conclusions: (a) that devachan, while nearer Reality when compared with the illusion of earth life, is nevertheless more a māyā than are the self-conscious and cause-producing experiences of this earth; for the devachanic dreams, however beautiful and spiritual they may be, are, after all, dreams; and (b) it is only in the nirvana, in which condition all māyā has been 'blown out,' that the spiritual monad tastes of Reality and is freed of its illusory dreaming which is none other than the vast experiences brought about by the peregrinations in manifested existence. And just so is it with the universe and its mahāmāyā.

We thus see that all the manifested worlds are *phenomenally* real, because they exist as an illusory, and therefore magical, activity of the cosmic mind, and because *essential* Reality is their background and source. It is important to grasp this point, because to look upon māyā as meaning the absolute nonbeing of the phenomenal is to wander wide from the true teaching. The phenomenal is illusory and yet based upon Reality, because flowing forth from it.

This is the reason that the doctrine of māyā has so easily acquired the meaning of magical illusion or the working of a magic power in nature. In several passages of the archaic Hindu philosophical books, certain cosmic divinities, such as Varuna or Indra, are clothed with magical powers of 'deception,' which passages point directly to the phenomenal universe itself as the product of the intelligent fancy of the cosmic imagination, dreaming forth the universe and all in it.

This is well exemplified in the following extract from the *Yoga-Vāsishtha-Rāmāyana* (ch. xii):

> During the reign of the great sleep of Mahā-pralaya, Brahm alone remains as Endless Space and Peace Supreme. And when It wakes again at the end thereof in the form of Chit (consciousness), It thinks unto Itself, "I am a speck of Light," even as thou imaginest thyself of any form thou pleasest during dreams. That speck of Light again assumes unto Itself Extension, "I am large." That mass, false in reality, becomes the Brahmānda. Within that Brahmānda, Brahm thinks again: "I am Brahmā," and Brahmā forthwith becomes the Ruler of a vast mental empire which is this world. In that first creation, consciousness took many forms; and the root forms that consciousness assumed in that Beginning — they persist unchangeably throughout the Kalpa. That is the Destiny which is the Nature and the Law of Things, while that primal consciousness shall last. It makes what are our Space and Time and basic elements. It makes them what they are out of *Asat*. That Destiny has also fixed the spans of human life, varying in various Yugas with variations in the grades of sin and merit.

The same thought is imbodied in several passages in the Purānas and Upanishads, in the *Rig-Veda,* and similarly in the *Bhagavad-Gītā.*[3]

We human beings are integral parts of the cosmic whole; and partaking as we do of all its characteristics and qualities, we follow the laws and functions of the universe of which we are offsprings. This is the reason why we are not only subject to māyā, but have THAT within us as our divine-spiritual nature, allowing us through evolutionary growth ultimately to become self-cognizant of the Real.

The glamor of the magic of māyā surrounds us on all sides; yet nonillusion, otherwise the cosmic noumenon, or the heart of Śūnyatā, is our own

97

inmost; and it is just this inmost which is alluded to by H.P.B. when she speaks of Alaya° as "the Universal Soul or Atman" — that which is nonphenomenal because it never dissolves away into illusion. Even our scientific researchers have come to suspect that physical matter is in itself illusory — "mostly holes." What we call physical matter is not substance per se, but only productions or manifestations of some underlying reality, compared with which our universe is śūnya, empty.

Some of the Mahāyāna writings enumerate eighteen ways of describing emptiness or Śūnyatā,[4] the whole purpose being to show the unreality or emptiness of everything in universal nature except the originating Reality. These are really a series of philosophical paradoxes, reminding one somewhat of the Greek school of Heraclitus, who was called "the Obscure" because of his intellectual subtlety in the stating of paradoxes showing both the pro and the con of philosophical principles.

It is constantly pointed out by Buddhist commentators that all the implications of the idea of emptiness can be grasped only through prajñā, or buddhic intuitive apprehension. Emptiness is not a speculative notion to be fitted into any category of logical thinking. It remains unattainable and unthinkable, for it is ultimate Reality, utterly beyond the confines of the world of manifestations. Hence it has become synonymous with the idea of Suchness (tathātā). Emptiness and Suchness may be said to

---

°Alaya is a Buddhist term used especially in Northern Schools and is virtually identical with the highest ākāśa, the summit of the anima mundi or cosmic soul. It is a Sanskrit compound formed of the negative particle a, and laya from the verbal root lī, signifying to dissolve, to disappear. Alaya should not be confused with ālaya-vijñāna, frequently found in writings of the Mahāyāna school. Alaya and ālaya are not the same. Alaya can be called mahābuddhi or cosmic buddhi, otherwise the Second Cosmic Logos; whereas ālaya means a receptacle, a dwelling, and is often used mystically for a treasure house of wisdom and knowledge. Vijñāna signifies discerning thought or reasoning power.

In the human constitution, ālaya-vijñāna corresponds to the reincarnating ego or higher manas, which is the storehouse of all the intellectual and spiritual experiences garnered by the human ego in each one of its incarnations. It is, therefore, the seat of the accumulated wisdom belonging to man's humanly spiritual nature; and is in one sense both the goal of his future evolution and, at the same time, because of the karmic seeds of destiny which it contains, the producer of reimbodiments. Ālaya-vijñāna is almost identical with the vijñānamaya-kośa of the Vedānta, literally thought-made sheath, and which is next to the highest or ānandamaya-kośa, sheath of conscious bliss, this last corresponding to buddhi; while the ātman is the summit of the constitution.

be the Mahāyāna perception of Reality. They are not to be conceptually reconstructed, but intuitively realized.

Turning again to the cosmic intelligence 'dreaming forth' the universe, we should remember that the Absolute, otherwise the cosmic mind, does not project itself totally as māyā, but only in the manner of 'dreaming' — that is, it does not totally *become* the phenomenal universe. This would be as incorrect as to suppose that the spiritual monad in man descends wholly into the human body at incarnation. Rather, it projects from itself a ray which, just because it is a portion and not the spiritual monad in its fullness, is a relative māyā when compared with its parent.

HINDU CONCEPTIONS OF MĀYĀ

THROUGHOUT THE ages man's genius has evolved various theories, philosophical, scientific, and religious, as to how the universe came into being. The differences, however, were mainly in the manner of presentation, for all the great minds of the past enunciated the same wisdom-doctrine, the same theosophy, which was originally taught to the first self-conscious human beings on this earth by mānasaputric entities from other planes. But as the ages rolled by, the primary meanings of these cosmic philosophies were lost sight of and only the mere words remained; and thus different schools of thought grew up, each following the more or less purely exoteric interpretation of the original religio-philosophical system to which it was attached.

For instance, some of the thinkers of ancient India taught the Ārambha doctrine, that the universe was created by some supreme intelligence out of material of a cosmic character previously existing in space. This school conceived of the universe as being formed by some vast individual divinity, and therefore as having had a 'beginning,' the essential meaning of the Sanskrit word Ārambha. The Christian scheme went still farther along the same line, and formed an entirely unphilosophical thought-structure of things in which an infinite personal God created the universe out of nothing. This was simply the Ārambha idea gone to seed. Yet those Hindu thinkers were right in the sense that every universe has its *periodic* beginnings and endings, although it was certainly not 'created' as the outer product of the will and intelligence of a supreme mind which acted in a supposedly irresponsible manner. The fact is that each universe is simply the karma or reproduction of its former self — a former universe thus preceding its own reimbodiment — and this repetitively through timeless duration, although progressive improvement is everywhere at work through the process of evolutionary growth.

Another school taught the doctrine of Parināma, which supposed the universe — any universe — to be emanated by a supreme cosmic intelligence from mind and substance flowing forth into manifestation from within itself. This particular idea of emanation° is thus far in accord with the

---

°Cf. *The Mahatma Letters*, p. 73.

esoteric tradition which, however, adds this point of high importance: that this supreme cosmic intelligence is but one of an infinity of other such intelligences, and does not exist alone and unique in frontierless space.

A third school, the Vivarta, sets forth as the substance of its doctrine that the universe is emanated from the divine as a change or modification of itself, and therefore as an impermanent, and hence a māyāvi, production. Here again we are in agreement with certain elements of their teachings. But the fault of this school seems to be that it avers that a portion of the divine essence actually does become an illusion, instead of recognizing that, while the manifested universe is indeed a temporary cosmic illusion, it is only relatively so because based on the substratum of Reality.

These three schools may be compared with science, philosophy, religion. The Ārambha with the scientific outlook; the Parināma with the philosophical vision; and the Vivarta with the religious manner of visioning truth.[5]

To recapitulate: the Ārambha is that view of the origins of things which, qualified as being scientific, envisions the universe as proceeding forth as a 'new' production of already pre-existent cosmic intelligence and pre-existent 'points' of individuality, what we would call monads rather than atoms. Although such a newly produced universe is recognized as being the karmic resultant of a preceding universe, the former 'self' of the present, nevertheless emphasis is laid upon *beginnings,* upon the universe as a 'new' production, much as scientists construe the universe to be.

The Parināma, while having many points of contact with the Ārambha, lays emphasis upon the coming forth of the universe as a production by powers and entities and substances unrolling from within, and thus bringing the universe into existence by a kind of emanational or evolutional conversion or unfolding.

The Vivarta system penetrates still more deeply into the cosmic mystery and fixes its attention upon the unending duration of the divine essence, which it considers as producing appearances° of itself through modifications of itself, or portions thereof, brought about by emanational evolution from within, these modifications being the cosmic mahāmāyā. Hence the entire objective universe, visible and invisible, is considered to be illusory because merely a collective modification, or series of modifications,

---

°The technical name for these appearances is nāma-rūpa — a Sanskrit compound meaning name-form, nāma equaling ideas or concepts, and rūpa meaning objectivization or images or forms in which these ideas manifest themselves.

of the productive divine essence, which last always remains itself, yet produces appearances of itself through objectivization by unfolding procession or emanational evolution.

These three schools still exist with greater or less variation in India, and their ideas have found currency elsewhere in the world. While they do have elements of truth in them, they seem to presuppose a 'creative' Supreme Intelligence which as an Individual works in a more or less human manner as a Creator or Former; all three are too anthropomorphic.

The theosophic view is to consider boundless Space as containing within its frontierless fields, and in every infinitesimal mathematical point thereof, inherent creative and formative life and substance; so that while in one part of the Boundless, visible and invisible, a universe may be coming into being, in another part another universe may be reaching its manvantaric end and preparing for its cosmic pralaya. Thus Infinitude is wrongly conceived when it is supposed at any time to be an active, creative, agent which emanates universes from within itself, for this implies willing and formative — therefore limited — action. The truth being that each such universe, as a spacial unit, although existing through eternity in the Boundless, nevertheless *brings itself forth* into manifestation because of inherent seeds of active individuality. This process of universes appearing and disappearing and coming into being because of their own innate individual life and consciousness and energy is one side of the doctrine of swabhāva° — characteristic self-production.

All such entities or beings — whether a universe or a life-atom peregrinating anywhere — are surrounded and pervaded by the encompassing mind, consciousness, substance and force of the limitless ALL. As H.P.B. expressed it: ". . . the incognizable Cause does not put forth evolution, whether consciously or unconsciously, but only exhibits periodically *different aspects of itself* to the perception of *finite* Minds."†

The point here is that the "incognizable Cause" is not an individual

---

°There was at one time a highly philosophical school in Buddhism called the Swābhāvika because of the insistence of its teachers that all entitative units or beings anywhere in time and space come into being and vanish because of inherent individual energies within themselves. These energies run the whole gamut of the cosmic Mystery, from the divine through the spiritual, intellectual, psychical, emotional, astral, to the physical. Thus far this school was at one with the esoteric philosophy; but for long centuries past the Swābhāvikas have greatly degenerated both in philosophical conception and understanding, so that today their school is virtually one of a disguised materialism.   † *The Secret Doctrine*, II, 487.

in the sense of being a creator, but is the vast illimitable cosmic ocean from which all arises, in which all forever is, and into which all entities finally return for their respective periods of rest and recuperation. It would be totally wrong to imagine boundless Infinitude as an individual heaving and rolling with waves of evolving life. All such notions of cosmic processes are finite, however colossal our human imaginations may take them to be. Infinity, Eternity, the Incognizable, cannot be said to evolve, because only finite things evolve, for evolution is a finite process. Evolution is but another way of expressing the operation of karma, i.e. the working out of karma and evolution are practically identical.

In the consciousness of beings of dhyāni-chohanic grade human evolution here on earth is a pure māyā, and in the consciousness of still more sublime entities, as far beyond the dhyāni-chohans as they are beyond us, even the dhyāni-chohanic evolution is a pure māyā. Nevertheless, evolution exists in the worlds of matter where māyā is supreme — for matter and māyā are substantially the same in meaning. Here evolution is supreme because karma is supreme, and hence evolution is a very real thing to us. It *exists* but is NOT.

When any entity or being awakens into manifestation, the process commences in every case by the beginning of emanation from within the hitherto 'sleeping' divine entity. This word emanation is from the Latin and signifies flowing out from, much as thought flows out from the mind, or as a river flows out from its originating spring. Emanation is continuously in process throughout the entire life term of any manifesting entity, great or small; and indeed every evolutionary advance is a growth achieved because of the emanating or flowing forth of powers, attributes, and faculties from the entity's inner being.

We may think of emanation and evolution as being almost if not exactly identical. In fact they are merely two manners of viewing the same process, whether cosmic or infinitesimal. Evolution signifies unfolding and thus releasing what is already pre-existent as unmanifested power and faculty within the entity. When emanation on any plane begins, at the same instant evolution likewise commences. Otherwise stated, once a quality or faculty begins to flow forth from the essence of the monad, from that instant it likewise begins to unfold its swabhāva or characteristic attributes. Now the exact opposite of evolution is involution: the rolling up or gathering in of whatever had previously been unrolled. Involution, therefore, is also the opposite procedure to emanation.

The entire manifested universe is, when compared with the divine, a mahāmāyā, produced by emanational evolution. However, to us finite beings, ourselves a māyā by contrast with the ineffable divine, evolution and emanation and all their works are real enough because our perceiving minds are themselves the products of these māyāvi processes. The esoteric philosophy may be said to teach an objective idealism: that the universe and all its manifestations and works are 'real' for those involved in it; but are māyā when contrasted with the utter and unlimited Reality from which the universe originally sprang forth as a cosmic monad, and into which, aeons hence, it will again return.

SPIRITUAL REALITY AND MIND-BORN ILLUSION

"VANITY OF VANITIES; all is vanity," said the preacher in *Ecclesiastes*. The Hebrew word here translated as 'vanity' is *hebel,*° which in general corresponds with the Sanskrit word māyā. This shows that the doctrine of illusion is not solely Hindu but is a part of the common philosophical and religious heritage of the human race.

As H. P. Blavatsky says in one of her letters: "We are a *Maya* in one sense all of us; but we are *realities* in our own sight, in space and time and so long as it lasts on our plane."† This is a profound truth, because māyā to māyā seems real enough; and although in our inmost essence we are divine and therefore integral parts of the cosmic Reality, yet in our manifested personalities we are distinctly māyāvi because impermanent and transitory *and* because we are imperfect. Herein lies the key not only to a correct understanding as to how māyā affects us, but also how we may find the pathway by which we may free ourselves from māyā and thus be at one with the Real and 'see' Truth per se.

The god within us, the immortal monadic spark of the cosmic fiery essence of utter Reality, is the source of all *our* truth and reality. The closer we *become* it and manifest its transcendent wisdom and power in our lives, the more closely do we approach its Reality. In this way we progressively free ourselves from the magical enchantment of the illusion in which we live, and which affects us because of the various imperfections of our sheaths of consciousness — our various 'personalities.'

As so truly stated in *The Secret Doctrine* (I, 145–6):

> . . . according to our teaching which regards this phenomenal Universe as a great *Illusion*, the nearer a body is to the UNKNOWN SUBSTANCE, the more it approaches *reality*, as being removed the farther from this world of *Maya*.

°This is also the name of one of the 'sons' of Adam — Abel, the female 'brother' of Cain. *Hebel* or *habēl*, meaning to be impermanent, to fade away; hence whatever is non-enduring, illusory.

†*The Letters of H. P. Blavatsky to A. P. Sinnett*, p. 253.

105

Hence the cause of human suffering is not in māyā itself, but in our own imperfections, and often deliberate mischoices to sink ourselves ever more deeply into the swirling waves of the illusory ocean of manifested existence. It is our willful perversities of thought and emotion, of appetitive instinct and attachment to things of sense, as well as our as yet not fully evolved intelligence, which prevent us from rising out of these waves of illusion into the clear and everlasting sunlight of the atmosphere of the god within us.

We are under the sway of māyās of many kinds: "Ye suffer from yourselves. None else compels" — as Sir Edwin Arnold puts it in his beautiful poem *The Light of Asia*. We are under the sway of māyā on the intellectual and psychological plane, and have forgotten our divine origin. We dream heavy dreams of matter because we are immersed in the illusions of imbodied existence, our brain-mentality being perhaps the greatest example of human māyā and thus the greatest sinner in us.

We may free ourselves from māyā in all its vast ranges by ever striving to cultivate the ātmic, the buddhic and the higher mānasic faculties within us, slowly rising to these superior planes of our constitution and living in and on them, which we can do even while imbodied. The first step is to be convinced in every part of our being that the heart or core of each one of us is a ray of the boundless Reality. As H.P.B. wrote:

. . . the miner knows what the gold will look like when extracted from the quartz, whereas the common mortal can form no conception of the reality of things separated from the Maya which veils them, and in which they are hidden. Alone the Initiate, rich with the lore acquired by numberless generations of his predecessors, directs the "Eye of Dangma" toward the essence of things in which no Maya can have any influence.[*]

This Eye of Dangma, as the Tibetans call the Eye of Śiva, is but another term for the interior spiritual organ of vision of the Buddha within us or, as mystical Christians would phrase it, of the immanent Christos. Indeed, it is precisely when some great human individual, through many lives of consciously striving towards the god within him, has become at one with the Christos or Buddha within him, that he then himself becomes this Buddha or Christos imbodied.

The only difference — albeit a most important and sublime one — between a Buddha and the ordinary man is that a Buddha has become

[*] *The Secret Doctrine*, I, 45.

self-consciously united with, and indeed the very imbodiment of, the dhyāni-buddha within him, otherwise the buddhi-manas of his own constitution. When this union of the initiate with the ātman-buddhi-manas or spiritual monad is more or less complete, then the Eye of Dangma functions in relatively full power and splendor, and such a man, who really then is a Buddha or a Christ, has virtual omniscience and omnipotence as regards all beings and things of the hierarchy to which he belongs.

In the far distant ages of the future, at the end of the seventh round of our present planetary chain, all those who will then have successfully made the goal will have become dhyāni-chohans. Of course, this culmination of human greatness at the end of the seventh round is not the end of all possible evolution for human monads, for future ages will carry the evolving monads to still greater heights of spiritual and intellectual achievement. Even then, there will be māyā, but māyā on a far more spiritual plane, which in turn will be transcended as the monads advance ever higher and higher on their everlasting pilgrimage. Thus it is that the different oceans of māyā, each being a series of cosmic planes, will be transcended one after the other, in the endless journey towards that ever unattainable Reality which we call Parabrahman.

Quoting once more from *The Secret Doctrine* (I, 638–9):

> In ancient Symbolism it was always the SUN (though the Spiritual, not the visible, Sun was meant), that was supposed to send forth the chief Saviours and Avatars. Hence the connecting link between the Buddhas, the Avatars, and so many other incarnations of the highest SEVEN. The closer the approach to one's *Prototype*, "in Heaven," the better for the mortal whose personality was chosen, by his own *personal* deity (the seventh principle), as its terrestrial abode. For, with every effort of will toward purification and unity with that "Self-god," one of the lower rays breaks and the spiritual entity of man is drawn higher and ever higher to the ray that supersedes the first, until, from ray to ray, the inner man is drawn into the one and highest beam of the Parent-SUN. . . . the single units of that humanity proceed one and all from the same source — the *central* and its *shadow*, the visible SUN.

The world illusion in which we live is really a most intricate and marvelously fabricated web of natural enchantment, a web woven by hosts of evolving entities surrounding us, by which we are deceived because our own imperfectly developed minds misinterpret the pictures they view. It is māyā without and māyā within. Nature in her differentiated and manifested aspects is, so to speak, a vast fata morgana, composed of innumerable minor yet similar mirages; nevertheless at the heart of this ever-active web of illusion, constantly in the weaving and thus constantly presenting ever-new aspects of illusion, there is Reality. Just as there is Reality at the core of every individual unit of the innumerable hosts of monads which in their incomprehensibly great masses combine and cooperate to make this enchanting mirage, so there is at the heart of each one of us the essential Real. It is therefore not only our duty, but the first step on the path to Reality, to keep our wandering illusion-creating minds steadily on the Light within us, and gradually, as the ages pass, make this Light the guiding star in our lives.

IV

Galaxies and Solar Systems:
their Genesis, Structure, and Destiny

Galaxies and Solar Systems:
their Genesis, Structure, and Destiny

THE UNIVERSE: A LIVING ORGANISM

> The Secret Doctrine teaches the progressive development of everything, worlds as well as atoms; and this stupendous development has neither conceivable beginning nor imaginable end. Our "Universe" is only one of an infinite number of Universes, all of them "Sons of Necessity," because links in the great Cosmic chain of Universes, each one standing in the relation of an effect as regards its predecessor, and being a cause as regards its successor. — *The Secret Doctrine*, I, 43

THE LIFE FORCES in a universe are incessantly working; not for an instant do they become motionless. Consequently, the universe, after passing through the stages of the invisible worlds, is born, reaches its culmination of material existence, but does not stop there, for at the moment when the acme of the curve is reached, the forces then move steadily on downwards, but nevertheless forwards.

A universe comes into being because a cosmic entity is imbodying itself; and a universe dies, as a man dies, because it has come to the point where the major part of its energies have already passed into the invisible realms. Universes imbody themselves just as human egos do. The same fundamental laws prevail in the great as in the small. There is no essential difference whatsoever. The differences are in details, not in principles. Death is only a change; life is only an experience. The one enduring thing is pure unalloyed consciousness, for it includes everything else.

Men commonly think that they grow to maturity and then stop growing, remain mature for a while and then begin to decline. There is no such stopping time. The forces composing the man, and making the man a being, are moving constantly along the same road which brought the child to birth, which brought the child to adulthood, and which carries the adult to death. From the instant when culmination of a man's faculties and powers in any one life is reached, decay begins, this 'decay' simply meaning that the inner man is already beginning to make his way and his new body in the invisible worlds.

Man is at home on many planes. He is at home, in fact, everywhere.

Our earth life is only one short arc of the circle of existence. How absurd it would be to say that any one particular place, such as our earth, is the standard by which to judge the entire pilgrimage of man. So too the imbodiment and growth of a universe, as well as its culmination and decay followed by its death, are caused by the cosmic entity's coming out from the invisible spheres into these material realms, imbodying itself in the substances thereof and thus building up a material universe, and then passing on; and when the passing on approaches its completion, the universe is in its stages of dissolution.

It is the same with a star or sun as it is with its parent universe. It is the same with any entity. Life is endless, has neither beginning nor end; and a universe is in no wise different in essentials from a man. How could it be, since man merely exemplifies what the universe imbodies as the primary law. The man is the part; the universe is the whole.

Look up into the violet dome of night. Consider the stars and the planets: every one of them is a life-atom in the cosmic body; every one of them is the organized dwelling place of a multitude of smaller life-atoms which build up the brilliant bodies we see. Moreover, every sparkling sun which begems the skies was at one time a man, or a being equivalent to a human, possessing in some degree self-consciousness, intellectual power, conscience and spiritual vision, as well as a body. And the planets and the myriads of entities on the planets encircling any such cosmic god, any such star or sun, are now the same entities who in far bygone cosmic manvantaras° were the life-atoms of that entity. Through the ages they trailed along behind, all learning and progressing. But farther along the evolutionary pathway, as their leader, was their parent, the source of their being.

By our actions we are constantly affecting the destiny of the suns and planets of the future, for when we, by bringing out the native powers of the god within, shall have become glorious suns shining in the cosmic deeps, then the nebulae and the suns around us will be the evolved entities who now are our fellow human beings. Consequently, the karmic relations

---

°Manvantara is actually a compound of two words, *manu-antara*, meaning 'between two manus,' and therefore applies technically to the period of manifested activity between the opening or root-Manu and the closing or seed-Manu of any globe. By extension of the idea it has come to have the general significance of the life term of any Egg of Brahmā, whether planetary, solar or galactic. Manu thus stands for the entities collectively which appear at the beginning of manifestation, and from which everything is derived.

that we have with each other on earth or on other globes of our planetary chain, or elsewhere, will most assuredly affect their destiny as well as our own.

Yes, each one of us, in far distant aeons of the future, is going to be a sun, resplendent in the spaces of Space. And this will be when we shall have evolved forth the divinity in the core of our being, and when that divinity in its turn shall have proceeded to still greater heights. Beyond the sun there are other suns, so high that to us they are invisible, suns of which our own sun is a divine attendant.

The Milky Way, a complete and self-contained universe, is, aggregatively, but one cosmic cell in the body of some supercosmic entity, which in turn is but one of an infinitude of others like itself. The great contains the small; the greater contains the great. Everything lives for and unto everything else. This is the reason why separateness has been called the 'great heresy.' It is the great illusion, for separateness is nonexistent. Nothing can live unto itself alone. Every entity lives for all, and the all is incomplete without the one entity, and therefore lives for it.

Boundless Space is our home. Thither we shall go, and there indeed we even now are. We are not only connected by unbreakable links with the very heart of Infinitude, but we ourselves are that heart. This is the still small path of which the ancient philosophers taught; the path of the spiritual Self within.

DAYS AND NIGHTS OF BRAHMĀ

The appearance and disappearance of the Universe are pictured as an outbreathing and inbreathing of "the Great Breath," which is eternal, and which, being Motion, is one of the three aspects of the Absolute — Abstract Space and Duration being the other two. When the "Great Breath" is projected, it is called the Divine Breath, and is regarded as the breathing of the Unknowable Deity — the One Existence — which breathes out a thought, as it were, which becomes the Kosmos. (See "Isis Unveiled.") So also is it when the Divine Breath is inspired again the Universe disappears into the bosom of "the Great Mother," who then sleeps "wrapped in her invisible robes." — *The Secret Doctrine*, I, 43

WHEN H.P.B. QUOTED passages from the archaic Hindu scriptures, such as the *Vishnu-Purāna*, about the cosmic Days and Nights as being the inbreathings and outbreathings of Brahmā° she was using a figure of speech. Brahmā may be described as an individualized aspect of the cosmic Oversoul or Brahman, the individual root-divinity of any cosmic unit, whether a solar system like ours, or some larger or smaller individual. Brahmā thus is the vivifying, expansive substance-consciousness of nature in its eternally periodic cycles of manifestation. It stands in true distinction to mūlaprakriti, or rather pradhāna, root-nature, which is the shadow or matter side of the cosmos.

Brahmā, generally speaking, is the cosmic divinity, although the word is likewise used in modern theosophical writings to signify the spiritual entity of which a planetary chain† forms the seven principles or, otherwise, is the imbodiment. Each globe of such a planetary chain — and on the larger scale this is applicable to the entire solar system — corresponds not only with one of the principles of the Brahmā of a planetary chain, but likewise each such globe is a focus or 'knot' in which the consciousness

---

°Cf. *Isis Unveiled*, II, 264–5; *The Secret Doctrine*, I, 368–78.

Brahmā is the masculine or personalized form of the neuter word Brahman (from the verbal root *brih* meaning to expand, to grow, to fructify), and stands for the spiritual evolving energy-consciousness of any cosmic unit such as a solar system, which is properly called an Egg of Brahmā.

†A planetary chain consists of seven (or twelve) principles or globes, of which only one is visible to us on this plane.

of that Brahmā is localized. Precisely in the same manner man in his own sevenfold constitution has his different knots or centers, in which the consciousness emanating from the god within him is localized and wherein it works. In fact, his inner god during its periods of activity in manvantara — in this case in human incarnations — is the man's Brahmā.

Every appearance of a solar system (and equally so of a planetary chain) into manvantaric manifestation is an outbreathing of its Brahmā or cosmic divinity; similarly every inbreathing of the same Brahmā means its pralaya or resting period, the disappearance into higher planes of the manifested being. It is exactly so with man: when imbodied on earth, he is like a pillar of light descending from the spirit downwards through all planes until the physical body is reached; when he dies and his constitution breaks up, the pillar of light gradually is indrawn from below upwards until it again reaches the spiritual realms, which means its disappearance from the lower cosmic planes.

Pralaya — from the root *lī*, to dissolve, and *pra*, away — is the generalizing term for the state of rest or latency between two manvantaras or life cycles, of whatever magnitude. During the great or mahāpralayas every individual or unit that was differentiated disappears from the phenomenal universe and is transformed into the noumenal essence which periodically and throughout endless Duration gives birth to all the phenomenal manifestations of nature. Pralaya, then, is the dissolution of the visible into the invisible, the heterogeneous into the homogeneous; in other words, the objective universe returns into its one underlying primordial and eternally productive cause, to reappear at the following cosmic dawn as a new universe, the karmic fruitage of the old universe, its former 'self.' To our finite minds, pralaya is like a state of nonbeing — and so it is for all existences and beings on the lower ethereal and material planes.

When a solar system appears out of cosmic latency at the end of its solar pralaya, and begins its manifestations from the spirit downwards into matter, it is the outbreathing of that respective cosmic individual or Brahmā. Similarly, when the solar manvantara is ended, all the parts and portions of the solar system gradually disappear from the lower planes and are withdrawn in serial order into the spiritual realms; there then ensues the solar pralaya, the inbreathing of that particular cosmic individual. Where formerly existed a sun with its planetary chains, we would see naught but 'empty' cosmic aether, such as that which now exists between star and star in the vast realms of the starry spaces.

Furthermore, pralaya and manvantara are but other names for the systole and diastole of a cosmos. The systole is the ingathering, the in-breathing, the disappearance of all that is, and the diastole is the reverse: the outbreathing or manifestation along the cosmic ladder of life from spirit to grossest matter of the planes of the expanding entity, whatever it may be — sun, planetary chain, or even a galaxy. Systole and diastole are also used for the sunspot periods which represent pulsations of the solar heart.

When a manifested entity on any one plane goes into pralaya, the life-atoms that it leaves on that plane are in their deep sleep which continues as long as the pralaya lasts. What science now thinks to be empty space is really cosmic aether in a state of pralaya; and every part of such miscalled empty space has from eternity in the past been, and will in the eternity of the future again be, the field for the appearance of manifesting entities.

Aether should never be confused with ether. They are as different both in substance and meaning as man's spiritual soul is from his astral body. Aether is virtually identic with the Sanskrit term ākāśa, both being the highest ranges of the anima mundi. Ether is the grossest or physical aspect of aether, and is often interchangeable with the astral light, which is the lees of the anima mundi or, what comes to the same thing, of aether. In the case of the auric egg of man, in its highest part it too is pure ākāśa or aether or the spiritual soul, and in its astral and physical parts it is the linga-śarīra corresponding to ether and lower astral substance, the physical body being the precipitate or deposit of these last.

During manvantara a cosmic entity, due to forces working from within outwards as well as from without inwards, is manifesting on the different planes of boundless Space; during its pralaya the same entity disappears from these planes, and its higher principles rest in unimaginable nirvanic bliss. Just so with man during life and after death, but on a much smaller scale.

Nirvana° is a state of complete, untrammeled consciousness, of absorption in pure kosmic Being, and is the wondrous destiny of those who

---

°Nirvana, a Sanskrit compound — *nir*, prepositional prefix meaning out or away; *vāna*, the past participle passive of the verbal root *vā*, to blow — literally meaning 'blown out.' So badly has the significance of the ancient Indian thought been understood, that for many years European scholars were discussing whether being 'blown out' meant actual entitative annihilation or not.

have reached superhuman knowledge, purity and spiritual illumination. It really is personal-individual identification with the spiritual Self — the highest Self. It is also the state of the monadic entities in the period that intervenes between minor manvantaras or rounds of a planetary chain; and more fully so between each seven-round period, or Day of Brahmā, and the succeeding Day or new kalpa of a planetary chain.

There are different degrees of nirvana; there is one so high that it blends insensibly with the condition of the cosmic hierarch of our universe. Nirvana has also been called the vanishing point of differentiated matter. The purely nirvanic state is the "laya of the Spirit in Parabrahman," an assimilation with Parabrahman, a passage of spirit back to the ideal abstraction of Be-ness which has no modifying relation with the manifested planes on which our universe exists during this manvantaric cycle.

Paranirvana is that which is 'beyond nirvana,' the period of kosmic rest or mahāpralaya — the Great Night of Brahmā — the condition which ensues at the end of the manvantara of the solar system, the Saurya manvantara.[6] Just as a man may attain self-conscious union with the divine monad which is the root of his being, thus attaining nirvana, so the solar system and all self-conscious entities within it, at the end of the Saurya manvantara, attain an exactly similar but far higher union with the hierarch of the galactic universe, and this we may describe as the paranirvana of the solar system.

Again, when the universal solar system has reached its manvantaric end and the Mahā-Saurya pralaya begins, then all the three dhātus — or generalized groups of cosmic planes which in their structural unity form any solar system as well as any universal solar system — are swept out of existence like so many dried leaves in an autumn wind, and naught remains except the 'fullness' of vacuity.

Every manifesting entity in the universe is a consciousness or monad. Thus our sun is a solar monad, a divine being in its higher parts; similarly every planetary chain is an individual, an entity of less spiritual magnitude than a sun, but a cosmic individual nonetheless. Every atom is likewise during its manifestation an imbodied individual — a god at its heart, a life-atom in the intermediate part of its constitution, a chemical atom in its body.

GENESIS OF A UNIVERSAL SOLAR SYSTEM

"The Central Sun causes Fohat to collect primordial dust in the form of balls, to impel them to move in converging lines and finally to approach each other and aggregate." (Book of Dzyan). . . . "Being scattered in Space, without order or system, the world-germs come into frequent collision until their final aggregation, after which they become wanderers (Comets). Then the battles and struggles begin. The older (bodies) attract the younger, while others repel them. Many perish, devoured by their stronger companions. Those that escape become worlds."   — The Secret Doctrine, I, 201

OUR SOLAR SYSTEM began in Space, in the womb of Aditi, the Eternal Mother, as a nebula — not by chance, but as one of the stages in its new imbodiment. As this nebula slowly moved in space, at its heart there began to be a condensation of its substance. This condensation became the sun, and a little later at various points within that nebula similar but smaller condensations of the nebular material occurred, and these became the planets.

Note the distinction as well as similarity between the terms Space and Aditi. Aditi is used for that particular portion of space which is or becomes the originant matter or cosmic womb from which any spacial unit such as a solar system or galaxy is to be born. Whereas Space can be used in this limited sense, it likewise can signify the Boundless; but it would be straining the meaning of Aditi to call it the Boundless or infinite Space, because neither the Boundless nor infinite Space can be looked upon as acting in an individualized or generative capacity. Aditi is often spoken of as Devamātri, the Mother of the Gods, because, as H.P.B. has it, "it is from her Cosmic matrix that all the heavenly bodies of our system were born — Sun and Planets."*

Let us raise ourselves in spirit to a portion of cosmic infinitude which science would call empty space; and then raise our minds upwards and inwards seven stages or planes until we reach the plane of cosmic spirit. All the planes through which our mind has passed form the manifested

---

*The Secret Doctrine, I, 99; see also I, 53, 356, 527; II, 527.

body or being of Aditi — a word which means 'frontierless.' As we remain in thought on this highest plane through aeons of cosmic time, our consciousness, having become an observer, grows cognizant of motion in the spirit-substance around us. A mathematical point or center seems to be condensing, begins to glow with light and take unto itself movement in circular or rotatory fashion, as well as movement of translation or progression.

As we watch in thought through the ages we see this center become duplicated and multiplied elsewhere in the substance-space around us: these other and apparently smaller foci doing just as the first point had done, glowing with unimaginable splendor and moving both circularly and in translation. We begin to notice that the so-called empty space, in which these various flashing points exist, itself becomes thoroughly active as spiritual substance; and, as still other ages pass by in our thought, we realize that we are observing the condensation or formation of a spiritual nebula, or a sea of flaming but heatless spiritual Fire in which the revolving points exist as living nuclei, each one formed around a laya-center. As time passes on, this spiritual nebula and all parts of it, both its fullness and the different nuclei, send emanations or flowing forces and substances from themselves down to the next lower plane of the body of Aditi, which plane in its turn is thus awakened by regular serial stages to manifesting nebular life. This progressing descent continues steadily through emanation upon emanation, so that every plane of the body of Aditi, or the universe, in its turn becomes a field of space or the stage of awakening existence and of innumerable living points, which are manifesting monads.

When the physical plane of space is reached, we begin to discern the same phenomena: faint wisps and streaks of light coalesce and become a luminous nebula, increasing in brilliancy as the ages pass, in which the living nuclei — or rather the emanations on this lowest plane reaching out from the original nuclei on the highest plane — again appear with their respective circular and translatory motions. Thus we have a nebula in its appearance on the physical plane.

The nebula itself slowly whirls in majestic rotation through long ages, the living nuclei gradually becoming more brilliant and more active in their manifestation on the physical plane. We then perceive that the largest of these living nuclei is really the beginning of our sun, and that the smaller nuclei have taken unto themselves movements as minor nebulae within the greater nebula, all of them being more condensed than the general field of the nebula itself. We see that the living substance forming the general nebula is slowly absorbed or sucked into the respective bodies of these nuclei. Finally we witness the birth of the physical plane of the solar system, with its attendant planetary chains in their first appearances on this cosmic plane.

We understand that both the sun and the planetary chains are manifold in character, extending from the spiritual down through all intermediate worlds to the physical cosmic plane. We notice that these nuclei assort themselves in such fashion that on the highest plane there is one globe, and on every succeeding plane there are two nuclei or globes, until we reach the physical plane where there is one nucleus or globe again — the 'reflection' on this plane of the highest globe on the spiritual plane. Every one of these nucleus-globes, itself being formed not only of the spirit and of the soul but also of the body of Aditi, is therefore as a cosmic unit seven- or ten- or twelvefold in character, according to the way in which we choose to count its different elements or principles.

What we may call the mechanics of the appearance of a universal solar system — first as a point or germ, which the Hindu writings speak of as a hiranyagarbha or 'golden seed' — should be understood clearly in order to avoid confusion. The appearance of the glowing hiranyagarbha on the highest of the seven planes of space really is a laya-center beginning to awaken to activity. This cosmic seed gradually expands as it unfolds, because of the pouring through the laya-center of the unfolding inner life principles from above downwards. As the ages of cosmic time flow by and this golden germ continues its expansion, it finally attains the dimensions of a nebula, filling all the space where it appears with 'cold light' or 'cold fire.' In this nebula, minor hiranyagarbhas or cosmic seeds slowly break through into manifestation, each one in its turn expanding and swelling and likewise being the beginning of the awakening into activity of a laya-center. We have thus a vast expanse of glowing but perfectly cool spiritual flame, which is the general nebula. Here and there in the substance of this nebula appear these minor foci or hiranyagarbhas, each one the seed of a future celestial body belonging to the universal solar system-to-be, and now in process of formation on this highest or seventh or spiritual plane of manifestation.

From time to time one of these minor hiranyagarbhas reaches the point in its emanational unfolding or evolution where, as said before, it takes unto itself movement of both rotatory and translatory character, because of the innate forces working through it — this dual movement making of each such minor hiranyagarbha a comet.

As the descent through the seven planes of manifestation continues through aeonic time, the surplus of life° on the descending arc finally reaches the lowest part of the highest or seventh plane, and breaks through into the highest part of the next lower cosmic plane. Here the same general run of unfolding activity takes place: first the appearance of the cosmic seed, which swells and expands and pours out from the laya-center, which is its heart, ever more and more of the forces and substances it progressively unrolls, so that in time on the lower cosmic plane a nebula is again formed like its parent on the superior plane.

The process continues through all the seven planes of manifestation until it reaches the lowest cosmic plane that it is possible for the karma of the unfolding universal solar system to attain; and this plane we call our material world, the lowest aspect of the universal Egg of Brahmā. On this material plane there first appears a cosmic comet which, having stirred in its far distant bed in space because of the awakening of the laya-center, begins to rush in erratic movements through the galactic spaces. Finally it reaches that portion of the galaxy to which it is karmically drawn — our own universal solar system, surrounded as it is by the zodiacal belt. Here it attains relative stability because of the balancing energies or powers of the twelve fohatic magnetisms flowing from the twelve constellations of the celestial zodiac.

The cosmic comet now has settled in space as a relatively circular disc of glowing light surrounding a globular center or heart, which latter is the developed hiranyagarbha that the cosmic comet has become. This heart in later aeonic time becomes the chief fohatic center of the universal solar system.

Movement is innate in any laya-center awakened into activity, because of the forces and energies and substances flowing downwards through it; and thus rotation is immediately inaugurated, a continuation of the rotatory movement of the cosmic comet, and this movement of the entire nebula, as it now is, continues until the end of the Mahā-Saurya manvantara. In the fabric of this nebula there appear the minor hiranyagarbhas, each one of which in turn, from innate powers of movement, takes unto itself both rotatory and translatory motion, and these minor foci in the

---

°Cf. *Fundamentals of the Esoteric Philosophy*, ch. XLV.

general nebula are the beginnings of what will in time become the planets.

From the primordial or first appearance of the universal solar system — from the first firing up of the laya-center in the deeps of galactic space, and passing through the stages of cosmic comet and later nebula — the various phases of the evolving and expanding entity, the universal solar system-to-be, are all marked by the glowing or shining of the cold flame, which Hindu philosophy calls daivīprakriti (literally, luminous substance).

Now even when the lowest cosmic plane has been reached, there is as yet no appearance of what we call *physical* matter — which comes only at the most unfolded stage of the evolution of the universal solar system. The cold flame, which is the appearance of daivīprakriti on the lowest cosmic plane, is in fact matter belonging to another subplane than that of our physical world, matter in its first and second highest conditions or states. It is, really, the same glowing luminosity that our sun even at present has, for what we see as our sun is physical matter in its two highest states; however, because the sun in its evolution has reached the lowest possible stage for the present Mahā-Saurya manvantara, it is surrounded by an aura or veil of matter somewhat more material, which matter is in its third stage of condensation downwards.

Here we have a paradox in that the sun itself is neither solid, liquid, nor gaseous; nor is it hot, although it is most emphatically glowing, and glowing with cold flame. Nevertheless there is 'heat' around the *outermost* veil of the sun, produced not by 'burning' or 'incandescence' but by the tremendous working of chemical and alchemical association and dissociation of the life-atoms which form the sun's outermost garment. All these garments of the sun are its vital aura and, in fact, are the grossest expression of the solar auric egg. The titanic energies producing the luminosity and splendor of the sun's aura are the manifestation of daivīprakriti on the two uppermost planes of the physical universe. Daivīprakriti itself is spiritual consciousness and intellectual light in its highest parts, and nebular and cometary luminosity when it touches the higher subplanes of our material cosmic plane.

During the Mahā-Saurya pralaya, the spiritual, intellectual, and higher psychical principles of a universal solar system exist in space in the incomprehensible activity of these higher principles, although the lower principles of such system are dispersed and dissociated. The life-atoms of these lower principles or elements hang in space in a condition which we may perhaps figurate as being 'frozen' in somnolence, and remain in such inactive condition during the long ages of that pralaya. But when the reimbodiments of its higher principles begin to take place as the descending life thereof reaches the lower planes and subplanes of space, these hosts of inactive life-atoms start to awaken into activity again, and are attracted to, and thus help to re-form, the lower principles and the body of this universal solar system.

Returning to the main theme of the reappearance of a universal solar system on the different cosmic planes, we find first the cosmic comet slowly expanding and gathering unto itself multitudes of waiting and 'frozen' life-atoms. Reaching its karmically destined locus in the galaxy, and passing by degrees through the stages of diffuse nebula and slowly rotating spiral nebula, it gradually assumes the form of the annular or ring nebula, and finally attains a spherical or egg-shaped form. Some magnificent photographs have been taken which show these different nebular shapes in various stages of their evolution. Indeed, our own galaxy or home-universe, could we see it from some outside point, would look like some of the flattened or disc nebulae that these photographs show so clearly.

Nature repeats her operations on all planes and in all ranges, high and low, inner and outer, for analogical action is the course of procedure of universal and all-permeant consciousness, which automatically follows the innate laws of its own being. Once a universal solar system or general Egg of Brahmā has reached its grossest or most materially evolved stage of emanational unfolding, then we have a universal solar system just like our own, consisting of a number of different solar systems collected together because of karmic descent and destiny.

Now the arc of ascent, which is the return to spirit of the Egg of Brahmā, is accomplished by a reversal all along the line of what took place on the arc of descent. Slowly through aeonic time, and from the very beginning of the arc of ascent, the universal solar system follows its long journey back to spirit. First, all the lowest portions of the lowest cosmic plane begin to involve, like an infolding scroll; when this has been rolled up, a similar procedure takes place with the next higher plane. This involutionary process continues through all the seven manifested planes until once again spirit is reached, the Mahā-Saurya manvantara is ended, and all the vast aggregate of the highest and higher principles and elements of the system enter into their paranirvanic and utterly inexpressible condition. Where formerly the universal solar system had existed in all the plenitude of its manifested powers and substances, there now is 'empty space.'

Although the ages be many and long, the time in endless Duration will arrive when once more the great drama of a 'new' universal solar system will begin, but on a series of cosmic planes higher than those of its 'old' self. All that was once X and Y and Z in the 'old' is now A and B and C in the 'new'; and thus by gradual stages up the galactic ladder of Being do all systems climb to destinies inconceivable by man.

Yet behind it all, and outside of all phenomenal appearances, however grand these may be, there is that Something, which the sages of archaic times reverently called THAT. We should ever keep in heart and mind as the ultimate intuition of truth, that whatever is 'appearance' is after all māyā. It is the incomprehensible, the unthinkable, the ever-enduring, which alone is eternal. It is this vast Mystery, of which we are all children, gods and men, universes and atoms, galaxies and aggregates of galaxies, which is the rootless root of our inmost essence, from which we all came, unto which periodically we all return.

THE CELESTIAL ZODIAC
AND THE BIRTH OF A SOLAR SYSTEM

H. P. Blavatsky says truly that our whole destiny, indeed the destiny of the solar system and of every planetary chain within it, is written in the zodiac, and naturally therefore in its twelve constellations, signs, houses, or mansions — all four names being applicable almost indifferently to the twelve parts into which the zodiac is divided.° These twelve houses, I might add, are not portions of our solar system, nor of our planetary chain.

The zodiac is that band of constellations which ancient astrology divided into twelve parts and which, seen from the earth, surrounds our solar system like a belt. Each of these constellations, together forming the twelve houses of the zodiac, is a cluster of stars karmically united by past bonds of destiny, each having its own characteristic swabhāva — in other words, its own spiritual electricity or fohatic magnetism. Thus the zodiac contains twelve different cosmic fohatic magnetisms, each one distinct from all the others, yet naturally all belonging to and enfolded within the still greater spiritual magnetism or fohat of our galaxy or home-universe.

In fact, every monad throughout infinity has its own characteristic spiritual magnetism, its own magnetic bipolarity, which is its individuality. No two men are identic: if they were they would not be twain but one. Every life-atom likewise has its own spiritual individuality or magnetism. Similarly, man's physical body, indeed his entire constitution, has a spiritual-magnetic swabhāva of its own, as has any organism such as a planetary chain or a group of stars like the constellations. Every zodiacal mansion also has its own swabhāva, and therefore its characteristic mahat or cosmic intelligence. In other words, the zodiac contains twelve different poles, i.e. polarities of spiritual-intellectual magnetism or fohatic electricity, each one producing its own type of influences in the outflow of its emanations around itself, and extending through space.

°Cf. *The Secret Doctrine*, I, 634, "Cyclic Evolution and Karma," and I, 647, "The Zodiac and its Antiquity."

The entire belt of the zodiac is a portion of the galaxy, a collection of constellations to which our solar system with all its attending planetary chains is karmically connected in an especial manner. This is the reason they are all grouped together in our home-universe.

Let us consider again the birth of a solar system. The time comes when the descending forces with their accompanying ethereal substances infill a dormant laya-center in the heart of the galaxy. Invigorated by these incoming life streams from higher planes, the cosmic seed of the future solar system rushes from its bed in space, and for ages pursues an erratic course throughout the galaxy, drawn hither and thither by the attractions of various stellar clusters or individual suns.

The Secret Doctrine (I, 203–4) gives the following graphic description of the cometary wanderings through the galactic deeps:

> Born in the unfathomable depths of Space, out of the homogeneous Element called the World-Soul, every nucleus of Cosmic matter, suddenly launched into being, begins life under the most hostile circumstances. Through a series of countless ages, it has to conquer for itself a place in the infinitudes. It circles round and round between denser and already fixed bodies, moving by jerks, and pulling towards some given point or centre that attracts it, trying to avoid, like a ship drawn into a channel dotted with reefs and sunken rocks, other bodies that draw and repel it in turn; many perish, their mass disintegrating through stronger masses, and, when born within a system, chiefly within the insatiable stomachs of various Suns. . . . Those which move slower and are propelled into an elliptic course are doomed to annihilation sooner or later. Others moving in parabolic curves generally escape destruction, owing to their velocity.

Also in the same work (I, 100), H.P.B. quotes from an ancient Commentary which states that Mārttānda, our sun, *"breathed (drew in) into his stomach the vital airs of his brothers,"* seeking to devour° them, and

---

°These devourings take place in all the ranges of cosmic life, but they are devourings of bodies, of vehicles, not of monads or egos. In the case of those comets which are irresistibly drawn into various suns and annihilated, due to karmic attractions from past manvantaras, they are failures only in the sense that they are insufficiently evolved or prepared to exist on our globe D plane. The failure is not because of any spiritual inadequacy of the monad. If the monads of a solar or planetary comet (or a human being, for the analogy is close), are thwarted in the process of seeking reimbodiment on this plane, it is solely the vehicles that are 'devoured,' for the monads or egos are instantly free and proceed once more to build a new cometary (or human) body.

It is well to remember that in the process of cosmic evolution, a sun not only tries to devour his younger brothers, the planets, but also endeavors to help them.

hence was exiled to the center of the kingdom, and that his younger brothers, the planets, wander around him in order to keep away from him until the time comes when they can safely approach him.

The cosmic germ or comet that does escape annihilation, continues pursuing its wanderings, and finally reaches its objective which, in the case of our own embryonic sun and its sleeping planetary chains, was the group of stellar clusters which we call the zodiac. More concretely, our embryo solar system, then a wandering pilgrim comet, reached the field of space within the galaxy where formerly, as a solar system, it had lived with its family of planetary chains. Once within the enclosing circle of the zodiac and henceforth subject to the mighty spiritual-magnetic fohatic emanations of a twelvefold kind, the pilgrim comet begins to settle in life. It then slowly passes from the cometary stage into the nebular stage, through the ages gradually increasing in size and growing more material and grosser in texture, because absorbing the countless multitudes of its former lower life-atoms which it had dropped on this plane when its previous existence as a solar system had come to an end.

As it passes through this process of concretion it accumulates all-various types of ethereal matter, partly from what science calls the dark nebulae which are but sleeping matter in the fifth, sixth and seventh states counting upwards; and thus by degrees it gathers unto itself, by accretion and attraction, increments of matter belonging to this plane.

Now relatively settled, it is enchained within the twelve polar fohatic attractions of the zodiac in the beginning of its existence as a nebula. It goes through various nebular stages, constantly growing more solidified, more condensed, glowing ever more brightly because of the Forty-nine Fires° working through it. When it has become a visible nebula, although still of matter not wholly of our physical plane but of ethereal matters belonging to the two or three highest conditions of physical matter — just like the substance of our visible solar orb — we discern within this vast

---

It is a paradox. In the case of ourselves, were we to approach the sun, our physical bodies would be annihilated with the rapidity of lightning, for they not only would be dispersed into atoms, but those very atoms themselves would be disrupted, torn apart. This is what is meant when it is said that the sun is a beneficent power but can also be an annihilator or 'devourer.' But the time will come when each one of us will enter the heart of the sun in perfect safety, and do so because the core of our own being is a portion of the solar essence.

°Cf. *The Secret Doctrine*, I, 291, 347.

nebula living nuclei spaced here and there within its field. The largest and most powerful of these in time becomes the body of the sun; the smaller nuclei are the respective planetary chains in the first of their rounds. Thus is a solar system begun, and thus is inaugurated the sublime life drama of the new solar manvantara.

After this stage has been reached, the substance of the nebula is slowly absorbed or swallowed up, partly by the sun and partly by the different smaller living nuclei which are the beginnings of the planetary chains. Each attracts and sucks in from the surrounding solar nebula those particular life-atoms which had belonged to it in the previous solar manvantara; in this way each living nucleus, whether solar or planetary, solidifies and strengthens its fabric or body.

During the course of the birth of a solar system, there are not only intense attractions among these different nucleus-globes, but likewise equally strong repulsions, due to the fohatic vitality of the living entity manifesting in and through each globe as its own Brahmā.

In the early ages of the formation of the solar system, before the present very beautiful and symmetrical condition of things in this system began, the sun, which was the largest of the then relatively condensed bodies in the nebula, began to pull hard on all other parts of the nebula, trying to gather these other smaller and inferior condensations into itself. There then existed an interplay of attraction and repulsion between center or sun and the outlying condensing points. This resulted in the beginning of the planetary revolutions about the sun. The planets fought against the mighty solar attraction, and there were battles in space between the sun with its terrific pulling power and the planets which attempted to seek safety in flight; and, as they could not free themselves from the gravitational pull — more accurately, the spiritual, psychomagnetic as well as physical influence — of the great sun, they turned around it, in circular and later in elliptical orbits, and thus was the solar system established.

RĀJA SUNS AND THE COSMIC EGG OF BRAHMĀ

THE DOCTRINE OF the spheres comprises the entire structure, characteristics and attributes, as well as the origin and destiny, of the solar system and all in it, including of course the scores of different planetary chains which together form the sun's kingdom. This doctrine has four different aspects which may be briefly described as:

1. The universal solar system, including a number of individual solar systems all subservient to the same Rāja sun.

2. Our solar system, a twelvefold solar chain, with its seven (or twelve) sacred planets which have our sun as their elder brother. This second aspect treats also of the spiritual-psychological influences which these planets° exercise upon our earth planetary chain, and the role they play in its formation.

3. The earth planetary chain per se, which aspect is primarily concerned with the circulation of the various life-waves through the twelve globes of the complete chain, and the manner in which this chain — as an instance of planetary chains in general — is built and formed.

Every planetary chain is the sevenfold (or twelvefold) constitution of a celestial being, whose abode is mainly in the highest globe, and whose vital influence and mind permeate every globe, and therefore every being or atom which goes to form the various globes of that chain. Just as man has his seven principles, so on the cosmic scale every planetary chain has its seven (or ten or twelve) foci or knots of consciousness, which are its respective globes.

°In this connection neither Neptune nor Uranus belongs to *our* solar system, nor indeed does the more recently discovered planet Pluto. These are what we may call 'captures,' intrusions, so to speak, into our solar system. These three planets belong to a solar system of their own, although equally with our solar system belonging to the universal solar system. It can happen in the economy and interacting relations of the cosmic Egg of Brahmā that certain planets of one solar system can intrude into visibility for the inhabitants of another solar system, because both belong to the one *universal* solar system; and when two such solar systems approach each other as regards position and evolutionary place on the cosmic planes, they are thus partially visible each to each because of similarity of vibrations.

4. That aspect of the doctrine which is, perhaps, the most mystical one of the four, and to which H.P.B. merely alluded when she wrote in closely veiled language:

> As to Mars, Mercury, and "the four other planets," they bear a relation to Earth of which no master or high Occultist will ever speak, much less explain the nature. — *The Secret Doctrine*, I, 163–4

There is a tendency to confuse the universal solar system with our solar system. The two are not one but different and in a sense quite distinct parts of the cosmic Egg of Brahmā.

Now the solar system which science recognizes is merely the physical portion of our cosmic Egg of Brahmā, and even then only that part of the physical portion which our senses can perceive. In reality our solar system exists on seven (or ten or twelve) cosmic planes, ranging from the highest or divine through the invisible worlds and realms down to our physical or prithivī cosmic plane. This cosmic Egg, then, is seen to be a vast aggregate of interpenetrating and interacting planes or worlds, each having its own particular planet-globes with their respective inhabitants in various degrees of evolutionary unfoldment, as well as different suns existing on these cosmic planes.

The ancient Greek mystics and later Gnostics, re-echoing the archaic teaching given in the Mysteries, properly spoke of this World Egg as a vast Pleroma or Fullness. We are thus entitled to conceive of the cosmic Egg as a 'solid,' of which by far the greatest part exists in the invisible worlds, and of which we cognize only imperfectly the physical part. This cosmic Egg is our universal solar system; and it contains not only our own solar system, but a number of others akin to ours because of ultimately identic origin and destiny. All these solar systems, interworking and interacting yet each one quite distinct from the others, are derivatives from a common primeval origin in far past cosmic manvantaras. Further, this cosmic Egg is presided over by one grand solar chain or spiritual sun which, because of its pre-eminence in age and spirituality, is called in the esoteric philosophy a Rāja sun,[7] a king sun, or a Rāja star.

In the second volume of *The Secret Doctrine* (p. 240) we find the following significant passage:

> This "central sun" of the Occultists, which even Science is obliged to accept astronomically, for it cannot deny the presence in Sidereal Space of a central

body in the milky way, a point unseen and mysterious, the ever-hidden centre of attraction of our Sun and system — this "Sun" is viewed differently by the Occultists of the East. While the Western and Jewish Kabalists (and even some pious modern astronomers) claim that in this sun the God-head is specially present — referring to it the volitional acts of God — the Eastern Initiates maintain that, as the *supra-divine* Essence of the Unknown Absolute is equally in every domain and place, the "Central Sun" is simply the centre of Universal life-Electricity; the reservoir within which that divine radiance, already differentiated at the beginning of every *creation*, is focussed. Though still in a *laya*, or neutral condition, it is, nevertheless, the one attracting, as also the ever-emitting, life Centre.

The "central suns" here referred to are the Rāja suns around which more than one minor solar universe turns. These Rāja suns or king stars are scattered through the boundless spaces of Space in virtually infinite numbers, and many are not in our physical world at all. However, there is of course no one central stellar body around which Infinitude revolves.

One solar system can pass its entire manvantara from beginning to end, enter upon and pass through its solar pralaya, and then begin a new solar manvantara, while other solar systems of the same cosmic Egg may or may not be doing the same thing. The time periods, however long for any individual solar system, are all relatively short when compared with the vast time periods of the universal solar system. Just as the planetary chains in our solar system have many reimbodiments during the solar manvantara, in like manner has our solar system many reimbodiments within the universal manvantara of the cosmic Egg of Brahmā.

Merely one facet of great cosmic mysteries is here touched upon, and we will understand this better if we remember that there are suns and suns. Some suns are manvantaric ultimates, ends for that manvantara of a majestic evolutionary unfolding which began in the dawn of our own galactic universe. There are other suns which instead of being at their manvantaric end are as it were at the beginning; and these are descending into matter instead of rising out of it. Both types of suns play their respective cosmic roles on the stage of manvantaric life; yet both have paths of activity which cross each other, functions which at times are identical; and both operate towards the common, to us humans utterly inscrutable, consummation of manvantaric time.

The life of the universal solar system is much longer than that of our solar system, with its sun and family of younger brothers or planets.

From time to time one of these planetary chains ends its seventh round and enters into its pralaya, while its principles begin to wander thereafter through space. In due course it is attracted back to its solar system as a planetary comet, which gradually finds its own sun, and pretty nearly, if not exactly, its own former orbit. So also our sun, or any other one of the suns in our universal solar system, will run its life period, peregrinate in and through the invisible planes through space, and return to this our universal solar system as a solar comet.

It is important here not to confuse the universal solar system with the system of the galaxy, which of course is likewise an immensely vaster system of suns which we could call perhaps the galactic system of solar systems. When, as above, I use the expression universal solar system in connection with our sun, I mean a particular group of solar systems closely assembling a vast chain of suns, of which only one sun, our sun, is visible to us on this cosmic plane.

Not only are all the other suns of our own universal solar system invisible, but likewise their respective planetary chains, because our vision is limited by our karmic development to this particular sub-subplane of a cosmic plane. Now a god with his consciousness developed on many subplanes of a cosmic plane possibly would see all the suns, and probably all the respective planetary chains of all those suns of our universal solar system. What a picture that would be!

REIMBODIMENT OF A PLANETARY CHAIN

The birth of the celestial bodies in Space is compared to a crowd or multitude of "pilgrims" at the festival of the "Fires." Seven ascetics appear on the threshold of the temple with seven lighted sticks of incense. At the light of these the first row of pilgrims light their incense sticks. After which every ascetic begins whirling his stick around his head in space, and furnishes the rest with fire. Thus with the heavenly bodies. A laya-centre is lighted and awakened into life by the fires of another "pilgrim," after which the new "centre" rushes into space and becomes a comet. It is only after losing its velocity, and hence its fiery tail, that the "Fiery Dragon" settles down into quiet and steady life as a regular respectable citizen of the sidereal family. . . .

What does Science know of Comets, their genesis, growth, and ultimate behaviour? . Nothing — absolutely nothing! And what is there so impossible that a laya centre — a lump of cosmic protoplasm, homogeneous and latent, when suddenly animated or fired up — should rush from its bed in Space and whirl throughout the abysmal depths in order to strengthen its homogeneous organism by an accumulation and addition of differentiated elements? And why should not such a comet settle in life, live, and become an inhabited globe! — *The Secret Doctrine*, I, 203–4

IN SEVERAL PARTS of her writings H. P. B. has pointed out that the evolutionary beginning in manifestation of any celestial body of whatever kind is a comet. This means that comets are of various kinds, whether or not they become a solar globe or a globe of a planetary chain; and there are other comets of far more widely varying types as regards ethereality or materiality. Yet every comet must pass through all possible stages of the inner worlds before it reaches this physical plane where it makes its first appearance as a tiny speck of light, gradually increasing in luminosity because of the exuded tail as it approaches the sun in its periodic or nonperiodic orbit around it. As a matter of fact, comets are invisible before they enter upon the highest subplane of this physical plane, and in all cases they may first be noticed as an almost ethereally luminous wisp of light.

The planetary chains in their origin were 'little suns'°— the difference between them and the sun being that the sun in the evolutionary unfolding of its spiritual nature and powers is far ahead of the planetary chains. An important point here is that a planetary chain manvantara is shorter in length than is the manvantara of the solar chain.

To illustrate: when the planetary chain of earth has reached the end of its manvantara, it dies and the inner principles of all its globes pass into their paranirvana. When the reimbodiment of this planetary chain is karmically destined to take place, the same descent of the higher principles through the inner worlds occurs as in the birth of a solar system. The new planetary chain is attracted to its own solar system, reaching it as a comet, periodically wandering into and out of its parent solar system, and even in and out of the deeps of the galaxy. This comet, the planetary chain-to-be, is attracted in several directions, but makes its way constantly towards that group of stellar clusters called the zodiac, drawn by spiritual-magnetic fohatic polarity. Finally it remains within our solar system, attracted to our sun around which it whirls in an orbit that in time becomes elliptical or perhaps circular. Thus, from being a cometary wanderer in the galactic deeps, it settles in life anew and becomes a planet in the first stages of its early rounds.

The question may arise as to the extent of the sun's control over the so-called periodic comets, because astronomy has shown that many of them travel into distant spaces, perhaps as much as thirty times the distance of Neptune from the sun, and it is likewise recognized that the cause of the periodicity of certain comets is the sun's attraction.

Now the aura or auric egg of any entity extends far beyond its physical vehicle. Hence the auric egg of a celestial body in its different layers has different limits of extension; the higher or more spiritual the layer the farther does it extend from its center, and the thicker or more material it is the less is its reach. The psychological, spiritual and divine layers of the auric egg of the sun are of immense extent, penetrating far into the galaxy, the divine actually reaching the galactic frontiers.

As all celestial bodies are in their essence living beings, expressions of monads, we see the reason why any comet which belongs to the sun's

---

°The name that the ancient Hindu writings give to the planets is ādityas, sons of Aditi; and although Aditi is usually said to have given birth to eight 'son-suns,' as alluded to in the Commentary quoted by H.P.B. in *The Secret Doctrine* (I, 99–100), at other times the number of ādityas is given as twelve.

family by karmic relationship is held in the attractive power of the higher layers of the sun's auric egg, no matter how far such comet may wander in or through the galactic spaces. In other words, the sun keeps control of its own comets, which are the periodic ones. Thus while the sun's kingdom on the lower planes comprises what is generally called the solar system, the reaches and therefore the attractive energy of the more spiritual layers of the sun's auric egg can operate by fohatic sympathy even upon comets which are wandering among the stars of the galaxy.

When completely manifested, a planetary chain consists of seven globes of form, or rūpa globes, in differing degrees of ethereality, and of five quasi-ethereal or arūpa globes — twelve in all. Now H.P.B., for reasons of simplicity, draws a veil over the five superior globes, and paints her marvelous word picture of the seven-globed planetary chain.

Every one of these globes, and each on its own plane, visible or invisible, begins its manvantaric career as a comet; so that we have physical comets as well as comets on each of the other six cosmic planes above our visible cosmic plane. Furthermore, each comet is formed around a laya-center — on whatever cosmic plane it may manifest — in order to concrete a globe around itself.

There are quite a number of comets belonging to the sun's family which show a most interesting attraction to the enormous planet Jupiter, and these are called by astronomers the 'comet family of Jupiter.' It might be asked what is the relationship between Jupiter and its comet family. There are two main causes for this attraction: the immense psychomagnetic or vital attraction of the planet itself; and the even stronger and more mystic influences of the Rāja sun 'behind' Jupiter.[*] We may say that the Rāja sun is the general, and Jupiter is the chief aide-de-camp. Furthermore, this group of comets is karmically connected with our universal as well as with our own solar system.

Let us now briefly sketch the building of a planetary chain, limiting our consideration to the comet whose destiny it is to build the lowest or globe D of our earth chain.

No comet when it first enters the highest subplane of a cosmic plane — such as our own lowest or physical cosmic plane — is formed of the gross matter of that plane, but is really ethereal matter 'breaking through' from the cosmic plane preceding or superior to it. Astronomers suppose that a comet is just ordinary physical gas which has aggregated unto itself

---

[*]Cf. *The Mahatma Letters*, p. 167.

a more or less large body of cosmic dust and asteroidal particles. Although this process does take place in ever-increasing degree, and especially so from the period when it has finally settled into its orbit, a comet in its first beginnings is essentially built of matter not belonging to our physical cosmic plane.

All celestial bodies are of spiritual origin. They are pilgrims — 'horizontally' through any one plane, and 'vertically' from the highest plane to the lowest. Here we find Plato's philosophical cross of spirit working in and on matter. Thus a comet is originally a solar or a planetary monad. It descends through the planes of space collecting its vehicles which it had thrown off after its previous imbodiment. When it reaches this plane it gradually becomes perceptible to us, and this is the beginning of its full septenary existence — just as a man's reincarnation as a full septenary being begins in the womb.

Now if such a comet successfully escape being caught and drawn into one of the suns that it passes in its interstellar journey towards our solar system, it enters into the field of the psychovital magnetic grip of the titanic forces flowing in and out of our sun. And being at one and the same time attracted to and repelled by our sun it is caught in this balance of forces — this bipolar character of gravitation giving to the comet its safety in its orbital circuits around the sun. Thereafter the comet becomes an individual member of our solar family, in this case globe D of our planetary chain. The other eleven globes of the chain to which this comet belongs are likewise entering their own beginnings of destiny.

It is the respective life forces from every globe of the moon chain,° or from the chain of any other planetary aggregate, which produce or become the respective laya-centers, the centers of resting energies. A laya-center is not a material thing. There is no laya-center where there is no individual, whether cosmic or human. A laya-center is not something which exists in space, to which life-forces (let us say from the lunar chain) flow. There is a chain laya-center containing within itself the globe laya-centers. Consequently there could be no globe laya-center until all the life essences and life energies from globe A of the lunar chain had left that globe a corpse. The aggregate of these life essences leaving globe A of the lunar chain became a laya-center.

Such a laya-center, being the spiritual-psychomagnetic vital essences of any globe of the planetary chain, must have location. Shall we say

°Cf. *The Secret Doctrine,* I, 170–4.

that it is located within or outside of our solar system? The latter. In the depths of cosmic space these laya-centers lie dormant, like sleeping germs of life. But the time comes when they reawaken to activity and feel the rising of impulses to a new manifestation — just as the human entity in devachan, when the time approaches for reincarnation, feels the faint uprisings of desire to come earthwards again. When this happens in a globe laya-center it begins to move and, gaining momentum, rushes forth from the cosmic depths, wandering in a more or less erratic fashion, attracted to this or that sun with which it has certain karmic affiliations, evading it, flying past it on the wings of destiny, attracted to some other sun, experiencing perhaps the same thing there; and, finally, drawn by stronger threads of affinity, it approaches our solar system, our sun then bringing and holding it within the confines of its own kingdom — a karmic return home.

The attractive power of the higher layers of the sun's auric egg holds within its sway the periodic comets properly belonging to the sun's family but which are wandering in the galactic spaces among the stars. Since not all comets are periodic, many of them for karmic reasons are only temporarily drawn towards our sun, whirl about it during their transit through our solar system, and then leave it to continue their wanderings towards the particular points in space which are their respective goals, each comet of this nonperiodic character being attracted by its own sun.

The mere fact that the sun with its attendant planets is itself in movement in no wise affects the pull exercised upon the periodic comets belonging to its family, because such psychomagnetic attraction is operative in and through the higher layers of the sun's auric egg. Thus we have the picture of our sun in motion through space affecting at every instant of time its own periodic cometary family, and so bringing about a constant modification of the individual movements of such comets.

Some of our periodic comets which wander among the suns of the galactic spaces are for a time karmically drawn to one or another sun in their immensely long pilgrimage, but always ultimately returning to our sun — unless they meet with the fate of being caught by some other sun and destroyed by its terrific powers. This cometary tragedy not infrequently happens, after which, and very quickly so far as cosmic time is concerned, such comet, being a failure, begins its effort at manifestation anew.

Every planet, if we look upon the higher part of its constitution as a planetary spirit, is both child and brother of the sun — brother, perhaps, is the better term. But when an entity thus born as a life-atom from the heart of the sun begins its evolutionary pilgrimage through time and space, it is as much an entity, distinct from the sun, as the sun itself is different and distinct from other suns. Each one of the planets, after the close of its pralaya, has a new reimbodiment as a nebula. Emerging from the deeps of stellar space, it is slowly drawn to the sun which was its chief in its previous chain-imbodiment. Such an entity reaching a solar system has then become a comet which circles around its own sun. There is now established an equilibrium of relations between the sun and the comet; and this comet, as the ages pass, becomes ever more and more dense and concreted, and at length settles into a regular orbit around the sun to which it has been drawn.

In due course of time a new planetary chain is fixed in its position in the solar system, finding its orbit in the almost identical locus which it had previously occupied as the former planetary chain. If its former globes, now moons, have not yet been disintegrated into their respective life-atoms, the new chain is attracted by and equivalently attracts these globe-corpses which now become its moons on the different planes, and together they thereafter pursue their orbits around the sun, until the moon finally dissolves into cosmic dust. Some planetary chains that are more advanced in evolution than our earth, and are more spiritual in character, have a happier destiny, for their moons long since had been dissipated. In other words, they are not afflicted with a kāma-rūpic moon or Dweller on the Threshold[8] as we are.

There are no fundamental differences between the occult processes at the birth of a planet and that of a human being. In every case there is a parent, the egg-bearer, and there is a parent, the bestrewer of seed. In every case there is a physicalization, a descent from the more ethereal to the gross realms of material existence. When the lowest point of the descending arc has been reached, there is a corresponding rise, leading the entity, whether world or human being, back to the spiritual realms. In the case of man, this occurs at death, and in rare individuals at initiation.

THE TWELVE FOHATIC MAGNETISMS

THE EARTH REPEATS the general structure, forces, and substances, of the solar system to which it belongs; and equivalently therefore of the zodiac, and on a still larger scale of the galaxy. Hence the earth actually has twelve different fohatic or spiritual-magnetic powers working through it, each of the twelve globes of our earth's planetary chain being the focus of one of the twelve magnetic poles both of the solar system and of the zodiac.

The signs of the zodiac are symbols which have come down to us from extreme antiquity; and in many parts of the world, such as Rome, Greece, Babylon, Egypt and Hindustan, the names of these signs, which are also given to the houses, are the same; in other parts of the world, as in China, the names of the houses differ completely from those modernly used in Europe and America. While the signs go by the same names as the constellations or houses of the zodiac, and their order is the same, the signs are not the same as the houses.

What then is the difference between the signs and the houses of the zodiac? The signs are the reflections on and in our earth of the twelve constellations or houses of the celestial zodiac. In other words, the twelve celestial houses reflect themselves in and upon our earth, each fohatic magnetic emanation from the zodiac producing its corresponding fohatic magnetic effect or reflection in our earth. The consequence of this is that our earth globe actually is electromagnetically controlled by twelve poles, i.e. six fundamental magnetisms, each of which is bipolar.

The *signs* of the zodiac therefore appertain to our earth alone; although it is of course true that the other planets of the solar system feel equally strongly the same twelve polar magnetisms, which reproduce themselves in these different planets, just as they do in our own planet. From another point of view, it becomes clear that the signs of the zodiac could be regarded as the twelve spheres of influence or kingdoms, permeating and surrounding and therefore controlling our earth globe. Although invisible and intangible, these spheres of influence, as definite portions of our earth and its atmosphere, retain their places geographically, as it were, and thus are segments of the zodiacal belt of the earth sphere.

139

By convention the signs begin with Aries at the vernal equinox, about March 20th, so that the sign Aries, being 30° in length, and each degree corresponding fairly closely with a day of 24 hours, will continue from March 20th to about April 20th. The succeeding day marks the beginning of the sign Taurus, which continues until the 20th of May; and so on throughout the year until the last degree of Pisces is reached in March. In this connection I might say that the precession of the equinoxes is brought about not merely as modern astronomical science explains it, but primarily because of the twelve fohatic magnetisms of the constellations of the celestial zodiac. Thus it is that the signs slide forwards — in 'precession' — through the celestial zodiac at the rate of about one sign in 2160 years, and 2160 × 12 makes 25,920 years, which is one of the Great Years of archaic astrology-astronomy. Each one of these periods of 2160 years is called in theosophical literature a Messianic cycle.

The diagram here given of the correspondences of the globes of our planetary chain with the signs of the zodiac shows how each globe is under the individual influence of one of the constellations. Otherwise stated, every one of the twelve globes of the earth chain is a focus of the particular fohatic emanation flowing forth from the constellation of the celestial zodiac with which it is in closest magnetic affinity; yet all twelve constellations likewise work in and through every one of the globes of the chain.

The movements in our solar system are so many (not only the sun as an individual having its own particular motions, but every planet likewise), that it would be a hopeless task to attempt to explain them all in detail. In the last analysis, each and every one of these different solar or planetary movements is directly referable to two main instrumental causes: (a) to forces of a psycho-spiritual character inherent in the individual or celestial body itself, together with (b) the constant and unceasing influence of the twelve fohatic magnetisms of the constellations of the zodiac. One of the most interesting of these movements is what astronomy calls the revolution of the line of the apsides of the respective planetary orbits.° In the case of the earth's orbit this brings about a slow

---

°The line of the apsides of the earth's orbit, for instance, is said by astronomy to stretch in both directions towards two constellations of the celestial zodiac, Sagittarius and Gemini, and to be moving steadily and slowly eastward at an estimated rate which will make a complete circuit in some 108,000 years. Of course the revolution of the line of the apsides of each different planet makes its circuit in its own time period.

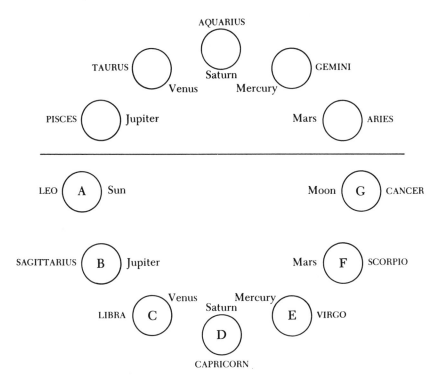

secular change or series of changes in the manner in which the constellational twelvefold magnetisms affect our planet, with which must be combined a similar but different change caused by the precession of the equinoxes in the direction contrary to that of the line of the apsides. There is a third most important movement, that of the inversion of the earth's poles, of a time period vastly longer than even that of the revolution of the line of the apsides.

All these various movements, whether of our earth or of any other planet, or of the sun itself, certainly partake of a mechanical character because they are movements of bodies; nevertheless within and behind them all is to be found the guidance and controlling power of lofty spiritual intelligences. It is precisely this working of mind upon the matter of the solar system which produces the beauty and regularity, the law and order, which have aroused the reverence of men of every age.

In this manner the earth in its motions carries along the signs, these being portions of itself; and from the twelve fohatic magnetisms of the celestial zodiac thus arises the shift of the signs with regard to and against the background of the constellations, producing not only the precession of the equinoxes, but other movements of the earth's axis. It is these other movements which bring about the extraordinary cataclysmic occurrences marking the endings and beginnings of root-races as well as of their main subraces.

THE GLOBE ZODIAC

It has been shown that the signs of the zodiac are located within the auric egg of our earth globe, and that they are not the same as the constellations of the celestial zodiac. It has also been stated that any planetary chain, as well as any globe thereof, is produced not only by its own monadic swabhāva, but that the twelve fohatic magnetisms of the twelve constellations are likewise intimately involved with these inherent magnetic swabhāvas in producing the planetary chains and their respective globes.

From this we see that the signs of the zodiac of any globe of any planetary chain are localized fields or foci, each such field being the portion of the auric egg of a globe which, in addition to its own swābhāvic magnetism, reflects the corresponding fohatic magnetism emanating from one of the constellations of the zodiac. Thus, a globe of a planetary chain is surrounded with its own twelvefold zodiacal ring, and each one of these fields is one of the twelve signs of the globe zodiac. We may picture to ourselves this twelvefold magnetism as flowing forth from the heart of the auric egg of such a globe, and spreading out into fan-shaped sectors, these forming the belt or ring comprising the twelve signs of the globe zodiac.

Now, because of the intermingling of these twelvefold zodiacal magnetisms with the twelvefold inherent magnetism of the swabhāva of any globe, we see that each sign of the globe zodiac is of a dual twelvefold character: (a) the magnetism of the swabhāva of the globe monad; and (b) the magnetisms of the twelve constellations of the celestial zodiac. Everything works with everything else, and this is the reason why the monads of the different classes are able to find their proper fields of evolutionary experience, not only on any part of the earth's surface, but also in any one of the sacred planetary chains of our solar system.

Furthermore, what the esoteric philosophy calls the lokas and talas° (i.e. the different worlds in which dwell and through which pass the evolving life-waves that circulate around any planetary chain) are actually

---

°For a fuller explanation of lokas and talas see p. 256 et seq.

built of and energized by the dual and compound magnetisms, thus putting each one of the talas and lokas in direct psychoelectric and psychomagnetic sympathy with the different magnetic emanations. Hence each such loka and tala is twelvefold in character, composed of a manifest seven and of the more spiritual five, very much as the twelve globes of a planetary chain are composed of seven manifest and five belonging to the arūpa worlds. In this connection, H.P.B. has an interesting passage in one of her letters:

> . . . each of the 7 globes or planets of our chain has such a dual septenary circle of RINGS — Saturn being the only half frank and sincere planet in this case.°

Entirely too much attention has been fastened upon the *words* here about Saturn and the so-called rings which surround it in the plane of its equator. What is really referred to is the dual series of manifested lokas and talas which are usually given as seven, the more spiritual lokas and talas being passed by in silence.

When we remember that the lokas and talas are actual worlds compounded of the blended magnetisms which build the planetary chains and their respective globes, we see what H.P.B. means when speaking of "a dual septenary circle of rings." Her reference to Saturn is but a way of stating that the Saturnian bhūr-loka and pātāla have collected an equatorial ring, which, because of the close interrelation between our physical globe and the globe of Saturn, is at least partially visible to us. Indeed, our earth is surrounded in outer space by a relatively thick and dense 'continent' of matter belonging to the solar system which we are not aware of because our eyes have been evolved to see through it.

It might be added that this question of the intermingling of the lokas and talas as building the structure of any globe of a planetary chain is one of the most difficult to understand. For instance, we have to keep clearly in mind that there are other life-waves, families of monads, besides our own human life-wave, which follow each other in periodic circulations around the globes of the planetary chain and, in doing so, pass in regular serial order through the various lokas and talas belonging to each globe. Moreover, every one of the lokas and talas of each globe is subject to, and under the respective and differing influences of, the twelvefold magnetisms or signs of that particular globe zodiac, from which the globes

---

°*The Letters of H. P. Blavatsky to A. P. Sinnett*, p. 245.

themselves are considered as compounded or individualized units of the chain.

To summarize: let us picture a monad, a cosmic germ or hiranyagarbha, beginning its period of manvantaric manifestation. This cosmic germ will eventuate, let us say, in a globe of some planetary chain, like our earth, in its very earliest stages of development. As the cosmic germ unfolds, it pours continuously forth from within itself all the various substances and forces which immediately upon their emanation coalesce with the twelvefold fohatic magnetisms of the general field of the solar system — these magnetisms issuing forth from the zodiac of the constellations.

As this cosmic germ of our earth unfolds into becoming a globe, it does so by the process of forming the various lokas and talas, two by two; and these worlds, or lokas and talas, are themselves formed of magnetic emanated substances. Thus was our globe built of the twelve pairs of lokas and talas, of which seven pairs are manifest and five pairs are unmanifest.

The auric egg of a globe is the general field or interpenetrating body of the spirit-substance which issues forth from and surrounds the heart of the cosmic monad or germ, and thus the auric egg enfolds and interpenetrates all the lokas and talas, including of course our physical globe earth, which is bhūr-loka and pātāla, considered as a pair. Every one of these worlds enclosed within the auric egg therefore has its own aspect, analogically speaking, of the globe zodiac of signs, just as our globe earth has; and each such sign on whatever plane, from the purely spiritual through all intermediate planes down to the gross physical, is the focus of the especial field of action of one of the constellations of the celestial zodiac, and therefore is known by the same name that the constellation has. Thus in a sense each of these different lokas and talas — each pair a world, and all combining to form the entirety of a globe — has its own zodiac of signs or twelvefold field of fohatic magnetisms.

145

AURIC EGG: COSMIC AND MICROCOSMIC

EVERY ENTITY HAS its own auric egg; and the higher the entity stands in evolutionary unfoldment, the more perfectly is the auric egg developed and the stronger is its function. The auric egg is by some supposed to be merely the vital aura (or astral-vital-material atmosphere) surrounding a living being; however, this is but its lowest expression, the physical body being actually the dregs of this vital auric atmosphere emanating from the auric egg.

In strict accuracy, the auric egg surrounds every portion of the constitution of an entity, and expresses itself on all the planes thereof in accordance with the laws and forces and substances pertaining to and active on any one plane. Each one of the different monads, which together form the complete constitution of any being, is surrounded by a knot or condensation of this living and intelligent aura — partly emanating from each monad and partly belonging to the general auric egg — which knot thus acts as a spiritual psychovital ganglion or nerve center for each plane and for the monad which it surrounds. All these different knots or foci of active consciousness, stretching from the divine to the physical, may be figurated as a pillar of light.

Thus the sun has its own individual auric egg through which, as in an electric field, operate the descending and ascending forces and substances which are continuously active and interblending in its constitution. Moreover, each one of the twelve globes of the solar chain has its own *individualized* auric egg, corresponding to the different monads in the human constitution. Precisely so with every planetary chain: every one of its globes, and in consequence our earth, has its individualized auric egg, yet the larger auric egg of the entire chain encloses them all.

The sphere of action or radiation of the divine and spiritual parts of any auric egg reaches to the stars of the galaxy, and possibly even beyond; while the range of action of the lowest parts of the auric egg of an entity extends little beyond the astral-physical vehicle. Thus, in the divine and spiritual parts of man's constitution, he is in actual 'touch' with all things over a sphere which reaches the stars; in his intermediate

146

or psycho-intellectual portions the extent of influence of the auric egg is much more limited, but nevertheless covers our solar system; whereas the range of influence of the lowest parts of his auric egg reaches scarcely farther than his astral-vital aura which surrounds his astral-physical body.

Again, what we call the solar kingdom — which comprises all space within the compass of the divine, spiritual and intellectual, and even psychomagnetic radiation of our sun — consists of the planetary chains belonging to our own solar system, and of the interplanetary fields of space likewise. Hence all these planetary chains are bathed in solar radiations of various kinds; but so tremendously powerful is the sun, even in its lowest parts, the physical orb and its garments, that its vital-astral-material radiation extends even to the physical limits of its kingdom.° Thus it is that the aura of the auric egg of every entity within our solar system reaches to every part of the solar domain: fully in the fields of the highest parts of the entity's auric egg; less in the intermediate parts; and only slightly so with the lower parts of its auric efflux.

Now it is just these individual but invisible spheres of influence flowing forth from the auric egg which, in the case of the planets, were called by the ancients 'crystalline spheres.' They did not take the word crystalline literally, any more than we ourselves look upon these spheres as being composed of actual glass or crystal. Their meaning was: spheres, totally invisible, yet compacted of vital-astral substance in their lower parts, and of spiritual and intellectual substance in their higher parts, which combined are the respective auric eggs of the different planets.

Furthermore, every one of the planets revolving around our sun has that sun as its center; and as the entire solar kingdom is substantial and therefore solid in a sense, each such planet, which really means each planetary chain and the auric sphere extending from it, is a substantial body with the sun at its center. Each surrounds the sun as an invisible sphere, the visible planetary globe being the nucleus or development of the laya-center on the physical plane of this particular minor Egg of Brahmā.

We thus have a picture of the Egg of Brahmā of our solar system

---

°It may be of interest to note that Mārttānda, also Mritānda, both names for the sun in Sanskrit literature, mean 'mortal egg' (from *mrita*, mortal, and *anda*, egg) — the reference being to the mortal or nonpermanent part of the Egg of Brahmā, i.e. particularly to the visible sun which is the physical vehicle of the solar Brahmā. In just the same fashion is man's body the mortal part of his constitution or auric egg.

147

as a complex and yet most harmoniously interworking and interblended system of 'crystalline' spheres, each sphere being the 'body' of a planet; and the common center of this aggregate of planets is the sun. From this it is not to be supposed that those segments of the sun's auric egg which are or contain its own signs of the zodiac are the sole controlling centers of the known or unknown planets; because each of the zodiacal signs of the sun, or of any of its globes, is particular to and individualized respectively for the entire solar chain and for each of its globes, of which our visible sun is one.

This leads us to a highly important point of esoteric astrology. While it is true that the twelve fohatic magnetisms of the celestial zodiac bathe every being and thing in our universal solar system, nevertheless they are a *diffuse* twelvefold auric ocean. In other words, while these constellational magnetisms powerfully and continuously throughout the manvantara affect every planet and globe in the universal solar system, yet the influences are general and diffuse rather than particular and direct. In the case of *our* solar system it is not only the sun, but all the planetary chains which affect our earth chain with their individual influences, these planetary spiritual-auric individualities being what the ancients called the kosmokratores or world builders of our earth and its chain of globes.

Likewise the twelve fohatic constellational magnetisms of the celestial zodiac are 'directed' by and through the sun and these other planets of our solar system. Thus the power exercised upon our earth and its chain by the other planetary chains is not only that of the individual swābhāvic influence of each such planetary chain and its globes, but both collectively and individually the sun and these other planetary chains direct and individualize the diffuse twelvefold magnetisms pouring forth from the celestial zodiac. Of course our own earth plays the same role on all the other bodies of our solar system that they individually play upon our earth, each contributing its own characteristic type of influence — a most suggestive picture of the interblending and interacting forces and substances ever at work throughout the entire manvantara of our solar system.

THE ASTRO-THEOGONICAL ASPECT OF THE COSMOS

EVERY CELESTIAL body that we can see is the physical manifestation on this plane of an indwelling cosmic spirit. The divinity manifesting through a sun is a solar spirit or god. The entity manifesting through a planet is a planetary spirit, the chief of its hierarchy.

The higher in the scale of life an entity stands, the more perfectly does it accord in its consciousness and in its will with the fundamental of the hierarchy of which it forms a part. The sun, for instance, having no arbitrary movements of its own, keeps strictly to its place in space through the ages and follows a regular path in its orbit among the other solar systems of the Milky Way. A planet or planetary spirit similarly is bound by the rules of the hierarchy of which it forms a part. It is, so to say, one of the cogs in the wheel of the cosmic mechanism.

Each starry entity has, as component parts of its constitution, what esoteric Buddhism calls: first, a dhyāni-buddha, then a celestial buddha, then a celestial bodhisattva, then certain intermediate elements, and finally the physical globe we see in the sky. Such a composite entity sends its influences or energies throughout the universe as rivers of living entities, life-atoms, composing in their aggregate a characteristic influence or force. These rivers of lives flow according to law, following certain definite paths or routes called the circulations of the universe or of the cosmos.

Every star as well as every true cluster of stars transmits to us its own particular range of vibrational energies. In fact, the stars, and to a less extent the planets, are the builders of the manifested universe — not merely of the physical bodies which flow forth originally from the physical bodies of the various celestial runners, but more particularly are they builders through the spiritual, intellectual, and psychical, as well as astral and vital, energies inherent in them and rooted in the invisible realms of the universe.*

---

*There are a number of Nordic myths regarding the making of the worlds, based on natural truths formulated in symbolic language by great Northern seers of the past. All of them have the touch of melancholy that seems to be inherent in the blood of the Norse people; and therefore in most of these myths of the formation

These rivers of lives — so far as they consist of the entities which reach this part of our solar system, when coming from the twelve constellations of the zodiac — are actually the twelve classes of monads, each of them being identical in essence with the controlling spirit of one of the constellations. In other words, each class of monads may be considered to be a corporate emanation from one of the constellations. We should distinguish carefully between the astro-theogonical aspect of this subject, and that which is commonly studied in so-called judicial astrology. These two aspects are based on the same facts of natural being, but they are two different ways of looking at them.

The constellations are in movement as much as any other aggregate entity is. The stars of any constellation, considered as individuals, are rapidly moving; and in vast spaces of time they will change their places in the sky. Nevertheless, these various groups of starry bodies are formed of stars or suns which are akin to each other in their spiritual roots.

The gods of all the ancient mythologies were looked upon as the powers of nature plus consciousness. This was the view taught to the multitudes; but in the Mysteries a very different one was taken. There, the old mythological legends and stories were explained, and the gods shown to be the divine causes of existence, the fountains of self-consciousness and enlightened will — guardians of the cosmic law and order. They were the causes of cycles in nature herself, the exemplification of order and time periods. Individual man himself is the physical expression of an overshadowing divinity; and the gods, when fully evolved, were known to be the overshadowing monads — now fully evolved into divinity, but in aeons upon aeons in the past they also were men, or beings equivalent in evolutionary grade to men. Such, in brief outline, was the teaching concerning the gods in the Mysteries of the European schools. In Greek mythology Phoebus Apollo or Helios was personified as the sun god; but in the Mysteries it was taught that behind the sun there is a living splendor, the root of whose being is a divine consciousness, and whose energies manifest in the solar forces.

of the world, there are references to one of the greatest mysteries of being — the self-sacrifice of the divinities in order that the worlds may come into existence. They give their bodies and of their 'lifeblood,' which latter flows forth and with the body becomes the world and all things.

There is a very holy mystery involved in this, taught in different forms as, for instance, in Hindustan and in Egypt, but all meaning the same: that the universe is kept going and preserved from destruction by the self-sacrifice of the highest gods.

Everything that is in the universe is in man, latent or active. This means that every influence coming from anywhere in universal space at some time or other streams through each human being. All the twelve characteristic influences of the zodiacal signs are in us as well as in every other entity, animate or so-called inanimate, for it is actually these influences which build up all things, according to pattern, according to karma. While the particular sign under which a person is born is dominant in that life, the influences of all twelve signs must work in man, for he would not be a complete human being were he deprived of the characteristic quality of any one of the twelve rivers of life flowing from the constellations of the zodiac.

Some of the starry constellations have a singularly beneficent influence upon earth, while others in a few cases have an influence which may be described as maleficent. But all things are relative. What is good for us may be evil for another planet, or vice versa. The earth in its turn exercises an influence not only upon the other planets of our solar family but also, by reaction, upon the sun, even as the sun acts directly upon this earth.

Moreover, every human being as well as every one of the globes of our earth planetary chain is under the particular governance or inspiration of one of the seven sacred planets; and this applies likewise to each of the seven root-races on any one planet. For instance, the first root-race, and similarly the first globe of the planetary chain, are under the influence of the sun, or rather that secret planet for which the sun stands. The second root-race and the second globe are under the influence of Jupiter. The third root-race and the third globe are under the influence of Venus. The planet dominating the destiny of the fourth root-race — the Atlantean — and of our own fourth globe in the planetary chain is Saturn, in close operative alliance with the moon. Our present or fifth root-race and the fifth globe on the ascending arc are under the especial dominance and control of Mercury. Strange as it may seem, the planet which will govern the destiny of the sixth root-race and the sixth globe is Mars.

The seventh and highest globe of the planetary chain, and also the seventh root-race of any globe, are both under the governance of the moon, or rather the secret planet for which the moon stands. The seventh race is the last before the evolutionary life-wave quits this globe. The seventh globe is also the last before the generalized and aggregate life-waves quit the planetary chain. In other words, both the seventh race of earth and the seventh globe of the chain are the gates of life; from the material standpoint, also the gates of death. In fact, every planet is a lord of life and of death, but it is the moon especially which in esoteric philosophy is called the lord, or sometimes the goddess, of life and of death.

While every root-race is under the particular control of one of the seven sacred planets, all the other six likewise cooperate, not only in building each globe of the planetary chain but also in affecting the destiny of each root-race. As it is written in *The Secret Doctrine* (I, 573):

> Hence the seven chief planets, the *spheres* of the indwelling seven spirits, under each of which is born one of the human groups which is guided and influenced thereby. There are only seven planets *(specially* connected with earth), and twelve houses, but the possible combinations of their aspects are countless. As each planet can stand to each of the others in twelve different aspects, their combinations must, therefore, be almost infinite; as infinite, in fact, as the spiritual, psychic, mental, and physical capacities in the numberless varieties of the *genus homo,* each of which varieties is born under one of the seven planets and one of the said countless planetary combinations.

The correspondences[9] given by H.P.B. are often taken entirely too mechanically. It is not the mechanism of these correspondences that is important. The important thing is to *understand the meaning;* the correspondences are merely hints, and were never supposed to be taken as being absolutes, as unveiling the whole truth.

I sometimes wonder if we are not going a little too far in making the earth and ourselves mere playthings of cosmic powers, influences or forces flowing to us from the zodiacal constellations. These powers or energies are undoubtedly facts; their influence on our earth and on all the other planetary chains is incalculably great. Yet we must never forget that every solar system — and every human being also — is an organic entity in itself, with an immortal monad within and behind it. The old astrologers used to say: the wise man controls his planets, the fool submits to them. The meaning is obvious: the indestructibly immortal monad cannot itself be fatally swayed by the universe around it, although its bodies and garments may be and are. Therefore, were all the universe pressing against a single monad, that monad would remain unharmed and untouched.

OCCULT PHYSIOLOGICAL STRUCTURE OF THE SOLAR SYSTEM

"The Sun is the heart of the Solar World (System) and its brain is hidden behind the (visible) Sun. From thence, sensation is radiated into every nerve-centre of the great body, and the waves of the life-essence flow into each artery and vein. . . ."

Thus, there is a regular circulation of the vital fluid throughout our system, of which the Sun is the heart — the same as the circulation of the blood in the human body — during the manvantaric solar period, or life; the Sun contracting as rhythmically at every return of it, as the human heart does.

— *The Secret Doctrine*, I, 541

IN OUR SOLAR system, which is an organic entity, there are various life streams, following well-defined paths within the structure of this cosmic entity, which may be called the "circulations of the cosmos." This phrase describes a wonderful natural process which is analogous to the circulations of the various fluids in the human body, whether these be material such as the blood stream, or quasi-astral such as the nerve aura.

Elsewhere more will be said about the outer rounds, and the rivers of lives which follow these circulations as among the sun and planets; yet it might be well now to enlarge upon what we may call the occult physiological structure of the solar system, which includes the circulations of the cosmos. What these circulations are could be illustrated by the electric and magnetic lines of forces which bind together in a closely knitted organic web planet with planet, and the planets with the sun. Electricity is universal throughout the solar system; so likewise is magnetism, its alter ego; and both are expressions on lower planes of the cosmic jīva or universal life force: first the jīva of the solar system, and secondarily the respective jīvas of the various planetary chains.

The electricities and magnetisms circulating in and through a solar system are the real causes of the forces of attraction and repulsion constantly at work in it. They function in such fashion that they attract the component bodies of a solar system, holding them in their respective orbital movements and at the same time, because of the polarity of these forces, bringing about repellent effects. Thus the different bodies of the solar system are kept apart, so that they do not collide or all rush to a common center, as they certainly would if the forces of attraction, whether electrical or magnetic, alone prevailed. In other words, both cosmic electricity and cosmic magnetism are manifestations of cosmic fohat, the Tibetan name for cosmic life or cosmic jīva. However, fohat is unimaginable apart from the indwelling and guiding cosmic mind or consciousness. As an ancient book quoted by H.P.B. so well expressed it: "Fohat is the steed, Thought is the rider."

Looking at the matter from another angle, electricity and magnetism are essentially *life, vitality* — yet always guided by indwelling mind. Thus the vitality of a cosmic being, evolved or unevolved, may in its most material aspects be called vital electromagnetism, and in its spiritual aspects the attractive and repelling operations of mind or consciousness.

Life, whether cosmic or enshrined within the vital sphere of a smaller organic entity, is a most protean thing in its multifarious and ever-changing manifestation. The very electric current which lights our cities and dwellings is an expression of cosmic vitality, as is the magnetism which attracts iron filings or plays so large a part at the poles of the earth. Even the influences that human beings exercise upon each other, such as sympathy, attraction or repulsion, are manifestations of the cosmic life, but working through us are therefore strongly affected by our individual characteristics.

The circulations of the cosmos are the arteries and veins of the solar system — considered as a living organism, as a cosmic individual — and are filled with, and actually composed of, the rivers of lives which are in constant movement in their passings from planet to planet and between planets and sun. In fact, the planets are actual organs within the body corporate of a cosmic entity, each organ fulfilling its own particular spiritual-magnetic function. Moreover, there are bodies circling around the interior of the sun, around its core, within what we perceive as the outer boundary of the solar orb. Truly, there are many mysteries connected with our sun.

Thus, by analogy, in man's physical body, and equivalently so as regards the monads of his entire constitution, each of the organs has its part to perform. Just as in our bodies there is a constant circulation of the vital essence imbodied in the blood and the nerve fluids, so in our solar system is there an incessant and tremendously powerful interchange of vital essences, every planet contributing to every other planet and to the sun, and the sun infilling them all in return with its own twelvefold forces and substances.

It would be difficult to imagine that the forces which leave or enter the sun do so haphazardly, without cause, or that they follow no particular channels. The circulations of the universe, so far as the sun is concerned, are the pathways of destiny used by the countless armies of the monads as they pass and repass on their journeys. These electromagnetic paths convey cosmic vitality which, like our blood stream, carries along with it innumerable multitudes of entities. All beings follow these pathways, for the universe is a living organism, threaded with its network of arteries and cosmic nerves, along which come and go all the migrating entities. As a matter of fact, these circulations have their beating heart in the central sun of our universe.

Now it is a very easy matter indeed for an adept, by using his will power and wisdom, to choose this or that route or channel by which he can pass from planet to planet, or from superior to inferior worlds, and vice versa. It is to this that Plato alludes in more than one of his writings, such as the *Timaeus,* and particularly *The Republic,* Book X, where he gives what is commonly called the Vision of Er, one of the least understood and most difficult passages of his books. Plato teaches in a rather figurative and mystical style, because he could not publicly put forth an actual teaching of the Mystery schools.

One thing of importance that we should constantly strive to avoid is to look upon ourselves as subject, and the solar system as object: in other words, to consider ourselves and the solar system or the planet, in or on which we may at any time be passing one of the phases of our aeons-long course of lives, as being separate and differently existing entities. In truth, man is throughout all his being an integral part of the universe. His vitality is not only derived from the universe which environs him and from which he receives further increments of 'life,' but in order to live and evolve he must return parts of his vitality to the source from which he got it.

These circulations of the cosmos are as fully active in the inner worlds as they are in our visible plane of the solar system. They are those invisible, but very real pathways, which are followed by the hosts of entities both before physical existence and after. In ancient literatures references can be found to the 'way of the gods,' the 'path of the fathers,' the 'path of the devas,' and we could rightfully add the 'path of the elementals,' the 'path of the dhyāni-chohans' — in fact, the path of any family or group of entities. They are also the pathways which are trodden by the dead, or by those re-entering imbodiment. The Hebrew Qabbālāh, for example, describes these circulations by the one word *gilgūlīm*, which means whirlings or revolvings, both of egos in their post-mortem peregrinations and of the pathways along which they revolve.

If we could realize what flows from star to star, and from star to our solar system and back again, and what passes throughout our solar system after coming to us from the stars, we would know the entire story of the genesis, nature, and destiny, not only of the solar system itself but of all its inhabitants. And those inhabitants are of many kinds, not merely planets and men, not merely comets and asteroids, but the vast, indeed numberless, hosts of living entities in all degrees of development from a single life-atom to the gods.

To summarize, then, the circulations of the cosmos are the spiritual-magnetic pathways of the solar system and are composed of rivers of lives; and every human being is one of these 'lives' in the particular river or life-wave to which he by his karmic destiny belongs for the time being. Just because man, both as an individual and collectively as the human hierarchy, is part and parcel of one of these rivers of lives, he will be obliged during the outer rounds not only to pass from planet to planet of the sacred seven known to the ancients, but likewise, because of the onflowing stream along these circulations, sooner or later to enter the sun — and in the course of time leave it on his return journey through the solar system via the various sacred planets, in due serial order. Thus it has been said by the great teachers that the sun is the majestic beating heart and ever-active consciousness of the solar system, whose regular and periodic pulsations are never-ceasing throughout the long ages of the solar manvantara.

CAUSATIVE NATURE OF CYCLES

THE DOCTRINE OF cycles is one of the most important in the entire cosmic range of the esoteric philosophy, because repetitive or rhythmic action is fundamental in nature. As a matter of fact, every being and thing that exists is an expression of rhythmic pulsation: we are not only the children of cycles greater than ourselves, but actually within our own beings imbody cycles because we are cyclical in all our life processes. The same rule applies with identical force to any entity in boundless Infinitude, whether a galaxy or an atom.

We perceive cycles by the recurrences of moving beings and things in our world, and are deluded into thinking that these repetitions are caused by some intangible entity called time, while in reality they are caused by the cyclical movements of the bodies or of the consciousness of entities. The revolutions of the planets around the sun is an example; they are not *caused* by time. It is the moving entities themselves which produce in us the time-illusion, due to our imperfect understanding of their operations in Duration. As one of the Stanzas of Dzyan says: "Time was not, for it lay asleep in the infinite bosom of duration" — because moving things were then no more.

A human being is a cycle; an atom is a cycle — in this technical sense. We say that the sun rises in the morning and sets in the evening, and we call it a cycle, a day. The time-illusion produced by the moving object — in this case our earth — gives us the notion that a day is produced by an absolute entity called Time, or is an integral part of such separate entity.

Cycles themselves are not caused as minor integrals of time by time. Where you have no space, there is no time; where you have no time, there is no space. Space is a substantial entity in occultism, and one of its māyāvi attributes is what we call time. As Space is eternally enduring, this is the cause of the time-māyā. That does not mean that time is nonexistent, but there is no absolute entity apart from things called Time, nor where there are no beings to perceive it.

All the various and varied phenomena of the infinitesimal worlds of physical chemistry; all the movements of nature everywhere, even astro-

157

nomical and meteorological phenomena, like storms, periods of drouth, electromagnetic outbursts such as the aurorae; the periodic epidemics of diseases — all these are rhythmic, because cyclical. The pulsing of the blood in the human body and the heartbeat manifest cycles as fully as does the sunspot period, or that of the precession of the equinoxes, or the whirlings of the rivers of lives along the circulations of the universe. The unending succession of manvantaras and pralayas, whether smaller or greater, rounds and obscurations, etc. — all are cyclical.

What is it in universal Being that sets in motion the various cyclical processes which make up the movements of the worlds? The *causes* of these interwoven cycles are to be found in the fact that the very swabhāva of the cosmic life is pulsatory, rhythmic.° Yet to state thus baldly that the cosmic life pulsates throughout eternity is incomplete until we add that such rhythmically vibrational activity is the imbodied expression of the movement of cosmic intelligence.

Now the cosmic life itself from the standpoint of structure may be looked upon as but an incomprehensibly vast aggregate of all smaller beings and things, each such comprehended entity or thing in itself, in its essence, being a droplet of the cosmic life and intelligence, and therefore imbodying its own relative portion of all the cosmic powers and faculties. Thus we have the vibratory and rhythmic movements of the cosmic life, *plus* all the other interwoven cycles of its incomputable hosts of entities, each one in itself of cyclical character. We have cycles within cycles: cycles within others still greater; or, conversely, cycles of increasing vibrational frequency running into the infinitesimal.

From this we see that every cycle is the life movement of the heartbeat and hence the mind-beat of some cosmic, subcosmic, or infracosmic being or entity. The whirling of a galaxy is an expression of the rhythmic life-pulses of the galactic hierarch throughout all its planes of being, and manifesting, astronomically speaking, on the physical plane as the cyclical wheelings of the galactic body. Similarly so in the world of the infinitesimals, such as the whirlings of the electronic bodies in the atom.

Cycles, then, irrespective of scale or magnitude or hierarchical plane, are the expressions of the pulsations of the life and mind of the hierarchical hosts — of the web of interblending worlds — which not only infill the universe, but actually *are* it. In short, cycles are the inherent rhythms of life.

°See the second fundamental proposition in *The Secret Doctrine,* I, 16–17.

CYCLICAL TIME PERIODS

SOME STUDENTS, after reading *The Secret Doctrine*, have spent years trying to apply the numerical keys given there in order to arrive at the exact length of the various kinds of Days and Nights of Brahmā. There may be little harm in such adventures, yet one could waste a great deal of valuable time in this kind of theorizing. If given the final keys, a clever mathematician might closely approximate the correct time periods, and apply them to ascertain when some karmic event might come to pass. But, in view of the highly imperfect moral evolution of mankind, such knowledge would be replete with danger. Suppose that it were possible for a man to calculate just what is going to happen to him in the next week or month or year. The chances are that he would immediately begin to make new and bad karma for himself in trying to forestall the working out of nemesis, and thus involve himself in a new karmic web highly perilous not only to his moral stability but even to his intellectual equilibrium. Mercifully has this branch of the esoteric philosophy been most carefully shrouded in mystery throughout the ages.

Nevertheless, it is good that we should realize that all nature, as Pythagoras so wisely taught, is built on numerical relations, harmonically interacting in inflexible mathematical connections. For this reason there has never been any attempt to veil the general teaching, and even in some cases actual time periods have been disclosed. For instance, in *The Secret Doctrine*, Volume II, pages 68-70, we have Brahmā's Age, called the mahākalpa, set down as 311,040,000,000,000 years; and one of Brahmā's Days as 4,320,000,000, with a Night of equal duration, so that such a combined Day-Night period is 8,640,000,000. Furthermore, the total of the four general yugas, together making a mahāyuga, is 4,320,000 years, and the full period of a manvantara is 308,448,000 years.

In examining the array of figures given by H.P.B., the difficulty lies in knowing just which manvantara or Day (or which pralaya or Night) is referred to. There are manvantaras of the entire solar system as well as of the planetary chain; and there are still smaller manvantaras, each one of which is the reign of a single Manu. Often terms are used which have different applications. For instance, the term 'solar system' may refer to our own planetary chain and its evolution. Thus seven chain-rounds of our earth chain might be called one solar manvantara *for our earth chain*, but the sun will be as lively as ever. When seven complete imbodiments of our planetary chain have taken place, that is a solar manvantara for our chain; for when a new manvantara for our chain shall again begin, a *new sun* will shine upon that chain; or, from the standpoint of our earth globe, we shall see that particular sun of the next higher cosmic plane of the solar chain on which our globe D will then begin to manifest.

A chain-round is a passage of the life-waves or families of monads from the highest globe through all the globes once. (When a chain-round passes through any one globe we call it a globe-round.) When seven such chain-rounds have been completed, that is a Day of Brahmā or planetary chain manvantara. Seven of these Days of Brahmā make a solar manvantara for this chain because, taking our globe earth as an instance, at the end of seven such planetary Days the seven subplanes of the cosmic plane on which our globe earth is will have been passed through and every experience gained therein. Then, in order to begin its new solar manvantara, the entire chain within our solar Brahmānda will begin its evolution on higher planes. And therefore a new sun will appear.

For the benefit of those who may be interested in numerical relations: the "full period of one *Manvantara*," mentioned by H.P.B.° as being 308,448,000 years, refers *in this usage* of the word manvantara to one half of a chain-round, which is the general time that it takes a life-wave to pass from the first globe (let us say globe A) of the chain to globe D, our earth. A similar time period is required in order to pass from the midpoint of our globe earth to globe G, let us say; so that one chain-round will take some 616,896,000 years. As the common teaching regarding the rounds gives their number as seven, when we multiply this last sum by 7, we obtain very closely the figure 4,320,000,000 years, which is one *complete* chain-manvantara, or one Day of Brahmā, the Brahmā in this case being the planetary chain Brahmā. The difference between this rough and ready calculation and the full period of 4,320,000,000 is due to the fact that the sandhyās (twilights) have been omitted.

Furthermore, when a planetary chain has completed its chain-man-

---

°*The Secret Doctrine*, II, 69.

vantara, there then ensues a rest period or Night of equal length — 4,320,000,000 years. In addition, the cosmic mahākalpa — here signifying the kalpa of our solar system or its complete manvantara or one Year of Brahmā — is composed of 360 of the solar Brahmā's Days, which are the planetary chain Days, as above alluded to. As there are a hundred of the solar Brahmā's Years in the full period of a solar mahākalpa (Brahmā's Life), this last figure must be multiplied by one hundred, and we thus attain the figure 311,040,000,000,000.

It has taken some 320,000,000 years since the first geological sedimentary deposits were made on our earth in the beginning of this fourth round, and this is but a trifle more than the "full period of one Manvantara," given by H.P.B. as being 308,448,000 years — which is but another way of saying the 'manvantara' of our fourth round inaugurated by Vaivasvata, the root-Manu of this round.°

The fact of the repetitive analogies in nature is the master key in making computations dealing with all these time periods. Just because the small reflects throughout its structure and its destiny whatever is the structure and destiny of the great, the same general mathematical rules will apply both to a microcosm — whatever it may be — as well as to a macrocosm, such as a solar system.

It might be as well to state here that the esoteric year contains 360 days, equal to the 360° of the zodiac, whether of the signs or of the constellations; and in a past period of the solar system our earth year was actually 360 days long. Since then, due to a number of cosmic interacting causes, under the governance of the fohatic magnetisms of the zodiacal constellations, the speed of rotation of the earth somewhat increased, so that the present year contains roughly 365¼ days. This acceleration has now probably reached its maximum, in which case the rotation of the earth will slowly again decrease and in time pass through and beyond the median point of 360 days, so that the year will then contain somewhat less than 360 days, possibly as few as 354. When this minimum period has been reached, the earth's rotation will again quicken slightly, and in time will pass through the median point of 360 days until

---

°If the reader will analyze the various passages in *The Secret Doctrine* regarding the different reigns of the Manus of our planetary chain as applied to the time periods of the seven rounds, he will better understand these numerical allusions. In particular see Vol. II, pp. 709–15, as well as pp. 307–9.

it reaches again its maximum. Thus it is that during the planetary chain's manvantara the average rotational yearly period is 360 days.

This is the reason that 360 days is recognized in occultism as the standard year; and many cultured nations, such as the Babylonians, Egyptians and Hindus, all famous throughout antiquity for their astronomical skill, used the 360-day period in their calculations for the length of a year. This is shown in the case of the Hindus by a passage in the very old astronomical work, the *Sūrya-Siddhānta*[10] (I, 12, 13), which first states the standard occult year of 360, and then refers to the year as consisting of 365¼ days more or less.

Modern scientists, scholars and mathematicians ascribe to the ancient Babylonians our present reckoning of 360° in a circle, each degree divided into 60', although this same practice was as well known in ancient India as it was in Egypt and elsewhere. Why? Simply because of the vast knowledge of occult astronomy and astrology in the archaic Mystery schools, wherein the 'standard' year was usually employed for secret calculations, as well as being also the basis of civil and economic computations.

RACIAL CYCLES AND YUGAS

WHAT TAKES PLACE within a race is but a copying of what takes place on grander scales elsewhere. Any planet, sun, or universe, has its own four periods of a length and magnitude corresponding to its life cycle. In Hindu cosmogony these are called yugas, their length in each case depending upon the scale of its arc, whether of a man or a sun.

The manner in which the great cycles in the evolution of a root-race are repeated in the small is an extremely involved one. The general rule is that the small repeats the great, that little yugas not only are included in the greater yugas, but repeat them on their own level. For example, our present fifth root-race, considered as a whole with all its minor subraces, is now in its kali yuga, which began over five thousand years ago at the death of Krishna, and will last into the future for about 427,000 years.

Now some of the minor cycles or yugas of this fifth root-race will be rising, and some will be falling, yet all interworking with each other and subject to the great kali yuga of the root-race. Thus, a minor yuga or race may be in its youth and rising to its flowering, yet, because it is included in the over-all kali yuga, will be subject to the general decline of the major kali yuga.

Every minor cycle, great or small, within the root-race is in its turn septenary and therefore has its own little kali yuga, and its numerical relations are about the same. Just as the great kali yuga is 432,000 years long, so a minor one may be only 432 years long, or 4320, or even 43,200. The Hindu or Aryan race, which was one of the very first subraces of our own fifth root-race, is now in its own racial kali yuga in addition to being in the longer kali yuga of the root-race. But it is striving to rise again, and will do so in the future. On a smaller scale, Spain is in its short kali yuga, as also Portugal. Italy has just ended a short kali yuga and is beginning to rise again.

Unfortunately, because our fifth root-race is a very materialistic one, heavily sunken in matter due to our fourth round, these rises are mostly along the lines of materialisms. Furthermore, the European general stock of races, which we might call the European subrace or family race perhaps, has been steadily rising since the downfall of the Roman Empire, and will continue to do so, with various smaller shocks and falls and risings again, for some six or seven or possibly eight thousand years more. And then there will be a rapid descent until its kali yuga is reached, a small kali yuga, when there will be a great European catastrophe of nature. This will be some sixteen to eighteen thousand years from now. This period will see the submersion of the British Isles. Most of France will be under the water, also Holland, some of Spain, a good deal of Italy, and other places. Of course all this won't take place in a night, for there will be premonitory signs, such as slow sinkings of the coast, great earthquakes, etc.

The main fact is that, although the fifth root-race as a whole is in its kali yuga which began some five thousand years ago, its subraces may be rising or falling, each one according to its own time periods; and each such subrace has its own little kali yuga repeated after the great one, bearing the same proportion to the entire length of any such small race that the great kali yuga does to the root-race.

Another name for yuga or cycle in Sanskrit is kāla-chakra, time-wheel. Just as a wheel revolves, so do the four yugas, the four time-wheels, following the numerical ratios of 4, 3, 2, and a period of pause; then again, the 4, 3, 2, pause, and so forth throughout the manvantaras. These same relative numerical ratios prevail in all divisions of nature. For instance, the globe manvantara can be subdivided into periods standing to each other in the relation of 4, 3, 2, pause or one, making the complete 10; and these can be called the satya yuga, tretā yuga, dwāpara yuga, and kali yuga, each with its rest period or sandhyā, of the globe manvantara.*

Using exactly the same principle of repetitive workings in nature, an entire round, passing through all the globes, can be looked upon as a time period which is divisible into the same relative numerical portions. So we can say that the four yugas apply to any unitary period in the flow of time: to a planetary round, a globe-round, a root-race, or even to the period of a human life.

To illustrate: a man is not in his kali yuga when he is in advanced age. His kali yuga is reached in his most active portion of life, his middle age, when he is in the full plenitude of his *physical* powers, but still

---

*Cf. *Occult Glossary*, pp. 184–5.

an infant as regards his higher powers. However, this fact did not apply to the early root-races, because they were on the downward arc and reached their kali yuga in their old age. Since we have passed the lowest point in our evolution and have begun to rise, our inner nature has evolved forth enough to make our later years, after our individual kali yuga period, a time of blossoming and realization. We now no longer die in the heyday of our physical age as did the early Atlanteans and the Lemurians. We live past the prime of physical activity, into the mellower, richer years, which older age brings. During the sixth and seventh root-races, curiously enough, our kali yuga will coincide with the rich point of our life, but we shall then be in the relative fullness of *all* our powers.

Applying these yugas or time cycles to the root-races: every root-race has its satya yuga, followed by its tretā, dwāpara, and kali yugas. Then comes a sandhyā or rest period, a junction point, after which comes the birth of the new race. The seeds of the succeeding new root-race spring into being; but the old root-race continues along, although no longer having the mastery of the earth. The reason is that with the opening of the satya yuga of the succeeding root-race, all the stronger, more advanced egos of the race then in its kali yuga take imbodiment in the new race; whereas the bodies of the decaying race are given over to less developed egos which enter them. As these bodies of the old race continue living and propagating through several succeeding ages, egos of less and less degree of evolutionary advancement enter them, until finally these bodies through slow degeneration will house only the least developed egos of the human stock. But the dying-out root-race lasts almost as long as it takes the succeeding root-race to reach its kali yuga.

Here we have the key to these numerical periods, as they are given in the Brahmanical computations. A root-race takes four yugas or 4,320,000 years to achieve its growth and its physical prime. The last tenth of this period is its kali yuga. Then the new race comes into being; just as on a smaller scale the sixth subrace of our present fifth root-race is already having its seeds of birth in the Americas, where also the seeds of the sixth root-race to come are now being laid, beginning now in *our* kali yuga, but as yet merely an adumbration of what it will be. When our kali yuga reaches towards its end, some 427,000 years from now, the seeds of the sixth root-race will then be fairly numerous. Meanwhile our fifth root-race will continue as bodies for inferior egos until this series of *bodies,* not of *egos,* through degeneration towards its end will finally be the vehicles for only the least developed egos of the human stock. From this we see that a root-race on this globe, during this fourth round in the past and up to the present, has taken something like 8,640,000 years to live from its seeds to its disappearance, though only half of that time — the mahāyuga or four yugas of 4,320,000 years — can properly be called the zenith of that root-race. The remaining 4,320,000 years represent its dying-out period.

As each root-race begins at about the middle period of its parent root-race, our own fifth root-race began to be born in the kali yuga of the fourth. The sixth root-race succeeding us will begin to be born in our kali yuga, upon which we are now entering. When a race begins, its forerunners are very few; they are strange people, and are considered almost as freaks of nature. By and by they find themselves in the majority, and that is when their root-race has become strong. It is the *egos* which make the root-races, and the egos really which make the yugas. What takes place in the great is repeated in the small: a root-race is but an analogy, a repetition, of a round; even of an entire solar manvantara. The life of a man is exactly the same: it is an analogy of a solar manvantara, of a round, of a globe-manvantara as well as of a root-race.

A root-race, then, from its seed to its death, since the beginning of the Lemurian or third root-race, has been running between eight and nine million years. If we reckon it in yugas, it is 8,640,000 years, but of this period only half, or the mahāyuga, can be properly called that root-race, as a beginning, growing, and mature entity. As pointed out earlier, the remaining or second mahāyuga is its slow disappearance, because the race becomes, as physical bodies, the receptacle of egos in a constantly decreasing scale of evolutionary advancement. Thus it is that we have amongst us today Atlanteans, but the egos inhabiting these degenerate 'Atlantean bodies' are much inferior to the best class of Atlanteans when Atlantis was in its prime. We have even a few of the ancient Lemurians amongst us, sorry remnants of once wonderful ancestors, for Lemuria was a magnificent race and continent in its day. These few 'Lemurian bodies' still going on and on — so called because they are of direct Lemurian descent — offer vehicles to the very lowest class of the human stock. Now these lower egos are not lost souls. They are simply the least evolved of human egos at the present time, and therefore trailers behind us. Each root-race contains the same egos that were evolving in the preceding root-race.

Turning again to the life cycles of the root-races as they relate to the yugas: the Lemurians and Atlanteans as a rule died quickly when their bodies, their lives, reached what we now would call the human kali yuga period. The reason for this was that they had not yet evolved sufficiently in higher intellectual power and spirituality. In other words, these early races died young because they had no old age of richness and fullness to look forward to.

We have passed in evolution that phase which was so noticeable in Atlantean times; and being in the fifth root-race and on the upward arc, we are slowly growing into the evolutionary stages of consciousness wherein the higher intellect and spirituality are becoming ever stronger with each hundred thousand years that pass, making the latter half of life, as time goes on, continuously richer of understanding and of feeling.

With the beginning of the fifth root-race the latter half of a man's life began to develop. Some day old age will be the years when he will be in the plenitude of his power, physical and intellectual and spiritual. It will then be the time when childhood and youth will be proportionately shortened, the reason being that man will come into self-conscious functioning of faculty far more quickly than now. This process will continue through the ages so that, when we shall have reached the seventh root-race on this earth during this fourth round, the latter half of life will be considered as the only part worth living. Bodies then will be stronger, more flexible, very different from what they are now in some respects: more vital, with greater resisting power, yet more ethereal. In those distant days a man's body before his death will be stronger than in what we would call his youth.

Although the Atlanteans died in what we would consider late youth or early middle age, the years that they lived were many more than ours. As time goes on, children will show a tendency to be born continuously more mature in interior faculties, as well as more mature in body, although not necessarily large physically. It was *bodies* which occupied the greater part of human life in the past. With us, things are beginning to reverse themselves. It will be the *inner man* — the mind, the spirituality — which will more and more show forth.

We live in a very interesting age. I do not think that in the recorded annals that are open to us at the present time there has ever been an epoch when serious-minded students of the ancient wisdom have had the opportunities that now are available.

167

Much has been said of the blackness of our age, the kali yuga, but it is just this stress and strain which are opening our hearts and tearing the veils away from our minds. It is the Iron Age, a hard, rigid cycle where everything moves intensely and where everything is difficult; but precisely the age in which spiritual and intellectual advancement can be made most quickly. In the Golden Age, in the so-called Age of Saturn, the era of man's innocence, everything moved smoothly and all nature cooperated to make living beautiful and pleasant; and there is something in our hearts that yearns to return to it. But it is not what the evolving ego longs for.

It is a strange paradox that the hardest and cruelest of all the yugas is the very one in which the quickest advancement can be gained. It is the opportunity time, the time of choice, when the most advanced egos will become the seeds of the succeeding great root-race. Thus will be born the satya yuga of the new race out of the kali yuga of the old, and in the distant future there will be even greater things than in the past. Once again the lives of men will be attuned to the inspiration of universal compassion and of wisdom, and the archaic teachings regarding the light which flows from the heart of the spiritual sun, which each man is in the inmost arcanum of his being, will again become the most precious heritage of the human race.

V

Hierarchies and the
Doctrine of Emanations

Hierarchies and the Doctrine of Emanations

OUT OF PARANIRVANA INTO MANVANTARA

It is the ONE LIFE, eternal, invisible, yet Omnipresent, without beginning or end, yet periodical in its regular manifestations, between which periods reigns the dark mystery of non-Being; unconscious, yet absolute Consciousness; unrealisable, yet the one self-existing reality; truly, "a chaos to the sense, a Kosmos to the reason." Its one absolute attribute, which is ITSELF, eternal, ceaseless Motion, is called in esoteric parlance the "Great Breath," which is the perpetual motion of the universe, in the sense of limitless, ever-present SPACE. That which is motionless cannot be Divine. But then there is nothing in fact and reality absolutely motionless within the universal soul. — *The Secret Doctrine*, I, 2

EVERYTHING, EVERY being or entity of the vast hierarchies that infill Space, is alive, is more or is less conscious, or self-conscious; and this is the case from supergod through all the intermediate hierarchical ranges of being down to the component parts of an atom. All have a consciousness side and a vehicle side, and both indwelling spirit and its vehicle are one composite unit. It is perfectly true that mechanics exist, whether in the cosmos or on the infinitesimal scale that prevails in the building of atomic structures, yet behind the mechanism are the living spiritual intelligences, the mechanicians. As H.P.B. writes:

The Occultist sees in the manifestation of every force in Nature, the action of the quality, or the special characteristic of its noumenon; which *noumenon* is a distinct and intelligent Individuality *on the other side of the manifested mechanical Universe.*°

Most of us, however, make too radical a distinction between these two aspects of the cosmic life structure, and this is understandable, because obviously there is an enormous difference between the car and the man who drives it. But in the universe there is no such sharp distinction in space and time between the spiritual mechanician and the mechanism which is its vehicle of expression. Here is where the mistake was made which brought about the birth of materialistic philosophies and those

---

°*The Secret Doctrine*, I, 493.

particular religions which teach of an extracosmic God working upon matter as his creature. There are no extracosmic gods anywhere. Whatever inspirits and invigorates a universe, or any component factor of it, lives in and works through it, precisely as the spirit and mind and psychical apparatus of a man form one composite whole working through his astral-vital-physical body.

The sun, the stars and the planets are not just material shells invigorated by spiritual entities having none other than a mere force connection with them. They are, like man, an incarnation of a spirit and a mind working in union through their own effluxes of force and substance, which are the lower parts of the constitution ending in the physical body. Every celestial body is essentially a divine being presently manifesting itself as a star or a sun or a planet.

If we understand the theosophical conception of emanation, we will have a key to many mysteries of the universe. Emanation signifies the flowing forth of all the lower stages of the hierarchical structure which we call cosmic planes or spheres. All this flowing out is from cosmic consciousness centers, and every such cosmic monad is essentially a god, from whose essence there emanate the veils or garments in which it clothes itself. These garments are the multiplicity of beings and things which make up the universe that we see. And exactly the same rule of emanational unfolding produces the various hierarchical grades of the constitution of any individual being or entity, from a star to an atom. So, at the beginning of a cosmic manvantara a universe is unrolled out into an expression of the substances and forces and consciousnesses *inherent in itself;* and thus does every hierarchical unit emanate from Parabrahman.

Evolution is but an aspect of emanational unfolding; from the instant emanation begins, evolution likewise begins its work. If we restrict the word emanation to the process of flowing forth from latency into active manifestation, then we can with logic restrict the word evolution to signify the immediate beginning of developmental growth, or the unfolding of inner faculty and organ from preceding and latent causal seeds. Actually, these terms are so much alike that it is difficult to distinguish between them.

It would be a mistake to say that Parabrahman by will or by an effort of its own consciousness emanates the universe or any hierarchical unit; or, similarly, that the Boundless by the action of its will and life unfolds a universe or hierarchy from itself. We would then be ascribing to Parabrahman or the Boundless action or acts which belong not to Infinity but to already manifested entities, such as cosmic or galactic monads. Parabrahman never acts, because Parabrahman is an abstraction. It is only beings and things that act; and both Parabrahman and the Boundless are but words signifying frontierless Space and beginningless and unending Duration.

Every cosmic entity coming into manvantaric activity does so from forces and powers and substances inherent in itself; arising out of its paranirvanic latency it begins its process of emanational unfolding in progressive stages towards evolutional development. Similarly with a man: it is no 'god,' nor the Boundless, nor Parabrahman, which brings about the reincarnation of a human being; but it is the awaking from latency into activity of innate powers and substances which ultimately results in the reclothing of the devachanic monad in its series of vehicular veils, ending with the physical body.

When a universe or any other entity begins its emanational unfolding from pralayic paranirvana into manvantaric activity, the stages progress 'downwards' into the ethereal and finally the material realms of encompassing space; but in its descent from spirit to matter, never does the highest *directly* drop through planes to lower planes. What happens is that first the divine awakens from its paranirvanic rest and clothes itself with a spiritual veil, mūlaprakriti or pradhāna, which then through cosmic time periods clothes itself in its veil of manifestation; and this last throws around itself, partly from forces and substances flowing forth from within its heart, and partly by accretions from surrounding space, still another encompassing vehicle or garment. This process continues until the emanating and evolving entity reaches its lowest or most material stage, which for it is its physical body, whether of a sun, a man, or an atom.

This idea is found in the *Bhagavad-Gītā* (ch. x) where Krishna says: "I established all this universe with portions of myself, yet remain separate." This means that the divine from its own effulgence of intelligence and life, its 'surplus of life,' clothes itself in garments of differing degrees of descending ethereality, finally reaching and composing the physical; the divine part nevertheless, and the spiritual, intellectual and higher psychical portions, remain above and unmoved *as essences*. Rays from each constitutional part sink into manifestation, infilling the lower cosmic planes with life and mind and consciousness appropriate to each plane thus formed.

The whole process of emanational unfolding can be likened to a column of light, pure spirit in its highest parts and physical matter in its lowest, with all intermediate stages of increasing substantiality in between. When the physical plane is reached, the process of descent ceases, and immediately there begins the process of ascent or of return to spirit, which is for any cosmic entity the grand *consummatum est.* The unfolding is the arc of descent, and the infolding is the arc of ascent.

Mechanics naturally are involved in emanation but, because we are dealing with beings and things and their common relations and interrelations, such mechanical aspects are entirely the productions of inner and inspiriting consciousnesses. In other words, because the universe and everything in it is alive throughout, cosmic life and mind or consciousness are the *real* factors and causal agents in producing, through emanation and evolution, the wondrous mystery of an imbodied universe and its component principles.

A universal solar system, coming into being from its paranirvanic latency, is born anew into manvantaric manifestation *from its own inherent and innate power.* It reproduces itself in the spaces of galactic space as a reimbodiment of all that it was in its last appearance therein, plus the enormous accumulation of experience gained before. This applies both in particular and in general to the reimbodiment of any individual cosmic body, such as a planetary chain, a globe or, on a smaller scale, to that of an inhabitant of a globe, or even of an atom.

All things take birth from within and express themselves outwards, run through the phases of their manvantaric cycles, and then are withdrawn and pass out of the realms of appearance or māyā, inwards and upwards into the spirit where they again have their nirvanic repose.

An egg is a good analogy: little by little the germ within awakens into activity, the enclosed chick slowly grows into shape and finally breaks through its shell. So it is with the universe coming into being; and that is why the ancient sages of Hindustan and others, such as the Orphics of archaic Greece, spoke of the cosmic Egg. No germ in an egg could ever follow the regular sequential stages of development unless that germ were filled full with forces and substances emanating from within itself, which really means flowing from invisible spheres outward into our visible sphere, and thus producing the imbodied entity.

The essence of this teaching of emanation is that all beings or entities on the higher planes of development are at one, and hence are virtually to be *identified* with the veils which they pour forth from themselves and which thus form their bodies. For instance, Brahman and pradhāna are not two, but one, these words merely meaning the two aspects of the entity unfolding itself into emanational growth. The Brahman is the consciousness side; the pradhāna is its enclosing veil of vital essence, really the stuff of mind, of spirit or of consciousness in which the monad enwraps itself. On the physical plane even our bodies are ourselves, very imperfect pictures of our inner being (and often an infernal nuisance to the higher parts of us), yet ourselves in our grossest aspects. But the heart of us, the monad, is our real Self; and all these bodies of ours, whether physical, astral or mānasic — with which from eternity we are karmically connected — are groups of life-atoms to which we have given birth and in which we clothe ourselves.

THE COSMIC SPIRIT IN PRALAYA AND MANVANTARA

WE ENTER NOW UPON the rather difficult subject of the nature of cosmic being in its state of mahāpralaya preceding the awakening therein of the activities of fohat and the consequent beginning of its evolutionary development into a fully manifested cosmos or universe.

When reading the passages from the *The Secret Doctrine* which follow, we should bear in mind that they refer to an individual universe, and never to Infinitude considered as being in a state of mahāpralaya, for that would be a philosophical absurdity. Infinitude has neither manvantara nor pralaya, for the simple reason that periods of divine or spiritual rest and periods of manifested evolutionary activity are appurtenant solely to *limited portions of Infinitude,* and therefore to universes, whether immensely vast in extent, such as a group of galaxies, or whether smaller cosmic units. It is only with regard to individual cosmic units that we could predicate time periods such as manvantaras and pralayas.

Manvantaric impulse commences with the re-awakening of Cosmic Ideation (the "Universal Mind") concurrently with, and parallel to the primary emergence of Cosmic Substance — the latter being the manvantaric vehicle of the former — from its undifferentiated *pralayic* state. Then, absolute wisdom mirrors itself in its Ideation; which, by a transcendental process, superior to and incomprehensible by human Consciousness, results in Cosmic Energy *(Fohat).* Thrilling through the bosom of inert Substance, *Fohat* impels it to activity, and guides its primary differentiations on all the Seven planes of Cosmic Consciousness. . . .

Cosmic Ideation is said to be non-existent during Pralayic periods, for the simple reason that there is no one, and nothing, to perceive its effects.

— I, 328

Light is matter, and DARKNESS pure Spirit.   — I, 70

The ray of the "Ever Darkness" becomes, as it is emitted, a ray of effulgent light or life, and flashes into the "Germ" — the point in the Mundane Egg, represented by matter in its abstract sense. . . . the noumenon of eternal and indestructible matter.   — I, 57

The Primordial Substance had not yet passed out of its precosmic latency

176

into differentiated objectivity, or even become the (to man, so far,) invisible Protyle of Science. But, as the hour strikes and it becomes receptive of the Fohatic impress of the Divine Thought (the Logos, or the male aspect of the Anima Mundi, Alaya) — its heart opens. — I, 58

Svâbhâvat, the "Plastic Essence" that fills the Universe, is the root of all things. — I, 61

"The radiant essence curdled and spread throughout the depths" of Space. — I, 67

THE ROOT REMAINS, THE LIGHT REMAINS, THE CURDS REMAIN, AND STILL OEAO-HOO IS ONE. — I, 68

The "Light" is the same Omnipresent Spiritual Ray, which has entered and now fecundated the Divine Egg, and calls cosmic matter to begin its long series of differentiations. The curds are the first differentiation, and probably refer also to that cosmic matter which is supposed to be the origin of the "Milky Way" — the matter we know. This "matter," which, according to the revelation received from the primeval Dhyani-Buddhas, is, during the periodical sleep of the Universe, of the ultimate tenuity conceivable to the eye of the perfect Bodhisatva — this matter, radical and cool, becomes, at the first reawakening of cosmic motion, scattered through Space; appearing, when seen from the Earth, in clusters and lumps, like curds in thin milk. These are the seeds of the future worlds, the "Star-stuff." — I, 69

THEN SVÂBHÂVAT SENDS FOHAT TO HARDEN THE ATOMS. . . .
It is through Fohat that the ideas of the Universal Mind are impressed upon matter. — I, 85

In its [Fohat's] totality, viewed from the standpoint of manifested Divine Thought in the esoteric doctrine, it represents the Hosts of the higher creative Dhyan Chohans. . . . By the action of the manifested Wisdom, or Mahat, represented by these innumerable centres of spiritual Energy in the Kosmos, the reflection of the Universal Mind, which is Cosmic Ideation and the intellectual Force accompanying such ideation, becomes objectively the Fohat of the Buddhist esoteric philosopher. Fohat, running along the seven principles of AKASA, acts upon manifested substance or the One Element, as declared above, and by differentiating it into various centres of Energy, sets in motion the law of Cosmic Evolution, which, in obedience to the Ideation of the Universal Mind, brings into existence all the various states of being in the manifested Solar System. — I, 110

It is one of the fundamental dogmas of Esoteric Cosmogony, that during the Kalpas (or aeons) of life, MOTION, which, during the periods of Rest "pulsates

177

and thrills through every slumbering atom" (Commentary on Dzyan), assumes an evergrowing tendency, from the first awakening of Kosmos to a new "Day," to circular movement. The "Deity becomes a WHIRLWIND." — I, 116–17

These extracts, and many similar ones, refer to the condition of a universe when it is resolved back into its highest and original cosmic elemental essence during the state of mahāpralaya, all the worlds having vanished out of the lower cosmic planes of manifested life. The universe has been inrolled upwards and inwards to its highest spiritual plane, where in the state of paranirvana all the hosts of manifested beings, from the supergods through the intermediate ranges downwards to ordinary life-atoms, pass cosmic ages in the dreamless 'slumber' which is, nevertheless, intense spiritual and superintellectual activity characteristic of the highest planes of the cosmic essence.

Such paranirvanic bliss lasts for "Seven Eternities," which is the vast period of time-space equivalent in length to the preceding mahāmanvantara. All manifestation has been swept out of existence. The inrolling of all the cosmic planes began first with the lowest plane, followed by the inrolling of the next higher one, the procedure thus continuing until finally the highest was reached, into which all the divine monads of the previous armies of evolving beings were ingathered, resting in paranirvanic consciousness untrammeled by any veiling garments of sentient lower existence. We may phrase the matter otherwise by saying that the auric egg of the universe or cosmos has been indrawn into the highest cosmic plane or element of the cosmic Egg, the Mahābrahmānda.

It may be well to call attention to one or two fundamental ideas of the archaic wisdom pertaining to the essential Being, rather than to the manvantaric existence, of a cosmic spirit. A cosmic spirit is for its own universe one and sole during mahāpralaya, because during this period manifestation is not; or, as it is expressed in the Stanzas of Dzyan, the Mother sleeps in dreamless peace and in utter unconscious consciousness of manifestation for seven eternities. This is looking at the subject from the standpoint of our worlds of manifestation, all the hosts of the galactic world existing manifestedly in their bewildering ramifications and differentiated varieties.

In reality, all such differentiation is a kind of death — the underworld — for the cosmic spirits within the universe, which universe nevertheless works and lives in and through its own anima mundi; whereas pralaya or mahāpralaya is the condition in which the spiritual-intellectual

178

life of the universe is at its highest, even the anima mundi having disappeared because having been indrawn into the cosmic monad.

Following the same line of thought, in ancient Egypt the *highest* aspect of the god Osiris was spoken of as a dark god, a black god, actually meaning, however, light so pure and intense that our manifested light is like its shadow.

On this subject, in response to the question: "Are the 'Great Waters' the same as those on which the Darkness moved?", H.P.B. answered:

It is incorrect in this case, to speak of Darkness "moving." Absolute Darkness, or the Eternal Unknown, cannot be active, and moving *is* action. Even in *Genesis* it is stated that Darkness *was* upon the face of the deep, but that which moved upon the face of the waters, was the "Spirit of God." This means esoterically that in the beginning, when the Infinitude was without form, and Chaos, or the outer Space, was still void, Darkness (*i.e., Kalahansa Parabrahm*) alone *was*. Then, at the first radiation of Dawn, the "Spirit of God" (after the First and Second Logos were radiated, the Third Logos, or Narayan) began to move on the face of the Great Waters of the "Deep." Therefore the question to be correct, if not clear, should be, "Are the Great Waters the same as the Darkness spoken of?" The answer would then be in the affirmative. Kalahansa has a dual meaning. Exoterically it is Brahmâ who is the Swan, the "Great Bird," the vehicle in which Darkness manifests itself to human comprehension as light, and this Universe. But esoterically, it is Darkness itself, the unknowable Absolute which is the Source, firstly of the radiation called the First Logos, then of its reflection, the Dawn, or the Second Logos, and finally of Brahmâ, the manifested Light, or the Third Logos.°

With regard to manifested light, if there be no things to reflect that light, no illumination could exist. We see the planets in the heavens because they intercept light, but we do not see the light itself as it flashes from the sun through space. There must be differentiation, i.e. objects, to bring about visible light. Therefore, light as we know it is vastly inferior to

---

° *Transactions of the Blavatsky Lodge*, pp. 90–1.

Hebraeo-Christian theology and literature refer to cosmic emanational unfolding as the Elohim moving on the "face of the Waters" in the first verse of *Genesis*. 'Elohīm actually is a plural noun meaning gods, although European scholars almost invariably translate it by the word God — a highly misleading translation as it succeeds in disguising, however unintentionally, the truth that the Elohim are the hierarchy of formative or demiurgic cosmic spirits extending from the highest cosmic plane down to the lowest Elohim of the physical plane. This Hebrew term corresponds to what in esoteric Buddhism is called the hierarchies of the dhyāni-chohans.

that utter glory of the spirit divine, totally indescribable and invisible to human beings. Light is in fact the efflux of a spiritual entity; one of the aspects of the vitality of a god — its psychovital fluid.

So we see that manvantara is a kind of death to the cosmic monad expressing itself through its beclouding veils of the anima mundi. It is a kind of deprivation, a sinking into the māyā of cosmic dreams; whereas pralaya is really the spirit of the universe fully awake on its own plane, because all is ingathered into it, and it is freely active in its own ineffably spiritual realms.

When evolution or manvantara commences, and the last moment of the cosmic pralaya is ended, the exactly reverse procedure takes place. There now awakens in the divine heart of the sleeping universe a purely abstract yearning to begin manifestation — a fact which is repeated ana- logically in the case of man. This desire for manifestation — expressed in Greek philosophy by Eros and in the Vedas as "Desire first arose in It" — shows itself in the highest cosmic plane as the awakening of the divine part of fohat guided by the divine mind of the 'sleeping' universe. When we speak of fohatic awakening, this is really but another way of saying that the supremely high classes of dhyāni-chohans begin to stir out of their ages-long paranirvana, thus bringing about the evolutionary unfolding of the cosmic elements as they proceed steadily downwards through the cosmic planes until finally the complete structural framework of the fully evolved universe appears once more.

In esoteric Buddhism, the nature of the cosmic stuff or essence sunken in paranirvanic rest during its mahāpralaya is called swabhavat, a Sanskrit compound which means not only self-essence but self-evolving; and this is cosmic stuff of a divine-spiritual character, out of which the universe is evolved. Swabhavat, therefore, is essentially abstract cosmic substance, but of a distinctly vital and spiritual-intellectual nature; and whether we call it the cosmic mother or womb, or the cosmic divine essence of nature, matters not at all, for these phrases are but different manners of attempting to describe what the spiritual essence of nature is during mahāpralaya.

We thus see that the urge awakening the sleeping universe to its new mahāmanvantara is guided by the divine thought of the universe, expressing itself through its divine, spiritual and intellectual as well as its essential magnetic energies, which energies collectively are called fohat.

When this divine thought begins to awaken into activity, it emanates rays of divine-spiritual intelligence which are sevenfold, or even twelvefold, and these are the cosmic logoi. These cosmic logoi, or what H.P.B. has once named the "Cosmic Sons of Light," are the primordial or highest dhyāni-chohans from whom stream, as the evolutionary unfolding of the cosmic planes proceeds, their own children-rays or minor logoi — all these minor hierarchies of dhyāni-chohans being the light side of the universe, otherwise called the Hierarchy of Light.

Finally, the divine thought is called in Hindu philosophical writings mahat, the universal mind, corresponding in man's constitution to manas, a ray from mahat. Higher even than mahat, we must envisage the still more sublime essences whose rays in man we call buddhi and ātman, and in the universe mahābuddhi or cosmic buddhi, and Paramātman or Brahman, respectively.

THE THREE LOGOI

THERE IS, PERHAPS, no single point of the esoteric philosophy about which cluster so many vague ideas as around the teaching concerning the logoi. The word logos, commonly used in ancient Greek mystical thought, was adopted by the early Christians, as for instance by John of the Fourth Gospel, and used with their own understanding of its meaning. Logos originally meant reason, and finally also came to mean word. Certain schools of Greek philosophy transferred it as a figure of speech to cosmic processes: in the beginning there was divine reason, divine thought, which in order to communicate life and intelligence within itself needed a vehicle, a 'word,' to pass itself on. And the word was produced by the functioning of divine reason, just as human speech is produced by the functioning of human reason or thought.

Now then, each hierarchy, each plane in other words, has its own three Logoi: the unmanifest, the partially manifest, and the manifest, or the First, Second, and Third Logos — although, because the entire universe is constructed of and in hierarchies which repeat each other on the different planes, an almost incalculable number of minor logoi exist in any universe as rays therefrom.

Considered as a triadic unity, the conception of the three primordial Logoi gave to the Christians their Holy Trinity, even if in somewhat distorted form; and the same concept gave to other religious and philosophical systems of antiquity the three individuals of their respective triads. Thus the First Logos, called by H. P. B. the Unmanifest Logos, is equivalent to the Pythagorean cosmic monad, the Monas monadum, which remains forever in what is to us silence and darkness — although it is the most utter and perfect light of the world. In the archaic Hindu Trimurti it is represented by Brahman; and in the Christian scheme by the Father.

This First or Unmanifest Logos is the Primordial Point or Ancient of Days of the Qabbālāh; and from one aspect, as when we are considering the very first stage in the opening drama of evolution, it is the primeval seed out of which all the hierarchy — imbodying all subsequent hierarchies — of the universe flows forth into manifestation. Such emanational evolution takes place through the First Logos clothing itself with a veil of spiritual light, which is at one and the same time cosmic intelligence and cosmic life, becoming the Second or manifest-unmanifest Logos, and to which different schools of philosophy gave different names.

In the ancient Pythagorean mystical system this Second Logos was the cosmic Duad, conceived of as a feminine power or veil of the First Logos or Monad of monads, while in Greek mythology it was spoken of as Gaia, the consort or veil of Ouranos or heaven, the First Logos. Similarly, certain mystical schools of the Orient spoke of the Second Logos as Pradhāna, the veil of Brahman or the First Logos; or again, as in esoteric Buddhism, as Alaya or mahābuddhi, which is the summit or root of cosmic ākāśa. The original Christian conception of the Trinity, as still held in the Orthodox or Greek Church, looked upon this Second Logos as a feminine power which is the Holy Spirit or Holy Ghost.°

This Second Logos, the cosmic womb of Space, being as it were the generative and productive field of lives, or seeds of life, brought forth the Third Logos. It was conceived of as the Son, as in the original Greek Christian scheme, the Third Person of the Trinity born of the Holy Spirit. In the ancient Brahmanical system it was Śiva born from the essence of Vishnu. Another name given in early Hinduism to this Third Logos was Brahmā, the Creator, the reproduction of Brahman, the First Logos, by and through the intermediary feminine power Pradhāna or the Second Logos.

With the cosmic appearance of the Third Logos, the evolutional un-folding of the universe has reached its third stage, and then and there begins the emanation of the innumerable minor hierarchies which, in their aggregate, compose the complex mystery of the manifold cosmos in all its interwoven activities and substances.

Many and various were the names given to the Third Logos by the philosophical and religious systems of antiquity. The Greeks gave this Third or formative Logos the title Demiourgos, a word mystically signifying the supreme cosmic Architect of the universe. This same idea always has been held by the Christians as well as by modern speculative Freema-sonry, as indicated by their title The Grand Architect of the Universe. In Hinduism another aspect of the Third Logos was called Nārāyana or Purusha, supposed to be involved in its accompanying cosmic veil, prakriti.

°Cf. H.P.B.'s article "Notes on the Gospel according to St. John," *Lucifer*, February and March, 1893.

Nārāyana means the cosmic man moving in and on the waters of Space (the cosmic waters of *Genesis*), and these cosmic waters, by the way, are but another name for the Second Logos, otherwise the vast womb of cosmic entities.°

In connection with the Logoi the following question and answer from the *Transactions of the Blavatsky Lodge* (p. 113) may be of value:

Q. What is the difference between Spirit, Voice and Word?

A. The same as between Atma, Buddhi and Manas, in one sense. Spirit emanates from the unknown Darkness, the mystery into which none of us can penetrate. That Spirit — call it the "Spirit of God" or Primordial Substance — mirrors itself in the Waters of Space — or the still undifferentiated matter of the future Universe — and produces thereby the first flutter of differentiation in the homogeneity of primordial matter. This is the Voice, pioneer of the "Word" or the first manifestation; and from that Voice emanates the Word or Logos, that is to say, the definite and objective expression of that which has hitherto remained in the depths of the Concealed Thought. That which mirrors itself in Space is the Third Logos.

There is an interesting series of ideas here relating to the Second Logos, the Voice, which in the Sanskrit is generally termed either Vāch or Swara. Both these words meaning Sound, or Breath in another sense, are used mystically for Voice — and occasionally for Word — and are invested with a feminine attribute because being the carrier or mother of the Third Logos.

To recapitulate: we have the cosmic ideation or cosmic Father, i.e. the cosmic thought, the First Logos. This surrounds itself with and reproduces itself in the Second Logos, which is the cosmic Mother, carrying within itself the essence of the First Logos or divine thought and reproducing it as the Third Logos, the cosmic Son or Word. Thus we have: Idea — First; Sound — Second; Word — Third, which last is the manifested or creative Logos of the universe. Therefore Vāch or Swara is the mystic Sound of the divine creative activity, the vehicle of the divine thought, of which the Word or Verbum is the manifested expression.

°Still another term in archaic Hinduism given to the Third Logos was hiranya-garbha — *hiranya* meaning golden, with the inherent sense of celestial or primordial or most beautiful; and *garbha* being a term which can be translated according to the context as womb or embryo or vital cosmic seed, this embryo existing in the womb of the Second Logos, and indeed itself sometimes called a womb because being the fecund source of all the seeds of the hierarchies which emanationally flow from it.

In applying Vāch or Swara to a human being, we find that either term corresponds in man's constitution to the buddhi born of the ātman, and reproducing the ātmic individuality from its buddhic womb as the manas. The same thought is found among several peoples, for example, among the Qabbalists, ancient and modern, who speak of Bath Qōl, the daughter of the Voice. Now this Bath Qōl was said to be the divine inspiration guiding some highly evolved human individual, whether it be prophet or seer; and signifies the manas of the man enlightened by the buddhi within him, the buddhic transmitting ray being Bath Qōl.

Turning again to the cosmic scale, we find ancient mystical Hebrew thought also referring to the divine Voice or Sound as being logoic in character, as instanced in *Job*, xxxviii, 4–7:

Where wast thou when I laid the foundations of the earth? declare, if thou hast understanding.

Who hath laid the measures thereof, if thou knowest? or who hath stretched the line upon it?

Whereupon are the foundations thereof fastened? or who laid the corner stone thereof;

When the morning stars sang together, and all the sons of God shouted for joy?

There is a distinct reference here to a very archaic thought that the world in all its cosmic planes was brought into being by sound, by singing, an idea likewise found among the ancient Druids and Germanic peoples. Here in *Job*, we see that the stars at the beginning of the manvantara, called the morning, sang together, at which time the sons of God, who were the divinities of the highest cosmic plane, shouted or sang the worlds into being.

As H.P.B. has written:

It is said that "Marcus had it revealed unto him that 'the *seven heavens*'. . . sounded each one vowel, which, all combined together, formed a complete doxology"; in clearer words: "the *Sound* whereof being carried down (from these seven heavens) to earth, became the creator and parent of all things that be on earth." (See "Hippolytus," vi., 48, and King's *Gnostics*, p. 200.) Translated from the Occult phraseology into still plainer language this would read: "The Sevenfold Logos having differentiated into seven *Logoi*, or creative potencies (vowels) these (the second logos, or "Sound") created all on Earth.°

° *The Secret Doctrine*, II, 563.

185

It is noteworthy that Swara in Sanskrit, in one of its significances, also means seven. This reveals an esoteric thought which the earliest Hindu writers attached to the term: that the cosmic Swara evolves itself forth into a series of seven sounds, each corresponding directly to one of the seven cosmic planes, thus giving each plane its own keynote or swabhāva. As for Vāch, this is often described as being śatarūpā, hundred-formed; and if we view the evolved universe as having *ten* cosmic planes, and each plane as being tenfold, we then have one hundred individual keynotes. Such a denary construction of the universe takes for granted the supreme cosmic plane of the unit by which it is linked with the Infinite, as well as the very lowest cosmic plane, which is the physical universe — the mere shell or carrier of all the others — thus making up the twelvefold universe mentioned by many ancient philosophers, including Plato.

If we apply the above to a solar chain (or a planetary chain of twelve globes), we see that every such chain is a manifestation of a logoic hierarch, which is its supreme logos. Each of the twelve globes of the solar chain is the product, and in a sense the dwelling, of one of the twelve rays from the solar logos or solar hierarch. The analogy with the constitution of man is perfect: our ātman is our supreme hierarch, and the different foci, in each of which dwells a monad, are the centers of the rays emanating from the ātman.

Taking again our sun as an instance in point, each one of the twelve rays emanating from this solar logos is in itself a minor logos, which in turn, being duodenary, is the solar ray guiding and watching over one of the sacred planetary chains. Every globe of such planetary chain is likewise the especial dwelling of one of the twelve minor rays in each such minor logos.

The Latin poet Martianus Capella spoke of the sun "whose sacred head is encircled with twice six rays." These rays represent the twice six powers or globes of the solar chain. There are, of course, as in the case of all the planetary chains, actually ten globes and two 'polar links.' Now these twelve powers of the sun are the twelve forces of the solar logos — the manifest solar divinity — and naturally they must have their own spheres of action as well as the appropriate substances through which to work. As a matter of fact, *they are themselves their own homes.* Even as a snail builds its own shell, they build their own dwelling places with a portion of themselves, remaining, notwithstanding, apart; as the spirit and the soul of a man remain apart from his body, in it yet above it, and in a true sense not of it. These twelve forces represent and are, in fact, the twelve planes of the solar system.

One of the mystic names of the sun in ancient Hindu literature is dwādaśātman, literally twelve-selved. Sūrya, the sun, is therefore stated to be both twelvefold and sevenfold. These twelve (or seven) selves can be looked upon either as individual logoi or, collected as a unity, as the solar logos or hierarch — very much as a ray of sunlight is composed of the seven colors of the spectrum — and are sometimes called ādityas, meaning born of Aditi, or Space; each such āditya or minor solar logos being the ruling spiritual genius of its planetary chain, and therefore its hierarchical chief.

In *The Secret Doctrine* (II, 29) we find:

"As it is above so it is below" is the fundamental axiom of occult philosophy. As the logos is seven-fold, *i.e.*, throughout Kosmos it appears as seven logoi under seven different forms, or, as taught by learned Brahmins, "each of these is the central figure of one of the seven main branches of the ancient wisdom religion"; and, as the seven principles which correspond to the seven distinct states of *Pragna*, or consciousness, are allied to seven states of matter and the seven forms of force, the division must be the same in all that concerns the earth.

In conclusion, then, remember that the First Logos is the cosmic consciousness, the summit or Brahman of any hierarchy, and these Brahmans are numberless in boundless Space. Every solar system is one such Brahman on the solar system scale; every galaxy represents or is one on the galactic scale; this is also the case with every planetary chain. Every human being has his own individual Brahman, the highest point of his being, his First Logos.

We are all children of the First Logos, life of its life, consciousness of its consciousness. The more we ascend into the higher parts of our being, the more we become self-conscious of our identity with it. Yet all these cosmic Brahmans, cosmic consciousnesses, 'First Logoses,' are offspring of the Boundless, "sparks of Eternity," coming and going throughout endless Duration. This is why Parabrahman is spoken of as being both conscious and unconscious, manifesting and unmanifesting, spirit and matter, because it is both and neither. It is both, because the Boundless gives birth to these points of its being throughout Infinitude and then receives them back — just as the spirit within us is that root which produces us, yet we are not it. We are but its feeble ray, which one day will be withdrawn into the Brahman within us, our First Logos. And therein the manifested being will lie latent for a time, but to reappear.

Thus are worlds born out of the depths of the Boundless and re-enter it, just as men are born from the Brahman within them, from their auric egg, and re-enter therein. When the solar system shall have come to its end, all beings whatsoever within it will be withdrawn into the Boundless for a still higher rest, to reissue forth again as logoic rays when a new cosmic drama of life begins.

FOHAT, THE DYNAMIC ENERGY OF COSMIC IDEATION

IN *The Secret Doctrine* (I, 16) H.P.B. gives in masterly fashion the essential character of fohat:

It is the "bridge" by which the "Ideas" existing in the "Divine Thought" are impressed on Cosmic substance as the "laws of Nature." Fohat is thus the dynamic energy of Cosmic Ideation; or, regarded from the other side, it is the intelligent medium, the guiding power of all manifestation, the "Thought Divine" transmitted and made manifest through the Dhyan Chohans, the Architects of the visible World. Thus from Spirit, or Cosmic Ideation, comes our consciousness; from Cosmic Substance the several vehicles in which that consciousness is individualised and attains to self — or reflective — consciousness; while Fohat, in its various manifestations, is the mysterious link between Mind and Matter, the animating principle electrifying every atom into life.

Fohat is a Tibetan as well as a Mongolian philosophical term, possessing the general meaning of cosmic life or vitality, ever guided by cosmic mind or intelligence. The verbal root *foh* is of Mongolian origin, and corresponds to the word buddha or even buddhi, or again to buddha-wisdom. Fohat performs its manifold wonders in weaving the web of universal being, because working through or directing it is the mahā-buddhi. This cosmic vitality represents in the universe what the prānas are in our bodies.

The reason the Mongolians spoke of the cosmic vitality in connection with thoughts properly ascribable to the terms buddhi, bodhi, etc., is that they refused to see in the symmetrical and harmonic structure of the universe that purely imaginary play of blind and soulless forces on dead matter which has been the bane of Occidental scientific thinking. To these early Orientals the universe was an expression of cosmic wisdom.

As a matter of fact, fohat, being the cosmic life in the sense of the vital flow or ethereal-vital fluids in a universe, is divisible into seven or ten principles or elements, each one a vitality with its own swabhāva, and their unity forming the generalized fohat of which H.P.B. wrote:

"Each world has its Fohat, who is omnipresent in his own sphere of action. But there are as many Fohats as there are worlds, each varying in power and degree of manifestations. The individual Fohats make one Universal, Collective Fohat — the aspect-Entity of the one absolute Non-Entity, which is absolute Be-Ness, 'SAT.' "Millions and billions of worlds are produced at every Manvantara" — it is said. Therefore there must be many Fohats, whom we consider as conscious and *intelligent* Forces.°

Primordial fohat, originating in the First Logos, is septenary or denary because the First Logos itself is seven- or tenfold. Hence fohat exists as a septenary or denary on every one of the planes of the universe. When the Second Logos unfolds itself from within the First Logos, fohat likewise follows each step of such emanation, thus reproducing itself as the cosmic vitality in seven or ten forms in the Second Logos. In exactly similar way does fohat reproduce itself in the Third Logos.

Now fohat is in the cosmos what the seven or ten prānas are in man; and as man's constitution has its prānas on every layer of his auric egg, so are the prānas of the cosmos the different aspects of fohat on the different planes. Just as in man the prānas are the vehicles for thought, feeling, emotion, and instinct, so on the cosmic planes fohat acts as the vehicle of cosmic ideation. Fohat is the steed, cosmic thought is the rider.

Fohat manifests in various forms, and electricity as we know it is one of its lowest manifestations. What vitality is in the human frame, electricity is in the framework of the material universe. They are manifestations of the same fundamental force. Mystically, cosmic electricity is the corporeal vitality of the entity in which we live and move and have our being. It is not a force by itself. There is no such thing in the universe as a force by itself, existing apart from other forces. It is a phase, a manifestation, of the fundamental of all things, which is consciousness. Gravitation actually is one of the manifestations of cosmic electricity and, equivalently, electricity is one of the manifestations of cosmic gravitation. Quoting again from *The Secret Doctrine* (I, 145):

. . . Fohat, the constructive Force of Cosmic Electricity, . . . has *seven sons* who are *his brothers;* . . . [these] represent and personify the seven forms of Cosmic magnetism called in *practical Occultism* the "Seven Radicals," whose co-operative and active progeny are, among other energies, Electricity, Magnetism, Sound, Light, Heat, Cohesion, etc.

Furthermore, just as vitality in a human body appears as cosmic-atomic electricity or the fohatic manifestation in the structure of every one of

°*The Secret Doctrine,* I, 143; see also I, 111–12.

the atoms which compose our body, so the vitality of the grand entity in which we have our being is the cosmic electricity. Lightning is electricity or the cosmic vitality manifesting at a certain spot and under certain conditions. It re-establishes the local electrical equilibrium. Similarly, when a balance of vitality is maintained in the human body, this means health; and when the equilibrium is disturbed, this means disease.

When things are not in equilibrium, electrically speaking, we have the very hot or the very cold days, the stormy days or the abnormally calm days. There is a constant change of direction in the movements and operations of this cosmic electricity. Lightning is one short segment of a circulation of the cosmos, and is very closely involved with certain vital currents between the sun and the earth and man and the earth, which pass through, and to and from, the earth and the meteoric veil which surrounds it. Magnetism is the alter ego of electricity, each a 'brother-son' of fohat. Fundamentally what we call gravitation, electricity and magnetism are all the same thing: three manifestations of fohat or the cosmic vitality as it appears in our physical section of the universe. This universe is not divided into grades separate from each other but is an organic whole, containing grades or stages passing into each other, from the invisible to the visible and passing still lower downwards into the invisible again. There are no radical divisions really except in a schematic sense.

Human beings have more to do with lightning than man has any conception of. If there were no animate entities on earth at all, electricity, manifesting in that particular way which we call lightning, would be an exceedingly rare phenomenon; but every point in space contains animate entities both visible and invisible to us.

In her *Theosophical Glossary*, H.P.B. has defined fohat as "the essence of cosmic electricity. An occult Tibetan term for *Daiviprakriti*, primordial light"; and in describing daivīprakriti, she gives it as "primordial, homogeneous light, . . . when differentiated this light becomes FOHAT."

There is a subtle distinction hinted at here. Daivīprakriti, meaning literally shining or divine prakriti or substance, is the original luminous force-substance, which Subba Row, an early theosophist and Brahmanical scholar, called the "light of the Logos"; fohat is the same light in a more developed state of manifestation. Thus, while in one sense the two are really the same, if we call ordinary electricity in its cosmic aspect daivīprakriti, then fohat, in this application, would be the more developed manifestations of cosmic electricity, such as lightning, the current that lights our houses, and the force of cohesion which holds the atoms together. Above everything else, daivīprakriti-fohat is active cosmic consciousness; daivīprakriti being the higher or spiritual or negative aspect, and fohat being the lower or active or positive aspect.

Each one of the three Logoi and its corresponding fohat is alive, is Life itself. Because the three Logoi are cosmic living beings, and because all the universe flows forth from them by a serial unfolding of hierarchies in their different emanations, the universe and all in it, including its physical body, is alive; so that from nebula and sun to electron and man, every entity in such universe is a *living being*, built of Life which is both substance and cosmic mind. Or, as H.P.B. graphically said: "The rays of the Logos vibrate in every atom."

ON THE GNOSTIC AEONS

DURING THE TWO or three centuries following the downfall of the esoteric system in Europe and its appurtenant Mystery schools — a downfall which had its incipient stages around the beginning of the Christian era — there came into existence quite a number of mystical and quasi-occult schools of thought, some of them containing no small portion of the then fading light of esoteric wisdom, others only feeble rays.

Among these schools thus rising into a temporary vogue were the different groups of the Gnostics, most of them commonly miscalled by Christian historical writers "heretical Christian sects," although, as a matter of fact, they were far less Christian than they were declining rays from the original centers of esoteric teaching in the Mediterranean world. Yet it is true that some of these Gnostic groups, for one reason or another and mainly through expediency, had certain avenues of *rapprochement* with the different Christian sects, probably in order that they might be allowed to live more or less in peace and to continue in relative safety their private studies.

The whole truth about these Gnostic sects has never yet been written. The Gnostic School of Simon was one of the most faithful in teaching some of the fundamental doctrines of the esoteric philosophy. Other Gnostic groups preserving elements of the archaic wisdom were those founded by Menander, Valentinus, Basilides, etc. Simon, because he taught in an age which, while avid and hungry for all kinds of occult and quasi-occult knowledge, was yet extremely critical and theologically unfriendly, obviously had to phrase his teaching in forms of speech that would not offend the dominant Christian power. Consequently, he abandoned very largely the sacred and ages-old phrases of teaching, and used manners of speech and illustrations which were often quite exoteric, and in certain cases were actually invented by him in order to conceal from the enemies of his school just what he really meant in his doctrines — the inner meaning of which was nevertheless perfectly comprehensible to his instructed followers.

The following somewhat lengthy extracts from H.P.B.'s E.S. *Instructions* give the Gnostic system of Aeons as taught by Simon:

Simon, as all the other Gnostics, taught that our world was created by the *lower* angels, whom he called Aeons. He mentions only three degrees of such, because it was and is useless, as explained in the *Secret Doctrine*, to teach anything about the four higher ones, and he therefore begins at the plane of globes A and G. His system is as near to occult truth as any, so that we may examine it, as well as his own and Menander's claims about "magic," to find out what they meant by the term. Now, for Simon, the summit of all manifested creation was *Fire*. It is, with him as with us, the Universal Principle, the Infinite Potency born from the concealed Potentiality. This Fire was the primeval cause of the manifested world of being, and was dual, having a manifested and a concealed or secret side. "The secret side of the Fire is concealed in its evident (or objective) side,"° he writes, which amounts to saying that the visible is ever present in the invisible, and the invisible in the visible. This was but a new form of stating Plato's idea of the Intelligible *(Noêton)* and Sensible *(Aisthêton)*, and Aristotle's teaching on the potency *(Dunamis)* and the act *(Energeia)*. For Simon, all that can be thought of, all that can be acted upon, was perfect intelligence. Fire contained *all*. And thus all the parts of that Fire, being endowed with intelligence and reason, are susceptible of development by extension and emanation. This is our teaching of the Manifested Logos, and these parts in their primordial emanation are our Dhyân Chôhâns, the "Sons of Flame and Fire," or higher Aeons. This "Fire" is the symbol of the active and living side of divine nature. Behind it lay "infinite Potentiality in Potentiality," which Simon named "that which has stood, stands and will stand," or permanent stability and personified Immutability.

From the Potency of Thought, Divine Ideation thus passed to *Action*. Hence the series of primordial emanations *through Thought begetting the Act*, the objective side of Fire being the Mother, the secret side of it being the Father. Simon called these emanations *Syzygies* (a united pair, or couple), for they emanated two-by-two, one as an active and the other as a passive Aeon. Three couples thus emanated (or six in all, the Fire being the seventh), to which Simon gave the following names: "Mind and Thought, Voice and Name, Reason and Reflection," the first in each pair being male, the last female. From these primordial six emanated the six Aeons of the Middle World. . . .

Thus we find in the system of Simon Magus that the first six Aeons, synthesized by the seventh, the Parent Potency, passed into Act, and emanated, in their turn, six secondary Aeons, which were such synthesized by their respective Parent. In the *Philosophumena* we read that Simon compared the Aeons to the "Tree of Life." " 'It is written,' said Simon in the *Revelation*,† 'that there are

---

°*Philosophumena*, vi, 9.

†"The Great Revelation" (*Hê Megalè Apophasis*), of which Simon himself is supposed to have been the author. — H.P.B.

two ramifications of the universal Aeons, having neither beginning nor end, issued both from the same root, the invisible and incomprehensible Potentiality, Sigê (Silence). One of these [series of Aeons] appears from above. This is the Great Potency, Universal Mind [or Divine Ideation, the Mahat of the Hindûs]; it orders all things and is male. The other is from below, for it is the Great [manifested] Thought, the female Aeon, generating all things. These [two kinds of Aeons] corresponding° with each other, have conjunction and manifest the middle distance [the intermediate sphere, or plane], the incomprehensible Air which has neither beginning nor end.' "† This female "Air" is our Ether, or the Kabalistic Astral Light. It is, then, the *Second World* of Simon, born of FIRE, the principle of everything. We call it the ONE LIFE, the Intelligent, Divine Flame, omnipresent and infinite. . . .

Simon's Third World with its third series of six Aeons and the seventh, the Parent, is emanated in the same way. It is this same note which runs through every Gnostic system — gradual development downward into matter by similitude; and it is a law which is to be traced down to primordial Occultism, or Magic. With the Gnostics, as with us this seventh Potency, synthesizing all, is the Spirit brooding over the dark waters of undifferentiated Space, Nârâyana, or Vishnû, in India; the Holy Ghost in Christianity. But while in the latter the conception is conditioned and dwarfed by limitations necessitating faith and grace, Eastern Philosophy shows it pervading every atom, conscious or unconscious. . . .

It thus follows that every rational being — called *Man* on Earth — is of the same essence and possesses potentially all the attributes of the higher Aeons, the primordial seven. It is for him to develop, "with the image before him of the highest," by imitation *in actu,* the Potency with which the highest of his Parents, or Fathers, is endowed.   — II

When H.P.B. refers to Simon's system of Aeons as starting "at the plane of globes A and G," the reader should remember that there are not just seven, but actually twelve different evolutionary stages of growth in the life history of an imbodiment of a planetary chain from its beginning to its end. She has passed over in relative silence the first five preliminary stages, and takes up the chain really at its sixth stage, which she calls the 'first.' The following diagram may make the matter somewhat clearer:

°Literally standing opposite each other in rows or pairs. — H.P.B.
†*Philosophumena,* vi, 18.

Primordial Stages°	{	1. Aetheric
		2. Etheric

Elementary Evolution	{	1. First Elemental Kingdom
		2. Second Elemental Kingdom
		3. Third Elemental Kingdom

The Seven Manifested Globes	{	1. Globe A fiery
		2. Globe B aery
		3. Globe C watery
		4. Globe D solid or earthy
		5. Globe E ethereal
		6. Globe F ethereal-spiritual
		7. Globe G quasi-spiritual

From this it is seen that preceding the evolution of the elemental kingdoms, which are the first to aid in building a globe on a plane, there are the aetheric and etheric stages, which really are the earliest cometary stage in its two chief divisions of development. Once these two primordial stages of preparation and quasi-materialization are ended, then the three main classes of elementals, which have been preparing themselves and have been separated and drawn into their three respective classes, begin their work of laying the foundations of a globe-to-be.

Again, when the three classes of elementals have built the outline of the globe-to-be, each class following when the preceding one has finished its work, the true globe commences its existence in what is here called the first round; because, by the time the three elemental kingdoms have completed their task, the different families of monads have become more or less segregated into their respective groups, and hence are ready to begin *their* rounds as life-waves.

From this time forwards, the seven rounds start and continue through serial progressions around all the globes of the chain; for it is to be noted that while the above description deals mainly with globe D, all the other

---

°Certain lower dhyāni-chohans blend their fluid or vital essence with the elementals of the higher four kingdoms of elementals and likewise with the life-atoms of the corresponding planes, thus providing the architectural ideation and guiding forces and energies upon which the lower three elemental kingdoms build in their turn. Cf. *The Secret Doctrine*, II, 233, footnote.

globes have been likewise evolving or coming into manifestation *pari passu* with it. A round begins in the highest of the twelve globes and proceeds regularly from globe to globe around the chain. This is but another way of stating that every globe unfolds from itself its surplus of life, or lives.

First of all we have the aetheric awakening into life of a laya-center, which, starting to move in its wanderings through space, gradually accretes to itself aetheric and etheric matter and thus slowly enters upon its second stage, the etheric; and when this stage is ended, the laya-center which is now manifesting as an ethereal comet, has just about become a member of the solar system to which its karmic destiny has inevitably drawn it back to imbodiment as a planetary chain-to-be. Once the comet is settled in its orbit around the sun as a highly ethereal globe in the first, or first and second states, of the matter of the physical cosmic plane, the three kingdoms of the elementals in serial order begin their characteristic activities,° and so gradually build a luminous and glowing or 'cloudy' body of very slight physical density, and of a type which probably our astronomers would describe as ethereally fiery. (The word fiery is used to suggest the glowing or luciform nature of fire in its first stages rather than the physical fire producing heat, as we have it on earth; electric substance might perhaps convey the idea somewhat better.) When this stage has been finished then the 'first round' starts, and it is with this round that H.P.B. begins her marvelous exposition.

The process of solidification or of materialization of the globes proceeds steadily until the middle of the fourth round, after which a re-etherealizing of the globe takes place, concomitant with and followed by the spiritualizing on the upward or luminous arc of the various families of monads which have been following or making these rounds up to the present point.

°Cf. *The Secret Doctrine*, I, 205–6, footnote:

"The seven fundamental transformations of the globes or heavenly spheres, or rather of their constituent particles of matter, is described as follows: (1) The *homogeneous;* (2) the *aeriform* and *radiant* (gaseous); (3) *Curd-like* (nebulous); (4) *Atomic, Ethereal* (beginning of motion, hence of differentiation); (5) *Germinal, fiery,* (differentiated, but composed of the germs only of the Elements, in their earliest states, they having seven states, when completely developed on our earth); (6) *Four-fold, vapoury* (the future Earth); (7) *Cold and depending* (on the Sun for life and light)."

THE DOCTRINE OF SWABHĀVA

THE URGE BEHIND evolution is not external to, but lies in germ or seed within, the evolving entity itself; both the urge and the seed arising out of one thing, and this is its swabhāva,° the selfhood or essential characteristic of the Self.

The doctrine of swabhāva has two basic aspects: first, the coming into being or existence through an entity's own innate powers of growth; and second, as a conception derivative from this, the inherent quality or character of an entity, so that whatever it is or does during the processes of its continuous expansional growth is along the lines of the forces and substances pouring forth from within its own heart, and all marked by the characteristic attributes of this fontal source.

In the case of man, his entire constitutional character is the compound swabhāva formed of the individual swabhāvas of his various monads. Each of these monads has its own character or type of individuality, and throughout the mahāmanvantara is unceasingly active in both an energic and a passive sense, pouring forth its own life essences from within. Since these different monads are in constant activity, which means in constant change, not only does the swabhāva of each individual monad undergo modification through evolution, but these modifications of necessity contribute to bring about equivalent changes in the complex general swabhāva of the human constitution. Hence, no swabhāva is eternally the same, never for even a fleeting instant utterly static; it is forever in course of modification or evolutionary change through timeless time.

As every swabhāva has its original source in the core of its constantly evolving monad, so every individual monad has its own swābhāvic spiritual magnetism, its individuality. Similarly so with every life-atom in the entire range of the universe. Furthermore, every group of individuals is collected together in a spiritual-magnetic swabhāva of its own; thus it is with man's physical body, or indeed his whole constitution, a nation or race, or even a group of stars such as the constellations of the zodiac. Variety is the

---

°A compound Sanskrit term, *swa* meaning self, and *bhāva*, becoming, coming into existence, signifying a continuous growth or change from state to state.

law of the universe, because it springs from the indwelling entity resident at the core of every living being, a ray of the everlasting monad in each.

A planet, for instance, is not only an entity by itself with a swabhāva or character different from that of other planets, but its inhabitants likewise partake to a certain extent of its individuality, as well as having a swabhāva of their own. Nature's fundamental laws, being universal, obviously must act throughout the universe; whereas nature's derivative laws, being largely the product of the indwelling spiritual entities of the cosmos which are the monads, vary according to time and place. We are, all of us, built of the same cosmic substances which exist everywhere. Our individualities are our respective swabhāvas, tones, numbers — call them what you like.

Hence every monad is a consciousness center with a definite swabhāva of its own, always in activity; and this activity, being spiritual-divine, is expressed on the lower planes by rays. Every monad thus irradiates forth from itself a continuous stream of energies of varying swābhāvic stamp, divine, spiritual, intellectual, psychic, etc. These rays penetrate the matter below them and surrounding them, and in this way produce the various phenomena in the beings in which they work. If these beings or vehicles are highly evolved and ready, so that they can manifest at once the powers of the monadic energy working within them, they do so, and the result is sublime. If, however, the vehicles are so low in the evolutionary scale that they can put forth but slightly some of the monadic qualities, then such slight manifestation is all that appears.

Of the multitude of rays that the monad is continuously sending forth, there is always one which is the highest. Every human being is an example. Around his core, which is this higher ray from his monad, are built the various vehicles or principles: the spiritual, the mental, the astral, the physical. Each one of these bodies is compounded of life-atoms, innumerable hosts of them, yet all having their own individual character, their swabhāva. Each such life-atom itself is a growing thing, and is a ray from the parent monad of the human being.

As the monadic essence or supreme hierarch of any spacial unit, whether a planetary chain, solar system or galaxy, emanates rays, every human being is 'born under' one or another of these rays. This statement as thus simply put is correct; but unfortunately there has been a good deal of mere guesswork and even foolish nonsense written about these rays, and how they affect and guide mankind, and how such or another individual 'belongs' to this or that ray.

It is of course true that every human being is a child of his own spiritual ray or parent star, but, as H.P.B. points out,° this star must not be confused with the merely astrological sun or star which marks the birth chart of a man. The spiritual ray here referred to is his highest and therefore first spiritual originant, whether it be the sun of our own solar system or one of the scores of billions of stars forming our glittering galaxy.

This does not mean that we are the only child of our parent star, as each such star has innumerable rays or children. It is something to think about, that the destiny of that star and our destiny are intimately related by swābhāvic or fohatic magnetism — and this will last as long as our present galaxy endures and, for all I know, even beyond that.

The matter of similarity and likeness among human beings does not mean that they come from the same monadic essence of any individual, but that they belong to identic planetary rays — in other words, that they are family rays from a grander monadic essence, a planetary monad. Human beings resemble each other. They are not as different from each other as they are different from beings occupying a state equivalent to humanity on the planet Venus, or on Mars or some other planet. But among ourselves, there are those who resemble each other still more closely than merely in similar traits; and these belong to the rays from the same planetary monad. A human 'Martian' does not have the same close similarity to a human 'Jovian' as he does to some other human being of the 'Martian' type, and so forth.

I would that I could write at greater length upon this matter of the rays if only in order to point out the mistaken conclusions of the many astralistic and psychistic authors who have written such flapdoodle about them; but it would take a volume to untangle all the errors.

Man as well as the universe is composite of distinct principles or elements, or tattwas, every one of which is itself divided into subprinciples, each having its own distinct swabhāva. Now if each principle contains all the swābhāvic energies of the others, why is it that we speak of one being superior or more spiritual than another? Why is not the sthūla-śarīra, the physical body, as lofty as the ātman?

In essence every one of the principles, cosmic or human, is as spiritual as any other; what makes one superior to another is not the essential substance out of which these elements or principles are composed, but

---

°Cf. *The Secret Doctrine*, I, 572–3.

the swabhāva which each manifests as its dominant note. The dominant characteristic of the ātman is spiritual selfhood; of the kāma, conscious fiery force or energy; of the manas, individualized intelligence or mind, etc.; yet each one has all the other six principles latent within itself.

Thus if a man, whose swabhāvic character is kāma, lives in the ātman part of it, he is living on a far higher plane than a man whose essential swabhāva is ātman, and yet lives in the lower portions thereof. Likewise, one who lives in the buddhi or higher manas of the kāma principle is really a nobler man than one who lives in the manas element of his constitution, but who at the same time is in the kāma part of his manas.

It is the principle in which we live that places us on the ladder of life. If we live in the ātman, the essential self, the divine part of any color, of any force, of any element, we are in the higher state of consciousness, and living far more nobly than a man who may be dwelling in the buddhi-manas, but on a very low plane of it. The thing is to strive to live in the highest plane where all is colorless glory. As soon as we descend into color, into distinct principles or tattwas, we descend into manifestation and differentiation producing a corresponding māyā and consequent ignorance. There is a divine kāma, there is a debased kāma; there is a divine buddhi, there is a human buddhi, which is its reflection. Every plane is subdivided and is patterned after its grand plane. Therefore, no matter in what station of life a man may be born, no matter to what ray he may belong, this does not place him. What places him is where his consciousness is focused. If it is focused upwards, rising into the ātman, into the colorless sphere, then he contains divinity. In the Absolute no one color, no one principle or tattwa, is more spiritual than any other, because all are born from the heart of divinity. When we come down into the worlds of differentiation, of existence, then we are obliged to make divisions.

One might ask: where on earth am I in this wilderness of swabhāvas and individualities and subprinciples, etc.? Granted that I am sevenfold, that I have seven ātmans or divinities within me, cooperating to make me what I am, as chemical elements cooperate to make an entity; but which part of this compound swabhāva is that which I know as I, that little unimportant part of me which is so aggressive?

We must remember that man is all his sevenfold being, from divinity downwards through all intermediate stages to the body. Where he centers his consciousness at any one time, in whatever particular layer of his auric egg, or in whatever swābhāvic center, that is the part which for the moment we may speak of as the I. The animal has it in his animal consciousness; we have it usually in our kāma-manas; the sages have it still higher, probably in the buddhi-manas; the Buddhas and Christs higher still, the divinities on a yet loftier stage.

We see here the tremendous import of this doctrine. A man can live in any portion of the entire range of his being *if he so wills*. He can center his consciousness, for a while at any rate, in whatever swābhāvic energy he desires and thereby gain inspiration and help from the energies of the universe, or he may center his thoughts and feelings in the lower energies; and, if he persist through many lives in loving evil and distortion, eventually he will sink to the Pit.

The hosts of monads are all learning, evolving entities, and they pass during the course of the revolving ages up and down through the immense cosmic planes. Each monad, originating in its primordial evolutionary development in a cosmic tattwa, must bear for long ages the fundamental impress of this cosmic tattwa as its foundation swabhāva; but as it rises through evolutionary modification or growth out of one cosmic plane or one cosmic tattwa into another, it does so because its swabhāva has likened itself unto the innate swabhāva of the new cosmic plane or tattwa into which it is entering. Furthermore, every swabhāva being compounded, we can, in our search for the 'first' swabhāva, pass upwards and inwards, so to speak, to its essence in order to find this primordial swābhāvic background; and in striving to do this we realize that there is always something higher still, still more recondite and immense, and that this something, apparently always unattainable, is an inexplicable x-quantity pouring forth from the very core of the monadic essence itself.

We may say, then, that every entity has the swabhāva of its divine monad, which it draws directly from its inseparable unity with the galaxy; that likewise there is in each one of us the swābhāvic core of the spiritual monad, which is of the spiritual essence of our solar system; that also we have within us as another swābhāvic core the human monad or reimbodying ego, which characterizes us as individual human beings and is of the spiritual essence of our planetary chain. Making the applications in proper order, we see that the most fundamental swabhāva within our compound swabhāva is the galactic swābhāvic core of us, which in its characteristic individuality lasts the longest and is the slowest to change; and even beyond that is the incomprehensible background of Infinity.

In exactly similar fashion, the swābhāvic essence of our spiritual monad, whose home is the solar system, lasts as a characteristic individuality longer than does the swābhāvic element of our reimbodying ego which belongs to the planetary chain. Yet all these swabhāvas, from the galactic down to the rather temporary swabhāva of the astral monad of a single human earth life, are evolving, and therefore in process of change towards inner and larger realms of cosmic life.

Man is therefore an intricate web of swabhāvas, each one of us having his own particular swabhāva complex. I might add here that were anyone to try to find out his own essential swabhāva or that of someone else — had he the power to do so — this would be an exceedingly dangerous thing. For if he were of unstable or weak moral sense, and yet had knowledge enough to know exactly the swabhāva or keynote of another person's character, it would be all too easy to subject that other to his will and thought and thus reduce him to the status of a willing or unwilling automaton or puppet.

Moreover, the monadic swabhāvas in our constitution are likewise modified by the different cosmic tattwas in and from which, and in serial order, they are born during the process of a manvantara, whether solar or planetary, so that at the same time any individual may have one of his monads ākāśic in its swabhāva, while another one of his monads may be either a taijasa (fiery) or a vāyava (airy) type; and others may be of still different tattwic characteristics. Our future destiny is to become self-consciously conscious on all the planes of our constitution, in all our swābhāvic tattwas which are in us, because we are microcosms of the encompassing macrocosm. When we reach such a condition of complete awakening we shall be fully self-conscious gods and, in fact, Silent Watchers or cosmic hierarchs — on a higher or lower plane of the environing universe — according to our destiny.

This is really a wondrous teaching, for it shows us the manner in which our whole constitution is enwebbed with the fabric of the universe. To change the figure of speech, a human being is somewhat like a sounding board, strung with seven chords like Apollo's lyre, across which sweep the winds of eternity, and the combined notes of these chords produce within him a cosmic symphony — each one of us being a living mystic lyre vibrating in sympathy with the Music of the Spheres.

203

SOUND, COLOR AND NUMBER

In Kosmos, the gradations and correlations of Colors and Sounds and therefore of Numbers, are infinite. This is suspected even in Physics for it is ascertained that there exist slower vibrations than those of the Red, the slowest perceptible to us, and far more rapid vibrations than those of the Violet, the most rapid that our senses can perceive. But on Earth in our physical world, the range of perceptible vibrations is limited. Our physical senses cannot take cognizance of vibrations above and below the *septenary* and limited gradations of the prismatic colors, for such vibrations are incapable of causing in us the sensation of color or sound. It will always be the graduated septenary and no more, unless we learn to paralyze our Quaternary and discern both the superior and inferior vibrations with our spiritual senses seated in the upper Triangle.

— H. P. B.'s E.S. *Instructions,* II

IT IS ONE OF THE fundamental teachings of the esoteric philosophy that every sound has its innate swābhāvic color, and, conversely, that every color has its inherent swābhāvic sound; and that, as a corollary, since both sound and color are expressions of rates of vibration, there can be no sound and no color without number, for every period of vibrational frequency has just so many units of vibration, which is equivalent to saying it is a number.

From this standpoint, when we speak of sound we at once imply both color and number; or, whenever we speak of color we imply sound and the vibrational number which manifests it; and equally so, whenever we speak of number, had we the eyes to see it and the ears to hear it, we should see the color as well as hear the sound corresponding to such number or vibrational frequency. It is to this that Pythagoras alluded when he spoke of the majestic harmony of the spheres.

Now as every atom in every object of nature, animate or inanimate, sings its own keynote and produces its own sound and has its own color and number, so every man, flower, tree, and every celestial body, is a play and interplay of sounds both loud and faint, interblending in a marvelous symphony, as well as being a beautiful intermingling of flashing and scintillating color. For instance, the auric egg of a man, because of the continuous activities of the prānic auras, is not only a mass of coruscating colors, but equally is a living organ producing harmonies of sound when the emotions, thoughts, and feelings are on a high plane, and horrible discord when they are characterized by hatred and other low passions.

For many decades astronomers have been intrigued by the varying shades of color which the vast stellar host presents; some stars are bluish, others are yellowish, still others reddish. The scientific idea is that the colors of the stars represent different ages in their evolutionary development. Be that as it may, and viewing the matter from another angle, it would be wrong to say that all blue stars are more spiritual than all red stars, merely because red is given as the color of kāma, and blue or indigo-blue as the color of the higher manas. For there is a spiritual red as well as a material red, and a spiritual blue as well as a material blue. Indeed, there are strong occult reasons for saying that for certain stars a reddish color would signify a more spiritual condition than the bright electric blue of certain others. The greater the intensity of vibration of light or radiation, the lower or more material in the scale that light is; and as the color of blue in our own octave of visible radiation is produced by a much higher frequency than is red, it is obvious that blue could signify a more material condition than the less intense vibration of red.

H.P.B. has stated that "the true color of the Sun is blue"° because its vital aura is blue. It is the real sun in the same sense as the vital aura of a human being is the real man; nevertheless the *real* man, the essential core, is the spiritual source of his merely vital aura. It would not be correct to say that the sun's vital aura is the interior sun; it is merely one of the coats or layers of its auric egg, and by no means one of the most interior. The blue force spoken of is the sun's vital aura intermingled, to some extent, with intellectual and spiritual energy, which flows forth from the sun continuously and in all directions. The sun is constantly pouring forth this blue energy in simply inestimable volume.

Other suns have other colors, which are the expressions of their complex swabhāvas. Likewise, could we hear the sounds which the various celestial bodies make as their natural expression, we would realize that each sun, each star, each planetoid, has its own characteristic keynote. Our scientists already are able to 'hear' certain stars, that is, to transform the light coming

---

°E.S. *Instructions*, II.

from a particular luminary into sound.° Curiously enough, when the moon's rays lighted upon the photoelectric cell used in these experiments, they sent forth moaning sounds, as of the tolling of great bells; but when the light from the bright star Arcturus flashed, it gave forth brilliant, scintillating sounds. If we could know the scheme of the correspondence of colors and sounds and numbers, we would be able to judge of the qualities of a sun or a star: for instance, dark blue would signify an intellectual sun; yellow, a buddhi sun.

The difficulty in attempting to determine to what specific ray or class any particular sun may belong by its color, is that our atmosphere affects colors very greatly as well as other things that come to us from the celestial bodies. The airy atmosphere surrounding our earth is a remarkable changer and a solvent to a certain extent. Our atmosphere is a transmuter as well as a transmitter. It deforms and actually changes the light — and therefore the sound — that comes to us from the planetary and solar bodies. Spectroscopic observation is by no means so reliable as has hitherto been supposed.

All the different colors of the solar spectrum originate in the sun and are represented on our earth in the form of light, in the form of forces — forces in the sun, every color of which is the outflow of a distinct swabhāva or individual energy, or solar logos. The sun is the vehicle of a divinity; whatever flows forth from it is rooted in the divine. There are seven (or twelve) solar forces or element-principles, and therefore seven (or twelve) swabhāvas making up the grand swabhāva of the sun. From these solar individualities, powers, forces, minor logoi, flow streams of substance-energy, combined in the light which we receive as daylight, white light. Pass this solar beam through a prism, and it will be broken up into its component colors. These seven rays of the spectrum are seven auric flows of vitality from the solar heart, and these swābhāvic energies combine to make light as we perceive it. Not one of the colors in essence is superior to any of the others. But on the plane of material existence, and having in view the work which each of the effluvia from the sun does on this scale of matter, we are bound to make distinctions and say that ātman is colorless, buddhi is yellow, kāma is red, and so forth. Yet all are divine in origin.

Every minutest portion of Infinity contains every essential element and force and swabhāva that Infinity contains. Likewise, every subdivision

---

°Cf. *The Mahatma Letters*, p. 170.

or subplane derives its own repetitive septenary from the surrounding universe. The microcosm simply repeats the macrocosm. In this connection we quote a somewhat lengthy extract from the E.S. *Instructions* of H.P.B. concerning the famous Tibetan invocation, *Om Mani Padme Hum:*

Know the corresponding numbers of the fundamental principle of every element and its sub-elements, learn their interaction and behavior on the occult side of manifesting nature, and the law of correspondences will lead you to the discovery of the greatest mysteries of macrocosmical life.

But to arrive at the macrocosmical, you must begin by the microcosmical: *i.e.,* you must study MAN, the microcosm . . . if we separate him for one moment from the Universal Whole, or view him in isolation, from a single aspect, apart from the "Heavenly Man" — the Universe symbolized by Adam Kadmon or his equivalents in every philosophy, — we shall either land in black magic or fail most ingloriously in our attempt.

Thus the mystic sentence, *"Om Mani Padme Hûm,"* when rightly understood, instead of being composed of the almost meaningless words, "O the Jewel in the Lotus," contains a reference to this indissoluble union between Man and the Universe, rendered in seven different ways and having the capability of seven different applications to as many planes of thought and action.

From whatever aspect we examine it, it means: "I am that I am"; "I am in thee and thou art in me." In this conjunction and close union the good and pure man becomes a god.

. . . in Tibet this sentence is the most powerful six-syllabled incantation and is said to have been delivered to the nations of Central Asia by Padmapâni, the Tibetan Chênrêsi.

But who is Padmapâni in reality? Each of us must recognize him for himself whenever he is ready. Each of us has within himself the "Jewel in the Lotus," call it Padmapâni, Krishna, Buddha, Christ, or by whatever name we may give to our Divine Self. The exoteric story runs thus:

The supreme Buddha, or Amitâbha, they say, at the hour of the creation of man, caused a rosy ray of light to issue from his right eye. The ray emitted a sound and became Padmapâni Bôdhisattva. Then the Deity allowed to stream from his left eye a blue ray of light which, becoming incarnate in the two virgins Dôlma, acquired the power to enlighten the minds of living beings. Amitâbha then called the combination, which forthwith took up its abode in man, *"Om Mani Padme Hûm"* ("I am the Jewel in the Lotus, and in it I will remain"). Then Padmapâni, "the one in the Lotus," vowed never to cease working until he had made Humanity feel his presence in itself and had thus saved it from the misery of rebirth. He vowed to perform the feat before the end of the Kalpa, adding that in case of failure he wished that his head would split into numberless fragments. The Kalpa closed; but Humanity felt him not within its cold, evil heart. Then Padmapâni's head split and was shattered into a thousand fragments. Moved with compassion, the Deity re-formed the pieces into *ten* heads, three white and seven of various colors. And since that day man has become a perfect number, or TEN. . . .

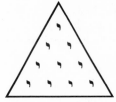

From Amitâbha — *no color* or the *white glory* — are born the seven differentiated colors of the prism. These each emit a corresponding sound, forming the seven of the *musical scale*. As Geometry among the Mathematical Sciences is specially related to Architecture, and also — proceeding to Universals — to Cosmogony, so the ten Jods of the Pythagorean Tetrad, or Tetraktys, being made to symbolize the Macrocosm, the Microcosm, or man, its image, had also to be divided into ten points. — I

Enough has been said to show that while for the Orientalists and profane masses the sentence, *Om Mani Padme Hùm,* means simply "O, the Jewel in the Lotus," esoterically it signifies "O, my God within me." Yes; there is a God in each human being, for man was and will re-become God. The sentence points to the indissoluble union between Man and the Universe. For the Lotus is the universal symbol of Kosmos as the absolute totality, and the Jewel is Spiritual Man, or God. — II

H. P. B. has beautifully expressed the sublime fact that our inner god is not only our highest link with the spiritual-divine universe, but is likewise the font whence streams into us everything that ennobles and purifies human existence. The more we become at one with this 'jewel,' the divinity at the core of our being, the more rapidly do we unfold in ever-expanding measure the grandeur that is within.[11]

ARCHITECTS AND BUILDERS

In every Cosmogony, behind and higher than the *creative* deity, there is a superior deity, a planner, an Architect, *of whom* the Creator is but the executive agent. And still higher, *over* and *around, within* and *without,* there is the UNKNOWABLE and the *unknown,* the Source and Cause of all these Emanations. — *The Secret Doctrine,* II, 43

Every form, we are told, is built in accordance with the model traced for it in the Eternity and reflected in the DIVINE MIND. There are hierarchies of "Builders of form," and series of forms and degrees, from the highest to the lowest. — *Transactions of the Blavatsky Lodge,* p. 98

NATURE IS ONE vast, living, inspirited organic entity, a true cosmic being — even when we limit the word nature to some particular range of the Boundless, such as our earth or solar system. In any organic entity every atom within it is connected with every other atom, and is not only an individual in itself, but likewise an integral part of the nature within whose sphere it has its being. All such 'atoms,' whether a sun, or one of the innumerable hosts of life-atoms, is thus derivative from the mother-substance of the environing nature; and this is true on all planes from the superspiritual down to the physical. Everything is interlocked and interworking with every other thing or being: just as the human body has its various aggregates of atoms and cells collected into organs, each such organ fulfilling its own purpose and function in the general organism. In similar fashion the nebulae, suns and planets, and the beings dwelling on the planets, are the various organs of some larger cosmic entity. But by far the greatest part of any such cosmic organism are the invisible and superior worlds and planes thereof, our physical plane being merely the grossest body that is inspirited and guided from within.

Every unitary being within nature, such as a sun or a planet, is in consequence an imbodied entity, divine in its highest parts, spiritual in the part subordinate to the divine, having an intellectual essence or mind, and all these manifesting through the lower garments, including the physical body. Thus every star is the expression of a divinity; for the universe

209

is imbodied consciousnesses existing in all-various and innumerably vast hierarchies, each possessing its own swabhāva.

Spirit at one pole, the higher or negative, and matter at the other pole, the lower or positive; and yet both fundamentally one. Matter is naught but the condensation of spirit, and therefore it is spirit living and working and 'sleeping' in the form of spirit.

The manifested universe, hanging as a pendant of evolution from the Formless and the Nameless, is subject to division by our human understanding into two interpenetrating and interlocking 'parts' — the light side, the spiritual or divine side of nature; and the night side, the matter or vehicular side. Now the light side we may call, although with great inadequacy, those portions of the manifested universe inhabited by the hierarchies of compassion and wisdom, which portions they actually *form and are*. The matter side is involved with and indeed made up of the many hierarchies of the cosmic builders, the masons of the world, which the mystic Greeks referred to as the kosmokratores, a word which may be translated both as world governors and world makers.

Just as in our building operations we have both architects and construction workers, so may universal nature be divided into two similarly general classes of cosmic beings. Of course, if we desire to be strictly logical, we shall find ourselves compelled to consider the architects of the universe as builders also; and yet there is the same important and natural distinction between them as there is in the human constitution between the ideative and directive human intelligence and the hosts of inferior monads and life-atoms through which the guiding and architectural mind of man works.

The builders of the universe are themselves in a sense architects in a minor fashion, for each one is an evolving entity and in cosmic time will become an architect. In fact, it is impossible to draw a line of demarcation between the two general classes, and we can do so only by excluding from our view the evolutionary future destiny of the builders and looking at the universe just as it is at any moment of time. What are now the cosmic architects were in former ages cosmic builders; just exactly as those who are now the cosmic builders will in future ages become cosmic architects, the places then vacated by them in the vehicular side of the universe being taken by other entities who are now inferior to the builders — the countless hosts of monads passing through evolutionary stages in those portions of the cosmic structure which to us are the lowest, the mineral and elemental kingdoms.

We thus have a picture of the universe which we can express in the words of the great Greek philosopher Heraclitus as being a cosmic entity in unceasing flux, "everything flowing" forwards and onwards to higher stages in evolution, and the places of those who have passed ahead immediately taken by inferior entities who are trailing along behind them. Hence, when we speak of the gods in the universe, we do not refer to certain beings who from utmost eternity have been gods and who in the future will forever and ever be gods, but we mean those fully self-conscious and ideationally active beings who form the hierarchies of light. Gods exist in almost an infinitude of different degrees on the evolutionary ladder of life, so that the lowest orders of the gods blend insensibly with the highest orders of the builders of the matter side of the universe. Again we see that the highest orders of the cosmic builders are themselves like gods and are indeed such to the lower orders of the builders.

The most important point here is that the architects represent the consciousness of the universe, and the builders the ethereal realms and the matter or substances of the universe. Both classes, the cosmic consciousnesses and the hosts of entities forming the matter side of nature, are cosmic monads. The only essential difference between them is that those monads which now have reached the condition of architects are far more evolved than are those other monads which are as yet only entities belonging to the substance side of being, which range all the way down the scale from the highest builders to life-atoms, elementals, and even ordinary atoms.

The entire universe, therefore, is built and formed of, indeed *is*, hosts of countless monads, and every monad is a consciousness point. Let us place in parallel columns two triads which H.P.B. discusses in *The Secret Doctrine:*°

CHAOS	GODS
THEOS	MONADS
KOSMOS	ATOMS

We see that each member of either triad corresponds to and is involved with its equivalent in the other triad. To illustrate: the gods find their spheres of activity in what the Greeks called chaos, the gods referring not so much to beings as to divine jīvanmuktas, consciousnesses so freed and with reaches so extended as themselves to be spacial in the abstract

°Cf. Volume I, 342 ff., 619 ff.

sense; Space, the container, giving birth to those beings who are living, conscious imbodiments of higher forces. The word chaos was chosen because suggesting conscious intelligence under higher direction. The monads similarly find their habitations in those other fields of space and consciousness which are aggregated under the one word theos; while the atoms find their spheres in the kosmos or structure of the manifested universe.

Considering each triad alone: the gods work through monads, and the monads, bearing within themselves the gods, work through atoms. Correspondingly, the esoteric chaos works in and through and by the divine carpentry of the manifested universe called theos which, in turn, bearing the abysses of chaos within itself, produces the manifested universe or kosmos. Thus on the matter side of nature, chaos (which is mūlaprakriti or pradhāna) works in and through the hierarchies of the builders which are aggregatively theos. These two combine to produce the vast kosmos instinct with evolving life as it is, and actually composed of innumerable monads in their present state of low evolutionary development.

If we now try to unify in thought these two triads and apply this coalesced picture analogically to the human constitution, we shall see that the highest part, the divine monad, is our inner god manifesting in and through its veil of consciousness, the mystical chaos or pradhāna of the human constitution. Similarly, our inner god expresses itself in and through the monadic sparks radiating from it, these sparks or rays being our different monads which work each one through its own spiritual garment, making the aggregated theos of our constitution. Again, our life-atoms on all the different planes work in and through their respective veils, the lower and less evolved atoms, which make the kosmos of the human constitution.

We have, therefore, the inner god working through the monads which in turn work through the life-atoms, forming as it were an upright stream of consciousness in man, while at the same time each of these three aspects works through its own garment to form the horizontal line of evolution of the human constitution. Hence the upright stream of consciousness traverses the horizontal and lower stream of consciousness, thus producing the mystic cross of which Plato guardedly speaks. This is the symbolical meaning of the cross in Christian theology: the Christos or spiritual ego of man 'crucified' in the realms of the matters of the human constitution.

By analogy, every universe has its inner god or supreme hierarch, which works through its countless monadic sparks radiating from it; these in turn work through their own rays or sparks, the life-atoms. Here we have the upright stream of consciousness on the cosmic scale. Likewise, the horizontal line of evolution is found in the inner god of our universe working through its pradhāna or prakritic essence; while its rays or monads work through the builders of the universe on all its different planes; and these cosmic monads, again, work through the elementals or cosmic life-atoms which find their secondary or horizontal line of evolution in the lower atomic entities which in their vast aggregate produce the kosmos.

Man is a microcosm of the macrocosm, and because he is an integral and inseparable part of the universe, we have an infallible key by which we may unlock the most recondite mysteries of space and time. This rule of course can apply in the inverse direction: once we understand the nature and characteristics and structure of the universe, we have thereby the cosmic master key by which we may unlock all the mysteries in man.

Our inner god is the architect of the building of the human vehicles through which it manifests. Just as our mind evolves an idea, forms a plan, makes a picture, and then uses will in order to corporealize it in certain material creations, such as a building, just so do the life forces, the will powers, and the spiritual and intellectual energies of the three higher classes permeate and stimulate the four inferior classes, and thus set them to work. Automatically, instinctively, the latter begin their activities according to the general cosmic plan. Why is it, for instance, that the ant or the bee follows each its own plan, building so symmetrically? What are these marvelous instincts in the lower creatures? They spring forth undoubtedly from within the creature; but what is that wonderful intelligence which seems to guide the instinct itself? It is the dominant thought of the spiritual planner as contrasted with the activity of the vital builder.

Let us relate these two fundamental hierarchies of architects and builders to the seven classes of monads (leaving aside for the present the uppermost five classes) who make man, build him, and complete him. These seven consist of two kinds of monads: the lower four are the builders, the masons, the workers; the three higher classes are the architects and planners, the evolvers of the idea which the builders follow. These two kinds of monads, as they work within the human being, form the two main divisions of his constitution: the three highest of the seven give to him his spiritual and intellectual principles; while the psychical, vital, astral, and physical parts come to him from the four corporeal classes of pitris, the actual progenitors of these lower principles.

The three higher are the spiritual and intellectual classes, the divine architects, the evolvers of the ideas; whereas the four lower classes, under the general name of lunar pitris or fathers, are they who work in the more material realms of existence and follow automatically the life plans which the spiritual classes have cast upon them in vital waves.

At the birth of a planetary chain the different globes thereof are built by these world builders, who had attained their spiritual and intellectual development in the preceding chain-manvantara. From another aspect, these world builders are of two general classes: first, the inner gods, looked upon collectively as a host of ten classes of monads at work in building any planetary chain; secondly, the spiritual influences coming to this planetary chain-in-building from the other planets and from the sun.

To repeat: higher than the world builders there are what the ancients called the architects, they who scheme the things to be; and in so scheming use thoughts, which are the spiritual elemental energies, the workers. And these thoughts are the hierarchies of the lower deities, such as the demigods, human beings, animals, the vegetable world, the mineral world, and so forth.

In the building of a planetary chain, for example, the dhyāni-chohans make the workshops from themselves, the product of their own being; much as a human being lives in his physical body, largely the product or flowing forth of the energies and substances within. It is the inner astral entity of the human constitution which fills the physical body, and this astral entity is the ultimate flowing forth from the spiritual body of the dhyāni-chohan, being composed of the streams of life-atoms. It is the matters and energies which flow forth from within, that build the worlds.

There are many classes of these world builders. There are many classes of the world architects. And above the architects there are other entities still more evolved, still more fully expressing the inexhaustible energies, powers and faculties of the inner god.

Space is boundless. Duration has neither beginning nor end. Time is but a fantasy of the human imagination cast on the background of eternal Duration. And in endless Time and through endless Space — inner and outer — passes the vast procession of the worlds and gods, demigods, men, beasts, etc. Movement always, with occasional breaks when sections of the procession drop out for a rest, and when that rest period is ended they take their place in the procession again, but at the rear.

In conclusion, the spiritual side of nature is composed of the hierarchies of light and compassion, and these hierarchies are monads which have been unfolded through evolution into expressing more and more of latent power and faculty and attribute, so that they have become the present self-conscious architects or true gods of the universe; whereas all the countless hosts forming the matter side, the vehicular side, or the class of the builders, are monads less awakened than are the general class of the gods or architects. By comparison, the monads forming the matter side of the universe are said to be 'asleep' — although of course this word covers ranges of consciousness from the highest of the builders, who are almost architects, down through all the grades to the relatively completely spiritually dormant life-atoms and atoms of the universe.

This is an exemplification of the Golden Chain of Hermes, stretching from the sublimest architect of the universe, the cosmic hierarch, and reaching as a vital flame down through all inferior entities to the lowest range of a hierarchical system. One cosmic plan, one cosmic life, one cosmic direction, one cosmic law.

THE LIPIKAS

Who are those highly mysterious agents of karma or occult agencies in nature to which H.P.B. has given the name of Lipikas,° taken from the Sanskrit?

Let me begin by quoting certain extracts from her writings. The first is from *The Secret Doctrine:*

There are three chief groups of Builders and as many of the Planetary Spirits and the Lipika, each group being again divided into Seven sub-groups. . . . The "Builders" are the representatives of the first "Mind-Born" Entities, therefore of the primeval Rishi-Prajapati: also of the Seven great Gods of Egypt, of which Osiris is the chief: of the Seven Amshaspends of the Zoroastrians, with Ormazd at their head: or the "Seven Spirits of the Face": the Seven Sephiroth separated from the first Triad, etc. . . .

The Lipika . . . are the Spirits of the Universe, whereas the Builders are only our own planetary deities. The former belong to the most occult portion of Cosmogenesis, which cannot be given here. Whether the Adepts (even the highest) know this angelic order in the completeness of its triple degrees, or only the lower one connected with the records of our world, is something which the writer is unprepared to say, and she would incline rather to the latter supposition. Of its highest grade one thing only is taught: the Lipika are connected with Karma — being its direct Recorders. . . .

The esoteric meaning of the first sentence of the Slokas is, that those who have been called Lipikas, the Recorders of the Karmic ledger, make an impassable barrier between the personal Ego and the impersonal Self, the Noumenon and Parent-Source of the former. Hence the allegory. They circumscribe the manifested world of matter within the Ring "Pass-Not." This world is the symbol (objective) of the One divided into the many, on the planes of Illusion, of Adi (the "First") or of Eka (the "One"); and this One is the collective aggregate, or totality, of the principal Creators or Architects of this visible universe.

— I, 127–9

°Lipika is formed from a verbal root *lip*, signifying to paint, to outline in colors, also derivatively to draw or to write — being a word adapted from the ancient usage of writing with a brush, as the Chinese do even today, thus signifying writing, transcribing, and hence recording.

The second extract is from the *Transactions of the Blavatsky Lodge:*

The Lipika proceed from Mahat and are called in the Kabala the four Recording Angels; in India, the four Maharajahs, those who record every thought and deed of man; they are called by St. John in the Revelation, the Book of Life. They are directly connected with Karma and what the Christians call the Day of Judgment; in the East it was called the Day after Mahamanvantara, or the "Day-Be-With-Us." Then everything becomes one, all individualities are merged into one, yet each knowing itself, a mysterious teaching indeed. But then, that which to us now is non-consciousness or the unconscious, will then be absolute consciousness.

Q. *What relation have the Lipika to Mahat?*

A. They are a division, four taken from one of the Septenates that emanates from Mahat. Mahat corresponds with the Fire of Simon Magus, the secret and the manifested Divine Ideation, made to witness to itself in this objective Universe through the intelligent forms we see around us, in what is called creation. Like all other emanations, they are "Wheels within Wheels." The Lipika are on the plane corresponding to the highest plane of our chain of globes.

— pp. 112–13

When H.P.B. points out that the Lipikas are "the Spirits of the Universe," she informs us at once that they are a hierarchy, septenary or even duodenary in their divisions, belonging to the very highest cosmic plane of a universe. They are not merely four, as might be supposed from one or two of her remarks to the effect that the Lipikas stand at the four quarters of the world. Actually, there are armies of Lipikas, the four quarters having reference to the polar magnetisms in any globe or chain or solar system, which cross each other producing the mystic North, South, East, and West. This is because of the concentration of focal energy-points at these quarters.

Each universe has its own hierarchy of Lipikas, which are to be radically distinguished both in their nature and in their functions from the lower hierarchies of demiurgic or world-forming beings, the builders. In fact, we may speak of the Lipikas as the highest group of the architects; and one of the reasons they are called the agents of karma is that, acting under the impulse of that universal and mysterious law, they lay down the architectural or karmic plan of the structure of a universe when it is coming out of its mahāpralaya. As soon as the Lipikas have outlined the plan and impressed it by cosmic ideation on the lower hierarchies of builders, these in turn immediately proceed in their labor of world-building.

The point here is that precisely because the Lipikas are the agents of karma, and the very highest group of the cosmic architects, they are the lofty intelligences almost automatically impressing cosmic ideation upon all 'beneath' them, it being obvious that both cosmic ideation and their own characteristics are typically expressive of the karmic history and background of such a universe. Hence the Lipikas, "Recorders of the Karmic ledger," are the cosmic agents responsible for circumscribing the manifested worlds with the various Rings-pass-not, which are merely the karmic boundaries defining and limiting the various spheres of action of the minor hierarchies and their included individuals.

The Lipikas, considered as the most powerful in their own universe, infill it with their combined intelligence and vital powers, so that all entities therein are continuously permeated by their essence. Consequently, whatever happens within such universe is instantaneously and forever 'recorded' or stamped upon the vital essence or fluids of the Lipikas. It is this fact that gives to them their name of Recorders, because they react to every thought, feeling, and action of all the multitudinous hosts of beings included within them; and thus the Lipikas carry indelibly engraved in their essences all that takes place in the hierarchies subordinate to their sway and which they enclose with their all-encompassing, vital-intelligent essence or substance. This is exemplified by the astral light of our earth, sometimes called the astral picture gallery. As the astral light is the linga-śarīra of the earth, it is completely within the vital essence and intelligent fluid of the Lipikas, just as is any other principle or element of our earth.

When the mahāmanvantara of a universe is drawing to its end, and the world is being progressively infolded into the higher cosmic planes, the time comes at the opening of the mahāpralaya when all subordinate beings and things have become at one with the highest hierarchies of the universe in and upon its highest cosmic plane. In other words, all entities have become at one with the Lipikas themselves, that is, are indrawn into their essence or substance. This consummation of karmic destiny is sometimes called the Day-Be-With-Us, when "everything becomes one, all individualities are merged into one, yet each knowing itself."

In relation to a smaller universe, such as our planetary chain, H.P.B. says: "The Lipika are on the plane corresponding to the highest plane of our chain of globes." As the Lipikas open a manvantara and close it, and are the first to appear and the last to vanish because of the

218

progressive unfolding and infolding at the beginning and end of every period of activity, they are the agents of karma because they carry all karmic seeds within themselves until the next manvantara or mahāmanvantara opens. And then, having thus recorded all the karma of a universe within themselves, they begin to emanate it *pari passu* with the evolving planes and hierarchies of that universe when its new mahāmanvantara begins.

We may look upon the grand hierarchy of the Lipikas as being composed of seven (or ten or twelve) grades or minor hierarchies. The three highest of these function particularly on the three highest cosmic planes — or on the three highest planes of any smaller universe such as a planetary chain or even a globe — whereas the remaining four subordinate grades of the Lipikas have especial functions on the four lower cosmic planes. Hence, as we are on globe D on the lowest cosmic plane, it is the four lower minor hierarchies of the Lipikas which affect us particularly and are the ones which record the karma of our four lower planes. It is for this reason that exoterically the Lipikas are referred to as being four in number only — thus stating occult truth under a veil or disguise. Actually these 'four' Lipikas individually are the four lower subgrades or minor hierarchies.

Every cosmic plane is an analogical repetition of all other planes, and especially of those above it on the hierarchical ladder. Even our physical cosmic plane has its Lipika host or Lipika hierarchy, originating on the highest or most ethereal subplane thereof; and it is the direct function and duty of these Lipikas to act as the highest architects in building and overseeing this physical plane, and as the karmic recorders of all that takes place in and on it throughout its various subdivisions.

It is just these Lipikas with their intelligent vital essence infilling and inspiriting any cosmic plane which produce what we call the laws of nature, and we thus see once more how karma, one of the most fundamental of such natural laws, and the Lipikas are interblended and indeed even coalesce into unity.

VI

Invisible Worlds
and their Inhabitants

PATTERN OF THE WORLD STRUCTURE

There are millions and millions of worlds and firmaments visible to us; there [are] still greater numbers beyond those visible to the telescopes, and many of the latter kind do not belong to our *objective* sphere of existence. Although as invisible as if they were millions of miles beyond our solar system, they are yet with us, near us, *within* our own world, as objective and material to their respective inhabitants as ours is to us. But, again, the relation of these worlds to ours is not that of a series of egg-shaped boxes enclosed one within the other, like the toys called Chinese nests; each is entirely under its own special laws and conditions, having no direct relation to our sphere. The inhabitants of these, as already said, may be, for all we know, or feel, passing *through* and *around* us as if through empty space, their very habitations and countries being interblended with ours, though not disturbing our vision, because we have not yet the faculties necessary for discerning them. Yet by their spiritual sight the Adepts, and even some seers and sensitives, are always able to discern, whether in a greater or smaller degree, the presence and close proximity to us of Beings pertaining to other spheres of life. Those of the (spiritually) higher worlds, communicate only with those terrestrial mortals who ascend to them, through individual efforts, on to the higher plane they are occupying. . . .

. . . such invisible worlds do exist. Inhabited as thickly as our own is, they are scattered throughout apparent Space in immense number; some far more material than our own world, others gradually etherealizing until they become formless and are as *"Breaths."*
— *The Secret Doctrine*, I, 605–6

THE ENTIRE PHYSICAL universe, in all its ranges of extension and multi-myriad forces and substances, is but the outer garment of the illimitable ranges of the invisible spheres and planes, rising in hierarchical stages into the Boundless.

This thought is not only a key to a correct understanding of the structure, visible and invisible, of any cosmic unit, but it has likewise a supreme ethical importance. It shows that man and the universe are not twain and different, but essentially one. Herein lies the basic explanation of karma: all that man is and does is bound up with the destiny of the universe, spiritual, ethereal, physical. In essence, what it is, he is; and therefore all his thoughts, emotions, and consequent actions are duly noted, even to the last details, by the karmic recorders, the Lipikas.

Many students find it difficult to understand the precise nature of cosmic element-principles and the lokas and talas, and their relation to the twelve major classes of monads. The first thing to bear in mind is that the invisible worlds are simply all those parts of the solar universe, and in a smaller degree of a planetary chain, which are invisible because composed of substances and forces either more ethereal or denser than are those which make up the physical plane. Our physical plane is but one out of twelve cosmic planes, each of which basically has its charac-teristic element-principle or swābhāvic aether. In other words, every one of these cosmic element-principles gradually evolves a world structure from within its own substances and forces, and this world structure consid-ered as a unitary whole is a cosmic plane. Now a cosmic plane, being its own cosmic element-principle unrolled into manifestation, has its spirit-ual, intermediate and physical-astral portions; and each such portion, when viewed as an individual minor world structure within the greater world structure of the cosmic plane itself, is a loka and a tala conjoined as a twin.

Briefly: the universe at the beginning of its manifestation unrolls itself from highest to lowest through all the intermediate grades as twelve elements or principles; then each element-principle unrolls itself into the different subplanes of a cosmic plane; and it is just these different subplanes which are the cosmic lokas and talas. These lokas and talas, therefore, can be called with equal truth the subgrades or minor worlds existing on any cosmic plane.

Let us return for a moment to the cosmic element-principles before these as individual units of the cosmic structure unfold themselves into planes and into the different lokas and talas. The cause of such manifesting into the varieties of differentiation lies in the fact that every cosmic element or principle is itself composed of unitary points of consciousness, and these are monads in their matrix — in and born of the cosmic element from which they came and therefore to which they belong.

These monads (which we may rather loosely refer to as cosmic life-atoms) are called cosmic elementals, because they are the first offsprings born directly from the respective cosmic elements. Since there are twelve cosmic elements, there are twelve fundamental classes of monads, ranging from the divine to the physical. Of course, each monad or consciousness center is a living, growing, learning entity; so that no matter what may be the cosmic element from which it originally springs, it is destined through evolution and the garnering of experience ultimately to blossom forth into a god. Beginning its career as an unself-conscious god-spark, a jīva — a cosmic elemental born from the cosmic element — its destiny is to pass through all intermediate stages of evolution until finally it becomes a full-blown god, a jivanmukta.

The general idea is that the cosmic element-principles themselves are vast armies of cosmic elementals or original monads existing on all the twelve planes of the universe, visible and invisible, and forming in their immense interlocking and interacting substances and energies the marvelous scheme of the world structure which is the solar Brahmānda, or Egg of Brahmā. The cosmic planes or, what comes to the same thing, the lokas and talas forming these planes, are actually built of the countless hosts of the twelve classes of the evolving monads. Every greater contains within itself an army of the smaller; or, inversely, every smaller unit lives within a greater unit which in its turn is but a component part of a unit still more vast; and so forth till the limits of the solar system are reached. And the solar system itself is but repetitively again a minor component in an entity still more sublime, which is our galaxy.

These twelve great classes of evolving monads not only exist on the twelve cosmic planes and in and through all the lokas and talas thereof, but also, because of past evolutionary karmic unfolding, *infill* the world structure, thus producing the different hierarchies of living beings from the highest to the lowest. Some of these monads are gods in our own world structure or solar system, and some are demigods; and others again are monads in a less evolved state of development, of which our human hierarchy is an example. We can carry the different minor hierarchies down below the human until we reach the three major classes of the elementals — down, not meaning underneath in the sense of position, but signifying younger monads.

A good analogy to the world structure may be found in the constitution of a human being. Here we have a septenary entity composed of substances and forces — which in the world structure we call planes — ranging from the divine to the physical, and on all intermediate grades; and each grade is a vast army of life-atoms presided over by its chief monad. Yet all parts of a man's constitution work together and interlock, in substance

225

and in action, in order to produce a sevenfold human being. On precisely the same analogical lines is a solar system composed; or a planetary chain or any one globe thereof, or indeed any atom of the numberless hosts of atoms making a globe. The solar system, just like man, is an entity having its own individuality, which is its hierarch; and this hierarch lives in and through all the forces and substances, all the planes and lokas and talas, of the solar system which is its expression, its constitution.

THE UNROLLING OF THE COSMIC ELEMENTS

Now, speaking of Elements, it is made the standing reproach of the Ancients, that they "supposed their Elements simple and undecomposable." Once more this is an unwarrantable statement; as, at any rate, their initiated philosophers can hardly come under such an imputation, since it is they who have invented allegories and religious myths from the beginning. Had they been ignorant of the Heterogeneity of their Elements they would have had no personifications of Fire, Air, Water, Earth, and Aether; their Cosmic gods and goddesses would never have been blessed with such posterity, with so many sons and daughters, elements born *from* and *within each respective Element.*   — *The Secret Doctrine*, I, 140–1

AT THE COMMENCEMENT of any universal manvantara when differentiation and manifestation begin, the great cosmic drama opens by the arising in the dormant hierarchical originants of a yearning for self-expression. This is the same sort of yearning that causes the awakening of the human ego in the devachan so that it may start its 'descent' into a new incarnation on earth. In this manner the universe unrolls or develops from within itself its various essences — often referred to as principles or elements — and always beginning with the highest and thereafter proceeding in regular serial or hierarchical manner. Each essence, once it is evolved forth from its predecessor, unrolls from within itself the essence which succeeds it in the building of the structure or fabric of the universe. Thus the divine essences produce from within themselves their offspring, the spiritual essences, and these in their turn produce the essences which succeed them in the world order; so that when this process is completed for that manvantara, we have the universe in all its planes ranging from the divine-spiritual down to the astral-physical.

The manner of this unfolding is such that each essence or element-principle not only contains within itself its own swabhāva, but likewise is the vehicle of the different swabhāvas of all the essences which have preceded it, and indeed of those which follow it; so that when the seventh (or twelfth) essence is reached we have the universe unfolded as an aggregate of webs of lives. This process is called differentiation or manifestation.

In different systems of religion or philosophy various names have been given to these essences or element-principles. However, any attempt to set in parallel columns the names of one system with those of others, while helpful as showing similar views, can be very misleading if these equated names are misconstrued as having exactly the same significances in all respects.

These principles or cosmic elements were called by Plato, and after him by Aristotle and other Greek writers, *stoicheia*, a word meaning 'things belonging together in serial order,' and used in the sense of the unfolding or unrolling of the cosmic essences, the lower from the higher and each from its own predecessor in time and space. As H.P.B. says in *The Secret Doctrine* (I, 461):

The στοιχεῖα, (Elements) of Plato and Aristotle, were thus the *incorporeal principles* attached to the four great divisions of our Cosmic World, . . . So close, indeed, that the hierarchies of those potencies or Forces have been classified on a graduated scale of seven from the ponderable to the imponderable. They are Septenary, — not as an artificial aid to facilitate their comprehension — but in their real *Cosmic* gradation, from their chemical (or physical) to their purely spiritual composition.

Proclus, a Neoplatonic writer and mystic, describes this process of emanational unfolding in the following suggestive manner:

That all the progression of the elements however, may become manifest to us, and the gradations of them, it is requisite that we should begin the theory of them from on high. These four elements therefore, fire and air, water and earth, subsist primarily, and uniformly according to cause, in the Demiurgus of wholes. . . . From these demiurgic causes, a progression takes place of these four elements into the universe, though not immediately into the sublunary world. For how can the most immaterial natures give subsistence without a medium, to the most material; and immoveable natures, to those that are in every respect moved? For the progression of things is nowhere without a medium, but exists according to a well-ordered gradation.°

Another Greek philosopher, Empedocles, used the word *rhizomata*, meaning roots, for these same cosmic essences, a term which H.P.B. also adopted.

°*On the Timaeus of Plato*, Book III, pp. 422–3.

The several schools of Hindu philosophy, such as the Sānkhya and the Vedānta, had their own special terms for these cosmic essences; and so again did Buddhism, especially the Mahāyāna. Yet all of them, while envisaging the same cosmic picture of unrolling essences, had each one its own manner of viewing them.

The Sānkhya term for these cosmic essences is tattwas,° looked upon as dual in character, and having an inner or more ethereal and an outer or more unfolded aspect. Their more ethereal aspect is called tanmātra, while their manifested aspect is called mahābhūta, so that tattwa corresponds to what in theosophical terminology is called an element-principle, tanmātra being equated with the principle and mahābhūta with the element. The Buddhists, on the other hand, instead of tattwas usually speak of dhātus.

Or, again, take two other terms used in the Sānkhya philosophy, prakritis and vikritis. In one sense, the prakritis mean almost the same as do the tattwas. Yet when analyzed more closely we see that the word tattwas should probably be reserved for the abstract cosmic essences themselves; while the word prakritis should be used for the various cosmic substances and their functions which we can best express as the 'producing power' within the tattwas. Thus prakriti, as signifying the unfolding

---

°Cf. *Fundamentals of the Esoteric Philosophy*, where I have given the following table of cosmic essences equated with the Brahmanic tattwas and the mystic Greek parallels, etc. Any such table, however, is more or less arbitrary, as others could be drawn up with equal accuracy from different standpoints:

	ESOTERIC LINE	BRAHMANIC TATTWAS	ELEMENTS	MYSTIC GREEK	
1.	Swabhawat	Ādi-tattwa	The ONE	First Logos	
2.	Ādi-buddhi or Ādi-buddha	Anupapādaka-tattwa	Spirit	Second Logos	DHYĀNI-CHOHANS
3.	Gods	Ākāśa-tattwa	Aether	Gods, Third Logos (Mahat)	
4.	Monads	Taijasa-tattwa	Fire	Daimones	
5.	Souls	Vāyu-tattwa	Air	Heroes	
6.	Atoms	Āpas-tattwa	Water	Men	PITRIS
7.	Bodies	Prithivī-tattwa	Earth	Beasts	

ELEMENTAL WORLD

8. _____
9. _____
10. _____

substance or ethereal matter inherent in every tattwa, brings forth from within itself the rivers of lives or cosmic elementals. The vikritis are a still further stage in cosmic evolution, and stand for the produced manifestations or differentiations of the prakritis — the multimyriad types of manifestation which each prakriti *becomes.*

Hence we have a tattwa as an abstract cosmic essence, and arising within itself is its productive substantial power, bringing forth its own swābhāvic ethereal substances and forces, and this is *its* prakriti. This prakriti in its turn unfolds itself into countless differentiations which, combined with all the other tattwas and prakritis and vikritis, produce the intricate web of the twelvefold universe.

Now the Sanskrit term mahābhūtas corresponds to what the ancient Greeks called the five cosmic elements, usually enumerated as aether, fire, air, water, and earth — these not being the ordinary elements familiar to us. These names were adopted because of certain attributes (vikritis) inherent in the physical or quasi-physical elements, in an attempt to describe the corresponding characteristics of the *cosmic* elements: earth implying solidity and expansion, water implying fluidity, fire suggesting vital heat, quick nervous energy as well as the stimulation of mental thought, etc.

There is an interesting point in connection with the term mahābhūtas, which literally translated means 'great have-beens' (*bhūtas,* coming from the verbal root *bhū,* to become), in that these mahābhūtas, when they are unfolded during the beginning of a cosmic manvantara, are exact reproductions of what these same cosmic elements were, each one, when the preceding manvantara had ended. The new universe, so far as the cosmic essences are concerned, can be likened to a watch which, having run down and again being wound, will begin to run anew from the exact instant which the hands indicated when the mechanism stopped.

When a universe is unrolled, through the unfolding of its component cosmic essences, it is called an Egg of Brahmā, and the hierarch of any such universe is the Brahmā thereof, living in his cosmic Egg, very much as the ātman of the human constitution is the Brahman thereof, living in the human auric egg, existent as it is on all the planes of man's constitution.[12]

It is of course true that even the cosmic essences, being formed as they are of incomputably vast hosts of monads, are themselves advancing in growth, because all their component monads are evolving. As one vast body of similar monads passes to higher things, their places are taken by other similar monads following in their train; and thus the cosmic essences of the universe are always there in their twelvefold stages, to unfold into new dramas of cosmic life — those monads which have graduated from one cosmic hierarchy passing onwards and upwards into the next hierarchy, and thus ad infinitum.

ELEMENTALS, OFFSPRING OF THE COSMIC ELEMENTS

> Fire, Air, Water, Earth, were but the visible garb, the symbols of the informing, invisible Souls or Spirits — the Cosmic gods to whom worship was offered by the ignorant, and simple, respectful recognition by the wiser. In their turn the *phenomenal* subdivisions of the noumenal Elements were informed by the Elementals, so called, the "Nature Spirits" of lower grades.
> — *The Secret Doctrine*, I, 461

EACH COSMIC ESSENCE or element, when it is evolved, is an immense aggregate of elemental lives, which in theosophical terminology are called elementals — inhabitants of the respective cosmic elements. In other words, the elementals of any one cosmic essence are its children and therefore belong to and themselves imbody the swabhāva of their parent. This is true for all the cosmic essences of the manifested universe, so that we have elementals springing forth from every one of the cosmic planes, from prithivī or earth, right on up to the highest or ādi-tattwa.

Another and more familiar use of the word elementals signifies beings or entities in the very beginning of their evolutionary growth in the scale of lives of a universe. If we apply this to the element-principles of man's constitution, we shall be able to make the appropriate applications to the cosmic scale. There are, for instance, elementals born of our buddhi, of our manas, others from our kāma, etc.

The word elementals may likewise be used for all entities beneath the human kingdom. More specifically, however, the term refers to the first entities that arise in and of the seven elements of nature before other more advanced entities come into manifestation. Thus on the hierarchical ladder we have: first, the three elemental kingdoms, then the elementals manifesting in the mineral kingdom, next those in the vegetable kingdom, then those manifesting as animals, followed by the 'perfected' elementals which we call human beings. The three elemental kingdoms are so designated because they are the first families or races of beings arising in the cosmic elements before any more evolved entity can manifest itself, and they provide the groundwork upon which the more evolved structure of a world is built by entities of higher kingdoms.

There are seven planes or kingdoms of nature, and these manifest in various forms. Looked at from one angle we call them lokas and talas; from another we say that nature is composite of seven tattwas and bhūtas, or seven principles and elements. The point is that every element contains all the other elements locked up within its heart, until the appropriate field and time in space come for the appearance of such latent elements.

The cosmic tattwas unfold in serial order and thus produce the hierarchies formed by the corresponding lokas and talas: beginning with the first or ādi-tattwa, the second or anupapādaka-tattwa emanates from it, the while retaining a certain portion of the first tattwa. From the second tattwa unfolds the third, ākāśa-tattwa, which contains not only its own dominant swābhāvic forces and substances, but likewise its portions of the second and also of the first cosmic tattwa. This continues down to the seventh and last. When the time of the cosmic pralaya approaches, the whole process of emanational unfolding reverses itself — the universe now begins the procedure of 'radiating' away or infolding itself.

Each one of these elements or kingdoms or realms or lokas — call them what you will — of inner and outer nature is filled full with its own populations, i.e. is composite of monads, monadic centers, varying in degree of evolution, ranging from self-consciousness to mere consciousness, down to passive unself-consciousness. Furthermore, the higher the scale of life, the greater and more spiritual do the inhabitants of these realms become. The highest are very powerful; some elemental beings are so high — not in evolutionary rank but in origin — that, being offsprings of one of the cosmic elements, they partake of the cosmic wisdom of which they as entities are life-atoms. There are other elemental beings whose origin is so low in the material spheres that they are instinctively antagonistic to human beings, some even fearfully malignant, not by choice, not by will, but by their character; on the other hand, others are friendly to the human race, even beneficent. A few have quasi-human form, but most are non-human in shape, some being gigantic in size, titans, with corresponding powers. The great majority of these elementals are only quasi-conscious.

There are many races and families of elementals, and also many subraces and subfamilies. They are, in fact, the building stones of nature. Nature itself is composed of them; for no entity anywhere can separate itself from the boundless All. They are the unevolved life-atoms of the several cosmic elements; and these beings have been alluded to under different names by mystical and initiated writers of various countries. The Fire

Philosophers of Europe said that there were four main elements of the universe, and that from these were born respectively: the salamanders of fire, the sylphs of air, the undines of water, and the gnomes of earth.°
These are but names, yet the idea thus set forth is perfectly true: from the essential elements of the universe are born the native entities belonging by essential characteristic to these elements.

Actually, these elements of the cosmos are seven, not four, but the three higher ones are never referred to in any detail in exoteric writings. The four usually spoken of are manifested or rūpa, possessing form; and the three higher classes are arūpa, formless. Consequently, some of these elements composing the very fabric of the universe are high; some are gross and material; there are also those of an intermediate type. Since there is a spiritual element and an intellectual, a psychological, an astral and a physical one, all going to form the general substance of the visible and invisible universe, the elementals originally springing from these seven mother-substances or elements partake in each instance of the swabhāva of the fountain of being out of which they are born.†

This is the reason that some of these elemental beings are of surpassing wisdom, because originating in the spiritual and intellectual planes of the universe; some are of exceeding malignity to man; there are those which are highly intellectual, while others are totally unintellectual; some are purely instinctual. All these adjectives are but words, applied to these elementals with the necessary reservations of quality and kind. In all cases they originate as the life-atoms of the mother-substances from which

---

°The sylphs or the nature spirits of the atmosphere, the vāyu-elementals, are popularly said to be the most dangerous to man, because they are on a plane which has close and intimate correspondences with the kāma range of the astral world. The gnomes, or prithivī-elementals, are less dangerous, because too heavy. The undines, or elemental beings of āpas-tattwa, are also less dangerous, because they are not as evolved as the sylphs. The fire elementals or salamanders, the beings born from the taijasa-tattwa, are likewise not as harmful because, though more evolved than the sylphs or vāyu-elementals, they are more intimately connected with the mānasic ranges of the astral world.

†Cf. *The Secret Doctrine,* I, 294, footnote:
". . . as man is composed of all the Great Elements: Fire, Air, Water, Earth and Ether — the ELEMENTALS which belong respectively to these Elements feel attracted to man by reason of their co-essence. That element which predominates in a certain constitution will be the ruling element throughout life. For instance, if man has a preponderance of the Earthly, gnomic element, the gnomes will lead him towards assimilating metals — money and wealth, and so on."

they come. As they are elemental beings, unconscious god-sparks, so to say, life-atoms of the original substances, they are devoid of a spiritual ego, or, to use H.P.B.'s words, "Elemental Beings void of Divine Spirit." Hence in popular language they have been called soulless, i.e. without an evolved soul; and this is generally true, because it is evolution alone which brings forth the hitherto unexpressed spiritual ego in men, or in beings equivalent to men. Divinity is as much at the heart of every elemental being as it is at the heart of a god. But until that core of divinity is evolved forth into manifestation, so that the entity is thereafter governed by the spiritual flame within as an ego, it is said to be without a spiritual soul.

Many interesting legends, stories, romances, have been written about the elementals, a few even describing the union of human beings with the beautiful and in some cases mechanically wise, yet soulless, elemental beings of the cosmos.° In Persian mythology even the Peris at the gates of Paradise cannot enter therein until they have evolved a self-conscious spiritual soul. They cannot enter heaven because they have no self-consciously aspiring center to attract them to the atmosphere of conscious spirit. They cannot pass because they cannot give the passwords. They do not know them, for already they have met their Ring-pass-not. It is only the stained and weary, but nevertheless successful, human pilgrim soul who can pass the final test at the portals of heaven, and enter in; and that test demands an evolved spiritual self-consciousness.

Now every elemental life-atom of one of these cosmic elements is an entity beginning its upward evolutionary journey toward self-conscious divinity. All these entities and all their manifold classes or races or families aspire to become men and will be in the next manvantara.† Not in this one, however, because the door opening into the human kingdom has closed for the present manvantara — the lowest point of matter having been reached by the evolving life-waves — and also because we have al-

---

°As an instance, cf. the mystical legend *Undine* by Baron de La Motte-Fouqué.

†The kind of manvantara referred to is the solar manvantara which, however, is an ambiguous term. As pointed out elsewhere, the term solar manvantara has two applications: first, to the entire life cycle of our sun and therefore of the entire solar system — usually called a mahāmanvantara; and second, to the life cycle of a single planetary chain, which is likewise called a solar manvantara, for the reason that each such life cycle, when beginning its course, enters upon a new cosmic subplane, and consequently a new sun, as it were, dawns for each such planetary chain-manvantara.

ready begun the ascent along the luminous arc, retracing our steps toward divinity. Each one of these elementals in future great manvantaras of the universe will become first a semiconscious entity, then a quasi-conscious entity or human being, and still later will evolve into becoming a god, a supergod, and so on forever.

We human beings were elementals in some far bygone cosmic manvantara, and we have evolved at present the first faint light of spirituality. However imperfectly it may be, we are already beginning to sense the working of the divine flame within, which is the influence of the inner god.

These elemental beings are constantly and throughout boundless Space springing forth from the seven mother-substances, and thus beginning their journey; while at the other end of the evolutionary pilgrimage vast armies of full-blown gods are passing over the horizon, following the cosmic pathway leading into an ever-enlarging splendor, and thus ever growing into something still more sublime. There is a constant life stream from elemental life-atoms to gods.

What, then, originates these life-atoms from the cosmic elements? Thoughts — thoughts of the supergods and gods; of daimones and heroes; of men and beasts — for thoughts are ensouled energies. And as nature is divided into seven elemental or cosmic substances, all classes of beings can trace their origin back to one or to another of these seven mother-substances or rivers of life.

In any solar system, as in our own with its seven (or twelve) sacred planets, these rivers of life express themselves by building up planets, each planet corresponding to one of the cosmic elements. We find this teaching imbodied in the Neoplatonic doctrines as expressed by Proclus:°

The Pythagoreans however say, that the elements may be surveyed in the heavens in a twofold respect, in one way indeed prior to the sun, and in another after it: for the moon is ethereal earth. . . . But they say that the planet Mercury is ethereal water, Venus air, and the sun fire. And again, that Mars is celestial fire, Jupiter celestial air, Saturn celestial water, and the inerratic sphere celestial earth. And thus speaking in a divided manner they make the extremes to be every where fire and earth, but conjoin the ethereal natures through media, viz. through Venus and Mercury: for both these have a collective and unifying power. But they conjoin the celestial natures, through Saturn and Jupiter: for

°*On the Timaeus of Plato*, Bk. III, p. 426.

through these that which is connective of wholes, and the commensurate, accede to all things. What we now say, however, is conformable to the history delivered by many [of the Pythagoric doctrines]. For that this mode of distribution is not Platonic, we may learn from this that Plato arranges the sun immediately above the moon, afterwards Venus, and then Mercury.

It is necessary therefore to understand, that all the elements are in each of the celestial spheres, since in the sublunary elements also, each participates of the rest. For fire participates of earth; since being moved with facility, it would most rapidly perish, if it was entirely without stability. And earth participates of fire; for being moved with difficulty, it requires heat to resuscitate and restore it. As this therefore is the case in these sublunary elements, much more must all the elements be in each of the celestial spheres, though some of the heavenly bodies participate more of fire, others of air, others of water, and others of earth.

There is the teaching in brief: mystic, wonderful, sublime. Just remember that each elemental, whether on the cosmic or microcosmic scale, is a learning, growing, evolving being. Its heart or core is a monad which, working through its spiritual elemental as its 'body,' produces from within itself its other veils. Man in a far past cosmic manvantara was such an elemental, and by gradual evolutionary growth he now has become a man; and as the human monad continues through the ages of future time to unfold from within its own essence its higher latent powers and faculties into self-expressive activity, man will evolve into becoming a god. Exactly the same is it with all entities in the scale of cosmic life: they are all learning and growing, each one having begun in some cosmic manvantara as an unself-conscious god-spark, and destined in the rolling of the wheel of life to become a self-conscious god, and from godhood to move forwards into ever-enlarging spheres of experience now beyond the utmost comprehension or intuition of man.

TATTWAS AND THE SEVEN SENSES OF MAN

The Tatwas stand in the same order as the seven macro- and micro-cosmic Forces; and as taught in Esotericism, are as follows:

(1) Âdi Tatwa, the primordial universal Force, issuing at the beginning of manifestation, or of the "creative" period, from the eternal immutable Sat, the substratum of All. It corresponds with the Auric Envelope or Brahmâ's Egg, which surrounds every globe, as well as every man, animal and thing. It is the vehicle containing potentially everything — Spirit and Substance, Force and Matter. Âdi Tatwa, in Esoteric Cosmogony, is the Force which we refer to as proceeding from the First or Unmanifested Logos.

(2) Anupadaka Tatwa, the first differentiation on the plane of being — the first being an ideal one — or that which is born by transformation from something higher than itself. With the Occultists, this Force proceeds from the Second Logos.

(3) Âkâsa Tatwa, this is the point from which all *exoteric* philosophies and religions start. Akâsa Tatwa is explained in them as Etheric Force, Ether. Hence Jupiter, the "highest" god, was named Pater Aether; Indra, once the highest god in India, is the etheric or heavenly expanse, and so with Uranus, etc., etc. The Christian biblical God, also, is spoken of as the Holy Ghost, Pneuma, rarefied wind or air. This the Occultists call the Force of the Third Logos, the Creative Force in the already Manifested Universe.

(4) Vâyu Tatwa, the aërial plane where substance is gaseous.

(5) Tâijas Tatwa, the plane of our atmosphere, from *têjas*, luminous.

(6) Âpas Tatwa, watery or liquid substance or force.

(7) Prithivî Tatwa, solid earthly substance, the terrestrial spirit or force, the lowest of all.

All these correspond to our principles, and to the seven senses and forces in man. According to the Tatwa or Force generated or induced in us, so will our bodies act.   —H.P.B.'s E.S. *Instructions*, III

This order of the cosmic tattwas is the one most generally given, yet occasionally vāyu and taijasa are interchanged as regards position. The reason for this is that each tattwa, being a cosmic plane or element, is septenary, and hence contains within itself all the other tattwas as sub-

tattwas, otherwise subplanes; yet of course each cosmic tattwa is characterized by its own swabhāva.°

For instance, certain mystic philosophers spoke of the very first sheath
of ādi-tattwa as being surrounded with its veil, just as Brahman is surrounded with its cosmic veil pradhāna, Brahmā with its veil prakriti, and
so forth. Furthermore, these Hindu philosophers called this veil, on account
of its concretion relative to the monad which it surrounds, by the name
earth, divine earth, divine prithivī. So we can look at anupapādaka-tattwa,
second in the regular serial order, as a kind of divine prithivī or 'earth'
for the consciousness which it surrounds, this earth being its body.

This is why the order of the tattwas is not always the same — one
writer giving their serial order as the universe unrolls itself from divinity
to the physical world; another considering a tattwa in its twofold aspect
as both principle and veil; and still another exchanging one or two of
the relative positions in the series in accordance with the viewpoint he
holds when writing.

Thus, in one or two cosmogonies, such as those of the ancient Hebrews
and of Thales, the Greek philosopher, the first appearance of things was
the cosmic Waters, the Waters of Space, this prakriti or surrounding veil
being regarded as aqueous in character; because when we look up into
the vasty deeps of Space, we can figurate them as 'crystalline waters'
as easily as we can 'air' or 'invisible fire.'

In connection with the seven senses of man, each of which is derived
from one of the seven elements or tattwas of which the universe is composed, H. P. B. has the following in her E.S. *Instructions:*

These seven senses of ours correspond with every other septenate in nature
and in ourselves. Physically, though invisibly, the human Auric Envelope (the
amnion of the physical man in every age of life) has seven layers, just as Cosmic
Space and our physical epidermis have. It is this aura which, according to our

---

°In the table on p. 229, I was referring to the taijasa-subtattwa, that part of the
cosmic vāyu which we may call the vāyu-taijasa; and, in similar fashion, to the
vāyu-subtattwa, that part of the cosmic taijasa which we may call the taijasa-vāyu.
For example, a man may belong by karmic characteristic to the taijasa-tattwa, yet
be passing through its vāyu phase, the taijasa-vāyu, and we could speak of him as
being for the time a vāyu individual. In this table we were considering the tattwas
in the serial order of their cosmic unfolding from the less to the more material, and
therefore taijasa preceded vāyu, because fire, even on earth, is more ethereal than
air. But there are other ways of looking at the unrolling of the universe out of its
inner substance.

mental and physical state of purity or impurity either opens for us vistas into other worlds, or shuts us out altogether from anything but this three-dimensional world of matter.

Each of our seven physical senses (two of which are still unknown to profane science), and also of our seven states of consciousness — viz: (1) waking; (2) waking-dreaming; (3) natural sleeping; (4) induced or trance-sleep; (5) psychic; (6) super-psychic; and (7) purely spiritual, — corresponds with one of the seven cosmic planes, developes and uses one of the seven super-senses, and is connected directly, in its use on the terrestro-spiritual plane, with the cosmic and divine center of force that gave it birth, and which is its direct creator. Each is also connected with, and under the direct influence of, one of the seven Sacred Planets. These belonged to the Lesser Mysteries, whose followers were called Mystai (the veiled), seeing that they were allowed to perceive things only through a mist, as it were "with the eyes closed"; while the Initiates or "Seers" of the Greater Mysteries were called Epoptai (those who see things unveiled). — I

Even the ordinary five senses that we have today are still imperfectly evolved. Each one is progressively growing more subtle, more capable of interpreting, through itself as a channel to the indwelling consciousness, the nature and functions of the universe outside. Remember that man is a stream of consciousness working in vehicles and building in those vehicles appropriate chambers and dwellings, doors and windows, so to speak, for manifesting its own powers and for receiving withinwards from the outside world the stimuli and the reactions which nature obliges it to receive.

Five senses hitherto have manifested themselves more or less perfectly; and they have been derived in the following order: first, hearing from ākāśa or aether; next, touch from vāyu or air; then, sight from fire or rather light, called tejas or taijasa; fourth, taste from āpas or water; fifth and last, smell from earth or prithivī. Of all these, taste is the grossest and most material; but the faculty of smell and its reactions upon the stream of consciousness are even worse than those of taste. Two more senses will develop in us and express themselves with an appropriate physical apparatus before the manvantara of this present round on this globe has run its course. All these senses are functions of the indwelling consciousness.

From the Middle Ages on, in a minor cycle, we have been moving up out of the prithivī-tattwa, successively into the water or āpas-tattwa, into the air or vāyu-tattwa, then into the fire or taijasa-tattwa, and now we are entering gently, slowly, into the aether or ākāśa-tattwa — very imperfectly it is true, mere forecasting of what will happen in the seventh race; still we have been and are passing through small cycles of all these, and inventions correspond. Human productions keep pace; and it will all depend upon man's genius whether these new discoveries be used for the purposes of heaven or hell. If for the latter, we shall go down, stifled and choked in our own evil effluvia. If they are used for purposes of beneficence, the whole of mankind will advance. The signs are all around us of a changing era, with the incoming of a new tide in human affairs.

After the downfall of the Roman Empire, men lived for the most part on land, in the prithivī-tattwa, scarcely going to sea at all. Then they began to travel more extensively and with greater cleverness over the waters — the āpas-tattwa coming to the fore. Next they started to use steam (vapor, 'air,' gas) — the vāyu-element; in later centuries taking to the air itself. Now with a rushing towards a culmination of airy experience, out of the air they are entering the more subtle tattwas. They are using, ever more extensively, fire (the taijasa-element), electricity, explosives, including all the various kinds of igneous horrors — connected with the air because rising out of it. Finally ether (ākāśa) is manifesting in the works of man as evidenced by wireless and the radio, etc. All of this shows that there are small cycles within greater cycles, repeating in general outline the processes of the greater ones.

The two future senses are almost impossible to describe, because the one following the present fifth, smell, has not yet even manifested its presence, except by an occasional instinct of its functioning. It will partake somewhat of the nature of the faculty or sense belonging to touch; but instead of being physical touch, it will be an interior sense, and the intuition of it, or the instinct of it, is occasionally found even among men today — shadows of coming events. Just as touch contacts the outer world, so will these two other senses on the ascending arc be on the same respective planes as hearing and touch; but, because they will exist in a more evolved entity, they will manifest themselves at first through an interior physical organ. An intimation of the sixth sense is what we call hunches that such and such a thing is right or wrong, or the thing to do or not to do. This is not intuition, however, for it is lower than intuition: it is a hunch or a feeling of things that are coming. It might in one sense be spoken of as a form of clairvoyance.

And the seventh sense, corresponding to hearing on the physical plane, will also be an ākāśic development. It will be the last sense to be brought forth by evolution in the physical body of man, and therefore will express an interior faculty, which will be awakened by contact with the lowest grades of the ākāśa. The nearest approach that we can arrive at as to what this faculty will be, leaving aside the nature and locality of the organ through which it will work, is intuition, fully developed as far as it can be on this planet in this manvantara: instant, always ready, functioning regularly, to be stopped or used at will.

Every faculty of sense, and therefore every sense organ as its expression in the body, is a faculty of our stream of consciousness; and no sense faculty can appear in evolution, and consequently no sense organ can show itself in the body, until that portion of the stream of consciousness has equivalently expressed itself. The Atlanteans, for instance, had in their beginning but an instinct of what smell is. They used this faculty almost unconsciously, even as men today are using the sixth sense and the sixth faculty almost unconsciously, and only occasionally are vaguely aware of it and say, "I had a hunch." The faculty passes from the invisible into the visible and creates for itself its appropriate organ, which develops exactly as the inner faculty evolves on its own plane.

It might be as well to add a few words here about the gunas, because they are sometimes confused with the cosmic essences or tattwas. The gunas or 'qualities,' commonly enumerated as sattva, rajas and tamas, are the three fundamental and universally potent modes of consciousness of the armies of beings which make the universe. From sattva flow forth the other two modes of consciousness, rajas or activity, and tamas or inactivity, generally speaking. Now the union of these two qualities, which do not neutralize each other but combine to form something superior to either, is what is meant by sattva — that which is 'real.' It is the condition in which the high gods live.

When the universe is in manvantaric manifestation, it is the rajas quality which predominates, although of course the tamas and likewise the sattva are both present. When the universe is in pralaya with the unending peace and quiet that then prevail, the predominating quality is highest tamas, yet rajas is present, albeit relatively latent. Thus in the Vedas as well as in the Laws of Manu it is stated that before manifestation begins the universe is in the tamas condition, in utter repose. Of course the highest principles of the universe are then in the sattva quality, while the rajas quality during pralaya is dormant.

Hindu philosophy in connection with its Trimurti or triad of Brahmā-Vishnu-Śiva, usually ascribes the sattva guna or characteristic to Brahmā; the quality of rajas to Vishnu; and the quality of tamas to Śiva. Yet in both manvantara and pralaya the sattva quality runs throughout all. Thus the gods while eternally active are nevertheless peaceful because filled with wisdom, and their motions are effortless activity, and their actions are wondrously quiet and undisturbed.

Furthermore, every one of the gunas — because the universe is fundamentally one, and all things in it are interblended and interacting — is itself threefold, otherwise we should have each of these three universal qualities existing absolutely separate and distinct from the other two, and this would make three absolutes. They are not absolutes, but all three are relative; and both rajas and tamas, when united and balancing each other without loss of individuality in either, manifest the presence of their common originant, sattva.

It has been customary among some Orientalists, who do not understand the esoteric meaning of these gunas, to speak of the tamas as being only sloth, darkness, evil, but this is quite wrong; for there is a sattva-tamas as well as a tamas-tamas; and the same type of observation may be made with regard to both the rajas and the sattva character or guna.

Thus it is that every one of the cosmic essences or tattwas is marked by the presence and inherent activity of the three gunas, each one acting in conjunction with the other twain. It should be the endeavor of all men to bring forth the sattva quality especially, for this means that instead of the frequent unbalance or bias of either rajas or tamas, both these qualities are in balance in the character and cooperating.

THE BIRTH OF A GLOBE

"Our Globe, as taught from the first, is at the bottom of the arc of descent, where the matter of our perceptions exhibits itself in its grossest form. . . . Hence it only stands to reason that the globes which overshadow our Earth must be on different and superior planes. In short, as Globes, they are in CO-ADUNITION *but not* IN CONSUBSTANTIALITY WITH OUR EARTH *and thus pertain to quite another state of consciousness. Our planet (like all those we see) is adapted to the peculiar state of its human stock, that state which enables us to see with our naked eye the sidereal bodies which are co-essential with our terrene plane and substance, just as their respective inhabitants, the Jovians, Martians and others can perceive our little world: because our planes of consciousness, differing as they do in degree but being the same in kind, are on the same layer of differentiated matter. . . . If he (meaning the objector) would perceive even the dim silhouette of one of such 'planets' on the higher planes, he has to first throw off even the thin clouds of the astral matter that stands between him and the next plane."*
— From a letter quoted in *The Secret Doctrine,* I, 166

As EACH COSMIC plane is divisible into seven or ten or twelve subplanes, there exists a close correspondence between the planes and the element-principles of the cosmos, the various cosmic planes being, in fact, *worlds* built of and in the corresponding element-principles. Every element-principle, being septenary or duodenary, contains within itself all the other element-principles; hence from each one of them can be ascertained in minor degree the nature and characteristics of all the others. The evolutionary plan consists in the gradual and successive emanations of the various element-principles from each other as the aggregated life impulse cycles downwards from one cosmic plane to the next. This is perforce repeated on a minor scale on every one of the seven cosmic planes, in the gradual and successive appearance in each of what might be called the correspondential sub-element-principle, as the combined life impulse passes from one subplane to the next lower one.

It follows from this, that each one of the seven rounds of a planetary chain, each of the seven (or twelve) globes of that chain, and every one

of the seven root-races of any globe thereof, has its predominating correspondence with one of the seven element-principles of the cosmos.

Let us take globe D of our planetary chain as an illustration of the
coming into being of any hierarchical unit through and in the seven cosmic
planes. This globe is on the lowest or seventh of the manifested cosmic
planes of our solar system, the prithivī plane; but this plane itself has
seven or even twelve degrees of ethereality — its subplanes, which again
are divisible into sub-subplanes after the same manner. As an instance
of how great are the differences between one subplane and the next, the
matter or prakriti of our physical plane ranges from the utter invisibility
of what we call ether to substances which our scientists assure us are
more dense than lead.

Now then, our globe D on this lowest cosmic plane, being itself
sevenfold in the degrees of its substance, *exists* (appears after various
manners) *on all that plane.* I do not mean to say that our physical globe
infills it, but that every part of globe D is on its corresponding sub-subplane
of the cosmic plane, each globe-phase corresponding to its own phase
of that plane. What applies to globe D applies of course to all the other
globes of the planetary chain, each on its own cosmic plane.

The question might arise as to how this series of correspondences comes
to pass. The answer lies in the correct understanding of the manner in
which the foundations of a planetary chain are built, globe after globe,
in and during the first round. This again can be illustrated by the case
of globe D, because the process involved is identical for all the globes
of the chain.

Our globe D in the first round, in its highly ethereal aspect, is on
the first, the uppermost, of the seven subplanes or phases of the prithivī
cosmic plane. It evolves thereon in the highest, or the quasi-spiritual,
phase of the prithivī cosmic element-principle. In the second round, globe
D will have evolved to the point of finding itself on and in the next
lower phase of the prithivī cosmic element-principle; otherwise stated,
it will have materialized to the extent of finding itself on subplane the
second, counting downwards. This should not be misunderstood as meaning
that globe D then is entirely on the second subplane of prithivī, having
completely left the first subplane. It would be far closer to truth to speak
of globe D as being (in the second round) in and on the second subplane
of the prithivī plane, but containing within itself the qualities and attributes
of the first subplane thereof. It has now evolved from within itself the

substances and energies which make it fit to appear on the second subplane of the prithivī plane.

In the third round, globe D will have descended to the third subplane of the prithivī cosmic plane. It will have evolved to the point of finding itself on and expressing the next lower phase of the prithivī cosmic element-principle, and will be then manifesting on the lowest of these three subplanes, meanwhile imbodying within itself the attributes and characteristics of the two superior subplanes. In the fourth round in which we are at present, globe D has reached the fourth subplane of prithivī, our globe's grossest state of matter in its present imbodiment. The downward cycling then ceases for our globe, and its reascent begins.

I am compelled to add here a word of warning in this very intricate subject of the subplanes, and sub-subplanes, of any cosmic plane. In the foregoing, I have sketched a mere outline of the descent of our globe D during its first four rounds, without attempting to be exact in description. However, were I aiming at strict accuracy, I should say sub-subplane instead of subplane. As a matter of fact, every imbodiment of a globe, which means the course of a period of seven rounds, takes place on one subplane of any cosmic plane such as the prithivī cosmic plane. Moreover, because each such subplane is itself septenary, therefore a round really is the touching and being in and on one of the subplanes of a subplane of the cosmic plane. In other words, in and on every cosmic plane, such as the prithivī cosmic plane, there are seven imbodiments of a globe, and consequently there will be seven respective moons.

What about subplanes 5, 6, 7? The diagrams given in *The Secret Doctrine* (I, 153, 172) of the globes of a chain on the different cosmic planes are excellent as suggestions, showing the descent into matter and reascent into spiritual realms; but these are graphs only, conveying ideas and evoking thoughts. If we were to take these diagrams as actual pictures, then we would have to say that subplanes 5, 6, and 7 are identical with subplanes 3, 2, and 1, each to each, and this is entirely wrong. It has already been stated that every cosmic plane is septenary, or denary, or duodenary, according to the manner of viewing it; and hence each subplane thereof, in addition to being itself seven- or ten- or twelvefold, is quite different from all the planes which precede or follow it.

Now when a globe has reached the fourth subplane — and the fourth in any series of planes or principles is always the grossest of the series — then the globe begins to ascend and thus to dematerialize itself, albeit very slowly. This ascent takes place through subplanes 5, 6, and 7, but in their more ethereal or higher sub-subplanes, so that when a globe finally reaches subplane 7, it does so in the most ethereal part of that subplane, which already is quasi-spiritual.°

I am only too keenly aware of the difficult nature of this thought, and feel almost in despair at finding adequate words with which to describe the serial evolution of a globe 'downwards' and 'upwards.' Nevertheless, there is one fundamental fact we can always bear in mind, namely, that every cosmic plane and, by analogy, every subplane thereof, has its quasi-spiritual, its intermediate, and its most material or concreted subplanes and sub-subplanes.

The following correlation of element-principles, globes, rounds, etc., given in tabular form, may help to clarify some of these technical points:

Cosmic Element-Principles	Globes of a Chain	Rounds of a Chain	Planes of a 12-fold Chain	Subplanes of any Plane
Ādi-tattwa	Highest globe of the twelve	1st Round	The planes of a twelvefold chain are virtually identic with the cosmic element-principles.	Analogy here shows that the subplanes of any cosmic plane repeat, each one, the general system of the planes of a 12-fold chain.
Anupapādaka-tattwa	Next globe on Descending Arc	2nd Round		
Ākāśa-tattwa	Third globe on Descending Arc	3rd Round		
Taijasa-tattwa	Globe A	4th Round		
Vāyu-tattwa	Globe B	5th Round		
Āpas-tattwa	Globe C	6th Round		
Prithivī-tattwa	Globe D	7th Round		

When we shall be on globes E, F, and G of the ascending arc, we shall then 'see' the corresponding globes of the descending arc, to wit, globes C, B, and A; but, as a matter of plain fact, we shall do so *only* when the globe or globes on which we happen to be on the ascending arc traverse the exact sub-subplane on which the globes of the descending arc then are.

There is one more point in connection with any fourth subplane in a series: those monads which have been descending with the bulk of any monadic class on the downward arc, and are unable for karmic reasons

°Cf. *Studies in Occult Philosophy*, pp. 56–62 and 94–101. —Ed.

to make the ascent along the ascending arc, take the 'downward path' at the grossest point — which is the middle point of the fourth subplane — and these unfortunate monads are those spoken of as 'failures.' They drop, and are left behind; and must wait for future manvantaras before they will be able to try again and, hopefully, pass the critical point of their evolution which is always the midpoint of a fourth round.°

What applies to globe D concerning rounds and globes, applies to every one of the globes of the planetary chain, each on its own cosmic plane. Now the combined life-waves, in making their first round, pass through the highest subplane (or sub-subplane) of each one of the four lower cosmic planes of the solar system to which the planetary chain belongs. In each one of these four lower cosmic planes, the life-waves, aggregatively, lay the foundations of a globe, any one of the then-in-the-making twelve globes of the entire chain.

To put it in a different manner: in the first round, the united life-waves form globe A on the highest or first subplane of the fourth cosmic plane — here following H. P. B.'s diagram. In the first round also, the combined life-waves form the foundations of globe B on the highest or first subplane of the fifth cosmic plane. In the same round, the combined life-waves form the foundations of globe C on the highest or first subplane of the sixth cosmic plane; and finally, they form the foundations of globe D, our own planet Terra, on the highest subplane of this seventh or prithivī cosmic plane.

On the ascending arc likewise, globes E, F, and G have their foundations formed by the combined life-waves. Then when the life-waves have reached the highest globe of our chain, the first round is ended. After the nirvana at the end of the first round, the second round begins. From this point the life-waves are now individualized to a much greater extent, and therefore peregrinate as individual waves, each such wave being really a family of monads. A life-wave on globe A, at the beginning of the second round, finds itself on the second sub-subplane of the fourth cosmic plane; it passes in karmic time then to globe B and finds itself on the second sub-subplane of the fifth cosmic plane; in due course it passes to globe C and to the second sub-subplane of the sixth cosmic plane; then again in kosmic time to globe D and to the second sub-subplane of the seventh or prithivī cosmic plane. Similarly, with respect to the

---

°Cf. *The Secret Doctrine*, I, 187–9, and *The Mahatma Letters*, pp. 86–8.

ascending arc, each life-wave finds itself on the appropriate sub-subplane of the respective cosmic planes upon which are located globes E, F, and G of the chain.

The same general scheme of emanational unfolding is followed in all subsequent rounds. Globe D is at present manifesting on the fourth sub-subplane of the fourth subplane of this prithivī cosmic plane, seeing that we are now in the fourth round. It follows likewise that during the seven rounds the life-waves pass through 49 sub-subplanes, all told, and the beings composing these life-waves thereby have the chance of evolutional unfolding on these different subplanes and of working out the destiny for which they came into active manifestation.

PLANES AND STATES OF CONSCIOUSNESS

The three upper are the three higher planes of consciousness, revealed
and explained in both schools only to the Initiates, the lower ones represent
the four lower planes — the lowest being our plane, or the visible Universe.

These seven *planes* correspond to the seven *states* of consciousness in
man. It remains with him to attune the three higher states in himself to
the three higher planes in Kosmos. But before he can attempt to attune,
he must awaken the three "seats" to life and activity.

— *The Secret Doctrine*, I, 199

MOST PEOPLE ARE inclined to look upon the seven planes or worlds in
any universe as lying one on top of another like a pile of books on a
table, or like the steps of a stair. This is, of course, an erroneous concept
and has arisen because of the attempt to portray these cosmic planes
in the form of a diagram, and thus as one on top of the other. However,
this is but a means of helping us to realize that the higher the plane
the more ethereal it is, and finally the more spiritual; and that the lower
the plane the grosser it is, and finally the more material.

Actually, the cosmic planes interpenetrate each other, inwards especially, as well as outwards; and the truth of this should be clear when we
remember the teaching concerning the auric egg, for instance, of a man.
Let us take the 'layers' of such an auric egg as being the exact correspondences of the planes in the cosmos. We immediately realize that
these layers are not one on top of another and rising above man's head
until they reach infinity, but are groups of life-atoms, all together composing the auric egg, and differing only in degree of spirituality or materiality.
Indeed, the analogy is extremely exact; for what the auric egg is in man,
with its many layers of atoms vibrating at different rates of intensity,
just that in the cosmos is the aggregate of the cosmic planes interpenetrating
each other — one plane being different from another because of immense
variations in vibrational rates, making one plane material, another ethereal,
and so forth to the highest plane.

Now from the very fact that the life-atoms are as units individuals,

250

each with its own highest or ātmic, and its own lowest or material (or it may be ethereal) vehicle, we see that a layer or plane is made by these life-atoms themselves; so that collectively, even the lowest of any such aggregate of life-atoms has likewise its ātmic or inmost fundamental being. Thus it is that the topmost layers of any cosmic plane are spiritual or divine; even the topmost subplane of the lowest cosmic plane, and this does not mean that it is spiritual-divine only when compared with all its own lower subplanes. In other words, the uppermost layers of *any* cosmic plane are spiritual per se; and as the succeeding layers unfold downwards, they thicken or grossen proportionally faster, the lower the cosmic plane is.

Despite all that has been stated, some may still picture the seven cosmic planes, or the seven principles of man, or again the different layers of the auric egg, as piled one on top of the other. Of course, in one sense, there is some truth in this, for one plane is emanationally unfolded in time and space from its superior plane. It is really the time-illusion which causes us to look upon each cosmic plane as being below the one which gave it birth.

The highest subplane of any cosmic plane is as high, *in its essence,* as the highest subplane of any other cosmic plane. Yet the lower the cosmic plane, the more rapidly concretion takes place as the hierarchy of that plane unfolds itself 'downwards.' Thus, with the lowest or seventh cosmic plane, its spiritual essence is as high as that of the first, second, or any other cosmic plane.

Here is the reason why we speak of the heart of the sun, of globe D of the solar chain, for instance, as being a particle of mother-substance in the sixth or even seventh state of this mother-substance, a subject we shall take up in more detail later. This means that all the different planes, instead of being actually one on top of another, are interblended and interacting, and hence there is a progression of life-atoms or monads not only from top to bottom and up again, but horizontally, as it were, on each plane.

The first or highest cosmic plane is the first or highest layer of the auric egg of the cosmos, or what we may call the cosmic ātman, the Paramātman. The second or next lower cosmic plane is in its highest in essence equal to the second ātmic subplane of the first cosmic plane or great ātmic plane. The third cosmic plane is in its highest in essence equal to the third ātmic subplane of the first cosmic plane; and so forth down the scale. Thus the ātmic subplane of the seventh or lowest cosmic plane is in its essence the same as the seventh or lowest subplane of the highest or ātmic hierarchy of the cosmos. It is, as it were, a reflection of the lowest sub-ātmic plane of the first cosmic plane. This is why every little life-atom, even on this physical plane, is a sevenfold entity, because possessing at its heart the essence of the first cosmic plane or highest ātman of the cosmos, plus the essences of all the intermediate five cosmic planes.

The highest ātmic plane of the cosmos therefore contains infolded within itself all the other lower ātmic degrees of the unfolded cosmos. For the highest unrolls itself into seven (or twelve), and out of these roll all the other ātmic essences of the lower cosmic planes. The ātmic subplane of the second cosmic plane we can call a derivative from the buddhi-ātman of the first cosmic plane; the ātman of the third cosmic plane would be a manas-ātman derivative of the first cosmic plane; and so on down the line of the unfolded cosmic hierarchy.

It may be of interest here to mention that the ancient Buddhist initiates divided the cosmic worlds and planes of any structural unit into three generalized groups or dhātus: the arūpa-dhātu, the rūpa-dhātu, and the kāma-dhātu.

Suppose we take our planetary chain and try to divide the seven cosmic planes on which its twelve globes are distributed into the threefold division of the dhātus. Then the lowest of the dhātus, the kāma-dhātu, can be looked upon as being the seven manifest globes, and the rūpa-dhātu as corresponding with the five higher globes of the twelve of our chain. The arūpa-dhātu or formless worlds would correspond to the three highest planes above the seven on which these twelve globes are, thus making the full number of the ten planes of the solar system. As a matter of fact, however, this allocation of the dhātus is somewhat arbitrary, because different distributions could be given with equal logic. All such divisions of the universe should be considered somewhat like diagrams: they are suggestive and are strictly accordant with nature's structure, but they are not hard and fast. H.P.B. herself gives another manner of allocating the globes by comparison with the seven globes of the Qabbālāh.*

The kāma-dhātu or desire-world refers to the planes and globes which are the worlds of more or less concreted materialization; the rūpa-dhātu

---

*Cf. *The Secret Doctrine*, I, 200.

or form-world refers to those planes of the solar system or of the chain and the globes on them, which are more ethereal; again the arūpa-dhātu or formless world comprises the planes which to us are not concreted matter, whether coarse or ethereal, but are purely spiritual and therefore to us formless. All these dhātus refer as much to the states of consciousness of the beings therein as they do to the planes and globes themselves.

Viewed from another angle, these three groups of cosmic planes may be described briefly as follows: the highest is the 'imageless' system or group; the intermediate is the 'image' system; and the third and lowest is the 'desire' system — the last meaning those planes or worlds where entities live in relatively material or grossly material vehicles with appropriate sense organs, brought about by as yet nonextinct desire or hunger for existence in spheres of matter.

Thus the kāma-dhātu system comprises our own physical cosmic plane with three others invisible to us, rising along an ethereal scale, and all together forming an aggregate of four planes of the cosmos on which we may place the seven globes of the planetary chain. Then follows upwards the next system of worlds or planes which comprises the rūpa-dhātu, a group system likewise seven in number, and graduating in ethereality and spirituality until the highest of this intermediate scale blends with the lowest of the arūpa-dhātu, which again is a group system of seven worlds or planes.

These three dhātus, ascending in steadily more ethereal ranges, form all the cosmic planes in any universal solar system; yet above them, there are other planes still more spiritual reaching into the divine, and in these last ranges of being are found those entities who have attained the nirvana. On the cosmic scale, the higher principles of a universal solar system reach these spiritual-divine ranges of being at the end of the Mahā-Saurya manvantara, and thus enter their paranirvana.

Now the outbreathings of Brahmā are from these paranirvanic spiritual-divine ranges of the galaxy, these outbreathings slowly descending through all intermediate planes until our physical world appears in the beginning of its manvantara as, first, a cosmic comet evolving to become a nebula, and ending as a universal solar system. When the Mahā-Saurya pralaya approaches, the reverse process of infolding or inbreathing begins to take place. The beings and energies and substances, commencing with the lowest cosmic plane, all gradually disappear within, like an infolding scroll, as the general life force of the universal solar system retreats ever higher and more inwards through all the planes of the trailokya,° ingathering each such plane and all beings on and in it, and thus finally attaining the imageless or paranirvanic realms of the divine principles of the galaxy.

What is nirvana or paranirvana for one class of entities may not necessarily be such for another class superior to it. In other words, the Ring-pass-not is not one particular plane or sphere, but varies with different classes of entities. As H.P.B. says with reference to the seven globes of our planetary chain as existing on the four lowest cosmic planes:†

These are the four lower planes of Cosmic Consciousness, the three higher planes being inaccessible to human intellect as developed at present. The seven states of human consciousness pertain to quite another question.

When H.P.B. states that the human intellect cannot ascend higher than the fourth macrocosmic plane — on which are the first and seventh globes of the planetary chain — this does not mean that we derive our origin from that plane, but merely that the higher part of our present constitution as a conscious entity cannot now ascend beyond it. Each one of us is Infinitude in the core of the core of the god within. Yet as a human entity, even with the loftiest and most sublimely developed human understanding, we cannot rise in thought and comprehension above the fourth macrocosmic plane. When we shall have passed out of ordinary humanhood into quasi-godhood, then we shall be able to reach in self-conscious thought and spiritual penetration even beyond this fourth plane.

The gods can ascend to the first or highest of the seven macrocosmic planes. But even they in their present state of godhood cannot go beyond the Ring-pass-not, which means the utmost limit of *their* consciousness and understanding. The wings of their spirit can carry them no higher,

---

°A Sanskrit word meaning three worlds, often used for the three dhātus. The correspondences between the trailokya and the similar parts of man's constitution are shown by the trikāya, or three vehicles, to wit, counting downwards, the dharmakāya, the sambhogakāya, and the nirmānakāya. The arūpa- or dharma-dhātu corresponds generally with the dharmakāya in man; the rūpa-dhātu with the sambhogakāya; and the kāma-dhātu with the nirmānakāya (and the physical body) of the human being. All three of these kāyas or vehicles are integral parts of the constitution of a man, and through initiation one may learn how to live self-consciously in any one of the three, both during life and after death. It should be noted, however, that the highest aspect of the dharmakāya is nirvanic, and thus it is often said that the nirvanī lives in the dharmakāya.

†The Secret Doctrine, I, 200.

no farther, no deeper, into the essence of Being. These expressions, high, deep, far, apply only to our physical universe, and are used because we have no proper words to express the spiritual fact of an ever-increasing penetration into the arcana of nature's heart.

When reading of the Ring-pass-not, we should remember that this Ring refers to the state or evolution of any individual entity. The Ring-pass-not of a god would mean that utmost extension of consciousness and vital activity which it in its divine power can attain; similarly, the Ring-pass-not of a buddha would be the buddha's utmost capacity to be conscious on and to act in his own farthest spiritual-vital sphere. In exactly identical fashion the Ring-pass-not of a man is that limit or frontier beyond which he, in his present evolutionary unfoldment, cannot go in consciousness or self-conscious action. Thus the Ring-pass-not does not mean so much any particular cosmic plane, but rather the entity's ability, beyond which it cannot *as yet* pass. For example, the beasts on earth today have merely direct consciousness and the merest unfoldings of self-consciousness as their Ring-pass-not; but humans have passed this Ring, because they have attained self-consciousness.

As H.P.B. writes in *The Secret Doctrine* (I, 131):

The chemist goes to the *laya* or zero point of the plane of matter with which he deals, and then stops short. The physicist or the astronomer counts by billions of miles beyond the nebulae, and then they also stop short; the semi-initiated Occultist will represent this laya-point to himself as existing on some plane which, if not physical, is still conceivable to the human intellect. But the full Initiate *knows* that the ring "Pass-Not" is neither a locality nor can it be measured by distance, but that it exists in the absoluteness of infinity. In this "Infinity" of the full Initiate there is neither height, breadth nor thickness, but all is fathomless profundity, reaching down from the physical to the "para-para-metaphysical." In using the word "down," essential depth — "nowhere and everywhere" — is meant, not depth of physical matter.

LOKAS AND TALAS

In this double progression *our World* — the only one we can judge by objectivity is no *one* distinct world, but a compound of two on each planet from which radiate the others from which our world or Earth radiated in her turn. Thus in the Ist Round on planet A, Humanity partakes of *Satya and Atala;* in the IInd Round — on Planet B it is *Tapas-Vitala;* IIIrd — *Janas-Sutala* — IVth Mahâr Rasâtala, etc. and on the progression of gradations in Races and sub-races it reflects according to ascent and descent, the qualities and attributes physical and spiritual of all and of each of those individually.

— *The Letters of H. P. Blavatsky to A. P. Sinnett*, pp. 252–3

FIRST OF ALL, the lokas and talas are not something distinct and separate from the entities or beings that inhabit them. As a matter of fact, these spheres or lokas and talas are virtually identic in fundamental essence with the principles and elements of a cosmos, and likewise with the planes of a hierarchy, whether that hierarchy be a solar system, a planetary chain, or a man.

As explained earlier, in the course of the unrolling of the worlds at the beginning of a cosmic manvantara, it is the cosmic elements, or element-principles, which appear first; then, taking a cosmic plane as an illustration, such plane unfolds or expands into its different worlds, and it is precisely these worlds or subplanes which are the loka-tala twins. Hence the terms subplanes, and lokas and talas, can be used more or less interchangeably.

The lokas may be called the principles or energies of a hierarchy and their corresponding talas its elements or substantial or material aspects. All seven lokas and talas are continuously interblending and interworking, and together form the universe with its various subordinate hierarchies. We may speak of a tala as the material aspect of the world where it predominates, just as we may consider a loka to be the spiritual aspect of the world where it is dominant. Every loka is coexistent with and cannot be separated from its corresponding tala on the same plane. By analogy, man's constitution is a hierarchy of its own kind, and therefore as such is a composite entity formed of lokas and talas.

The accompanying diagram sets forth the seven manifested cosmic planes with the twelve globes of a planetary chain as well as the lokas and talas traversed by the life-waves in the different rounds; and on a still smaller scale of magnitude, the sub-sublokas and sub-subtalas in relation to the races of any one globe of the chain, such as our earth. This diagram shows that our present human life-wave, now on globe D, is on the lowest or seventh cosmic plane, or in bhūrloka-pātāla; and that because we are in the fourth round, we are in the fourth world of the loka-tala system, maharloka-rasātala; but since we are also in the fifth root-race of this fourth round, we are in the svarloka-talātala world.

The dual septenary of interacting and interblending lokas and talas may be looked upon, at least from one viewpoint, as the spiritual and the vehicular poles of a universe. In our own solar system, they represent the evolved and evolving worlds or subplanes of every one of the seven cosmic planes, on which are distributed the twelve globes of our planetary chain. Because of the repetitive structure of the solar system, each globe has all the lokas and talas, which we may call its sublokas and subtalas.

Furthermore, it will be noticed that the talas are especially allocated to the arc of descent, that the lokas and talas balance each other in globe D, the turning point of our chain, and that the lokas are especially allocated to the ascending arc. The actual meaning is that the lokas are the luminous arc, or rather that procession of nature and of entities in which spirit predominates; while the talas are the shadowy arc, or that procession of nature and of beings in which matter predominates. This should not be misconstrued to mean that there are no lokas on the descending arc, and no talas on the ascending arc. The point is that the talas are particularly unfolded on the descending arc, and the lokas are relatively recessive there; whereas on the ascending arc the lokas are particularly manifested and the talas relatively recessive. Every loka has its corresponding twin or tala; and each such pair is inseparable, although there are times when either the loka or the tala quality is the more manifest.

What distinguishes each of the twelve globes is the fact that the loka and the tala of the cosmic plane on which the globe is placed are for that globe the dominant or strongest in effect. For instance, we are on the lowest or seventh plane of the solar system. Therefore, our loka and tala are the bhūrloka and the pātāla of the solar system; but as we are in the fourth round, the combined influences of maharloka-rasātala are likewise very strong in us, yet interacting with bhūrloka and pātāla and working through these last as overtone qualities, to use a musical expression.

Now let us take globe B. Following the septenary scale, we will say that globe B is talātala and svarloka combined; but, on account of the globe's being on the tala-side, the descending, material side, talātala is stronger in effect than is the svarloka part of globe B. Or take globe E which has bhuvarloka working and interblending with mahātala, but here the bhuvarloka quality is more pronounced.

We note that the highest cosmic plane is a union of satyaloka and atala. Again the second cosmic plane is a combination of taparloka and vitala working together; like the positive and negative poles in electricity, one cannot separate these. Yet at any period of time, or at any moment of evolution, or on any part of the racial arc, either a loka or a tala is more predominant than is its opposite tala or loka.

Continuing downwards, the third cosmic plane is where janarloka and sutala interblend and work together. On the fourth cosmic plane maharloka and rasātala are jointly predominant — and it is just on and in this fourth plane of the manifest seven planes where the grossest aspects, the greatest density, are found. Next, we have the fifth cosmic plane formed of svarloka and talātala; and then the sixth cosmic plane imbodying bhuvarloka and mahātala; and finally, we reach the bottom of the descent in the seventh or lowest cosmic plane imbodying bhūrloka and pātāla, the lowest loka-tala twin of the hierarchical series.

Therefore we may rightly say that every one of the globes of a planetary chain is the imbodiment of the swabhāva of its predominant loka-tala twin. Yet all the other lokas and talas are expressing themselves in each globe likewise. As each globe is sevenfold (and indeed, tenfold and even twelvefold), so the cosmic planes and the lokas and talas are likewise seven-, ten- or twelvefold in characteristic swabhāva. To illustrate, the highest globe on the first cosmic plane is satyaloka-atala and, being seven-fold, it includes all the other lokas and talas, but in the satyaloka-atala condition: they are all represented therein in latency, held there in seed, not yet expressed in manifestation.

Following down the diagram we get a picture of a universe expanded, unfolded, in spheres of consciousness, in globes, cosmic planes, otherwise called lokas and talas, until finally we reach globe D, our earth. We call it bhūrloka-pātāla, because it is an expression of the bhūrloka-pātāla

D′ ATALA ◯ SATYA-LOKA		1
C′ VITALA ◯	**E′** ◯ TAPAR-LOKA	2
B′ SUTALA ◯	**F′** ◯ JANAR-LOKA	3
A RASĀ-TALA ◯	**G** ◯ MAHAR-LOKA	4
B TALĀTALA ◯	**F** ◯ SVAR-LOKA	5
C MAHĀTALA ◯	**E** ◯ BHUVAR-LOKA	6
D PĀTĀLA ◯ BHŪR-LOKA		7

EXTENDED DIAGRAM OF THE SEVENTH COSMIC PLANE
(Applicable to each of the other planes after making the necessary
changes for rounds and races)

	ROUNDS		RACES		
	Atala-Satyaloka		Atala-Satyaloka		
SUBLOKAS	Vitala	Taparloka	Vitala	Taparloka	SUB-SUBLOKAS
	Sutala	Janarloka	Sutala	Janarloka	
	Rasātala	*Maharloka*	Rasātala	Maharloka	
	Talātala	Svarloka	*Talātala*	*Svarloka*	
	Mahātala	Bhuvarloka	Mahātala	Bhuvarloka	
	Pātāla-Bhūrloka		Pātāla-Bhūrloka		

PRESENT HUMANITY OF EARTH:

7th Cosmic Plane:	Pātāla-Bhūrloka
4th Round:	Rasātala-Maharloka — subloka
5th Root-race:	Talātala-Svarloka — sub-subloka

259

characteristics. Likewise the sun that we see is the bhūrloka-pātāla of the solar chain. The visible planet Venus is also the bhūrloka-pātāla of the Venus chain, and so on for all the other planets.

Analogy is the master key — simply because nature is built that way, is consistent with herself, is coherent with her own parts and powers, and therefore what the great contains, the small part of that great *must* likewise contain. Applying this to the lokas, we may deduce that, whether the universe is divided into seven, ten or twelve parts, every portion of it will have the same number of characteristics. In the septenary scale, each loka and tala manifests its powers in seven different degrees of strength, and therefore we have seven times seven lokas and talas, making in all forty-nine loka-tala twins.

THE HUMAN LIFE-WAVE IN THE LOKA-TALAS

These [lokas and talas] are worlds — to their respective inhabitants as much *solid* and *real* as our own is to us. Each of these, nevertheless, has *its own nature*, laws, senses — which are not *our* nature, laws or senses. They are not in space and time *for us* — as we are not in space or time — for them, as the 3-dimens. world suspects the 4-dimensional, so the latter suspects the existence of our *lower* world.

— *The Letters of H. P. Blavatsky to A. P. Sinnett*, p. 249

IN CONNECTION WITH the evolution of peregrinating entities in and on the seven manifested cosmic planes, and therefore functioning in the different lokas and talas, it is important to remember that the cosmic planes, and coincidentally the lokas and talas, may be looked upon from two different viewpoints: (a) in the *evolutionary* sense as signifying the progressive and continuous unfolding of powers and faculties; and (b) in the sense of cosmic planes and lokas and talas considered as being the unfoldings of the cosmic structure from the standpoint of densities and corresponding etherealities.

Evolution proceeds from the spiritual through all intermediate planes in what we may call a direct line until we come to the end of the evolutionary arc, as is shown by the paradigm of the globes of a planetary chain; and then when the bottom of the arc is reached, the ascent towards spirit begins, but nevertheless the evolutionary progress is continuously forwards. The evolving life-waves progress steadily around the planetary chain and through the different globes, first on the downward arc, and then, making the turn, they rise along the ascending arc until spirit is again reached — the life-waves continuously unfolding from within themselves all possible powers, faculties, attributes and qualities, which the evolutionary journey involves.

Referring now to the lokas and talas, evolution begins for the classes of monads in the satyaloka-atala and moves straight forwards until the bhūrloka-pātāla, or full flowering of the evolutionary capacity in the monads, is achieved. Yet the densest cosmic plane, and appropriately the densest loka and tala, is the fourth in the series of planes and lokas

261

and talas. Beginning with the fifth plane and its corresponding loka-tala twin, and thereafter proceeding on the rising scale, the density grows proportionately less and the ethereality more pronounced, so that when the evolving monads reach the end of the sevenfold evolutionary journey in the bhūrloka-pātāla, they do so as evolved spiritual monads with the flowering of faculty and attribute, but in the ranges of the bhūrloka-pātāla which are highly ethereal and relatively spiritualized.°

To illustrate: when our human life-wave shall have reached the seventh root-race in *this round, on this earth,* it will be in more ethereal conditions (because in the higher parts of bhūrloka-pātāla) than our life-wave was when in the fourth root-race, corresponding to the maharloka-rasātala of our globe and our racial evolution. Again, when our human life-wave shall have reached the *seventh round* on the highest or seventh globe — using the sevenfold system — we shall be at the end of all possible evolution

---

°It may not be easy to grasp these involved and paradoxical statements with regard to the fact that evolution, although proceeding as it were in a straightforward line from its beginning to its manvantaric end, and thus working in and through the hierarchical series of lokas and talas, nevertheless, considered as a process, has its grossest and coarsest expression in the middle of such serial progress — in the *fourth* phase, whether of lokas and talas or of globes.

I have on several occasions pointed out that the fourth in a series, such as the fourth principle in man, is the grossest. On exactly analogical lines of reasoning, the grossest globe of the seven manifested globes is the fourth, our globe D; and again the fourth root-race, the Atlantean, was the most grossly material of our present racial manvantara on this globe during this fourth round. In other words, root-races first, second, and third, ran down a steadily descending arc, the life-wave reaching its culmination of coarse animal materiality in the fourth root-race. Since then we have begun the ascending arc, we of the present fifth root-race thereby experiencing a steady, albeit slow, etherealization and even spiritualization of ourselves as well as of surrounding nature.

As stated above, evolution considered as a process moves steadily forwards, constantly unfolding from within the evolving monads what is latent therein, so that the acme of evolutionary perfection is reached in the seventh stage which, for this evolutionary reason, we call the highest. Yet when we look at this evolutionary course from the standpoint of 'falling into matter,' i.e. from the standpoint of changing densities, we see that the *fourth* stage is where the grossest and the densest evolutionary episode takes place. Applying this rule to the journeying of the monads through the lokas and talas, we see that we reach the culmination of evolutionary flowering of attribute and faculty in the highest subplanes of the bhūrloka-pātāla, which are really semispiritual — at any rate highly ethereal; yet before we reach this seventh stage we must pass through the coarsest and most grossly 'animal' of the lokas and talas, the maharloka-rasātala.

in the present chain-manvantara, and shall be in the satyaloka-atala ranges of ethereality. Then the individuals of our life-wave who shall thus have run the race successfully will be ready to take their nirvana as relatively evolved dhyāni-chohans — virtually a race of minor buddhas.

In brief, we should keep in mind that evolution proceeds as it were in a straightforward and direct line, from the highest to the lowest, makes the turn and returns to the highest spheres; but that the greatest densities and grossness of world systems, or lokas and talas, are found in the manifested fourth phase — again following the septenary system.

If the monad were to return to the identic state in which it began its peregrinations, this would simply be a returning to the unself-conscious state of the monad or jīva. But this is not the case; we evolve forwards in a steady line, and eventually reach the highest point as self-consciously individualized entities. In other words, in order to have a field of action and of consciousness appropriate and fit for the highly developed and evolved jīvas to work in, nature provides these manifested planes; and the return to divinity, which ultimately takes place at the end of a manvantara of whatever magnitude, is a re-entrance not into the former conditions but into the highest planes as evolved self-conscious beings. For instance, we do not come down the chain to the fourth subplane of the bhūrloka-pātāla and then recede upwards through the identic planes until we reach the former planes or conditions, because that would simply be like the English saying: "The king of France and his forty thousand men drew their swords and put them up again." But we go steadily forwards through all the seven planes or subplanes of whatever cosmic plane; and the result of this is that after the downward arc is ended and the rising towards spirituality begins, it is not backwards but forwards — forwards through the planes not yet traversed, but in the higher and more spiritual portions of those planes.

To repeat once again: the fourth plane and the fourth loka-tala twin are the grossest in the series, and the planes which precede and those which follow are more ethereal in both directions from it. Otherwise stated, planes or loka-tala systems become denser and denser until the fourth of each is reached, then rise again into more ethereal planes and loka-tala systems, although evolution proceeds in a 'straight course' steadily forwards in its process of unfolding faculty and power and attribute.

Just here is a significant point. Considering the twelve globes, we see that bhūrloka plus pātāla is a reflection of satyaloka and atala, a shadow of spirit cast 'down' into the waves of the seventh cosmic plane. Also the talas grow more tala-like as we follow them down the scale — more and more tala-istic, so to speak. In a similar manner, each loka on the upward swing is more spiritualized than the one immediately beneath it until we reach the highest, the 'loka of Reality.'

In satyaloka-atala, the highest tala and the highest loka combine into or rejoin the monadic essence of the planetary chain. The differentiation so marked on the lower planes ceases here and, because of this, the two blend into or become one. Contrariwise, in the lowest or globe D of the chain, we have the most evolved tala called pātāla, uniting with and becoming the alter ego of the most fully expressed loka, bhūrloka. The thought is extremely interesting; because we find on the uppermost plane the highest loka and tala melting into virtual identity; and on the lowest or seventh cosmic plane, the lowest loka and tala likewise blending into almost indistinguishable unity — but in a manner opposite to the nondifferentiation found in the highest, for in the lowest loka-tala and in the lowest globe is produced the greatest development of innate substance and force, quality and attribute, characteristic and potentiality.

However, the globes of a chain — otherwise, the lokas and talas forming each globe — do not remain throughout the chain-manvantara on the same cosmic plane to and on which they respectively belong or are situated. For these globes themselves in the course of the ages pass downwards through the cosmic planes until the evolutionary bottom of the arc is reached, and then rise upwards until each globe reaches the spiritual planes again, preparatory to a new chain-manvantara.

Each loka and tala as a twin represents the bipolarity of each world; and it is just this interaction which enables the evolving monads to bring forth what lies latent within them. Actually, as we have seen, the lokas and talas are themselves built of monads of varying degrees of evolution; and it is these less developed monads composing the structural framework of the worlds, or lokas and talas, which provide the living vehicles or bodies, whether cosmic or subcosmic, in which the more advanced monads live, evolve, and carry out the purposes of their karmic destiny.

Hence even a human being can, if he will evolve from within himself the ability to do so, be in sympathetic touch with the spiritual powers which rule our universe; and he does so by placing his center of self-consciousness in the loka-tala corresponding to the inner plane of being in which he desires at the time to be.

The lokas and talas should really be thought of as *worlds or spheres of consciousness* of varying degrees of ethereality and spirituality. We should not imagine for a moment that a man lives solely in the bhūrloka-pātāla, just because his physical body happens to be in that loka-tala. Let me give an illustration that may perhaps show how two individuals, living on the same cosmic plane, and therefore in the same loka-tala system of that plane, nevertheless have, each one, an inner life in a loka-tala world different from that of the other. A and B, let us say, are friends. They may be sitting in A's study, they may be walking on a street, or they may be in the country resting on a grassy bank. The one man is a musician; the other is a scientist. Now both men are on globe D of our chain and on the seventh cosmic plane and therefore in bhūrloka-pātāla. But, because both belong to our present fifth root-race, they are also under the overtone influence of svarloka-talātala; in addition, because as a life-wave we are in the fourth round, they are subject likewise to the overtone influence of maharloka-rasātala. It is precisely these common coefficients, or these common faculties of consciousness, which enable them to understand each other, to be friends despite the great inner differences of character — of swabhāva.

Nevertheless, while these two men are together, the mind and inner consciousness of A, let us say, is in one of the higher loka-tala systems, possibly even temporarily in janarloka-sutala; yet at the same instant, the mind and inner consciousness of the other man may be in its own maharloka-rasātala. Just here is the secret key that the adept frequently employs when he wants to communicate with interior realms. He raises his consciousness out of bhūrloka-pātāla, and puts it into the loka-tala wherein he desires to function.

INTERWEBBING OF LOKAS AND TALAS

THERE IS NO NEED whatsoever to boggle over the differences as among planes, lokas and talas, and principles and elements; because when we look at the *essence* of all these various things we find they are identical, being but different manners of viewing Space in its manifestations.

Man, being a microcosm, repeats by analogy throughout his structure whatever the macrocosm or universe contains. We already have learned that man's seven principles are but another way of looking at the different layers of the auric egg, and that actually these layers correspond closely to the lokas and talas of the universe. These aggregates of layers, or principles and elements, when considered each one as a unity, correspond to the planes of the cosmos.

Neither the layers in the auric egg, nor equivalently the lokas and talas in the cosmos, occupy the same space, although in both macrocosm and microcosm they interpenetrate and are centered around the individual entity. I mean that the more ethereal, and even more so the spiritual, lokas and talas of a cosmos, or the more ethereal and spiritual layers of a man's auric egg, extend outwards and inwards as an aura or atmosphere surrounding the entity; so that while the lowest lokas and talas and the lowest layers of the auric egg are virtually the physical vehicle, either of the cosmos or of man, the higher lokas and talas and the higher layers of the auric egg extend far beyond their physical vehicles. It is just these far-flung auras which keep an entity in constant spiritual and psychovital touch with other entities of its own kind: with other parts of the universe in the case of a cosmos, and with other parts of the world in the case of a man.

In this lies the real meaning of the teaching that the spiritual entity continuously flowing through the laya-center has rays extending far beyond the more material vehicles, which in the lowest vehicle radiate scarcely further than its own circumscribed limits. In other words, the inner realms of man (or of a globe) are the various planes or spheres of the auric egg. This thought is imbodied in the *Vishnu-Purāna*, one of the Brahmanical works:

The sphere of the earth (or Bhūr-loka), comprehending its oceans, mountains, and rivers, extends as far as it is illuminated by the rays of the sun and moon; and to the same extent, both in diameter and circumference, the sphere of the sky (Bhuvar-loka) spreads above it (as far upwards as to the planetary sphere, or Swar-loka). The solar orb is situated a hundred thousand leagues from the earth; and that of the moon, an equal distance from the sun. At the same interval above the moon occurs the orbit of all the lunar constellations. The planet Budha (Mercury) is two hundred thousand leagues above the lunar mansions; Śukra (Venus) is at the same distance from Mercury; Angāraka (Mars) is as far above Venus; and the priest of the gods (Brihaspati, or Jupiter), as far from Mars; whilst Saturn (Śani) is two hundred and fifty thousand leagues beyond Jupiter. The sphere of the seven Rishis (Ursa Major) is a hundred thousand leagues above Saturn; and, at a similar height above the seven Rishis, is Dhruva (the pole-star), the pivot or axis of the whole planetary circle. Such, Maitreya, is the elevation of the three spheres (Bhūr, Bhuvar, Swar) which form the region of the consequences of works. The region of works is here (or in the land of Bharata).

Above Dhruva, at the distance of ten million leagues, lies the sphere of saints (or Mahar-loka), the inhabitants of which dwell in it throughout a Kalpa (or day of Brahmā). At twice that distance is situated Jano-loka, where Sanandana and other pure-minded sons of Brahmā reside. At four times the distance between the two last lies the Tapo-loka (the sphere of penance), inhabited by the deities called Vairājas, who are unconsumable by fire. At six times the distance (or twelve Crores — a hundred and twenty millions of leagues) is situated Satya-loka (the sphere of truth), the inhabitants of which never again know death.°

— II, vii, pp. 225-7

In other words, the field of influence of bhūrloka, our earth, reaches little farther than its atmosphere; bhuvarloka has an atmosphere or aura extending to the sun, although actually it is the world or loka next within the earth; and svarloka within bhuvarloka is a world still more ethereal or spiritual, having an aura which reaches even to Dhruva, or the polar star.

We could have no connection with beings outside ourselves, or with other globes or planets or even our sun, unless there were these atmospheric carriers or auric rays, both on our plane and on other planes. Just as a magnet has its field or atmosphere reaching beyond itself, so all these lokas and talas have their respective atmospheres.

Take our earth or our solar system: the highest lokas and talas of

---

°The ranges or individual distances of the planets from each other are not to be construed as being astronomical units; the references are mystical not spacial.

either are its points of contact with other spacial units throughout infinity. The more ethereal and more spiritual lokas and talas of our earth keep it in intimate magnetic and all other kinds of contact not only with the other globes of our chain, but likewise with the other planetary chains of our solar system; and the same great law applies to the interwebbing of our solar system with other solar systems of our galaxy.

We see from the foregoing that our *spiritual* principles are universal, which means that our ātma-buddhi links us with the whole universe; similarly, the cosmic ātman of our solar system is universal in extent, interwebbing it with the entire galaxy. This wondrous fact is the basis for the statement in Hindu philosophy that the essence of man, his ātman, is identical with the paramātman of the universe.

When we succeed in allying ourselves with the higher principles of our constitution and learn to think and feel and act self-consciously therein, we gain self-conscious immortality° for the duration of the planetary chain — billions of years; for we then are jīvanmuktas. Of course when the planetary chain reaches its end, such liberated monads, not having been able to go higher into still vaster realms of self-conscious cosmic life, must follow nature's law and have their nirvanic period of rest.

In this connection we might well ask ourselves whether the lokas and talas that make up the fabric of the twelvefold sun are identic with those of a planetary chain or of a globe. Or again, do the lokas and talas of our earth derive their essence and energy from the sun, the sun stepping these down, as it were, from the lokas and talas of a galaxy? If this is so, does a man embrace or contain the loka-tala powers of a galaxy?

The answer in brief to each of these questions is yes. Our solar system is a unitary individual, and therefore it has its own lokas and talas on the solar scale. Being and living therein, it is obvious that the lokas and talas of a planetary chain, or of any globe thereof, are *fundamentally* identic with those of the solar chain, yet preserving their own respective individualities. So too the lokas and talas of our galaxy comprise within their being the minor lokas and talas of any solar system in that galaxy. Hence we see that the lokas and talas of our own solar system are individual worlds, yet contained within the encompassing grander system of the galactic worlds, precisely as the lokas and talas of a planetary chain, or

---

°This is what K.H. referred to as "panaeonic immortality" in *The Mahatma Letters*, pp. 129, 131.

of any of its globes, are encompassed by the greater loka-tala system of the solar chain. It is a case of wheels within wheels. In the same fashion all the life-atoms, on whatever plane, which go to make up the constitution of a man, are individual entities, yet included within the larger human entity.

While the answer to the above questions is in the affirmative, it must be qualified with the statement that each smaller individual world, or loka-tala twin, is surrounded by and suffused with the life-essence of the greater loka-tala system in which it lives. Thus we cannot say that the smaller system is identic with the greater, because the greater and the smaller are each one an individual; nevertheless, so far as fundamental essences go, they are identic on the grand scale. The differences which exist between lokas and talas, whether on the macrocosmic scale, or on that of a planetary chain or globe, pertain to rates or frequencies of vibration.

Therefore even man contains within his constitution, as the very basis of his being, not only the loka-tala powers and substances of our galaxy, but likewise of our solar system as well as of our globe D, earth. More than this, being himself an individual, he combines all these grander loka-tala powers with his own loka-tala powers and substances.

This beautiful fact of nature allows man, by going into the arcana of his own being, to come into identic vibrational relations with all other parts of the universe, and thus feel and *know* himself to be at one with all that is. Just here is the sublime cause of morals, and the reason why all the great sages and seers of the past have taught that ethics are no merely human convention, but are based on the structure of the universe itself: when a man injures another, in very truth he injures himself.

MONADS, CENTERS OF CONSCIOUSNESS

The "Three-tongued flame" that never dies is the immortal spiritual triad — the Atma-Buddhi and Manas — the fruition of the latter assimilated by the first two after every terrestrial life. The "four wicks" that go out and are extinguished, are the four lower principles, including the body. . . .

Just as milliards of bright sparks dance on the waters of an ocean above which one and the same moon is shining, so our evanescent personalities — the illusive envelopes of the immortal MONAD-EGO — twinkle and dance on the waves of Maya. They last and appear, as the thousands of sparks produced by the moon-beams, only so long as the Queen of the Night radiates her lustre on the running waters of life: the period of a Manvantara; and then they disappear, the beams — symbols of our eternal Spiritual Egos — alone surviving, re-merged in, and being, as they were before, one with the Mother-Source. — *The Secret Doctrine*, I, 237

EVERY MATHEMATICAL point of Space is a consciousness center, a monad — an 'individual,' the final point which cannot be divided any more, the vanishing point. Consider what this thought means. In everything around us — all the materials in a building, the substance of all our bodies, the atoms, molecules, electrons, all so-called mathematical points, whether of the air, the world, the surrounding space of inner planes, upper and lower — the same rule applies, for Space is a vast congeries of points of consciousness.

We are surrounded by very material things, by every kind of entity; for instance, in our own world by chemical composites: stone and wood, water and plants and flesh, and what not. All these are formed of monads, ultimately. If we press the search ever farther and deeper inwards, as far as we can go, we realize we shall never reach an end; yet the mind at last obtains a point of support which it calls a mathematical center, the core of the core of an entity — and that is the monad, a spiritual individual with divinity at *its* heart. In this connection the ancients spoke of the Waters of Space, each droplet or monad emanating from the environing Ocean of Consciousness and ultimately returning to it. Or, as the Lord Buddha is stated to have said, the "dewdrop slips into the shining Sea" — to emanate from it again at the beginning of some future manvantara. The Monas monadum, signifying the cosmic monad, is simply the aggregated monads of which it is at once the parent and final goal. It in its turn is but a minute monad in a supercosmic entity still more vast.

However deeply the mind plunges into the abysses of thought, it will never reach anything more than an ever-expanding consciousness of itself: the ultimate Self, the god within, the ātman. This is the monad. This is the perpetual individual, the spiritual individuality, the indivisible part of us. The heart of the monad, its superior fountain of life and intelligence, is a divine monad, the inner god. But the word monad is used in a general way for a variety of consciousness centers in man. There is the spiritual monad, offspring of the divine monad; there is the human monad, offspring of the spiritual monad; there is the vital-astral monad, offspring of the human monad. All these together form the human constitution. Each such monad, no matter what its grade, is an evolving entity. All that we are as human beings we derive ultimately from the monadic essence which is surrounding the inmost. Our spiritual intelligence, our instincts for noble thinking, for kindly and brotherly action, the impulses to compassion which fill our hearts, the love which so dignifies us, the loftiest intuitions which our nature is capable of — all these are derivative from and rooted in the monad. The spiritual monad, which is the 'heart' of the reincarnating ego, is itself rooted in the divine monad or inner god, the deathless part of us. Without the influence or rays from the monad streaming into our human consciousness, we should be merely human beasts. The monad would be there, though inactive, and we should indeed be humans, but spiritually darkened and unawakened.

Now the soul, which is an aggregate entity just as a monad itself really is, is simply the clothing or the psychomental veil of a monad which is passing through that particular phase of its everlasting peregrinations through periodic time and hierarchical space. This monad's expression on any plane is a soul. The soul, in turn, works through *its* own vehicle, whether an ethereal or a physical one. Mystically, the physical body itself may be called an aggregated monad of the physical plane, because it is formed of mathematical points, little lives or monads of which the soul is the Monad of monads of this particular bodily hierarchy; while the monad above the soul is again its supermonad or Monas monadum.

This is a wonderful mystery: the universal nature of consciousness.

It shows the fallacy of having our ideas crystallized, of keeping them pigeonholed. In matters of consciousness one cannot do this. We must keep our ideas fluid like ether — indeed, like consciousness itself! The consciousness of a man, for instance, is all over his body, yet has its different foci or points of special activity in the bodily organs. (It is possible for one's consciousness to be localized in an organ, or even in a point, in the body; but it requires the expenditure of great energy to do this.) By analogy, we see how the consciousness of the cosmic monad is universal, and how we are all in it throughout eternity, constantly increasing and expanding our consciousness in it, which really means evolving our conscious selves.

The universe expresses its inner powers, faculties and structure by means of alternating periods of world-manifestation and world-rest. At the beginning of each manvantara, it begins unfolding what is within; and when that manvantara finally ends, all the monads of the different hierarchies and classes in the universe have, each one, gone up a step on the endless ladder of cosmic life. Thus, considered as an individual, there is no beginning and no end of a universe, except insofar as the stages of its expanding growth are concerned, the periods of manifestation and pralaya — just as a human incarnation has a definite beginning and a definite ending at what we call birth and death; but the inner spiritual consciousness streams onwards and forwards forever.

One thing a human being cannot ever do is to annihilate himself, because, as an individual droplet of the cosmic Sea, he is an individual monad continually pouring forth, somewhat like an artesian well, ever-enlarging streams of consciousness from within.

A monad begins its evolutionary course in any one of these great manvantaras at the bottom. It cannot begin elsewhere, because one cannot *climb* a ladder by starting at the top and going downwards. So it is with monads: they enter upon the manvantara at the beginning of things. They do so as bare monads, and gradually unfold around themselves sheaths of consciousness, each one appropriate to the sphere through which it is at the time passing, these sheaths being composed of still less evolved monads trailing after the chief monad — children monads to which it had given birth in past manvantaras. But the core of each such monad beginning its new mahāmanvantaric evolution is a monad that came from the previous mahāmanvantara.

Thus the monads at the beginning of the manvantara enter the three

272

elemental kingdoms, and proceed on up the scale to the gods. But whence come the three elemental kingdoms? From the monads at the heart of every such elemental. Every being — god, demigod, man, subhuman entities of all classes — each one is essentially a monad passing through that particular phase of its evolution. All impulses originate in the monad. All substances flow forth from the heart of the monad. All consciousness resides in the core of the monad, all thoughts in their ultimate origin spring forth from the flow of consciousness arising in its fountainhead.

All these entities, from the elementals on up to the gods, and so on forever, are vehicles expressing different phases of the long, long evolutionary journey of the monads through space and time. A god is as much such a vehicle as is a man, only far greater in spiritual quality. Similarly an elemental is a vehicle of a monad. Can we ever reach an ultimate, an absolute ending, by going deeper and deeper into the heart of the heart of the monad? Never; for its root is Infinity.

Certain monads by the end of the previous mahāmanvantara had already evolved so far that at the beginning of the new mahāmanvantara they have little to learn in its *opening* stages, and therefore pass very rapidly through these lower stages. But their children monads, rays from themselves, spring into active manifestation at the beginning of such a new mahāmanvantara, and in consequence must go through all the lower stages as their new schoolrooms of experience.

The 'graduated' monads are, each one of them, a Monas monadum; and these are the guides and spiritual helpers of the less developed monads, their own children, trailing along behind. This is the essential thought of the doctrine of the Hierarchy of Compassion.

The ancient Hindus spoke of an 'anu,' which means infinitesimal or atomic; hence it is a monad in its lowest ranges of cosmic expression. When we say monad, do we give to it magnitude, volume or bulk? No, because our mind instinctively recognizes it as a point of consciousness, an infinitesimal, whose essence nevertheless is universal since it is a droplet of the universal consciousness. A monad (literally 'one') cannot ever be divided; it is an individual, yet it is all-embracing because its heart is Infinity. The beginning of a circle is likewise its ending; similarly, Infinitude is the ultrainfinitesimal. The spirit or self within us catches and understands this thought, because it contains it; but the brain-mind, with its insistence upon dimensions, will not catch it because it is not evolved enough. Yet even the brain-mind itself is an as yet unexpressed monad.

This is why the ancient Hindu philosophers called anu by the name of Brahman, for Brahman is both the universal and the ultrainfinitesimal. The dewdrop is not different from the shining Sea, and when it returns to the fount from which it came, it has become one with the water of its source. That is what consciousness is and does; this is what body and form are not and do not. We should try to think in terms of consciousness, in terms of understanding. If we conceive of the monad as having physical size we shall never get the essential idea, because we are then giving it limitations which do not belong to it. The phrase "it becomes one with the water" does not signify that the monadic essence producing the dewdrop coalesces with the water. The dewdrop is the physical vehicle of the inner monad and, just as our human bodies do, breaks up into its component particles which are distributed throughout the prithivī-tattwa of nature; but the monad remains the individual, the indivisible center of consciousness, and in good time will gather together again its life-atoms and reproduce the dewdrop that was and now again is — the 'resurrection of the body,' as the Christians would phrase it.

Thus the jīvanmukta or freed monad rebecomes at the closing of the manvantara the Brahman from which it originally emanated as a ray, but does not coalesce unto eternity with that Brahman, for at the opening of the cosmic drama of the succeeding manvantara the monad issues forth again, and enters on its new peregrinations in realms higher than those from which it had previously been freed as a jīvanmukta.

As one of the "Sacred Ślokas" quoted in The Secret Doctrine (II, 80) has it:

"The thread of radiance which is imperishable and dissolves only in Nirvana, re-emerges from it in its integrity on the day when the Great Law calls all things back into action."

The word anu, the smallest imaginable particle of matter, has much the same indefinite meaning that atom has in modern philosophical and scientific thought. Jīva means life, also a living entity. Let us then coin a term for the soul of an anu and call it a jīvānu, a 'life-atom,' a life-infinitesimal, the 'soul' of the chemical atom. Superior to it, actually its parent, let us place a paramānu (parama, meaning primordial, first in order). Thus we have anu, the atom; jīvānu, the life-atom; paramānu, the supreme atom or atomic monad.

The paramānu or atomic monad lasts through the whole cosmic manvantara without diminution of power or cessation of consciousness. The life-atom or jīvānu lasts only for a certain period of time within the cosmic manvantara. Like our physical body, the anu is even more transitory and fugitive. Thus when a life-atom and an anu reach their term, the paramānu or atomic monad has to imbody itself again, take a new life-atom and a new aggregate of infinitesimals making a new anu.°

Similarly with man: our monad lasts through the whole cosmic manvantara. Our soul or reincarnating ego, which correspondentially is the human life-atom within us, lasts for the duration of the planetary chain; but our bodies last only for one earth life. Thus we have the analogies: paramānu, jīvānu, anu; monad, reimbodying ego, body; or, in the Christian scheme, spirit, soul, body. Every manifested entity everywhere, on inner or on outer planes, here or anywhere in boundless Space, is constructed on identical lines. Its heart, the core of itself, is an individual or a monad, a spirit, a god, which has its soul and its bodies.

When we say that a paramānu lasts through the whole cosmic manvantara without diminution of power or cessation of consciousness, we are considering the paramānu as the monadic essence of an atom; but this does not imply that this atomic monadic essence is as highly unfolded in its innate divine and spiritual faculties and powers as is the monad of a divinity. Both a paramānu and a divine monad are in essence one; yet a paramānu is, as it were, latent or sleeping, in comparison to the divine monad which is fully expressing its transcendent powers and is, in all probability, the monadic essence of some jīvanmukta.†

Another method of classifying the three main divisions of man's being is according to the three classes of the indriyas as given in Hindu philosophies. They are considered to be the organs or channels, or rather the instruments by which the ego expresses itself in and through its sheaths of consciousness: the buddhīndriyas, jñānendriyas, and karmendriyas. From the theosophical standpoint, the buddhīndriyas, as the word buddhi shows, are what one might call the organs or means of spiritual consciousness, apperception, sense and action; the jñānendriyas are those innate organs

---

°I am here using these Sanskrit terms in their strictly etymological sense, and hence in a manner somewhat different from that employed in the two Hindu schools of Atomic Philosophy — the Nyāya and the Vaiśeshika — which have endowed these words with specific meanings of their own.

†The Secret Doctrine, I, 610–34.

and functions of consciousness which pertain to the intellectual, mental, and psychical parts of the human constitution; whereas the karmendriyas fall naturally into place as the astral-vital-physical organs of sensation and of action on our plane, such as the ear, the skin, the eye, the tongue, and the nose.

To understand the esoteric philosophy it is best to forget bodies and to grip the essential consciousness of ourselves. The fatal error of Western thought in all its departments of religion, philosophy and science is that it concentrates on the body-aspects, therefore on the transitory, the ever-changing. We have forgotten that the way by which to understand ultimates is by facing and studying them; and the ultimate of ultimates is the divine Selfhood, essential consciousness.

THE MONADIC CLASSES

The MONAD emerges from its state of spiritual and intellectual unconsciousness; and, skipping the first two planes — too near the ABSOLUTE to
permit of any correlation with anything on a lower plane — it gets direct
into the plane of Mentality. But there is no plane in the whole universe
with a wider margin, or a wider field of action in its almost endless gradations
of perceptive and apperceptive qualities, than this plane, which has in its
turn an appropriate smaller plane for every "form," from the "mineral"
monad up to the time when that monad blossoms forth by evolution into
the DIVINE MONAD. But all the time it is still one and the same Monad,
differing only in its incarnations, throughout its ever succeeding cycles of
partial or total obscuration of spirit, or the partial or total obscuration of
matter — two polar antitheses — as it ascends into the realms of mental
spirituality, or descends into the depths of materiality.

— *The Secret Doctrine*, I, 175

EVERYTHING IN THE universal cosmos consists of twelve principles or
elements; or, if we are thinking of the consciousness side, the hierarchies
of consciousness, we look upon them as the twelve classes of monads.
In other words, when our universe first came into being and proceeded
in its evolutionary stages of unfolding, it unrolled itself into twelve 'folds'
or divisions, each being a plane or principle or a class of monads. If
instead we use the septenary scheme, we do so only because for the time
we are limiting ourselves to the seven manifested spheres from *their* highest to *their* lowest; similarly, when we speak of ten, we have in mind the
manifested seven with the divine monad, triune in character, hovering
above it. When we refer to twelve, we are viewing the *whole*, high and
low, no part or portion omitted.

Each monad of whatever class is, in its origin, a cosmic elemental
because born of one of the cosmic elements or principles. Circumgyrating
and whirling through the kingdoms of nature and along the pathways
of karmic destiny, each such monad brings forth from within itself the
locked-up characteristics, faculties and powers which, as they appear,
slowly raise the evolutionary status of the evolving monad into an ever-
enlarging field of consciousness and activity. Finally the evolving monad

277

becomes a man, destined to become in future ages a full-blown god.°

Let us consider for a moment the relation of the different classes of monads in and to the manifested world around us. Those monads — and I am referring now to the evolution of beings progressing forwards — which have unfolded one element or principle are natives or inhabitants of what we call the elements per se. It is customary in occultism to speak of these inhabitants as falling into three elemental kingdoms: the elementals of the spirit of an element; those of the intermediate ranges; and the elementals belonging to the lowest triad of such cosmic element.

Those monads which have unfolded two principles we call in their aggregation the mineral kingdom; those which have unfolded three principles compose the vegetable kingdom, while those which have unfolded four are the animal kingdom. The human kingdom has unfolded, at least to some degree, five principles out of the twelve. We shall not be really complete human beings until the end of the fifth round, when manas, so far as it is possible, will then be fully developed in us. At the present time, being only in the fourth round, and yet in the fifth race on the fourth globe, we are a kind of animal-human, the fourth element or kāma manifesting in us almost more strongly than does the fifth or mānasic principle.

Those, again, who unfold six elements in themselves are the highest mahatmas, the bodhisattvas; and those fully enlightened by ātman — when all six principles or elements have been to some relatively large degree unfolded within themselves — are called Buddhas or Christs, or by some similar descriptive name. Those monads who have unfolded, or who in the future will unfold, seven elements with relative fullness in themselves, are the gods. Similarly, those who unfold ten of the cosmic principles are the cosmic hierarchs, the Silent Watchers, who have nothing more to learn for the remainder of their respective manvantaras. Whereas those who have unfolded all twelve cosmic principles within themselves, and are thus self-conscious on every plane or in every aspect of their being,

---

°"It would be very misleading to imagine a Monad as a separate Entity trailing its slow way in a distinct path through the lower Kingdoms, and after an incalculable series of transformations flowering into a human being; in short, that the Monad of a Humboldt dates back to the Monad of an atom of hornblende. Instead of saying a 'Mineral Monad,' the more correct phraseology in physical Science, which differentiates every atom, would of course have been to call it 'the Monad manifesting in that form of Prakriti called the Mineral Kingdom.'" —The Secret Doctrine, I, 178

are those divine entities who manifest as universes — including inner spirit, intermediate ranges, and encompassing cosmic body.

From the foregoing we see why at times it is necessary to speak of seven, ten or twelve, when referring to principles or elements or cosmic planes. But all methods of division are somewhat arbitrary, in that one could with equal truth speak of three-principled creatures or beings, or even of four- or five-principled, etc.

Every monad, high or low, in boundless Space, contains *every* element that all other monads do; but all have these common principles unfolded in differing degrees and according to classes. Some have unfolded many of their principles; others, only a few; still others, such as human beings, are approaching the midpoint, where the buddhas and the gods stand. When we view the universe in its totality we think of ten, or even of twelve, elements; or, when we consider only the lower or manifest aspect, we speak of seven, which is perhaps the most common because so practical in teaching. This is probably why H.P.B. so strongly emphasized the septenaries in the universe, although she frequently pointed to other principles or elements, superior to the manifest seven, as belonging to divine or superdivine ranges.

The Secret Doctrine treats of the different classes of monads — and the hierarchical stages and evolutionary grades which they occupy in the cosmic life and structure — from a very mystical standpoint, by distributing the seven monadic classes in and through the twelve zodiacal divisions.

It is obvious that the number twelve can be divided into two groups of six. Now this manner of distributing the manifest seven over and into the twelve is as follows: the lower hexad is left undisturbed, and the lowest of the six individuals of the upper group forms the link uniting the lower with the upper hexad. Thus the lower six *plus* the lowest individual of the upper six make the manifested septenary, whether applied to cosmic planes, to classes of monads, or to lokas and talas. Furthermore, this lowest of the upper six includes all the other and superior five members of the upper hexad, thus giving us again the number twelve.

Another similar scheme is that of the ten, divided into the lower septenary and the highest triad, the latter hovering over the septenary, as it were, yet strictly to be considered as inspiring, because residing in, the uppermost unit of the lower septenary.

These seven classes of monads, which imbody in themselves the supernal five classes, are so interestingly, even if somewhat vaguely, described in

The Secret Doctrine, ° that I quote here the following pertinent passages:

The hierarchy of Creative Powers is divided into seven (or 4 and 3) esoteric, within the twelve great Orders, recorded in the twelve signs of the Zodiac; the seven of the manifesting scale being connected, moreover, with the Seven Planets. All this is subdivided into numberless groups of divine Spiritual, semi-Spiritual, and ethereal Beings. . . .

The highest group is composed of the divine Flames, so-called, also spoken of as the "Fiery Lions" and the "Lions of Life," whose esotericism is securely hidden in the Zodiacal sign of Leo. It is the *nucleole* of the superior divine World. . . . They are the formless Fiery Breaths, . . .   — I, 213

The second Order of Celestial Beings, those of Fire and Aether (corresponding to Spirit and Soul, or the Atma-Buddhi) whose names are legion, are still formless, but more definitely "substantial." They are the first differentiation in the Secondary Evolution . . . they are the prototypes of the incarnating Jivas or Monads, and are composed of the Fiery Spirit of Life. It is through these that passes, like a pure solar beam, the ray which is furnished by them with its future vehicle, the Divine Soul, Buddhi. These are directly concerned with the Hosts of the higher world of *our* system. From these twofold *Units* emanate the *threefold.*
                                                                              — I, 216

The *Third* order corresponds to the *Atma-Buddhi-Manas:* Spirit, Soul and Intellect, and is called the "Triads."

The *Fourth* are substantial Entities. This is the highest group among the *Rupas* (Atomic Forms). It is the nursery of the human, conscious, spiritual Souls. They are called the "Imperishable Jivas," and constitute, through the order below their own, the first group of the first septenary host — the great mystery of human conscious and intellectual Being. . . .

The Fifth group is a very mysterious one, as it is connected with the Microcosmic Pentagon, the five-pointed star representing man.   — I, 218–19

The fifth group of the celestial Beings is supposed to contain in itself the dual attributes of both the spiritual and physical aspects of the Universe; the two poles, so to say, of Mahat the Universal Intelligence, and the dual nature

---

°We must remember that H.P.B. was writing for lay readers; and this accounts for the many and various quasi-exoteric facts drawn by her from the literatures of the world. To one who has not studied comparative religion and philosophy, the wealth of material adduced by her in support of her statement that these monads are found mentioned in the different world literatures, makes these passages extremely complicated, and to many minds they read almost like hodgepodge. Thus unless the student hold on like grim death to H.P.B.'s essential train of thought, he finds his mind drawn hither and yon; and this is one reason why these pages have been so badly understood, or passed over by some as almost incomprehensible.

of man, the spiritual and the physical. Hence its number Five, multiplied and made into ten, connecting it with *Makara*, the 10th sign of Zodiac.

The sixth and seventh groups partake of the lower qualities of the Quaternary. They are conscious, ethereal Entities, as invisible as Ether, which are shot out like the boughs of a tree from the first central group of the four, and shoot out in their turn numberless side groups, the lower of which are the Nature-Spirits, or Elementals of countless kinds and varieties; from the formless and unsubstantial — the ideal THOUGHTS of their creators — down to the Atomic, though, to human perception, invisible organisms. . . . The Celestial Hierarchy of the present Manvantara will find itself transferred in the next cycle of life into higher, superior worlds, and will make room for a new hierarchy, composed of the elect ones of our mankind. Being is an endless cycle within the one absolute eternity, wherein move numberless inner cycles finite and conditioned. Gods, created as such, would evince no personal merit in being gods. Such a class of beings, perfect only by virtue of the special immaculate nature inherent in them, in the face of suffering and struggling humanity, and even of the lower creation, would be the symbol of an eternal injustice quite Satanic in character, an ever present crime. It is an anomaly and an impossibility in Nature. Therefore the "Four" and the "Three" have to incarnate as all other beings have. This sixth group, moreover, remains almost inseparable from man, who draws from it all but his highest and lowest principles, or his spirit and body, the five middle human principles being the very essence of those Dhyanis. Alone, the Divine Ray (the Atman) proceeds directly from the One. When asked how that can be? How is it possible to conceive that those "gods," or angels, can be at the same time their own emanations and their personal selves? Is it in the same sense in the material world, where the son is (in one way) his father, being his blood, the bone of his bone and the flesh of his flesh? To this the teachers answer "Verily it is so." But one has to go deep into the mystery of BEING before one can fully comprehend this truth.   — I, 221–2

Taking then these seven classes of beings, we can make an analogy with the seven principles of man or of the cosmos, and again with the seven cosmic planes. Thus the first or highest class of the seven monadic groups corresponds with the ātman in man or the paramātman in the cosmos; the second class corresponds with the ātman-buddhi in man or the mahābuddhi of the cosmos; and in similar fashion, we find next in serial order the third class of monads corresponding in man with ātman-buddhi-manas; the fourth class with ātman-buddhi-manas-kāma; and so forth, running down the scale until we reach the seventh or lowest class of monads which corresponds with ātman-buddhi-manas-kāma-prāna and the linga-śarīra plus the physical body or sthūla-śarīra.

Now while each one of these seven classes of monads is a group in itself, corresponding by analogy with a cosmic plane, in fact actually forming and *being* that cosmic plane, nevertheless we notice that every subordinate class of monads contains within itself all superior classes — exactly after the manner in which the universe is unrolled from its highest principle or cosmic plane, downwards through all the series, thus building the structure of the cosmos. Each class of monads, although being itself divided into seven (or twelve) subclasses, *as a group* can be thought of as a cosmic individual family composed of seven submembers; exactly as a cosmic plane, considered as an individual, is itself divisible into a like number of subordinate planes. This fact of the septenary nature of each class of monads provides the immense and amazing variety of the monads existing in any one class.

We likewise observe that, just as in the unrolling of the cosmic planes (in order to form the compound structure of the universe), or in the emanation of man's lower six principles from his ātman, each contains within itself all the preceding or superior planes or principles; so in like manner each of the seven classes of monads contains within itself all the preceding or higher classes.

There is in man a representative monad from every one of the seven monadic classes, their union thus putting him in touch or in inseparable common life essence not only with all the seven cosmic planes, but also with the entire septenary of these monadic groups. Yet man is self-conscious in his present evolutionary stage only on this lowest (to us) cosmic plane. This is because the human monad, or his kāma-mānasic essence, is wakened to self-consciousness on *this* cosmic plane, and he is functioning self-consciously in *its* third from the top (or fifth from the bottom) principle or monadic class.

Finally, as said, these seven classes of monads are the inhabitants of the respective seven cosmic planes. Each such plane (taking the highest as an instance in point), because of the subordinately septenary nature of the class of monads appurtenant to it, contains not only the most evolved monads which belong to it by evolutionary development, but likewise undeveloped monads native to that highest plane — because of their karma in the manvantara — in and from which plane they begin their aeons' long evolutionary journey. This is explained by the fact that such highest cosmic plane, or highest class of monads, is itself septenary, with the divine-spiritual at one end and the lowest subordinate class at the other.

THE TRIPLE EVOLUTIONARY SCHEME

THE PARAGRAPHS CITED below from *The Secret Doctrine* (I, 181) are replete
with occult facts, although unfortunately many students have construed
them so literally as to miss the major part of H.P.B.'s intent. Having
in mind the seven or more classes of peregrinating monads, they then
come upon her reference to "a triple evolutionary scheme," and wonder
if this is not a contradiction. There is no contradiction of any kind.

It now becomes plain that there exists in Nature a triple evolutionary scheme,
for the formation of the three *periodical Upadhis;* or rather three separate schemes
of evolution, which in our system are inextricably interwoven and interblended
at every point. These are the Monadic (or spiritual), the intellectual, and the
physical evolutions. These three are the finite aspects or the reflections on the
field of Cosmic Illusion of ATMA, the seventh, the ONE REALITY.
1. The Monadic is, as the name implies, concerned with the growth and
development into still higher phases of activity of the Monad in conjunction
with: —
2. The Intellectual, represented by the Manasa-Dhyanis (the Solar Devas,
or the Agnishwatta Pitris) the "givers of intelligence and consciousness" to man
and: —
3. The Physical, represented by the Chhayas of the lunar Pitris, round which
Nature has concreted the present physical body. This body serves as the vehicle
for the "growth" (to use a misleading word) and the transformations through
Manas and — owing to the accumulation of experiences — of the finite into the
INFINITE, of the transient into the Eternal and Absolute. —
Each of these three systems has its own laws, and is ruled and guided by
different sets of the highest Dhyanis or "Logoi." Each is represented in the
constitution of man, the Microcosm of the great Macrocosm; and it is the union
of these three streams in him which makes him the complex being he now is.

When we consider the evolution of man through the ages, it is as
correct to say that all his seven principles and his various monads evolve
as it is to say that his evolution takes place as a "triple evolutionary
scheme," to wit, his spirit evolves, his soul evolves, his body evolves.
It will be seen that in the above extract H.P.B. was simply dividing the
seven monadic classes into three general groups: (a) those monads which

are typically spiritual in swabhāva and in position on the ladder of life; (b) those which are, by swabhāva and evolutionary unfolding, intellectual or typically mānasic; and (c) the group which aggregatively are the monads more or less completely sunken in the material or physical realms of nature.

Thus then, the human constitution is divisible into three monadic groups: an upper duad, an intermediate duad, and a lower triad.° The two highest monadic classes — those farthest advanced in evolutionary growth — form what H.P.B. describes as the spiritual or the monadic, corresponding to the upper duad (ātma-buddhi) in the human constitution.

The second group, corresponding to the intermediate duad (manas-kāma) in man, comprises the two particularly mānasic classes of monads: the typical solar devas or agnishwātta pitris, otherwise the mānasa-dhyānis; and the lower solar devas which are the higher lunar pitris. In other words, these latter are agnishwātta pitris of a lower class, albeit of solar characteristics, which were evolving intellectual monads of lower degree on the moon.

Thirdly, the three monadic classes of the lowest group form what H.P.B. calls the physical, and correspond to the lower triad (the vital-astral-physical) in the human constitution. These three classes consist partly of monads typically terrestrial because closely connected by karmic destiny with globe D of our planetary chain, and partly of the monadic life-atoms exuded or emanated from the lowest part of the veils of the lunar pitris, which life-atoms in their aggregate are the 'shadows' or chhāyās or astral doubles of the lunar pitris, just as man's linga-śarīra is his astral double.

Now when the lunar pitris, during the course of their evolutionary growth as the early 'humans' on this globe D in the present round, clothed themselves in these astral veils — the thickened effusion of their own vitality pouring forth from the auric egg — these chhāyās or astral bodies served as the original 'physical' bodies of the 'human' stock in the first root-race. The terrestrial life-atoms collected around these chhāyās and thus aided in the consolidating process of the 'human' linga-śarīra in those earliest times of human evolution on this globe during this fourth round. Hence our present physical bodies or sthūla-śarīras are the thickened and concreted chhāyās of the lunar pitris.

We see that the three periodical upādhis mentioned above are the three groups of monads corresponding to the spirit, soul and body of man,

---

°Cf. *Fundamentals of the Esoteric Philosophy,* ch. XLVI.

the union of these three streams in him making him the complex being he now is. While "each of these three systems has its own laws, and is ruled and guided by different sets of the highest Dhyanis or 'Logoi,'" nevertheless in our system they are "inextricably interwoven and inter-blended at every point."

From the foregoing the distinction between agnishwātta pitris and lunar pitris should be clearer. The agnishwātta pitris are those monads which in former planetary chains rose from unself-conscious god-sparks into the human status, and passing through the human status attained mānasic divinity. On the other hand, the lunar pitris, often called the barhishads, although *in essence* solar devas precisely like the agnishwātta pitris, had not yet reached the 'human' status on the moon, but they have attained it on our present planetary chain — hence the lunar pitris are now we humans.

For the bulk of mankind this great event took place during the third root-race, when the mānasaputras or 'sons of mind' awakened the latent intellectual and psychical faculties in the then relatively unself-conscious human stock of that root-race, it being their karmic obligation so to do. These mānasaputras or agnishwāttas thereafter continued their evolution in their own realms, while the lunar pitris, being thus stimulated or awakened, pursued their evolutionary course from about the middle of the third root-race onwards as self-conscious thinking individuals.

Every monad, of whatever class, and no matter what may be its state in evolution at any time, is in its essence a non-fully expressed divinity or god. Therefore we, having now in our constitution these different monads, are very composite beings, each one of these monads being itself a learning, growing entity, destined in future ages, if at present below the human status, to become a man; and if above the human, to go still higher.

In the future, and following nature's rule of action, it is we who will at the end of the seventh round become mānasaputras or agnishwāttas of one of the lower classes of this group; and, when our planetary chain imbodies itself anew, it is we who shall then perform the role of illuminating or awakening those monads which *now* amongst us have not yet evolved forth the human status, being at present the higher groups of animals.

I have touched upon the manner in which the lunar pitris, during the first root-race on this globe D during this fourth round, exuded or projected their shadows or chhāyās, which were nothing more than their astral bodies, the vital-astral and quasi-physical forms in which they were then imbodying themselves. This exuding simply means that the lunar pitris had reached the point in their evolution when their astral vehicles were more or less fully developed, so that they formed actual bodies in and through which the lunar monads worked, exactly as our human monads today live in and work through our present physical bodies. Once this stage in the evolving of the lunar pitris had been reached, and once their chhāyās or astral bodies had become concrete enough to manifest in the 'physical' world, from that moment the terrestrial matter and forces of this globe aided in the thickening of these chhāyās. This process continued until actual physical bodies were produced, which steadily became grosser and heavier until the middle point of the fourth root-race — the most material point possible in this fourth round. From that time on our bodies have been very slowly but continuously etherealizing themselves, so that we of the fifth root-race have bodies less gross than those of the Atlanteans or fourth root-race. This process of the etherealizing of our sthūla-śarīras will go on without interruption, so that at the end of the seventh root-race on this globe D during this fourth round, our physical bodies will be closely akin in texture and appearance to the quasi-astral bodies of the first root-race.

When H.P.B. speaks of the astral doubles of the lunar pitris being exuded or projected, she uses this graphic expression for the reason that a man's astral and physical vehicles are more or less doubles or reflections of what the inner man is. Thus, our physical bodies are but the feeble reflections of what we as human egos really are. It is utterly erroneous to consider this phrase astral doubles to mean that the lunar pitris detached from themselves astral forms which, thus separated, evolved into human beings.

Now, how can we relate the above to the statement in *The Secret Doctrine* (II, 1), that seven groups of humanity appear simultaneously?°

As regards the evolution of mankind, the Secret Doctrine postulates three new propositions, which stand in direct antagonism to modern science as well as to current religious dogmas: it teaches (*a*) the simultaneous evolution of seven human groups on seven different portions of our globe; (*b*) the birth of the *astral*, before the *physical* body: the former being a model for the latter; and (*c*) that

---

°The author's comments on this question were later published in *Studies in Occult Philosophy*, pp. 260–2. — Ed.

man, in this Round, preceded every mammalian — the anthropoids included — in the animal kingdom.

This refers to the fact that human evolution opened on this globe D in this fourth round by the simultaneous appearance, on seven different parts of the land surrounding the north pole, of seven embryonic astral 'humanities,' these being the seven classes of lunar pitris. It is from these original humanities, forming the beginnings of the first root-race on this globe in this round, that all the later human races came. These astral humanities had their geographical zones on what H.P.B. calls "the Imperishable Sacred Land," the first continent, surrounding and including the north pole and extending, like the leaves of a lotus, somewhat southwards from the pole in seven different zones. These primordial life centers or simultaneous races were as distinct as the seven globes of the planetary chain are from each other. The esoteric doctrine thus teaches a polygenetic and not a monogenetic origin for mankind.°

There are, strictly speaking, ten classes of pitris: three arūpa or relatively formless, called the agnishwātta or kumāra class who were solar beings; and the other seven, the rūpa, or those having form, who were the lunar pitris. Of these seven classes, the three highest were also relatively arūpa, while four were distinctly rūpa. It is the lunar pitris who, coming to this globe from the preceding globe C of our planetary chain, appeared — when the time for human evolution on this globe began — on the north pole in their seven classes, awakening the śishtas or seeds of the humanities left on this globe D when the preceding round, ages and ages previously, had ended.

It is not quite accurate to speak of these seven astral humanities as

---

°It does not teach the descent of mankind from a single pair, from an Adam and an Eve. The Hebrew story does not really refer to one man called Adam and one woman called Eve, originally a rib in Adam's body, but is a generalized way of speaking of early mankind — not meaning the first root-race but the middle of the third root-race on this globe in this round. The rib is a reference to the separation of the androgynous humanity of that period into two sexes; and 'rib' is only *one* translation of the Hebrew word, which signifies a 'side' or a 'part.' This account reminds one of the mystical and quasi-historic narrative given by Plato in his *Banquet* or *Symposium* (§ 190), where he spoke of the original mankind as being of globular form, strong and mighty, but wicked in temperament and in ambition; so that Zeus, in order to curb their evil-doing and to diminish their strength, cut these beings into two, much as one would divide an egg with a hair.

seven races, for this word races in this instance could be misleading. I would liefer speak of them as seven embryonic astral mankinds, each one of them being the production of one of the seven classes of the lunar pitris. It was especially the four lowest classes of lunar pitris which gave to these original mankinds their physical form.

Such was the opening of the drama of present human evolution on this fourth globe in this fourth round. From that time onwards, the seven astral humanities began their evolutionary development as the first root-race, and continued it, each on its own zone, until the time came for the appearance of the second root-race. By then the seven original mankinds had mixed and had disappeared as separate individual humanities. The first root-race then merged itself into and became the second root-race. Already in the first root-race, and among the seven astral embryonic humanities of that very early time, seven grades or differences appeared in evolutionary development from the lowest mankind upwards to the highest or seventh, which even then showed the beginnings of self-conscious and thinking man.

Now these seven primordial humanities were much more ethereal at first than was this globe D on which they appeared, although the globe at that time was considerably more ethereal than now. With the exception of the relatively few who had attained a certain degree of self-consciousness, because belonging to the highest class of the lunar pitris, the great majority of these early seven astral mankinds were unself-conscious and therefore 'mindless.' They were the more or less concreted astral bodies projected by the lunar pitris: boneless, skinless, and without internal organs as we know them. They were embryonic men in a state of consciousness which can be likened only to that of a heavy daydream; likewise they had no moral sense, and in consequence there was no sin among them because there was no conscious mind to imagine sin and to do it. Morally, they were as irresponsible as the just-born child, although the analogy is not very close.

To summarize: the seven embryonic mankinds were actually the astral bodies of the seven classes of the lunar pitris, the lunar monads, each class of which was attracted by karma to its own geographical zone. However, it was only the lowest four classes of lunar pitris which formed and shaped, by projecting their own astral shadows or bodies, the then physical bodies of these earliest humanities.

Thus is a man composite — composite of the divine grandeur of a galaxy, the solar splendor of the mānasa-dhyānis, as well as the transient energies of the lunar pitris. What a pathway we have before us! As *humans* we are finite entities; our human stage is but a finite event, a transitory phenomenon in the field of endless Duration; as *humans* we have not been evolving through eternity. Evolution is one of nature's laws, and evolution per se, considered as an abstract idea, is eternal; but no entity, no thing which exists, is eternal.

In the present cosmic manvantara we humans sprang forth as seeds of life, unself-conscious god-sparks, from some entity which had preceded us in evolution and of which we are the offspring, and in which we move and live and have our being. As we ourselves, along with all other entities, evolve into divinity, we too shall cast forth from our being god-sparks, that is, elementals, which in their turn will begin their long pilgrimage through the succeeding manvantara and finally themselves reach divinity.

Even the gods themselves, by contrast with endless Duration, are no more permanent than we are: a flash of life and they are gone, but to reissue forth in the next cosmic manvantara on a higher plane. We, not as men, but as the monadic essence within us, are the children of Eternity, particles of the Boundless. We began in this cosmic manvantara a new life experience, a new pilgrimage in higher spheres and on higher planes, in a nobler world than that in which the monadic essence manifested in the preceding manvantara.

In order to know all about this present universe, this present hierarchy, we must pass through every part of it from the most spiritual to the most material, and then rise along the ascending arc to rebecome what once we were, *plus* — and here is the value of evolution — all the assimilated fruitage of the experiences gained: the strengthening of inner fiber, the bringing out of new treasuries within our essential being.

Reincarnation exemplifies the idea. We have our experiences in one life, evolve a few steps along the path, bring out somewhat of what is locked up within us, take our devachanic rest, and then begin a new period of evolution — a new incarnation on earth. Here we see precisely the same law: a man in any one incarnation has not been evolving eternally. He is therein a new event, a new production, with its beginning and its end.

This monadic essence of each one of us is a divine thing, is an eternal producer, an inexhaustible fount of life and intelligence and consciousness, all different facets of the same fundamental consciousness-life-substance.

At the end of the preceding mahāmanvantara we finished our evolution there as dhyāni-chohans, 'lords of meditation,' gods, and went into our paranirvana, the cosmic rest, and passed aeons in that period, only to reissue forth again as unself-conscious god-sparks in the *new* stage of life, in the new and higher hierarchy — the child of the preceding hierarchy just as we are children of our own Self.

And such dhyāni-chohan, the fruitage of the preceding manvantara, is what we now call our inner god. We are it and yet different from it. We sprang from it as a new seed of individualized life in the beginning of the present mahāmanvantara; and it is the destiny of each one of us to become an inner god for some future psychical monad, issuing from the heart of that inner god in the next cosmic manvantara. I am my inner god and yet am its child.

VII

The Doctrine of the Spheres

THE HEART OF THE SUN — A DIVINITY

> The most mystic of discourses inform us, that the wholeness of him (the sun) is in the superior cosmic realms; for there a solar cosmos and a complete light subsist, as the oracles of the Chaldaeans affirm.
>
> — PROCLUS, *On the Timaeus of Plato*, iv, 242°

EVERY MONADIC ESSENCE, every monad, no matter where or in what period of time, is a learning entity, always advancing from the less to the more perfect. In any one cosmic manvantara it begins its evolutionary journey as an unself-conscious god-spark, passing through all the phases and experiences which that particular manvantara contains, and finishes as a fully perfected god.

During the course of our evolution in the various cosmic manvantaras as they succeed each other, it is part of our destiny ultimately to become a glorious sun in space — more particularly its soul or spirit, not so much its physical body, be it visible or invisible. And every such sun is composed of monads less evolved than it, godlings and atom-souls in the many degrees of their evolutionary development.

The spirit of our sun is surrounded by an army of these godlings not as old as itself, yet in many cases they are great spiritual beings when contrasted with men. In their turn these young gods are composed of other less evolved beings, although of a spiritual character; and so forth throughout the solar hierarchy until the physical body of the sun is reached, which contains atom-souls formed of light. These atom-souls, unself-conscious god-sparks, are all evolving continuously, and will with all other entities be ready to begin a new and higher cycle of experience at the opening of the new solar manvantara.

The constitution of the sun, just like that of a man, is built of monads, of atom-souls, which are pilgrims on the pathways of the spaces of Space, each one at its heart a god. Consequently, when our sun in distant cosmic times shall have become something still more wondrous, the atom-souls and monads which make up its vehicles now — and which form in part

---

°Cf. Cory's *Ancient Fragments*, p. 266 (2nd ed., London, 1832).

even the physical splendor that we see — will have become suns. Our present sun by then will be the divine essence infilling a galactic universe; and its atom-souls, and the younger gods and spiritual beings now belonging to and surrounding it, will be scattered through that universe as stars and suns, nebulae and planets.

The sun is immaterial in its higher parts. This does not mean that there is no matter there, for the sun is surrounded with veils of ethereal matter which produce our sunlight. What we see is the physical expression or reflection of a cosmic god — literally.°

The heart of the sun is a particle of mother-substance which is pure spirit. H.P.B. points to this by quoting from a private commentary:

> *The real substance of the concealed (Sun) is a nucleus of Mother substance. It is the heart and the matrix of all the living and existing Forces in our solar universe. It is the Kernel from which proceed to spread on their cyclic journeys all the Powers that set in action the atoms in their functional duties, and the focus within which they again meet in their* SEVENTH ESSENCE *every eleventh year. He who tells thee he has seen the sun, laugh at him as if he had said that the sun moves really onward on his diurnal path.*
>
> — *The Secret Doctrine,* I, 290

The heart of the sun is a dhyāni-buddha.

Now there is no contradiction in saying in one breath that the heart of the sun is a particle of mother-substance and that it is also a dhyāni-buddha. It is merely voicing two aspects of the same fundamental verity. The term dhyāni-buddha refers to the solar monad itself or the higher triad of the solar divinity; whereas the expression, "the heart of the sun is a particle of mother-substance," has reference to our visible orb, globe D of the solar chain. This particle of mother-substance (otherwise, spirit-matter, pradhāna or mūlaprakriti) is the substantial although spiritual focus in and through which the dhyāni-buddha of the sun lives and expresses its powers. Similarly, every one of the other globes of the solar chain has as its spiritually substantial heart such a particle of mother-substance through which the same solar monad manifests.

°Cf. *The Epinomis,* § 6, one of the "doubtful works" of Plato:
"For it is possible to conceive correctly that the whole Sun is larger than the whole earth, and that all the stars, which are borne along, possess a wonderful size. Let us then take into our thoughts what would be the method of any nature in causing so great a bulk to revolve for ever for the same time that it revolves at present. Now I assert that a god would be the cause, and that it could not be possible otherwise."

Furthermore, every globe of our earth chain is the dwelling and vehicle of a planetary spirit, and yet all the globes form a unity through which the still more evolved monad of the entire chain works, just as in man his divine monad exists in and works through all the subordinate monads of his constitution. We find here again the law of nature's composite structure, so that solar chain and earth chain, and man himself, are each one a microcosm repeating analogically what exists in the macrocosm. Thus every globe of the solar chain is an entity with its own seven element-principles, and each globe is ruled over and inspired by its own minor solar monad, all nevertheless being under the governance and supreme control of the still more sublime monad of the solar divinity.

That which we call the sun is but a physical reflection, a reflected essence of the real sun which to us is as invisible as air. What we see is merely the spiritual-electromagnetic flame of the working of the titanic energies and forces which the sun essentially is; and we perceive all this on the physical plane and imagine it to be the sun.° It is the sun's lowest, grossest aspect; yet even this aspect is only quasi-material or, rather, ethereal. In other words, the sun that we see is physical matter in its fifth, sixth, and seventh degrees of ethereality, these being the three highest degrees of matter on this physical cosmic plane.

Now it would appear that some students have taken the statement that the physical sun is but the reflection of the real sun, the solar monad, in a strictly literal sense, as when one speaks of seeing his reflection in a mirror; and thus have obtained the totally erroneous idea that what we see is not the sun at all but a kind of magical optical reflection cast in some mysterious way by the real sun which is situated somewhere

---

°Cf. *The Secret Doctrine*, I, 541.

It may be of some slight interest to include here the following passage from the *Vishnu-Purāna* (Bk. II, ch. viii), as it proves conclusively that the ancient Aryans knew the globular form of the earth and taught the heliocentric system. However, it was a secret temple-teaching in their days, and therefore was carefully veiled and often purposely contradicted.

"The sun is stationed, for all time, in the middle of the day, and over against midnight in all the *dwipas* [continents], Maitreya. But, the rising and the setting *of the sun* being perpetually opposite *to each other*, — and, in the same way, all the cardinal points, and so the cross-points, — Maitreya, people speak of the rising of the sun where they see it; and, where the sun disappears, there, *to them*, is his setting. Of the sun, which is always *in one and the same place*, there is neither setting nor rising; for what are called rising and setting are *only* the seeing and the not seeing the sun."

else in space! The sun *is* a reflection (much as the physical man is the reflection of the inner man), real enough to our physical eyes, yet not the *real* sun, which is invisible, a spiritual being, indeed a god, and therefore existing on a far higher plane than the physical plane of our solar universe.

Our sun is the globe D of the solar chain *as it appears on our subplane,* the fourth of the physical plane of the solar system. We should remember that the solar chain consists of seven or twelve globes, exactly as our earth chain does. The solar globe D is, in a certain sense, therefore, on *all* the subplanes of the physical plane of the solar system; in other words, it has an appearance, a certain form and certain qualities and attributes which are visible on, because belonging to, each one of the seven subplanes of this physical plane. Here again our sun as it appears on each such subplane is a reflection of the true sun on that subplane, and thus enlightens all the different planetary and other bodies existing in and on this physical plane of the solar system, whether we see them or not.

Now the solar globe D in *its* essence is a focus or mass of physical plane matter in this matter's highest or first state if we count downwards, or in its seventh state if we count upwards. This core of highly ethereal or even spiritual substance of the physical plane of the solar system surrounds itself with its veil of glory, *its* prakriti, which bears the same relation to it that prakriti does to Brahmā. This veil of the solar heart is therefore the matter of this physical plane of the solar system.

Again, this veil or second appearance of the heart of the true physical sun in its turn is surrounded by its own aura or veil, which is the third step downwards towards materialization. This third appearance likewise surrounds itself with its own auric garment; and it is this fourth veil of the heart or mother-substance of the physical sun which we see.°

We can continue in the same serial descending steps, with a new veil or reflection at each step until we reach the seventh and last stage of the physical sun, which is far beneath our own fourth subplane of the physical plane of our solar system, and is therefore as much outside the powers of our sense perception as is the highest substance of the sun.

°Cf. Plotinus, *On Gnostic Hypostases,* ix:

"No one therefore, will admit that light to be the sun, which proceeds from, and shines about it. For this light originates from the sun, and permanently surrounds it; but another light always proceeds from another prior to it, until it arrives as far as to us and the earth. All the light, however, which is about the sun, must be admitted to be situated in something else, in order that there may be no interval void of body after the sun."

From another standpoint, we can look upon the reflection of the physical sun that we see as its aura, i.e. its vital fluid surrounding and enclosing it so that it appears to us as a globe of splendorous light. In fact, we can say that it is that particular layer of the auric egg of the sun which is on the same subplane on which our earth and we as physical human beings are.

What I have stated with regard to the solar globe D applies, *mutatis mutandis*, to every one of the seven (or twelve) globes of the solar chain. Each one has the same series of appearances or veils on the cosmic plane on which it is.

It is these teachings that H. P. B. had in mind when quoting the following passage from the private commentary spoken of before:

Matter or Substance is septenary within our World, as it is so beyond it. Moreover, each of its states or principles is graduated into seven degrees of density. SÙRYA (the Sun), in its visible reflection, exhibits the first, or lowest state of the seventh, the highest state of the Universal PRESENCE, the pure of the pure, the first manifested Breath of the ever Unmanifested SAT (Be-ness). All the Central physical or objective Suns are in their substance the lowest state of the first Principle of the BREATH. Nor are any of these any more than the REFLECTIONS of their PRIMARIES which are concealed from the gaze of all but the Dhyan Chohans, whose Corporeal substance belongs to the fifth division of the seventh Principle of the Mother substance, and is, therefore, four degrees higher than the solar reflected substance. As there are seven Dhâtu (principal substances in the human body) so there are seven Forces in Man and in all Nature.
— The Secret Doctrine, I, 289–90

The same facts are hinted at by K. H. in *The Mahatma Letters* (pp. 164–5):

The fact is, that what you call the Sun is simply the reflection of the huge "store-house" of our System wherein ALL its forces are generated and preserved; the Sun being the heart and brain of our pigmy Universe, we might compare its *faculae* — those millions of small, intensely brilliant bodies of which the Sun's surface away from the spots is made up — with the blood corpuscles of that luminary — though some of them as correctly conjectured by science are as large as Europe. Those blood corpuscles are the electric and magnetic matter in its sixth and seventh state. . . . We *know* that the *invisible* Sun is composed of *that* which has neither name, nor can it be compared to anything known by your science — on earth; and that its "reflection" contains still less of anything like "gases," mineral matter, or *fire,* though even we when treating of it in your civilized tongue are compelled to use such expressions as "vapour" and "magnetic matter.". . . The Sun is neither a *solid* nor a *liquid,* nor yet a gaseous glow; but a gigantic ball of electromagnetic Forces, the store-house of universal *life* and *motion,* from which the latter pulsate in all directions, feeding the smallest atom as the greatest genius with the same material unto the end of the *Maha Yug.*

The time may not be too far distant when science will discover that the interiors of the various suns are not at all existing in conditions of incomprehensibly intense heat, although it is probably true enough that the outermost ethereal layers of the suns possess a certain amount of heat of their own, as a result of chemical processes. The heart of any sun is a most marvelous alchemical laboratory in which occur molecular, atomic, and electronic changes which it would be utterly impossible to reproduce in any of our chemical workshops.° The interiors of the suns are not superheated imaginary furnaces, chemical or alchemical or otherwise, and the future will see intuitions of this great truth dawning upon the minds of our scientists. Every sun is the outward vehicle of an indwelling spiritual and intellectual presence — the solar logos — having its sublime dwelling place in the hidden recesses of the solar chain. Our sun is a cosmic atom and, just as every atom on the infinitesimal scale, it is ensouled by its own spiritual-intellectual 'life-atom,' at the core of which there resides a divine monad of stellar origin and character.

°Cf. H.P.B.'s reply to the question, "Is the sun merely a cooling mass?" published in *The Theosophist,* September 1883, pp. 299–301.

SUNSPOTS AND THE CIRCULATIONS OF THE SOLAR SYSTEM

The Sun is the heart of the Solar World (System) and its brain is hidden behind the (visible) Sun. From thence, sensation is radiated into every nerve-centre of the great body, and the waves of the life-essence flow into each artery and vein. . . . The planets are its limbs and pulses. (Commentary)
— The Secret Doctrine, I, 541

WHAT ARE THE SUNSPOTS? Similarly, one might ask, what are the pores of the human skin? The sunspots are the outer mouths of channels through which the rivers of lives go forth from and re-enter the sun. They are the openings (if we do not distort this word too greatly) through which the sun expels to the remotest corners of its system its accumulated store of solar vitality; and it is this vitality which gives life to all things within the sun's aura, which extends even to the farthest boundaries of the solar system. It is through the sunspots again that the solar 'blood,' the solar energy, electricity or psychomagnetism, returns to be purified in the heart which sent it forth some twelve years previously.

The sunspot periodicity is usually reckoned at 11.2 of our years; but it has been found that this is not always exact. Strictly speaking, the cycle of sunspots is ten years, but the current of vitality which governs it requires another year to pass through the sun, and still another one for its return through the sun, which makes twelve years all told. Each cycle is a vibration, a new beat of the pulse of the sun. The sun is a heart, a beating heart; in another sense, it is a brain. There is a temptation to use the words heart and brain literally, and such usage wanders not far from fact. But it is not the physical globe which is the true head and heart, except insofar as the physical universe is concerned. The real head and the real heart, coalescing and working as one, are the divinity behind and above and within the physical vehicle of our glorious daystar.

The statement that the sun is both the heart and the brain of the solar system may seem puzzling, because in the human body they are two different organs. In biological science, however, there are entities known which have no such distinct organs, combining in one what in our body is separated into two. The living cell is such an example; and from a certain standpoint our visible solar orb is a cosmic living cell. Even in ourselves the flow of substances and energies from our spiritual monad through the astral body into the physical body is really a stream of consciousness, which because of its functioning brings about our relatively high degree of development in the evolutionary scale; and this stream is divided into two currents, one the mānasic, and the other the buddhi-prānic which has its locus in the human heart. Similarly the same stream of consciousness flowing from the spiritual monad includes other attributes or functions which need their corresponding organs in our bodies in order to express themselves; and so it comes about that we have a stomach and a nervous system and an arterial circulatory system, and so forth.

Thus our sun contains and expresses the solar manas, its brain, and also the solar buddhi-prāna, its heart; and just as in man's physical body heart and brain work in coordination, although through two distinct organs, so in the sun do heart and brain work coordinately but in a union of these two functions of the solar monad.

In the distant aeons of the future we shall lose the physical body that now we possess; we shall then have egg-shaped or globe-shaped bodies of glowing light, in which will abide both heart and mind of the entity, each separate and yet both coalescing in operation as one. We shall be highly intelligent entities, far more so than now — far more intellectual and far more spiritual.

As H.P.B. explained it:°

If the "Adepts" are asked: "What then, in your views, is the nature of our sun and what is there beyond that cosmic veil?" — they answer: *beyond* rotates and beats the *heart and head* of our system; externally is spread its robe, the nature of which is not matter, whether solid, liquid, or gaseous, such as you are acquainted with, but *vital* electricity, condensed and made visible. . . . Undoubtedly were the "robes," the dazzling drapery which now envelopes the whole of the sun's globe withdrawn, . . . our whole universe would be reduced to ashes. *Jupiter Fulminator* revealing himself to his beloved would incinerate her instantly. But it can never be. The protecting shell is of a thickness, and at a distance from the universal HEART that can hardly be ever calculated by your mathematicians.

As the heart and brain of its entire system, the sun sends a twelve-faceted life into every atom of its own solar universe of which we form

---

°*The Theosophist*, September 1883, p. 300.

an integral part. The sun is pre-eminently a giver of life. Cosmogonically, it is our elder brother, and not at all our physical parent as scientific speculations would have it; yet it is also in a vital sense our father-mother, because through the sun come down the invigorating life streams from systems and worlds above ours. And our planet Terra, as well as all the other planets, receives its own share of these life-giving streams, precisely as every individual atom and every entity does on the microcosmic scale, while at the same time receiving them individually from the inmost of the inmost within itself. The sun is a storehouse of vital-electric energies and, as the great pulsating heart of its system, vitalizes and informs the endless hosts of beings under its systemic sway.

In one of the most illuminating passages from her pen, H.P.B. writes in *The Secret Doctrine* (I, 541–2):

> Thus, there is a regular circulation of the vital fluid throughout our system, of which the Sun is the heart — the same as the circulation of the blood in the human body — during the manvantaric solar period, or life; the Sun contracting as rhythmically at every return of it, as the human heart does. Only, instead of performing the round in a second or so, it takes the solar blood ten of its years, and a whole year to pass through its *auricles* and *ventricles* before it washes the *lungs* and passes thence to the great veins and arteries of the system.
>
> This, Science will not deny, since Astronomy knows of the fixed cycle of eleven years when the number of solar spots increases, *which is due to the contraction* of the Solar HEART. The universe (our world in this case) breathes, just as man and every living creature, plant, and even mineral does upon the earth; and as our globe itself breathes every twenty-four hours. . . . It is similar to the regular and healthy pulsation of the heart, as the life fluid passes through its hollow muscles. Could the human heart be made luminous, and the living and throbbing organ be made visible, so as to have it reflected upon a screen, such as used by the astronomers in their lectures — say for the moon — then every one would see the Sun-spot phenomenon repeated every second — due to its contraction and the rushing of the blood.

The periodicity of the sunspots coincides with the mean periods not only of the planets nearest the earth, but of all the planets of our solar system — those which are visible as well as the scores of planets which are invisible. As our sun is the pulsing heart and the sensitive brain of our solar world, consequently every movement of its heart is intimately related to and in exact synchronous accord with every other movement, great or small, which takes place within the members of its solar family.

Every celestial body, be it sun, nebula, comet or planet, is the manifestation of a god. All these divine beings — cosmic, solar or planetary — are organs or members within the life of the spiritual sun, the supreme divinity of our solar system. In using these terms, gods, cosmic or planetary spirits, etc., no reference is made to the physical body of any celestial orb, whether we see it or not, but to its indwelling life, its indwelling spiritual, intellectual and vital essence. The solar system, from one standpoint, can truly be looked upon as a vital-mechanical organic entity, functioning in its physical and astral aspects as a mechanism, but a mechanism which is, nevertheless, ensouled by spiritual beings greatly varying in evolutionary degree.

The giant planet Jupiter, especially in its time periods, has a particular relation to the cycle of sunspot maxima and minima. Jupiter's year is some twelve (11.86) of our years. There is a large body of most interesting facts showing the connection between the sunspot cycles and the orbital periods of the planets, for their respective 'years' are as precisely geared together, both causally and effectually, as are the interlocking wheels of some intricate physical mechanism. When we remember that our sun is at once the heart and the brain of our solar system and that it is both a giver as well as a receiver of the vitality of that system — and of those far higher powers and potencies thereof which we call spiritual, intellectual and psychical — we can perhaps picture the relations of sunspot periods to the respective planetary 'years.'

Doubtless the mathematicians or astronomers of the future will discover this close cyclical relation of the planetary 'years' with the sunspot periods; possibly the rule of the lowest common multiple will be a hint to those of a mathematical bent of mind in discovering how the planets work together with the sun towards a common ultimate destiny in the evolutionary scheme.

Now in and out of these sunspots steadily flow — and at certain periods in veritable inrushes and outrushes — not only streams of lives, but their involved masses of psychomagnetic-vital powers. These rivers of lives are intimately connected with the planetary periods in which the respective positions taken by the planets at different times (what astrologers would call aspects) mark critical points in the interlocking celestial mechanics of the solar system. The term celestial mechanics does not here refer to mere mechanisms, but applies directly to the circulations and interblendings of the various planetary magnetisms, coalescing with the magnetism of the sun itself.

The great as well as all smaller cycles on earth are the effects of cosmic causes, which causes at the beginning of their operations are marked by the positions of the different planets in their orbits and by their aspects to the sun. It is stated in ancient Hindu books that at the opening of kali yuga certain planets, including our earth, were grouped together in one of the zodiacal signs, aspecting certain other planets, thus powerfully affecting the sun which in turn likewise reacted upon such grouping.[13] This took place at the end of the dwāpara yuga and the opening of the kali, which important event was marked in history by the death of the avatāra Krishna.

When it is said that every planet in the solar system has its individual influence on the period of the sunspots and, conversely, the sunspot cycle is intimately connected with and influences the vital activities of all the planets, visible or invisible, this does not imply that either the visible or the invisible planets have attributes of inferiority or of superiority. Visibility simply means that our eyes, because of having evolved on this plane, can see certain celestial bodies belonging to this plane: just as our eyes can take in a certain range of electromagnetic vibrations which we call light. There are other ranges of electromagnetic vibrations which we sense as heat; and still others which are the X rays, cosmic rays, etc.

The sunspots may be described as windows through which we may get a vague glimpse into the temple-body of a living god, thus seeing a little way into the dark invisible heart of the sun. We may think of them as channels, openings or vents, which serve for the entrance into the sun, and for the ejection from it, of rivers of lives of many grades. Every monad of all the countless myriads which infill the solar system, must pass again and again at cyclic periods into and through the solar heart, and come out therefrom; just as in the human body, every atom of every molecule of every drop of blood must pass into and through the heart, and leave it again to pursue its destiny along the circulations of the body.

What brought the sun into being in the beginning? What governs its course? What is the cause of its incessant outpouring of energy? To begin with, there is a suggestive passage in *The Mahatma Letters* (p. 168):

The sun gives *all* and takes back *nothing* from its system. The sun gathers nothing "at the poles" — which are always free even from the famous "red flames" at all times, not only during the eclipses. . . . Nothing can reach the sun from *without* the boundaries of its own system in the shape of such *gross* matter as

303

"attenuated gases." Every bit of matter in all its *seven* states is necessary to the vitality of the various and numberless systems — worlds in formation, suns awakening anew to life, etc., and they have none to spare even for their best neighbours and next of kin. They are mothers, not stepmothers, and would not take away one crumb from the nutrition of their children. . . . For indeed, there is but one thing — radiant energy which is *inexhaustible* and knows neither increase nor decrease and will go on with its self-generating work to the end of the Solar manvantara.

Every sun is a living entity, and it derives from within itself its streams of energy, which it is so unceasingly pouring into space through billions and even trillions of years. Atomic dissociation may, from a mechanical point of view, account to a certain degree for the *modus,* but does not explain the origin of the solar energy, all of which on its way outward feeds the entire solar system with life, with spirit, with psychical powers. For however great may be its physical influence, it is very minor as compared with the enormous part that the sun plays in the invisible realms. The vitality, the intellectual power, together with the spiritual energy that the sun ceaselessly emanates, are all derived from the god which is its heart. And this god should not be thought of as being solely at the core of the physical sun, but rather as being in the invisible realms and spheres. So, too, the real man does not dwell in his physical body, for it is but the reflection of the real man who lives and acts and, strictly speaking, moves in the invisible parts of his constitution.

Energy or force and matter are fundamentally one. What is force to us is substance on a higher plane; what is matter on our plane is force or energy on a plane inferior to ours. Deduction: could we trace the reach of the energies flowing forth from the sun and extending to the outermost bounds of its kingdom, and could we do this by rising to a higher plane, we would see the 'empty space' of our solar system as one vast substantial body. And could we glimpse this apparently substantial energy through a telescope, from some distant planet circling round some distant star, we would see it as an 'irresolvable nebula.' This would be simply the flood of energy, of life, of vitality, of substance, pouring forth from the heart of the sun, and returning to it in regular cyclic intervals through the circulations of the cosmos — the pathways which all entities follow in passing from planet to planet, and from planet to sun, and from sun on their returning journey to planet: a circulation truly of the lifeblood or life essence of the solar system.

SOLAR AND TERRESTRIAL MAGNETISM

The two poles are said to be the store-houses, the receptacles and libera-
tors, at the same time, of Cosmic and terrestrial Vitality (Electricity); from
the surplus of which the Earth, had it not been for these two natural
"safety-valves," would have been rent to pieces long ago.
                                                   — *The Secret Doctrine*, I, 205

THERE IS A VERY close connection between the sunspot cycle and terrestrial
magnetism, particularly at the two poles of the earth, although there exists
a very important difference of quality in the respective polar magnetisms.

To use the ancient metaphor, there is a Door of Horn and a Door
of Ivory through which enter and leave the earth, not only celestial
influences, but also the souls of men and other beings. Mystical Greek
and Roman writers said that through the Door of Horn came and went
one class of entities and influences, while through the Door of Ivory an
opposite class came and went.° The Door of Horn is the portal of ingress,
the north pole; and the Door of Ivory or south pole is the earth's vent
or door of egress. All things that are good, elevating, and spiritual, belong
to the north pole; and all things that are evil, degrading, and unclean,
pertain to the vent of the earth, the south pole.

The eleven-year sunspot cycle affects each of the planets of the solar
family through their north and south poles. The magnetism which reaches
us from the sun — physical, astral, as well as mental — enters the earth
through the north pole; it then follows certain circulations within and

---

°Cf. Virgil, *Aeneid*, VI, 893–6:
"Two gates there are of sleep, of which the one is of horn, whence easy exit
is given to the true shades, but the other shining in white ivory; thence the Manes
send deceiving dreams skywards."
Also Homer, *Odyssey*, XIX, 560 *et seq.*:
"Stranger, verily dreams are hard, and hard to be discerned; nor are all things
therein fulfilled for men. Twain are the gates of shadowy dreams, the one is fashioned
of horn and one of ivory. Such dreams as pass through the portals of sawn ivory
are deceitful, and bear tidings that are unfulfilled. But the dreams that come forth
through the gates of polished horn bring a true issue, whosoever of mortals beholds
them."

around the earth, and leaves it at the other pole. All these magnetic circulations pass around the equator a certain number of times, whether they be brief or of longer duration.

The earth follows very closely the breathing of the sun, very closely indeed, because the entire solar system is an animate organism of which the planets are the organs. It is likewise true that the earth has many periodic circulations smaller than the sunspot cycle, such as the lunar cycle, but these pertain more particularly to the intimate family life of the earth. All movements throughout boundless Space are cyclical in character, whether they last for an infinitesimal fraction of a second or as long as the cosmic manvantara itself. Everything is cyclic. The life of a firefly is as cyclic as is the life of a human being or the periodic revolution of a planet around the sun.

Terrestrial magnetism is of course connected with the nature and characteristics of the aurora borealis at the north pole as well as the aurora australis at the south pole — both the geographic and the magnetic poles at either end of the earth being involved. The aurorae are manifestations of the psychomagnetic vitality of the earth, and are most intimately linked with the sun, and particularly with the sunspots and, in a somewhat less close relationship, with the seven sacred planetary chains. They are psychomagnetic phenomena, and therefore we must never regard them as *merely* electric and magnetic displays or outbursts.

As a matter of fact, both aurorae are very much involved with the peregrinations of the simply numberless hosts of monads constantly entering and leaving our globe, yet doing so at certain stated periods in far greater numbers or masses — as inrushes and as outrushes; and the auroral displays, i.e. the psychomagnetic and vital outbursts, usually come about during these periods of inrush and outrush.

The auroral phenomena, being so closely associated with the mysterious operations of the terrestrial vitality, are connected with some of the most occult facts concerning the destiny of the earth as well as of all its families of monads. I might add that were it not for the relief given by these psycho-electromagnetic effluxes and influxes, our mother-globe would suffer catastrophes of the most appalling kind. Like earthquakes, however disastrous these at times may be, the auroral discharges in one of their functions dissipate what would otherwise become an overaccumulation of magnetic and electric energy within the earth; and thus they save it from catastrophes so terrible — physical, psychical and astral — that research in all recorded history could find no parallel to what would occur if such dispersion of energy did not take place.

These currents of magnetism and of vitality manifest not only at the poles, but likewise at what are known as the four cardinal points: north, south, east, and west. Hindu mythology speaks of them as the four Maharajas, and these are represented both in our physical world and in the entire solar system.

What are the cardinal points? Do such points actually exist in space, to which the sun and the planets of our solar system conform directionally? Why is it that the plane of the ecliptic contains within itself all the planets of our solar system, and why does it pass through the sun?

It is the spinning earth itself which produces the cardinal points so far as this globe is concerned, and this rotation is caused by the entry into it at its north pole of spiritual and psychomagnetic energies; for electricity, and magnetism perhaps especially, pursue a circuitous or serpentine path, somewhat like that of a spiral, and the entity through which it flows follows the circular impulse given to it and therefore whirls or rotates.

But this is not all. The poles of the earth point at various times to different parts of the celestial sphere — the abysses of space surrounding us on all sides. The pointing of the north pole is caused by the attracting influences emanating from that quarter of the celestial sphere towards which that pole may be directed at any time. This pointing gives us the cardinal north, and its direct opposite the cardinal south, with east and west at right angles to them. You may remember that in more than one of the *Dialogues* of Plato, that great initiate describes the cosmic cross, which Greek manuscripts usually show as having somewhat the shape of the Greek cross. This is the cross in space on which the cosmic consciousness is 'crucified.'

The cardinal points per se are not at all four limited concrete points in space, i.e. four centers of force or energy to which the earth is attracted especially by its north pole. The opposite is the case. All the points of the vault of space considered as a sphere are pointed to in serial rotation by the earth's north pole. The instinct to point arises from within the earth's inner constitution, but at the same time the north pole is attracted by the influences emanating from the spacial sphere. The cardinal points therefore result from the mutual and interchanging influences between earth and the twelve main directions of space.

The earth as a magnet is infilled with the solar energies streaming continuously from our daystar through the entire solar system. This solar magnetism is septenary and enters the earth in the region of the north pole. Certain elements of this magnetism pass directly from pole to pole through the center of the earth, while other parts sweep around or over its surface, but always from north to south.° Furthermore, there are crosscurrents which this solar magnetism follows in its circulations in and around the earth, and these crosscurrents, although flowing from the north pole, take a slanting or oblique direction, always from northeast to southwest, pursuing their course around the earth and swinging back again to the north pole.

If we could see these lines of magnetic force, they would appear to us as streaming in from outer space, impacting the earth at its north pole, rebounding thence and sweeping around all the surface of the globe, towards the south pole — where a portion is sucked in and returns to the north pole, again to be sent forth. Thus the circulation continues. But not all the magnetism is sucked in at the south pole; a portion of it streams outwards, cone-like, into space, and ultimately returns to the sun from which it came.

°There are certain currents which flow more strongly or with greater volume at night, and others do so during the day. These currents affect man very little indeed when he is standing, for then he is awake; his body is highly charged with the magnetic energies flowing forth from within his own being, from the mānasic and astral-vital vehicles of his constitution, and these are powerful enough during the day to offset — not neutralize — the solar currents as these follow their pathways around the earth.

At night things are very different. The body as a rule is tired and its individual magnetic energy is greatly reduced. Consequently the body is much more subject to the solar electromagnetic currents of energy. That is why it is best to sleep with the head towards the north or northeast, so that the body may be in corresponding polarity of circulation with the magnetism of the earth as it passes from pole to pole. The head is the positive pole and the feet form the negative pole, just as the north pole of the earth is positive and the south pole negative.

THE TRIADIC LIFE OF FATHER SUN

> It must be remembered that every cosmogony has a *trinity* of workers
> at its head — Father, spirit; Mother, nature, or matter; and the manifested
> universe, the Son or result of the two.   — *Isis Unveiled*, II, 420-1

THE LIFE OF THE SUN, considered as a unity, infills the whole of its kingdom
with the vital effluxes flowing forth from all parts of the solar chain.
This solar life for the time being we may consider as septenary, the three
higher aspects or planes being spiritual, and the four lower planes being
ethereal, of which the lowest parts are concretely physical. The upper
triadic life-consciousness of the sun is often spoken of as Brahmā-Vishnu-
Śiva, corresponding to what in the human principles are ātman-buddhi-
manas. Hence this triad is relatively arūpa, and itself flows forth from
the highest parts of the solar constitution, thus making the tenfold (or
indeed twelvefold) fullness of the solar being.

Such a triad, usually recognized as being solar in essential character,
was known in all the ancient religious and philosophical systems under
different names. These various triads are not all referable to the same
cosmic planes; nevertheless, a lower triad corresponds on its own planes
with a triad conceived as being on superior planes. For example, the
Egyptian triad of Osiris-Isis-Horus has similarities in many respects both
to the Hindu triad of Brahmā-Vishnu-Śiva and also to the Christian Trinity.
Yet, plane for plane, this last triad is a more perfect correspondence with
the Parabrahman-mūlaprakriti, Brahman-pradhāna, and Brahmā (Purusha)-prakriti of Hindu philosophy: the Father corresponding with Parabrahman-mūlaprakriti; the Holy Spirit or Holy Ghost with Brahman-
pradhāna; and the Son with Brahmā (Purusha)-prakriti.

It may be said in passing that this order of the so-called procession
of the Trinity — Father-Holy Spirit-Son — is that of the earliest Christian
thought, to which the Greek Orthodox Church, faithful to the pagan
tradition from which Christianity came, has always held. However, the
Church of Rome from even an early period has preferred to consider
the two latter Persons of the Trinity as proceeding from the Father in

the order of first the Son and then the Holy Ghost, and this has been accepted by the various churches of the West. This difference in viewpoint was one of the main causes of the theological schism between the Greek Orthodox and the Roman Church and brought about the *filioque* controversy — a Latin word meaning 'and from the son' — the idea being that the Holy Ghost proceeded from the Father *and from the Son.*

All these triads are really solar in character when they are properly understood. As a matter of fact, Parabrahman-mūlaprakriti and correspondentially the Father of the Christian Trinity are the First Cosmic Logos; Brahman-pradhāna and likewise the Holy Spirit are the Second Cosmic Logos; and Brahmā (Purusha)-prakriti and the Son are the Third Cosmic Logos. On the other hand, the Egyptian triad of Osiris-Isis-Horus really originates in or emanates from the Third Cosmic Logos, just as does the Hindu triad of Brahmā-Vishnu-Śiva.

These observations are made solely for the purpose of showing an accurate series of correspondences of solar gods as taught among various ancient peoples. Even though all these triads have reference to *our* solar system only, they would apply with perfect propriety to the universal solar system, in which case of course they would be conceived of as being of far greater magnitude and sublimity.

The facts of nature are equally true on different planes, the system of triads being as much a fact in the divine and spiritual as it is in the intellectual realms. Making, however, an application of thought directly to our solar system, we can see that all these triads as they were revered in their respective times and countries are virtually the same solar triad differently named, and are derivatives from the Third Cosmic Logos, the Third Logos of our solar system. Furthermore, because of the analogical structure of the universe, their correspondences in the human constitution are: ātman, ātman-buddhi, buddhi-manas.

All such triadic unities are reflections or reproductions by analogy of the still higher cosmic triad which, because of its deeply abstract character, was rarely, if ever, worshiped by the populace as these reflected triads were. This highest cosmic triad was referred to only occasionally, as Pythagoras did when he spoke of the cosmic monad as being forever in "silence and darkness" — meaning that it was beyond all ordinary human conception.

To illustrate: any cosmos or universe is a ten-principled being, the three highest principles forming the supernal triad, from which emanates the lower septenary (or manifested units) of the decad. This septenary in turn is formed of an upper triad and a lower quaternary — and it is just this upper triad which was envisaged when the ancients spoke of their triadic divinities, such as Brahmā-Vishnu-Śiva, Osiris-Isis-Horus, Father-Holy Spirit-Son. This second triad is thus seen to be the reflection of the first or supernal triad of a cosmos or Brahmānda.

It is of interest to note that the second Person of virtually every one of these triads has been pictured in the exoteric religions and mythologies as being of a feminine character, as is Isis in the Egyptian triad. In fact, the same feminine characteristics of the second Individual originally applied to the Christian Trinity, for the Holy Spirit or Holy Ghost, although appearing masculine in name or title, was originally considered to be a feminine cosmic power or influence.[14] It was only when Christianity became dogmatic and crystallized in theological forms that the feminine character of the second Person became distinctly masculinized.

Even in the Hindu triad of Brahmā-Vishnu-Śiva, while Vishnu is commonly considered to be a masculine type-form of divinity, many of his attributes and functions are feminine, so that the spirit of the idea prevails despite the fact that the gender of the name of the second Person is masculine.

Now these different triads may be considered either as the feminine spirit emanating from the first Individual and in turn, because infilled with the seeds from above, giving origin to the third Individual; or as three coordinate and mutually interacting aspects of the cosmic life. Thus in the human constitution we may look upon buddhi as emanating from ātman and in turn giving birth to manas, in serial order; or we may look upon all three, ātman, buddhi, manas, as acting coordinately and at the same time as the higher triad of man. The first shows their derivation in origin; the second how they cooperate in unitary action.

The triadic life of the solar system expresses itself as Father Sun, our solar system in its entirety being a solar monad of which the sun is the heart. Father Sun is the spiritual part of that heart. It is this threefold spiritual energy which produces the sun; it is not the sun which originates it. The solar divinity, although manifesting through its chain of twelve globes, dwells apart in the heart of each one of them, much as the soul of man dwells apart in the core of the human being.

Father Sun, then, is a convenient expression which adequately describes several points of teaching. Not only does it have direct reference to the solar divinity of *our* solar system, but it can also be used on certain occasions for what H. P. B. called the "astrological star" of a man:°

The star under which a human Entity is born, says the Occult teaching, will remain for ever its star, throughout the whole cycle of its incarnations in one Manvantara. But *this is not his astrological star.* The latter is concerned and connected with the *personality*, the former with the INDIVIDUALITY. The "Angel" of that Star, or the Dhyani-Buddha will be either the guiding or simply the presiding "Angel," so to say, in every new rebirth of the monad, *which is part of his own essence*, though his vehicle, man, may remain for ever ignorant of this fact.

The spiritual star, on the other hand, "the star under which a human Entity is born," involves a sublime mystery. It is that particular sun or star in our home-universe or galaxy of which man's divine monad is the offspring, and with which star in consequence the man is connected in most intimate spiritual relations throughout the virtual eternity of the galactic manvantara.

At other times, when speaking of the solar divinity, I have used this term Father Sun in the sense of the peregrinations on the outer rounds of the spiritual monad in, through, and from the solar chain which includes all its globes. Just as the human father contains in his body, as passing through it, the life germ, to become in the proper environment the beginning of the body of the child-to-be, so does the sun receive into itself all the spiritual and indeed other monads in its kingdom (and therefore likewise does globe D of the solar chain, our visible sun), and after due course of time send them forth again to complete their outer rounds along the circulations of the cosmos. Insofar as our sun's visible globe is concerned, these rivers of lives or streams of monads enter it at its north pole and are expelled from its heart through the sunspots.

The heart of Father Sun is a ray of the Absolute, using the word Absolute in the theosophical sense. Father Sun, could it manifest the full influence and power of this divine ray, would indeed have every faculty, every power, that the universe enshrines. Not only Father Sun, but each human being, has this divine ray within, its inner god. In the case of the sun, what we see is but the physical encasement, a ball of cosmic forces, electricity and superelectricity. A sun is also full of psychical and

---

°*The Secret Doctrine*, I, 572–3.

spiritual forces, each according to its own plane, for there is the inner sun and the outer sun.

This solar divinity is the spiritual and intellectual parent of all the numberless hosts of entities throughout the solar system. From it we came in the far, far past; and to it we shall return in the far distant future, when the evolutionary course of our solar system shall approach its term. When the last cosmic moment comes, the entire solar system — gods, monads, and atoms, sun, planets, and the various moons, as they then shall exist — will suddenly vanish as a shadow that passes along a white wall and is seen no more.

The cause of all this is the withdrawal of the vitality from every atomic entity throughout the range of the solar cosmos; and once the vitality is gone, the whole structure falls to pieces, disappears, and the solar system with all its hosts of entities passes into paranirvana.° There it will remain until the hour strikes on the cosmic clock for a new solar system to emerge from the womb of Space — the child, the reimbodied entity, the karmic consequence of the solar system that was.

In his treatise *On Isis and Osiris* (ix), Plutarch, the ancient Greek philosopher, biographer and initiate, at one time priest of the Delphic

---

°When scientific thinkers speculate on the alleged dying sun, and wonder when it will be extinguished through loss of heat, as they think, they might find a hint or two in the words of H.P.B.:

"No, we say; no, while there is one man left on the globe, the sun will not be extinguished. Before the hour of the 'Solar Pralaya' strikes on the watch-tower of Eternity, all the other worlds of our system will be gliding in their spectral shells along the silent paths of Infinite Space. Before it strikes, Atlas, the mighty Titan, the son of Asia and the nursling of Aether, will have dropped his heavy manvantaric burden and — died; the Pleïades, the bright seven Sisters, will have upon awakening hiding Sterope to grieve with them — *to die themselves for their father's loss.* And, Hercules, *moving off his left leg,* will have to shift his place in heavens and erect his own funeral pile. Then only, surrounded by the fiery element breaking through the thickening gloom of the *Pralayan* twilight, will Hercules, *expiring amidst a general conflagration,* bring on likewise the death of our Sun: *he will have unveiled by moving off the* 'CENTRAL SUN' — the mysterious, the ever-hidden centre of attraction of our Sun and System. Fables? Mere poetical fiction? Yet, when one knows that the most exact sciences, the greatest mathematical and astronomical truths went forth into the world among the *hoi polloi* sent out by the initiated priests, the Hierophants of the *sanctum sanctorum* of the old temples, under the guise of religious fables, it may not be amiss to search for universal truths even under the patches of fiction's harlequinade." — *The Theosophist,* Sept. 1883, p. 301

313

Apollo, tells us that over the portal of the Temple of Isis in Egypt the following mystical words were engraven in everlasting stone:[15]

[Isis] am I; all that was, all that is, all that ever will be. And no one of mortals has ever discovered my garment.

As will be noticed, our rendering of this famous inscription differs somewhat from the one usually given: "... and no mortal has ever lifted my veil." This is an important difference, because it introduces a new significance to the meaning of the Greek phrase, really more close to the deep esoteric sense of this majestic declaration. It is noteworthy that Plutarch ends this inscription after the words "discovered my garment," whereas Proclus, the well-known Neoplatonic philosopher, says that it also contained the further words:°

The fruit that I brought forth became the sun.

There are two explanations of this statement. The first is that the eternal wisdom or Sophia, which has always been, now is, and always will be, is the virgin-mother of initiates: a mother always fertile, always bringing forth a constant, uninterrupted series of buddha-like men. This is the ancient wisdom, a wisdom ever enduring, a representation in human terms of the operation, structure, and very nature of the universe — divine, spiritual, astral and physical. Such was the mystic Isis.

What is the fruit that this wisdom is continually yielding by a process of becoming, of growth, of evolving forth what is within? "Sons of the Sun" — a literal truth! For as every human being in the core of his essence is a sun, destined in future aeons to become one of the stellar host besprinkling the spaces of Space, so even from the very first instant when the divine-spiritual monad begins its peregrinations throughout universal Being, it is already a sun in embryo, and is furthermore a child of some other sun that then existed in space. Initiation brings forth in the neophyte this inner, latent, stellar energy from the womb of the virgin-mother, Sophia, the ancient wisdom, who is at once the 'mother,' 'sister,' 'daughter,' and 'wife,' of the man-god whom initiation thus brings to birth. Here is the key to the mystery of the virgin birth.

The second significance of this ancient inscription is the following: Isis, particularly in her more mystical aspect as Neith or Nephthys, is

---

° *On the Timaeus of Plato*, I, 82.

the cosmic ākāśa, eternally virgin yet ever giving being to the universes which begem the skies. From the deeps of Space — the cosmic ākāśa, the virgin Isis — are born the suns; for the cosmic goddess-mother of any solar system can truly be made to say: "The fruit that I brought forth became the sun." Such a sun is the seed — even as the acorn is the seed of an oak — for future hosts of solar gods. Osiris is the cosmic spirit in its energic aspect, at once the 'father,' 'brother,' 'husband' and 'son' of the goddess Isis, the other aspect of the cosmic spirit; just as the fiery spirit of life, no matter where it may be, even in a seed, is the impelling force which brings out the evolutionary tendencies lying latent within. Therefore is Osiris called the cosmic seed, and Isis is the divine mother of it.

There is a third way of looking at this profound Egyptian teaching wherein Isis signifies the mystical moon, and the children of the moon are each one of them on the way to becoming a sun.

Every one of us is a child of the sun: from it we issued forth in the far distant aeons of the past, and to it we shall return in the far distant aeons of the future, but will do so as gods. Through initiation, if a man pass successfully the tests, his spirit will wing its way from earth through moon and planets to the portals of the sun, penetrate to its heart, then deeper still into the invisible realms and regions, and return finally to his entranced body, waiting for him, and kept alive by the sublime magic of the Hierarchy of Wisdom and Compassion. For a short time thereafter his face will shine with light, his body with splendor; and this is the meaning of the archaic saying that after the three days' trance the "man's face shone with glory," and he appeared as if he were "clothed with the sun."

Yet in order to pass the portals of the sun we must first learn to pass through the portals of our inner god, our inner spiritual sun. For verily there is a portion of our constitution which is composed of solar substance. How could the spirit-soul of man pass the portals of the sublimest entity of our solar system — pass them self-consciously and with safety — unless that spirit-soul itself were of the same essence and being as that of the sun? Anything inferior to the sun, when approaching it closely, would be annihilated. None can enter the sun who is not already a full-grown child of the sun: of the same essence, of the same quality or substance, and therefore possessing potentially the same titanic energy. We sprang from it, and we shall return to it before our pilgrimage in the solar system is fully complete. Back to it we shall go, and then we shall surrender

315

the solar part of us to the sun from which we received it. In each one of the seven sacred planets, as we wing our way sunwards, we shall leave what we took from it: dust to dust, Moon to Moon, Venus to Venus, Mercury to Mercury, Mars to Mars, Jupiter to Jupiter, Saturn to Saturn, Sun to Sun — and then each one will return to his parent star, a 'parent star' only because that star is HIMSELF.

THE TWELVE SACRED PLANETS

It is then the "Seven Sons of Light" — called after their planets and (by the rabble) often identified with them — namely Saturn, Jupiter, Mercury, Mars, Venus, and — *presumably* for the modern critic, who goes no deeper than the surface of old religions — the Sun and Moon, which are, according to the Occult teachings, our heavenly Parents, or "Father," synthetically. Hence, as already remarked, polytheism is really more philosophical and correct, as to fact and nature, than anthropomorphic monotheism. Saturn, Jupiter, Mercury, and Venus, the four exoteric planets, and the three others, which must remain unnamed, were the heavenly bodies in direct astral and psychic communication with the Earth, its Guides, and Watchers — morally and physically; the visible orbs furnishing our Humanity with its outward and inward characteristics, and their "Regents" or *Rectors* with our Monads and spiritual faculties. In order to avoid creating new misconceptions, let it be stated that among the three *secret* orbs (or star-angels) neither Uranus nor Neptune entered; not only because they were unknown under these names to the ancient Sages, but because they, as all other planets, however many there may be, are the *gods* and guardians of other septenary chains of globes within our systems. — *The Secret Doctrine*, I, 575

ARCHAIC OCCULTISM knew that our complete solar Egg of Brahmā contains many more planets — i.e. planetary chains — than those which astronomers are acquainted with; and more suns than our own brilliant daystar. Hence in my earlier writings I have called our solar universe in its fullest occult sense the universal solar system; and used the term solar system for our *own* sun and the planetary chains which belong to its kingdom.

There are literally scores of planetary chains in the universal solar system, and others in our *own* solar system that we do not know of, some of which in either case are much higher than our earth chain, and some much lower. Likewise there are many planets belonging to our Rāja sun, some of them inhabited, some man-bearing like earth, some bearing no men, and yet we do not see them because they exist on cosmic planes either superior or inferior to our own. There are planetary chains of which we do not see even the lowest globe, for the reason that it is above our cosmic plane; just as there are planetary chains so far beneath us that even the highest globe of these chains is below our cosmic plane. For instance, if a planetary chain has its fourth globe on the sixth cosmic plane, counting downwards, we cannot see that fourth globe because we are on the *seventh* cosmic plane — another plane of cosmic substance.

Yet all these many planetary chains are as fully component parts of the universal solar system as our earth is, or as are Venus, Mars, Jupiter, etc. Each such chain, however invisible it may be to us, is an integral part of the living cosmic organism of chains playing their respective roles on the various stages of the cosmic life; and they are, all of them, the habitats of sentient beings — some of them far higher in evolutionary development than we, some of them far inferior.

Now this large number of planetary chains is divided into septenary (or duodenary) aggregates consisting each one of seven (or twelve) planetary chains. Each such aggregate of chains composes therefore a cosmic family, the members of which are karmically united and closely bound together in a more or less identic future destiny when the universal solar system shall have reached its term of manvantaric existence.

In *our* solar system the seven planetary chains with which our earth chain is karmically most intimately linked were known among the ancients as the Seven Sacred Planets.[16] They have aided in building and therefore have subsequently influenced the evolutionary course of the earth from the time when it was a globe of ethereal light in space; and will continue to watch over it, astrologically speaking, until its final course is run, and it projects itself anew — all its life powers and forces — into the new laya-centers. Thus each one of these seven planets, as an individual, has acted very strongly on a corresponding globe of the seven globes which compose the manifested planetary chain of our earth.

These seven planets and our earth chain are much more closely connected among themselves than they are with the innumerable hosts of other celestial bodies (or chains), whether existing in the universal solar system or on the still larger scale of the kosmos. It is these sacred planets — or rather their spiritual rectors or governors — which are what certain Greek philosophers called the kosmokratores, world builders or world rulers; and their combined action, in connection with the supervising spiritual powers of the solar logoi, originally built our planetary chain. Each controlling spiritual planetary or rector is the mystical parent of one of the globes of our earth chain: not wholly its physical or even its

318

spiritual parent, but its mystical parent by karma — otherwise its leader, guide or overseer.

As a matter of fact, there are not only seven but twelve sacred planets, although, because of the extremely difficult teachings connected with the five highest, only seven were commonly mentioned in the literatures and symbols of antiquity. However, reference is made in places to twelve spiritual planetaries or rectors, which were known as the Twelve Counsel Gods and called in the Etrusco-Roman language Consentes Dii — 'Consenting or Cooperating Gods.'* Thus it is that each one of the twelve globes of our earth chain has as its overseeing 'parent' one of these twelve planetary rectors. This shows clearly enough that the ancients, at least the initiates among them, knew of more planets in our solar system than the seven or five commonly spoken of.

The seven sacred planets are those which we know as Saturn, Jupiter, Mars, the sun (which stands as a substitute for a secret planet very near the sun and which we may perhaps call Vulcan), Venus, Mercury, and the moon (also reckoned as a substitute for a secret planetary chain).† Some astrologers are beginning to suspect the existence of such a planet near the moon, and one or two of them have even given to it the newfangled name of Lilith — taken from Rabbinical legend as signifying the quasi-animal and first 'wife' of Adam.

The moon, although intimately connected with human destiny and with the earth, as well as performing certain other very occult functions,

---

*They were also known as the 'Superior Deities.' Quintus Ennius, the father of Roman poetry, gave their names in these lines:

"Iuno, Vesta, Ceres, Diana, Minerva, Venus, Mars,
Mercurius, Iovi', Neptunus, Volcanus, Apollo."

†Cf. *The Secret Doctrine*, I, 575, footnote:

"These are planets accepted for purposes of judicial astrology only. The astro-theogonical division differed from this one. The Sun, being a central *star* and no planet, stands in more occult and mysterious relations with *its* seven planets of *our* globe than is generally known. The Sun was, therefore, considered the great Father of all the Seven 'Fathers,' which accounts for the variations found between *seven* and *eight* great gods of the Chaldean and other countries. Neither the earth nor the moon — its satellite — nor yet stars, for another reason — were anything else than *substitutes for esoteric purposes*. Yet, even with the Sun and the Moon thrown out of the calculation, the ancients seem to have known of *seven* planets. How many more are known to us, so far, if we throw out the Earth and Moon? *Seven*, and no more: Seven primary or principal planets, the rest *planetoids* rather than planets."

is not one of the sacred planets mentioned by the ancients and recognized in archaic occultism, for the simple reason that — in addition to this lunar chain's being dead — it is the twelvefold Dweller on the Threshold of the earth chain. The importance, however, of the function that the lunar chain has in relation to our own chain cannot be overstressed.

We thus have the seven planetary chains, two of which are invisible, respectively Vulcan and the secret planet named in connection with the moon; and there are four other invisible planetary chains mentioned in *The Mahatma Letters* (p. 176) under the mere letters "A, B, and Y, Z." These four, with the seven enumerated, make eleven, to which we may add the solar chain, forming the full number of twelve. These planetary chains are those which especially recognize our sun as their ruler, and therefore they form the main members of its kingdom. It is the constant intercourse of various kinds carried on among the eleven or twelve celestial bodies of our solar system which brings about the rebuilding of the planetary chains when they, as individuals, pass out of imbodiment, undergo their pralayic rest and reimbody themselves as new chains, the offsprings of their former selves. The cosmic highways by which the intercourse is accomplished are the circulations of the cosmos.

These circulations are carried on, not by hap or by hazard, but from sphere to sphere, from world to world, from plane to plane, by and through individual consciousnesses, whether these be gods, monads, souls or atoms, working in and through and in fact composing the various elements. More particularly in our own solar system this is brought about through the intermediaries of the sun and its family of planets, especially by and through their respective worlds, the lokas and talas.

Thus the seven planets are sacred *to us*, because they are the transmitters from the sun of the seven primal spiritual and other forces of the solar cosmos to the globes of our chain. The seven principles and seven elements, whether of our own constitution or of the different globes of our chain, spring originally from this sevenfold inrushing and outrushing life flow. The seven planets which *we* call sacred are those which are, as it were, the upādhis (bearers, carriers) *to us* of the seven solar forces. They are all 'higher' in this *one* sense of the term than is the earth, although the earth chain performs the same functions of reciprocity to these other planetary chains. They provide the earth with spiritual, intellectual, psychical, astral and vital, and even physical powers, and thus in a certain way oversee our destiny; they are all most closely connected with the human

320

race and with the development of all entities of whatever grade or class. As expressed by H. P. B.: °

> The next step will be for the modern astronomers to discover that no mere change in atmospheric temperature accompanying the conjunctions of planets affects human destinies, but a far more important and occult power, the magnetic sympathy between the various planetary orbs. Astrology may have fallen into contempt under the influence of improved modern science, but undoubtedly the time is coming when it will again have the attention it deserves and recover its ancient dignity as a sublime science.

The formative energies of these sacred planets work together with and are reinforced by the general field of forces and energies which the entire universe of the stars transmits to us. This does not mean, of course, that the earth planetary chain has no individuality of its own, for it has. But that individuality can imbody itself in the planet only through a laya-center, when it receives the help in building and in composition supplied by the various influences transmitted to it from the sacred planets, as well as from the ocean of energies and forces in which it is bathed and which ocean is the efflux or aggregative emanation of the starry host.

It is the same with the human body: it receives and incorporates into itself a certain amount of material through the emanations of other human beings, which it absorbs partly through endosmosis and partly through the intaking of food. Nevertheless it is built up or composed mainly of the substance-energy flowing forth from the reincarnating ego. Similarly does a planetary chain or a globe act. Its main substance or atoms, its main composition, comes from itself through the laya-center. But it draws into itself other energies and atoms flowing from its family of sacred planets, which are closely attuned to it in karmic destiny. It is precisely these particular planets of the many scores of planets (most of them invisible) within the universal solar system, which compose *our* solar family. This solar family forms a larger chain of planets around and through and in which the life-wave passes in its outer rounds. (The inner rounds take place through any one chain made up of its one physical globe and the other eleven globes.)

We do not refer here merely to the physical bodies of the seven sacred planets — doubtless each physical globe has its own so-called astronomical

---

° *The Theosophist,* February 1881, p. 104.

forces, such as gravitation and magnetism — but more especially to the inner powers and influences emanating from the ensouling divinities of these planetary chains. In the case of our earth: although of course the globe itself has life — the vital cohesive and indeed repulsive force which keeps it together and brings about its various phenomena of chemical and other action — nevertheless it is the prānic energies of its planetary spirit which ensoul it. Thus the life of any individual globe is the ultimate vital manifestation of its planetary spirit, which infills the globe because of the all-permeant life flow emanating from the planetary, and containing energies of spiritual, psychical and intellectual character also.

In her scholarly article entitled: "Star-Angel-Worship," H.P.B. says:°

Every planet according to the esoteric doctrine is in its composition a *Septenary* like man, in its principles. That is to say, *the visible planet is the physical body* of the sidereal being the *Atma* or Spirit of which is the Angel, or Rishi, or Dhyan-Chohan, or Deva, or whatever we call it. This belief as the occultists will see . . . is thoroughly occult. It is a tenet of the Secret Doctrine — *minus* its idolatrous element — pure and simple.

One of the main reasons why the seven, or rather twelve, planets are called sacred is because they are, as individuals, the dwelling places of the twelve essentially spiritual forces emanating as minor logoi from the supreme logos of our sun. As pointed out in previous chapters, there are twelve chief rays or forces which make and inform our solar chain, their vehicle; and they are the twelve minor logoi of our solar system. Each one of these logoi, hence, is the rector, the spiritual genius, the archangel if you will, of one of the twelve sacred planets, and uses that planet as its principal 'nerve center.'

The following diagram illustrates the correspondences which exist between the sacred planetary chains and the signs of the zodiac on the one hand, and the twelve globes of our own planetary chain on their respective cosmic planes on the other hand. The reader will see for himself that the seven sacred planets — or rather five of them — are given both on the upper three cosmic planes and 'reflected' on the lower three. This manner of repeating these five planets is more or less a blind. Yet it is based on the occult fact that, while there are twelve individual cosmic or zodiacal magnetisms working in and through our solar system, they

---

°*Lucifer*, July 1888, p. 364.

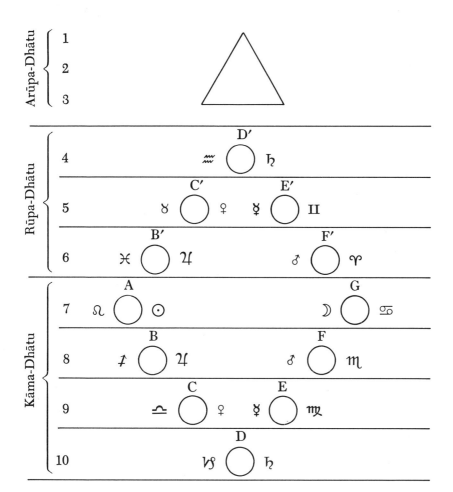

SIGNS OF THE ZODIAC

♈ — Aries   ♎ — Libra
♉ — Taurus   ♏ — Scorpio
♊ — Gemini   ♐ — Sagittarius
♋ — Cancer   ♑ — Capricornus
♌ — Leo   ♒ — Aquarius
♍ — Virgo   ♓ — Pisces

PLANETS

☿ — Mercury
♀ — Venus
☉ — Sun
☽ — Moon
♂ — Mars
♃ — Jupiter
♄ — Saturn

323

are more accurately viewed as being six fundamental magnetisms each having its positive and negative pole; so that every one is really dual, the six expressing themselves as the twelve 'manifested' magnetisms. Furthermore, as every one of the sacred planets is the house or principal nerve center of one of these fundamental magnetisms, otherwise called minor logoi, these sacred planets are reproducible in a diagram in double, i.e. the five positives reflecting their negatives, thus making ten, five above and five below the fourth manifested cosmic plane. Here we touch upon one of the reasons why the ancients regarded the sun and the moon as substitutes for two secret planets.

Just as the sacred planets are world builders with respect to our earth's planetary chain, in precisely the same way our planetary chain is a kosmokrator aiding particularly in the building and guidance of one of the other planetary chains; but also aiding generally in the building and guiding of *all* the other planetary chains of our solar system.

Action and interaction prevail everywhere throughout our solar cosmos; everything therein being interlocked and interworking. As an instance: the planet Mars is built by its particular group of seven or twelve planetary chains, itself being the eighth of *its* ogdoad; and our earth chain is one of these. There are other similar groups of sacred planets formed of visible and invisible planets belonging to our universal solar system; and in these groups of chains neither our earth nor any one of its family of sacred planets is a specific unit, although belonging of course in a general way to all the groups of twelves which compose the universal solar system. Our sun is but one of several other suns in our universal Egg of Brahmā, and these other suns — each with its own family of planetary chains — are invisible to us because being on other planes of the universal solar system.

With regard to Uranus and Neptune: Uranus is a member of the universal solar system, but does not belong to *our* solar system, even though as a true planet it is closely linked with our sun both in origin and destiny. The only sense in which Uranus can be considered as a member of our solar system is the purely astronomical one, in that Uranus is under our system's influence so far as the revolutions of its physical globe around the sun are concerned.

Neptune, on the other hand, is not by right of origin in this solar manvantara a member either of our solar system or of the universal solar system. As I have explained in my *Fundamentals*, it is what is called a capture, which event changed in one sense the entire nature of the universal solar system, and will remain with us until the karmic time shall come for it to leave.° It has been captured in the same sense as some of the planets have captured moons. Suppose we were to say that in some past aeons of time a comet, approaching the truly planetary stage of evolution, passed sufficiently close to the gravitational attraction of the universal solar system on its own plane of being to be captured, and that due to the interplay of various forces it settled into an orbit around the sun, and then long aeons later our astronomers discovered it and named it Neptune! It would be correct to look upon Neptune as such a captured comet. Likewise, the planet Pluto is a capture.

Now comets, as discussed earlier, are merely the first stage in the evolutionary history of all planets, and of all suns too, for that matter; because there are planetary comets and solar comets and cosmic comets, i.e. comets which become planets around a sun, and comets which become suns.

Since Neptune is a capture, it has no direct connection with the twelve houses of our zodiac, after the manner of the true planets of our solar system. Nevertheless, Neptune does influence the system as a whole, and very strongly, and will continue to do so as long as it remains one of the bodies revolving around the sun. Not only does it change the entire polarity of the system, but also it affects everything within the solar cosmos by that fact alone, and therefore exercises an influence, astrologically speaking, upon all men, upon all beings and things on earth. Yet it is an 'outside' influence, although strictly karmic of course. Neptune is a septenary (or duodenary) living entity through whose veins there courses the same cosmic lifeblood that courses through ours. It is a planetary chain exactly as all other celestial bodies are, but we see only that one globe of its chain which is on the same plane of perception as we are.

Thus we see how all the planetary chains throughout the solar system, whether our own or the universal, work together, aid each other, and how those in a single sun's kingdom interbuild each other — all working out their common destiny. Our solar system is indeed alive throughout: a living organism, an organic entity.

°Cf. *The Secret Doctrine,* I, 102, footnote:
"The true Eastern Occultist will maintain that, whereas there are many yet undiscovered planets in our system, Neptune does not belong to it, his apparent connection with our sun and the influence of the latter upon Neptune notwithstanding. This connection is *mayavic,* imaginary, they say."

NATURE AND CHARACTERISTICS OF THE PLANETS

For even great adepts (those initiated of course), trained seers though they are, can claim thorough acquaintance with the nature and appearance of planets and their inhabitants belonging to our solar system only. They *know* that almost all the planetary worlds are inhabited, but can have access to — even in spirit — only those of our system; and they are also aware how difficult it is, *even for them,* to put themselves into full rapport even with the planes of consciousness *within* our system, but differing from the states of consciousness possible on this globe; *i.e.,* on the three planes of the chain of spheres beyond our earth. Such knowledge and intercourse are possible to them because they have learned how to penetrate to planes of consciousness which are closed to the perceptions of ordinary men; but were they to communicate their knowledge, the world would be no wiser, because it lacks that experience of other forms of perception which alone could enable them to grasp what was told them.

— The Secret Doctrine, II, 701

EVERY PLANET INTRINSICALLY is in a different evolutionary stage and has a different spiritual characteristic from every other planet; it stands, at its root, on its own spiritual plane, and during its entire evolutionary course in its present pilgrimage that one spiritual plane will remain unaltered. In addition, one planet may be ahead of or behind another in evolutionary time; although it may be, essentially, higher or inferior spiritually.

Thus, there are two ways of considering evolutionary advancement: one, when referring to an older planet-hierarchy of larger cosmic experience; and the other, when referring to a planet, which though younger in cosmic experience, may be more advanced in its present imbodiment as regards number of rounds already passed through. For instance, we are told that Jupiter is in essence or in age of cosmic experience spiritually far more advanced than is the planetary spirit either of the earth or of Mars; and yet in this solar manvantara Jupiter in its *present* imbodiment is less advanced in its cycle of seven rounds than the earth is in its own cycle. Again, the earth as compared with Mars is, essentially, a grosser planet; and in evolution, also, it stands at a lower or more material point of its own planetary cycle than does Mars in its planetary cycle.

Venus is farther along in the number of rounds run through in *this* solar manvantara than the earth, and therefore is more advanced in this sense; but the planetary spirit of earth is nevertheless spiritually more advanced because older in number of cosmic manvantaras.

The basic rule is as follows: the nearer the sun, the more advanced is the planet in its evolution, and consequently the more evolved are its burden of living beings. The farther from the sun, the more ethereal and in one sense the more spiritual are the planets, but less evolved in their respective planetary manvantaras.

Therefore, Mars is more ethereal than the earth; Jupiter more so than Mars; Saturn more than Jupiter. But Jupiter is more evolved in its planetary evolution than is Saturn; Mars more than Jupiter; the earth more than Mars, and Venus more than the earth.

The reason is that the sun, while being the vehicle of a god, is also in its physical expression the very focus of the life force of the solar system, and consequently is the place where the life-pulse beats most strongly. We see this also in human beings: where health is physically most robust in the animal sense of the word, spirituality is usually recessive. The analogy is not exact but it will give the general idea. Therefore too close a neighborhood to the sun means being deluged with the physical vitality which the sun pours forth exhaustlessly from its lowest part.

The 'men' on Venus, for instance, are much more intelligent than are the men on earth, but they are not as spiritual nor as ethereal — and ethereality and spirituality do not necessarily mean the same thing. Venus is in its last round, and that is why, although nearer the sun than the earth, it is less dense because its substance has been slowly dematerializing as the planet advanced along the ascending arc of its evolution.

We discern the planet Venus, although it is in its seventh round while we are only in our fourth round, because the physical body of Venus is on our cosmic plane, albeit in the first subplane or highest state of matter belonging to our plane. Remember that each cosmic plane of substance is divided into seven subplanes. We are all on the seventh or lowest cosmic plane; but we of earth are on its fourth subplane.

When we of this earth globe D speak of Venus, we speak of course of globe D of the Venus chain — that globe which we can see. As Venus is near the end of its globe-manvantara and is already slightly self-luminous, the root-race at this time evolving on globe D of Venus is either the sixth or the seventh of its present seventh globe-round.

327

The statement that Venus is more material than the earth is to be taken in the sense of its being a younger planetary spirit, and not as signifying merely a difference between gross matter and ether — although of course the matter in which a planetary spirit enwraps itself corresponds to its state of evolution. Venus is grosser than the earth, yet its humanities are more evolved as regards the higher mānasic qualities.° On the other hand, because it is in its seventh round, and the earth is in its fourth round, even the matter of which globe D of the Venus chain is composed is more ethereal than is the matter of globe D of the earth chain. Essentially the earth is older than Venus; and therefore even the earth's grossest matter is now more ethereal than was the grossest matter of the Venus chain when Venus was in *its* fourth round.

While Venus is in its seventh round, that does not mean that the life-waves on all the globes of the Venus chain are in the seventh round. It so happens that the life-waves circling on globes A, B and C, and doubtless on one or two of the higher globes, are in their seventh round; nevertheless the life-waves of globes E, F and G of the Venus chain, as well as its highest globes, are not yet in their seventh round because the seventh-round life energies of the Venus chain have not completed the full round, having passed only through the globes of the descending arc and reached globe D of the Venus chain.

When the earth and its inhabitants shall have reached the seventh round, they will stand somewhat higher spiritually and ethereally than the planet Venus and its inhabitants today. But, relatively speaking, the men on earth of that far future time will be somewhat inferior in intelligence to the inhabitants of Venus as they are now. Intelligence is gained by the balanced union of spirit with matter; then manas the child is born out of the element latent and inhering in both spirit and matter.

A number of astronomers at different times have noticed spots of light on Venus, and they must have been most excellent observers. The statement has likewise been made by their critics that if such lights were actually seen, they could not be due to the sun, nor to reflected light, but must spring forth from some strange occurrence on or in the planet itself. And that is true for there are areas on Venus which will one day probably be discovered to be artificially illuminated.

Moreover, Venus, being in its last or seventh round, emanates an auric light which is visible to our eyes. Some astronomers have observed this;

°Cf. *The Secret Doctrine,* I, 602.

some have tried to deny its possibility because they cannot explain it. This light does not come, however, from its 'godlike' inhabitants — they could be called godlike only as a courteous expression — who intellectually are far more godlike than we are, although they are grosser. The 'phosphorescence' arises in the vital force of the planet itself. The earth towards the end of its seventh round will be probably somewhat more luminous than Venus is today.

Actually, every self-contained entity from atom to god, including all entities on earth and the other planets, and on and in the suns, is surrounded by an auric atmosphere which is seen as light by those who have developed the percipient faculty. The mere fact that we cannot see this light does not authorize us to deny its existence. The sun in its splendor is an example of one celestial body whose light we are very much aware of. Furthermore, every human being, had we the eyes to sense it, would seem like a globe of light — light spreading from every part of his body, flaming from his eyes, pouring forth from his mouth, from every inch of his skin. In the same way, every planet is encircled by an auric light. Even the moon, dead body as it is, is surrounded with its own phosphorescent light; just as decaying stuff is sometimes phosphorescent, although this is usually ascribed to some other cause. However that may be, every self-contained entity irradiates energy all the time, and light is but a form of energy; and could we perceive this energy visually, we would see light.

One is reminded here of the ancient Buddhist saying:

> Shining Venus trembles afar,
> Earth's Higher Self, and
> With but one finger touches us.

Venus is a very interesting planet. It is perhaps the most closely connected with the earth in a number of ways; and it has been said that wherever Venus goes, there goes the earth also, and vice versa. As phrased in *The Secret Doctrine* (II, 30–1):

Venus is the most occult, powerful, and mysterious of all the planets; the one whose influence upon, and relation to the Earth is most prominent. . . .

According to the Occult Doctrine, this planet is our Earth's *primary*, and its spiritual prototype. . . .

"Every sin committed on Earth is felt by Usanas-Sukra. The Guru of the Daityas is the Guardian Spirit of the Earth and Men. Every change on Sukra is felt on, and reflected by, the Earth."

329

In pondering upon the evolutionary status of planets, we should not confuse spirituality with ethereality. Things ethereal belong to matter; things spiritual belong to spirit. The inhabitants of earth are more spiritual than the inhabitants of Saturn and Jupiter, because they are more evolved, farther along the pathway, although the Saturnians and the Jovians are much more ethereal than we are. Our humanity and our earth are on the ascending cycle, beginning the luminous arc; therefore as we advance in spirituality both our earth and we shall likewise advance in the sense of becoming more ethereal.

These remarks are made from the standpoint of the different positions in evolution that the various planets occupy in the evolutionary scale. There is another way of looking at the matter of spirituality as appertaining to the planets, and this is what we might call their *essential* spirituality. Thus Saturn or Jupiter may be intrinsically of a more spiritual swabhāva than are the planets closer to the sun, although the latter, as said, are evolutionally more advanced. It is somewhat like two men: the one whose swabhāva is less spiritual may nevertheless in his own evolution be on a minor arc of ascent, while the more essentially spiritual man may be making a minor descent in his evolutionary course.

As pointed out, the general rule is that the nearer a planet is to our sun, the more gross and dense it is physically. If an inner planet is less dense than an outer planet, it means that the inner planet has reached a more advanced point in its planetary evolution. Furthermore, the planets as they advance in age draw nearer to the sun. Although the sun is the dwelling of a god, nevertheless, so far as matter is concerned, its vital magnetic and electric power is so enormous by comparison with the relatively tiny bodies of the planets, that its vital force alone on account of its sheer magnitude coarsens the planetary bodies.

Please remember that our physical sun is that globe of the solar chain of twelve globes which corresponds to our globe D of the earth chain. The substance of this physical or fourth-plane sun is the prakriti of this cosmic plane in its three highest subplanes or elements; that is to say, the heart of our visible sun is a portion of the mother-substance of this lowest cosmic plane, which heart is surrounded by its veil of substances, and this again is surrounded by *its* veil of substances — the third on the downward scale. And it is this last veil which is the dazzling auric stuff surrounding the sun. We can draw an analogy between the three solar substances and the three highest principles in man: thus, our sun's heart corresponds to our ātman, its veil to our buddhi, and the next lower veil to our manas.

All planets go through their phase of material existence, have their temptation, just as we of earth have had and shall have. Of course, the higher a planet stands on the ladder of existence, the fewer are the deviations or winding pathways that the entities follow in their long pilgrimage. There have been planets, however, whose humanities have 'failed,' in the sense that such planets with their teeming humanities did not make the grade, and went backwards — it was karma, part of their evolutionary unfoldment so to do. But these are very rare cases.

Mercury is just emerging from obscuration, to begin its last or seventh round. This planet is even more mysterious than Venus, and in many nations of antiquity has been closely associated with the after-death teachings of the Mysteries. The Sanskrit name for Mercury is Budha (wisdom), which planet the Greeks called Hermes, the particular overseer of mystics and the "conductor of souls" to the Underworld.°

The Secret Doctrine (II, 44–5) contains this illuminating passage:

The men of Budha (Mercury) are metaphorically *immortal* through their Wisdom. Such is the common belief of those who credit every star or planet with being inhabited. . . . The Moon being an inferior body to the Earth even, to say nothing of other planets, the terrestrial men produced by her sons — the lunar men or "ancestors" — from her shell or body, cannot be immortal. They cannot hope to become real, self-conscious and intelligent men, unless they are *finished*, so to say, by other creators. Thus in the Purânic legend, the son of the Moon (*Soma*) is *Budha* (Mercury), "the intelligent" and the Wise, because he is the offspring of Soma, the "regent" of the visible Moon, not of Indu, the physical Moon. Thus Mercury is the elder brother of the Earth, metaphorically — his stepbrother, so to say, the offspring of *Spirit* — while she (the Earth) is the progeny of the *body*.

The intramercurial planet Vulcan, as astronomers have named this to them hypothetical body, has its orbit between Mercury and the sun. According to the teachings of esotericism, it became practically invisible during the third root-race after the fall of man into physical generation. As we have now reached on the ascending arc the degree of plane-development corresponding to that of the third root-race, the planet Vulcan should begin to show itself again in a relatively short cyclic period. Even today,

---

°Cf. *Fundamentals of the Esoteric Philosophy*, ch. xviii.

while it is generally invisible on account of what we may call its ethe-reality, if searched for by telescope it might be seen, under favorable conditions, crossing the solar disk.

On March 26, 1859, astronomers observed a dark body transiting the sun; however, that body has not been seen since. Still, there are other reasons, such as the perturbations in the orbital elements of Mercury, which have convinced some astronomers that there actually does exist an intramercurial planet. Vulcan is in a certain sense the highest psycho-logically of the seven sacred planets, even though not the least dense.

As for the planet Mars, its physical sphere is younger than the earth, but presently it is in obscuration. It is more than merely 'asleep,' for the great bulk of its living entities have moved on to higher globes of the planetary chain of Mars. However, certain beings were left there when its globe D went into obscuration. These are the śishtas, 'remainders,' i.e. those who serve as the seeds of life on any planet, until the returning life-wave in the next globe-manvantara shall find these bodies waiting and ready for their use. At present, the vital essences of the Mars planetary chain have left its physical globe D, having ended their third round there-on, and have gone to its other globes. There is a mystery with regard to Mars, and that is why H.P.B. in a certain passage° on the seven sacred planets mentions only four (Saturn, Jupiter, Mercury, and Venus), and merely hints at three more. Like the sun and the moon which are substi-tutes for two secret planets, Mars — to a certain extent — is in the same category.

The subject often comes up as to whether there is life on the different planets of our solar system, i.e. various kingdoms corresponding to the kingdoms of the earth. How could there be such a thing as matter without life; how could the component elements of any entity or thing hold together if there were not a unifying and cohesive energy — and that energy is life. Matter itself is condensed life, concreted electricity, and electricity is but a form of life. There is no such thing as lifeless substance anywhere. It is not matter first and then life as a fragile fruit of it, but life comes first, life universal; and matter only occasionally appears as a mushroom growth.

On our little dust heap that we call earth, we see nothing but matter, which in reality is the most unsubstantial thing that the intellect cognizes.

°The Secret Doctrine, I, 575.

We give to it the primal place as the foundation of the universe, whereas in very truth matter is but a passing phase of life. Consider what matter is, mostly holes, vacancies, empty spaces, a mere play of cosmic energies, foam on the Waters of Space, as transient and as impermanent. Life-Consciousness-Substance, the cosmic triad, is one: not three things, not three essential entities, but one with three faces. °

On all the planets there are phases of life, just as there are on our own planet here, the parent of our physical bodies. On every one of them there is or will be a serial line of ascending degrees of entities: three elemental kingdoms, a mineral kingdom, something corresponding to our vegetable kingdom, and again to our animal kingdom, and on some of the planets a kingdom corresponding to the human. For life itself is everywhere because it is the very basis of things: it is gravitation, it is cohesion, thought, body, spirit, mind, ego — it is everything. As *The Secret Doctrine* (I, 133) has it:

> The refusal to admit in the whole Solar system of any other reasonable and intellectual beings on the human plane, than ourselves, is the greatest conceit of our age. All that science has a right to affirm, is that there are no invisible Intelligences living under the same conditions as we do. It cannot deny point-blank the possibility of there being worlds within worlds, under totally different conditions to those that constitute the nature of our world; nor can it deny that there may be a certain limited communication between some of those worlds and our own.

And again in the second volume on page 702:

> Since no single atom in the entire Kosmos is without life and consciousness, how much more then its mighty globes? — though they remain sealed books to us men who can hardly enter even into the consciousness of the forms of life nearest us?

People are far too prone to imagine that life on other planets (when it is recognized to exist) is exactly as on earth, so that the 'men' on Jupiter, for instance, would have bodies of human flesh and would breathe our particular kind of air. But a very little thought shows that such a conclusion is an absurdity. The inhabitants of the other planets — those which are

---

°In this idea is the basis of the Christian Trinity: not three gods, but one God, and yet verily three 'Persons' — a fact when properly understood, but a ludicrous collocation of words when not understood.

inhabited at the present time — must have forms strictly related to and fitted by evolution for their particular planet. They would be very various indeed, and we might not easily accept those beings as intelligent, sensitive and conscious. Some may be flat, some spherical, and some long; the inhabitants of Mercury having, perhaps, the nearest resemblance to us, while those of Jupiter are probably the most diverse in form from us. The inhabitants of Venus, which is an inhabited planet at the present time, are doubles, ovoid in shape. Venus is superior to earth: both naturally and spiritually. The inhabitants of some of the planets move by floating, while those of other planets of our solar family do not move at all; they are fixtures somewhat as trees are with us, and yet are highly intelligent, conscious beings.

The inhabitants of other planets would look like monstrosities to us, simply because our understanding is too feeble to grasp their evolutionary history — and indeed, so far as that goes, we do not even know our own evolutionary history. On the other hand, we men of earth, for instance, would be like developed beasts to the inhabitants of Mercury, repulsive in shape and horrible in the uses to which we put our faculties.

Jupiter's inhabitants are much more ethereal in physical structure and texture than those of earth or Venus, but much less evolved than either. We could describe them as aeriform or igniform; huge entities, as perfectly at home on their own planet as we are on ours. Conditions on Jupiter are such as would prevail on a planet which is passing through an evolutionary stage which the ancients would have called the 'element of fire.' However, at the present time it has almost completed that stage and is very near to the critical line dividing that from the element of air.°

There are some wonderful mysteries connected with Jupiter. It is one of the least dense of the planets of our solar system, surpassed in physical ethereality only by Saturn. Physically speaking, many of its characteristics closely resemble those of the sun; in fact, Jupiter is an infant sun, in

---

°Cf. *The Mahatma Letters*, p. 167:

"Your science has a theory, I believe, that if the earth were suddenly placed in extremely cold regions — for instance where it would exchange places with Jupiter — all our seas and rivers would be suddenly transformed into solid mountains; the air, — or rather a portion of the aeriform substances which compose it — would be metamorphosed from their state of invisible fluid owing to the absence of heat into liquids (which now exist on Jupiter, but of which men have no idea on earth). Realize, or try to imagine the *reverse* condition, and it will be that of Jupiter at the present moment."

the sense of 'small' sun. There is liquid on Jupiter, but of a kind that would be unrecognized in our laboratories. We would need to study alchemy, and to know its principles well, in order to understand the properties of this Jovian liquid. Jupiter's atmosphere is very heavy and very dense, in comparison to that on earth. It has a relatively heavy core, but of a fluidic character.

The light that we receive from Jupiter is almost entirely reflected sunlight; but also, in a minor degree, results from the glowing nature of that planet. However, this glowing is not because of its highly progressed stage, but is due to its fiery character. In other words, its self-luminosity has a physical cause, whereas the self-luminosity of planets such as Venus is in a certain degree due to an auric light which they themselves radiate.

In one of his letters to A. P. Sinnett,° K. H. speaks of the powerful influence of a Rāja sun on Jupiter; and that this sun is not yet what astronomers would consider a physical body. Could they see it through their instruments, they would discover it as a practically dimensionless point — a laya-center so far as the physical plane of our solar system is concerned, and yet this Rāja sun is vastly greater in volume than Jupiter. Their close relationship has a strong bearing upon the question of the so-called 'physical characteristics' of the surface of Jupiter, particularly

---

°Cf. *The Mahatma Letters*, p. 167:

"The whole of our system is imperceptibly shifting its position in space. The relative distance between planets remaining ever the same, and being in no wise affected by the displacement of the whole system; and the distance between the latter and the stars and other suns being so incommensurable as to produce but little if any perceptible change for centuries and millenniums to come; — no astronomer will perceive it *telescopically*, until Jupiter and some other planets, whose little luminous points hide now from our sight millions upon millions of stars (all but some 5000 or 6000) — will suddenly let us have a peep at a few of the *Raja-Suns* they are now hiding. There is such a king-star right behind Jupiter, that no mortal physical eye has ever seen during this, our Round. Could it be so perceived it would appear, through the best telescope with a power of multiplying its diameter ten thousand times, — still a small dimensionless point, thrown into the shadow by the brightness of any planet; nevertheless — this world is thousands of times larger than Jupiter. The violent disturbance of its atmosphere and even its red spot that so intrigues science lately, are due — (1) to that shifting and (2) to the influence of that Raja-Star. In its present position in space imperceptibly small though it be — the metallic substances of which it is mainly composed are expanding and gradually transforming themselves into aeriform fluids — the state of our own earth and its six sister globes before the first Round — and becoming part of its atmosphere."

335

the dense, concealing cloak of 'vapor' which, according to astronomers, is supposed to surround it.

It should be borne in mind that every globe of a planetary chain is surrounded during its globe manvantara with a thick veil of meteoric dust, most of it very fine, some of it, however, consisting of more or less large bodies. Take Venus, for instance, or Mercury: each is surrounded with its own meteoric veil which acts in one sense as a cushion, thus forming a protection to the planet. For that reason, we do not see the real face of Venus or Mercury. Globe D of Mars — which we see — has no such veil at present, because the vital essence of that planetary chain has left globe D for its superior globes.

The meteoric veil is the seat of very great electromagnetic forces continuously at work. It is this "meteoric continent" surrounding our own globe which is responsible for some seventy per cent of our heat. Forces emanate from the solar heart and reach the meteoric veil encircling the earth, and arouse electromagnetic currents, producing a part of our meteorological phenomena. Such things as storms are caused mostly by electromagnetic action and reaction between the innate prāna or vital forces of the earth and its meteoric continent — a fact pointed out by K.H. in the same letter (p. 161) when he wrote that "every atmospheric change and disturbance was due to the combined magnetism of the two great masses between which our atmosphere is compressed."

There is a close analogy between the coils of a dynamo and the earth whirling within its surrounding continent of cosmic dust. As said, the great climatic changes of the earth, such as the glacial periods, are directly due to this continent of cosmic dust. Even such things as strong winds, electrical storms or heavy rains, the aurorae borealis and australis, and the changes in temperature, can ultimately be traced to the electromagnetic interchanges between the earth itself and this spherical continent or veil of meteoric dust.

The secrets concerning the true nature, structure, characteristics, and movements of the planets of our solar system have not yet been discovered. One of these days astronomers are going to find that those movements, as they are now understood, are largely māyāvi, illusory, strange as this may sound.

ASTEROIDS, METEORS, AND COSMIC DUST

Not all of the Intra-Mercurial planets, nor yet those in the orbit of Neptune are yet discovered, though they are strongly suspected. We know that such exist and *where* they exist; and that there are innumerable planets "burnt out" they say, — in *obscuration* we say; — planets in formation and not yet luminous, etc. . . . Science will *hear* sounds from certain planets before she *sees* them. This is a *prophecy.*
— *The Mahatma Letters*, pp. 169–70

WHAT IS THE NATURE and destiny of the asteroids which revolve around the sun between the orbits of Jupiter and Mars? Briefly, they are the remnants of dead worlds, although it is perhaps nearer the truth to say the remnants of *a* dead world, a dead moon, the parent of a then future planetary chain. The great gap between Mars and Jupiter, which is now to a certain extent occupied by the asteroids, will be the locus of the orbit of a planet which even at the present time is on the descending arc, coming out of the more ethereal and therefore invisible realms on to this physical plane of our universe. This new planet, in the course of its materialization into a physical planet more or less resembling the other planets of our solar system, will gather into itself most of the asteroids as they now exist.

Of course, evolution in the solar system moves with what is to human beings great slowness. Millions of years will pass before this future planet will be first perceived in our physical universe as an ethereal translucent body somewhat resembling a comet. Prior to this stage, it will be a comet slowly settling into an elliptical orbit around the sun, in the ring now occupied by the asteroids.

Before our earth began its first round in this planetary chain, it too found its orbit (somewhat farther from the sun than now, however), which was then occupied by vast numbers of asteroidal bodies, tiny planets each one, some large and some small. In many cases these were the remnants of the earth in a former manvantara even before the moon was a living planet.

All meteorites, meteors — all intercosmic dust in other words — are but the debris, the residue, of old and dead worlds. They are all destined to some cosmic dust heap where they will be broken up and ground over in nature's wonderful laboratories.

Every mathematical point of being, therefore every atom of matter, every electron of every atom, is simply a monad passing through a temporary phase of its aeons-long evolutionary pilgrimage, this phase being a manifestation as a particle of material substance. In the far distant future every such monad will have become a full-blown god; but before it reaches the divine stage, of necessity it will have to pass through all intermediate stages, one of these being the mental. Every particle of substance, no matter how gross it may be at any one time, is on its way to becoming mānasic substance.° Remember that matter and energy — spirit and substance — are fundamentally one; hence matter is but one phase of certain hosts of monads which are presently passing through the matter stage of their long evolutionary journey.

Meteorites are simply old matter in process of decomposing into cosmic dust, later to be used in building up other new worlds. But every atom which composes a meteorite will have its time, as evolution through the cosmic ages proceeds, to become a thinking entity.

Reverting to the nature and characteristics of the asteroids, it may be said that while the majority of them are fragments of a former planet which had its orbit between Jupiter and Mars, thousands of them have been drawn together by various attracting influences so that they now circle around the sun in the space occupied by the asteroid swarm.

Thus far the esoteric teaching is not essentially different from that of modern science, although indeed many astronomers are doubtful that the majority of these asteroids could be the fragments of an exploded or broken up planet, apparently because any such explosion would be inadequate to account for their present large number and the tangle of their orbits which differ so greatly from each other.

As a matter of fact, a great many of the asteroids are captures from the abysses of outward space, and really are fragments of worlds which formerly existed in solar systems other than our own; and these fragments, for almost innumerable ages, had been wandering through interstellar space until they happened to be captured by our sun and its family of planets.

Now when the planet-to-be shall have reached a sufficient degree of physicalization, it will slowly gather unto itself most of these erratic

---

°Cf. *The Ocean of Theosophy* by W. Q. Judge, ch. viii.

asteroidal wanderers around our sun, and they will thus help to build up its future physical body.

There is a certain analogy between the manner in which a planet attracts unto itself meteors from outer space (as our earth does by the millions daily) and the way in which the human body continuously draws to itself millions of life-atoms, giving them temporary harbor and then ejecting them when they have served their purpose, after which they are again attracted to some other body. Thus the life-atoms follow their peregrinations or transmigrations both through the different planes of being and along the spaces or fields of any one such plane.

These asteroids have been attracted to this zone of the solar system because of the already manifesting psycho-electromagnetic pull of the planet which is descending into manifestation and will have its orbit between Jupiter and Mars. This fact means a former karmic relationship between the planet-to-be and most or all of the present asteroidal swarm.

An intriguing passage in *The Secret Doctrine* (II, 700) bears, among other things, on the subject of asteroids:

Unconsciously, perhaps, in thinking of a plurality of inhabited "Worlds," we imagine them to be like the globe we inhabit and peopled by beings more or less resembling ourselves. And in so doing we are only following a natural instinct. Indeed, so long as the enquiry is confined to the life-history of this globe we can speculate on this question with some profit, and ask ourselves what were the "Worlds" spoken of in all the ancient scriptures of Humanity, with some hope of at least asking an intelligible *question*. But how do we know (*a*) what kind of Beings inhabit the globes in general; and (*b*) whether *those* who rule planets superior to our own, do not exercise the same influence on our earth *consciously*, that we may exercise *unconsciously* — say on the small planets (planetoids or asteroids) in the long run, by our cutting the Earth to pieces, opening canals, and thereby entirely changing our climates. Of course, like Caesar's wife, the *planetoids* cannot be affected by our suspicion. They are too far, etc., etc. Believing in esoteric astronomy, however, we are not so sure of that.

A good deal more could be said about these matters, but as they pertain to exceedingly difficult phases of the doctrine of the spheres, it will be sufficient to say here that there is no accident or chance happening anywhere in the universe, whether in the great or in the infinitesimal. Everything takes place according to strict rules or karmic courses of action, which must be understood as originating in intelligences guiding and directing the magnetic sympathies between beings and beings, and things and things.

THE MOON

When a planetary chain is in its last Round, its Globe 1 or A, before finally *dying out*, sends all its energy and "principles" into a neutral centre of latent force, a "laya centre," and thereby informs a new nucleus of undifferentiated substance or matter, *i.e.*, calls it into activity or gives it life. Suppose such a process to have taken place in the lunar "planetary" chain; . . . And now it will be easy to imagine further Globe A of the lunar chain informing Globe A of the terrestrial chain, and — dying; Globe B of the former sending after that its energy into Globe B of the new chain; then Globe C of the lunar, creating its progeny sphere C of the terrene chain; then the Moon (our Satellite) pouring forth into the lowest globe of our planetary ring — Globe D, our Earth — all its life, energy and powers; and, having transferred them to a new centre becoming virtually *a dead planet*, in which rotation has almost ceased since the birth of our globe. The Moon is now the cold residual quantity, the shadow dragged after the new body, into which her living powers and "principles" are transfused. She now is doomed for long ages to be ever pursuing the Earth, to be attracted by and to attract her progeny. Constantly *vampirised* by her child, she revenges herself on it by soaking it through and through with the nefarious, invisible, and poisoned influence which emanates from the occult side of her nature. For she is a *dead*, yet a *living body*. The particles of her decaying corpse are full of active and destructive life, although the body which they had formed is soulless and lifeless. Therefore its emanations are at the same time beneficent and maleficent — this circumstance finding its parallel on earth in the fact that the grass and plants are nowhere more juicy and thriving than on the graves; while at the same time it is the graveyard or corpse-emanations, which kill. And like all ghouls or vampires, the moon is the friend of the sorcerers and the foe of the unwary. . . .

Such is the moon from the astronomical, geological, and physical standpoints. As to her metaphysical and psychic nature it must remain an occult secret in this work, . . .   — *The Secret Doctrine*, I, 155–6

THE MOON HAS BEEN called the Lord and Giver of Life; it likewise has been called a dead planet and the producer of death. Are these statements contradictions, or are they, more truly speaking, two sides of the same coin? It is a fact that some drugs can prolong life, and can even bring life back, but if improperly used can deal death and bring about disease. Food can kill, and yet food keeps us alive. Life is full of seeming contradictions which are in reality paradoxes.

As the giver of both physical and astral life, the moon is also the transmitter of the lower mental and psychical vitality. But it is full of all the energies of death as well. It is a decaying body. Every atom that leaves the moon rushes earthwards, impregnated with the lunar influences. The effect of the moon in these respects is deleterious and even death-dealing. And yet, if it were possible suddenly to remove the moon from the skies, annihilate it and its influence, within twenty-four hours we would see ninety-nine per cent of our plant and animal life, including man, wilt and die out. At the same time we would see weird and uncanny forms of growth coming into existence overnight. Love, for instance, gives life, and love also can give death. The lunar vitality not only stimulates the grosser forms of our physical existence, but can likewise by that very action cause decay and disease in other parts of the human constitution.°

Our moon has also been referred to as the Dweller on the Threshold of this earth, much as the kāma-rūpic phantom haunts the human being in certain unfortunate cases where the previous life (or lives) has been strongly influenced by evil thoughts and passions. Just as a Dweller, whose whole nature is corrupt and whose emanations are of death, is constantly, although automatically, suggesting thoughts of depravity, and urging the man to commit evil, so likewise our moon haunts our earth. It is a dead body, a decaying entity, and therefore filled with low life energies. The very life in it causes its decay; for a corpse decomposes on account of the life in it tearing it asunder. Decay itself is a manifestation of life

---

°Cf. *The Secret Doctrine,* I, 386–403; see also p. 537 where H.P.B. comments on the 'Nervous Ether' of Dr. Richardson:

"This 'Nervous Ether' is the lowest principle of the Primordial Essence which is *Life.* It is *animal vitality* diffused in all nature and acting according to the conditions it finds for its activity. It is not an 'animal product,' but the living animal, the living flower or plant are *its* products. The animal tissues only absorb it according to their more or less morbid or healthy state — as do *physical* materials and structures (*in their primogenial State — nota bene*) — and henceforward, from the moment of the birth of the Entity, are regulated, strengthened, and *fed* by it. It descends in a larger supply to vegetation in the *Sushumna* sun-ray which lights and feeds the moon, and it is through her beams that it pours its light upon, and penetrates man and animal, more during their sleep and rest, than when they are in full activity."

in its disintegrating energy rather than in its composing and building energy. Hence, the moon is the Dweller on the Threshold of the earth. It was our former habitat, which through ages and ages of the lunar manvantara we filled with evil magnetism, and this magnetism still holds the moon together; and because it is attracted to the earth by reason of affinity it continues to haunt our globe and its inhabitants. It sends forth emanations night and day, which rush by magnetic attraction to their own kind on earth, permeating our globe through and through. Its effluvia are maleficent, so far as men are concerned, for they arise in a disintegrating body. The moon has all the psychomagnetic energy of a decaying corpse; and, being a cosmic body, its emanations and powers of radiation are therefore very great.

The crater-like markings of the moon are due to the processes of disintegration arising out of its core: pustules, so to say, freeing the inner gases and other things springing out of the moon and finding their vents through these so-called craters. Blessed will be the humanities of that future time when the moon is finally quite vanished through the dissociation of its atoms into blue ether.

What we see when we look up into the starry spaces is the astral body, the kāma-rūpa of the physical moon that was, aeons and aeons ago, which physical body is now disintegrated into impalpable cosmic dust. We perceive this kāma-rūpic phantom, because our physical earth is one subplane higher than that on which the physical body of the moon was. Were our scientists by some magic to be transported to the moon, even though they would be able to see it almost as clearly as they see our earth, I do not believe they would find it easy to walk about on its surface, for it is not quite hard enough for easy walking.

More specifically, we do not see the physical vehicle of the moon that was, when that moon *lived* as the fourth globe of its chain, but rather the kāma-rūpa of globe D of the lunar chain that was, because we now have senses built to cognize what takes place on a subplane one degree superior to the subplane on which the physical body of globe D of the lunar chain was aeons ago. In other words, the physical vehicle of our globe D is on the astral subplane of the globe D of the former lunar chain.

Remember, however, that there are seven (or twelve) moons, and every one of them is at present the kāma-rūpa of its corresponding globe which is now 'dead,' gone, disintegrated into its component elements; and the six (or eleven) other moons belong of course to the other and higher planes of the lunar chain that was, in the same way that our higher globes belong to the higher planes of our earth chain.

The moon ran its seven rounds just as our own planetary chain will, and at the end of its seventh round it died and left its physical body behind, which ages ago decayed into cosmic dust. But the moon chain was not a good chain of life; it was a vicious chain, and we humans are among those who made it so. The kāma-rūpa of the moon will have disintegrated into its component atoms and vanished before the earth will have attained the seventh round or the last stages of its evolutionary progress in this present planetary manvantara.

As said, the moon is the lord and giver of life, as well as the cause of the death of human beings and of all other organic entities on earth. The moon also has a marked effect on the processes of disease, being the origin of the influences under which all diseases begin and run their course, culminate and either kill the body or pass out of it. Its emanations furnish the field, so to say, in which diseases begin their work. Paradoxically, the moon is also the source of healing, and this part of its power it derives from the sun; but it may not be the best thing for the individual to have the moon heal, either. It is the sun which is the great physician of the earth and of the solar system. Yet the sun itself can likewise kill. An excess of sunlight is as bad in its way as no sunlight at all. And so it is with the moon: excess of lunar light will cause putrefaction, decay, ultimate death. But the lunar light likewise stimulates growth if the balance is otherwise preserved.

In ancient mythologies the moon is sometimes referred to as the Lord of Birth, or the Lord of Generation, and at other times as the Moon-Goddess who presides over conception and the birth of children. In some countries it has been considered to be a predominantly masculine influence, as among the ancient Latins who referred to the moon as Lunus; whereas in later times when the feminine aspect was emphasized it was called Luna. Whether the moon, as in the Hindu legend, be personified as Soma, a masculine deity, or as Artemis or Diana by the Greeks and Latins, matters not at all. This merely signifies that in one case the masculine influence has been more particularly stressed in the mythological stories about the moon; and in the other, the feminine.

Since the moon is the gate of both life and death, in practically all countries of the world and in all ages the conception and growth, not only of animals, but indeed of all entities on earth, were looked upon as being directly under the lunar influence, psychically as well as physically.

There are great mystical secrets connected with the influence of the moon on marriage and gestation, and H.P.B. tells us that it were better for the human race were this more fully understood.° It may be said that no marriage should be consummated in the waning moon, but always between new and full moon towards the time of full moon. Furthermore, marriages should take place in the springtime, whether of the northern or of the southern hemisphere, the reason being that then the whole of nature is burgeoning with the new life running through all things. The ancient Attic Greeks even had a month which they called Gamelion, meaning the month of marriage, corresponding to our January-February.

The suggestions given above apply to all other spheres of man's activity. When the conditions are appropriate and you have time to choose it is always better to undertake anything of importance, such as the carrying out of a plan of high import, a journey, and so on, when the moon is waxing. Try to avoid the "dark fortnight," as the Hindus express it, which is the period of the waning moon. Begin your enterprises — commerce, study, professional work, farm work, it does not matter — after the moon is new and while it is growing towards full. Nature is then expanding and growing with you. It is a good rule to follow; but there are times when a man, a true man, should not wait but should act immediately, and act powerfully too, quite irrespective of what the moon's phases may be.

It is the moon that controls the initiatory cycle, and it is considered evil to do certain things when it stands in certain quarters of the sky, and holy to do them when it stands in other quarters. Only very great urgency will permit a violation of this rule, for it is based on operations of nature herself. As the sun gives light and inspiration to the spirit, so the moon — which in one very real sense is our evil genius, and in another very real sense an aid — governs the initiatory cycle; and the difference in these respects between the master of white magic and the master of black magic is that the former overmasters the conditions and controls them for an impersonal and holy end, and the other for a personal and evil end.

In regard to this dual influence of the moon, the one of darkness and decay, and the other of light and life, H.P.B. wrote:

°Cf. *The Secret Doctrine,* I, 228-9.

A "soma-drinker" attains the power of placing himself in direct *rapport* with the bright side of the moon, thus deriving inspiration from *the concentrated intellectual energy of the blessed ancestors.* This "concentration," and the moon being a store-house of that Energy, is the secret, the meaning of which must not be revealed, beyond the mere fact of mentioning the continuous pouring out upon the earth from the bright side of the orb of a certain influence.

This which seems one stream (to the ignorant) is of a *dual nature* — one giving life and wisdom, the other being lethal. He *who can separate the former from the latter, as Kalahamsa separated the milk from the water, which was mixed with it, thus showing great wisdom — will have his reward.* °

These are mystical thoughts, and they explain in part why the greater initiations take place always, where possible, during the light half of the moon; this is a matter of natural law, of circumstances which rule the conditions. It is not only at full moon that they take place; they begin at the instant of new moon, and continue until the moon is full, when they cease. When the moon is full, it is on the side of the earth opposite to the sun. This means that both sun and earth are pulling on the moon, drawing from it the soma drink, the lunar nectar. To those who are not ready, who are not strong enough to drink this nectar of the gods, death ensues. To those who are prepared, the soma drink is no longer lethal but gives life.

The moon not only gives life, but it likewise looses the arrows of death.† And he who can separate the life aspect of it from the death aspect is indeed a wise man. The moon is a reservoir of solar influences, what H.P.B. calls the "intellectual energy of the blessed ancestors," of the solar Lhas, as they are spoken of in Tibet. These influences the moon transmits to us, precisely as our brain-mind is the transmitter of the influences of our spirit. The inner spiritual sun of man sends forth its emanations, its rivers of rays, which are transmitted to the brain through the intermediate function of the soul. Thus the moon is the soul, the sun is the spirit, and the earth is their child, the body.

The relationship of moon and earth is so close, so far-reaching, that it affects every atom of the entire body of the earth: more, of every globe of the earth planetary chain as well as of the lunar chain.

° "Thoughts on the Elementals," *Lucifer,* May 1890, p. 187.

†Cf. *The Secret Doctrine,* I, 396–7.

THE PLANET OF DEATH

Moreover, shells of this nature [lost souls] do not remain for any great length of time in the atmosphere of this earth, but like straws floating near a whirlpool get caught up by and dragged down in that terrible Maëlstrom, which hurries off the failures towards disintegration, in other words to the planet of matter and death — the mental as well as the physical satellite of our earth. — *The Theosophist*, Sept. 1882, p. 312

THIS SOMBER PLANET is what at different times has been called the Planet of Death, or the Eighth Sphere, or the realm of Māra. As a globe it is slowly dying, and therefore is in its last round. It is almost a corpse, and is properly called, in two ways, the Planet of Death. It is of material so dense, so heavy, that we, with our relatively ethereal bodies and the relatively ethereal physical substance around us, do not perceive it as a material sphere. However, there are rare occasions when, due to a number of converging causes including the materializing influence of the moon, certain individuals may catch a glimpse of it in the moon's neighborhood. The reason that we do not see it is that very gross or material substance is as invisible and as intangible to us as is highly ethereal or spiritual substance, because both planes are different from our physical plane.

Further, this Planet of Death has a retrograde motion of rotation. As a matter of fact, every planet or globe in the solar system, visible or invisible, at different times in its planetary manvantara, slowly changes the position of its axis of rotation, so that the axis has a secular movement of inclination, slowly increasing (or decreasing) through the ages. Thus it is that at one time the axis of our earth is upright — the plane of its equator coinciding with the plane of the ecliptic — and then there is springtime over all the globe throughout the year. At other times the poles of the earth, i.e. of the axis of the earth, are parallel with the plane of the ecliptic, or with the earth's own orbit. This secular movement of inclination continues until what is the north pole points, so to speak, downwards, and the south pole upwards. The poles then have become inverted; and the movement of inclination continues until finally the north

THE PLANET OF DEATH

pole resumes its former upright position in space when considered in relation to the plane of the ecliptic.

An inversion of the poles usually brings about great continental readjustments, with consequent karmic changes in the destiny of human races, such as those which took place in the long career of the fourth root-race, the Atlantean. It should be obvious that a slow secular movement of change in the earth's axis takes millions of years; and an inversion of the poles brings about a retrograde rotation of the thus inverted globe. The Planet of Death or the Eighth Sphere is in such an inverted condition, and therefore its rotation is retrograde.°

The Eighth Sphere is a very necessary organic part of the destiny of our earth and its chain. Just as in a great city the sewers form a most important part of the organization for public health and convenience, and we have designated places where refuse is disposed of, similarly in the solar system there are certain bodies which act as vents, cleansing channels, receptacles for human waste and slag.

The Planet of Death has been given this name because it is the dread sphere to which utterly corrupt souls finally descend, although it is not hell in the Christian sense, because there is no similarity in its functions to the exoteric horrors of the theological place of punishment. But when a human soul has lost its link with its inner god, and is therefore cast off because it is no longer a fit and receptive channel for the spiritual life flowing from its inspiriting divinity, it then is discarded, much as the body may slough off particles of itself which have become useless and dead. Obviously such a lost soul or discarded psychologic entity must find its own proper habitat. It cannot go floating around aimlessly forever in the astral world or kāma-loka, because its propensities or attractions are too gross even for the vile and filthy ranges of the kāma-loka itself. It therefore sinks into the Planet of Death or the globe of Māra to which its own heavy material magnetism drags it, where it is dissipated as an entity from above, which means from our globe, and is slowly ground over in nature's laboratory.

In *The Mahatma Letters* (p. 171), this is graphically described:

Bad, irretrievably bad must be that *Ego* that yields no mite from its fifth Principle, and *has* to be annihilated, to disappear in the *Eighth Sphere*. A mite, as I say, collected from the Personal Ego suffices to save him from the dreary

---

°Cf. *The Secret Doctrine*, II, 352–3.

Fate. Not so after the completion of the great cycle: either a long Nirvana of Bliss (unconscious though it be in the, and according to, your crude conceptions); after which — life as a Dhyan Chohan for a whole Manvantara, or else "*Avitchi Nirvana*" and a Manvantara of misery and Horror as a —— you *must not* hear the word nor I — pronounce or write it. But "those" have nought to do with the mortals who pass through the seven spheres. The *collective* Karma of a future Planetary is as lovely as the collective Karma of a —— is terrible.

This is the outline of the teaching, although there are many and various exceptions pertaining to individual lost souls. However, precisely because the lost soul is an aggregate of astral-vital-psychical life-atoms concreted around a monad as yet scarcely evolved, this monad, when freed from its earth veil of life-atoms, thereupon begins in the Planet of Death a career of its own in this highly material globe.

Finally, the whole subject is complicated by the fact that the Planet of Death is in its last round, and that in consequence its 'normal' inhabitants are not to be confused with these monads dropping among them from our earth globe. The truth is that while the Planet of Death receives these fallen monads and cares for them according to those laws of nature which prevail and operate in the Eighth Sphere, it receives them as imperfectly evolved entities and treats them as such; which simply means that they are 'failures' which in the next globe reimbodiment of the Planet of Death will have to begin their evolution in an inferior capacity.

Quoting again from *The Mahatma Letters* (p. 87):

Now there are — there *must be* "failures" in the etherial races of the many classes of Dyan Chohans or Devas as well as among men. But still as these failures are too far progressed and spiritualized to be thrown back forcibly from their Dyan Chohanship into the vortex of a new primordial evolution through the lower kingdoms — this then happens. When a new solar system is to be evolved these Dyan Chohans are (remember the Hindu allegory of the *Fallen Devas* hurled by Siva into Andarah who are allowed by Parabrahm to consider it as an intermediate state where they may prepare themselves by a series of rebirths in that sphere for a higher state — a new regeneration) born[e] in by the influx "ahead" of the elementals and remain as a latent or inactive spiritual force in the aura of the nascent world of a new system until the stage of human evolution is reached. Then Karma has reached them and they will have to accept to the last drop in the bitter cup of retribution. Then they become an *active* Force, and commingle with the Elementals, or progressed *entities* of the pure animal kingdom to develope little by little the full type of humanity. In this

348

commingling they lose their high intelligence and spirituality of Devaship to regain them in the end of the seventh ring in the seventh round.

But enough of this. Always remember that we are sons of the Sun, even if we did pass through the moon and played on that stage of life — as Shakespeare might have said — such antics as made the gods weep. Yet we are rays from the solar Lhas, and ultimately, after many manvantaric ages, we shall return to Father Sun, and pass the solar portals into our spiritual home.

349

LIFE-WAVES AND THE INNER ROUNDS

Every Spiritual Individuality has a gigantic evolutionary journey to perform, a tremendous gyratory progress to accomplish. First — at the very beginning of the great Mahamanvantaric rotation, from first to last of the man-bearing planets, as on each of them, the monad has to pass through seven successive races of man. . . . Each of the seven races send seven ramifying branchlets from the Parent Branch: and through each of these in turn man *has* to evolute before he passes on to the next higher race; and that — *seven times.* . . . The branchlets typify varying specimens of humanity — physically and spiritually — and no one of us can miss one single rung of the ladder. . . . Please, bear in mind, that when I say "man," I mean a human being of our type. There are other and innumerable manvantaric chains of globes bearing intelligent beings — both in and out of our solar system — the crowns or apexes of evolutionary being in their respective chains, some — physically and intellectually — lower, others immeasurably higher than the man of our chain.   — *The Mahatma Letters,* p. 119

THE INNER ROUNDS ARE the journeyings of the evolutionary life-waves or families of monads around the globes of a planetary chain. There are actually twelve such life-waves passing from globe to globe, but we shall confine our remarks here to a consideration of the seven rūpa or manifest globes, or rounds, or life-waves, etc., leaving aside the upper five or arūpa globes with their life-waves. Thus each of the seven planetary life-waves, when passing from the first to the last globe of the seven, goes through each one in turn, beginning with A and closing with G.

On each globe the evolutionary waves make seven gyrations or turns, each of which is a root-race. These seven root-races begin with the lowest and end with the highest evolutionary degree on any one globe of the planetary chain. Between any two globes, as the life-wave passes from one globe to another in any one round, there is an interval of relative quiet or repose, which is too low in type to be called a nirvana, and yet too high to be called devachanic; and this interglobal interval is in duration about one tenth of the time passed on any one of the seven globes during each round.

The rounds likewise signify changes of consciousness as the hosts of human entities pass from globe to globe, either on the descending or shadowy arc, or on the ascending or luminous arc. Each passing from globe to globe signifies either a further descent into material existence, or a further rise out of material existence into a more spiritual state, and therefore into a more spiritual sphere. Nevertheless, the rounds themselves also are actual transfers of the hosts of entities from one globe to the next, not unlike the migrations of birds. Birds when beginning their migration first rise into the air, then they whirl around for a while, following a leader who finally finds the direction, and off they go. They leave the places where they had lived, only to return when the proper season comes again. Flock after flock of birds thus take wing to other parts of the earth; and in a closely similar manner do the families of entities living on our globe at the end of the globe-round wing their way to the next higher globe of the planetary chain. It is in each case an actual transfer, although it also means a coincident changing of consciousness.

The human host is not the only life-wave passing around the planetary chain seven times from globe A to globe G. There are several different evolutionary life-waves following each other serially in time and therefore in space. When our human life-wave shall have reached its seventh race on earth in this fourth round, and shall have gone through the interglobal period of rest and on to globe E, then after a short time, cosmically speaking, its place on globe D will be taken by another life-wave composed of a host of evolving monads; and this will occur before we as a life-wave shall have finished our sojourn on globe E.

As has been already stated, there are seven main classes of monads in seven different stages or degrees of evolutionary growth. The highest, when entering upon a new planetary chain, enters globe A — which the three classes of elementals had already formed in space around a laya-center — and therein begins to help build that globe. When the work of this monadic class is completed on globe A, by means of seven turns or root-races, then comes the second class of monads which starts to build on the foundation laid by the first monadic class.

Meanwhile this first class of monads begins to pass to the next globe on the arc of descent, globe B. When the second class of monads on globe A has finished its evolutionary course, consisting of seven gyrations or root-races, it is succeeded by the third class of monads, the second class then proceeding to globe B. So accurately adjusted are the times

351

of evolution on the cosmic clock, that when this takes place the first class of monads will have finished its work on globe B and will pass on downwards to globe C; and so on all around the chain of seven globes, all seven classes of monads following each other serially. Each globe has a certain interval of rest before any succeeding evolutionary life-wave follows on.

In connection with the entities or circling life-waves of those globes superior to our globe D, it might be of interest to add here that because these globes on the ascending arc are so much more evolved — both in types of entities living there and also in spiritual status — the very 'beasts' on globes F and G, and almost so on globe E, are hundreds of times higher than men are on this earth.

Each class of monads as it passes to the next globe leaves behind it, as seed for the next round, śishtas or remainders which will serve as the first vehicles for the first incoming monads on that globe. The life-waves, after having passed around the chain in that round, have their nirvana between globes G and A, and then begin the next manvantaric round.

K. H. in one of his letters to A. P. Sinnett called a round "the passage of a monad from globe 'A' to globe 'Z' (or 'G') through the encasement in all and each of the four kingdoms, viz., as a mineral, a vegetable, an animal and man or the Deva kingdom." The phrasing "from globe 'A' to globe 'Z' (or 'G')" is exceedingly significant, for it gives a hint of the existence of more globes than the manifest seven.° H. P. B. herself, because of the difficulty for people in those days to understand even the septenary idea, was forced to hide, except to the intuitive, the existence of the upper five globes of a chain.

A monad at its heart is a monadic essence, a continuing entity. Now the statement that the monad in its evolutionary progress from an unself-conscious god-spark to self-conscious divinity must pass through each one of the kingdoms, does not mean that these kingdoms exist before the monads which composed them brought them into being. Rather it means that the life-wave of monads expresses itself, initially, as the first kingdom of the elementals, next, as the second and then as the third elemental kingdom; it continues as the mineral, vegetable and animal kingdoms, and seventhly, as the human or deva kingdom, and finally as the three classes of the dhyāni-chohanic kingdoms. Once these kingdoms are es-

---

° *The Mahatma Letters*, p. 80.

tablished on earth, or on any other planet or celestial sphere, the fertile field is there for evolution to pursue its courses farther; and the monads come and go on their peregrinations therein.

It is the first round which marks the actual evolutional appearance of true globes, the five preliminary stages of developmental formation having been the work of the three elemental classes and of the primordial pre-elemental two stages. During this round, the monads had to build from the ground upwards all the foundation structure upon which the later superstructure was to be erected. In so doing, as they themselves were the builders, they became the monads which built the embryonic globes of the shadowy globe-chain. All the classes of monads without exception must begin at the beginning and run through all the experiences in that first chain-round to its end. This produces the ten classes of monads thus cooperating to build the globes, forming at the end of such first round the twelve globes in their embryonic shape or form.

After the first round the method of the monads in entering the globes is very naturally changed, because they find the śishta vehicles already waiting for them from the preceding round, in which the monads simply need to imbody without having to build their bodies from the ground up as had to be done during the first round. In reality, however, there is no change; it is rather a taking up again of their evolutionary development on a globe at the point where it was dropped when a particular family or life-wave of monads had left that globe during the preceding round — not a change in method, but merely a continuation of evolution in bodies already waiting.

Thus, in the first round, do the various kingdoms from the elemental to the dhyāni-chohanic come into being; and upon leaving any globe of the planetary chain, they leave behind them the śishtas to await the second round of the same life-waves. On each globe, therefore, after the main life-wave has gone to inhabit the next globe, there are left śishtas of all the different classes of monads.

Now the first life-wave, reaching the laya-center which becomes globe A, contains within itself all the other life-waves; so that after the first entering life-wave has run its seven rings or root-races on globe A, it unfolds from itself the second life-wave which takes its place, and the surplus of the first life-wave passes to globe B. This surplus — which is not the projection but rather the globe B aspect of itself — must not be regarded as being merely a superabundance of animal vitality, for every

353

higher contains within itself that which it unfolds on a lower plane. After all, this surplus of lives is really a river of peregrinating monads in all-various stages or degrees of evolutionary development, which, when considered as a unit, is indeed flowing life. This means that each passage of a life-wave from one globe to another brings forth into its proper cosmic field of manifestation the attributes and characteristics which it was impossible to unfold during the preceding globe. In other words, within the first globe all the other globes are encapsulated,° so to say, because they could not come into existence unless they were contained in the first. Thus we have seven surpluses of lives forming globe A, six forming globe B, five forming globe C, and so on around the chain.

In exactly the same way the animals came into being from the human stock — the surplus of life pouring itself forth from the human reservoir. We have the human line continuing in its genetic purity, although evolving from age to age, and meanwhile throwing off the stocks which were unevolved within it, stages inferior to the human, each unit of such inferior surplus being a learning entity, destined at some future period to pass through the human stage. This has reference to the unfolding process which took place on the downward arc; but when the bottom of the arc is reached, evolution and emanation cease, and the reverse process or involution along the ascending arc starts. The 'outbreathing' in this its minor application ends, and the 'inbreathing' begins.

Every seed is the body of an evolving entity, of a psychical life-atom, an elemental. Of course, every life-atom has everything in it *essentially* that a man or a god has. Yet no life-atom can express on any one plane more than its then evolved capacities permit, any more than a man today can be a god because he has not yet evolved forth the god within him. In the human body every vital cell, every reproductive germ, contains

---

°The Mediaevalists had a strange theory which they did not understand and which has been rejected by science. They called it encapsulation. The idea was that Mother Eve in the Garden of Eden held encapsulated in her womb all the seeds of the human race, which she passed on to her children, the families of which in their turn held encapsulated the seeds of future generations, passing them on to their children; and so forth. When properly interpreted, this is what H.P.B. meant when she spoke in *The Secret Doctrine* (I, 223-4) of the unmodified germ plasm — Weismann's theory.

Here again the Christians anthropomorphized the esoteric doctrine, thus distorting it. As a matter of fact, not only the animal kingdom, but the vegetable, mineral, and even the three elemental kingdoms, came forth from the primal human, the 'Ādām Qadmōn. They were all encapsulated within him, and he brought them forth.

within itself the potentiality not only of the divinity latent within it, but also numerous lower quasi-psychical life impulses which, could they find expression, would produce an inferior creature, whether it be an elephant, a giraffe or even some biological 'sport.' The reason why such cells in man today do not evolve forth new animate stocks is that the evolutionary urge has faded out for the remainder of this round, and involution has taken its place.

Now the expression surplus of life may likewise be used in connection with the growth of a seed into a plant. Out of the seed flows forth the surplus, in the *technical* sense, of life that the seed contains: first the green shoot, then the stem and branches and leaves, and finally the fruit producing other seeds. Surplusage here means that which flows forth from what is locked up within. The growth of a man from a human germ is also descriptive of this process: out of the seed comes the embryo, which enters the world as a child and grows to adulthood, by unfolding from within the hitherto latent powers and faculties of mind and heart, the moral and spiritual attributes.

Thus we see that, after the life-waves have formed globe A in any one round, the surplus of life is not merely what is left over in the ordinary sense, but actually is the greater part, the immense life, attributes, powers and faculties stored up in globe A, which cannot manifest there because that is not their field, and so they pass down to and unfold globe B, the next stage. When globe B has unfolded to a certain extent in the first round, the same surplus of life passes down and unfolds globe C. And so on all around the chain.

When round the first is completed, there is no longer this rolling out, no longer an evolution of what is within as regards *unmanifested* globes, because now they are on the scene. They are there. And when the life-waves enter the chain anew for the second and all subsequent rounds they merely follow the pathways that have been laid down, evolving of course, unfolding the surplus of life in themselves, but not for the building of the chain, except as further improvement upon previous stages.

This surplus of life is exactly what the ancient Stoics meant when they spoke of spirit unrolling from within itself the next element or plane in the cosmos which, let us say, was aether; and when spirit and aether were unrolled, the surplus of life passed down and formed the third, or spiritual fire; and then in serial order: air, water, earth. After that the universe was completed.

Now when the first round is ended, the globes, otherwise the mansions or houses of the planetary chain, are built each one on the highest subplane of its own cosmic plane of the solar system. Henceforth all subsequent rounds up to the seventh, or last, *are* the different cycling families of monads entering into the houses or mansions, and conditions of existence, which are ready and waiting for each class of monads as it appears on a globe in its turn in the series.

When the twelve embryonic globes of this shadow-chain in the first round are formed, on which the vehicles thus built live by force of repetitive habit, the way becomes familiar to the journeying pilgrim monads so that at each recurrent appearance of the life-wave the progress through the lower realms becomes ever more rapid. Therefore, once a monad has evolved forth from itself faculties and powers so that it can manifest as a human being, its progress through the lower kingdoms in any later cycle is very quick indeed. There is a perfect analogy in the growth of the microscopic human seed through its embryonic and fetal stages and on to adulthood. The reincarnating ego is not self-consciously active in the embryo, but becomes self-conscious on this human plane when the child first manifests signs of intelligence and of inner faculties. Just so with the ten or seven classes of monads as they pass through the various kingdoms.

The monads — which we essentially are — have now reached a stage in their evolutionary journey when the pathway forwards becomes slow and difficult again, because we are passing from humanity into godhood. Dhyāni-chohanship is the next great stage that we shall reach, as the monad of each one of us evolves forth more and more of the divine faculties and powers within us. Slowly the human race in the aeons of the future will advance to a nobler humanity, and in time there will be no men and women as such; we will be but 'humans' on the way to becoming gods. First, we shall be human dhyāni-chohans, and then at the end of the seventh round we shall leave our earth's planetary chain as fully evolved dhyāni-chohanic entities.

Those beings now expressing themselves in the human kingdom on our earth manifested in the beast kingdom on the moon. When the earth reimbodies itself as a new planetary chain we humans shall be the dhyāni-chohans or gods of the future planet which will be the child of this earth. The beings now in the beast kingdom will then be the men of that planet; and as our karmic bonds with that kingdom are very strait and close, so will they be on the planet-to-be.

When our humanity shall have attained the ultimate degree of development possible on this earth, it will likewise have attained the ultimate possible in this series of seven rounds. But the earth itself at the end of the seventh round will be passing through the stages of death, becoming the moon of the next planetary chain. This future chain will comprise the entirety of the hosts of life-atoms — spiritual, intellectual, psychical, astral, and physical — which now animate the twelve globes of our present planetary chain.

The monadic essence must pass through every grade or condition of matter belonging to the planetary chain to which it is attached, beginning with the spiritual, descending through the ethereal, and finally passing through the material states, before the monad begins again its upward cycle on the luminous arc. The purpose of this is that the monadic essence, although a god in its inmost being, shall obtain experience in these new phases of the evolution of the life-stream. But that part of the monadic essence which absorbs this experience is not the monad itself, but rather a projection of it called the ego, an imperfect ego coming over from the previous planetary chain.

To recapitulate: the monad at the beginning of every reimbodiment of a planetary chain — because it is a part of that chain unto eternity, although the chain itself is evolving — must pass through all the lower kingdoms, thus helping to form them. On the second round it passes through these kingdoms much more quickly because the road is ready. On the third round it moves still more rapidly through the lower kingdoms, but more slowly in the higher. In identic fashion the reincarnating ego finds itself obliged to enter the human womb as a life-spark; and it must pass through all the phases of gestation, although it itself is essentially a spiritual being. It must do this in order to build up a human body in which it can work, yet it stands apart from the embryo, which it merely enlivens with a portion of itself.

If we think of the passage of the monad through the globes and during the rounds as a process of gestation, then we can look upon the monad as finally being born into its own ethereal spheres after the end of the seventh round. As said, the development of the embryo is a good illustration. Here we have the case of a spiritual being needing to pass through all the kingdoms of nature in the human womb: the mineral, vegetable, animal, and finally human, before it can build for itself a body to work with on this plane. In the far future the human monad will no longer

357

have need of bodies of flesh, but, living then on highly ethereal planes of the kosmos, it will fashion for itself correspondingly ethereal vehicles. Furthermore, these bodies of ours are in themselves also evolving entities, ultimately in their turn to become monads.

When the monadic ego has finished its seven rounds, it leaves the planetary chain as a dhyāni-chohan, a planetary spirit, to become one of the army of guides of the humanity and lower entities of the next planetary chain. In that new chain, these dhyāni-chohans will not have to go through every condition of matter therein, except in the first round. When the monadic egos, the monads, have passed through the first round, they have then gained sufficient experience of the new conditions of matter to enable them to assume their position as guides and spiritual heads of the hosts of less evolved beings trailing along after them.

It is these less evolved entities which will have to pass through every phase or degree of material substance of that new planetary chain; and the highest class of these imperfectly evolved egos, in their turn, when the seven rounds of the future planetary chain shall have been completed, will leave it as dhyāni-chohans. Meanwhile, we shall have passed to a destiny still more sublime than that particular condition of dhyāni-chohanship which we shall have attained at the end of the seven rounds of our present chain.

Of course, the manifold states of material substance are not in themselves different from the lower monadic entities evolving in and through a planetary chain, but are in fact the vast aggregate host of these monadic beings themselves. Matter per se is an illusion. The essence of matter is the host of the monadic essences which are dormant or quasi-dormant, in the various conditions of material substance. Matter and the monadic hosts are therefore one; and these monadic hosts in the core of their being are pure consciousness. Hence matter per se has no actual existence, but is merely the product of these hosts of monadic essences — a subject at once mysterious and wonderful.

All the seven globes of any planetary chain are compact of these virtually incomputable armies of monads in their various degrees of evolutionary development. The mineral kingdom on our earth, for instance, is naught but a host of monads passing through that particular stage of consciousness. A somewhat higher class of monads composes the vegetable kingdom, and one still more advanced works through the beast kingdom. A host still more evolved composes the human kingdom, above which is the army of the dhyāni-chohans, who were the human beings of the planetary chain of the moon.

Furthermore, our very bodies are built of hosts of monads passing through that grade of their evolutionary growth; for our bodies are but higher animals. It is the splendor of the buddhic light shining from the heart of the monad which makes the human soul a growing, evolving entity — originally sprung from the monad, but destined at the end of the seven rounds of this planetary chain to blossom from an unself-conscious god-spark to self-conscious divinity.

To summarize: there are three evolutionary streams of life going on at one and the same time through eternity, whether it be in a cosmos, a sun, a planet, a human being, or an atom. And these are the spiritual, the psychomental or intermediate (which in man is the human soul), and the astral-vital-physical. Fundamentally the three are one — a trinity, the same ultimate life, the same ultimate substance; and yet the highest gives birth to the intermediate, and the intermediate throws forth from itself its own child, the vital-astral, which in turn is imbodied in the physical.

For three and a half rounds the general tendency of all the globes of the planetary chain is towards a greater degree of materialization; during the second half of the seven-round period there is a corresponding rise towards dematerialization, an etherealization of all the globes and of all their entities and inhabitants and things.

In the first round the life-wave passes through all the globes from A to G, the descent of the entities occurring through globes A, B, C, and through half of our globe D's life cycle. Then there begins a reascent to spiritual realms along the ascending arc through the second half of globe D, and through globes E, F, and G. The second round and third round repeat this process, through planes and worlds of an ever more material type and character. The fourth round is the last round of the process of materialization, that descent lasting until half of the life-evolution on our globe D is reached. Then begins a reversal towards a progressive etherealization, a general ascent taking the place of the former gradual slipping down through the preceding three and a half rounds.

We are now in the fourth round, and have passed the critical period which occurred during the fourth subrace of the fourth root-race on globe D in this round. We have already begun to ascend, although we have not yet left our fourth-round globe; and the next three rounds will be a continuous and ever gradual movement towards the spiritual again.

359

Nevertheless, during each of the three rounds to come there will be a descent through the globes until our earth is reached, and then an ascent along the remaining globes. But in each subsequent round the descent to globe D will be of a somewhat higher or more spiritual type than was the preceding one.

A globe is therefore seen to be evolved by a dual process of involution and evolution They work together and at the same time, every step in evolution being likewise a step in involution. The elemental powers forming the energies of a planetary chain as they descend into physical substance, are at once an involution of spirit and an evolution of matter proceeding concurrently and continuously. On the ascending arc, it is an involution or disappearance of matter and an evolution of spirit, the opposite of what took place on the downward arc. These are but two sides of the same thing. You cannot discover evolution working apart from involution, nor is involution ever found anywhere working apart from evolution. Consequently we cannot say that in the building of the latter half of the fourth globe — our earth — and of globes E, F, and G, and on up the ascending arc, evolution is the only or even predominant quality or force at work. We can only say that on the ascending arc spirit evolves and matter involves, just as on the downward arc matter evolved and spirit involved.

Every entity lives in the greater life and consciousness of some other entity from which it was born. Nothing exists unto itself alone. Everything is interlocked and permeated with something else, with another entity's vitality, mentality, spirituality, will, and body. As we humans are formed of minor entities, which are the life-atoms composing our various vehicles, so we are the life-atoms of an entity still more sublime. Our higher attributes — the inner light, vision and power, all that belongs to the spiritual part of us — remain as forming the structure through which the higher consciousness of the monad streams. Yet these inner attributes themselves are evolving equally with the lower. This can hardly be understood unless we grasp the nature of consciousness which is the fundamental of the cosmic structure. All else — matter, energy, change, progress, dormancy, the state of being awake — are but phases or events in this wondrous story of consciousness.

360

INTERPLANETARY AND INTERGLOBAL NIRVANA

When the universal spirit wakes, the world revives; when he closes his
eyes, all things fall upon the bed of mystic slumber.
— *Vishnu-Purāna*, Bk. VI, ch. iv

WHAT HAPPENS TO THE various families of monads when the end of a
round is reached on globe G and their nirvana begins? As a matter of
fact, after leaving *any* globe each class of monads enters into a short
nirvanic period of rest and spiritual assimilation before it enters the succeeding globe.° This process is repeated until the topmost globe of the
twelvefold chain is reached — when the next round begins. The important
point here is that upon leaving globe G, which already is a quasi-spiritual
globe, the different classes of monads enter the arūpa globes, where
conditions of life — and increasingly so as the monads ascend — become
more and more typically nirvanic. The same principle in reverse applies
to the monads on the downward arc when they enter globe after globe,
each globe becoming more material and physicalized.

When a life-wave, which is but another name for a family of monads,
leaves any globe, that globe then and there enters upon a period of
obscuration until the next life-wave reaches it and awakens it again. These
interglobal periods which the monadic classes experience are not all of
the same length, but vary according to the time that the life-wave has
spent on the globe which it has just left. For instance, when our life-wave
leaves globe D, after having passed, let us suppose, some thirty million
years thereon, then one tenth of that period would be our interglobal
nirvana before we as monads would begin to imbody ourselves on globe
E. The rule is that the interglobal nirvanic rest is on the whole one tenth
of the time that the life-wave has just passed on the globe.

Actually, our life-wave on this globe D during this fourth round passes
a good deal more time than thirty million years — all these time-periods

---

°This interval of rest is often rather loosely referred to as an interplanetary nirvana,
whereas it should really be spoken of as an interglobal nirvana.

have been carefully veiled as regards their respective durations. Indeed, if we were to take the entire period from its first beginnings here until its very last endings, a much longer time would be required, because we have to take into account the forerunners, the body of our life-wave, as well as the stragglers or trailers. The passage of a life-wave through any one globe of a planetary chain, such as that of our human host through our present globe D, takes therefore hundreds of millions of years; and such a passage is called a globe-manvantara.

Furthermore, a life-wave does not remain the same length of time on every globe, for not only do the life-waves differ in spirituality and materiality, but the higher the globe the shorter is the *imbodiment* period upon it. The reason for this is that the spiritual and intellectual faculties are then more strongly aroused and do not yearn for material things or imbodied existence. It is the same rule which applies to the devachanic interludes: the more spiritual and intellectual the ego, the longer is its devachan — so long as the devachan is still needed; the grosser and more materialistic the individual, the shorter is the devachan, and hence the more numerous are the imbodiments on a globe during the passage of the life-wave to which it belongs. From the foregoing it is seen that no life-wave 'jumps over' from one globe to the next; in every passage there is always an interglobal nirvana of differing lengths of time.°

When the life-wave on its round through a planetary chain leaves a globe, that globe so abandoned for the time being does not go into pralaya — which means disintegration — but into obscuration, a period of dormancy. Thus when we shall leave this fourth globe and go to the next higher globe on the ascending arc, globe E, our earth will for a long time go into its obscuration. However, it will not remain resting during the full period in which our own particular life-wave ascends through globes E, F, and G, and through the upper five globes, has its own nirvana between globes G and A, and then undertakes the descent through globes A, B, C, until our present globe D is reached again. After a few tens of millions of years, following the departure of our human life-wave from this globe, the life-wave succeeding us in the procession

---

°We should bear in mind that there are several kinds of manvantaras, pralayas, and obscurations. For instance, there are cosmic or universal manvantaras, solar manvantaras as well as planetary chain manvantaras. There are also manvantaras for the rounds, globes and races; and when we come down to human beings, there is the individual manvantara which we call an earth life.

of entities will make its appearance on earth, and then go through its seven root-races.

Obscuration simply means that a planet at certain times in its evolution is more or less barren of humanities. Periods of activity occur when the humanities appear in full flower on the respective globes. Our present human racial stocks are not the only life-wave which lives on earth. In fact, our globe D has several 'humanities' or Manus — several life-waves perhaps is a better word — evolving on it, one after the other. As explained, when our life-wave leaves, our globe D will go into obscuration for a certain period; and then a new life-wave will come rolling in, composed of its armies of beings very closely like ourselves, but not identic. By that time our human life-stocks will be on globe E.

It is like a room in a hotel. I am traveling and I spend a night in it, and then I leave. Let us say that the room remains empty for a few hours. But soon some other man is given my room, my globe, and stays there for a night and part of a day. This room does not remain vacant until I go back to the same hotel, perhaps after a year or two. So the families of monads, the life-waves, follow each other in serial order around the globes of the chain; and when a particular life-wave reaches a globe, that life-wave begins to flower: its time has come to run through its root-races.

There is an analogy between the life-waves entering their nirvana, and the human soul entering its devachan in the bosom of the spiritual monad. After every chain-round the monads go into their interplanetary nirvana; similarly, after each globe-round the monadic classes undergo an interglobal nirvana. Where do the nirvanīs go when they leave globe G? Are they just wandering vaguely in empty space like motes in the sunbeam? No; for, as pointed out, those monads who enter their nirvana after quitting globe G pass through the five upper globes before they come down again for each new round.

However, it is not the divine and spiritual parts of our constitution which pass into nirvana, for they are already, as it were, beyond that state, but it is the human monads: the nirvana is for them what the devachan is for the human soul after death. The tradition is that when the bodhisattva becomes a buddha, the buddha enters nirvana, he is wiped out; but that does not signify annihilation. What is left behind is that portion of the bodhisattva which in its turn is a monad and again will become a buddha leaving behind a bodhisattva-śishta.

There are several kinds of nirvanas, each being a state of consciousness. Now the divine and spiritual parts of an entity such as a man, are, when in their own native condition of consciousness, in a typically nirvanic condition; but the 'nirvana' into which the lower monads enter is not that higher condition of consciousness characteristic of the divine and spiritual entities.

The reason that there is a temporary nirvana between every round is that the monads which attain full self-consciousness on globe G (as we shall when we reach it at the end of this present fourth round) are not yet sufficiently evolved to have full self-consciousness on the three still higher cosmic planes; just as the human soul when it dies is not yet evolved enough to become self-conscious on planes higher than its own consciousness, and therefore sinks into the devachan where it remains until its rebirth on earth.

At the end of the seventh round, however, when the monads leave globe G, they will probably be sufficiently more evolved to be self-conscious on the first of the arūpa globes of the upward arc, possibly the second, almost certainly not the third — simply because the consciousness of that globe is too great. The monads will lapse into unconsciousness before they reach it because they have not evolved from within themselves the spiritual powers or organs to be self-conscious thereon; just as the human soul after death sinks into dreams. We are unconscious in these higher realms because we have not yet learned to live self-consciously in the grander parts of our constitution; when we have learned to do that we shall be self-conscious when we sleep, and therefore conscious when we die. Furthermore, a part of the constitution of every human being, as it travels on its upward path during its post-mortem peregrinations through the spheres, must traverse the globes on the ascending arc of our planetary chain. It has an imbodiment or contact on each one of such globes, at least once.

All these families of life-waves finally gather together like homing birds on the topmost globe of the twelvefold chain; or, if we were considering only the sevenfold chain, we might say globe G. But, because nature repeats her operations everywhere, there must be on any one of the globes, before it goes into obscuration, an assembling of all the life-waves — not in fullness, however, because there are always forerunners as well as trailers.

Thus, there is a globe-manvantara for A, a globe-manvantara for B, then C and then D; and when a life-wave has gone all around the chain, that is one chain-round for it. On each of these globes there are all classes of life-waves. There are the forerunners of our human life-wave, and there is also a numberless host of entities trailing behind, young beings on the evolutionary pathway, younger by manvantaras than the seventh race of the seventh round will be. This seventh and last race of the present manvantara of our planet will leave it then as dhyāni-chohans — gods.

The forerunners, called fifth and sixth rounders, are those advanced egos who, because of past relatively perfected experiences on the moon chain, are more evolved than the bulk of the life-wave. It is a simple thing: we have all grades of men, from the most unevolved on up to mahatmas and buddhas. The forerunners who are now in our fourth round are those individuals who, when they get the chance, leave the earth and run ahead; they forerun us, which merely means that while we are laboring along back of them on globe D they already have rushed ahead of us up the globes and down again in their fifth round. The sixth rounders are those rare flowers of the human race who are still more evolved than the fifth rounders; they have gone around twice ahead of us. But these last are few; they are as rare as the buddhas, as "rare as is the blossom of the Udumbara tree."°

The case of the trailers is quite the contrary. Many of these will not enter into active evolutionary experience on this planetary chain, which therefore means on this globe, when it shall have attained its fullness of completed evolution; for then this globe will begin to die. Those following in our wake now, and who will likewise be following us then, will pass into their nirvana just as we shall, awaiting the next planetary chain; and on that new chain-to-be, still trailing after us, will come these hosts upon hosts of minor entities inferior to us in evolutionary development. At the end of the seventh round, all the inferior entities composing the hosts of life on our planet will go into their own nirvana, but on a much lower nirvanic plane than that in which the life-wave as a whole (which will then consist of dhyāni-chohans) will be. If everything were perfected as regards the earth and all its hosts of inhabitants at the end of the seventh race of the seventh round, there would be no possibility of future reimbodiment. Everything and everybody and the planet itself would have attained paranirvana; and many, many solar manvantaras would pass before the urge to reimbodiment was felt anew.

°*The Voice of the Silence,* p. 39.

But such is not the case. The entities and things that are less evolved than the seventh-race humanity in the seventh round are still imperfect, therefore possessing both good and evil in them; and necessarily they bring back into the next reimbodiment all that they are themselves. There will be entities immediately inferior to the seventh race of the seventh round followed by other hosts still more imperfect trailing behind along the evolutionary pathway to the very deeps of material existence.

Let us consider our own globe D. We are in the fifth root-race. We have to run through two more root-races before our globe goes into obscuration. But the animals are here also, as are the plants, the stones, the three elemental kingdoms, all these life-waves cooperating and making the life around us. There are also representatives of some of the dhyāni-chohanic kingdoms amongst us, invisible to us, but that is simply because they are higher than we. We know of a few on the lower globes, and we call them mahatmas, chohans, and by other names. Christians speak of them as angels; but these chohans are amongst us, forerunners of their regular life-waves. Therefore on our globe D towards the manvantara's ending every one of the different life-waves must have its representatives here, and all must be ready to wing their way in serial order, each in its turn, to globe E before globe D goes into obscuration.

When I say that representatives of every one of the seven or ten life-waves gather together like homing birds on a globe before it goes into obscuration, it does not mean that every one of these life-waves or monadic classes is on such globe in that life-wave's *fullness*, although this last fact approaches reality on the highest globe of the twelvefold chain, where there is a rest before the new round begins.

As the earth is but the physical body of a seven- or twelvefold entity, the rest periods of such a composite being are likewise composite in character. When a planetary chain dies, each of the elements of its constitution — that is, the hosts and multitudes of life-atoms, and quasi-conscious, self-conscious, and fully self-conscious beings — goes into its respective nirvana. But the planetary chain itself, considered as an entity, does not enter a planetary nirvana, but rather goes into a planetary devachan. What is nirvana for the component inhabitants of a planetary chain is but the devachan of that chain, or rather of the globes forming that chain.

Similarly is it with the human being, for nature's primal law of analogy runs throughout. When a man dies, the human monad is in a nirvanic state for a period. But the god within, for that period, is not in that nirvanic state. And, thirdly, the human soul is in its devachan.

Our earth is lower in the scale of its individual evolution than is the average humanity inhabiting it, although the spiritual entity, of which the earth is the physical expression, bears the same relation to its humanity that the human soul bears to the composite atoms of the lower part of the human constitution. Now some may wonder whether this statement refers to the earth as globe D of our planetary chain, or to the chain as a whole. While it applies to our globe earth in particular, it can refer by analogy equally well to every other globe of our planetary chain. The fact is that each such globe, from the evolutionary standpoint, is less advanced than the 'humanity' of the evolving egos which at any time inhabit it or, otherwise stated, pass through it during the course of the rounds through the globes of the planetary chain.

In this connection I am reminded of a certain passage in *The Mahatma Letters* (p. 94):

The correspondence between a mother-globe and her child-man may be thus worked out. Both have their seven principles. In the Globe, the elementals (of which there are in all seven species) form (a) a gross body, (b) her fluidic double (*linga* sariram), (c) her life principle (jiva); (d) her fourth principle kama rupa is formed by her creative impulse working from centre to circumference; (e) her fifth principle (animal soul or *Manas*, physical intelligence) is embodied in the vegetable (in germ) and animal kingdoms; (f) her sixth principle (or spiritual soul, Buddhi) is man (g) and her seventh principle (atma) is in a film of spiritualized akasa that surrounds her.

Now I would like to point out that K. H. had in mind here the sevenfold nature of the *physical* sphere of the earth only, and was not dealing as I was with our globe earth as a cosmic septenary, containing as it does all the seven element-principles of the universe from the cosmic ātman down to the globe's sthūla-śarīra. K. H. was concerned only with our globe's terrestrial sthūla-śarīra, with *its* seven elements and principles. As every one of the principles is in itself sevenfold, even the sthūla-śarīra is a septenary entity; and of this sevenfold characteristic of our physical plane, we human beings form the buddhi life-atoms during our transit.

In identical manner, man's sthūla-śarīra may be divided into seven principles formed of portions of all the parts of his constitution expressing themselves *on the physical plane* in and through his body. For instance,

FOUNTAIN-SOURCE OF OCCULTISM

in the human body all the seven species or classes of elementals form its grossest physical matter, its fluidic double, and its life-principle or prāna; whereas the fourth principle of the physical body is a portion of the element of kāma working through it; its fifth principle is the brain-mind's psychomagnetic activity; its sixth principle is the reflection in the body of man's higher human soul; and the body's seventh principle or ātman is the ākāśic auric fluid surrounding the human body, i.e. the auric egg of man in its lowest or most material aspect.

While the planetary spirit of our earth is farther along the evolutionary ladder of life than is the humanity inhabiting it, nevertheless the earth as a globe is less advanced in physical evolutionary development than is the human body of flesh, relatively soft and quasi-astral when compared with the earth's rocky and metallic sphere.

I might add here that the relation which the planetary spirit of our globe earth — considered as a cosmic septenate — bears to the different 'humanities' evolving on and through our globe is of a distinctly hierarchical character; and the same relation holds with regard to all the other globes of our planetary chain. Indeed, the same hierarchical relation exists with respect to the planetary spirits of the sacred planets through which the evolving 'humanities' pass during the course of the outer rounds.

ŚISHTAS AND MANUS

The most developed Monads (the lunar) reach the human germ-stage in the first Round; become terrestrial, though very ethereal human beings towards the end of the Third Round, remaining on it (the globe) through the "obscuration" period as the seed for future mankind in the Fourth Round, and thus become the pioneers of Humanity at the beginning of this, the Fourth Round. Others reach the Human stage only during later Rounds, *i.e.*, in the second, third, or first half of the Fourth Round. And finally the most retarded of all, *i.e.*, those still occupying animal forms after the middle turning-point of the Fourth Round — will not become men at all during this Manwantara. They will reach to the verge of humanity only at the close of the seventh Round to be, in their turn, ushered into a new chain after *pralaya* — by older pioneers, the progenitors of humanity, or the Seed-Humanity (*Sishta*), viz., the men who will be at the head of all at the end of these Rounds. — *The Secret Doctrine*, I, 182

COMPARATIVELY LITTLE has been written in theosophical literature about the śishtas, their characteristics and the very important function they play in nature.

The Sanskrit word śishta comes from the verbal root *śish*, to leave, to remain behind, so that its past participle means remainder, left behind, etc. Now it is interesting that śishta may also be derived from the verbal root *śas*, to discipline, to rule, to instruct, this past participle meaning disciplined, well regulated, and hence learned, select, wise, etc., and therefore superior or chief. It is rather curious how the past participle of each of these verbal roots imbodies meanings which the esoteric doctrine shows as being the characteristic qualities of the śishtas themselves.

The śishtas thus are the highest representatives of a life-wave, otherwise of a monadic class, left behind on a globe of a planetary chain when that globe goes into its obscuration. When a life-wave finishes its seven races on a globe, the greater part of it passes on to the next globe during the round, but leaves behind its highest representatives who are the śishtas, the remainders, left there to provide the same life-wave, on its return to the same globe, with the seeds of life enabling it to multiply itself again.

Now the śishtas must not be confounded with the Manus. In various

369

passages of *The Secret Doctrine*, H.P.B. speaks of the Manu that begins the evolution of a life-wave on any globe as then being a root-Manu, and of the Manu that remains behind when the life-wave leaves a globe as being the seed-Manu. This shows clearly that the Manus and the śishtas are very intimately connected, so much so that in certain aspects they are identical; yet they are not identical all along the line.

The life-waves, as already stated, pass around the globes of the chain one after the other, so that the first class which appears on the evolutionary scene is the first elemental kingdom, and when it has run through its seven rings or root-races, the second elemental kingdom does the same, followed in its turn by the third; and when this last has completed its rings, then come the monads of the mineral kingdom which run through their septenary gyrations, to be followed by the vegetable, the animal, and the human kingdom and, finally, by the first, second, and third dhyāni-chohanic kingdoms.

When any one of these ten kingdoms leaves a globe in order to pass to the next globe around the chain, it leaves behind its most fully evolved individuals as śishtas, and the globe thus quitted has a brief period of obscuration, after which it awakens to the flowing into it of the first representatives of the succeeding life-wave or kingdom. Meanwhile the śishtas of the preceding kingdom remain on the globe until the great majority of their own life-wave, which is now passing along the other globes on its round, returns; and then these śishtas feel the incoming or influence of their own life-wave returning, and respond by proper increases in numbers, thus providing the vehicles in which the bulk of the life-wave will in time imbody itself as the first root-race of the new round on this particular globe.°

It would be a mistake to imagine these śishtas as either evolving rapidly,

---

°In her magazine *The Theosophist* (March 1886, p. 352), H. P. Blavatsky writes that in the Vedas "it is said that at the end of each *Manvantara* comes the *pralaya*, or the destruction of the world — only one of which is known to, and expected by, the Christians — when there will be left the *Sishtas*, or remnants, seven Rishis and one warrior, and all the seeds, for the next human 'tide-wave of the following Round.' "

In a footnote to this she explains that, according to the Hindus, these eight persons are named śishtas because they are the only ones left after all the others are destroyed. Then she adds: "This is the orthodox version. The secret one speaks of seven Initiates having attained Dhyanchohanship toward the end of the seventh Race on this earth, who are left on earth during its 'obscuration' with the seed of every mineral, plant, and animal that had not time to evolute into man for the next Round or world-period."

or as having no evolutionary progress whatsoever, for both these supposi-
tions are incorrect. Although the śishtas when left behind are always very
much less numerous than the bulk of the life-wave, being the highest
representatives of their life-wave, nevertheless they do continue to evolve,
but at a much lower rate than takes place when the life-wave proper
is on the globe; so that during the hundreds of millions of years before
their own life-wave comes again, they slowly evolve and regularly reproduce themselves, albeit in a quasi-passive state or condition.

In the human kingdom, these śishtas are imbodied reincarnating egos,
and of course die and are reborn again and again, the individual egos
having exactly the same post-mortem destiny that they always had had.
Furthermore, the human śishta-group — which will serve more or less
accurately as an illustration for all other śishta-groups — does not remain
numerically fixed, for the simple reason that it is constantly receiving
a gradual increment in numbers because of forerunners, individuals who
outrun their life-wave and thus again reach the globe on which the
śishta-group is, but more quickly than does the main body of the life-wave.
These śishtas, in our case the fifth rounders (and very rarely the sixth
rounders), remain behind because they have already run through their
fifth round, and therefore do not need to repeat it; as a matter of fact
they cannot go on in their evolutionary development until the life-wave
catches up to them. Hence it is that the śishtas continuously, albeit slowly,
increase in number, and somewhat more rapidly with each passing million
of years until the life-wave reaches their globe again.

I have been speaking here about the śishta-groups left on the different
globes of our planetary chain during any round; but nature, because of
her analogical structure and operations, has śishtas of other kinds than
the globe-śishtas. There are śishtas, as an example, which pass over from
one dying chain to the next imbodiment of the same chain, and hence
it is that these śishta-groups are called the seeds of life, or the root-śishtas,
which open the manvantaric drama in the first round on globe A of the
new chain-imbodiment.

Being śishtas no longer of evolving life-waves from globe to globe
of a chain, these śishta-groups from one chain-imbodiment to the next
are not so much individuals manifested in bodies as what I at times have
called monadic spheres or monadic eggs.° Indeed, the human ego while

°Cf. *Fundamentals of the Esoteric Philosophy*, ch. XLII.

in its devachan may likewise be considered as a monadic egg or sphere because, in its blissful dreaming within the spiritual monad — clothed as the devachanī is in its auric egg — it is really a sort of monadic egg out of which will grow the man-to-be in the next earth life. Of course what is said here about the monadic egg of the human kingdom applies equally well, in principle, to the śishta-groups of all the other nine kingdoms or monadic classes between chain-imbodiments.

Thus when the new chain is forming it is always the highest representatives of all classes which, combining with the elementals of their own class or variety, become as it were the ideative 'architects' impressing the architectural plan upon these elementals so that these last can do their respective labors in building the globes of a chain. Once this architectural scheme, with the help of the elementals, is ideated forth, then the lower representatives of each different kingdom begin to manifest and in turn do *their* respective labors of preparing the differing types of groundwork into which the highest representatives again, and later in due course of time, manifest themselves.

As for the Manus, the following selections from the writings of H.P.B. give the essence of the teaching:

Vaivasvata Manu (the Manu of our own fifth race and Humanity in general) is the chief personified representative of the *thinking* Humanity of the fifth Root-race; and therefore he is represented as the eldest Son of the Sun and an *Agnishwatta* Ancestor. As *"Manu"* is derived from *Man*, to think, the idea is clear. Thought in its action on human brains is endless. Thus Manu is, and contains the potentiality of all the thinking forms which will be developed on earth from this particular source. . . .

Manu is the synthesis perhaps of the Manasa, and he is a single consciousness in the same sense that while all the different cells of which the human body is composed are different and varying consciousnesses there is still a unit of consciousness which is the man. But this unit, so to say, is not a single consciousness: it is a reflection of thousands and millions of consciousnesses which a man has absorbed.

But Manu is not really an individuality, it is the whole of mankind. You may say that Manu is a generic name for the Pitris, the progenitors of mankind. They come, as I have shown, from the Lunar Chain. They give birth to humanity, for, having become the first men, they give birth to others by evolving their shadows, their astral selves. . . . But, as the moon receives its light from the Sun, so the descendants of the Lunar Pitris receive their higher mental light from the Sun or the "Son of the Sun." For all you know Vaivasvata Manu may

372

be an *Avatar* or a personification of MAHAT, commissioned by the Universal Mind to lead and guide thinking Humanity onwards.

— *Transactions of the Blavatsky Lodge,* pp. 77–8

Manu declares himself created by Virâj, or Vaiswanara, (the Spirit of Humanity), which means that his Monad emanates from the never resting Principle in the beginning of every new Cosmic activity: that *Logos* or UNIVERSAL MONAD (collective Elohim) that radiates *from within himself all* those Cosmic Monads that become the centres of activity — progenitors of the numberless Solar systems as well as of the yet undifferentiated *human* monads of planetary chains as well as of every being thereon. Each Cosmic Monad is "Swayambhûva," the SELF-BORN, *which becomes the Centre of Force, from within which emerges a planetary chain* (of which chains there are seven in our system), and whose radiations become again so many Manus Swayambhûva (a generic name, mysterious and meaning far more than appears), each of these becoming, as a *Host,* the Creator of his own Humanity. — *The Secret Doctrine,* II, 311

As the word *manu* is a derivative from the Sanskrit verbal root *man,* to think, to reflect upon, a Manu, therefore, is at one and the same time a thinking individual and an army of minor individuals or 'thinkers' which compose it. Our physical body is an individual and yet is composed of an immense number of smaller individuals, each one a distinct unitary entity, and yet absolutely belonging to and comprehended by the body as a whole. Now this is an exact description of what a logos is in cosmic magnitudes. In other words, that which a cosmic logos is in the cosmos — being at once the cosmic Purusha as well as an army of subordinate monads composing it — that on the smaller scale of a chain or a globe is a Manu.

H.P.B. expressed this fact in her own inimitable way:

If all those Manus and Rishis are called by one generic name, this is due to the fact that they are one and all the manifested Energies of one and the same LOGOS, the celestial, as well as the terrestrial messengers and permutations of that Principle which is ever in a state of activity; conscious during the period of Cosmic evolution, unconscious (from our point of view) during Cosmic rest, as the Logos sleepeth in the bosom of THAT which "sleepeth not," nor is it ever awake — for it is SAT or *Be-ness,* not a Being. It is from IT that issues the great unseen Logos, who evolves all the other *logoi,* the primeval MANU who gives being to the other Manus, who emanate the universe and all in it collectively, and who represent in their aggregate the *manifested* Logos. Hence we learn in the "Commentaries" that while no Dhyan Chohan, not even the highest, can realise completely "the condition of the preceding Cosmic evolution," "the Manus retain a knowledge of their experiences of all the Cosmic evolutions throughout Eternity." — *The Secret Doctrine*, II, 310

A Manu, then, is a minor logos, either of a globe or of an entire chain, according to our scale of magnitude; and is humanity both as an individual and as the vast number of egos of the human host which in their inclusive aggregate compose the Manu. Hence we may speak of a life-wave beginning its evolutionary course upon a globe as a root-Manu, out of which will proceed in due course of time the seven root-races; and, equivalently, we may say that the same life-wave when it leaves a globe is the seed-Manu, passing forwards on its round through the other globes and becoming again the root-Manu when it reaches that globe once more.

As said before, the Manus and the śishtas, while very closely linked, are not identical, for the śishtas are the most advanced individuals of the seed-Manu; and it is these śishtas which become the seeds of life when their Manu reaches their globe again and becomes the root-Manu. The Manu therefore includes not only the main body of the life-wave but the śishtas also.

In the light of the preceding paragraphs, it will be easier to understand the teachings as imbodied by H.P.B. in the following passage from her article, "The Septenary Principle in Esotericism." Speaking of the septenary law and of the innumerable allusions to it throughout ancient literatures, she asks "Who was Manu, the son of Swayambhuva?", and answers by explaining that:

The secret doctrine tells us that *this* Manu was no man but the representation of the first human races evolved with the help of the Dhyan-Chohans (*Devas*) at the beginning of the first Round. But we are told in his *Laws* (Book I, 80) that there are fourteen Manus for every Kalpa or "interval from creation to creation" (read interval from one *minor* "Pralaya" to another); and that "in the present divine age, there have been as yet *seven* Manus." Those who know that there are seven rounds, of which we have passed three, and are now in the fourth; and who are taught that there are seven dawns and seven twilights or fourteen *Manvantaras;* that at the beginning of every Round and at the end and on, and between the planets there is "an awakening to *illusive* life," and "an awakening to *real* life," and that, moreover, there are "root-Manus" and what we have to clumsily translate as "the seed-Manus" — *the seeds for the human races of the forthcoming Round* (a mystery divulged, but to those who have passed

374

their 3rd degree in initiation); those who have learned all that, will be better prepared to understand the meaning of the following. . . . Just as each planetary Round commences with the appearance of a "Root-Manu" (Dyan Chohan) and closes with a "Seed-Manu," so a *root* and a *Seed* Manu appear respectively at the beginning and the termination of the human period on any particular planet. It will be easily seen from the foregoing statement that a *Manu-antaric* period means, as the term implies, the time *between* the appearance of two Manus or Dyan Chohans; and hence a minor *Manuantara* is the duration of the *seven* races on any particular planet, and a major manvantara is the period of one human round along the Planetary chain. Moreover, that, as it is said that each of the seven Manus *creates* 7 x 7 Manus, and that there are 49 root-races on the seven planets during each Round, then every root-race has its Manu.

— *The Theosophist*, July 1883, p. 254

Thus we see once more the fundamental unity of all that is and the unbreakable natural bonds uniting us with everything that the universe contains. None of us can advance or pursue our pilgrimage alone — not one of us. We take along with us, bound into all the parts of our constitution, countless hosts of entities evolutionally inferior to us; and precisely in the same manner, but on a different scale, all of us are united by inseparable bonds with the spiritual beings superior to ourselves in the cosmic hierarchy. We must all go forwards together, as we have been doing through all past time; and into all future time we shall be progressing unitedly as a host of monads, like a vast cosmic river of lives.

VIII

Gods - Monads - Life-Atoms

WHO ARE THE GODS?

Esotericism, pure and simple, speaks of no personal God; therefore are we considered as Atheists. But, in reality, Occult Philosophy, as a whole, is based absolutely on the ubiquitous presence of God, the Absolute Deity; and if It itself is not speculated upon, as being too sacred and yet incomprehensible as a Unit to the finite intellect, yet the entire philosophy is based upon Its divine Powers as being the source of all that breathes and lives and has its existence. In every ancient religion the One was demonstrated by the many. In Egypt and India, in Chaldea and Phoenicia, and finally in Greece, the ideas about Deity were expressed by multiples of three, five, and seven; and also of eight, nine and twelve great Gods which symbolized the powers and properties of the One and Only Deity. This was related to that infinite subdivision by irregular and odd numbers to which the metaphysics of these nations subjected their ONE DIVINITY. Thus constituted, the cycle of the Gods had all the qualities and attributes of the ONE SUPREME AND UNKNOWABLE; for in this collection of divine personalities, or rather of symbols personified, dwells the ONE GOD, the GOD ONE, that God which, in India, is said to have no Second: "Oh God Ani (the Spiritual Sun), thou residest in the agglomeration of thy divine personages."

These words show the belief of the ancients that all manifestation proceeds from one and the same source, all emanating from the one identical principle which can never be completely developed except in and through the collective and entire aggregate of its emanations.

— H.P.B.'s E.S. *Instructions,* II

IT IS PROBABLE THAT no theme is so enwrapped in hazy obscurities as that of the gods of the various nations. In fact, even scholars — while acquainted with the religious, philosophical and mystical literatures of antiquity, as well as with the scriptures of those Oriental peoples who are still polytheistic in their belief — would be hard driven to give a clear-cut statement as to just what these gods were and are. The reason is that Occidentals for some two thousand years have abandoned all polytheistic thought for a somewhat illogical monotheistic conception of nature, and so are wholly out of sympathetic understanding with what these ancient and modern peoples consider their gods or goddesses to be.

Now it would be quite misleading to suppose that either the devas

379

of Hindu mythology, or the gods and goddesses of the ancient Mediterranean peoples and their neighbors, are all fully self-conscious divinities inspiring and more or less controlling nature. They would be far better understood if we called them the powers of nature, including under this definition the divine, the semidivine, and all the ethereal, astral, and astral-physical entities which not only infill, but actually compose, our universe.

The esoteric philosophy, however, when speaking of gods, conceives of beings who, from their origin and by their characteristics and functions, are typically inhabitants of the highest cosmic planes. These gods are divisible into two classes or groups which are, so to speak, the extremes of the divine powers of nature, these extremes being the septenary classes of the divinities considered (a) *at their origin,* and (b) as *full-blown self-conscious beings* active on the light side of nature and on the divine-spiritual planes.

When a universe is beginning to unfold itself, there arise into activity, automatically as it were, beings on the highest cosmic plane (the only one then in existence) which are born from the very stuff or essence of that divine cosmic plane itself. These, class (a), are what we could call cosmic divine elementals; born of the substance or essence of the mūla-prakriti of the cosmic unit, they are divine and divine-spiritual in type or character, gods after a fashion, although elemental divinities just beginning their evolution in this universe, and not yet full-blown gods or highly evolved jīvanmuktas.

Class (b), on the other hand, more truly corresponds to what the Western mind conceives divinities to be. They are those relatively fully evolved gods who had reached divinity on the divine and divine-spiritual planes at the end of the *preceding* mahāmanvantara; and because they have so far advanced on the evolutionary ladder of life that they are native to those realms, they come forth contemporaneously with the group of cosmic elementals described under (a). Now those of group (b), while being full-blown divinities, are, nevertheless, 'failures' in the sense that they had not evolved sufficiently far at the end of the preceding mahāmanvantara to leave the present universe and enter into a higher one, and consequently they have karmic links obliging them to take part in the new mahāmanvantara of the universe now in process of opening its cosmic drama of life.

Thus the cosmic elementals are borne forwards into activity and begin the work of building the new universe under the spiritual and intellectual guidance of the true divinities or divine powers, the latter coalescing with the former and guiding their activities. As all these entities of both groups are, or at least become, sevenfold, such coalescence takes place in the points of mutual joining or similarity of swābhāvic substance. In *The Mahatma Letters* (p. 87), K.H. speaks of this event and the coalescence of the self-conscious divinities with the newly aroused elementals as bringing about the first formation of a cosmic unit.

The gods are no mere abstractions; they are entities, incomparably more 'entified' than we are. They are examples of pure, individualized consciousnesses, while we are examples of entities whose consciousness is scarcely realized by ourselves. The gods live in their own spiritual realms, in bodies of spiritual texture, or in what to us would be bodies of light; just as to entities lower than we *our* bodies would seem to be built of light — and so in fact they are. To us it is flesh, because our senses are of the same substance.

What form have the gods? They have such forms as karma and evolution have given to them. What form have human beings? Such forms as karma and evolution have given to us. The great difference between a man and a god is that the gods are quasi-universal in their vital and consciousness-spheres, while men are extremely restricted in the spheres of their vitality and consciousness. On the other hand, the main similarity between them is that both god and man hold within their vital sphere other entities of a lower degree. The gods are countless. New gods are continuously being added to the host, while others are advancing into a still higher class of divinities. But every god contains within the realm of his auric egg — which includes his vitality and his consciousness, his intellect and his buddhic energy and his ātman — a whole vast range of less evolved beings.

Consider the body of man with its multitudes of life-atoms and physical atoms, and remember at the same time that a large number of such physical atoms within their own atomic system have inhabitants, many of which are sentient, conscious, self-conscious, thinking entities. Yet man comprehends them all within the sphere of his vital influence. His is the dominant vitality which permeates and holds them all together as an entity. Similarly, we are human life-atoms living in the auric egg, in the vital sphere, of a divinity.

Stars, comets, planets, and nebulae — all are entities, vital phenomena, gathered together in and encompassed by the vitality of some super-divinity. And thus it is throughout Space endlessly.

Mere size has naught to do with consciousness. Some of the electrons of certain atoms are inhabited, and some of these inhabitants are fully as intelligent and self-conscious as we are. They think, they feel, they aspire. They are the 'humans' of those infinitesimal worlds. In the other direction, think of the wondrous spaces that we call our universe; the billions of suns which compose the Milky Way, most of them probably having planets around them, many of which are inhabited.

We on this little electron of our own solar system atom are in the same position in relation to the cosmic divinity in which we have our being, as the infinitesimal entities are to us. It is our vitality, our intelligence, our individuality, it is the energies and powers and forces welling forth from the heart of us, which give life and evolutionary direction to these infinitesimal beings living within us. They are our children. There is nothing separate in boundless Infinitude. Everything is interwoven with everything else. And this fact is the basis of the greatest teaching of occultism — the fundamental essential oneness of all that is.

Now as every universe, of whatever grade or magnitude in Space, is overseen and inspired by an originating ātmic divinity — or cosmic hierarch° — we may look upon all these divinities as rays or logoi from this cosmic hierarch, very much as the life-atoms on any plane of a man's auric egg can be looked upon as rays or individuals flowing forth from one or another of the different monads of his constitution.

°The cosmic hierarch is likewise called the supreme Silent Watcher of our universe, and this should throw light on just what a Silent Watcher is on any other plane.

EVOLUTIONARY JOURNEY OF THE MONADS

MONAD IS A GENERAL term for a variety of consciousness centers, whether in the constitution of a man or of a universe. In man, a microcosm, there are a number of monads: the divine monad or inner god, the spiritual, the human, and the vital-astral monad, each being the offspring of the monad immediately superior to it. No matter what its grade, every monad is a learning, evolving entity.

Man is composite, wholly mortal in his lower aspects, and unconditionally immortal only in the monadic essence, his inner god. From this monadic essence all his sevenfold nature evolves and manifests various phases of the stream of consciousness which man essentially is. The spiritual monad forms around itself a veil, a body, in which it can express certain parts of its energies on a lower plane, and this again exudes from itself a less ethereal vehicle, a soul, which enables the spiritual monad to manifest on a still lower plane. And so the process is repeated serially, these garments of light becoming progressively grosser until we reach the linga-śarīra or model-body which, in its turn and as the last effort, exudes forth and builds the physical body. In this way are man's sheaths of selfhood unfolded.

We humans are but evolved life-atoms, and in comparison with beings higher than ourselves, our spiritual natures are but life-atoms living in and of the essence of the higher gods. Thus there exists an intimate communion between the gods and men, because in these greater and vaster cosmic spheres we are evolving life-atoms of that sublimer stage.

Not only is every being an expression of an individualized divinity, its inner god, but all these inner gods are under the sway of, and living in and forming a part of, some greater divinity, itself but a part of a superior host collectively aggregated within the life-sphere of some divinity still more sublime; and so on ad infinitum. At every step we may say with Paul of the Christians: "In It we live and move and have our being." The supreme hierarch of the cosmic hierarchy includes within its body corporate this vast aggregate of inner gods, much as our body contains all the life-atoms which compose it. In boundless Space, there are an infinite number of such cosmic hierarchies.

Every one of us, in aeons upon aeons in the far distant past, was a life-atom continuously forming a part of the body, or of the intellectual portion, or of the psychical range, of the constitution of some entity who now is a divinity — our own supreme hierarch — and we are trailing along behind as part of that divinity's 'family.' These supreme hierarchs, infinite in number, form the inhabitants of the divine-spiritual universe; just as we in our relatively little sphere of consciousness and energy are the inhabitants here. We are gods to the life-atoms which enter our bodies; and to the higher gods, into whose vehicles and spheres of life we enter, we are life-atoms.

Gods or monadic essences, monads, egos, souls, life-atoms, atoms — these form a descending series. First, a monadic essence or god clothes itself with its monad, which in turn clothes itself with its ego; this again enwraps itself with its soul, which clothes itself with one particular life-atom around which are grouped by karmic attraction other minor life-atoms, likewise emanated by the originating monadic essence. Thus every monad is derivative from its parent god, yet its future destiny is to unfold itself into a god. This apparent inversion of teaching will not seem so difficult to understand if we remember that as soon as a monad becomes a god, through an unfolding of its latent faculties, it then and there begins to emanate its own child monad and the hosts of minor children monads which in their aggregate furnish it with its various vehicles — all of this reproducing the above-mentioned series from gods to atoms.

A monad entering our hierarchy starts its existence as an unself-conscious god-spark, and then flowering out through humanity it attains divinity and ends its career in that particular manvantara as a full-blown god. It would be absurd, as pointed out by H.P.B.,° to say that the monad of an atom of hornblende, through the long ages, by wriggling in and out of other minerals, and in and out of vegetables and heaven knows how many kinds of beasts, finally wriggled into a man. That is not the idea. The statement which, by the way, was written by one of her teachers, was made in an endeavor to set forth that the old quasi-Darwinian theory of evolution, as meaning a constant accretion of things becoming at length a self-conscious center, was wrong.

Evolution does not mean a continual accretion of experience upon experience upon experience. Evolution means *a flowing out from within:*

°Cf. *The Secret Doctrine,* I, 178.

the unrolling, the unfolding, of what is already within. Character, individuality, self-conscious energy, self-conscious power, all come from within. The core of every entity, whether god, monad, man, or atom, is in essence a divinity. In the gods it is a still higher divinity; in human beings it is a god. This is the monadic essence.

The statement of the Lord Buddha that nothing composite endures, and consequently that as man is a composite entity there is in him no immortal and unchanging 'soul,' is the key. The 'soul' of man is changing from instant to instant — learning, growing, expanding, evolving — so that at no two consecutive seconds of time or of experience is it the same. Therefore it is not immortal. For immortality means enduring continually *as you are.* If you evolve you change, and therefore you cannot be immortal in the part which evolves, because you are growing into something greater.

Hence the monad of an atom of carbon or any other mineral is not the same thing as the monad of a Shakespeare, a Newton or a Plato. The essence in each case is identic, but not the monad. It is this essence which projects a ray or extends a portion of its energy in and upon the astral realm, which energy thus at its tip becomes the astral monad — itself a mere phase of the energies and capacities inherent in the monadic essence. The next phase, and speaking now in aeonic periods, is the human monad. When the human phase of the monadic essence passes, we shall have become spiritual monads. When this spiritual phase passes, we shall then have become the monadic essence itself, and thus shall have returned home as a full-blown god.

The teaching in *The Secret Doctrine* was an endeavor to uproot the mistaken idea that the little, everlasting, and unchanging hard atoms, as the atoms of the chemistry of that day were supposed to be, were our monads. The monads are vital entities, centers of consciousness quivering with life, changing incessantly and continually growing. And so it is quite wrong to picture any monad as an identic unchanged monad through the past ages: through the minerals, through the vegetables and through the animals. What we must figurate is a monadic essence divine in character, belonging to the spiritual-divine world, which continually manifests certain portions of itself in lower realms — from the lowest to the highest — of that universe. As Krishna says: "I established this whole Universe with a single portion of myself, and remain separate"° — separate, yet

---

°*Bhagavad-Gītā*, ch. x.

385

the 'single portion' is not detached in the sense that it is an amputated ray, as if the sun could send out a ray and lose it. The sun remains separate from its ray, yet the ray remains a portion of the sun.

The monadic essence, because it is the root of everything that flows forth from it, is like the sun shining upon the evolving entity derived from it — the many monads which are its rays. But if we think of such an entity as radically separate, progressing along an absolutely distinct path from other entities, we shall wander far afield.

Every monad or soul is in a certain sense an entity destined to evolve to the spiritual stage of its parent monadic essence. As the human child grows up to be like his father, sprung from the father and yet different, another individual, so is it with any monad. The human soul, for example, is destined to develop into a spiritual soul, because already latent in and overshadowing the human entity, is a Buddha or Christ, itself destined in time to flower out as a dhyāni-chohan, a god; for a dhyāni-chohan is the very heart of a Buddha or Christ.

Dhyāni-chohan is a term taken from the Mahāyāna Buddhism of Central and Northern Asia, and is a generalizing expression very much like the word gods. Indeed, the very highest classes of dhyāni-chohans are identical with the gods, while all the lower or intermediate classes run down the scale of the cosmic structure, thus including demigods and other self-conscious entities of still inferior grades, until we reach beings like us, who are what one might call embodied dhyāni-chohans of a lower grade, for such we truly are in our buddhi-mānasic parts. It would be wrong to speak of the elementals as dhyāni-chohans, for the significant meaning of dhyāni is a self-conscious individual of a more or less spiritual character who to us seems to be involved in lofty 'contemplation,' i.e. in what Hindu philosophy calls dhyāna. Hence, all the different grades of dhyāni-chohans more properly belong to the higher parts of the cosmic hierarchical structure. The lower portions of this structure are the three general classes of the elementals, the various kinds of nature-sprites (elementals slightly evolved), and the grades of beings higher than the nature-sprites up to and including the human kingdom. Above the human kingdom, which is marked by self-consciousness and the beginnings of spiritual dhyāna, begin the lowest groups of the dhyāni-chohans, the highest classes of which are gods.

LIFE-ATOMS, THEIR ORIGIN AND DESTINY

. . . Occultism does not accept anything inorganic in the Kosmos. The expression employed by Science, "inorganic substance," means simply that the latent life slumbering in the molecules of so-called "inert matter" is incognizable. ALL IS LIFE, and every atom of even mineral dust is a LIFE, though beyond our comprehension and perception, because it is outside the range of the laws known to those who reject Occultism. "The very Atoms," says Tyndall, "seem instinct with a desire for life." Whence, then, we would ask, comes the tendency "to run into organic form"? Is it in any way explicable except according to the teachings of Occult Science?

"The worlds, to the profane," says a Commentary, "are built up of the known Elements. To the conception of an Arhat, these Elements are themselves collectively a divine Life; distributively, on the plane of manifestations, the numberless and countless crores of lives. Fire alone is ONE, on the plane of the One Reality: on that of manifested, hence illusive, being, its particles are fiery lives which live and have their being at the expense of every other life that they consume. Therefore they are named the "DEVOURERS." . . . *"Every visible thing in this Universe was built by such LIVES, from conscious and divine primordial man down to the unconscious agents that construct matter."* . . . *"From the ONE LIFE formless and Uncreate, proceeds the Universe of lives."* — The Secret Doctrine, I, 248–50

EVERY MONAD IS literally a creative center, continually pouring forth from its heart a stream of life-atoms born within and from its own essence. And each such life-atom has as its own core an as yet unexpressed god. There is not a mathematical point in infinite Space which is not such a life-atom.

More specifically, a life-atom is an astral monad, which merely means a phase of the spiritual monad itself operating by remote control in and on the astral plane. A ray or projection of the native energy of the spiritual monad thus passes through all intermediate planes of matter and consciousness until it reaches the astral, and there it forms an infinitesimal whirl, a vortex, in the astral substance. This is the astral monad, called monad because, with the essential monadic consciousness, it participates directly along this ray or extension of the monadic energy on the astral plane. The physical atom in its turn is similarly formed by the operation in physical matter of a ray from the astral monad; and the fundamental of the physical atom, according to science, is electricity.

Thus we can trace the root of the life-atom back along this ray of energy to the monadic essence. Every life-atom therefore is such a potential divinity, for the inner god is at the core of it. Every atom of chemistry is such an extension of an astral monad; and the various chemical elements, now reckoned to be some one hundred, are simply the different classes of the ten general families or orders into which matter divides itself, each of these orders being subdivided into ten subfamilies.

Life-atoms, or what the ancient Hindus called paramānus or primal anus, are the 'souls' of the chemical atoms which disintegrate as our physical bodies do. A life-atom is a manifestation of a jīva; a jīva is a monad; and the heart of a monad is indestructible, because it is divinity itself. The very atoms of our body are the identic ones that formed our last earthly vehicle. These same atoms in the next incarnation will make the body that then we shall have; and this applies not only to our physical body, but to all the sheaths of consciousness of our sevenfold constitution. Each one of these sheaths is formed of life-atoms, these jīvas making up the hosts of entities composing the complete man through which the inner god works. Some of the Upanishads speak about Brahman seated at the heart of the atom — that Brahman which is smaller than the smallest, and greater than the greatest, encompassing the universe.

Such then are the life-atoms. All matter, all substance, is composed of them and of nothing else. They are the building stones of the universe. They are composite of consciousness in the core of each, manifesting in its two forms of energy and will — for energy and will are themselves forms of consciousness, the ultimate Reality.

Every life-atom originating in the supreme hierarch of any hierarchy has a tremendous evolutionary journey to perform. Beginning in the highest stages, it slowly, as the ages roll by, descends the arc of shadows into the matter formed of other similar life-atoms which have preceded it on their 'downward' way; and this journey continues until the pilgrim life-atom reaches the lowest possible point of its own hierarchy — but only of that hierarchy, because that is where it is undergoing its typical evolutionary experience. Then, having reached this point, it begins the reascent along the luminous arc, until at length it reattains union with its divine essence, the god within.

During this evolutionary process it passes from unself-consciousness through manifold and all-various stages of experience to relative self-consciousness, then to full self-consciousness, evolving into impersonal consciousness, and finally merging into divinity — now no longer a mere god-spark but a god, one of the co-laborers in the great work of the building of worlds.

Everything is composed of life-atoms, from the superspiritual to the inframaterial. To those who accept without question the appearance of things, relying solely on their outer sense perceptions, inanimate matter may seem lifeless, or at best asleep. But the physical life-atoms are very lively little entities, constantly at work, even when we are sleeping. Were they to stop for the fraction of a second, our bodies would vanish. As a matter of fact, the physical life-atoms are more intensely at work than are the life-atoms of spiritual things. They are aggressively active, as all matter is.

Intensive movement is a sign of matter; consequently the less there is of it, the higher the entity is. Peace, tranquillity and quiet are the insignia of greatness; and it is so in the spirit as it is in material things. The great things are accomplished in the quiet, in the silences.

All the various monads which make up the composite nature of man evolve forth from themselves children monads which form their successive vehicles, the outermost being the physical body built of physical life-atoms which are the atoms of previous incarnations simply because they have been our children in other lives. During each lifetime we are not only pouring them forth, but absorbing them, for there is a constant interchange of atoms. In addition, a great many of the life-atoms, hosts of them, that form our physical vehicle have flowed forth from us as new 'creations.'

Man's sevenfold constitution, including every organ of his body, is composed of life-atoms of varying degrees of evolution. A life-atom may be the vehicle of a god in a lower sphere which for karmic reasons it must at least reach toward and touch. For instance, the human brain may contain at times life-atoms which are the fingers of a divinity reaching down into our material sphere and seeking the most evolved physical matter that it can find, which is the human cerebral substance, wrapped as it is during earth life in a veil of ākāśa.

This is karma for the human being who can contain such life-atoms in his brain-substance; but it is, as it were, unmerited. Absolutely everything that happens to a man is his karma; but here is an instance where we can say that the individual by his free will did not really cause this god to choose a life-atom in his brain; and yet it happens because his karma made him a fit vehicle for this. The man receives the benefit.

It is also true that the brain can harbor life-atoms of a diabolical character which bring suffering. This too is karma because the man's past acts have made him a vehicle for such life-atoms. Nevertheless, it is unmerited suffering for him because he did not with his will choose to bring these diabolic life-atoms into his body. Hence, there may be life-atoms in the brain or in other vital organs which actually could be characterized as being in nature diabolic — or again, spiritual or divine.

Linked with the foregoing is the teaching regarding the peregrinations of the monads on the other planetary chains which they visit during the course of the outer rounds. Many have wondered whether the monads are imbodied on the globes of the various planetary chains, and whether their bodies correspond in size to that of the globe they visit. Let me repeat just here that bulk has no occult importance whatsoever where consciousness per se is concerned. A being but slightly evolved may have a body as huge as the earth, while its thoughts may have a compass but slightly larger than itself. A god can live in a life-atom, yet its thoughts may roam infinitude.

Now the monads peregrinating from chain to chain or from globe to globe are composed of families coming not only from our earth chain, but likewise from the other planetary chains and their respective globes. There are monads peregrinating from and to the planet Venus or the planet Jupiter, from and to Mars, etc. Many of these reach our own chain during the course of their rounds. They *must* do so because our earth chain is a station on the road that the monads follow along the circulations of the cosmos, some taking one form or imbodiment, others taking other forms or imbodiments. Some of these monads are highly evolved in character, some are spiritual beings, some are demigods. Others, from our human standpoint, are diabolic.

Every life-atom of every entity, born in and from the heart of the monadic essence, forever after is the child of that monadic essence, just as the human soul is the more or less developed child of the spiritual monad. In the beginning of their evolutionary journey in man, these children monads manifest first as the life-atoms of the lower parts of the human constitution; and then, throughout the many minor manvantaras that succeed each other, they grow from small to great, from great to greater, and find their ultimate destiny for the solar manvantara as liberated jīvanmuktas, dhyāni-chohans, gods.

As we cannot become a man until we have learned everything that is beneath manhood, so the life-atom of a dhyāni-chohan, destined to become a man, that is to say a reincarnating ego, must in time bring forth from its own heart the locked-up potencies of divinity. Even such a life-atom, such an elemental, such a dhyāni-chohanic thought, must descend into matter in order to learn from the experiences of material existence and to struggle out of that existence as a man. What kind of a god would it be that knew nothing of the material half of the universe?

All nature proceeds after one rule. Every entity, then, may be said to originate in the life-substance of some dhyāni-chohan as a life-atom; and thence it begins to evolve by descending slowly into matter. When it reaches the deepest depths of the arc of that particular hierarchy, it begins to turn upwards and becomes a complete man, which will develop into a monad or a god — not by accretions of growth from outside, but by bringing forth what is locked up within itself; and thereafter, when it attains the state of the monad of a dhyāni-chohan, it becomes a cosmic spirit.

Do we flatter ourselves that the thoughts we think are our own creations? The mind of man is merely the channel through which thoughts pass in transit. While it is true that a monadic essence, the god within, gives birth to the reincarnating egos, these latter begin their evolution as dhyāni-chohanic atoms, elementals, thoughts, if you like; and 'thoughts' is not so bad a term, for a thought is an entity. It is ensouled, it persists in time, it has individuality; and each such thought or elemental center of consciousness appears in the psychospiritual atmosphere surrounding a monadic center. It originated in the vital substance of a dhyāni-chohan, simply because every point in boundless Infinitude is a monad, either active or dormant.

Hence a thought-elemental existing as a life-atom in some dhyāni-chohan belongs and is attached to it through all the aeons of the future; and as that dhyāni-chohan itself evolves, similarly will its hosts of life-atoms sent forth from it at different times grow through infinitude, and forever follow along after it and compose its train of lives.

Every monad in our home-universe, which means everything within the Milky Way, is an atom, so to speak, a particle of the spiritual essence belonging to the life — the individual vital essence — of a cosmic entity still more sublime. We ourselves are life-atoms, children monads, of a cosmic divinity, just as our bodies are composed of young life-atoms beginning their journey to the gods. There are multitudes of such glorious beings in boundless Space, so we must not call any one of them 'God.' This very concept gave rise to the idea that we are all 'children of God' — the early Christians had the original thought, but soon lost the key.

These children monads are by no means all of contemporaneous birth date. Furthermore, they are in all degrees of evolution, some beginning for this manvantara, some already old in it, and others not yet evolved forth from the monadic essence. Out of this host of children monads a very much smaller aggregate has attained an evolutionary stage approximating the human, and of this a still smaller number are human beings. These last, of course, are not all living on earth at the same time, as some may be in the devachanic state, and others in the intermediate phase.

It should be clear that we are responsible for the evolution of the atoms of our bodies throughout all future ages. In other words, the evolution of the life-atoms, not only of our physical vehicle, but of the other sheaths through which we express ourselves, is dependent upon our thoughts, our feelings, our aspirations, our very life. So in future cycles, as we and they evolve to greater and greater heights, shall we continue as their guides and instructors, even as we in turn have ours.

The spiritual part of the human being is the hierarch, the Silent Watcher, of all the smaller lives which compose the vehicles through and in which this higher nature of man expresses itself. These smaller lives are offsprings from the fountain of vitality welling up in the heart of the spiritual being of man. And as the human being advances, so do these come trailing along behind, evolving, and entering a constantly greater life and expanding consciousness. Ultimately the spiritual entity, the superspiritual part of man, shall have become the expression of some cosmic being — a sun or star; and what are now the life-atoms of a man, as these exist on all the planes of his sevenfold constitution, shall have become the intermediate constitution of that cosmic divinity, as well as the visible star and the other minor bodies surrounding it, like the planets. When this event of cosmic magnitude to the superspiritual nature of man shall have taken place, the less evolved life-atoms, clustering around the more highly evolved, shall furnish the bodies, inner and outer, of the minor entities circling around the solar god.

We are but spiritual and intellectual atoms — atoms of the consciousness of the hierarch of our universe. From that hierarch we take our origin, and to it we shall return, only to begin, in the next cosmic manifestation, a larger pathway of evolution. Even as the atoms forming man's body are of his very essence and being, psychomagnetically drawn to him because they originally came from him, just so are we atoms of this cosmic entity, our supreme hierarch — itself but one of countless heads of hierarchies, for the universe is filled full with gods, and everything is interlinked and interblended with everything else. The consciousness of this celestial hierarch is our fountain of inspiration, and is that everlasting guiding light which permeates every atom of our being. It is the cosmic life-intelligence.

Everything in the solar system ultimately springs from the sun which, as said, is not so much the parent as the elder brother of the other bodies of its kingdom. This becomes more easily understood when we bear in mind that every life-atom, even those composing our physical body, is a part of us, lives in us, and yet each one of them is the expression of its own individual monad — a monad which in its core is just as glorious and high as our own, but whose vehicle is not as highly developed as ours.

The human body is more fit to express the monadic essence than is the life-atom fit to express the essence of its monad or inner god. Once we humans, individually speaking, were manifesting in simple life-atoms — all sons of the sun as well as brothers of the sun. Each one of us, although forming a part of the solar essence, is nevertheless in his inmost part a divine being; and in the future, if we follow the path faithfully to the end, we shall become a glorious sun in the cosmic spaces. We shall then be a manifesting god in our inmost part and a sun will be our body.

HEREDITY AND THE LIFE-ATOMS

Now the Occultists, who trace every atom in the universe, whether an aggregate or single, to One Unity, or Universal *Life;* who do not recognize that anything in Nature can be *inorganic;* who know of no such thing as *dead* matter — the Occultists are consistent with their doctrine of Spirit and Soul when speaking of *memory* in every atom, of *will and sensation.* . . . We know and speak of "life-atoms" — and of "sleeping-atoms" — because we regard these two forms of energy — the kinetic and the potential — as produced by one and the same force or the ONE LIFE, and regard the latter as the source and mover of all. But what *is it* that furnished with energy, and especially with *memory,* the "plastidular souls" of Haeckel? The "wave motion of living particles" becomes comprehensible on the theory of a Spiritual ONE LIFE, of a universal Vital principle independent of *our* matter, and manifesting as *atomic energy* only on *our* plane of consciousness. It is that which, individualized in the human cycle, is transmitted from father to son.   — *The Secret Doctrine,* II, 672

THE SELF-CONSCIOUS part of each human being is the hierarch of the multitudes of atoms composing his body. Their evolution is concurrent with ours; but naturally each such life-atom or elemental soul, while involved in the general karma and destiny of the human entity to which it belongs, nevertheless follows its own individual pathway within the ocean of influences and forces which compose the field of action of the man. In other words, every elemental soul has its own especial line of evolution involved in the greater encompassing field of activity of the human hierarch, of which each and all such elemental souls form the vehicle. We ourselves were such elemental atomic souls at one time, passing through the various vehicles which we call 'atoms.' Every physical atom imbodies an elemental on its way to becoming human, not merely by the stimulation of environment and by the cyclical abrasions of karmic time, but by developing the latent capacities locked up within the core of such an elemental soul.

As said, in each succeeding earth life we pick up the same physical life-atoms which were ours in former incarnations because they are our children and are impressed with our karma; in a sense they are the bearers of our physical karma. These physical life-atoms, however, do not differ from any other life-atoms except in evolutionary grade. We pick them up not only when we are born, but also during our life, and indeed before birth; in fact, we are gathering in and ejecting them hourly, daily — all the time. The reunion of the physical life-atoms to the reincarnated entity is inevitable. We have to take up the life-atoms whose faces we have dirtied in the past, and wash them clean. It is a part of our karma, and we may be thankful that it is so; for if we had to work with those belonging to someone else, we would be in a very disagreeable situation indeed.

It is true that life-atoms from each of us are passing through the bodies of others constantly, but they are only in transit. They learn from us, and we learn in a sense from them; but it is on our own physical life-atoms that we mostly feed and it is through these that our bodies grow. We take in from food, water and air, and by absorption through the pores of our skin and otherwise, very few alien life-atoms as compared with the hosts of our own children life-atoms, left behind on this plane during our last incarnation.

Our life-atoms are not so much attached to us as they are integral parts of our stream of karmic existence, prānic children of the Brahman within us. This means that we have practically the same body that we had in our last life: somewhat evolved, somewhat improved to be sure. And the bodies of our friends and relatives — how is it that they are familiar to us? The causes lie in the instincts, in the latent memory, and in the familiar attraction, of the life-atoms, for all these causes are at work and in a sense keep our hearts and minds attached to matters of earth. We see, therefore, how greatly we are enchained, held down, how our soaring and aspiring spirit is crippled thereby.

This whole subject involves the so-called problem of heredity. Every human being has more than a mere physical heredity; he has an astral, a psychical, an intellectual, a spiritual and, indeed, a divine heredity. Being the child of himself, and being at present the parent of what he will be in the future, his heredity is simply the resultant of the chain of causation flowing forth from what he was before on any plane. There-fore, also, whatever he thought or had feelings about, will of necessity have its consequences and shape his character accordingly. In *The Secret Doctrine* (II, 671-2), H. P. B. writes:

The latter (Occultism) teaches that — (a) the life-atoms of our (*Prâna*) life-prin-ciple are never entirely lost when a man dies. That the atoms best impregnated with the life-principle (an independent, eternal, conscious factor) are partially transmitted from father to son by heredity, and partially are drawn once more together and become the animating principle of the new body in every new incarnation of the Monads. Because (*b*), as the *individual* Soul is ever the same, so are the atoms of the lower principles (body, its astral, or *life double*, etc.), drawn as they are by affinity and Karmic law always to the same individuality in a series of various bodies, etc., etc.

Heredity is not merely the return of the prānic atoms from previous lives, carrying with them the impress given to them by the ego during those lives, but it is also the characteristic of a life stream carried from parent to child through the life-atoms. Life-atoms are of seven different grades or classes of evolutionary advancement, each manifesting in its own appropriate sphere of activity: the three elemental classes working and manifesting in the elemental kingdoms; the mineral life-atoms in the mineral kingdom; the vegetable life-atoms in their kingdom; the beast life-atoms manifesting in the animal kingdom; and the human life-atoms — each one the embryonic or germinal dwelling of a reincarnating ego.

Furthermore, each one of these seven main classes of life-atoms is subdivided into subordinate families. Thus the one general class of human life-atoms contains all the varieties which eventuate in the different families or types of mankind. By this I do not refer to body only, color, complexion, length of nose, etc., but rather more to the possibilities of variety in psycho-astral personality. Moreover, these seven general classes of life-atoms are representative on the physical plane of the seven main classes of monads.

A large part of heredity, of the stream of consequences, is carried on from generation to generation by the life-atoms. The other part of heredity is that which the parents bring into the equation. But no life-atom ever goes into an inappropriate environment. It goes only to that environment towards which it is psychomagnetically attracted: like unto like, life after life.

Similarly, there is a succession of incidents or karmic effects in any strain, whether animal, vegetal, human, or other. It is this succession of event after event, forming the links in the chain of causation, which we call heredity. It is because of this chain of causation, and of the almost unlimited tendencies and capacities lying latent in the life-atoms out of which all things are built, that the breeders, whether of animals or of plants, can produce the interesting varieties that they do. For example, our fruits and cereals were all developed in Atlantean and early Aryan days from wild plants. Some of these variations actually become new species: they last; they produce their own kind. This can be done because in every life-atom there is virtually an infinitude of possibilities of change in direction, and the breeders simply provide a new environment allowing hitherto latent tendencies to express themselves. It is this fountain of vitality or life within each life-atom which brings about the vast diversity of entities around us.

Human beings, however, provide much more than merely a home or environment for their children. Life is not a matter of chance or fortuity — these are but words covering human ignorance. Whatever is, is the result of a chain of causation. Why do certain children come to certain parents? Every child is drawn to the environment and to the life streams of parents which are the most akin to the incoming soul's own vibrational rate; call it a kind of psychomagnetic attraction to a milieu which has the greatest affinity to the reimbodying ego's own karmic requirements, to his own characteristics, in other words. The consequence of this is that the parents are much more than mere channels through which a reincarnating ego enters this sphere, and much more than mere human automata which provide a 'good or bad' environment.

THE DOCTRINE OF TRANSMIGRATION

The question is asked if there is any basis for the popular but erroneous doctrine in the East that souls transmigrate into animal and inanimate forms. The origin of the belief is probably due to teachers informing disciples that the atoms used by the soul while in any body are impressed with the character and acts of each soul, and that the soul has a duty imposed on it to so live, think, and act that all the atoms used in the material body shall progress equally with the Ego and not be given a downward tendency, for if such downward tendency be given, then when death comes the atoms fly to lower forms and are there degraded, and also, in that sense, the man has gone into lower forms. Of course the human ego cannot go into a lower form. It must be remembered as a grave, a weighty, thing, that each atom in the body is conjoined with *a life of its own*, and has a consciousness peculiar to itself. These lives are a class of elementals and hence are the carriers of much of our character to any forms they may go to. It is similar to lighting many candles at one flame. They live in us and derive from us a character, and as they enter and leave us every instant our duty is plain. For by means of these atoms and lives we are actually carrying on the work of evolution, and are as members pledged to the Higher Self, bound to aid in evolution with good intent, or liable to heavy karma if we aid in degrading atoms which are to be used by our fellowmen and succeeding races.
— W. Q. Judge's E.S. *Suggestions and Aids*

WHEN DEATH COMES and the human ego passes into its devachan, all of the vehicles in which it was imbodied in its earth life break up, and the life-atoms of which these sheaths were built go to those environments and conditions to which they are psychomagnetically attracted. This is the gist of the doctrine of the transmigration of life-atoms which has been generally misunderstood to mean that the human soul descends at death into the bodies of animals. That idea is not true; it is not a natural fact.

The basic rule is that during the intervals between earth lives the physical life-atoms of a human being transmigrate through and within the kingdoms of nature. The individual elements or souls of these atoms, considered from the evolutionary standpoint, are not as far progressed as are the animal souls of the beasts. As a matter of fact, when the human

398

body breaks up at death and the life-atoms composing it begin their transmigrations, they are attracted to those bodies or entities, be they human, beast, vegetable or mineral, to which their own rates of vibration at the time draw them. It is all a case of psychomagnetic attraction.

If a man during his life has lived an exceedingly material existence, hordes of his life-atoms will be attracted to the bodies of swine, sloths, tigers, dogs, fish, heaven knows what! Or they may go to help build the bodies of the plants. There is no real degradation in this. Each such elemental is an infinitesimal entity, and passes through even a chemical atom much in the same way as a comet might pass through our own universe, drawn thither by attraction. There is no chance in nature at all. Everything is karmic, great and small. And these life-atoms reimbody themselves innumerable times before they are attracted back by the dominant magnetic pull of the reincarnating human ego to whom they belonged in the preceding earth life. Then they join together and build up the new body in which that returning ego finds its habitat in the next life on earth.°

There are some human beings who are not only so animal in tendencies and in emotional and psychical biases, but who also are so strongly attracted to what we might call the beast-existence, that after they die — and after the 'second death' or separation of the reincarnating ego from the kāma-rūpa has taken place — the energies still informing this kāma-rūpa are so powerful in the passionately psychical and grossly material sense of the word, and hunger so for renewed existence, that it is not uncommon for these bundles of passions and tendencies to inform the bodies of some of the beasts.

This is not a transmigration of the *human soul*, because that soul had fled long since and gone to its devachan. But the remaining part is so low in the human scale that all its instincts are beastwards and the life-atoms composing this bundle of appetites are attracted to those animal entities whither their own impulses impel them to go. From this it should be clear that there is no such thing as a human soul's reincarnating naturally in the body of a beast.

Now then, the process of the reimbodiment of a human monad begins with the vitalizing of a life-atom, which grows into the human embryo,

---

°See the important article: "Transmigration of the Life Atoms" by H.P.B. in *The Theosophist*, August 1883, pp. 286–8.

and is finally born — unless, for compelling karmic reasons, it is unable to advance farther in its growth than the stage of a life-atom, thus being obliged to try again for human rebirth. It is not the higher triad which reincarnates, for it does not enter the body, although its influences are in the body, touch the heart and brain, and especially fire the brain with the divine flame of thought. While the upper triad is above the body, hovers over it, it is the lower part or the psycho-astral monad which actually reincarnates, that is, enters into the physical body. As the reincarnating ego descends through the spheres on its way to another incarnation on earth, it picks up in each different realm or world, through which it had previously ascended, the hosts of life-atoms that it left behind there. It re-forms these into the same outer veils of itself that it had had before, and thus builds up the human constitution before actual physical rebirth takes place — the same life-atoms on every plane and of every principle of the human constitution. Thus it is the personality which reincarnates, while the individuality merely 'over-lightens' (overshadows is the popular word) and fills that personality with its own divine fire — at least with as much as the personality can receive of it.

Just as our bodies are built of the very life-atoms that formed our physical body in our last incarnation, so is this the case not only with the linga-śarīra and the psycho-kāmic principles, but likewise with the mānasic and buddhic principles. Every life-atom is stamped with its own predominant impulse, for which, however, we as humans are strictly responsible. Hence the justice of karmic operations.

In brief, the reincarnating ego as it issues forth from the monad builds around itself veils or bodies, each one appropriate to the principle which such a veil covers, and thus the entire septenary constitution of man is finally completed when the descending entity through its lowest veils touches, and by the touch quickens, the human seed — and the baby is born a few months later.

Writing of the mystery of human consciousness and the inherent potencies of physical cells, H.P.B. says in *The Secret Doctrine* (I, 219):

> This inner soul of the physical cell — this "spiritual plasm" that dominates the germinal plasm — is the key that must open one day the gates of the terra incognita of the Biologist, now called the dark mystery of Embryology.

This has given rise to the question as to whether the 'spiritual plasm' is the life-atom. No, the spiritual plasm is the monadic essence, the spiritual characteristic which works through the reincarnating ego. The life-atom belongs to the astral plasm. There is heredity on all planes: spiritual, intellectual, psychical, astral and elemental or physical, and there are hosts of life-atoms corresponding to each one of these planes.

Further, a life-atom is not the germ cell. The human germ cell contains an untold multitude of life-atoms. A life-atom is an infinitesimal entity, smaller even than the electron; and there are astral infinitesimals which are each one the focus, the channel, through which works the entirety of the ethereal and spiritual forces. In other words, the life-atom is the undeveloped house or temple of all the higher parts of the constitution of the human being-to-be; and this life-atom will be drawn psychomagnetically to the proper environment, and there will form a part of the germ cell of the father.° This germ cell — with its latent seed of growth in it and being formed of other life-atoms of less progressed type destined to build the future body of this particular life-atom — will be passed to the mother; the union of the two cells occurs, and embryonic growth begins.

How does the returning ego find that seed of life from and around which its future physical body is to be built? How does it attract to itself just that one seed of life from among the incomputable number of life-atoms which belong to other egos awaiting rebirth? It would be an inexplicable riddle if an incarnating entity had had no natural or self-attraction to one out of many trillions or quadrillions of such human life seeds. No reincarnating entity could be so attracted unless that particular seed belonged to it as an off-throwing of its own vitality in some former life.

The seed of life does not belong either to the father or to the mother. It belongs to the reincarnating entity itself and, as it enters our sphere, is the first seed to awaken under the attraction of the psychomagnetic flow of the vitality of the reincarnating entity, surrounded as that entity is with its psychomagnetic atmosphere or auric egg. This seed of life, having passed through the body of the father into that of the mother, is one of the transmigrating life-atoms originally springing from the reincarnating ego itself. At this moment of destiny, this life-atom is ready and waiting, and the auric psychomagnetic atmosphere of the reimbodying

---

°The rule applies with equal accuracy to all other entities such as the beasts and the plants.

ego catches it, surrounds it and begins to flow through it, causing it to grow and to develop by the accumulation of similar life-atoms belonging to the last life of the now returning entity — to become finally the body of the little child.

It is quite impossible for these seeds of life to make a mistake in their attraction to the parents from whom the body of the returning ego is to be born. They move with infallible regularity, precision, and accuracy, for the simple reason that their movements are karmically automatic, and are not the result of the choosing of a fallible human mind. In the last analysis, the life-atoms are moved by the great forces of the universe, and hence they follow their instincts, their psychomagnetic attractions, exactly as the magnetic needle points to the north. It makes no mistakes; it does not point at one time to the west and at another time to the southeast. So also do the life-atoms act automatically under rigid karmic causal motivations.

In the case of twins or triplets, the life-atoms of each child are closely alike, but nevertheless quite distinct, for each one is a human individual and is built, physically speaking, of life-atoms of its own type, quality, and psychomagnetic character.

Every entity takes its origin in a vital germ, a life-germ, the heart of which is a life-atom; in fact, every human body is built up of such life-atoms, through and in which the more evolved human soul is working. Most of these particular life-atoms belong, as its children, to that evolving soul, which itself is the offspring from the vital essence of the human monad. But there pass through every human being other life-atoms, almost countless in number, which do not spring either from his body or from his soul, but transmigrate through human bodies according to certain natural laws of attraction and repulsion; and each such life-atom is awaiting its turn and time and place to be a possible vehicle for the beginning of a new human body.

THE CAUSE OF DISEASE

Science teaches us that the living as well as the dead organism of both man and animal are swarming with bacteria of a hundred various kinds; that from without we are threatened with the invasion of microbes with every breath we draw, and from within by leucomaines, aerobes, anaerobes, and what not. But Science never yet went so far as to assert with the occult doctrine that our bodies, as well as those of animals, plants, and stones, are themselves altogether built up of such beings; which, except larger species, no microscope can detect. . . . Each particle — whether you call it organic or inorganic — *is a life*. Every atom and molecule in the Universe is both *life-giving* and *death-giving* to that form, inasmuch as it builds by aggregation universes and the ephemeral vehicles ready to receive the trans-migrating soul, and as eternally destroys and changes the *forms* and expells those souls from their temporary abodes. It creates and kills; it is self-generating and self-destroying; it brings into being, and annihilates, that mystery of mysteries — the *living body* of man, animal, or plant, every second in time and space; and it generates equally life and death, beauty and ugliness, good and bad, and even the agreeable and disagreeable, the beneficent and maleficent sensations.   — *The Secret Doctrine,* I, 260–1

LIFE-ATOMS ARE intimately connected with the causes and manifestation of disease. Both health and disease are karmically the consequences of the characters and tendencies which we ourselves have impressed upon the life-atoms composing the various sheaths in which we, the human egos, are clothed during earth life: impressed upon them by our thoughts, our feelings, our desires and our habits. This does not mean, however, that a man has now a photographic duplication, as it were, of his last physical body with the same diseases that he may have been suffering from then. Predisposition to health or disease, shape of body, and physiog-nomy, are all matters of karmic change, of evolution.

A man in one life may have a disease and exhaust the karmic causes which brought it about, and in the next life be perfectly free from it, or he may not be free — it all depends upon his karma. We have the same life-atoms and the same astral monad as before, both of course modified according to the karma previously engendered. The karma of these life-atoms and of this astral monad is simply brought over from the past life, and begins anew from the very point at which that life was closed. Life is continuous; but as all things change, including the very life-atoms of our body, and as our soul has changed for the better in its devachan by absorbing its experiences, so the new man is indeed the old man, yet is in a sense new.

We have now practically the same body that we had in our last life. Nevertheless, as a general rule — save in certain instances due to karma, as in the cases of those who die in childhood or in early youth — the reincarnating ego is born into a different race when it returns to earth, into a different era, into different surroundings. The life-atoms are identical, but they change necessarily, just as last Monday is not the same as the Monday to come, although we are the same person.

How about the growth and change even in one life of a human being? Has a full-grown man the same contour that he had as the newborn babe? And yet it is the same individual, the same life-atoms. Is the child the same as the adult man? Yes and no; the same body, but how different! So it is with succeeding lives. Just as the child grows into the adult by slow stages, so does a man pass from incarnation to incarnation, continuously the same in essential being, although in each new life undergoing a change, let us hope, for the better. We are making ourselves now very largely what we shall be ten years hence. We may have conquered a disease that we are today suffering from, or we may have a disease then that at present we do not have. In either case we ourselves are responsible. Disease, therefore, is the working out of karma, for everything that comes to a man is the consequence, the flowering, of seeds sown in the past.

Our physical life-atoms, being our children, partake of our swabhāva, and respond to our thoughts and feelings, to our example; but it does not necessarily follow that a man whose present life has been marked by high endeavor and by noble characteristics should in the next earth life have a healthy body. The contrary of this is too well known: noble-minded men and women who are frail and sickly, and, on the other hand, vicious characters who have healthy bodies. How is this to be explained?

In the case of a fine and unselfish character who has a weak physical vehicle, he has won his freedom so far as the inner man is concerned; but so far as the life-atoms are concerned which he still has to use, he has not yet cleansed them of the preceding stain which that same spirit-soul brought upon them. But in time when the cycle of a frail physical body will have passed, then the man will be able to shine in splendor.

It is likewise true that some corrupt and evil human beings have bodies of physical beauty, but this is rare. More often, it is the *unadvanced* human souls who possess bodies of physical perfection, simply because the fire within is not yet aroused, and neither consumes nor enflames the body. Genius usually appears in a weak and often decrepit body because the inner fire is too strong for it, and can tear the body to pieces when it does not distort. Yet, if one were given the choice, who would not liefer be a genius, particularly a spiritual genius, even with a weak body, than an individual whose soul is spiritually dead — or as yet wholly unawake!

To say that selfishness is the cause of all disease is too general a statement. To be more specific, it is the form of selfishness called passion, whether conscious or unconscious, which is the fruitful cause of disease — unconquered violent passion, such as hatred, anger, lust, etc. Any such passion, mental or physical, shakes the lower constitution of man; it escapes from the control of the guiding hand of the higher part of his being, changing the direction of flow of the prānic life-currents, condensing them here, rarefying them there. It thus interferes with the normal, easy workings of nature, which in this connection means health. In fact, selfishness is at the root not merely of most disease, but of most evil-doing, and both are originally caused not by unconquerable but by unconquered passions.

The symptoms of disease, which only too often are treated as being the disease itself, are not infrequently the efforts of the forces of health to throw the poison out of the body. A disease should be understood as a purifying process because the end will be a cleansing. It should be welcomed in the sense of a quiet understanding of the situation, and without either fear or an attempt to complicate or hinder the process. But many people have an idea that the curing of disease consists in damming it back, shutting the doors against its egress out of the system. Such damming back, however, allows the roots of the disease to take firmer hold and spread and accumulate energy, so that when it reappears — as it inevitably will for its roots have not been extirpated — its reaction upon the body is more violent than it would have been if the disease had been allowed to take its course. As W. Q. Judge has written:

. . . diseases are gross manifestations showing themselves on their way out. of the nature so that one may be purified. To arrest them through thought ignorantly directed is to throw them back into their cause *and replant them in their mental plane.*

This is the true ground of our objection to metaphysical healing practices, which we distinguish from the assumptions and so-called philosophy on which those methods are claimed to stand. For we distinctly urge that the effects are not brought about by any philosophical system whatever, but by the practical though ignorant use of psycho-physiological processes.°

There is an ethical side to all this which has not been sufficiently touched upon. In many instances diseases may be a heaven-sent blessing: they cure egoism, they teach patience, and bring in their train the realization of the need for living rightly. If we with our ungoverned emotions had bodies which could not be diseased, they might well be weakened and killed by excesses. Diseases actually are warnings to reform our thoughts and to live in accordance with nature's laws.

A new cycle in medicine entered the world in the latter half of the nineteenth century: no longer were human beings dosed until they died with mighty draughts of this and mighty potions of that. Doctors were beginning to see that it is nature that cures, and that the wise physician is a guide and an eliminator rather than a doser. Nevertheless, because of the still imperfect knowledge which physicians have, diseases in their acute stages often kill. Their course is too rapid for the human system to withstand the strain. On the other hand, the medical practitioners of the distant future will understand so well what diseases are, and the methods of curing them — indeed, how to prevent them — that they will lead a disease out so gently that it will appear to vanish while actually it is manifesting itself, even as the body today very often throws off a sickness by its own unaided powers.[17]

As I have already said, there is no certain knowledge as to the meaning and cause of disease, with the result that new systems of medical practice are constantly being introduced. For example, some advocate the use of stimulants and narcotics; others, eliminative and suppressive measures, with respect merely to symptoms. I might add that there is more justification for these and other methods in vogue in certain of the regular schools of medicine, than there is for those opposed to all medical practice, such as the schools of so-called mental or faith healing. It is a very dangerous thing indeed by the use of affirmations and denials, or by methods of

°*The Path*, September 1892, p. 190.

intense psychologic thinking, to dam back elemental forces working their way outwards through the human constitution. Consequently, however imperfect medical science may be today, it nevertheless treats the body with material means, which are the least harmful.

The ancient wisdom has some points of agreement with the "sects of deniers," as H. P. Blavatsky neatly called them; for instance, the teaching that a bright and cheerful spirit is a good thing to have; again, that life should be faced with an attitude of courage, and with an appeal to the spiritual energy inherent in the universe. But these are mere isolated points of agreement. There are other things which are impossible to accept, such as the notion that matter does not exist. If we were to deny the existence of matter, we should be obliged to deny the existence of spirit also, because spirit and matter are the polar antitheses of each other. Above all, there is the question of the concentration of personal interests around the individual, and the strenuous attempt at getting help for oneself, which is so contrary to the true spiritual ideal. If a man, in order to seek relief from some affliction, uses the spiritual powers of his being and tries to drag them down into the material world, he is proceeding in a direction opposite to nature's evolutionary flow, which is upwards. The rule is to raise, not to debase. Such action is a swimming against the current; and this is where the system of the healers or deniers is basically wrong.

We must remember that everything that happens to a man is the working of karma, and that diseases are the result of inharmonious thoughts and emotions of this or of a past life now working themselves out through the body. More particularly, all diseases are brought about through the instrumentality of elementals. This is the ancient teaching, and was the belief of the entire world until the West, in its supreme wisdom, began to look upon this consensus of opinion of the human race as founded upon superstition.

In the New Testament, due to its faulty translation arising out of a misapprehension of what those early Christian writers intended to say when they wrote these tracts, diseases are ascribed to the operation of devils or demons — a mistranslation which is grotesque. These *daimonia*, as the Greek word runs, are simply the lowest order of animate and sensate creatures — commonly called in theosophy elementals — forming the lowest step of the hierarchical ladder of which the highest is the condition of spiritual existence of as well as an actual world inhabited by the gods.

Between elemental and god there is a wide range of difference in evolutionary progress, but no difference in essence or in origin, man occupying an intermediate stage on this ladder of life.

All diseases, therefore, from epilepsy or cancer to a common cold, from tuberculosis to a toothache, from rheumatism to any other physical ailment, are brought about through elementals working as the instruments of the karmic law. And the same applies to mental diseases: an outburst of anger, a raging temper, persistent melancholia, and the manias of various kinds, all are elemental in origin. Homicidal mania is an example in point; essentially it is quite *un*human as well as being *in*human — it is elemental. In this case an elemental has control of the human temple, and has for the time being dispossessed the rightful human dweller therein. Such a state is due to weakness and self-indulgence.

Epilepsy is likewise due to an elemental, which is a nature spirit, an energy center, a consciousness center, of an unevolved kind which in this case has usurped temporarily the position normally occupied by the human soul in the body. Epileptics, in actual fact, are 'moon-struck' when they suffer an attack. In this connection it may be of interest to note that one of the ancient Mesopotamian gods, spoken of in the early Christian and Jewish scriptures, is Beel-Zebub, usually translated as "Lord of the Flies." Zebub does mean flies, but the fly is mystically symbolic of an astral animate entity, and hence was taken as representative of the character and antics of the elementals. Therefore, Lord of Flies simply means Lord of the Elementals — of the elemental forces and powers; and that lord is the moon.

In antiquity and during the Middle Ages, epilepsy was known as the "sacred illness" on account of its marked psychological element which contrasts it so strongly with other more purely physical afflictions. It was believed that elementals of a higher grade, possessing a larger psychological sphere of activity, were concerned in the "falling sickness." This thought also prevails throughout the Orient, as in the South Sea Islands where things which are sacred in any sense are called tabu, forbidden, and considered to be under the special protection of the elemental spirits of nature.

Epileptic seizures are in reality no worse than any other outbreak of disease, for, as indicated, every disease can be traced to the same causes: an originating series of thoughts and emotions, eventuating in the present life in a distortion and an inharmonious interaction of the prānic currents in the body. According to the character of the emotions and thoughts, so is the disease.

In regard to cancer, there is one fundamental cause branching into two: deep-seated selfishness, first; and next, acting on this general background, unregulated emotionalism, the causes of which may have been sown ages back in other lives. The combined power of these two vital-astral currents weakens or even destroys resistance, and so directs the currents of life that they leave certain portions of the body where they are naturally in check, and center on others where they run riot. However, by control of the emotions and by self-forgetfulness, it is possible to help nature modify the course and development of the disease. Many more people would suffer from cancerous growths on the body if nature did not automatically gather together its forces of resistance — intellectual, emotional, moral, physiological, and what not — and thus cause the body to react so strongly that the resistance wards off the attack.

Many things regarding the human body are great mysteries, simply because we do not know enough about our evolutionary history. For example, we should understand cancer better if we realized that all growths, malignant or benign, are physiological memories of the method of propagation which the early third root-race used unconsciously. Then such growths were normal and natural; now they are abnormal at best and malignant at the worst. Then they were caused by the natural currents of life running true and strong; now they are caused by the same currents of life running strong in a wrong minor direction — wrong because occurring out of evolutionary time.

There is, however, a sure preventive of all diseases which partake of both a physiological and a psychological character, and that is the practicing of the age-old virtues, such as the pāramitās.

As diseases are the karmic result of past errors of living, of working inharmoniously with nature, the way of health is to work with nature; and this is possible because we are an integral part of it. Every sage and seer has taught the way. The method is voiced again and again in every great religion and philosophy. But no true sage or adept ever interferes with the karmic law, for they are the servants of that law and manifest it in their works among mankind. In some senses also are they the bringers about of the karmic law; for thereby is natural equilibrium achieved and evolution advanced. Thus are they healers of the souls of men. Heal the soul and you heal the body.

MAN IS HIS OWN KARMA

Karma-Nemesis is the synonym of PROVIDENCE, minus *design*, goodness, and every other *finite* attribute and qualification, so unphilosophically attributed to the latter. An Occultist or a philosopher will not speak of the goodness or cruelty of Providence; but, identifying it with Karma-Nemesis, he will teach that nevertheless it guards the good and watches over them in this, as in future lives; and that it punishes the evil-doer — aye, even to his seventh rebirth. So long, in short, as the effect of his having thrown into perturbation even the smallest atom in the Infinite World of harmony, has not been finally readjusted. For the only decree of Karma — an eternal and immutable decree — is absolute Harmony in the world of matter as it is in the world of Spirit. It is not, therefore, Karma that rewards or punishes, but it is we, who reward or punish ourselves according to whether we work with, through and along with nature, abiding by the laws on which that Harmony depends, or — break them.

Nor would the ways of Karma be inscrutable were men to work in union and harmony, instead of disunion and strife. For our ignorance of those ways — which one portion of mankind calls the ways of Providence, dark and intricate; while another sees in them the action of blind Fatalism; and a third, simple chance, with neither gods nor devils to guide them — would surely disappear, if we would but attribute all these to their correct cause. With right knowledge, or at any rate with a confident conviction that our neighbours will no more work to hurt us than we would think of harming them, the two-thirds of the World's evil would vanish into thin air. Were no man to hurt his brother, Karma-Nemesis would have neither cause to work for, nor weapons to act through.   — *The Secret Doctrine*, I, 643

KARMA IS THE HABIT of universal being, which so works that an act is necessarily followed by a result — a reaction from surrounding nature. The very core of this doctrine is that every thought and deed sets up an immediate chain of causation, acting on every plane to which that chain of causation reaches. But what is this primordial habit of nature, which makes it react to an arousing cause? Cosmically speaking, it is the will of the spiritual beings who have gone before us and who now are as gods, whose will and thought direct and protect the type and quality of the universe in which we live.

But there is no God outside of us which dictates what our destiny or fate shall be. We are free agents, children of the universe, gods going through the sublime adventure of cosmic life. Having free will, intelligence and consciousness, dwelling in a universe of which we are inseparable parts, we are in our inmost essence Parabrahman, and yet in all exterior garments of consciousness we are individualized.

Hence karma is not something outside of us; we are our own karma. We, essentially speaking, are the spiritual part of ourselves; the material or elemental, the psychical and the intellectual, are but aspects of our constitution through which our essential self acts. These subordinate parts are bound to follow the current of the life stream as it flows forth from the fountain within — from which originate will, consciousness, understanding, and all the other spiritual qualities and energies, such as love and compassion.

To look at the matter from a somewhat different and more familiar point of view: would you expect that the divine part of you would suffer the karma of what the physical body did? Or that your inner god would be a bondslave to what the prānic life-atoms of your astral body do, or to what your brain-mind or emotions may impel you into? Obviously not. We prepare for ourselves the destiny that we are, or will work through, and we do this from within our spiritual nature wherein ultimately originate all karmic activities. Thus whatever happens to us, we bring about either consciously or unconsciously: we have made ourselves what we are now, and are making ourselves what we shall be in the future.

There is an organ in the brain through which act the elemental karmic energies urging an individual into this or that pathway of action and thought and emotion. This has been called the 'third eye,' or the 'eye of Śiva,' and physically it is the pineal gland, the organ that expresses and carries over into the physical body the karmic urges which will impel us to follow this or that course of action, eventuating in either weal or woe. In this regard H.P.B. writes in *The Secret Doctrine* (II, 302):

Now that which the students of Occultism ought to know is that THE "THIRD EYE" IS INDISSOLUBLY CONNECTED WITH KARMA. The tenet is so mysterious that very few have heard of it.

This is a very difficult thing to explain. We are our own karma. That is all we are. We are the effect in our entire constitution of what we were at the preceding instant of time. We are an aggregate of forces, a composite entity with our own characteristics, tendencies and impulses, all of which form and compose us, even to the very shape of our body — all this is our karma, because we and our karma are one.

What causes or controls destiny? Which part of us exercises the greatest sway over what we shall be in the future? It is the higher part; and the lower part is at once our vehicle and our stumbling block. Therefore, as we are naught but an expression of ourselves, an expression of our karma on all the planes, we carve our own future as we have our present and past. We do this by will, by choice, by discrimination — all belonging to the higher part of us which functions as best it may through its own organ, the pineal gland. And this, as said, is as indissolubly connected with karma as it is with each of us, recording succeeding steps in choice and discrimination — or lack of these.

We learn through our faults. Sorrow, pain and suffering are our best teachers. But let us not seek to be 'good'; the man who seeks to be 'good' is exercising one kind of spiritual selfishness, for he seeks something for himself. The roadway to the mountaintop is impersonality; for the truly and spiritually impersonal man never does an evil or a selfish deed. If he did he would be personal. Were the impersonal man to turn a deaf ear to a cry for help, to pleadings of compassion and pity, his impersonality would be but a mockery.

He whose vision is clear, whose heart is at peace, whose mind is tranquil, seeks neither for good nor for evil; his whole being is set on the supernal light within. As long as there are good men in the world there will be evil men, and vice versa. The salvation of the human race is coming about, not by a craving for good and to be good, but by a yearning, which passes all ordinary understanding, to be impersonal, self-forgetful, so that almighty love and compassion, which hold the universe in their keeping, can stream through the human heart without any barrier of the lower selfhood.

Karma, like everything else, manifests in energies, varying in strength. The strongest normally come forth first. Every karmic consequence comes into action at its appropriate time and place. No karma can be turned aside. It may, indeed, be dammed back temporarily, but out it will come some day. Actually, the damming back brings about an accumulation of karma: of other karma of a closely connected type which therefore will increase the action of the karma thus held back.

Nor can we excuse ourselves for a wrong action merely by saying:

"How could I help it? It was my karma." This is cheating ourselves with words. When we act, we act from choice and make new karma, deliberately directing our mind and consciousness in thought and in action. Is our choice also karmic? Of course, for everything we think or do is karmic; but we can change our karma at any moment by making new and giving easier direction to the old, for we have created energy through our spiritual nature. At any instant of time, man has the divine faculty of free choice; to strike out along new avenues of effort, which the fields of nature provide for him constantly. The universe is limitless in extent; and the consciousness of man is not only coeval with the universe, but spiritually coextensive.

A strong man makes a strong impress on surroundings, on circumstances, on other men; and the reaction upon him is correspondingly forceful. Feckless individuals make a very weak impression, and the reaction is correspondingly weak. Now the man who has a powerful will, inevitably acts powerfully in all that he does; and whether for weal or for woe there will be an equivalent reaction. Consequently, the higher a man goes along the evolutionary pathway, the more careful must he be.

All karma works from within outwards; it originates within and simply expresses itself on the physical plane. It is man who makes his own karma, because in doing so he makes himself. *Man is his own karma, his own destiny* — the destiny he incurs is the one which he has carved for himself, and he does so by making himself, by making his character. What he does, he does from himself, and nature's reactions will fall upon him. There is karma of many kinds: mental, psychical, emotional, vital, astral, physical; and there is individual or personal karma as well as collective karma. We have to partake of the karma of the world, of our race, our family, our solar system, and of our universe, because we have put ourselves where we are — none else.

Man can achieve so high a status in spiritual evolution by unfolding from within himself his inner powers in accordance with cosmic law, that he thereby becomes a direct and self-conscious collaborator in his own sphere with the cosmic laws. Doing nothing contrary to the natural order, there is no reaction from nature upon him, and thus he may be said to have "risen above karma," insofar as the term karma applies to his own evolution and character and activity as a man.

The spiritual nature is not acted upon by any exterior karma except that of the universe of which we are an inseparable portion, and then only because we have our being as a monadic essence in the aggregative essence of some greater entity. But our own personal karma never acts upon the spiritual plane because that plane is the wellspring from which it flows forth. When a human being has reached the evolutionary stage of being wholly impersonal, he makes thereafter no new *personal* karma. Consequently, he no longer weaves around himself a web of personal destiny. He becomes an impersonal servitor of his spiritual superiors.

There is, of course, *impersonal* karma, because karma means the sequence of cause and effect arising out of what an actor thinks and does; but the statement that when one has reached divinity, or even as a human being has become truly impersonal, he weaves no more karma, means that no longer do the bonds of personality enchain him. He is freed from them, living as a worker and collaborator of natural law. Yet the *universal* karma of cosmic Being is the ultimate background of activity of the karma of any individual, because he is inseparable from the universe. The highest god is as much subject to universal karma as is the humblest ant climbing up a sandhill only to go tumbling down again.

When man has reached quasi-divinity because he has become at one with the divine-spiritual nature of his own hierarchy, he is no longer under the sway of the general field of karmic action in that hierarchy. He has become a master of its life, because he is an agent of its inmost impulses and mandates. Thus it is that a man may rise above the karmic sphere in which he finds himself, while remaining within the hierarchical karma of cosmic Being.

IS KARMA EVER UNMERITED?

A STRANGE MISCONCEPTION has arisen that there can be unmerited karma. This is probably due to a misunderstanding of H.P.B.'s and of W. Q. Judge's statements that unmerited *suffering* is undergone by all creatures, not only men but the animals, possibly even the gods. There are a number of converging lines of thought which bear upon this question, as well as upon the fact that all *karma* is merited.

First of all, the universe is imperfect because it is composed of imperfect entities which are evolving — in fact, the universe *is* these entities. This means that it has a light side consisting of the more progressed entities, and a dark side consisting of those less evolved. Evil therefore, or the dark side of nature, is imperfection, there being no such thing as absolute evil in the universe.

Further, we know that because we are in the universe and are evolving beings we learn from each other, we act and react upon each other. Good actions elevate us and by so much help not only ourselves but others to progress. The Lord Buddha said, if we think evil, suffering and pain follow, exactly as the wheel of the cart follows the foot of the ox which draws it. Every hierarchy is comprehended within the vital sphere of some greater hierarchy; equally so an atom in a man's body is comprehended within the hierarchy of the atoms of his physical constitution. The consequence is that we are suffering in a certain sense from what the gods do, within whose hierarchy we have our being; just as the atoms of our body are subject to all things that the body does. And if the human will causes this body to commit a wrong, the atoms within it necessarily suffer a corresponding action upon them.

Let us go a step farther. Any entity, because it is identical in substance and essence, in energy, destiny and origin, with the hierarchy to which it belongs, has all the qualities, powers, faculties and substances of this hierarchy and therefore of the universe. Man has free will because the universe has. Every monad, because it springs from the heart of the universe, has its quota of free will, and thus is individually responsible for what it does.

415

We have now the very interesting situation that evil arises out of a conflict of free acting wills: the gods acting among themselves to keep the universe in balance; all subordinate hierarchies acting among themselves to keep their part of the universe in order; men forming a minor hierarchy acting among themselves to carry out their individual destinies. Consequently, whatever happens to a man at any time, in whatever place, is always karma, the result of a preceding cause.

Thus we are subject to the karma of the universe; to the laws which control the solar system, and to the laws which control our planet. We are subject to the laws which affect us all as belonging to the human race; to the government of our country because we are born there; and likewise to our own family karma. Then, most individually, each man suffers in his body or in his mind according to his own thoughts and acts.

Now let us take the question of unmerited suffering, pain, misery, which we must distinguish from the natural fact that everything that happens to us is karma. As we have said before, there is really no unmerited karma, but there is unmerited suffering to various parts of our constitution. To illustrate: I have free will. I strike out a new pathway in life because I receive an inspiration; it is like a revelation to my soul. I change my whole course of conduct. Can I do this without receiving reactions? Of course not. I certainly will affect my family and friends. I will also strongly affect myself, especially my mind and body; but many of these effects are not deliberately planned by me, and in this sense the body receives unmerited suffering. Even the mind may receive suffering that it, as the mind-vehicle, did not merit. Viewed in this way we are always receiving unmerited suffering. But out of it all we learn, we grow stronger, we evolve more quickly.

Unmerited suffering and pain we do experience, but in time we recognize them as karma because the 'revelation' spoken of above came to us when we had arrived at the point in our evolution when the god within could touch our mind and show us a new path. For example, some men deliberately bring suffering and pain upon themselves in order to help the world. They have not merited this suffering as retribution for past evil acts, but they make up their mind that cost what it may they henceforth are going to help the world. And here we have the explanation of the mystery which Christians call the sacrifice of Jesus.

Every buddha does the same, every chela also: he deliberately takes a course of action leading to the gods, but does so for the sake of the world. He acts strongly upon his fellow human beings by this new path he has taken. He raises the whole human race by the strength of his character, by the wondrous and beautiful thoughts he puts into the minds of his fellow men. Here we have a case not of unmerited suffering but of unearned joy, which others receive because one man has chosen the path he did! We thus see that there is unearned or unmerited happiness and joy, just as there is unmerited suffering and pain — but merited or unmerited, whatever may befall anyone at any time, is karma.

Nature is balanced with exceeding delicacy, and nothing is accidental or fortuitous. The animals, plants and minerals are our younger brothers, and therefore we as men, as self-conscious, moral — or immoral, alas — influences on this earth, will be held strictly accountable for all that we think and do. Even the suffering of animals, whether due to human cruelty or neglect, or to other causes such as being preyed upon by other animals, is karma. But how can an animal be made responsible for its actions if it has no real self-consciousness? While the suffering of the animals is karma, it is not largely derivative from their inner nature; they are not morally responsible, as men are. Hence for them there is no moral retribution, although they are involved in the general karma of the races of beings on earth, in what we might call the earth karma.

In their origin the animals are the offspring of men, and even today are deeply rooted in the astral life of mankind because their inner constitutions are mainly built up of the life-atoms that men are constantly throwing out. Their karma is to a great extent apparently unjust because they have not earned, morally speaking, the suffering that they endure. In a sense they are victims, because they are composite even physically of the life-atoms originating in men, who thereby have made themselves responsible in large degree, spiritually and morally, for the sufferings of the animal kingdom. This is a karma which man will have to work out, not the animals.

Nevertheless the beasts are not *wholly* free from karmic responsibility, for every psycho-astral monad — the center around which the beast-body is built — is the reflection of a spiritual monad, coming out of past eternities of manvantaras in which that spiritual monad made for itself karma not exhausted when those manvantaras ended. And consequently these monads have come into the present manvantara with these distant karmic stains imprinted into the very fabric of their being. The same observation applies to the plant and to the mineral kingdoms.

417

In each animal, as in each man, there shines the visible but feeble radiance of a divinity at its heart. In the animals this glory shows only the faintest glimmering of its power. They are on the way towards humanhood, even as we are on the pathway to becoming gods.

I might add that the unmerited sufferings of the animals can be traced to two causes: first, the actions done by them in this or in some earlier life; and second, the things that they did in a previous solar manvantara. For they were living their careers then much as we men do. Just as the reincarnating ego of man must for a time lose its sublime self-consciousness during its embryonic stage before it can become a man again, so even the animals have been full-grown self-conscious entities in a former manvantara, which was much less evolved than this one, on a lower cosmic plane. So too we men on this present cosmic plane are passing through a period of our evolution which is far lower than the one we had attained in a previous solar manvantara when we were gods.

We see how difficult this whole question of karma is. It is all wrapped up with various other teachings. As H. P. B. says, there is not a misshapen day in our lives, there is not a sorrow or a pain, or contrariwise not a joy or a delight, which cannot be traced back to our thoughts and actions in this or in a former life.

It is true that the present personality is in no wise responsible for the acts of any past personality, because it is an entirely new thing, different in every respect from each and every one of those which preceded it on the karmic chain of lives. This being the case, there is indeed apparent injustice in the suffering that each personality unquestionably experiences, in that it must face the results of the misdeeds of its predecessor which it itself did not do. This is one side of the matter. And the other side is that there is no break in the chain of consequences, no disruption of continuity in the karmic line of effects: one personality follows the immediately preceding one as inevitably, as fatefully, as one hour follows another — different from it, yet the same.

Nevertheless, each personality is a new man with a new brain in a new time, speaking a new language, knowing nothing of what brought this or that result upon him; therefore suffering apparent injustices, or receiving apparent fortune, subject to all the so-called whims of fate and destiny. Is the man different from the boy? Absolutely different — in form, qualities, capacities, outlook; but the background of both is the same. Through all runs the stream of the individuality which does not change.

From this standpoint, he is in no wise different. The man is merely the resultant of the boy. There is no break in the chain of causation; no real karmic injustice in that the man should be held accountable for what the boy did, good or bad.

There is no enduring, everlasting soul which passes from life to life dipping, as it were, into human bodies alien to it. The idea is a phantasm of the imagination. But there *is* consciousness expressing itself in manifold forms, each incarnation being but the karma, the fruit, of that which immediately preceded it. This is what Gautama Buddha meant by his teaching that an eternal and immortal soul existing within a man, and after his death existing eternally in the heavens, is an illusion; for all that remains of a man at death is his karma. What a man is at the instant of physical dissolution *is himself*, that is to say his karma, the result of what he was the previous instant. Not one of us is the same in every identic respect that we were one second ago; much less are we now what we were a year ago.

There is another angle to the matter of unmerited suffering. I am reminded of H.P.B.'s statement in *The Key to Theosophy* (p. 161) where she says that after death the reincarnating ego receives only the reward for the unmerited suffering which it has undergone in the life just past. It is the man's karma because it happens to him, and there is no such thing as unmerited karma if we mean uncaused at some time in the past by the individual unto whom it occurs. Yet when she called his suffering *unmerited*, she was speaking here only in connection with the devachanic rest, and the reward he would receive for the sorrows and trials he had experienced in his life on earth.

In the Lord's Prayer occurs the phrase: "Lead us not into temptation, but deliver us from evil." An extraordinary statement from the Christian standpoint, which has never been explained by any theologian. Now just here is the heart of the meaning of what H.P.B. refers to. The Christos or the Buddha within a man, in other words the higher part of the re-incarnating ego, will at times lead the imperfect human ego, the higher astral monad, into temptation. If the human ego falls into the temptation, it suffers. The suffering is karmic. But that human ego did not deliberately in the beginning plan to do the acts which brought about the suffering. Recompense comes to it in the devachan, but the responsible center — in other lives or in this life — is the reincarnating ego.

Man ordinarily lives in the kāma-manas, which is not the reincarnating

419

ego, this being the buddhi-manas. Now these are two distinct monads: one is the spiritual monad or reincarnating ego, and the other is the human monad or higher astral monad which is a very imperfectly developed entity. It carries over from its previous life a certain amount of karmic responsibility, but only insofar as its limited powers have acted. The reincarnating ego, on the contrary, carries over from former lives a far heavier load of responsibility; it is continually 'tempting' the human ego into courses of action, some for its good which bring it joy, others for its good which the human ego regards as suffering because it has very little sense of humor. Many of our difficulties become not merely tolerable but actually pleasant when we change our attitude towards them.

However, karma must not be misconstrued to mean that we should ever remain passive or without compassion when others suffer or are in danger, on the wholly fallacious plea that: "Oh, it is only his karma, he has deserved it, let him work it out, he will learn by it and grow stronger." While this is true in principle, to bring it forth as an excuse for inactivity in a time of need is diabolic, and can be traced back directly to the malevolent insinuations of the dugpas of the human race, whose teachings find easy lodgment in the minds of selfish and heartless people. The teaching of all the Buddhas of Compassion is the direct contrary, and was expressed in H.P.B.'s beautiful words in *The Voice of the Silence* (p. 31): "Inaction in a deed of mercy becomes an action in a deadly sin." Karma will indeed exact every atom of retribution for the passive attitude of him who sits idly by when another is in need of help.

GOOD AND EVIL

No more philosophically profound, no grander or more graphic and suggestive type exists among the allegories of the World-religions than that of the two Brother-Powers of the Mazdean religion, called Ahura Mazda and Angra Mainyu, better known in their modernized form of Ormuzd and Ahriman. . . .

The two Powers are inseparable on our present plane and at this stage of evolution, and would be meaningless, one without the other. They are, therefore, the two opposite poles of the *One* Manifested Creative Power, whether the latter is viewed as a Universal Cosmic Force which builds worlds, or under its anthropomorphic aspect, when its vehicle is thinking man. For Ormuzd and Ahriman are the respective representatives of Good and Evil, of Light and Darkness, of the spiritual and the material elements in man, and also in the Universe and everything contained in it.

— H. P. Blavatsky, *Lucifer*, March 1891, pp. 1-2

WHAT IS GOOD? What is evil? Are they things-in-themselves, or are they conditions through which entities pass? Good is harmony because relative perfection, and evil is disharmony because imperfection; and these two, good and evil, insofar as we are concerned, apply solely to our hierarchy. Our 'good' is 'evil' to the entities existing in a superior hierarchy. Evil signifies a state of an entity or group of entities in greater or less degree opposing the forwards-moving evolutionary stream of life.

Whence comes the evil in the world, if the divine which is mightier than evil is everywhere? One would think from such a question that evil is an entity, a power or a force, which flows forth from the heart of some thing or being. On the contrary, it is merely the condition of an evolving entity which has not yet fully manifested the latent divinity at its core, and thus is inharmonious with its environment because of its imperfection.

Good is not created. Evil is not created. They are two poles of the same thing. There is no Devil in the universe, wrongly supposed to be the creator and arbiter of evil. Equally so, there is no God, wrongly supposed to be the creator and arbiter of good. It is all a question of growth. Human beings are evil entities when compared with the gods. The gods in their turn could be called evil by entities still loftier than they.

Good is not spirit, evil is not matter, the nether pole of spirit, because that would be saying that matter is essentially evil, which it is not. Evil, whether spiritual or material, is whatever is imperfect and passing through a phase of growing to something better. Neither matter nor spirit is in one or the other condition *absolutely,* and for eternity. A spiritual entity is evolving just as much as any material entity. Nevertheless, because spirit and spiritual beings are nearer to nature's heart, they are, collectively speaking, more perfect, therefore less evil than matter and material entities.

Evil per se does not become good per se, that is, one state does not become another state, the truth being that it is the evolving entity which passes from one state into another. Both good and evil are conditions of growth. This calls to mind the ancient theosophical — and Christian — expression concerning entities existing in a state of "spiritual wickedness."° Obviously, if those entities, although belonging to the spiritual realms, are imperfect and inharmonious there, they are 'evil' in that state. If entities, belonging to the state which we call relative perfection, exist harmoniously with surrounding beings, then they are entities of spiritual good. Harmony, law, order, peace, love: all these are conditions of entities who are in accord with the onward-flowing current of evolutionary growth. Such entities are more nearly at one with the heart of Being, and therefore endure.

It is the balance of spiritual and material existences — the natural course of universal being — which gives the diversity in the universe. There is no power (or powers) which keeps the universe either all good or all bad; for it is neither the one nor the other. Vast hierarchies are the universe, hierarchies on the invisible planes and likewise on that cross section we call our physical world; and it is the differences in evolutionary degree attained in these hierarchies and in the hosts of entities composing them which provide the vast diversity that the universe manifests. It can at no time be either all good or all bad, for it is perpetually advancing; and this marching army is without beginning and without ending.

A tidal wave comes in upon the land and sweeps twenty thousand human souls into the waters and drowns them. Is there therefore evil

---

° *Ephesians,* VI, 12.

in the world? What brought that catastrophe about? Or again, an earthquake shakes down a city, and more than a hundred thousand perish. Is that evil per se? The earthquake is an event, as is the tidal wave. Nature's law is that effect succeeds cause. Nature is strictly harmonious at its core and through all its parts, and all its movings are towards a restoration of harmony — which is equilibrium. What we sow, we shall reap. Nothing happens by chance. And if a person is caught by a tidal wave or killed in an earthquake, it is because he himself by his past karma has put himself in those surroundings. He is reaping what he has sown.

We should have a lunatic universe were karma nonexistent, if men could wreck the lives of others, and then escape scot free. Nature is not so built. Man is a god in his inmost and, because he is linked with the divine elements as well as with all the other elements of the universe, what he does, nature reacts against. He has free will, and so reaps the consequences of all that he thinks and does and is. A man who works for brotherhood and kindliness has all nature's evolutionary stream with him; this brings strength and light and induces a cosmic expansion of his inner faculties. The man who works for hate, for selfish ends, who sets his puny will against the evolving river of lives, has all nature's incalculable weight pressing upon him. Such action on his part is imperfection, inharmony, and therefore evil.

Universal nature in manifestation is dual in character, divided into consciousness or the light side and matter or the dark side. Quoting from *The Key to Theosophy* (p. 112):

Light would be incomprehensible without darkness to make it manifest by contrast; good would be no longer good without evil to show the priceless nature of the boon; and so personal virtue could claim no merit, unless it had passed through the furnace of temptation.

The ancient Zoroastrian religion strongly emphasized this duality, and this conception was very early taken over by the Christians.° But when the cosmic unit passes into its pralaya, then good and evil vanish and are resolved back into the ineffable oneness of cosmic divinity — to lie latent until the new term of manifestation as a universe begins.

Throughout the cosmos we see that evil is the conflict among entities, arising because of their as yet imperfectly developed spiritual powers.

°Cf. *The Secret Doctrine*, I, 411–24, "Demon est Deus Inversus."

Applying this to man and his works, the conflict of human wills and intelligences which strive against each other, produces disharmony, pain, disease, and all the host of evils. Yet when we learn the lesson that our interests are one instead of diverse, we shall work together in a constantly increasing ratio as our spiritual understanding unfolds.

Again, on the universal scale, cosmic evils arise from the different strivings and conflicts of the prakritis in nature with their respective inhabitants. Matter — the seven prakritis — is not evil per se, but crystallized or condensed spirit; and the prakritis are simply incomputably vast numbers of monads individually unawakened or unevolved and hence functioning in nature as fields of material or prakritic extent. When a universe, through evolution of all its variously differentiated prakritis, shall finally reach spiritual levels, these differentiations will merge into the spiritual unity of the cosmic monad, thus bringing about the grand *consummatum est*, when duality vanishes into unity.

The following passage in *The Mahatma Letters* (p. 401) gives a further key:

. . . discord is the harmony of the Universe. . . . each part, as in the glorious *fugues* of the immortal Mozart, ceaselessly chases the other in harmonious discord on the paths of Eternal progress to meet and finally blend at the threshold of the pursued goal into one harmonious whole, the keynote in nature सत् [Sat].

Thus, in its essence, matter is as divine as spirit, for it is merely the shadow or vehicular side of spirit.

424

Correlations of
Cosmic and Human Constitutions

THE AURIC EGG, ITS NATURE AND FUNCTION

EVERY BEING OR THING throughout the universe, and indeed the universe itself, has, or rather *is*, its own auric egg. Its primal substance is the ākāśa of which the cosmic ether is the grossest aspect. This ākāśa concretes itself progressively from its highest to its lowest part, so that the auric egg in its most material aspect is but slightly more ethereal than the physical body, and is in fact astral substance. It is fundamentally life; it is not only the seat of the prāṇas or life-forces, but the auric egg is itself concreted life, for ākāśa is life, and life is ākāśa.

The auric egg originates in the monad which is its heart or core, and from which, when manifestation begins, it emanates forth in streams of vital effluvia. On the different planes which the auric egg traverses as a pillar of light, from the ātmic to the physical, each such auric or prāṇic effluvium is a principle or element, commonly reckoned in man as seven in number. When the auric egg is viewed on any one plane of the human constitution, we discover that this plane or 'layer' not only corresponds to, but actually *is*, one of the unfolded six principles of man; it would appear to be ovoid or somewhat egg-shaped in outline, and to be a more or less dense, extremely brilliant, central portion surrounded by an enormously active interworking cloud of prāṇic currents. If we look at the sun we get a sublimely beautiful picture of what the solar auric egg is on this plane, and this gives some idea of what the auric egg of a human being looks like when considered on any one of its six planes or layers emanated from the ātmic or monadic source.

These immensely active and interworking clouds or vital effluvia are actually the prāṇas of the auric egg on any one plane expressing themselves as auras. Thus, in illustration, all the prāṇas in and of man's astral-physical body are simply the vital auras of his physical being, and similarly so on any other layer of his constitution.

The auric egg, originating in the ātman or the true naked monad, flows forth from the heart of the monad, clothing itself first in its highest veil, the substances and energies of buddhi. As the consciousness stream descends farther into manifestation, the buddhic auras with the ātmic energies working in and through them produce manas, the second veil or garment; and this in its turn flows forth in the next auric attribute, the kāma, including its various substances and forces, until finally the physical body is formed from the matters and forces of the astral auric egg as its lees or dregs.

Each such layer or plane of the stream of consciousness called the auric egg is emanated from a center or core which itself is a child monad emanated from its superior, and so on upwards until we reach the ātmic monad again, out of the heart of which all flows. Thus, each of these children monads aids in producing in its fullness the whole auric egg of a septenary being, by pouring forth from within *its* heart the particular swābhāvic prānic essences belonging to itself as a monad on that plane.

All manifestations of human life, from gestation to death, originate in the auric egg, and pass out through the physical body. Every part of the body, every different organ, is a deposit from an equivalent layer of the auric egg. Blood, as an illustration, is the physical representative of what in the auric egg manifests itself as the vital streams. It is concreted or materialized vitality, and the various cells with which it is filled represent on this plane the as yet unevolved life-atoms which exist equivalently and causally in the auric egg. Just as blood is the dregs of the prānic streams flowing through the auric egg, so is the physical brainstuff the dregs of the mānasic substance which composes a part of the auric egg, i.e. a deposit from those layers of the auric egg in which the mānasic principle functions.

Mentality thus originates on the mental plane of the auric egg, spiritual thought and impulses on the spiritual planes, animal impulses on the grosser planes. The astral body has its source in the auric egg also; and even the physical body is a deposit of it, being but the shell of the auric egg — born out of it, built up from its life, and deriving therefrom all its vitality.

It is through their auric egg that the spiritual adepts (and even the Brothers of the Shadow) perform the wonders which they can work, for it is the center of their vitality. An adept in these mysteries, by the power of will and by wisdom, could surround himself with a cloak of invisibility — a concealing veil of part of his auric substance — so that he could pass through a crowd in broad daylight, and be totally unseen. Again, he could so harden or strengthen his auric egg as to cast around himself an impenetrable garment that nothing known to man could pierce. Neither bullet nor sword could pass this protecting veil of ākāśa, which nevertheless is so ethereal that it is utterly invisible. And yet, because it is composed of pure energy, it is the same, fundamentally, as pure substance. The atoms composing the bullet or the sword are unable to penetrate it, for to those atoms this protecting veil is made incomparably denser by the strength of will of the one who so shields himself, or someone else. It is by a knowledge of the powers and energies latent and residing in the auric egg that an adept, by using his will, can also levitate himself or, on the other hand, make his body so heavy that fifty men could not lift it.

The size of the auric egg is not always the same. When it is in full manifestation, the prānic essences poured forth from the different centers are greater than when it is in a state of inactivity. Thus, after death, the auric egg — otherwise the constitution — shrinks very considerably as concerns the reach of the prānic auras, and this is especially the case in its lower layers, which break up into their component atoms and are dissipated. In fact, mere size or extension of an auric egg has nothing to do with the intrinsic functions of consciousness; for when a monad is in certain spiritual states, as happens after death, the extent of the prānic or vital outflow may be at times infinitesimal in character. This, however, does not apply with equal force to the spiritual and divine layers of the auric egg, for these, being relatively immortal, are not affected in any especial degree by the death of a being such as a man.

Thus we see that the auras of a man's astral-physical body are merely those portions of the prānas which during incarnation surround the body as a mist or shining cloud; and these auras are invariably characterized by marvelously shifting and changing scintillations and flashings of color.

In principle, then, the higher the layer in the auric egg the far-ther-reaching are its various prānic auras, so that actually the higher layers are characterized by auric extensions which range far beyond the limits of our own planetary chain, to the sun and other planets — indeed, the reach of the auric egg in its divine aspects embraces in varying degrees of power and largeness different parts of the galaxy. It is just by these 'touchings' or 'contacts' of the auras of the different layers that we inter-weave our vitality with the beings and things that surround us, and this on all planes of our constitution. And herein lies the cause of the ordinary sympathies and antipathies that we are constantly experiencing: our prānic auras touch or contact the world around us, enabling us to become cog-nizant of our environs by means of our sensory apparatuses both outer and inner.

As a matter of fact, no entity could cognize any other entity in the universe unless his auric egg reached that entity. We could not see the stars unless our auric egg were already there, and transmitted to us along the pathways of the ether the touch that we have of those distant objects. There is actually no such thing as action at a distance, to quote the favorite phrase of the scientists of our grandfathers' day. *All* things are connected together everywhere, not merely those that are in the vicinage of each other. Every human being is as closely and straitly allied with Sirius or with the Polar Star as he is with his own skin, and his divine essence extends even farther.

The sun, for example, may be said to 'feel' and to 'embrace' whatever is contacted by its rays flashing forth from itself; and it is precisely the intellectual and spiritual and divine reach of the forces and energies of the auric egg of the solar chain, linking themselves in eternal and unbreakable bonds with the surrounding galaxy, which thus permits the solar chain to come into contact with the galaxy, its home. Indeed, the reason that one man can understand another is that the mānasic layers of the auric egg of the one touch and interweb with those of the other, thus bringing about intellectual contact; and when there is such synchrony of vibration, we have intellectual sympathy and understanding; but when the mānasic wavelengths are not of the same frequency, we have the cases of inability of men to understand each other, antipathetic feelings, etc.

However, let us not be too literal and falsely imagine that here is a reason for indulging in hatreds as being 'according to natural law,' or some other such tommyrot. Of course, we should try to synchronize our 'vibrations' with those of others — not by descending to a lower level than our own best, but by endeavoring through impersonal will and spiritual aspiration to apply the grand old rule of cosmic ethics that love harmonizes all things, that hatred is always destructive. It is our duty to replace antipathies by the sympathies that we can in fact *always* attain to by rising to higher planes of feeling and thought. This is possible because all monads, in their own high status, are permanently on the plane of spirit, and hence vibrate in harmonic and synchronous spiritual rhythms.

No sensitive man can go into a crowd without being strongly affected by its emanations — an efflux of vitality which leaves every human being constantly, day and night — and these emanations literally poison the outer layers of the auric egg. However, help is afforded by nature's automatic closing of the doors of entrance, and thus the auric atmosphere receives protection. Just as the pores of the skin involuntarily close and open — a process which aids in keeping the body healthy and in preventing the entrance of disease — so are there certain psychic adjustments, automatic in type, which take place in one's auric atmosphere when in crowds.

Now if one were strong enough in love and in universal sympathy, as the higher adepts are, he could enter safely into places heavily charged with the emanations of matter and evil, and do so with perfect security to inner health, because his auric egg, on account of its innate purity, would then automatically close its 'pores' against such emanations; the heart and the mind meanwhile expanding in compassionate understanding so largely as to see hid beauty and to sense *natural* sympathy even with one's most uncompromising foe, because we are all united on the higher planes of our being.

From the foregoing, we can see the reason for H.P.B.'s statement°
to the effect that the prānas are the direct emanations from an ātmic layer of the auric egg, and similarly so from the ātmic essence of the different children monads in the human constitution. Furthermore, it is the auric egg as a whole which is the actual ever-enduring compound vehicle of man considered as a peregrinating entity. It is in his auric egg, in its many and various planes or layers, that a man throughout eternity lives and moves and has his consciousness, and all the other attributes and faculties and powers that characterize him in any one of the many episodes of his immensely long evolutionary journey.

In connection with this last thought, we should remember that the size of the auric egg is of no importance, because during incarnation it is variously extensive, while after death its prānic auras may all be withdrawn into the heart of the different monads from which they originally emanated. Thus, on any one plane, such as the astral-physical, the auric egg may be infinitesimal in extent, possibly even smaller than an anu or an atom; and at the same time in its spiritual and divine reaches coextensive with the universe. This explains the phrase in the Upanishads which describes Brahman as "smaller than the atomic, vaster than the universe."

° *The Key to Theosophy,* p. 176.

MONADS, EGOS AND SOULS

THE VARIOUS SOULS, element-principles, and egos, which are all comprised in the constitution of a human being, are of necessity enwrapped within the layers of the different substances and energies which form the auric egg, itself the field of evolutionary activity. Indeed, the whole work of evolution is conducted in and upon the auric egg, because all its layers are modified or refined in consequence of the growth and change taking place in the monadic centers.

I will endeavor now to be more specific as regards the terms monadic essences, monads, egos, and souls. Monadic essence has been commonly used to signify the essential or divine substance of a monad, of which the monad is an individualized expression in time and space. Hence, monadic essence is virtually equivalent to the term god, there being as many gods as there are monads. We have thus the series: gods (or monadic essences), monads, egos, souls (or vehicles); and this series is likewise chronological in that from the god emanates the monad, from the monad the ego, from the ego comes the soul, and from the soul the body. It is to this that H.P.B. alludes in *The Secret Doctrine* when, in giving the three fundamental bases of consciousness and the structural framework of the universe, she speaks of "Gods, Monads, Atoms."

Taking up next in order the term ego, we can briefly describe this highly important part of a man, on whatever plane of his constitution it may be native, as the stored-up fund of conscious evolutionary experience acquired during the continuously repetitive imbodiments of a monad in the worlds of manifestation. As an illustration, the reincarnating ego is the gatherer and the storehouse of all the spiritual and intellectual experiences gained by the human monad in its many incarnations — and it is just because of this fact that the experiences garnered by the ego after the death of man were called by H.P.B. the 'aroma' of a spiritual and intellectual and nobler psychical character, treasured up after each life on earth.

The term soul we can define as the sentient, sensitive vehicle or garment, itself of living substance, with which the ego surrounds itself during any imbodiment. Another term for soul is body — not necessarily a body of flesh, but any vehicle in and through which, and on whatever plane of the human constitution, an ego may be expressing itself. Hence the usage of the various terms, spiritual soul, human soul, animal soul, and even physical soul — meaning the body of flesh.

Thus we have the divine-spiritual stuff or essence, itself a god, which when expressing itself as an individual on the next inferior plane we call a monad; such monad expresses itself on the plane on which it may be manifesting through its appropriate mānasic garment or egoic focus which is its ego; and each such ego in its turn surrounds itself with its own prānic auras or characteristic veil of living substance and sensitive stuff, its soul.

Man being a microcosm of the macrocosm, we can by analogy understand the constitution of a universe by transferring to a cosmic scale these points of teaching concerning the constitution or auric egg of man. We then infer that a universe has its monadic essence, its cosmic monad, its cosmic ego as an individual, and likewise its cosmic soul or anima mundi.

The following two diagrams are symbolic representations of certain structural and interpenetrating parts of nature, and should not be read as exact or photographic pictures, but only as suggestive of related entities or qualities.

We notice in this diagram six centers or ātmic foci, each one triadic, and each such triad containing its respective monad, ego, and soul, enclosed by the auric egg, the seventh and 'universal' element or principle in this scheme. Furthermore, the septenary auric egg is represented as a pendant hanging from the kosmic or galactic Paramātman, the supreme self or hierarch of the galaxy, which in its turn is a pendant from the irradiating superkosmic focus, itself symbolic of an indefinite group of galaxies. Indeed, this focus at the top of the diagram can likewise stand for the limitless fields of Infinitude, for it is obvious that any such group of galaxies merely suggests innumerable other such galactic groups in endless Space.

The straight line originating in this irradiating focus is an attempt to show the individuality of the superkosmic monad which, running like the sūtrātman or thread-self through all things, links all together in permanent and inseparable unity. Pausing a moment on this sublime thought, we see that the fundamental essence of every being and thing in the galactic aggregate of hierarchies originates in the superkosmic monad; and hence even the smallest life-atom in such a hierarchy is irradiated by and is the same in essence as the hyparxis or supreme of the supreme in the galaxy.

This diagram is not drawn up specifically on either a sevenfold or a twelvefold basis; rather it sets forth in a generalizing way the relations and interrelations of the different monads, egos and souls in man and, analogically, in any cosmic unit, and also their connections with the human principles. As to their relation with the globes of the earth chain and the sacred planetary chains of the solar system, it is as follows: Paramātman is kosmic or galactic; Ātman is cosmic or appurtenant to the solar system; Jīvātman, to the sacred planetary chains; Bhūtātman, to the earth planetary chain; and Prānātman, to globe D alone. By analogy the same interrelations will apply by increase of magnitude to the universal solar system. The Ātman and the Jīvātman constitute together the inner god of man's constitution. One could say that the superdivine principles in man, or, equivalently, in another sense, the five highest and secret globes of a planetary chain, are the respective links with the divine principles of our solar system and through this last with the galaxy.

Sanskrit names are given for the three higher triadic foci or ātmans in the human constitution, but the three lower foci are grouped under the one term Prānātman, since there exist no proper terms to describe the particular ātmic quality which belongs to the beast monad and to the astral-physical monad, these two lowest foci having not yet evolved forth sufficient egoic manifestation. Nevertheless, it is the destiny of both the beast monad and the astral-physical monad in a future manvantara to bring forth from themselves an ātmic focus. When this happens, each will have advanced: one step higher for the beast monad, and two steps higher for the astral-physical, each thus becoming what in the diagram is called a psychic monad.

This shows the fluidic character of these different egos and souls, for each one during the long, long evolutionary pilgrimage will 'move up' into the next higher 'plane.' The astral-physical monad will become a beast monad, the latter in due course will unfold from itself the already latent psychic monad, which in evolutionary time will become a mānasic monad, and so forth for the remaining two monads. However, such advancement in evolution does not mean that any monad 'moves up' a step by mere accretions to itself from outside, but only that that which is already latent within will unfold ever larger measures of its own sublime monadic essence.

434

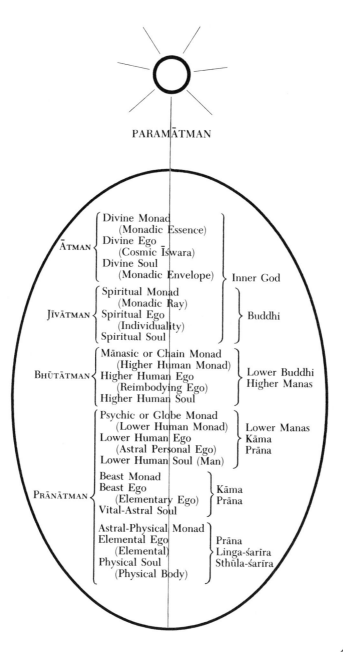

PARAMĀTMAN

ĀTMAN
{
Divine Monad
  (Monadic Essence)
Divine Ego
  (Cosmic Īśwara)
Divine Soul
  (Monadic Envelope)
}
Inner God

JĪVĀTMAN
{
Spiritual Monad
  (Monadic Ray)
Spiritual Ego
  (Individuality)
Spiritual Soul
}
Buddhi

BHŪTĀTMAN
{
Mānasic or Chain Monad
  (Higher Human Monad)
Higher Human Ego
  (Reimbodying Ego)
Higher Human Soul
}
Lower Buddhi
Higher Manas

PRĀNĀTMAN
{
Psychic or Globe Monad
  (Lower Human Monad)
Lower Human Ego
  (Astral Personal Ego)
Lower Human Soul (Man)
}
Lower Manas
Kāma
Prāna

Beast Monad
Beast Ego
  (Elementary Ego)
Vital-Astral Soul
}
Kāma
Prāna

Astral-Physical Monad
Elemental Ego
  (Elemental)
Physical Soul
  (Physical Body)
}
Prāna
Linga-śarīra
Sthūla-śarīra

For the benefit of those whose minds are fond of connections in teaching, I may add that this diagram indicates that for an individual human being we should place the dhyāni-buddha of his constitution in the topmost triadic focus, but with constant links in and with the second triadic focus; the dhyāni-bodhisattva in the second of these foci but with links in and with the third triadic focus; and that when such a dhyāni-bodhisattva in a man becomes the mānushya-buddha it is therefore seated in the third focus, but with links in and through the fourth triadic focus, thus enabling the mānushya-buddha to manifest his glorious powers and faculties on our globe D. When our life-wave shall have moved to the next globe, or indeed to any other globe during a chain-round, the same teaching applies to such new globe-habitat of the life-wave and the human individuals thereof.

This first diagram also contains many hints as to just which portions of the constitution of a human being belong to our globe D, or to our earth planetary chain, or again to the sacred planetary chains, and likewise which portions of a man's constitution make the inner rounds, and which ones make the outer rounds.

The second diagram given here is analogically the same in general as the first one, but differs enormously in particulars. The proper way, therefore, of studying these two schematic constructions, on the one hand of a cosmic unit, and of a human being on the other, is to do so on the lines of nature herself, taking each instance as it is, and not trying to force analogies. We can liken a cosmic unit, such as a solar system, to the ocean of intelligent life with its psycho-vital-astral structure which surrounds us, and from this cosmic ocean there flow forth in manifold ways innumerable tiny rivulets, each being identical with its cosmic parent in fundamental force or substance, yet not identical either in function or in consequent action, and usually not in framework. Just as the oceans of earth are the ultimate source of the rivers of the globe and of the streams and brooks which enchant our landscapes, all finally returning to the oceans from which they came; and just as these minor streams or 'rays' are identical in substance and in other ways with their great parent, but are not identities in locality, function or attributes; so exactly do all the hosts of microcosmic units, such as we men, derive from the cosmic ocean, being as it were the 'rays' or rivulets therefrom, and destined ultimately to return to the cosmic Paramātman at the close of the mahā-manvantara.

PARABRAHMAN – MŪLAPRAKRITI
Amūlamūla; The Boundless; The 'Rootless Root'

PARAMĀTMAN
Brahman-Pradhāna; Kosmic Monad; Monas Monadum
First or Unmanifest Logos

ĀDI-BUDDHI
Alaya; Mahā-Buddhi; Cosmic Buddhi;
Ākāśa or Pradhāna; Root of Mahat;
Higher Seat of Anima Mundi or Cosmic
Aether; Source of Monads; Second Logos

MAHAT
Cosmic Mind, Intelligence, Consciousness; Manifest
Purusha-Prakriti; Cosmic Source of Individual In-
telligences, such as Egoic Monads, etc. Third or
'Creative' Logos

COSMIC KĀMA
Field of beginnings of Manifest Cosmic Entities, such as
Solar Chains, Planetary Chains, Comets, etc., including
manifesting Nebulae, each expressing an Egoic Center

COSMIC JĪVA
Source of individual Elementals and their unfolded
Prānas, therefore of unfolded or unexpressed Monads

ASTRAL LIGHT
Cosmic Ether: the Fields of action of the various
classes of Elementals

STHŪLA-ŚARĪRA
Physical Universe
'Reflects' or carries all the above

437

Now if we make false analogies, all we shall finally succeed in doing will be to project upon the cosmic unit merely an image of ourselves as we are at the present stage of our evolutionary pilgrimage. We should simply be building in our minds a picture of the cosmic unit as being an immensely enlarged man, and thus almost automatically we would attribute to such imaginary cosmic being our own weaknesses and particularized varieties of imperfect development — all of which is absurd, and would lead us into the same fatal fault that many of the exoteric religions fell into when man created his personal Gods.

THE AURIC EGG AND MAN'S PRINCIPLES

THE FOLLOWING PASSAGE, from H.P.B.'s E.S. *Instructions* (III), deals not only with our human principles and what she calls their transitory aspects, but also with the auric egg:

Speaking metaphysically and philosophically, on strict esoteric lines, man as a complete unit is composed of Four basic Principles and their Three Aspects on this earth. In the semi-esoteric teachings, these Four and Three have been called Seven Principles, . . .

THE ETERNAL BASIC PRINCIPLES.

TRANSITORY ASPECTS PRODUCED BY THE PRINCIPLES.

1. *Âtmân,* or Jîva, "the One Life,' which permeates the *Monadic Trio.* (One in three and three in One.)

1. *Prâna,* the Breath of Life, the same as *Nephesh.* At the death of a living being, Prâna, re-becomes Jîva.°

2. *Auric Envelope;* because the substratum of the Aura around man is the universally diffused primordial and pure Âkâsa, the first film on the boundless and shoreless expanse of Jîva, the immutable Root of all.

2. *Linga Sarîra,* the Astral Form, the transitory emanation of the Auric Egg. This form precedes the formation of the living Body, and after death clings to it, dissipating only with the disappearance of its last atom (the skeleton excepted).

3. *Buddhi;* for Buddhi is a ray of the Universal Spiritual Soul (ALAYA).

3. *Lower Manas,* the Animal Soul, the reflection or shadow of the Buddhi-Manas, having the *potentialities* of both, but conquered generally by its association with the *Kâma* elements.

4. *Manas* (the Higher Ego); for it

As the lower man is the combined

°Prâna, on earth at any rate, is thus but a mode of life, a constant cyclic motion from within outwardly and back again, an out-breathing and in-breathing of the ONE LIFE, or Jîva, the synonym of the Absolute and Unknowable Deity. Prâna is not abstract life, or Jîva, but its aspect in a world of delusion. In the *Theosophist,* May, 1888, p. 478, Prâna is said to be "one stage finer than the gross matter of the earth." — H.P.B.

proceeds from Mahât, the first product or emanation of Pradhâna, which contains *potentially* all the Gunas (attributes). Mahât is Cosmic Intelligence, called the "Great Principle."* product of two aspects: physically, of his Astral Form and psycho-physiologically of Kâma Manas, he is not looked upon even as an aspect, but as an illusion.

The Auric Egg, on account of its nature and manifold functions, has to be well studied. As Hiranyagarbha, the Golden Womb or Egg, contains Brahmâ, the collective symbol of the Seven Universal Forces, so the Auric Egg contains, and is directly related to, both the divine and the physical man. In its essence, as said, it is eternal; in its constant correlations and transformations, during the reincarnating progress of the Ego on this earth, it is a kind of perpetual motion machine.

As given out in the *Secret Doctrine*, the Egos or Kumâras, incarnating in man, at the end of the Third Root-Race, are not human Egos of this earth or plane, but become such only from the moment they ensoul the animal man, thus endowing him with his Higher Mind. Each is a "Breath" or Principle, called the Human Soul, or Manas, the Mind. As the teachings say: "Each is a Pillar of Light. Having chosen its vehicle, it expanded, surrounding with an Âkâsic Aura the human animal, while the Divine (Manâsic) Principle, settled within that human form."

Ancient Wisdom teaches us, moreover, that from this first incarnation, the Lunar Pitris, who had made men out of their Chhayâs or Shadows, are absorbed by this auric essence, and a distinct Astral Form is now produced for each forthcoming Personality of the reincarnating series of each Ego.

Thus the Auric Egg, reflecting all the thoughts, words and deeds of man, is:

(*a*) The preserver of every Karmic record.

(*b*) The storehouse of all the good and evil powers of man, receiving and giving out at his will — nay, at his very thought — every potentiality, which becomes, then and there, an acting potency: this aura is the mirror in which sensitives and clairvoyants sense and perceive the real man, and see him *as he is*, not as he appears.

(*c*) As it furnishes man with his Astral Form, around which the physical entity models itself, first as a foetus, then as a child and man, the astral growing apace with the human being, so it furnishes him during life, if an Adept, with his Mâyâvi Rûpa, or *Illusion Body*, which is not his *Vital* Astral Body; and after

---

*Remember that our reincarnating Egos are called in the *Secret Doctrine* the Manasapûtras, "Sons of Manas" (or Mahât) Intelligence, Wisdom. — H.P.B.

death, with his Dêvâchânic Entity and Kâma Rûpa, or Body of Desire, (the Spook).°

In the case of the Dêvâchânic Entity, the Ego, in order to be able to go into a state of bliss, as the "I" of its immediately preceding incarnation, has to be clothed (metaphorically speaking) with the spiritual elements of the ideas, aspirations and thoughts of the now disembodied Personality; otherwise what is it *that enjoys bliss and reward?* Surely not the *impersonal* Ego, the Divine Individuality. Therefore it must be the good Karmic records of the deceased, impressed upon the Auric *Substance,* which furnish the Human Soul with just enough of the Spiritual elements of the ex-personality, to enable it to still believe itself that body from which it has just been severed, and to receive its fruition, during a more or less prolonged period of "spiritual gestation." For Dêvâchân is a "spiritual gestation" within an ideal matrix state, a birth of the Ego into the world of effects, which ideal, subjective birth precedes its next terrestrial birth, the latter being determined by its bad Karma, into the world of causes.†

We should note that in this passage only four basic principles are mentioned: ātman, its auric envelope, buddhi, and manas — the last really being the higher manas; and three transitory aspects: prāna, linga-śarīra, and the lower manas or animal soul. Certain students have wondered about this, and also why the second principle is given as the auric envelope; and, again, why kāma does not enter into the picture.

First, kāma is inherent in every one of those four basic principles and their three aspects, because, in the human constitution, it is representative of cosmic kāma — the universal and fundamental principle-attribute which is the intrinsic force or energy of the universe. For we should always remember that every one of the seven principles in man, whether a basic principle or an aspect, is itself septenary.

These four principles are considered 'basic' because they are the highest and therefore the most powerful and enduring in the entire constitution of man. They survive the great drama which takes place at death leading to the dissolution of the lower quaternary, or what H.P.B. calls the three aspects plus the physical vehicle — these lower three aspects being reunited only preceding and at the time of the next reincarnation. This applies

---

°It is erroneous to call the fifth human principle "Kâma Rûpa." It is no Rûpa, or form at all, until after death, but stands for the Kâmic elements in man, his animal desires and passions, such as anger, lust, envy, revenge, etc., etc., the progeny of selfishness and matter. — H.P.B.

†Here the world of effects is the Dêvâchânic state, and the world of causes, earth life. — H.P.B.

441

with equal force and propriety to the constitution and 'death' of any cosmic entity, such as a planet or a galaxy.

By placing the principles in parallel columns H. P. B. suggests that each of them has its particular corresponding aspect on earth during the lifetime of a complete septenary man. To illustrate: various prānas in man correspond with the ātman; for, when traced back to their ultimate origin, the prānas will be found to be emanations from the ātmic monad. In similar fashion, the linga-śarīra is coupled with the 'auric envelope' enclosing the ātman as its spiritual aura; and likewise the third aspect or lower manas, the animal soul, is in the imbodied man the reflection of his buddhi. We can carry the analogy one step farther by pointing out that, just as manas is the focal center of the egoic human individual, so it has its correspondence on earth in the sthūla-śarīra, which is the focus of the powers and faculties making the physical man an individual separate from others.

Now all these principles and aspects, and indeed everything in the human constitution, are enclosed within the auric egg, which is at one and the same time the aggregated effluvia from all the different monads and, because of this, the conjoined representative expression of the forces and energies of the septenary imbodied human being. Yet, when death ensues, the lower part of the auric egg, because built largely of the effluxes from the aspects, dissipates in that part of the astral light which is called the kāma-loka of earth; although even here the more ethereal life-atoms or appurtenant forces and substances are drawn upwards into latency to become the tanhic° elementals in the higher parts of the auric egg enclosing the permanent basic principles mentioned by H. P. B. Hence, the auric egg, because continuously functioning and perennially enduring, in one sense is the most important of all the principles or parts of the human constitution. Outside of anything else, it is the field, or composite fields, of the different phases of human consciousness on all its septenary planes. Thus at each new incarnation the various 'aspects' are formed out of the substances and forces of the auric egg — even the physical body or sthūla-śarīra being the dregs or lees, so to speak, of the auric egg through and by means of the linga-śarīra, itself a condensed emanation of the lower layers of the auric egg.

Further, H. P. B. points out that the māyāvi-rūpa, or body of thought

---

°Tanhā, a Buddhist term signifying "thirst for life."

and feeling projected by the adept at his will, is formed of the substances and energies of appropriate layers of the auric egg; and just because all such projections of the auric substance are for temporary purposes, the māyāvi-rūpa possesses its name, 'illusion-body.'

It is from the auric egg that the actual rūpa or shape which surrounds the devachanic entity is formed, so that we can properly speak of this part of the auric egg, vibrating with the relatively spiritual consciousness of the devachanī, as being the field for the play of its consciousness. These layers of the auric egg, which we may perhaps rather graphically call the 'body' of the devachanī, give to the devachanic ego the illusion that it is in a beautiful spiritual vehicle. The kāma-rūpa after death, whether before or after it becomes the spook, is likewise formed of the appropriate substances drawn from the lower layers of the auric egg.

From the foregoing we see how very important is the role that the auric egg plays in the human constitution, for it not only is the field of all the different ranges of consciousness of the imbodied man, but it is likewise the ethereal and astral and even spiritual substance or auric envelope out of which are formed every one of the vehicles of the human entity including his linga-śarīra, his māyāvi-rūpa, his devachanic auric shell, and his kāma-rūpa after death.

There are two basic ways of viewing man: one, as being compounded of the seven cosmic elements, as H.P.B. at first presented it; and the other, as being a composite of interacting monads or centers of consciousness working in and through and by means of the instrumental aid of the seven cosmic elements which give to man his seven principles.

What, then, is the distinction between the different monads in man and the seven principles, and what are their respective functions? This very question was at the bottom of the dispute between H.P.B. and Subba Row. Subba Row followed the teaching of the Brahmanic esoteric school in fastening attention on the monads, looking upon the universe as a vast aggregate of individualities; while H.P.B. for that time of the world's history saw the need to give to the inquiring Western mind, then taking a materialistically scientific bent, some real explanation of what the composition of the universe is as an entity — what its 'stuff' is, and what man is as an integral part of it. Now the seven principles are the seven kinds of 'stuff' of the universe. The higher part of each kind is its consciousness side; the lower part of each is the body side through which its own consciousness expresses itself. Yet every mathematical point in boundless

Space can really be looked upon as a monad, because the universe is imbodied consciousness collectively; and imbodied consciousnesses or monads individually.

Our scientists say that the universe is built up of chemical elements amounting to around one hundred, these together making up the stuff of the universe, divided into so many minor stuffs. Just as the chemical elements form the body of the universe, which nevertheless forms the clothing of hordes of consciousness-beings, humans among them, so in exactly the same way the seven principles of both cosmos and man, ultimately reducible to one causal principle-spirit, are the sevenfold stuff of which the universe is built throughout.

Now then, what are these seven (or ten) principles? That is the point which was so important to bring out in H.P.B.'s time. A background of divinity clothing itself in spirit, these bringing into birth the light of mind; and the light of mind, coworking with the other principles and elements thus far evolved, brought forth cosmic desire; and so on down until we reach the sthūla-śarīra. (This word, by the way, does not mean physical but rather substantial or concreted body on whatever plane, whether physical, spiritual or divine; sthūla simply means compacted, gross.) As the universe is built of radiations, light and energy, these radiations, manifesting in a graded scale, can from one point of view be considered as forces; but when they become enormously concreted, they become gross stuff, which the higher forms of radiation nevertheless continuously work through.

Every mathematical point of space is a monad, a point of consciousness, because all Infinity is infinite consciousness. Therefore every point of Infinity must be a consciousness-center, a sevenfold monad, which has its ātman, buddhi, manas, right on down, because the universe is built of these seven stuffs reducible to one causal stuff — spirit, consciousness, ātman. I emphasize this point because we must not have our minds confused with the idea that the seven principles are one thing, and the monads are something else which work through the principles as disjunct from them. That is wrong.

Every one of the seven principles or elements of a monad can represent one of the cosmic planes, and is itself sevenfold. For instance, there is an ātman of the kāma, a buddhi of the kāma, and so forth throughout the range of element-principles or stuffs. What differentiates one man from another, or a man from a beast? The differences do not lie in their respective seven principles, because these enter and form the compound constitution of all entities, but arise from the relative degree of evolution of the individual monads. The human monad is far more evolved than is that of an animal or of a plant, or than are the highly unified monads which, due to their relative stages of development, distinguish granite from marble or sandstone.

The seven principles which compose man — ātman, buddhi, manas, kāma, prāna, linga-śarīra, sthūla-śarīra — are identic with those which compose our solar cosmos, man's seven principles interblending and interacting in more or less the same fashion as the cosmic principles do. For instance, just as the astral light of our earth is its fluidic astral double, so in man the linga-śarīra is the astral double of the human body; and just as the various cosmic prānas are the compound vitality of our globe, so is the compounded prāna of the human constitution the element of vitality in man.

For purposes of study the constitution of man may be viewed in various ways. Thus, when we are considering the after-death states, we can divide man's constitution into a lower triad, made up of his physical body, fluidic double and prānic vitality; into an intermediate duad formed of the interworking manas and kāma; and then into a spiritual duad, formed of ātman veiled in its own especial sheath of consciousness, buddhi.

Even our physical body has its own septenary composition formed almost wholly of the seven classes of elementals working on the physical plane, these seven classes or grades being derived from nature's fundamental elements. The linga-śarīra is likewise formed of these same seven classes of elementals, distributed into their seven different types; and man's prānic elements are composed of the seven classes of elementals in their own prānic characteristics. Indeed, all the sheath-aspects of every one of man's sevenfold principles are formed in a similar manner. Further, every principle or element of man is subject, more or less, to the one immediately superior to it, and is likewise more or less well controlled or governed by the highest and all the higher principles attempting to manifest through it.

MANY MONADS IN MAN

IT IS NOT A MERE figure of speech when we speak of man as having in his constitution different monads. A monad means an indivisible center of life-consciousness-substance, a spiritual ego. Therefore man has within him a divinity, a Buddha or Christos, a mānasaputra, a human being, an astral entity; and he is housed in an astral-vital-physical body. All these collectively make up his constitution, through which the sūtrātman or thread-self extends from the inmost core of the universe — through all these different monads, from the highest downwards till it touches the physical brain. For man is both legion and unit. The Silent Watcher in him is the dhyāni-buddha, an actual, entitative, living ego of divine type.

The sūtrātman — the term signifying a thread or ray or current of consciousness emanating from a monad — traverses whatever is below it, which thus forms its field of action, and finally touches and acts upon the appropriate organ or organs in the physical body. The fundamental sūtrātman — to wit, the ray from the divine monad — passes through all the layers of the auric egg of the human constitution, thereby forming the backbone of the septenary human being around which are gathered, and interplaying with it, the other subordinate monads, each one of which rays forth its own minor sūtrātmic emanation.

To particularize, we have in man the sūtrātman of his own humanhood, emanating from the mānasaputric or human ego overenlightened by and enclosed within the comprising essence of the divine monad, its Father in Heaven. Similarly, and on a much lower plane, we could speak of the as yet feebly developed sūtrātman of the vital-astral monad. It is the aggregation of these interworking sūtrātmic activities in man which makes him the compound entity he is, with one sūtrātmic channel into his own *human* monadic consciousness, another sūtrātman along which he can rise into his spiritual monadic consciousness, and still another by means of which he can ascend to commune with his own individualized inner god.

Another and more familiar explanation is that the sūtrātman, or thread-self, passes from life to life, on which the serial reincarnations are strung like beads on a string. The term as thus used is succinctly described by H.P.B. as the monad or the ātman-buddhi-manas in the human constitution; in other words, we may say that the sūtrātman is the reincarnating ego.

Now, then, the human ego is one of those particular monads as yet relatively unevolved. Above it there is the spiritual monad, and above that there is the divine monad. For karmic reasons any one of us happens to be a certain stream of consciousness, a sūtrātman; yet you or I as human individuals are the human monad. As such, we are only in the intermediate part of that stream of consciousness which is our constitution, whose upper part links us with Infinity, and whose lower part enables us to learn on this plane.

The divinity in the solar system is both one and an army, of which we are component parts. It has a life-consciousness-substance-energy, which flows through all of us, and is our substantial, conscious background; and all that particular range of monads or egos which forms the stream of consciousness of any one of us is spiritually housed in this solar divinity in whom we have our being.

When our human monad shall have brought out from within itself its undeveloped powers, it will become a spiritual monad, and we shall be buddhas. We shall then work through what is now the animal nature in us, which then will be human. Each monad will have stepped up a degree, and be more highly evolved. Or take any portion of man's constitution, such as the evolving human ego: it will become a spiritual ego, and afterwards a divine ego; and yet at the same time shot through and through with forces streaming down into man from egos superior to him, of which he is the child. This is the esoteric basis for the old saying, that at the flame of a candle you can light all the fires of the world, and the flame is undiminished. Consciousness is just like that.

There is one point concerning the different classes of monads which seems important to mention here. It deals with the individual monads of whatever class as being, on the one hand, those merely monadic consciousness-points which are monads in potency and fact but as yet relatively unevolved; and, on the other hand, those already highly developed spiritual entities evolving on their own planes which are in full possession of their monadic faculties and powers.

Strictly speaking, a monad is an 'independent' spiritual or divine entity in continuous evolution on its own plane; in other words, a relatively full-blown god. Only of a life-atom can it be said that it is a mere consciousness-point, although, again, every life-atom on whatever plane is but the manifestation of its own parent monad, connected with it by a ray of consciousness or sūtrātman. So that we have the monad in its realm, then the ray issuing forth from it and running 'downwards' through the intermediate realms or spheres, to find its terminus on whatever plane it may be as a life-atom, which then clothes itself with its own effluvia, thus forming the physical or chemical atom, the sthūla-śarīra of the life-atom.

The monad of a beast or of a mineral, or, again, of a man or of a buddha, is a divinity living and evolving throughout the manvantara on this its own spiritual or divine plane; hence every individualized entity in the lower realms, from elemental or life-atom to the highest god, is but the expression on its own plane of its indwelling parent monad.

Every life-atom in the human constitution not only helps to build it structurally, but likewise is the expression therein of its own *individual* parent monad, such parent monad on its own plane being in all likelihood the equal in dignity and spiritual unfoldment of the highest monad in man's own constitution. Everything interpenetrates and interblends with everything else, and thus aids in building its framework, in 'feeding' it, and in enabling it to express itself. It is a case of all for one and one for all; and I might add in passing that this is the inner significance of the teaching concerning universal brotherhood.

In addition to the immense multitude of life-atoms which compose man's constitution, there are the particularly evolved monadic foci or centers which we may call the monadic hierarchs, one for each of the seven or twelve 'planes' of the human constitution. As an illustration, the buddhic monad is really not a life-atom, but is the buddhic focus in us surrounding itself with its outflowing waves of effluvia forming its auric envelope. This auric envelope, however, is composed of buddhic life-atoms, largely children of this monad, but likewise the field for the play and interplay of other buddhic monads peregrinating through it, exactly as most of the atoms in the physical body are also the vital-astral atoms of monads coming in and going forth on their peregrinations.

Similarly, our solar system is filled mainly with the effluvia from the sun, but it is likewise the field for life-atoms coming from cosmic space, thus providing an electromagnetic field connecting sun with sun, or solar system with solar system; or, on the smaller scale, the twelve mansions of the zodiac with our sun. Human beings are likewise interconnected by psychovital, magnetic, and physical bonds, by exchanging life-atoms which do not belong to us but are peregrinating through us. It is the same on every plane of the human constitution. Each contributes its quota to that part of the auric egg to which it has an affinity: the buddhic life-atoms to the buddhic, the mānasic to the mānasic, and so forth.

It should be borne in mind that each ray from a divine monad is not merely a portion of it, but likewise passes *through* and *from* that divine monad as a monadic focus itself. The divine monad is composite in its high vehicles on the divine plane, these vehicles being 'atomic'; they are the descending rays or monads which pass through and from the divine monad in order to become manifesting monads in the constitution of a man and thus collaborate in building that constitution. The divine monad is, as it were, a monadic sun, a 'creative' or emanative focus of these rays which in a sense are of its own characteristic divine essence; and yet they are not of the monadic essence of that sun but pass through it, this ātmic sun being thus their temporary host or container. Each such ray in itself is a monad, destined to evolve into a being of the nature of the divine monad, its parent.

This is what K.H. referred to in *The Mahatma Letters* (p. 89), where he says that each such monadic focus is a creative center which we can call A, B, etc.; each giving birth in its turn to offsprings A^1, B^1, etc.; these latter in turn giving birth to A^2, B^2, and so forth.

When we loosely describe the different monadic classes as being un-evolved, latent, germinal, etc., we are not speaking of the monads them-selves, but only of their respective vehicles, some of them but slightly developed, others fully efficient instruments. The monads, *as monads*, are, each one of them, a spark or droplet of the essence of the monadic essence of the universe — or it may be of a sun or a planetary chain — each such 'highest essence' being of the very substance and nature of the ātman out of which the monads belonging to it emanate. We may think of a monad per se as a divine or spiritual elemental, because belonging by its origin to the highest cosmic element, i.e. to the hierarchy's ātman or paramātman. Thus an elemental, of whatever class, is an emanation or a spark from the cosmic element-principle from which it emanates; and this applies even to the lowest elemental classes which we have called life-atoms.

It might be asked what our relationship as a human life-wave is to the hierarch of our planetary chain. To answer this is not as easy as may appear on the surface. The difficulty lies in the fact that the human life-wave, considered not as a unit but as a vast number of individual entities, is composed of monads which as a class have reached the human stage in their evolution and therefore are linked together by tremendous bonds of karmic sympathy. Actually, however, the monads of our life-wave when traced to their parent-sources are found *not* to be, all of them, derivative from *one* hierarch. Certain monads are derivatives of the chief planetary spirit or the hierarch of our earth planetary chain; others are to be traced back to the hierarch of one of the other sacred planetary chains.

The life-wave as a whole is passing through our present earth chain as the cosmic station in which we are now living and evolving; but, because we are cosmic pilgrims, when the time comes for us as a life-wave to pass to some other one of the sacred planetary chains, we shall then for long aeons live and work in the auric egg of the hierarch of that planetary chain; and thus along the arc and the immense periods of the grand outer rounds.

Similarly, but on a smaller scale, as long as our human life-wave is undergoing its evolutionary pilgrimage on our present globe D as a station, we shall be held within the protecting and guiding hospitality of the minor hierarch which oversees our globe D; and when we pass to the other globes of this chain in regular serial order, we shall for millions and millions of years at each such station live in the auric egg of the respective hierarchs of these other globes.

Now a few words with regard to the statement elsewhere made by me that we as humans are higher evolutionally than is our globe D, earth. The truth is that the spiritual parts of the planetary spirit of globe D are higher in evolution than the spiritual monad of any human being; but we human beings as such are higher than our globe D which is the outermost veil of our globe's planetary spirit. In other words, the human hierarchy represents a rather more evolved stage on the ladder of life than has been attained by the earth, because at the present time we are the manifestations in quasi-astral, almost gelatinous bodies, of life-atoms of a spiritual type, which stage the globe, considered as an entity, has not yet attained. Human beings collectively thus represent the buddhi-mānasic quality of the earth.°

°Cf. *The Mahatma Letters*, p. 94.

LOST SOULS AND THE LEFT-HAND PATH

> Antaskarâna is the name of that imaginary bridge, the *path* which lies between the divine and the human Egos, for they are *Egos*, during human life, to rebecome *one* Ego in Dêvâchân or Nirvâna. This may seem difficult to understand, but in reality, with the help of a familiar, though fanciful, illustration, it becomes quite simple. Let us figure to ourselves a bright lamp in the middle of a room, casting its light upon the wall. Let the lamp represent the divine Ego, and the light thrown on the wall the lower Manas, and let the wall stand for the body. That portion of the atmosphere which transmits the ray from the lamp to the wall, will then represent the Antaskarâna. We must further suppose that the light thus cast is endowed with reason and intelligence, and possesses, moreover, the faculty of dissipating all the evil shadows which pass across the wall, and of attracting all brightnesses to itself, receiving their indelible impressions. Now, it is in the power of the human Ego to chase away the shadows, or sins, and multiply the brightnesses, or good deeds, which make these impressions, and thus, through Antaskarâna, ensure its own permanent connection, and its final reünion with the divine Ego. Remember that the latter cannot take place while there remains a single taint of the terrestrial, or of matter, in the purity of that light. On the other hand, the connection cannot be entirely ruptured, and final reünion prevented, so long as there remains one spiritual deed, or potentiality, to serve as a thread of union; but the moment this last spark is extinguished, and the last potentiality exhausted, then comes the severance.   — H.P.B.'s E.S. *Instructions,* III

In studying H.P.B.'s writings we must remember that she often had to invent words and phrases which would express with fair approximation the highly mystical terms of the Secret Language and of other ancient Oriental tongues in which the doctrines of the esoteric philosophy were imbodied. She herself explains the difficulties of teaching the individuals of her day, who had not the remotest conception of the sevenfold nature of man nor of the after-death conditions. There were then no words or terms in which to describe what had been for thousands of years typically doctrines of the Sanctuary.

For example, the two quite distinct types of entities, 'lost souls' and 'soulless men,' were more or less fused together in H.P.B.'s descriptions of the different destinies that ensued to men who follow the left-hand path; and very frequently she referred to both categories under the inclusive phrases 'soulless person' and 'second death.'

Lost souls are those human entities who, through a series of lives of almost uninterrupted evil living, and because of lack of aspiration towards their god within, have become so heavily involved in the lower quaternary, with its intense and unceasing attractions to absolute matter, that the 'link' or antahkarana connecting the personal man with the spiritual man has been snapped, thus freeing the spiritual monad, and leaving the personal ego relatively completely involved in the energies and substances of matter. Hence lost souls are human beings divorced from their higher natures.

Soulless men, on the contrary, are still septenary human beings, in whom the spiritual nature is but feebly or only occasionally active; they are not *ensouled* by the spiritual life flowing forth from the spiritual soul. Soulless people are exceedingly common, for they comprise all who pass their lives almost entirely absorbed in the emotions and thoughts of the mere personality, in its whimsies and wants and its restricted outlooks and selfish egoisms. Obviously this does not mean that they have no soul, but merely that the spiritual soul is not functioning within them accurately and continuously, due to their own lack of inner yearning.

A continued series of lifetimes of such 'soulless' living could and very probably would result in the dread destiny of the loss of the soul. For when the spiritual soul finds no fit habitat in its series of personalities, and the personalities have no attractions spiritwards, there will result a breaking of the antahkarana, thus producing a lost soul. From this we see why there is the utmost need of cultivating the higher nature by aspiring towards it and by living the life in accordance with the mandates received from within, and by letting no single day pass without some inner spiritual yearning. The daily aspiration to live an ever better and increasingly higher life is true yoga and will finally result in making one more fully ensouled. Indeed, chelaship is just this and nothing more. Chelas are more ensouled than average men, mahatmas more ensouled than are their chelas, and the buddhas still more so than the mahatmas. When a man is fully ensouled, he is then an incarnate god.

Now the destiny of those human beings who have become lost souls is dreadful almost beyond description. Quite outside of the awful inner agony that they suffer, the mental torture and psychic pain and horror which overwhelm them, they can become veritable human devils wreaking evil upon their fellowmen and, because of their own despair, joying in it. Meanwhile, they themselves are rushing downwards with increasing velocity with each new reimbodiment and finally are drawn to the Pit or Planet of Death and, dropping therein, pass out of the earth's sphere of attraction and are heard and seen no more. In the Pit their destiny is, because they are failures, to be broken up as *human* remnants and to be ground over and over in this one of nature's laboratories.

The statement has been made elsewhere that the astral monad can become so degenerate, humanly speaking, that it is attracted to the lower kingdoms. And as we have just said that the lost soul enters the current of fate which carries it to the Pit, it may be asked, what is it then that goes to the Planet of Death if the astral monad disappears first in the bodies of the beast kingdom, then in the plant world, and finally in the mineral kingdom?

The answer lies in the fact that man is composed of a group of monads, each one of which follows its own pathway through the ages; and therefore when karmic destiny falls heavily upon any one of these monadic centers, that center rises or falls to the sphere towards which its attractions draw it. Do not confuse the astral-vital monad of the man with the human monad. When we speak of a lost soul we mean a human soul, the human monad. After death the astral monad has one destiny for itself, the human monad has its devachanic interlude, the spiritual monad has its peregrinations through the spheres, the divine monad re-enters the bosom of the divine. That which goes to the Eighth Sphere or Planet of Death, sometimes called Māra, is the degenerate lost human soul. Thus abandoned not only by its spiritual part but also by its human soul part, the *vital-astral* soul enters the beast and the vegetable kingdoms. It has to do so. It cannot rise, the link with the above having been snapped. It is a derelict and drifts like a bit of flotsam in the astral light and naturally seeks the spheres which are most attractive to it.

Remember that a monad in the beginning of a world projects from itself a ray, and does so because of the karma of a past universe impelling it to manifest once more all the karmic seeds that it carries within itself. This ray passes through multiform and manifold experiences in matter, building up slowly through the ages an ego; and should this ego — sprung forth from its monadic parent and therefore having its parent's qualities — choose the left-hand path, it then begins to 'descend' towards the sphere of absolute matter and spiritual death, which means that when a black magician reaches the Eighth Sphere the remaining faint glimmering of the monadic ray has been withdrawn. There remains naught but a soul-shell, which falls apart into its component atoms, atoms that are withdrawn into the womb of nature with the rapidity of lightning once the last flickering gleam of the monadic ray has gone. This monadic ray is withdrawn into its monadic parent and remains there in its nirvana for aeons and aeons.

Meanwhile the monad sends forth another ray. What really once *was* is not destroyed. But the evolutionary work must be done all over again. A new ego must be built up. New peregrinations and transmigrations through the lower kingdoms of nature must follow before a new ego, a fit temple for the monadic divinity, is again evolved.

Yet even for the lost souls, although the antahkarana has been broken, there is yet a chance for reunion with the god within, at least in the beginning and before the distance between the inner god and the personality has become too great. Even a single desperate spiritual thought or yearning will be enough to draw together again the dissevered portions of the human constitution and thus, happily, enable the reunited upper triad and the lower quaternary to rebecome the full septenary entity. Should such reunion take place, it may become permanent, provided that thenceforwards, by intense upward striving, the personal man knits ever more closely the higher personal aspects into the webbing of his spiritual being. Should, however, the lower nature finally prove the stronger, then the rupture again takes place and with even less possibility of reunion than before.

All the archaic scriptures and philosophical schools have references to beings on spiritual planes who are centers and workers of evil. There are in the spiritual realms beings who are distinctly evil because falling or descending to lower regions through their attractions thither; and in certain cases they are of characteristically evil power, and even possibly possess such power in large measure. This somber and dread fact of nature was the basis of what became a superstitious legend in Christianity about "evil angels" or "beings of spiritual wickedness."

Many have found it difficult to reconcile the idea of an entity's being spiritual and at the same time evil. As said earlier, good and evil are not things in themselves, but are relative *conditions* or ways of life which entities create or follow and in which they consequently live. Hence a

454

spiritual or quasi-spiritual entity who has reached a certain evolutionary stage in spiritual realms, but in whom the instinct for harmony, altruism, etc., gives place to the attractions of the nether pole of those realms, thus bringing about disharmony, egoism, and selfishness, may be considered as being spiritually evil. Any being or entity on whatever plane, whose tendencies are towards the nether pole, is 'evil' *in its own surroundings*, and therefore can be productive of similar 'evil' to others. Every plane or world of the universe has its upper and lower poles, the light side and the night side of nature.

Alluding more specifically to human beings, there are two kinds of evil-doing: one caused by ordinary weakness in character; and the other by deliberate choice, where evil seems a flowery path and the fruits of selfish victory are considered as of larger worth than to walk with the gods. This is the path of the Brothers of the Shadow. It is the *direction* of action of our choice and will, which determines whether we shall become a black or a white magician. It matters not what the stage of progress may be that we have reached: if our direction is to the 'left,' we belong to the dark forces; and if the choice is to the 'right,' we belong to the forces of the sun. The division line is this: when we work and live for self, we are on the left-hand path; when we work impersonally for all, we are on the right-hand path.

Now when a being has willfully chosen the path of the shadows, it means that he has chosen with each day that passes to try to cut off one more feeble gleam from the spirit within. It is a mania with him. It is spiritual suicide; just as in the case of some other maniacs, he knows what he is doing, and yet he wills to do it.

There are certain human beings, although corrupt enough to desire to do evil in the world and to tempt others, and who love to see a fellow man fall and suffer, who yet feel an inner glow of gladness when the one so tempted refuses to succumb. This is one of the curious psychological paradoxes of human character. There are indeed beings who take a horrible delight in causing pain to others; yet even while they do it there may be remorse in the soul, a yearning for the one who is in torture and tempted, to turn and to stand up and to refuse. The Brothers of the Shadow are of many degrees, of many kinds, just as are the Brothers of Light. Indeed, there are human beings among us who are Brothers of the Shadow unconsciously to themselves! They have no noble permanent thoughts which fill their minds, and few unselfish impulses which touch

455

their hearts. Hence they are said to live in the shadows. Then there are other Brothers of the Shadow by profession and by knowledge, who have chosen the path of evil-doing, of the dark wisdom of matter.

It should be remembered that, so far as the *spiritual* principles or faculties are concerned, the Brothers of the Shadow have no hold upon any human being, sane or insane. Their work is in seduction: *a man falls from within.* There is the secret. The hosts of Light govern and control the hosts of the Shadow, although the former never interfere with the destiny of the latter, strange as it sounds. The Brothers of the Shadow, contrariwise, have no hold on the Sons of Light, but actually receive from the hosts of Light their very life which they use and abuse.

The Brothers of the Shadows, who have deliberately chosen evil, are our worst foes. They are often men and women of charming personality, apparently loving and unselfish, sometimes seemingly devoted friends. Were they repulsive, their evil work of disintegration and of the bringing of misery upon the race, would kill itself. They succeed by wiles, by temptings; never by being repulsive and horrible, for evil succeeds at times only on account of its fictitious beauty.

Men do not fail through the works of others; they fail from within themselves. The Brothers of the Shadow work by temptation, by mental pictures, by suggestion, by quoting scripture, by appealing to their victims' vanity as if their plea were made to the high virtues, by playing upon their egoism, and by arousing ignoble passions. Innocence is no sufficient protection. Gain knowledge, seek for wisdom; strengthen the heart by love, and learn to forgive — nothing acts to reduce evil so quickly as trusting and following these ancient rules. The methods of the black magicians vary, and these Brothers of the Shadows are of many grades and degrees; they range from high and evilly illuminated beings of "spiritual wickedness" down the scale which ends in their victims who have been ensnared in ignorance of the danger that they run.

The fate of the unfortunate Brothers of the Shadows is annihilation; for they have set their wills against the evolutionary current rising in nature's heart and flowing through every atom; and thus their structure of selfhood is ultimately worn away. But preceding this final stage of annihilation nature's currents sweep them into the eddies of dense matter which are the portals of Tartarus or avīchi.

The ultimate fate of the Sons of the Sun, of the Brothers of Light, is divinity, self-consciously realized: an expansion of self into sublime impersonal selfhood, when the personal becomes the impersonal, when the rushlight becomes the splendor of the sun. Such is the destiny of the white magician: to become a cooperator with the ever-enduring laws of nature; and these laws are the actions on this plane of the working of the wills of the gods, reflecting cosmic consciousness.

In theosophical literature reference is often made to the "moment of choice," particularly to that one which will take place at the midpoint of the fifth round. A similar moment of choice applies to the middle of the fourth round, which took place ages ago at the midpoint of the fourth or Atlantean root-race.

In the fifth round manas will undergo its especial evolution, and there will come a time when the evolving races will reach a stage where they will be subjected to two contrary attractions both at their mānasic maximum: the attraction towards the higher spiritual nature opposing the pull towards matter. This will occur, so far as this globe D is concerned, at the middle point of the fourth subrace of the fourth root-race of the fifth round. There and then will come the supreme choice of the evolving egos. If they find the attractions to the nether pole, towards absolute matter, to be too strong, they will be drawn to or towards the Pit in the worst cases; or if the pull is less strong, they will sink into utter intellectual oblivion and must wait their turn for future evolution until the new imbodiment of our chain. But if, on the contrary, spirit prevails over matter, the evolving egos will keep the link unbroken with the spiritual soul within them, and thus be able to go forwards to the succeeding sixth and seventh rounds. They will reach the culmination of the present chain-manvantara as dhyāni-chohans, imbodied human buddhas, with the light of ātman, of the inner god, shining in and through them.

This moment of choice is not something which will come upon us suddenly and unexpectedly when we are fifth rounders, but is a 'moment' which will have been in the making for aeons previously, even from the fourth round. We are right now making our characters to be fit or unfit to meet in safety that moment of choice when it comes upon us — as it infallibly will.

457

OCCULT PHYSIOLOGY

True knowledge is of Spirit and in Spirit alone, and cannot be acquired in any other way except through the region of the higher mind, the only plane from which we can penetrate the depths of the all-pervading Absoluteness. . . . If man by suppressing, if not destroying, his selfishness and personality, only succeeds in knowing himself as he is behind the veil of physical Mâyâ, he will soon stand beyond all pain, all misery, and beyond all the wear and tear of change, which is the chief originator of pain. . . . All this may be achieved by the development of unselfish universal love of Humanity, and the suppression of personality, or *selfishness*, which is the cause of all sin, and consequently of all human sorrow.

— H.P.B.'s E.S. *Instructions*, I

IT IS WITH RELUCTANCE that I deal with occult physiology, not at all because knowledge of whatever kind is wrong, but because of the very real danger of the misuse of teaching concerning the human body and its various organs, chakras, nādīs, etc. It is precisely these relatively unimportant facts of occult physiology which seem to exercise on the perverse minds of some people a sort of psychic fascination, as if it is with the body and its functions and organs that the really sublime teachings of the esoteric philosophy mainly deal — when in fact they almost totally ignore the body, for it is regarded as a merely temporary or māyāvi vehicle of the higher attributes of the real man.

Not alone in the West does this craving for knowledge of the secrets of the human frame have currency; for innumerable ages the masses of the East, as for instance in India and China, have been just as greatly addicted to running after powers, self-advantages, and the acquiring of influence over others. There are all too many who want to know the mysteries of these various nādīs, chakras or ganglionic force-centers, for selfish gain; and not a few for the purpose of strengthening the body or stimulating certain of its organs so that straightway such knowledge may be misused or perhaps even prostituted to evil and soul-destroying ends.

Is it any wonder, then, that all the great teachers from immemorial time have taught their chelas or disciples to concentrate undivided attention upon the really great powers and functions of the spiritual, intellectual, and higher psychical parts of the human constitution?

In India, due to ages of high philosophical teachings, these truths are far better known than they are in the West; yet most of the Oriental countries are simply overrun with the practices of a quasi-occultism, whose proponents in India are the lower classes of yogins or fakirs. Most of their whole life is given up to a study and practice of the elaborate rules for psychophysical development contained in the hatha-yoga as well as in the often infamous tāntrika works. But in India the dangers of these works are more or less clearly appreciated by educated people and those who have been trained in the loftier branches of philosophical thought, whereas in the Occident there is little if any such protective knowledge.

Any attempt to apply to his own body what one may read in these exoteric tāntrika or hatha-yoga works, by breathing exercises or otherwise, and thereby evoking secret powers or stimulating the body in usually illicit directions, is fraught with the very gravest peril — involving not only the risk of the loss of physical health or power, but likewise possible loss of mind. Pulmonary tuberculosis is one of the most common results of such dabbling, and one of the least harmful, for there are others far more serious, such as cancer, which could readily follow upon a disturbance of the equilibrium of the prānas through an attempt to arouse into abnormal activity one or another of the chakras.

The attention should not be fastened upon the body and its organs, but should be centered upon the higher nature where, by aspiration and spiritual yearning, the individual may awaken his spiritual-intellectual and higher psychical capacities which in most men lie latent from birth until death — partly through ignorance of their existence, and partly through inherent laziness which most have no desire to overcome. Consequently these observations are by way of attempting to elevate our notions of what the body is: a wonderful psychophysical mechanism, an instrument of the spiritual monad within.

The human body as a microcosm may be looked upon as containing every power or attribute or energy in the solar system. In other words, all the seven (or twelve) logoic forces that originally emanate from the sun, and pass in and through the various sacred planets, are transmitted to us as human beings and directly to the physical body. Thus each one of these solar logoic forces has its corresponding focus or organ in the human body, and these are the chakras.

There is a complete science regarding the chakras, but it is mostly studied by the black magicians, or by those who are unconsciously aspiring to become such, because what they want is to gain 'powers.' Even chelas are not allowed to cultivate the powers of the chakras by concentrating upon them. In fact, most chelas are not interested in these nerve centers, many not even knowing the names of them. Because they have become evolved men, they simply use the powers which flow through the chakras, precisely as we use our brains and our wills, although most people do not know which portion of the brain is the organ of the highest part; and most men do not know through what part of the body the spiritual influence flows, and yet we use it. This is rāja-yoga, jñāna-yoga, kingly union, wisdom-union.

The powers that we need we shall acquire by living the life. The powers that the unfortunate hatha-yoga seekers long for, and occasionally acquire in small degree, almost invariably work moral mischief with their natures, and psychical and physical harm to their constitutions, because they have gained these powers before they are able to control themselves. The way of jñāna-yoga and rāja-yoga is the path of a man who is a king in his own right by the spiritual divinity within him.

Six chakras and their respective seats are commonly named in most exoteric Hindu writings. These are the ganglia or foci wherein six of the different prānas have their centers of activity and gather in volume, each one in its own chakra. Now the names for these chakras not only vary, but likewise their respective positions in the body are not always uniformly given. Moreover, in most cases, the seventh is entirely omitted; yet, in one sense, it is the most important of all.

Hereunder is a list of the seven chakras, in a somewhat different and more correct form, with a translation of the Sanskrit names:

1. *Mūlādhāra:* 'root-support'; the regions around the pubis, including the generative organs. Under the governance of the planet Saturn.

2. *Svādhishthāna:* 'own seat or base'; the umbilical region generally. Under Mars.

3. *Manipūra:* 'jewel-stream'; the region of the epigastrium; the solar plexus. Under Jupiter.

4. *Anāhata:* 'individual, single'; the heart and its region, strongly affecting the lungs. Under Venus.

5. *Viśuddhi:* 'complete purity or clarity'; the region of the forehead between the eyes, including the organs of vision and the optic nerves. Under Mercury.

6. *Agni* or *Agnīya:* 'fire or fiery'; the pituitary body in the skull. Under the Moon.

7. *Sahasrāra:* 'thousandfold or thousand petaled'; the pineal gland in the skull. Under the governance of the Sun.

As said, this list varies somewhat from the one usually given. For instance, the anāhata is occasionally said to be located in the throat or neck (as is the udāna among the prānas), at other times at the root of the nose, and still again, as shown above, in the region of the heart. Furthermore, the manipūra and the svādhishthāna are often interchanged in position by different writers; which proves the lack of knowledge even in the tāntrika writings of the real and proper locations of some of these chakras and even of their names. Agni or the sixth chakra is sometimes called ājñākhya, and said to occupy the region of the fontanelle; the word means 'commanding or willing,' a fair description of the occult function of the pituitary body.

As already explained, these seven chakras are the foci or knots or condensations of the seven differently functioning prānas or vital streams in the human physical vehicle, each prāna having its respective chakra. Although only five prānas and six chakras are named exoterically, actually there are ten or even twelve prānas in man's constitution, and they find their respective outlets or functional organs in ten or twelve seats in the human body.

We should bear in mind that each of the chakras is a focus for one of the solar logoi as this logoic force passes through its planetary transmitter to the human physical vehicle. In exoteric Hinduism these forces are often spoken of as rays; for instance, sushumnā is referred to as one of the seven principal rays, i.e. logoic energies, of the sun. This ray has its seat or focus of action in the spinal cord, rooted as this is in the chakra at the lowest part of the body called mūlādhāra, and running upwards along the tubular cavity of the spinal column to end in the brain, more exactly in the chakra therein called sahasrāra or the pineal gland.

Now on each side of the central tube of the spinal cord are located respectively idā (called Ilā in Vedic literature, the consort of Budha, god of wisdom) and pingalā. Hindu writers are not unanimous with regard to the respective positions of idā and pingalā, because many place pingalā on the right of sushumnā and others on the left. All three are called nādīs, a Sanskrit word signifying tubular vessel. The meaning of pingalā is reddish brown, and idā implies refreshment, the higher vital and stimulating spiritual essence; whereas the sushumnā represents the solar vitality modified by lunar influences.

Hence the spinal column and the accompanying sushumnā in its tubular vessel with pingalā and idā, are the main channels of the psychovital economy of the body, with which all the chakras are intimately connected by the nervous and sympathetic systems as well as by the blood vessels. In occultism the spinal column is not only an organ, but it is actually threefold in its functions, being the foundation of the prānic vitality of the body, driven by the kāma of pingalā and more or less controlled by the higher mānasic or directing attributes of idā. This is why the adept at will and with his great knowledge can use these various nādīs. It may be added that the 'soul' leaves the body at death through the brahmarandhra at the summit of the skull, which last is in intimate connection with the three tubular vessels of the spinal column, and therefore with the sahasrāra and ājñā, these two chakras being the pineal gland and the pituitary body respectively.

Due to the tremendous activity of these three nādīs of the spinal column and the immense role they play in the economy of the physical body, they are destined to manifest as a double spinal column in the human beings of the far distant ages to come, for then idā and pingalā will have developed into cartilaginous or semi-bony structures, i.e. two spinal columns connected by the central nādī or sushumnā, which now is surrounded by the vertebrae of the spinal column.

Furthermore, the bodily chakras are the extensions or representatives of their respective principal foci or 'roots' in the brain and various appurtenances thereof contained in the skull, whether of the cerebrum or of the cerebellum. This is H.P.B.'s meaning when she says: "Our seven Chakras are all situated in the head, and it is these Master Chakras which govern and rule the seven (for there are seven) principal plexuses in the body, besides the forty-two minor ones to which Physiology refuses that name."[*]

Every artery and every vein, as well as every tiny capillary, in the human body can technically be called nādīs of the blood; and it is with reference to this that certain exoteric works of tāntrika or hatha-yoga physiology speak of their number as being 72,000 — which may or may not be accurate but which actually refers to every kind of 'tubular vessel' or nādī in the human body.

---

[*] E.S. *Instructions*, III.

The blood of a man or of a beast, or indeed the sap of the plants, is a deposit of the prānic vitality suffusing throughout the physical body and emanating from the different sources of the seven (or ten or twelve) prānas in the auric egg. Thus blood really is the prānas condensed; whereas we may call the nervous fluids the condensed psychomental vital fluids of the higher portions of the auric egg expressing themselves on the astral and physical planes.

There is a constant and unceasing exchange and interchange of ethereal substances and forces between idā and pingalā, and between these two and sushumnā, and through these last again with all the other chakras and nādīs, which is as much as saying with the sympathetic and/or nervous systems in the body and also its reticulated structure of blood vessels.

As by far the larger part of these Hindu writings are strongly influenced in one way or another by the tāntrika thought, I again emphasize the warning to leave the chakras and their respective prānas alone, because very serious peril to both mental and physical health will almost certainly be incurred by foolish yoga experimentation with them, such as attempting to control the breath. No one was more keenly aware of the situation than was H.P.B., who wrote in her E.S. *Instructions:*

> He who has studied both systems, the Hatha and Râja Yôga, finds an enormous difference between the two: one is purely psycho-physiological, the other purely psycho-spiritual. — III

When we correlate all these physiological functions with the cosmic powers, we recognize that every human being is truly a miniature universe; and that every element and force in the solar system and therefore of the sun itself has its respective focus in man, in his auric egg, and hence in his astral-physical frame. This sublime truth can give spiritual dignity to our thoughts, and lead us to regard our bodies as temples of the god within us.

X

The Hierarchy of Compassion

The Hierarchy of Compassion

THE SILENT WATCHERS

The *Arhats* of the "fire-mist" of the 7th rung are but one remove from the Root-Base of their Hierarchy — the highest on Earth, and our Terrestrial chain. This "Root-Base" has a name which can only be translated by several compound words into English — "the ever-living-human-Banyan." This "Wondrous Being" descended from a "high region," they say, in the early part of the Third Age, before the separation of the sexes of the Third Race. . . .

He is *the* "Initiator," called the "GREAT SACRIFICE." For, sitting at the threshold of LIGHT, he looks into it from within the circle of Darkness, which he will not cross; nor will he quit his post till the last day of this life-cycle. Why does the solitary Watcher remain at his self-chosen post? Why does he sit by the fountain of primeval Wisdom, of which he drinks no longer, as he has naught to learn which he does not know — aye, neither on this Earth, nor in its heaven? Because the lonely, sore-footed pilgrims on their way back to their *home* are never sure to the last moment of not losing their way in this limitless desert of illusion and matter called Earth-Life. Because he would fain show the way to that region of freedom and light, from which he is a voluntary exile himself, to every prisoner who has succeeded in liberating himself from the bonds of flesh and illusion. Because, in short, he has sacrificed himself for the sake of mankind, though but a few Elect may profit by the GREAT SACRIFICE.

It is under the direct, silent guidance of this MAHA — (great) — GURU that all the other less divine Teachers and instructors of mankind became, from the first awakening of human consciousness, the guides of early Humanity. It is through these "Sons of God" that infant humanity got its first notions of all the arts and sciences, as well as of spiritual knowledge; and it is they who have laid the first foundation-stone of those ancient civilizations that puzzle so sorely our modern generation of students and scholars.

— *The Secret Doctrine*, I, 207–8

THE HIERARCHY OF COMPASSION is divisible into almost innumerable minor hierarchies, running down the scale of cosmic being from the supreme hierarch of our solar system through all intermediate stages and infilling every one of its planets, until finally its representatives on this physical plane are found on the different globes of the planetary chains. It is built of divinities, demigods, buddhas, bodhisattvas, and great and noble men, who serve as a living channel for the spiritual currents coming to this and every other planet of our system from the heart of the solar divinity, and who themselves shed glory and light and peace upon that pathway from the compassionate deeps of their own being. Little do men know of the immense love, the divine impulses of compassion, which sway the souls of those who form this Hierarchy of Light. They have made the great renunciation, giving up all hope of personal evolutionary progress, it may be for aeons to come, in order to remain at their appointed tasks in the service of the world. Unrecognized, unthanked, they work steadily on, watching others go past them as the slowly moving river of lives sweeps along in unending flow.

On our earth there is a minor hierarchy of light. Working in this sphere there are lofty intelligences, human souls, having their respective places in the hierarchical degrees. These masters or mahatmas are living forces in the spiritual life of the world; and awakened minds and intuitive hearts sense their presence, at least at times.

Consider the wonderful work in which labor those who have preceded us. They are revealers in the sense of unveilers, for they are the initiators, the handers on of light from age to age. Those of the order of the buddhic splendor, of wisdom and compassion, copy among us what takes place in spheres supernal, for there are revealers among the gods themselves. And with these immortals, as we conceive them to be, there is likewise a training school, and a passing on of light from manvantara to manvantara. The old Hermetists were right: what is above is the same as that which is here below, and what is here below is but a shadow, a reflection, of what is above.

At the summit of the Hierarchy of Compassion is the Silent Watcher. He has renounced all; in utter self-sacrifice he waits and watches with infinite pity, reaching downwards into our own sphere, helping and inspiring, in the silences of spiritual compassion. The Silent Watcher remains at his post from the beginning to the ending of the manvantaric life cycle, nor will he move from that post of cosmic compassion until the last thread of destiny of that hierarchy has been spun. He is called the Silent Watcher because he watches and guards through the age-long manvantara in what to us seems to be a divine silence.

This Wondrous Being is the spiritual bond and link of the various bodhisattvas and buddhas of the Hierarchy of Light, both with superior worlds and with us and the lower beings of our round. He is the chief of the spiritual-psychological hierarchy of which the masters form a part. He is the ever-living human banyan from which they — and we too — hang as leaves and fruit. From this Wondrous Being originally come our noblest impulses through our own higher selves: the life and aspiration we feel stirring in our minds and hearts, the urge to betterment, the sense of loyalty and troth — all the things which make life bright and beautiful and well worth living.

We are taught that, as far as great spiritual seers know, the same hierarchical pattern exists on every globe, on every man-bearing planet of every sun in the infinitudes of Space. There is over each one a master teacher, and in each case he merits the term which H.P.B. uses, namely, the "Great Sacrifice," because from boundless compassion for those lower in the scale of evolution he has renounced all hope and opportunity of going higher in this manvantara. He can learn nothing more of this hierarchy, for all knowledge pertaining to it is his already; but he remains behind for aeons as the great inspirer and teacher. He has sacrificed himself for all below him.

Just as the hierarchies in the universe are virtually infinite in number, so are the Wondrous Beings or Silent Watchers, because every one is such only for the series of lives in its hierarchy. There is the Wondrous Being who is the supreme spiritual chief, the Silent Watcher, for the Brotherhood of Compassion. There is one for our globe, who is identic in this case with the hierarch of the Brotherhood of Compassion. There is also one for our planetary chain, and one for each of its globes; there is likewise one for our solar system, whose habitat is the sun, and one for our own home-universe, and so forth forever.

Each such Silent Watcher is the fountain, the parent, of a hierarchy of the Buddhas of Compassion. They are really the ones from which flow forth into the universe those majestic operations of consecutive and never-failingly accurate action which we call natural laws. It is the movement of their will and consciousness which expresses itself thusly, and therefore are they said to be engaged in a perpetual battle — a human metaphor — with the forces of pure matter, with the Mā-mo. This is a general term covering the dark and sinister spirits and operations of nature, which are merely the workings of hosts of monads of the cosmic life climbing slowly upward, but still plunged in the deep spiritual sleep of material existence. The battle of these Silent Watchers is the holding of the laws of life in orderly consequence, so that all go well, and the Light die not out from the universe.

Following the same rule of repetitive action in nature, there is a Silent Watcher for every man, his own inner god — the buddha within him — which is the core of his being, the origin of the fundamental law or consciousness of his hierarchical structure. And there is a Silent Watcher for every atom. As the entire framework of kosmos is built throughout on correspondences and repetitives, there are no absolutes anywhere, and everything is strictly relative to everything else. The divine of one hierarchy is actually grossest matter to another far superior hierarchy; but within one and the other the repetitive rules apply very strictly, because nature has one general and *throughout-repeated* course of action.

It is obvious that these Silent Watchers are of many grades. The one for our globe D of the earth chain, for instance, is still human, for, although the farthest advanced of humanity, he is not yet evolved out of the human into the god stage. There are planetary spirits, Silent Watchers, who occupy a grade intermediate between divinities and men. There are Silent Watchers among the gods, and some of these manifest themselves as suns — not only as the heart of a sun, the god behind the glorious star which is its garment, but likewise in a sense as that garment, in the same way that a man is not only the spirit and the soul of himself, but also his vehicle; he being thus a physical, psychical, spiritual, and a divine man.

It is likewise true that a greater Silent Watcher is the head of the minor Silent Watchers which he leads, just as the Silent Watcher of our globe, who is a human demigod indeed, but yet a man, is the guardian of our humanity. It is in this Being that our roots of individual consciousness originate, much as the various offshoots of the banyan tree derive their primal origin from the parent trunk which now lives with its children as an equal, yet first among equals. The ever-living human banyan alluded to by H.P.B. is not an incarnated man. It is in fact the Mahāchohan°

°A chohan, a mahāchohan, a dhyāni-chohan, of necessity is a man, or has been a man, either of this earth or in some past manvantara. It is not accurate, however, to speak of the Mahāchohan as having been, in some far past manvantara, a divine being who came to earth in order to help mankind, for he has gone through the human stage as an evolving entity, and is still human. We now are passing through lower degrees of the human stage. In far distant aeons of the future, even before this planetary chain shall have reached its manvantaric end, we too, as a human host, shall become dhyāni-chohans; and before that, we shall attain the lofty stage which the Mahāchohan now occupies. The word Mahāchohan is a title, just as is Buddha or Christ. There are great mahāchohans, also those of inferior degree, but the one of whom we are here speaking is the supreme chief, the lord and teacher of the Brotherhood of adepts, and through them of us.

of this earth, an entity who was a man in far past ages, in former manvantaras in fact. He is the loftiest of the Buddhas of Compassion, the supreme guide and teacher of the hierarchy of the Great Ones at the present time, the channel through whom pass the sublime inspiration and life flowing from the Silent Watcher of humanity.

The higher self of each one of us is an ever-living human banyan, the source of a multitude of human souls which have been sent forth as branches, which themselves take root in the material world; and these human souls in their turn grow through ages-long evolution to become spiritual banyans, each of them sending out new roots, new branches, but all derivative from the parent tree. Therefore this ever-living human banyan may be called the parent heart of the mahatmas.

When we call this hierarchical Wondrous Being our highest self, our Paramātman, we mean that it is the primeval or originating seed from which we grow and develop into composite entities. From it we spiritually spring. Or we can consider it, *in one aspect,* as a sheaf of divine light separating into innumerable monads and monadic rays in a manvantara; and, when the pralaya comes, again withdrawing and drawn back into itself, now enriched and ennobled, through its countless hosts of manifested monads and monadic rays, by the individualizing experience that these have gained. The innumerably various consciousnesses increase in power and glory and self-cognition by means of the lives through which they have passed within the life of the greater being.

Some speak of our inner god as if that were the divine ending of us. Yet its realms of consciousness are but the beginning of other realms still more divine, reaching ever deeper and deeper into the womb of Infinitude, because the ladder of life extends endlessly.

Let me try to illustrate: in future ages when the spiritual selfhood of a man will have become, say, a solar divinity, he will be a Silent Watcher of that solar system — its apex, its head, heart and brain, ruling all the hosts of entities which infill that solar system. They will all be his children; now they are life-atoms in his physical body, also of course in his linga-śarīra, kāma-rūpa, manas and in his spiritual part. As an individual he will have no more to learn in that Egg of Brahmā, which will then be himself greatly expanded. In other words, all the beings that now compose him, that help him to express himself on all his planes, will themselves have grown into many kinds of entities: atoms, vegetables, animals, men, demigods, etc. — call them angels, archangels, powers, principalities, for

471

the name does not matter much. He himself will be the Silent Watcher, one who will stand in all his solar splendor throughout innumerable aeons, learning no more in the world which then will be his body, his self-expression — living for the sake of the lives who had sprung forth from him, as sparks from a central fire. Of course, in his still higher parts he will be learning on planes correspondingly higher; but half of his attention, of his life, intelligence, and possibilities for individual growth as a god, will be devoted to the hosts composing the lower elements of his being. He cannot, will not, advance one step and leave a single life-atom behind him abandoned, on the long, long, evolutionary trail, because this would be impossible. This is partly karma, and partly pure compassion. Such is the sublime destiny of us all.

Let us take another example, the Silent Watcher of our planetary chain. When our solar system began, our planetary chain was there among the "sons of God" — the god was Father Sun, and the sons were the divinities in and around it — and the highest being of our chain, the most progressed planetary spirit of that same planetary chain as it was in the preceding solar manvantara, now reimbodies itself as the leader, the coryphaeus, of our present chain. Furthermore, throughout all the many reimbodiments of our planetary chain during the solar manvantara, that one planetary spirit will be our Silent Watcher. It has, so to speak, to drag the heavy weight of the whole planetary chain hanging like a multiple pendant from it, but never for an instant wishing to free itself from the multitudinous hosts composing that chain, ourselves among them.

A third example, on the human plane, is the upper triad of man's constitution, ātma-buddhi-manas — call it the Christ-monad or inner Buddha, if you will — his own individual Silent Watcher. It is himself, and yet not himself. In this thought lies the true significance of a Silent Watcher: the solitary spiritual entity who will not go higher alone, and who reproduces as from a source every new reimbodiment of the man as a human soul. This is brought about by means of the ray from this Silent Watcher within man.

As the Pythagoreans phrased it, the highest triad remains in "silence and darkness," and verily is the root of our being. It is silence and darkness to us; but actually our human life is the darkness. In its own being this upper triad is supernal light, unspeakable glory, and its silence is such to us only because our ears are not trained to hear what there takes place.

Another instance of a human Silent Watcher is the spiritual head of

472

all the adepts who have ever lived on this globe, who now live, or who will live in the future: the one whom they all recognize as their spiritual father, a man and yet a demigod, because a god imbodied in a highly advanced man's soul. He is an actual imbodied being, although not necessarily possessing a body of flesh. It may well be that he is imbodied as a nirmānakāya, more likely than not; a nirmānakāya is a complete man minus the lower gross triad. This entity, the Silent Watcher of our globe and its humanity, is on earth.

This Wondrous Being is the hierarchical Brotherhood of adepts of our planetary chain, begun in the fourth round on our globe at about the middle period of the third root-race — which was the period when humanity was beginning to be self-conscious and ready for the receiving of light. The descent of this Being from a high plane, from globe A by way of globes B and C, was rather a projection of energy than a descent of an imbodied entity downwards. It was a visitation in our underworld,° undertaken for the sake of helping those beings living in its 'shadows.'

Now this Wondrous Being is a dhyāni-buddha. Interlocked in his vital essence, streaming forth from him as from a sun, are innumerable rays, and these various children rays are human egos. Like the banyan tree, this Wondrous Being sends forth tendrils of the spirit which reach down into the substantial fabric of the universe in which he lives, and there take root; and because of receiving from him the life essence, they themselves become banyan trees, growing up in their turn. In other words, they achieve full evolutionary growth, spiritual and intellectual and psychical maturity, and then send forth other new tendrils 'downwards,' which take root, thus building up new trunks, etc.

One of the most beautiful teachings of theosophy is that this Wondrous Being came from a "high region" as a visitor to us, living in what was to him the underworld, and dwelling for a time amongst us as the primal master-spirit of the human race — a Being at once one and many — a mystery.

°Underworld is a technical term meaning any world inferior to that on which the higher being lives. There is no one absolute underworld — even globe A is an underworld to a higher globe.

THE THREE VESTURES

IN THE SEVENFOLD constitution of every manifested being, not only of man but of the gods, are 'three vestures,' known in esoteric Buddhism as the trikāya, to wit, the dharmakāya, the sambhogakāya, and the nirmānakāya. It is, however, only in the more advanced humans (or in beings equivalent to them) that these vestures become *self-consciously* active and functioning.

In every being this threefold essence has a common identic origin, and this fountainhead is the Wondrous Being who is at the same time 'the One and the Many,' manifesting throughout the hierarchy in a succession of beings emanating from itself, and therefore existing and functioning both as an individual and as an aggregate in the dharmakāya, the sambhogakāya and the nirmānakāya states from the beginning of the great cosmic manvantara until its end.

The highest aspect or sub-entity of the Wondrous Being is the First Logos or primal spirit, called Ādi-buddha, ādi meaning primeval. It is this Ādi-buddha that is in the dharmakāya state: that of pure consciousness, pure bliss, pure intelligence, freed from all personalizing thought; it is that spiritual body or condition of a being in which the sense of soulship and egoity has vanished into the universal or hierarchical. The second aspect of the Wondrous Being is called the dhyāni-buddha, and is carried by the sambhogakāya, meaning participation-body, because the buddha in the sambhogakāya state still retains its consciousness as an individual, its egoship. The third aspect or sub-entity is the mānushya-buddha, meaning human buddha, so named because born in a human body for compassionate work among men; at will or need, he lives and works in the nirmānakāya, about which a very wonderful doctrine exists. In one sense it is the highest of the three aspects on account of the immense, willing, self-sacrifice involved in the incarnation into human existence. It is along the line of the dhyāni- and the mānushya-buddhas that the wisdom-teaching of the ages is mystically handed down to mankind through their representatives on earth, the Brotherhood of adepts. They constitute the spiritual-psychological aspect of the Wondrous Being, and are the Hierarchy of Compassion, called by the Greeks the Golden Chain of Hermes.

In such noble humans as the mahatmas — although less so than in the various grades of bodhisattvas and buddhas — not only are these three vestures self-consciously active and functional, but these exalted men can at will shift their center of consciousness almost completely from the one to the other.

Now when the self-conscious ego chooses to center its consciousness in the dharmakāya, and if this choice has been *definitely* made, its nirvana is irrevocable, for from that moment the lower parts of the constitution are cast off and the buddha-adept rises into the nirvana state where he remains for ages — until the end of the cosmic manvantara. Thus do the Buddhas of Compassion attain the dharmakāya condition, which gives them the right to enter nirvana; but they renounce it, and a few of them remain in the sambhogakāya, though many choose the nirmānakāya. The Pratyeka Buddhas, on the other hand, deliberately strive to "attain the sublimity of the dharmakāya" and therein remain sunken in selfish spiritual bliss and isolation until the next cosmic manvantara opens.

The sambhogakāya is the intermediate vesture, and is the state of those grand beings who for various karmic reasons partake to a certain extent of the wisdom and unutterable bliss of the dharmakāya, yet are held by karmic bonds of sympathy with the multitudes of suffering beings trailing behind, and thus to a degree are functional in the nirmānakāya as well.

Those beings who have become self-consciously functional in the nirmānakāya, choose this vesture in order to remain in contact with mankind; for the nirmānakāya condition enables them to exercise a steady and continuous influence of a highly spiritual and intellectual kind in human affairs, and also to give direct aid when karma permits.

The bodhisattvas invariably choose the nirmānakāya vesture when their initiatory rank enables them to do so, although a few of them for karmic reasons which even with their great wisdom and will they cannot control, find it needful to assume the sambhogakāya. When the karmic causes have worked themselves out, they either reincarnate and later assume the nirmānakāya vesture, or assume it immediately.

I might mention that the three vestures can be correlated to the three dhātus of Buddhism, these dhātus being respectively the spiritual realms, the intermediate or higher manifested worlds, and the lower cosmic sub-planes on which we humans are presently living. Thus the dharmakāya belongs to the arūpa-dhātu; the sambhogakāya to the rūpa-dhātu; and the nirmānakāya to the kāma-dhātu.

Likewise these three vestures correspond to the three divisions of the human constitution — broadly spoken of in the West as spirit, soul and body — which the adept or initiate on rare occasions when the need arises can separate one from the other without killing himself. The dharmakāya, then, corresponds to the higher triad, ātma-buddhi-manas (or rather higher manas here); the sambhogakāya to the higher manas conjoined with kāma and the higher ranges of prāna; and the nirmānakāya to manas-kāma-prāna and the astral garment that these three exude from themselves. Since the nirmānakāya is living in the astral worlds, he obviously needs an 'astral body' corresponding to the plane on which he is active. Furthermore, his higher manas and buddhi are of course functional within him, although his self-conscious field of work is in the manas-kāma-prāna, just as the self-consciousness of man today is largely centered in the kāma-manas and the lower principles, yet the higher principles are more or less functional in him.

All such statements, it is to be remembered, are merely crutches of thought and therefore we should not permanently anchor our thinking to any particular manner of viewing these correspondences. As a matter of fact, the nirmānakāya comprises everything except the lowest triad, that is, the body, the physical-astral prānas, and the linga-śarīra. It includes the sambhogakāya and the dharmakāya to boot; but the center of consciousness is for the time being placed in the particular nirmānakāya quality of consciousness itself.

It is not possible for even the adept to be self-consciously functioning in fullness in all three vestures at one and the same time; but he can choose at will in which one he wishes temporarily to function. Whatever may be the one he chooses to work in at any given time, the ātmic stream of consciousness is always pouring through him. Hence, such separation or temporary concentration of self-consciousness in one of the vestures does not mean that the vesture thus selected is broken off from the remainder of the constitution, for such a rupture would bring about dissolution of the whole constitution and spell complete death to the adept.

The teaching concerning the trikāya is one of the sublimest in the entire range of occultism. It is in order to bring forth into self-conscious functioning this living threefold buddhic essence in the constitution of every human being, that the masters of wisdom and compassion, when on the threshold of nirvana, renounce that lofty state and return to guide and teach men.

476

THE DHYĀNI-CHOHANIC HOST

The truths revealed to man by the "Planetary Spirits" (the highest Kumâras, those who incarnate no longer in the universe during *this* Mahamanvantara), who appear on earth as Avatârs only at the beginning of every new human race, and at the junctions or close of the two ends of the small and great cycle — in time, as man became more animalized, were made to fade away from his memory. Yet, though these Teachers remain with man no longer than the time required to impress upon the plastic minds of child-humanity the eternal verities they teach, their spirit remains vivid though latent in mankind. And the full knowledge of the primitive revelation has remained always with a few Elect, and has been transmitted from that time up to the present, from one generation of Adepts to another. As the Teachers say in the *Occult Primer:* "This is done so as to ensure them (the eternal truths) from being utterly lost or forgotten in ages hereafter by the forthcoming generations." . . . . The mission of the Planetary Spirit is but to strike the *key-note* of Truth. Once he has directed the vibration of the latter to run its course uninterruptedly along the concatenation of the race to the end of the cycle, he disappears from our earth until the following Planetary Manvantara. The mission of any teacher of esoteric truths, whether he stands at the top or the foot of the ladder of knowledge, is precisely the same: as above, so below. — H.P.B.'s E.S. *Instructions*, III

THE CLASSES OF SPIRITUAL beings which infill our solar system are twelve in number, often however referred to as ten, of which three are spoken of as residing in the silence, and seven as being manifested. As H.P.B. wrote in *The Secret Doctrine* (II, 77):

Occultism divides the "Creators" into twelve classes; of which four have reached *liberation* to the end of the "Great Age," the fifth is ready to reach it, but still remains active on the intellectual planes, while seven are still under direct Karmic law. These last act on the man-bearing globes of our chain.

The four highest of the twelve classes of monadic or spiritual entities are the highest classes of the gods. The fifth class are entities who stand on the threshold of divinity, and may be regarded as quasi-divine; these are the various grades of the higher buddhas, whether Buddhas of Compassion or even the highest Pratyeka Buddhas. They are lofty spirits, liberated dhyāni-chohans, above the lower seven grades of manifested beings. This fifth class composes, collectively, the link by which all the lower septenary manifested universe is held as a pendant from the divine realms. As the apex of any one hierarchy blends into the lowest plane of the one superior to it, there must be links between them, connecting agencies, hierarchies of beings serving as intermediaries. It is this fifth class of lofty beings which directly links us with the gods. Their place in nature is in fact the realm of the Silent Watcher.

The remaining seven classes of monads or cosmic spirits — dhyāni-chohans of many grades and degrees — are commonly divided into two groups: the upper three, and the lower four. Those of the upper three of this septenary host of spiritual beings are spoken of as the dhyāni-buddhas and it is they who comprise the Hierarchy of Compassion. They are the intelligences impelling the builders, i.e. the dhyāni-chohans of the lower four, into action. It is the interacting of the energy-substances between these two lines which together comprise the totality of all evolutionary processes within our kosmos. These two lines should not be confused. The dhyāni-buddhas are the architects, the overseers who provide the model, lay down the plans, and their work is carried out by the inferior grades of dhyāni-chohans called the builders, who receive the creative impress from the beings of the luminous arc, and carry it out. The builders not only work in, but actually form, the outer or material kosmos, and are (in one sense) the lower principles of the dhyāni-buddhas who compose the inner kosmos. Now each of these two lines is septenary: there are seven classes of dhyāni-buddhas, and seven classes of the inferior grades of dhyāni-chohans.

The acme of any hierarchy is its seed, its root, the originating life center from which the hierarchy hangs as a fruit from a bough of the Tree of Life. This rule prevails throughout the universe and consequently the origin and fountain of the life of all the dhyāni-buddhas is the summit of that particular hierarchy to which they belong. It is this summit of a hierarchy we sometimes call, 'He who watches in silence': a phrase similar to the expression, 'lords of meditation,' i.e. dhyāni-chohans.° This does not mean that these lofty spiritual beings pass their time in doing nothing but meditating, in the human sense of the word. They are spoken

---

°Cf. *Fundamentals of the Esoteric Philosophy*, chs. xxix and xl.

478

of as 'lords of meditation' because that is the manner in which the human mind mystically conceives them to be. Actually, on their own plane they enjoy a state of high spiritual activity and are collaborators in the great cosmic work with the higher gods. Another reason why they are so named, is that the dhyāni-chohan at the heart of each one of us, our own inner god, is conceived by us as an entity meditating in the silence through the ages, awaiting the time when this inner Buddha, this immanent Christos, shall be enabled to bring up to its own spiritual state of power and wisdom our struggling human soul.

If some of the beings living on the electrons of the atoms of our body were to think of the human consciousness, which is their fountain of existence and vitality, I doubt not that these infinitesimal thinking entities would regard us as lords of meditation. Our human life is lived on a scale much slower, much more majestic, than is their frenzied existence; and consequently the duration of a single human thought, fleeting as it seems to us, would be to them a state of consciousness of immense duration. Similarly we human beings living our own frenzied little lives in comparison with the majestic time periods of godlike entities, can conceive of them only as plunged in a state of deep spiritual consciousness, each phase or thought of which to us seems to be ages long. And higher even than these lofty beings are other ranges of entities still more sublime.

A full-blown dhyāni-chohan was aeons upon aeons ago, in other solar manvantaras, a life-atom; and every one of the hosts of life-atoms that compose our entire constitution on all its planes and in all its principles is in its outer self a dhyāni-chohan-to-be and at its heart of hearts a fully developed dhyāni-chohan — although as yet unexpressed. So man is not only *one* essence, which is already a dhyāni-chohan, but is also a host, a vast and almost infinite multitude of unevolved dhyāni-chohans. Even his human soul is on its way to evolving forth dhyāni-chohanship.

The human life-wave at the end of the seventh round of our planetary chain will have become a dhyāni-chohanic host, a race of gods, ready to take their flight into the interior spaces of Space. Man will have blossomed forth into a self-conscious god, not yet 'God,' or the summit of the hierarchy to which he belongs by karmic descent, but *a* god. He will have become a planetary spirit, a dhyāni-chohan, one of that wondrous host of spiritual beings who are the perfected men of former manvantaras. When we first started on this pilgrimage in this manvantara, it was these dhyāni-chohans, our own spiritual lords, who opened the path for us, who

479

guided our uncertain steps as we became men, incarnations of our higher selves. When we became *self*-conscious, we began to guide ourselves, and to work consciously with them according to our evolution.

The agnishwāttas° or solar Lhas are another aspect of this chohanic host. The agnishwātta pitris belong to the higher triad of the manifested seven which work directly in and through man. And it is precisely because we are straitly allied with this solar hierarchy, in fact belong to it, that we have these links of psychological and intellectual and spiritual connection with the solar divinity, Father Sun.

Indeed, we are Sons of the Sun or solar pitris in our higher parts. Or, more accurately still, we shall become such when the agnishwātta-energy, a fully developed Son of the Sun, now overshadowing each of us, will have worked the spiritual marvel within us — raised us to its own stature. Every human being is the temple of a ray of the solar splendor, here not referring to the physical sun alone, but to the auric egg of the inner sun which is an indwelling divinity giving to the manifested sun the light and life which it sheds throughout its kingdom.

Most of the Egyptian kings, as shown on the cartouche of many of them, bore as one of their titles the dignity of Son of the Sun. In the earliest days of Egypt, where this was a truly royal salutation, it signified an actual passing, by initiation in the fourth degree, of the inner constitution of man out of the sphere of earth and across the planetary spaces, until one had entered the portals of the sun and, spiritually speaking, had come into communication with the lord and giver of life of the solar system.

There were other countries also which followed and retained the ancient rites and therefore the titles; and frequently in their older literatures, and sometimes in their more modern writings, we find the identic initiatory expression used, Son of the Sun. The ancient Egyptian kings, and the mystics of all peoples who passed through this wonderful rite, trod that pathway and returned true saviors of their fellow men.

°*Agnishwātta* is a Sanskrit compound: *agni*, fire and *svad*, to taste or to sweeten; hence it means those who have tasted of or been tasted by fire — the fire of suffering and pain in material existence producing great fiber and strength of character, i.e. spirituality. This word 'taste' likewise has the meaning of becoming one with. Thus to taste of fire is to become at one with it: the fire-part of one's nature is the part in which the monadic essence is at the time manifesting itself around an egoic center. From the standpoint of occultism, the term agnishwātta signifies an entity who has become through evolution one in essence with the aethery fire of spirit. The agnishwātta pitris are our solar ancestors as contrasted with the barhishads, our lunar ancestors.

The mānasaputras° are likewise dhyāni-chohans. There are seven classes of these mānasaputras, just as there are seven classes of agnishwāttas. In fact, the agnishwātta-energy and the mānasaputra-energy are two aspects of the same cosmic beings. The incarnation or entrance of these mānasaputras into the as yet mentally unawakened humanity, of the middle and later third root-race of this fourth globe during this present fourth round, took place in seven stages, according to the seven classes of the mānasaputras. It took ages before all the humanity of that period became self-conscious. The highest class of the mānasaputras incarnated first, so that the human vehicles in which they imbodied were not only the first to become self-conscious, but likewise were the greatest humans of that far distant period; and the least advanced mānasaputras were they who entered the lowest human vehicles, which were also the last in time to become self-conscious.

The entrance of the mānasaputras into the then still unself-conscious vehicles was a karmic act, and corresponded in racial history to the entrance of mind into the human child today. The one is racial, the other is individual; but the rule is the same. This event occurred when mind, the ability to understand, was unfolded. Or, as it is expressed in *The Secret Doctrine*, the mānasaputras descended and taught; they came from the higher and invisible realms and incarnated in the as yet senseless brain, and men thenceforward were self-conscious, thinking, intelligent beings. As a babe in its earliest years is not strictly human in the sense that mind, the reincarnating ego, is not yet manifesting its powers, so likewise was the condition of the human life stream preceding the middle point of the third root-race: the human vehicles were there, but mind was asleep.

These mānasaputric entities were not entirely extraneous from the beings into which they poured their divine flame of intelligence. The fact is that the time had come in the ages-long cycling of the pilgrims' journey when their lower psychical and physical apparatus had through evolution been raised to the point where their higher part could manifest itself even on this physical plane, and thus make out of the then dreamy and quasi-conscious entities self-conscious human beings.

Nevertheless these mānasaputras, our own higher egos, did come from other spheres. The two statements are perfectly consistent, because the

°*Mānasaputra* is a compound: *mānasa*, mental, from the word *manas*, mind, and *putra*, child — offspring of the cosmic mahat or intelligence, which latter has always been described as the fire of spiritual consciousness.

481

essence of a man is by no means bound by the limitations of his physical body. His higher ego, the mānasaputra working in him even at the present day, lives in another sphere than that of his brain, and is itself but a veil of the still higher spiritual parts of the monadic essence.

Each one of us, as a human being, as a reincarnating mānasaputra, draws the origin of that part of his constitution from the solar divinity. And when, through initiation combined with strong spiritual striving upwards, we attain self-conscious communion with this solar flame dwelling in our heart, then we of right can bear the title Son of the Sun.

As all mānasaputras and all agnishwātta pitris are dhyāni-chohans, they are therefore practically identical. The difference is that the agnishwātta element emphasizes that portion of their nature which relates to their having become at one with, and channels for, the manifestation of the cosmic fire, the fire of spiritual being; whereas the mānasaputra stresses the fact that they have become identified or at one with that part of their own inner core whose element is the fire of spiritual consciousness.

Kumāra° is still another name for these gods or cosmic spirits, and constitutes a third aspect of the same host of beings. Each hierarchy, whether it be sun, planet, or man himself, is an aggregate of monads, all connected together by unbreakable bonds — not of matter or of thought, but of the essence of the universe. They are intrinsically one, just as every ray that springs from Father Sun is of the same fundamental stuff, and yet they are different as individuals. The monads are kumāras higher even than the agnishwāttas and mānasaputras. The agnishwāttas or mānasaputras are called kumāras because, as compared with us, they are beings of spiritual purity. Of these three terms, kumāras is the most general, and could likewise be applied to other hierarchies of beings which cannot technically be called mānasaputras or agnishwāttas.

While these three names appertain to the same class of beings, each has its own significance. An unconscious god-spark begins its evolution in any one mahāmanvantara as a kumāra, a being of original spiritual purity, as yet untouched by matter. When the evolving entity has become a fully self-conscious divinity, it then is an agnishwātta, for it has been purified by the working through it of the spiritual fires inherent in itself.

°A Sanskrit word: *ku*, with difficulty, and *māra*, mortal; the idea being that these spiritual beings are so lofty they pass through the worlds of matter, i.e. become mortal, only with difficulty. Cf. *Occult Glossary*, pp. 2–4.

When such an agnishwātta assumes the role of a bringer of mind to a lunar pitri in which a ray from it incarnates, it then, although in its own realm an agnishwātta, functions as a mānasaputra.

No man can be a complete human being unless he possess within himself spiritual, intellectual, psychical, vital, astral, and physical elements; and, furthermore, unless he be connected by the three higher — thus forming the ten — with his inner god. We are now the evolved lunar pitris; in other words, we as human souls are the lunar pitris become what we at present are, considerably evolved from the time when we came from the moon.

Of the seven classes of lunar pitris the four lower are the builders, the laborers so to speak; the three higher are the architects, the planners, the evolvers of the idea which the builders follow. These three higher classes of dhyāni-chohans or lunar pitris we may speak of, first, as the highest buddhas. The second class is the sons of mind, the mānasaputras or agnishwātta pitris — lunar pitris also because, although they come from the sun, they do so through the moon. The third class we may refer to merely as dhyāni-chohans. These three are the spiritual and intellectual classes, whereas the four lower classes, grouped under the general name of barhishad pitris, are they who work in the more material realms, following automatically and instinctively the life plans which the spiritual classes have cast upon them in vital waves.

THE AVATĀRA — A SPIRITUAL EVENT

THE DOCTRINE OF THE avatāra° is a deeply mystical one. It will lead us, perhaps more than any other teaching, to a realization that wonderful indeed are the mysteries hidden behind the veil of the outer seeming. An avatāra is a spiritual transitory event. It comes as a blinding light from heaven into the world of men, passes athwart the sky of human affairs, and vanishes. There will be many avatāras in the future, as there have been many in the past.

The avatāra is a magical composition, a putting together of spiritual, psychical, astral, and physical elements. Just as is an ordinary human being, it is composed of three bases: spirit, soul, body; but instead of being a man — a reincarnating ego with a long karmic past stretching back into the infinitudes of duration, and with a long karmic future ahead of it — the avatāra is a temporary union of these three elements, in order to produce a more or less permanent spiritual and intellectual effect among men. It is a sublime feat of the highest white magic deliberately brought about by the masters of wisdom and compassion, in order to introduce into our human atmosphere the direct influence and energy of a god.

The avatāra has no past and no future because it possesses no reincarnating ego in the sense that a complete human being does. The intermediate nature of an avatāra is loaned by a very highly evolved human being of buddha-type. Lord Gautama the Buddha was the one who furnished his own psycho-spiritual apparatus to the avatāra Śankarāchārya in India, and also to Jesus the Christos. Neither of these two had any past or future karma, in the usual meaning of the word. The avatāra, as such, is an illusion, a pure māyā, and obviously it is impossible for an illusion to reimbody itself. Yet, strangely enough, it is this māyā which does a wonderful work in the world. The divinity is no māyā, the buddhic element is no māyā, the body is no māyā, but it is the combining of these three into a temporary union which is the māyā.

The following extract describes graphically, yet succinctly, the main

---

°Avatāra is a Sanskrit word meaning 'descent,' from *ava*, down, and *trī*, to 'cross over.'

characteristic of the nature and function of all avatāric beings, but especially of the upapādaka avatāras.° It is taken from papers left by H. P. B., which were published after her death as a so-called third volume of *The Secret Doctrine:*

There is a great mystery in such incarnations and they are outside and beyond the cycle of general re-births. Rebirths may be divided into three classes: the divine incarnations called Avatāras; those of Adepts who give up Nirvâna for the sake of helping on humanity — the Nirmânakâyas; and the natural succession of rebirths for all — the common law. The Avatâra is an appearance, one which may be termed a special illusion within the natural illusion that reigns on the planes under the sway of that power, Mâyâ; the Adept is re-born consciously, at his will and pleasure; the units of the common herd unconsciously follow the great law of dual evolution.

What *is* an Avatâra? for the term before being used ought to be well understood. It is a descent of the manifested Deity — whether under the specific name of Shiva, Vishnu, or Âdi-Buddha — into an illusive form of individuality, an appearance which to men on this illusive plane is objective, but it is not so in sober fact. That illusive form having neither past nor future, because it had neither previous incarnation nor will have subsequent rebirths, has naught to do with Karma, which has therefore no hold on it.

A Buddha of Compassion can incarnate in a human body whenever he so wills, but this they very rarely or perhaps never do, because nature's spiritual mechanisms are so delicately adjusted that they come at certain

---

°It is a matter of some historic interest that one early Christian sect was called by its opponents, Docetists — from a Greek word meaning appearance or semblance, because it taught that Jesus was a mere 'appearance' among men, clearly a distorted reflection of the original meaning of the avatāra doctrine when applied to upapādaka avatāras. These Docetists went entirely too far, however, for they claimed that even the body of Jesus was an illusion, and that therefore he himself was not crucified, but an 'appearance' of him only was so punished — a curious tangle of fact and fiction and twisting of esoteric allegory. It is of course true that the orthodox party were even more at fault in this matter than were the Docetists, for they claimed that Jesus was born of a Virgin, was one of the Persons of the cosmic triad, and, equally foolishly, that it required one of the Persons of their Trinity to save humanity from the consequences of sin which the unfortunate human race had been created by infinite wisdom and prescience to commit.

This is not written as an apologia for the Docetists, nor as approving their views; but solely to point out that in an important early Christian sect the essential teaching concerning upapādaka avatāras had not been wholly lost sight of.

cyclic times in racial history. Nevertheless their great influence is flowing out from them constantly, permeating the human heart and stimulating the human intellect — at least whenever the divine visitor is welcomed. It is they who are the sublime hope of the human race, the inspirers and teachers of mankind. They are the nirmāṇakāyas in their different stages; and to this day the nirmāṇakāya of him who is known as Gautama remains on earth, and is known by great initiates and mahatmas; and he teaches and inspires and initiates in earth's most holy spot, an unknown district of Central Asia, known in mystic records as Śambhala. There the great initiations take place. There are the Buddhas born, and reborn.

A buddha is one who has ascended the rungs of the ladder of life one after the other, and who thus has attained buddhahood, which means human plenitude of spiritual and intellectual glory, and who has done all this by his own self-directed exertions along the far past evolutionary pathway. An avatāra, on the contrary, is a flaming spiritual splendor which passes across the horizon of human history, stays for a while, and then disappears. An avatāra comes at certain cyclical periods, when evil is running strong in the world and virtue is fading from men's hearts; then there occurs a descent or imbodiment of a divine being, which in the spiritual realms is ready and waiting. But in order to make contact with the sphere of human life, an unusually evolved and holy intermediate vehicle or principle is necessary to step down the divine current. This intermediary is furnished by a Buddha of Compassion in order that the imbodying divinity may shine through and thus illumine still more strongly this loaned intermediate nature of the Buddha which thereupon incarnates in a human seed.

When the avatāra vanishes the body is dissipated, and the loaned part returns to the Buddha — yet to say that it 'returns' would give a wrong idea, because it suggests that it had been separated from the Buddha, which is inexact. It *is* the Buddha; but after the death of the avatāra, the Buddha then is in full possession and use of all his faculties, instead of being in the position of having loaned the noblest portion of his psychical apparatus. The divinity receives back to itself its divine ray, the projection of its essence which it had sent forth into the avatāra composition. As a tongue of flame from a fire will leap forth and then recede, so does the divine ray flash back to its divine source — and this is instantaneous, for the action of the spirit is quicker than thought.

UPAPĀDAKA AND ANUPAPĀDAKA AVATĀRAS

THERE ARE REALLY two kinds of avatāras: the upapādaka and the anupapā-daka, and the distinction between these avatāric 'descents' is seen in the Sanskrit words themselves. *Upapādaka* means 'caused to follow along or according to,' 'caused to occur.' *Anupapādaka* is the opposite of this, '*not* caused to follow along,' etc., and consequently may be translated as one who does not go or come according to a line of succession; hence, not signifying a messenger in a line of messengers, each passing the torch of Light to the hand of his successor.

The upapādaka class of avatāric beings is almost unknown popularly, and scarcely even suspected in the philosophical schools of India and elsewhere, whereas the anupapādaka is fairly well understood as being a 'descent' of a portion of a divine being into a human individual for the purpose of carrying out some great and lofty objective in the world. The upapādakas, quite rare in human history, are called such because they are caused to follow along or to occur by the swabhāva of the psychological instrument through which the avatāric ray functions, much as a ray of brilliant sunlight streaming through a stained-glass window is caused to be the color of the glass. In other words, the divine ray, although having its own swabhāva, nevertheless is *de facto* modified in its expression by the strong characteristics and individuality of the Buddha's psychological apparatus through which it works; and thus is said to be upapādaka.

Now the anupapādaka avatāras are much more numerous since this class includes all the various modes by which a divine ray manifests itself in human life. The term anupapādaka was somewhat paraphrased by H.P.B. as "self-born of divine essence," and this exactly describes the nature and type of this class of avatāra in any world where such manifestations take place.

As instances of the anupapādaka class, there are, first, the dhyāni-buddhas, self-born from the womb of the cosmic intelligence, and never-theless appearing through their own inherent spiritual swabhāva and urge. Again, the various kinds of true logoi are likewise anupapādaka avatāras in a sense, and indeed the dhyāni-buddhas are rays from such logoi, although these dhyāni-buddhas themselves are of anupapādaka character. As other examples of somewhat different types of anupapādakas, we may point to those fairly rare cases of surpassing human spiritual and intellectual genius, where the dhyāni-buddha of the man himself inspires or infills by its direct radiance the man's *own* psychological apparatus; and perhaps the most noteworthy of this type of anupapādaka avatāric descents are the mānushya-buddhas, such as Gautama the Buddha.

All this teaching regarding the avatāras is typically esoteric and therefore was only pointed to by H.P.B., and then usually in rather ambiguous terms and even sometimes in language which, while correct, is a 'blind.' In her *Theosophical Glossary* (p. 44) — a posthumous work which never underwent her correcting hand — she states that "there are two kinds of avatars: those born from woman, and the parentless, the *anupapâdaka.*" Now the anupapādakas are indeed "parentless," for they are divine rays arising in the bosom of the divine monad and streaming downwards in their various descents in order to do their work in the world through their reflections or representatives on earth — i.e. their own human vehicles. It is the much rarer cases of the upapādakas who are "born from woman"; and just here is the blind, for naturally, as far as physical bodies go, any human being who is an anupapādaka avatāra likewise must work through a body born from a woman.

The point here is that the upapādaka avatāras are really 'creations' of a sublime and lofty white magic. Śankarāchārya was one, as was Jesus; and these two alone, with their greatly differing characteristics, show that the upapādakas vary among themselves.

The wide range of the anupapādaka class includes all the different individuals who send a radiance from themselves through their own lower constitution. Hence they extend all the way from the dhyāni-buddhas and logoi down to those great men and women who are *inspired* each one by his or her inner god. Examples of avatāras which are anupapādaka are very numerous in history, and are often mentioned in religion and philosophy. We may cite the long line of the true mānushya-buddhas, of which Gautama was one. Tsong-kha-pa of Tibet, who lived in the fourteenth century of the Christian era, was a sort of minor anupapādaka mānushya-buddha likewise. Krishna was another example of an anupapādaka avatāra.

The 'second coming' of Christ — not of Jesus but of the Christ-spirit —

alludes to the universally held belief that Ādi-buddha or the Christos, the Logos, manifests itself from time to time in the world. In other words, the 'second coming' is simply a new manifestation of the Logos, the Christos. As Krishna says in the *Bhagavad-Gītā:* °

> Whenever, O descendant of Bharata, a decline of duty comes into being — a springing up of unrighteousness — then, indeed, I emanate myself.
> For the preservation of the righteous, for the destruction of the evil-doers, for the sake of establishing Duty, I take birth from age to age.

Here we have Krishna, the type-avatāra of Hindustan, implying that he comes at different times into the manifested world as an avatāric energy at the beginnings of descending or materializing cycles in human experience. He spoke in his divine capacity as being one of the gods who inspirit and invigorate our universe. It is obvious from the reach of this teaching that many gods can and do have avatāric manifestations. The one who was in Krishna as the divine essence may have manifested as an avatāra many times before, and inevitably will manifest again; and the same divinity which worked through Jesus must have sent a divine ray into other human beings in the past, i.e. into other avatāric entities, and will do so again.

In a way every human being's own inner god, who is a spark of the cosmic spirit, could say the same words as those ascribed to Krishna. For the average man today, buffeted as he is by the winds of destiny because he has no spiritual holding-power, it would be a manifestation resembling that of an avatāra if his inner divinity — the heart of his re-incarnating ego — were to express itself more or less continuously through his consciousness, and therefore through his physical brain. When such an event happens, we have a buddha — one no longer an ordinary human being, but one glorified.

A buddha is one who, during past ages, through self-directed evolution, has evolved forth the god within himself. Working for all that is, he advances steadily towards godhood; and it is this utter self-sacrifice of the human being, of the most lofty type conceivable, which makes of a buddha so holy and exalted a being. That is why any Buddha of Compassion is considered in the esoteric philosophy to be even above an avatāra. Nevertheless, so far as rank goes, the avatāra stands higher. We should not confuse mere rank with evolutionary development. Nothing on earth

---

°Chapter iv, ślokas 7–8.

stands higher in evolution than the Buddhas of Compassion, for they are the very imbodiment of wisdom and love. It is they who form the Guardian Wall around mankind.

The avatāra is a most sublime event in the spiritual history of mankind — like the coming of a great light for purposes esoteric and wonderful; but the light comes and passes; while a buddha continues his noble work forever, time without ending. But they really cannot be compared. The buddha assists the coming of the avatāra. Both come at cyclic periods: the avatāras usually at the beginning of a downward cycle, the buddhas at the beginning of ascending as well as descending cycles.

As said earlier, the dhyāni-buddhas are all anupapādaka; yet they themselves (whether we count them as seven or as ten or twelve) were divine avatāric rays from the Ādi-buddha, the Logos, which Buddhist mystical writings call Avalokiteśvara. Avalokiteśvara itself is thus the synthesis or origin of the dhyāni-buddhas radiating from it; and, furthermore, is a grand logoic avatāra of the anupapādaka class.

Now, in a certain sense, every buddha, as being a manifestation of the spiritual efflux of a dhyāni-buddha, is an anupapādaka avatāra. Every time a human being unites himself with his inner god, even if it be momentarily, he becomes for that brief period an anupapādaka avatāra — self-made or self-born. He is not necessarily made so by initiation, nor by an act of white magic as the other class of avatāras is. For the same reason every buddha may be said to be an anupapādaka, a self-born avatāra, because he is allied with the dhyāni-buddha, the celestial buddha. For the time being he becomes the vehicle or channel through which this celestial buddha, his own inner divinity, manifests with relative fullness. In such case it is more than the buddha's own spiritual ego at work.

I have elsewhere stated that all of the mānushya-buddhas, the racial buddhas, are, each one, the representative or reflection on earth of his respective dhyāni-buddha. For example, Amitābha, the dhyāni-buddha, radiated the inner god of Śākyamuni called Gautama the Buddha; and the same Amitābha radiated the inner individual buddha or inner god of Tsong-kha-pa. Now this fact alone establishes a very intimate or personal connection between Gautama the Buddha and Tsong-kha-pa. I quote here the significant passage from *The Secret Doctrine* (I, 108) which bears directly upon this matter:

Esoterically, however, the Dhyani-Buddhas are seven, of whom five only have hitherto manifested, and two are to come in the sixth and seventh Root-races.

They are, so to speak, the eternal prototypes of the Buddhas who appear on this earth, each of whom has his particular divine prototype. So, for instance, Amitâbha is the Dhyani-Buddha of Gautama Sakyamuni, manifesting through him whenever this great Soul incarnates on earth as He did in Tzon-kha-pa. As the synthesis of the seven Dhyani-Buddhas, Avalôkitêswara was the first Buddha (the Logos), so Amitâbha is the inner "God" of Gautama, who, in China, is called Amita (-Buddha). They are, as Mr. Rhys Davids correctly states, "the glorious counterparts in the mystic world, free from the debasing conditions of this material life" of every earthly mortal Buddha — the liberated Manushi-Buddhas appointed to govern the Earth in this Round. They are the "Buddhas of Contemplation," and are all Anupadaka (parentless), *i.e.*, self-born of divine essence.

Each one of these seven dhyāni-buddhas is the spiritual guide or Manu for one of the seven globes of our planetary chain, and during each round on any such globe, the mānushya-buddhas respectively appearing in the seven root-races are all the anupapādaka 'reflections' of the dhyāni-buddha of that globe.

There has been a good deal of rather gushy and vapid writing in certain circles about the coming of the next Buddha, whom Buddhists everywhere expect to come in the due course of the cycling ages, and whom they have called Maitreya — a Sanskrit word which can be translated as the Friendly. Now just when the Buddha-Maitreya is to appear is known only by the mahatmas themselves, and by those higher than they; but it certainly will not be for many thousands of years. The reason for this is twofold: (a) the Buddha-Maitreya in his manifested *fullness* of power will be the racial buddha of the seventh root-race on this globe in this fourth round; and (b), a minor racial buddha appears in every one of the seven great subraces of a root-race; and hence the Buddha-Maitreya who is expected to be the next buddhic avatāric manifestation among men will be that particular minor mānushya-buddha, called 'Maitreya,' who will appear at the end, or the seventh and last part, of our present great subrace and therefore at the beginning of the succeeding great subrace — and this is many, many thousands of years distant.

AVATĀRAS OF MAHĀ-VISHNU AND MAHĀ-ŚIVA

The Buddhists have always stoutly denied that their BUDDHA was, as alleged by the Brâhmans, an Avatâra of Vishnu in the same sense as a man is an incarnation of his Karmic ancestor. They deny it partly, perhaps, because the esoteric meaning of the term "Mahâ Vishnu" is not known to them in its full, impersonal, and general meaning. There is a mysterious Principle in Nature called "Mahâ Vishnu," which is not the God of that name, but a principle which contains Bîja, the seed of Avatârism or, in other words, is the potency and cause of such divine incarnations. All the World-Saviours, the Bodhisattvas and the Avatâras, are the trees of salvation grown out from the one seed, the Bîja or "Mahâ Vishnu." Whether it be called Âdi-Buddha (Primeval Wisdom) or Mahâ Vishnu, it is all the same. Understood esoterically, Vishnu is both Saguna and Nirguna (with and without attributes). In the first aspect, Vishnu is the object of exoteric worship and devotion; in the second, as Nirguna, he is the culmination of the totality of spiritual wisdom in the Universe — Nirvâna, in short — and has as worshippers all philosophical minds. In this esoteric sense the Lord BUDDHA *was* an incarnation of Mahâ Vishnu.

This is from the philosophical and purely spiritual standpoint. From the plane of illusion, however, as one would say, or from the terrestrial standpoint, those initiated *know* that He was a direct incarnation of one of the primeval "Seven Sons of Light" who are to be found in every Theogony — the Dhyân Chohans whose mission it is, from one eternity (aeon) to the other, to watch over the spiritual welfare of the regions under their care.   — From papers left by H.P.B., and published after her death as 'S. D., III.'

THE ULTIMATE SOURCE of an avatāra is in a Rāja sun; but actually the spiritual part of an avatāra is a ray from a god, an inhabitant of our own solar system; and more particularly this divinity is a portion of the solar spiritual essence. In India these gods thus belonging to our sun and its system are collectively called by the generic name of Vishnu, although equally they could be called Śiva.

One of the oldest mythologic Hindu legends tells how Vishnu plunges into the 'waters' in the form of a boar and holds up the earth on his tusks. The story is found in some of the literary works of the Vedic cycle as well as in the *Mahābhārata* and the Purānas. In its earliest forms, the avatāras of a deity are ascribed to Prajāpati, the father of mankind and of the beasts, the vegetation and all the mineral world; in other words, to Brahmā. Later forms of the story as given in the Purānas attribute ten avatāras to Vishnu, the Sustainer. These range from the fish-avatāra, through the tortoise, the boar, the man-lion, the dwarf, and so forth to Krishna, the eighth incarnation, and on up to and including the tenth, called the Kalki-avatāra. Each succeeding avatāra in the world order is in a higher grade of beings than the preceding one. The Kalki-avatāra has not yet appeared, and this incarnation represents what the Occident popularly speaks of as 'the coming of the Messiah' — when all wrongs shall be righted, and when righteousness and justice shall be firmly established on earth.

All these legends are based upon facts of nature, but they are told in mythological form, so that unless one has the key to them they are difficult to understand. Some of these zoologico-mythologic figures are very interesting. For instance, in Babylonia and in Persia, also in Greece, the horse symbolized the sun; the bull and the cow were symbols of the moon. Similarly, in Hindustan, the boar which plunges into the 'waters' of space and lifts up the earth upon his tusks, and so bears it for the remainder of the manvantara, signifies not only the fourth-plane physical vitality, but likewise the cosmical vitality which infills and sustains the earth, rooted as this vitality is in the spiritual life of the god of our solar system.

In the two classes of avatāras we may qualify perhaps some as avatāras from Mahā-Vishnu, and others as from Mahā-Śiva. The following thought may be helpful: men differ among themselves in character, some being aggressive, others being thoughtful and retiring; and still others, although essentially good and constructive in action, nevertheless produce results by the overthrow of evil. These last we might call human rays or very minor avatāras of Mahā-Śiva, for these men are destroyers in the sense of regenerators. Other kinds of men, on the contrary, are preservers of the good already existing, its guardians and protectors: equally high, equally strong, as the former class, and serving an equally beneficent and lofty purpose in the world. These we may call very minor avatāras of Mahā-Vishnu.

Thus the avatāras of Mahā-Śiva are the regenerators by action; and

493

the avatāras of Mahā-Vishnu are the preservers not so much by the action of overthrowing evil but by saving and stimulating the good already existing. Krishna was an avatāra of Vishnu, while Jesus, from the very little we know of him, was, in my judgment, an avatāra of Śiva; and I might add that there does not appear to be any alternation in the successive appearances of the avatāras of Śiva and of Vishnu.

In one very true sense the ancient Brahmans were right in regarding Gautama the Buddha as one of the avatāras of Vishnu. In a sense still more recondite, perhaps, the Lord Buddha might be called an avatāra of Śiva. Nevertheless, he may be looked upon as a partial incarnation of that aspect of the life of our solar system which the Hindus called Vishnu — one of the triadic elements of the heart of the sun. Viewed esoterically, Vishnu is not a personal god but an individualized divinity, one of the three loftiest of our solar system which form the apex or crown of the ethereal sun, the other two being Brahmā and Śiva.

The union of a great and noble man with a cosmic divinity is the kind of avatāra that the Buddha Gautama was: he had raised himself so high spiritually and intellectually that, by a tremendous effort of will and aspiration, he could reach with his consciousness into the very heart of the Vishnu-energy of our solar system, and thereafter 'step down' that divine energy to his fellow men. This thought is a wonderful key. Here is a man with ages and ages of past karma; destined to have ages and ages of future spiritual karma; and always rising on the evolutionary path to ever loftier peaks of achievement; and even at the present time able to reach up by a supreme effort of his buddhic being and connect with the Vishnu-energy.

JESUS THE AVATĀRA

THE AVATĀRAS APPEAR at different cyclical periods, and sometimes these periods overlap. For instance, Śankarāchārya of India and Jesus of Nazareth came quite close together, being separated by an interval of about five hundred years. As to the historical date of Jesus, H.P.B. has pointed out that he lived a good hundred or more years before the accepted beginning of the Christian Era, and there is some faint evidence that the great Syrian avatāra was born during the time of the Jewish king, Jannaeus, who reigned 104–77 'B.C.'

Now, as has just been explained, no avatāra can reincarnate or return, because such reincarnation would mean that the unusual magical conjoining of these particular three elements would have to occur again and be the identic individual who lived before — and this does not happen. There is, however, one reincarnating element in the avatāra, and that is the human part, the intermediate soul-apparatus, loaned by one of the Buddhas of Compassion in order to form the link between the divinity and the body, so that the ray from the divinity may stream through the buddhic soul and thus reach the brain of the human body.

It is possible for the Great Ones to send forth from themselves a portion of their psychomental vitality — a portion of their human consciousness — and to fix it in the psychological apparatus of some other human being. In Tibet this is called Hpho-wa, a transference of consciousness and of will, of which the simplest manifestation is thought transference.°

Since the buddha reaches his stature by means of reincarnation, i.e.

°Please do not confuse Hpho-wa, the transference of consciousness, which also means will power and consciousness, and a sense of surrounding circumstances and locality, with a transference of the mere personality. The transference of a master's thought, however, is so nearly identical with the transference or passing of himself to another part of the world in the māyāvi-rūpa, that it is often difficult to distinguish between the two, because the māyāvi-rūpa actually is the projection of the individuality. All the man is there, except the physical and astral and vital elements, which are left behind; and therefore obviously it is also a projection of consciousness and of thought. It is the Hpho-wa in the highest stage; the Hpho-wa in the lower stage is merely the projection of one's thought, an extreme degree of thought transference.

by means of learning the lessons of life, he becomes a master of the powers and energies of the human constitution, and among these is the ability to project himself out of his body. The buddha knows when an avatāra is due to appear, and he invigorates the human seed which will produce the child-body of a karmically and hereditarily pure type. At the appropriate time, the buddha projects his soul and inspirits the growing embryo with the spiritual fire of his own soul. Later in the life of the child the connection is made between the buddha-soul in the body and the waiting divinity, when the buddha raises himself by will and aspiration until, as it were, the divine ray is caught and held. And thus is formed the union of the divinity above, the buddhic soul-splendor, and the pure body — and this union is an avatāra. The state of the buddha remains normal, yet deprived of a portion of his human consciousness which is abstracted away by his own will and serves as the vehicle for the avatāra.

Jesus, for example, in his *human* aspect was Gautama the Buddha: a man who, through incarnation after incarnation in ages past, had risen to his lofty pinnacle of spiritual grandeur through self-devised efforts. This is the reason that certain theosophical writers have spoken of Jesus as having attained the buddhic stage in his evolution in previous lives. But this has reference only to the intermediate element of the avatāric being, the psychological or soul-apparatus of the Lord Buddha, and not to the avatāra which, as such, has no past or future karma.

One may ask, how about the life germ, the human seed, which in ordinary circumstances would have grown up to be the body of a Jewish boy, had that no previous karma? Yes, of course, everything is karmic; even a seed has its own kind of karma. What happened was this: the Buddha's psychological apparatus took possession of this growing life germ before the reincarnating ego, which under normal circumstances would have incarnated in that body, had time to involve itself with that germ.

As regards the overshadowing of the divinity, this is rather an illuminating, a glorifying: it was to this that Jesus on the Cross really alluded, when there came, as alleged in the New Testament, the wonderful cry, *Eli, Eli, lama sabachtani* — a Greek rendering of the Hebrew phrase — which has been badly mistranslated: "Oh, my God, my God, Why hast thou forsaken me!" This is not the translation of these Hebrew words. If the verb 'forsaken' had been used in this cry, it would have been *'azavtānī;* but it was, as recorded *shabahhtānī*, which means 'thou dost glorify me.'

Now when we remember that Christians for fifteen hundred years or more have taught that their Gospels were inspired by the direct action or presence of the Holy Ghost, and therefore written under 'plenary inspiration,' and hence infallible; and when we find perfectly good Hebrew words which have been mistranslated, we can only suppose that there was something that faced the theologians in these passages which to them was inexplicable; so they attempted to obfuscate. The Christian apologists simply make the matter worse by stating that these words are Chaldaean or Aramaic, Shemitic tongues closely akin to the Hebrew. It has never yet been shown that the Hebrew verbal root 'āzab becomes shābahh in Chaldaean or Aramaic, with the meaning to forsake. For shābahh signifies to glorify — the very word found in the New Testament and mistranslated as 'to forsake.'

The original writers of the passages° in which this mistranslated phrase occurs in the Greek of the New Testament unquestionably knew something of the ceremonies of initiation as these took place in Asia Minor. We know, for instance, that the Church Father Origen, whom I personally believe to have had a great deal to do in helping to frame the present Canonical Gospels, was at least a partial initiate in the esoteric mysteries of Greece.

A neophyte passed through two phases in the initiatory trial: one was the experiencing of the agony of the temporary withdrawal of the god within, at which time he was left deprived of his spiritual guidance, to meet and conquer the difficulties and probing tests of initiation and of the underworld. He had to *prove* that as a man alone he could stand and face the tests and conquer them. As you can see, it was a moment of the most intense suffering in which all the human part of the tortured man uttered the cry: "Why hast thou abandoned me?"

The second phase came after the man had proved that his sole human ego had wakened its own inner monadic divinity which then came into operation as a guide and protector; and when this happened he could then cry in the ecstasy of successful realization, "Oh, god within me, how thou dost fill me with glory."

Now the writers of the two passages — they are almost identic — evidently omitted a previous passage referring to the agony of abandonment, but retained the Hebrew words of the cry of glory, the exclamation

°*Matthew* xxvii, 46; *Mark* xv, 34.

of successful achievement. Yet the Greek translation of it renders it as the cry of abandonment.

Or, perhaps, was this tangle of words and meanings arranged by these original quasi-initiate Christian writers in order to show to posterity that there was a mystery involved which could not be openly explained, but which should be investigated? I think that these two verses give in metaphor the sketch of what took place in the initiation chambers; and the writers chose as a type-figure the glorious individuality of the man-avatāra Jesus, and wove around him what they wanted to say under mask of the drama of initiation. As a matter of fact, the incident never happened on a cross of punishment, as the Gospels recite the story, turning a symbolical incident of the Mysteries into a pragmatical punishment. Jesus, later called the Christos, was never crucified in that manner.

The whole event simply describes one of the most wonderful of the initiation ceremonies — the raising of a great man to divinity, the entrance of a god into the superior man, so that the humanity of the man became lost in the divinity which illuminated him, being an example of the theopneusty becoming the complete theopathy.° From that moment he became the channel of the divine working through him, a true Christ. This occurred when physical maturity had been gained, and when certain initiations had been passed through. Then when the body was laid on a cruciform couch after months of preparation, the psychological apparatus of the Buddha by a supreme act of will raised itself into union with the waiting divinity — the divine poured in splendor into the man, and the avatāra became!

This does not mean, however, that Jesus had not begun his work long before. He was a high initiate, a master, in training for the avatāra event, but it was after that event that his real teaching was given to his inner school.

An avatāra and his existence and his work, when these are properly understood, are all combined in the word itself, for in its use it refers

---

°These are Greek technical terms taken from the ancient Mystery teachings. The theopneusty or 'inbreathing of a god' occurred at the sixth initiation when the candidate felt the inbreathing or inspiration of his inner god coursing through his entire being for a shorter or longer period. The theopathy or 'suffering of a god' was the seventh or highest initiation of all, when the candidate had become an absolutely selfless instrument of the divine, both within and without, so that literally he 'suffered' absorption or at-oneness with his own flaming divinity. (Cf. *Fundamentals of the Esoteric Philosophy*, ch. xxxv.)

particularly to the 'descent' or 'passing down' of the divine influence. In this lies the mystery of the Christ. There are, in fact, avatāras among the gods also. And there are such things as avatāras in the beast world — not the anupapādaka or self-born avatāras as exemplified among men, but the white magical avatāras like Jesus, Śankarāchārya, and others.

The whole existence and being and work of the avatāras come about because they are involved as part of the efforts of the hierarchy of the Buddhas of Compassion. Thus, it is an act of compassion which impels — karmically also of course — the buddha to loan a portion of his own constitution and thereby to have it karmically colored, for which condition the buddha thereafter is responsible, because such loan was an act of his own will. The divinity on its own plane, naturally, is likewise proportionately responsible.

An avatāra usually happens in our world when a divinity is passing through initiation, and a human being provides the vehicle to enable it to descend into what is an underworld to the divine spheres. When a human being on our plane undergoes a corresponding initiation, the man descends into the underworld where a denizen thereof cooperates to lend its thinking conscious vehicle in order to allow the human monad to manifest and work there.

In some of the Apocryphal Christian Gospels there are legends about the descent of Jesus into the underworld and preaching to the "spirits in chains"* — the chains merely meaning the karmic bonds of a realm of matter lower than ours, the chains of the underworld, the chains of evil-doing. We humans are spirits in chains to a divinity in its own sphere who enters our sphere and tries to teach us.

The entire story of Jesus is an esoteric mythos — not a myth in the ordinary meaning of the word, but a story having a wonderful background of truth, and expressed in mystical or metaphorical style. In other words, the narratives of the New Testament are but a record of an initiatory cycle. Some of the parables ascribed to the great human avatāra are direct teachings taken from the Mystery schools of Asia Minor, and when rightly understood, they are seen as garments veiling a sublime truth.

One such parable is that of Jesus and the fig tree: "And when he saw a fig tree in the way, he came to it, and found nothing thereon, but leaves only, and said unto it, Let no fruit grow on thee henceforward

---

*See also *The First Epistle of Peter* (iii, 19).

for ever. And presently the fig tree withered away" (*Matthew*, xxi, 19).

In the ancient schools of the Hither East, and also in some other parts of the Orient, trees were always metaphorically representative of a system of esoteric doctrine — sometimes also of the teacher thereof. The fruit which the tree brought forth were the good works done and the success attained in following the spiritual life which this esoteric school had, or was supposed to have had.

Therefore a fig tree — the favorite symbol of the day in that part of the world — which brought forth no fruit signified a mystical school which had failed. The spirit, the light, had abandoned it, and there remained naught but the flourishing exoteric organization: the tree indeed with its outer life, but without fruit. According to the misworded manner of speaking, Christ is said to have 'cursed' the fig tree because he found no fruit on it when he hungered. The Mystery school had failed: the Christ-spirit of humanity could find no lodgment therein, hungering as that Christ-spirit constantly does to benefit others; and so what remnant of the life of the tree was there, finally was withdrawn, and then the school withered and died.

The Christians, in the very beginning of their era, were an esoteric school in that part of the world, but in no long time they degenerated from that standing. The spiritual life which their great founder had instilled into his immediate disciples soon left, leaving nothing but the dead ashes of the past, fugitive memories which quickly faded from the consciousness of the men of that time.

Another example of teaching by metaphor is found in the story of the Star of Bethlehem. Actually, there was no such star, although there is always an unusual collocation of the sun and moon and planets, astrologically speaking, near the time of birth either of a buddha or of an avatāra. The occult character of the Christian mythos cannot be better proved than by this legend of the star which guided the Three Magi to the stable in Bethlehem, where the infant Jesus lay. "We have seen his star in the East, and have followed it hither," is the substance of what the three Wise Men are stated to have said; yet it is ludicrous to suppose that one of the stellar orbs of heaven wandered through the earth's atmosphere in order to guide three individuals into the little town of Bethlehem, and then 'stood still' over the stable.

The two words star and East are sufficient to show the true meaning here. The 'star' is just that one to which H.P.B. alludes in *The Secret*

Doctrine (I, 572–3), where she mentions two kinds of stars: one, the astrological star presiding at a man's birth; and the other 'star' which is the man's inner spiritual or rather divine prototype or source in the galaxy. The word East is likewise a philosophical term, often employed in the phrase 'the mystic East,' and commonly signifies esoteric wisdom or occult knowledge. So that the alleged statement of the three Wise Men simply means that "by occult wisdom we have found out that an avatāra is soon to appear among men, and we know what is the guiding divinity or star of this new spiritual luminary which we have followed."

THE POWER OF ĀVEŚA

IN THE ANCIENT occult literature of Hindustan frequent mention is made of āveśa,° a technical and mystic word signifying the power possessed by initiates, whether of the white or of the black schools, to enter into the body of another, and to occupy and use it. The power of so doing is of course neither good nor bad in itself, but becomes beneficent or maleficent according to the manner in which this magical ability is used or misused.

On the rare occasions when an adept of the right-hand path, or a white magician, uses this power for the purpose of employing the body of another, he never in any circumstances whatsoever overpowers or destroys or evilly affects the will or the life or the body of the other. Rather he brings his own psychological and prānic characteristics into synchronous and sympathetic vibration with those of the one whose vehicle he so uses; and in this manner the psychological apparatus and vitality and body of the individual thus used are in no sense injured but, if anything, actually refined.

The black magician, or adept of the left-hand path, on the contrary, invariably overpowers or enslaves the will and the psychological apparatus and the prānas of the one whose vehicle is so used, and always to the lasting detriment and injury of his victim. Furthermore, the white adept without exception has the willing consent or acquiescence of the one who thus loans him his vehicle; whereas the black magician rarely ever gains such consent, and, even should such unwilling consent be forced, the effects are always bad.

One very important point should be mentioned here, for it explains a certain mystery connected with H.P.B., and indeed with any other chela who at times may loan himself or herself — i.e. the lower parts of the constitution — for use by the intelligence and will of the chela's teacher.

°A Sanskrit compound formed of the preposition ā, meaning approach or towards, and of the verbal root viś, signifying, to enter, to pervade, and hence to possess. The root viś has another form vish, of almost identic meaning, and from this comes the name Vishnu, the second divinity of the Hindu Trimurti.

This important point is that because the adept synchronizes his swabhāva or individual characteristics with those of the chela in this instance, the natural effect of this is that almost infallibly the adept's own characteristics or style of writing or manner of speech are to a large extent modified by and become closely similar to those of the chela whose vehicle he is using. We thus see the chela, in giving his teacher's words, unconsciously and automatically influencing his teacher's style and characteristics by his own.

As an illustration: at those times when H. P. B. loaned her psychological apparatus and lower principles to the use of her teacher, he accommodated or synchronized his own mental and psychological characteristics to hers in order not to injure hers; in fact, he raised and clarified them for the time being. Yet the result was, that when the objectives in view were produced — whether it was a letter or a writing or whatever — it all sounded or looked like H. P. B.'s own, but immensely improved, clarified — very much as H. P. B.'s own higher self would have expressed itself had it then been working free and unfettered through the H. P. B. human apparatus.

Now by the use of the āveśa power, many very strange and astounding things can happen and have happened in the occult history of philosophical and religious movements. Indeed, the magicians of ancient days could animate statues; and this accounts for the fairly large number of literary records and legends about statues of the gods or of heroes having been caused to wink, or nod the head, or even to speak. The occult rationale of this marvel lies in the fact that all matter, such as wood and stone, is composed of molecular and electronic particles which, although usually held in equilibrium, are nevertheless perfectly fluid when considered as aggregates of electrons and atoms and molecules moving with vertiginous speed. Thus when the all-powerful will and intelligence of the adept are thrown into the electric fluid controlling these molecular and electronic movements, such movements can be, at the will of the operator, changed to bring about a moving of portions of the hitherto 'inanimate' body — such portions being rendered for the time plastic.

This fact also accounts for the so-called moving stones of ancient story, or for the statues of the gods moving and speaking over possibly quite long periods of time. Of course this magical feat could be stopped by destroying the material object thus 'enchanted,' for such destruction obviously meant the rupture of the molecular cohesion of the object when it was broken or reduced to powder or burned — with the material object destroyed, the magic itself perforce ceased, there being then no material vehicle for the magical energy to work through.°

In the degenerate days of Atlantis the misuse of āveśa was very prevalent, the black magicians being notorious for the wicked practices and frauds worked by them upon the humble, thoughtless, and often trusting multitudes.

Both the white and the black schools of the Atlantean race used this power to 'produce,' among other things, automatic or self-moving entities, and indeed these were as common as modern machinery is today. As an instance, H.P.B., quoting in *The Secret Doctrine* (II, 427, footnote) from an ancient manuscript, speaks of the Atlantean sorcerers employing some specially produced automata as servants, doing the heavy and humble work; and of other automata, who were really 'animated machines,' employed as guardians on the one hand, or warners of danger on the other hand, very much as modern science has learned to understand and to use the thermometer, the barometer, the photoelectric cell, etc.

All these automata were soulless in the human and proper sense of this word, for they had neither conscience nor integral mind, being merely machines animated by magic to do particular duties or to perform certain important scientific functions. Plato mentions in one of his famous *Dialogues* the existence and employment of such automata by the inhabitants of the island of Poseidonis, a portion of old Atlantis.

The process by which the adept brings his will and intelligence to bear by making exteriorizations from himself is, as said, called Hpho-wa, a term likewise covering the projection of the māyāvi-rūpa by the adept. There are many ways in which this power, which can be as terribly evil as it can be divinely beneficent, can be employed.

°Cf. "Animated Statues" by H.P.B., *The Theosophist*, Nov. 1886.

THE TIBETAN LAMAISTIC HIERARCHY

Among the commandments of Tsong-Kha-pa there is one that enjoins the Rahats (Arhats) to make an attempt to enlighten the world, including the "white barbarians," every century, at a certain specified period of the cycle. Up to the present day none of these attempts has been very successful. Failure has followed failure. Have we to explain the fact by the light of a certain prophecy? It is said that up to the time when Pban-chhen-rin-po-chhe (the Great Jewel of Wisdom) condescends to be reborn in the land of the P'helings (Westerners), and appearing as the Spiritual Conqueror (Chom-den-da), destroys the errors and ignorance of the ages, it will be of little use to try to uproot the misconceptions of P'heling-pa (Europe): her sons will listen to no one. Another prophecy declares that the Secret Doctrine shall remain in all its purity in Bhod-yul (Tibet), only to the day that it is kept free from foreign invasion. The very visits of Western natives, however friendly, would be baneful to the Tibetan populations. This is the true key to Tibetan exclusiveness.

> — From papers left by H.P.B. and published after her death as 'S.D. III.'

BECAUSE OF THE FACT that H.P.B. made so many allusions in the course of her writings to Tibet and to the Lamaistic hierarchy there, and to the so-called incarnations of the Buddha, etc., I write the following to serve as a warning against confusing the teachings of exoteric Tibetan Buddhism and Lamaism with the esotericism of the wisdom-religion.

The succession of the Lamaistic hierarchy since the time of Tsong-kha-pa in the fourteenth century is a real one, the principle of which is comprised in that deeper Buddhism which is really esoteric Buddhism.°

° There is even today, and it has been so since the time of Gautama the Buddha himself, an esoteric line of teaching in Buddhism, despite what may have been said, even by H.P.B. herself, partly to conceal the truth and partly to reveal it. This esoteric Buddhism is no different in any essential respect from the esoteric teaching lying in the background of every great religious or philosophical system, and therefore it is identic with the theosophia of the archaic ages. It was precisely this archaic theosophia which H.P.B. had in mind when she referred to the occult meaning of the different Buddhist doctrines. Both *The Secret Doctrine* and *The Voice of the Silence* contain innumerable references to this secret wisdom, her *Voice* especially being replete with teachings as well as names belonging distinctly to the esotericism of the Buddhist philosophy.

As is fairly generally known, the Tashi Lama and the Dalai Lama are the two heads of the Tibetan state.° Neither one is a reincarnation of the Bodhisattva Śākyamuni; but the succession beginning with Tsong-kha-pa *is* a transmission of a 'ray' in each case of the line of Tashi Lamas derivative from the spiritual Mahā-guru whom H.P.B. called the Silent Watcher of this globe. There is an important distinction to be drawn between successive reincarnations of Gautama and the successive imbodiments of rays from an identic source in the Hierarchy of Compassion.

It is indeed a transmission in serial line of a ray from the Buddha: but the Buddha in this instance is not the Bodhisattva Gautama, but the dhyāni-buddha of whom the Bodhisattva Gautama himself was an incarnated ray — and the noblest and most complete since the beginning of our fifth root-race.

Now, even the Tibetans, with the possible exception of the Tashi and Dalai Lamas themselves, look upon this transmission in succession as being repeated reincarnations of Gautama the Buddha. But this is erroneous; and it is just the point where the confusion occurs. The higher members of the Tibetan hierarchy, including the Khutukhtus, are as well acquainted with the esoteric facts in this matter as was H.P.B. This has been the case up to the present, and there seems no reasonable doubt that the succession will go on until human vehicles are found to be too imperfect to carry on this line. In former ages an identic succession of true teachers existed in other parts of the world, and this was the basis for the mysterious stories current in the ancient literatures telling of hierarchies of initiates continued through the ages because of being linked with the Mahā-guru.

°Dalai Lama is a compound term of Tibetan origin — *dalai*, being a corruption of *ta-le*, signifying ocean or sea, and *lama* carrying the meaning of superior — meaning the Superior Ocean or Ocean of Majesty, the word majesty having a spiritual as well as an official significance. Ocean or sea, according to H.P.B. (*The Secret Doctrine*, II, 502), has reference to the 'sea of knowledge' which has been traditionally cherished, and which remained for ages where now stretches the Gobi or Shamo desert. Dalai Lama is the official title used mainly by Chinese and Mongols in connection with the highest dignitary of the Gedun Dubpa Monastery of Lha-ssa, the city of the Lhas, the sacred city of Tibet. The Tibetans refer to this chief official as Gyal-wa Rim-po-che, the Most Excellent Sovereign.

The Tashi Lama is the highest dignitary of the Tashi-lhünpo Monastery at Shigatse, and bears the title of Pan-chen Rim-po-che, the Most Excellent Jewel Teacher; Tibetan tradition places the Tashi Lama as being spiritually higher in inner rank than the Dalai Lama.

Making certain allowances for the exaggerations of fancy and the mistakes of past Tibetan philosophical history, and having the esoteric keys in mind, it is not too much to say that at least the higher and more philosophical teachings of even exoteric Lamaism are as near an approach to an exoteric presentation of some of the doctrines of archaic theosophical occultism as can be found on the earth today.

The Dalai Lama is considered to be the executive official head of the Tibetan hierarchy, and the Tashi Lama to be the main teacher and repository of the mystic secrets of Tibetan Buddhism. Furthermore, the Dalai Lama is supposed to be the tulku or human imbodiment of certain of the characteristics of Avalokiteśvara, the merciful Governor of the World; whereas the Tashi Lama is supposed to be the tulku of the dhyāni-buddha Amitābha — 'boundless wisdom.' The Tashi Lama and the Dalai Lama are copies, in the esoteric and exoteric government of the Buddhists of Tibet, of what is actually the form of spiritual government in operation at Śambhala.

Now both Avalokiteśvara and Amitābha (Tibetan: Chenrezi and Ö-pa me, respectively) are cosmic entities or powers, Avalokiteśvara really being the entitative buddhi of cosmic kāma or boundless love and compassion, whereas Amitābha is the cosmic dhyāni-buddha or cosmic essence representing the wisdom or intelligence of the solar universe.

Exoteric Lamaism speaks commonly of five dhyāni-buddhas to which various names are given; esoterically there are of course seven or even ten; and these dhyāni-buddhas are both cosmic entities and the rays or reflections of these cosmic originals which manifest in man as monads. Now the main monadic essences or 'buddhas' in the human constitution as well as in the constitution of the cosmos, are the following: Ādi-buddha, Amitābha-buddha, Avalokiteśvara, Amitāyus.

Ādi-buddha,° meaning Original Primordial Buddha, corresponds from one angle of vision to the First or unmanifest Logos.

Amitābha, meaning Unbounded Light or Unlimited Glory, corresponds

---

°In esoteric Tibetan Lamaism, Ādi-buddha is likewise called Vajradhara (Tib. Dorje-chang) and Vajrasattwa (Tib. Dorje-sempa). *Vajra* is a Sanskrit word having various meanings such as diamond, thunderbolt, and indeed anything which in mystical thought partakes of the nature of durability, utmost clarity, immense power and impersonality; and hence it is to this that H.P.B. refers when she speaks of the Diamond Soul. *Dhara* means possessor or holder; and *sattwa*, of the essence of. (Cf. *The Voice of the Silence*, p. 83)

to the Second or manifest-unmanifest Logos, and thus also to Alaya. It is from the bosom of Amitābha that radiate forth those spiritual-intellectual rays or monads which in the Brahmanical system are often called kumāras, agnishwāttas, and mānasaputras.

Avalokiteśvara° corresponds to the Third or manifest Logos. In exoteric Tibetan Lamaism it is often called Padmapāni, meaning lotus-bearer or even lotus-born; but in esotericism, Padmapāni is a name given to the spiritual-intellectual power radiating from Avalokiteśvara, the Third Logos.

Amitāyus signifies Unlimited Life or Boundless Vitality, with distinct reference to that part of the cosmic hierarchy of our solar system which manifests itself throughout as intelligent, unifying, and all-encompassing vitality issuing from the heart of the sun.

The key to the mystery of the intricate and much misunderstood doctrine of the 'incarnations of the Buddha' in Tibet lies in this: every human being contains within himself, as formative parts of his constitution, a ray from every one of the seven or ten cosmic essences of and in the solar universe; so that, for example, his higher manas is a ray from the cosmic Amitābha and the spiritual and divine part of his kāma is a ray from the cosmic Avalokiteśvara.

Thus these incarnations are not the actual reimbodiments of the Buddha called Gautama (who himself was a ray from the cosmic Amitābha, which ray worked through his own inner dhyāni-buddha, itself this ray from the cosmic Amitābha). But *when they occur in fact and not merely in theory*, these Lamaistic incarnations are in very truth instances of men who, because of high evolutionary advancement and occult training, manifest at least some portion of one or another of the dhyāni-buddhas within and belonging to each such man. For this reason the Tibetans regard the Tashi and Dalai Lamas as tulkus respectively of Amitābha and of

---

°This word is usually mistranslated by Orientalists as 'the down-looking Lord,' probably because exoteric northern Buddhism generally speaks of Avalokiteśvara and its rays as the Great Lord of Pity. Such translation, while giving the idea of the characteristics and functions of Avalokiteśvara, nevertheless sins not only against Sanskrit grammar, but against the intrinsic significance of the Buddhist philosophy. The name is a compound: *ava*, below or down; *lokita* is the past participle passive from the verbal root *lok*, to contemplate, to view, to be aware of, and thus signifies seen or manifest; while *īśvara* means lord. Hence Avalokiteśvara, when properly rendered and understood means, 'the Lord who is seen below' — i.e. the manifest appearance (or appearances) of the spiritual energy of the Third Logos working in our world, and showing itself as harmony, regularity, order, compassion, etc.

Avalokiteśvara. This also applies to the cases of minor incarnations of the 'living Buddhas,' as European travelers call them when referring to the many instances of Lamaistic story showing that this or that individual is 'an incarnation of the Buddha.' It simply means that these minor lamas are claimed to be — let us hope they actually are — 'incarnations' of one or of another dhyāni-buddha.

The truth is that all these references to dhyāni-buddhas so common in Tibetan religion and mythology, are either to cosmic entities or, more often, to the spiritual monad in man; and because human beings themselves belong as individuals by their evolutionary swabhāva to one or to another of these cosmic essences, therefore a 'living Buddha' is said to be an incarnation either of Amitābha, or of Avalokiteśvara, or again of Amitāyus, etc. From this it is clear that such 'incarnations' are by no means limited to the chief official Lamas of Tibet, but can take place in minor instances; yet only when the individuals are genuinely initiated and highly evolved. Such high initiates, however, are exceedingly rare. One of these was the great Tibetan religious and philosophical reformer Tsong-kha-pa, who purified the degenerate Buddhism of his time and founded what is now known as the Gelukpa sect, often called the Yellow Caps, the official ecclesiastical and dominant power in the Tibetan hierarchy.

Every man on earth has different monads in his constitution, each one of which the Tibetan philosophy calls a dhyāni-buddha; and each such dhyāni-buddha manifests through an effulgence from itself, which is its human or mānushya-buddha. Very few human beings are sufficiently evolved as yet to express even the human buddha within themselves; when they do so, one of those grand figures appears, such as Gautama Śākyamuni. There are of course minor buddhas who are the bodhisattvas, and I may say here that the bodhisattva doctrine in occultism is fully as important as are the teachings concerning the buddhas. It is the glorious line of bodhisattvas appearing frequently through the ages who largely form the noble Brotherhood of nirmānakāyas of which the Brotherhood of adepts is partly composed, and of which the Buddha Gautama in his more human or bodhisattva aspect is a member.

Thus, every human being, containing or being in his higher parts a dhyāni-buddha, has or is likewise a mānushya-buddha and hence has the potentiality of becoming an active bodhisattva among men; and all initiations are directed to the point of raising men into bodhisattvahood for the benefit of the world and everything that is.

Tibetan Lamaism is the only representative at present on earth of a *system* which, throughout human history, oral or written, has been in existence in every land and among every race of people. Recorded history is usually silent, or very nearly so, about these ancient systems of philosophical and religious thinking and their schools of philosophy and training, because these were largely kept secret from the populace, very much as the existence of the Brotherhood of the mahatmas was almost unknown until H.P.B. brought it to the attention of mankind and received the guerdon of martyrdom for her self-denying sacrifice.

Any such system when operative in purity is, so to say, an extension on earth of the spiritual-psychological Hierarchy of Compassion, which we may call the spiritual banyan of our planetary chain with its overseeing Silent Watcher.

We thus see that Tibetan Lamaism contains noteworthy elements of occult truth, mixed with a great deal of sheer exotericism both in thought and in practice; and on the fringes of the Tibetan plateau Lamaism has again sunken almost to the level at which Tsong-kha-pa found it when the degenerate Buddhism of his time had largely fallen into sorcery and black magic due to the infiltration into it of the native Bhön practices.

In Tibet the people as a general rule are still spiritually unspoiled, although exceedingly crude in many ways; and thus they have preserved some of the teachings of the archaic wisdom, however exotericized they have become. But precisely what takes place in Tibet, and is recognized as incarnations in human beings of spiritual rays from cosmic sources working through their own seven principles, can occur — and indeed has occurred — in other parts of the world whenever human vehicles, through occult training and spiritual purity, are fit and ready to receive.°

In former ages, such knowledge was common to humanity, but it has been absolutely forgotten in the West. The Druids had more or less the same teaching; it exists even today in rather vague form among the Druses of the Lebanon of Syria. It was as well known in ancient Persia among

---

°The words shaberon, khubilkhan, khutukhtu, etc., found in *Isis Unveiled* and elsewhere, are in common usage in Mongolia, and even in other parts of Asia, such as Siberia. Their meaning varies and the words are often wrongly applied to mere sorcerers or spiritistic mediums. As originally used in Tibet, these and other similar terms referred to minor cases of incarnations; and some hundreds of years ago, and perhaps in a very few cases even at the present time, could properly designate genuine initiates.

the Zoroastrians as it was in Egypt. Many Greek mystics taught the same, as for instance in the Neoplatonic philosophy, and Greek history often records the fact that this or that man had been inspired by Apollo or by Mercury, or that one or another woman had been infilled with the virtue of Juno or Venus. In India this tradition is a commonplace, the greatest examples of such spiritual cosmic ray imbodiments being the avatāras.

What has taken place in the past is but significant of what will take place in the future; so the present, which is but a dividing line between past and future, must likewise know instances of spiritual imbodiments.°

° See the following articles by H.P.B.: "Lamas and Druses," *The Theosophist*, June 1881; "Reincarnations in Tibet," *The Theosophist*, March 1882; and "Zoroastrianism in the Light of Occult Philosophy," *The Theosophist*, June and July, 1883.

FIFTH AND SIXTH ROUNDERS

Every "Round" brings about a new development and even an entire change in the mental, psychic, spiritual and physical constitution of man, all these principles evoluting on an ever ascending scale. Thence it follows that those persons who, like Confucius and Plato, belonged psychically, mentally and spiritually to the higher planes of evolution, were in our Fourth Round as the average man will be in the Fifth Round, whose mankind is destined to find itself, on this scale of Evolution, immensely higher than is our present humanity. Similarly Gautama Buddha — wisdom incarnate — was still higher and greater than all the men we have mentioned, who are called Fifth Rounders, while Buddha and Sankaracharya are termed Sixth Rounders, allegorically. Thence again the concealed wisdom of the remark, pronounced at the time "evasive" — that "a few drops of rain do not make the Monsoon, *though they presage it.*"   — *The Secret Doctrine*, I, 162

EVER SINCE THE existence of the Brotherhood of adepts and masters came to the attention of the Western world, particularly after the publication of some of their letters in the 1880s, students have been puzzled by some of their references to fifth and sixth rounders. The theme has already been dealt with in an earlier chapter, but in order to clarify it still further, the following remarks are added.

A fifth rounder is one who has already attained the state of consciousness which the average member of the human race will attain during the fifth round on this earth. A sixth rounder is one who has reached the state of consciousness which the average human being will attain during the sixth round. The human life-wave, with its many grades of evolutional unfolding manifesting in the various types of humanity, is not alone and single, but in reality is but one of the ten families of life-waves that are making the rounds of our earth planetary chain. For instance, there are hosts upon hosts of entities preceding us in evolutionary progression, the forerunners, and there are likewise hosts upon hosts following in our wake, the trailers.

On our planetary chain there are other families of entities, not only presently on earth but on the other six globes, so that we humans, the

512

beasts, the vegetables, the minerals, and the elementals, are not the only hosts on this chain as it now is.

When all the seven or ten hierarchies finally reach globe G during the first round, they gather on that globe all together, it being the last globe of the manifest seven; and here they all finish the first round simultaneously before the interplanetary nirvana begins.

Starting with the second round, all the lines of evolution or activity now having been laid, and nothing having to be instituted from the ground up, the progress of the life-waves is relatively faster for those which are the most evolved. The effect of this is that some smaller hosts of monads, and individuals too, run through their evolutionary course much more rapidly, and thus precede the general body of the seven evolving hierarchies. This is why we have fifth rounders now among us, although we as a human host are in our fourth round.

When our life-wave shall have moved on to globe E the śishtas of the human kingdom will be the highest or next to the highest representatives of their life-wave. They will be really fifth rounders, with a very few sixth rounders appearing among them at long intervals of time. This means that they are not called upon to make, then and there, what is for our human life-wave its fifth round because they have already made it, through their character and quality as forerunners: they have outrun the bulk of their life-wave. Exactly the same observations apply to the sixth rounders, who are the buddhas. These sixth rounders — those whose spirituality is so high, and whose innate capacity acquired through long aeons of experience is so great that they go ahead even of the fifth rounders — are very, very few in number. Gautama the Buddha is said to have been the only *fully developed* sixth rounder in recorded history.

Now how is this inner evolution achieved? Obviously, in every collection or group of entities, there are some who are behind; then the intermediate majority, and finally some who are ahead. These last are the elder souls, those who have strived the hardest and conquered most of self, for true self-knowledge comes from intelligent self-control in every thought and act. When death occurs, these forerunners follow the same course that all excarnate entities do, only they do so *self-consciously*. They perform an individual round of their own through the planetary chain, first by ascending along the luminous arc until they reach the highest globe; then after a relatively long nirvanic rest they descend through the globes of the descending arc until they again reach globe D or our earth;

and because they have thus made a round ahead of the life-wave, they are fifth rounders when they return to our globe.

They progress through experiences gained on the different planes of the other globes and by having in each of those globes various imbodiments; and these experiences are built into the fabric of the soul as character. It is a continuous and natural inner growth, which is none other than an ever-greater manifestation of the monad, the inner god. In other words, on these other globes these peregrinating monads undergo self-conscious experiences, instead of being, as is usual with reincarnating egos, enwrapped for the entire period between earth lives in a long devachan. From this it should be clear that the evolutional development of the fifth and sixth rounders is not achieved solely by training, initiation or self-study during incarnations on this globe D. However indispensable all these methods are, it would be utterly impossible to become a genuine fifth or sixth rounder in these ways alone.

A sixth rounder is one who, in advance of the human life-wave, has evoked into operation the buddhi or sixth principle within him, because it is in the sixth round that buddhi will receive its evolution; while the fifth rounder is one who has awakened into more or less full expression the fifth principle within himself, the manas. We humans, being in the middle of the fourth round, are still in process of evolving our fourth principle, kāma.

The sixth rounders are so few that we may state definitely that a true sixth rounder is always a buddha, or one equivalent to a buddha. The whole being of the man is filled with the glory of the god within him. However, there are many fifth rounders among us even today, but they are not by any means all on the same level of fifth-round unfoldment: there are the advanced ones, those less advanced, and those who have just become fifth rounders. If these peregrinating souls are so far advanced that they can find the spiritual, intellectual and psychical strength within themselves, they continue without interruption the process of self-conscious imbodiments on the other globes for one round more, and thus when they reach earth again they do so as sixth rounders.

It may be of interest to quote the following passage from one of K.H.'s letters* written in answer to a question of A.P. Sinnett's as to whether a fifth-round man, if he "devoted himself to occultism and became an adept, would . . . escape further earthly incarnations?"

___

*The Mahatma Letters, p. 117.

No; if we except Buddha — a sixth round being, as he had run so successfully the race in his previous incarnations as to outrun even his predecessors. But then such a man is to be found in a *billion* of human creatures. He differed from other men as much in his physical appearance as in spirituality and knowledge. Yet even he escaped further reincarnations but on this earth; and, when the last of the sixth round men of the third ring is gone out of this earth, the Great Teacher will have to get reincarnated on the next planet. Only, and since He sacrificed Nirvanic bliss and Rest for the salvation of his fellow creatures He will be re-born in the highest — the *seventh* ring of the upper planet. Till then He will *overshadow* every decimillennium (let us rather say and add *"has overshadowed already"* a chosen individual who generally overturned the destinies of nations. See *Isis*, Vol. I, pp. 34 and 35 last and first para. on the pages).

As far as known the human race has not as yet produced a seventh rounder, a forerunner ahead by three rounds of the general life-wave. The majority of the mahatmas are either very far advanced fifth rounders, or hovering on the line of passing into sixth roundership; their chelas are fifth rounders less advanced.

The forerunning monads — in addition to passing in more or less self-conscious reimbodiment after death through the other globes of our planetary chain, and thus attaining fifth roundership — were already, when leaving the moon chain, evolutionally more advanced than the majority of their fellows. During the course of their rounds on our present earth chain, and beginning even during the third round, these forerunning reimbodying egos began to feel so strongly the working within them of spiritual and intellectual qualities and faculties, that they left, as it were, the vast flock of the egos in the human life-wave, and took imbodiment on the different globes of the chain in advance of the mass of egos. This precedence in evolutionary status is then kept even when the bulk of the human life-wave in its turn reaches its fourth round, so that these forerunners may actually be by that time in their fifth round, and in a few cases even in their sixth round.

Writing on this subject in 1882, K.H. made the following explanation:[*]

The scheme with its septenary details would be incomprehensible to man had he not the power as the higher Adepts have proved of prematurely developing his 6th and 7th senses — those which will be the natural endowment of all in the corresponding rounds. Our Lord Buddha — a 6th r. man — would not have

---

[*]*The Mahatma Letters*, pp. 96–7.

appeared in our epoch, great as were his accumulated merits in previous rebirths but for a *mystery*. . . .

And now as man when completing his seventh ring upon A has but begun his first on Z and as A dies when he leaves it for B, etc., and as he must also remain in the inter-cyclic sphere after Z, as he has between every two planets, until the impulse again thrills the chain, clearly no one can be more than one round ahead of his kind. And Buddha only forms an exception by virtue of the *mystery*. We have fifth round men among us because we are in the latter half of our septenary earth ring. In the first half this could not have happened. The countless myriads of our fourth round humanity who have outrun us and completed their seven rings on Z, have had time to pass their inter-cyclic period begin their new round and work on to globe D (ours). But how can there be men of the 1st, 2nd, 3rd, 6th and 7th rounds? We represent the first three and the sixth can only come at rare intervals and prematurely like Buddhas (only under prepared conditions) and that the last-named the seventh are not yet evolved!

Speaking generally, the "mystery" means that these rarest few, destined to become sixth rounders even in the fourth round, are aided and individually guided by certain dhyāni-chohanic beings who not only foster these forerunning egos, and protect them, but do so even when those egos undergo the various initiations through which they must pass. This mystery imbodies the further fact that these forerunners are helped to make full and self-conscious imbodiment on each one of the globes of our planetary chain, thus enabling them to gather the experiences that the bulk of the fourth rounders can attain only when the main life-wave reaches these different globes.

BUDDHAS AND BODHISATTVAS

Now bend thy head and listen well, O Bôdhisattva — Compassion speaks and saith: "Can there be bliss when all that lives must suffer? Shalt thou be saved and hear the whole world cry?"
— *The Voice of the Silence*, p. 71

THERE ARE CERTAIN beings whose love is so all-encompassing, whose self-abnegation is so great, whose sense of unity with the One is so relatively complete, that at a certain period of their evolution they turn back on the path and become beneficent forces in the spiritual and intellectual life of humanity, sacrificing their own advancement for aeons upon aeons to come, and enduring what is to them little less than a living hell, in order to help by remaining as a spiritual fire in the atmosphere of a planet or of a solar system. These are the Buddhas of Compassion.

All nature bows in reverence and awe before them; for they stand higher than the gods whom otherwise they would have joined and gone beyond.

The Great Ones of the earth live for the world, in it but not of it, linked with it by their own act of mighty compassion; and they will enter no permanent nirvana until humanity, through the natural course of evolution, shall have progressed to the point of no longer needing the spiritual stimulation that is given by the Buddhas of Compassion.

Greater love hath no man than that he give up his life for his brother. But when the Buddha of Compassion gives up everything that he is, gives up all individual advancement, in order to go back into the murk of the physical sphere to help and save humanity, there indeed is divinity itself at work!

The Pratyeka Buddha, on the other hand, is one who strives after and achieves buddhahood for himself. He raises himself to the spiritual realms of his own inner being where he enwraps himself, not heeding the call to return and help mankind. He is a very pure and holy individual; otherwise he could not possibly reach nirvana. But he is so completely absorbed in the beauty and glory and wonder of the spiritual spheres, that that very beauty is like a veil which beclouds his eyes and dims

517

his memory of the struggling hosts of beings behind him. Though exalted, the Pratyeka Buddha does not rank with the unutterable sublimity of the Buddha of Compassion.

The Buddha of Pity puts all that lives before himself in the measure of importance; the Pratyeka, the Buddha 'for self alone,' puts *himself* before all that lives. Both are on the right-hand path; but the one lives for the world, and the other lives for himself in the world for the purpose of gaining individual nirvana.

If we were to perform a deed of mercy solely in order to stifle something within or to be more at peace with ourselves, then in the last analysis this would be selfish; it would exemplify just what a Pratyeka Buddha is. Yearning for self-advancement is spiritual selfishness. No one who has ever felt stirring in his heart a self-forgetful glow of pity, of universal love, the instinct of self-sacrifice for others, could ever conceive that all this is a moving of the soul based upon mere self-interest. The ideas are as utterly apart as the two poles.

The Pratyeka Buddhas and the Buddhas of Compassion in a certain sense may be likened to the old fable of the tortoise and the hare. The Pratyekas are like the hare; they leap forward into the future and win for themselves a glorious place in the spheres. But the Buddhas of Compassion remain behind in order to accomplish the noblest work that it is given even unto the gods to do — to lead the army of those less evolved than they: to lead them to the Light, to the Great Peace; and although their individual progress seems slower than that of the Pratyekas, nevertheless the time will come when the Buddhas of Compassion will pass beyond the Pratyekas, who will be found crystallized in their spiritual purity and, for the time being, unable to advance farther.

But, because the Buddhas of Compassion have renounced the personal self for the Self of the universe, the very heart of the universe is active within them and thus their progress will actually be accelerated. When, in the far distant aeons of the future, the Pratyekas emerge from their nirvanic state, they will have to begin a new path of evolution as learners, whereas the Buddhas of Compassion will already by then be far ahead of them.

Do the Buddhas of Compassion have no joy in their work? Indeed they do, for their hearts are at peace, knowing they are allied with the gods, and that through them flows the stream of illumination from the Silent Watcher. They are the Great Helpers, helping always whenever karma permits, which means the karma of the individual, whether it be a human being or a race.

Each one of us is an unexpressed buddha, even now. It is our higher self, and as we conquer in the battle with self — for that is our only impediment, strange paradox, because it is the pathway we must tread — as we conquer the self in order to become the greater self, we approach with every step nearer and nearer to the 'sleeping' buddha within. And yet truly it is not the buddha which is 'asleep'; it is we who are sleeping on the bed of matter, dreaming evil dreams brought about by our passions, egoism and selfishness — making thick and heavy veils of personality around the buddha within.

H.P.B. has called the Buddhas of Compassion the very incarnation of wisdom and love, the two greatest elements in the universe: wisdom, which is supreme vision, knowledge from recollections of eternities past, and utter acquiescence in and forming part of nature's laws; and love, impersonal and majestic, leading to the sacrifice of self even when on the very threshold of nirvana.

It may be at first very confusing to hear about so many gods, dhyāni-chohans, buddhas, bodhisattvas, and what not. But it need not be so if we remove the old idea from our minds that the gods are one family of beings, and men are some other and quite distinct family. We are children of the gods, literally, embryo gods; and the gods who now are, were once men. What the dhyāni-buddhas are to the dhyāni-bodhisattvas, the human buddhas are on this plane to the human bodhisattvas. The rule is the same.

Every dhyāni-buddha or 'buddha of contemplation' has his mind-born sons, so to speak, his spiritual offspring, who are the dhyāni-bodhisattvas. Let me illustrate: when a teacher arouses the soul in a man and leads him to a greater, nobler life, that now understanding man is then a bodhisattva of his teacher. The teacher has transplanted a portion of his own life-essence, a part of his own mind, into the life of the disciple, thereby awakening within him the mānasaputric fires. This is what the dhyāni-buddhas do to other high entities on their own plane; they have their pupils in whom they arouse the bodhisattvic faculty, the buddhic splendor, thus bringing about the coming into being of the dhyāni-bodhisattvas, and, later, the human or mānushya-buddhas.

Similarly so on the human plane: when the mānushya-buddhas find fit disciples, they inspire them, infill them with holy spiritual and intellectual fire, so that when these pupils themselves are relatively complete in spirituality, they become mānushya-bodhisattvas, on their way to becoming mānushya-buddhas. And this is so because the buddha-light is awakened within them; each one feels the god within himself, and from that moment he knows neither pause nor rest until he too attains human buddhahood.

Concerning the various kinds of buddhas: one common procedure and structure runs throughout, so that if we understand the nature and function of one class of buddhas, we shall understand in outline the entire range of the teaching. For instance, every round is under the governance of a dhyāni-buddha who is divisible into seven 'children,' making the mahā-buddhas of the seven globes. Each one of such mahā-buddhas is again divisible into seven 'children,' making the racial buddhas.

Of the two buddhas appearing in every root-race — one towards the beginning and the other towards the middle or the end, depending upon circumstances — one of them is particularly devoted to the root-race as a race. The same buddhic influence, however, working through the especial racial buddha, manifests itself in quite a large number of bodhisattvas, all belonging to the same race, who may be called minor buddhas; and these appear at periodic intervals during the race. Gautama the Buddha was such a bodhisattva in and through whom the racial buddha manifested its transcendent power. These bodhisattvas usually are also the individuals who appear at the beginning of every so-called Messianic cycle, which averages some 2,160 years.

The buddha who appears about the middle or towards the end of a race is the particular buddha of the following root-race, who thus appears a little ahead of his own time in order to guide, in collaboration with the racial buddha himself, the end of the race towards coalescing and connecting with the succeeding root-race.

GAUTAMA THE BUDDHA

IN ALL THE ANCIENT religions possessing an esoteric[18] or mystical side, there are teachings or suggestions centering on the one thought that somewhere in the world there exists a spiritual energy or intelligence, who is mankind's guardian and friend. He is often alluded to as the Chief of the adept-seers of the ages, who is intimately connected with the spiritual principles which guide and inspirit the universe. H.P.B. speaks of this mysterious individual as the Great Initiator.

Now, to refer to this individual as Gautama the Buddha would in a sense be quite correct, because the spiritual influence of the Great Initiator was there; and yet, to look upon this individual merely as a human being is to wander wide from the truth. His ray, a part of his intelligence, on certain occasions, rare and far between in a great root-race, appears as a buddha in a human body. But the buddha is not the mere physical man, who is only the outward garment and the channel through whom the light and the teaching come. The real buddha is an inner entity (though not exactly the spiritual entity within each man), which serves as a channel through which stream the influences, the will power, the intelligence, of some being still more sublime — the Great Initiator.

Gautama the Buddha was a man. He is at present a nirmānakāya. The higher ego of the entity which last manifested itself as Gautama the Buddha works through this nirmānakāya; and this higher ego is the Buddha, the transmitter of the spiritual intelligence of the Great Initiator.

It is to Gautama the Buddha, thus considered, and the power working through him, that the teachers of H.P.B. referred when they used phrases such as "He to whom we owe allegiance," "He whose word is our Law." As one of the two racial Buddhas of our fifth root-race — the second Buddha being Maitreya, still to come millions of years hence — he will continue to watch over and protect this root-race. He is the origin, the founder, of every great spiritual religious or philosophical movement begun at any time during our root-race. It is he who is the Chief of all the adepts, the Lord, the Chohan; and it is before him, and in his presence, that the seventh and greatest initiation of all takes place.[19]

On account of his connection with the avatāra Jesus, the Buddha was closely associated with the founding of Christianity. Through infinite compassion, he lent himself to the work of the avatāra Jesus, thereby linking himself inevitably and forever with the karma that flowed forth from it; but that does not mean that all the evil that has been wrought, and such good as has been done, by Christians and the Church since the passing of Jesus, fall with dead weight upon Gautama the Buddha. This would simply be voicing the old theological and utterly mistaken interpretation of the doctrine of vicarious atonement. The karmic law will call to account the evil workers themselves.

This is what is meant: Gautama the Buddha, the noblest sage who has lived within millions of years, even he, with his godlike wisdom, made minor mistakes in his life. In his spiritual yearning to give truth, light, love and peace to men, on several occasions he opened the doors a little too widely. Therein lies always a great psychical and spiritual danger. In order to correct what he had overdone, he became the intermediate part of the avatāra Jesus (just as he had some hundreds of years earlier provided the intermediate part of the avatāra Śankarāchārya), thereby to a certain extent rectifying what he, Gautama the Buddha, in his boundless love for mankind, had done.

In Gautama Śākyamuni, as a man, there were several different elements functioning: (a) the ordinary individual who was a great and splendid man; (b) inspiring him was the incarnate bodhisattva, although the mānasaputric essence, belonging to that grand human being as a monad per se, had not yet been fully awakened; (c) enlightening this bodhisattva within Gautama was the buddha; and (d) inspiring and enlightening that buddha — a spiritual flame working through the bodhisattva in the man — was the dhyāni-buddha of our round, working of course through the dhyāni-bodhisattva of this globe D.

All this may seem very complicated, but it really is not. We have, first, a spiritually evolved human being in whom the native mānasaputric essence was partially awakened, thus providing a field of consciousness for its individualization as the incarnate bodhisattva. Then the monadic essence working through this incarnate bodhisattva was individualized as the buddha, these elements forming the various monadic centers mainly active in Śākyamuni. In addition to this, and because the incarnate bodhisattva allowed the ray from the inner buddha to manifest itself, there was the reception even into the human consciousness of the still more spiritual ray from the fourth-round dhyāni-buddha, in its turn traveling to the human buddha by means of the globe dhyāni-bodhisattva.

This dhyāni-buddha might be described as the 'outside' spiritual influence working through the human buddha; and the buddha and the bodhisattva and the partially awakened mānasaputric essence form the triad in the constitution of Gautama Śākyamuni acting to produce the mānushya-buddha.

When Gautama, whose personal name was Siddhārtha, left his home, according to the beautiful story, and went out in search of light, in order to attain human buddhahood for the sake of the "salvation of gods and men," he brought first into relatively full activity the bodhisattva within himself. The ordinary man, grand as he was, nevertheless was utterly subordinated to the bodhisattva within him, which could then manifest and express its noble faculties, enlightened by the buddhic ray. Yet this becoming at one with his inner buddha was still not enough for the purpose in mind, because this particular human incarnation of the man called Siddhārtha was to be the vehicle of the minor racial buddha, who would watch over our fifth root-race.

In the exoteric literatures of Buddhism it is stated that every human or mānushya-buddha, such as was Gautama, is the counterpart on earth of a celestial buddha, its spiritual-divine origin. It is the celestial buddha, the dhyāni-buddha, who sends forth from himself the ray, the energy, the spirituality, the will, the intelligence, all of which, manifesting through the spiritual-human vehicle, produce the mānushya-buddha.

It is also the Buddha who, during his entire administration which lasts from the beginning of the fifth root-race until the Maitreya-buddha succeeds him, helps to bring about the appearance of an avatāra at certain cyclical periods. The reason for this is that a divinity requires a psychological apparatus as pure and strong as that of a buddha for its manifestation. In fact, the energy emanating from a divinity would probably wreck the psychological apparatus of an average mahatma, although he is far above the general run of mankind. There are great mysteries involved in this question of buddhahood.

Even in physical appearance, when the Lord Buddha manifested as Gautama, he was very different from other men. Not only did he radiate kindness, love, disciplined strength, peace, and brilliant intellectuality, but, it is said, he was almost unhumanly handsome and looked like a god; and yet his son, born before buddhahood was consciously attained, was but a fourth rounder, although a good and noble man. Rāhula was his name.

The incarnation of a buddha is not a descent from devachan as is the case with ordinary men. Every human being is a compounded entity. There is a god in him, a spiritual ego, a human ego, an animal nature, and the physical body which expresses as best it can the bundle of energies surging through and from within the auric egg. Now each of these elements is itself a learning entity on its upward way. The self-consciousness, the sense of egoity, is there; but above that is the sense of cosmic unity, which is the atmosphere and consciousness of the inner god, a celestial buddha. Hence, as there are in a man a celestial buddha, a human buddha, a human soul working through an animal body, it is apparent that many strange things may take place if circumstances are right, and that the conditions of incarnation of a buddha must *de facto* be very different indeed from the reincarnation of an ordinary man. And so it was in the case of Śākyamuni.

The Prince Siddhārtha of Kapilavastu, who later became the physical vehicle of a buddha, was a spiritually evolved human being, and therefore a fit vehicle to express the higher element in his nature, the mānushya-buddha, itself the vehicle of the celestial buddha — the loftiest part of such an exalted constitution. Hence the man was born, passed through all the usual phases, but because he was overshadowed by the buddhic splendor, he was a wonder-child. He married. Rāhula was born. A little later came the first inner light of dazzling splendor. Understanding began to come to the human part of this compounded entity, and then the mānushya-buddha took control. The human thereafter was subordinated to the spiritual; and Prince Siddhārtha left his home and became a wanderer — which merely means that he withdrew from the world, so that the human part of him might be trained to become a fully conscious channel for the manifestation of the mānushya-buddha within.

So it was that finally, after striving in self-imposed discipline and spiritual yearning and inner conquest, under the sacred Bodhi tree, the wisdom-tree, the full illumination came, as the legend runs, and the mānushya-bodhisattva called Gautama Śākyamuni attained buddhahood. This incarnate bodhisattva became the willing and perfect psychospiritual instrument through which his inner buddha could express itself. When the buddha-state had been attained, we find the buddha working through the bodhisattva, which itself works through the awakened man; thus exemplifying the activity of the three higher monads in a human constitution: to wit, the spiritual, the bodhisattva or mānasaputra, and the evolved human. And this is exactly what each one of us someday will have the lofty privilege and joy of becoming — provided that we run the race successfully.

Until eighty years of age the Buddha lived and taught: initiated, helped, comforted, inspired. When the body which had served him so well became feeble with the passing of the years, the Buddha 'died' — according to the exoteric teaching.°

The truth of the matter is that at that time the buddha within Gautama Śākyamuni entered into the nirvanic condition, leaving the bodhisattva still active and working through the aged physical frame. Nirvana, in this case, really meant that the celestial buddha entered into its native cosmic realms, its work for the time being ended, and left behind the human illuminated by the mānushya-buddha splendor, the inner buddha. The buddha-part of him had 'died' for the world, i.e. had done its work and had passed into the nirvana, therein to await its succeeding task at the end of this fifth root-race, when that same buddha-spirit will again enlighten a new bodhisattva-man.

For twenty years after the nirvana was attained, Gautama the Buddha lived among his initiates, and taught and initiated; and at the age of one

---

°Certain passages in the *Mahā-Paranirvāna-Sūtra* briefly give a very important teaching regarding death, by applying the process by which it takes place to the passing on of the Buddha-Gautama himself, as a type-figure. They speak of this process as the 'ascent' of the Buddha's consciousness through several planes, and of its 'descent' again, and this three times in succession. Now physical death takes place in all human beings in exactly the same fashion, although in the case of the great sages this is modified by their high spiritual standing.

The higher portions of the human constitution do not break away from the physical body with one single wrench of the golden cord, but this is preceded by a rising of the consciousness into the higher planes of man's constitution, a momentary pause there, then a descent till the consciousness reanimates the physical brain for a few seconds, and at this instant the eyes may open for a moment or two. Then the consciousness ascends once more and, after another brief pause, is again drawn back into the entangling attractions of the astral and physical worlds, and again perhaps for a fleeting instant the physical brain becomes momentarily conscious. Then for a third time the consciousness ascends, but more strongly now, and after another short interval it descends again, but very weakly this time, the consciousness perhaps registering a feeble contact with the physical plane; and after a very brief span, unconsciousness, complete and utter, supervenes: the golden cord of vitality is snapped, and the inner man is free. The ante-mortem panorama immediately precedes the period of the first ascent.

hundred, his body finally died. The body was cast off, and the entire entity as a mānushya-buddha remained as a nirmānakāya,° and so lives today, the channel, the vehicle, through which pour energies deriving from the spiritual center of our solar system. Hence he is the channel of the Great Initiator, the guardian and protector of every great world religion or world philosophy founded during our fifth root-race, and will continue so to be and to act until the Buddha-Maitreya comes in the course of the cycling ages.

The difference between this great sage and ordinary men is that in Śākyamuni the higher parts of his constitution were more or less fully working through the 'man,' at least as fully as is possible for any human being who is a sixth rounder. When he had undergone his sixth sublime initiation, from that moment as a 'man' he 'died,' but continued to live on. In other words, he taught after this episode for twenty years in and through the initiated and therefore glorified human part of his constitution; but no man can undergo the sixth initiation, which is the time of the Great Renunciation — much less the seventh — and 'return' to the world of men as he was before.†

°A nirmānakāya can live in any vehicle that he may choose to form by his will and thought; and similarly he has the power and the wisdom to choose the inner plane or planes on which to live. In all cases, however, the 'body' of the nirmānakāya is formed from his own auric egg; that is, the process of forming such thought- and will-body amounts to a temporary thickening by kriyā-śakti of the outer layers of the adept's auric egg; such 'body' being formed to correspond in quality and attribute with the inner plane that is chosen as the 'world' in which the nirmānakāya dwells.

Every nirmānakāya is a mahatma, minus the lower triad; but not every mahatma is a nirmānakāya. There are mahatmas who are incarnated; and, obviously, because living in the physical-astral-vital vehicle, they are not nirmānakāyas. Some of the mahatmas of the lower degrees have not yet reached the point in their evolution where they find it advantageous to their sublime work to drop the lower triad of their constitution and to live as nirmānakāyas.

†In order to understand the esoteric meaning of what the nirvana of Gautama the Buddha really was, we must remember that there are nirvanas of different kinds and of different grades of sublimity. In renouncing nirvana, the choice was made by the human part, the bodhisattva on its way to becoming a buddha in the future. But the highest part of the Buddha must enter nirvana, it cannot recede; it has gone beyond the point of spiritual existence where a choice to remain behind is possible. This explains the exoteric teaching that the Buddha enters nirvana from which there is no return for the highest part that does enter nirvana; whereas the real teaching is that the human soul of the Buddha, the bodhisattva, is the part which makes the great renunciation and turns back in the spirit of compassion to help all that lives.

The meaning therefore is that the higher part of his constitution, to wit, the human ego within him, had now re-become a buddha and had entered a nirvana; but the lower part of his human or intermediate nature still functioned on earth as a glorious bodhisattva — in this grand and beautiful fact we see the meaning of many exoteric Buddhist statements that a buddha leaves a bodhisattva behind in order to carry on the work. So then, to be a buddha means that one's highest part is in the nirvana, and that one's higher human part, which is buddhi-mānasic, lives on as a teacher, as a bodhisattva-nirmānakāya. Then there is the physical body with its vital-astral apparatus which finally dies.

Now Śākyamuni, upon attaining buddhahood at and during his sixth initiation, re-entered a nirvana. This could be otherwise phrased by saying that the spiritual monad within him entered or became a dharmakāya, whose consciousness is nirvanic and too pure and loftily spiritual to permit any contact with our gross spheres of life and matter. All the remainder of the constitution of the Buddha then and there, after such initiation, chose to enter the nirmānakāya condition; while that part of Śākyamuni's constitution which was intermediate between the spiritual monad and the higher portions of the human ego, went into abeyance as the sambhogakāya, i.e. non-manifesting because not 'chosen.'

The important point of teaching here is that certain highly spiritual human beings who undergo successfully the sixth initiation choose the sambhogakāya instead of the nirmānakāya, as for instance the Pratyeka Buddhas, for in their case the highest part of their constitution becomes the dharmakāya, all the higher intermediate portions become the sambhogakāya; the nirmānakāya 'choice' is not made, and thus in their isolation these pure but spiritually selfish individuals lose all contact with the world and its forces, and all desire to help those less advanced.

After the Buddha's physical death at the ripe old age of one hundred years, the bodhisattva, who was really the now enlightened Siddhārtha, remained, as said, in the earth's atmosphere as a nirmānakāya, that is to say, a complete but glorified man in the full possession of all faculties, characteristics and principles of his constitution, except the physical body, with the linga-śarīra and grosser prānas.

The expression 'in the earth's atmosphere' is correct as far as it goes, but it is incomplete. One could state the situation with even greater accuracy by saying that the bodhisattva as a nirmānakāya withdrew from ordinary physical contact with men and the earth and its affairs, but maintained intimate and watchful and overseeing relations with them from inner planes — the bodhisattva-nirmānakāya, formerly known on earth as Śākyamuni, being a resident of that extremely mysterious part of the earth's surface, protected and guarded against outer intrusion, wherein are found some of the greatest members of the occult Brotherhood, Śambhala.

OUR SPIRITUAL HOME

Śambhala is the secret home of the great Brotherhood of mahatmas and their chiefs, from which center at certain times in the history of our fifth root-race come forth mandates for spiritual and intellectual work among men. It is an actual district in a mystical region of the earth known to none but those whose training calls them there, and is described as a place of great beauty, surrounded by a range of the majestic Himalaya mountains. No force engendered by human genius can penetrate into this spiritual center, for it is protected by ākāśic barriers. From the end of the fourth root-race of mankind it has been held inviolate against aggression of any kind. Many have endeavored unsuccessfully to identify this mystical locality with some known modern district or town. In the Purānas and elsewhere it is stated that out of Śambhala will appear the Kalki-avatāra of the future.[20]

It is precisely because the Buddha-Gautama was the Buddha destined to appear in our fifth root-race, that his destiny and duties are closely linked with our present root-race until its end; and thus he remains in mysterious seclusion in Śambhala, yet, as the chief of the Brotherhood of adepts, in constant spiritual and intellectual and psychical touch with mankind.

This center is karmically one of the earth's destined spots for the future. It is significant that one of the arteries, so to speak, of the earth's fountain of life passes through or under it. In this connection, H.P.B. in *The Secret Doctrine* (II, 400) quotes from the Commentaries on the Book of Dzyan, as follows:

It [the water of life] *gets purified* (on its return) *to her heart — which beats under the foot of the sacred Shambalah, which then* (in the beginnings) *was not yet born. For it is in the belt of man's dwelling* (the earth) *that lies concealed the life and health of all that lives and breathes.*

Then she comments in a footnote:

It is the blood of the earth, the electro-magnetic current, which circulates through all the arteries; and which is said to be found stored in the "navel" of the earth.

529

Furthermore, Śambhala has two aspects to it: the spiritual and the geographical.

It has been said that the spiritual home of our race is primarily in the sun, and in the foregoing I have referred to that sacred inaccessible district of Tibet as the central home of the masters. Now there is a third spiritual home, an intermediate locality, between the sun and the Tibetan Śambhala. Allusions to this third and most holy spot on earth may be found in all the great exoteric religions, and this spot is the summit of what in the Hindu Purānas is called Śveta-dvīpa, Mount Meru or Sumeru. It is the north pole of the earth, so chosen not for its geographical qualities, if such there be, but on account of its astronomical position. Of this region H.P.B. wrote in *The Secret Doctrine* (II, 6):

> This "Sacred Land" . . . is stated never to have shared the fate of the other continents; because it is the only one whose destiny it is to last from the beginning to the end of the Manvantara throughout each Round. It is the cradle of the first man and the dwelling of the last *divine* mortal, chosen as a *Sishta* for the future seed of humanity. Of this mysterious and sacred land very little can be said, except, perhaps, according to a poetical expression in one of the Commentaries, that the "pole-star has its watchful eye upon it, from the dawn to the close of the twilight of 'a day' of the GREAT BREATH."

Thus the stages or 'floors' of mankind's spiritual home are three: the ground floor is the beautiful and mysterious region of Śambhala; the next is the mystical north pole, geographically identical with the north pole of the earth, but mystically quite different; and the highest floor is the sun. On these floors live three separate classes of entities, with all of which the human race is in strait spiritual and intellectual union. From manhood we pass to mahatmahood, from mahatmahood we pass to quasi-divinity, and from quasi-divinity we become gods.

Life itself is a sublime adventure, a constant series of veils, beyond which the pilgrim passes, the one after the other. And each evolutionary initiation is a revelation in the sense of an unveiling, although strangely enough this means a re-veiling. And why? Because every time we receive a new light we are temporarily blinded by it, the increase in knowledge blinds us for the time being to all that is still higher. And we have to live through the new revelation until we learn that it is a re-veiling, and then we pass on to a higher revelation.

On the other hand, there is revelation in the sense of un-veiling, and this is initiation. Initiation is, in very truth, inspiration, and all the light side of nature is eternally at work in unveiling, in giving to ready souls, human and other, help and light, in fostering aspiration in the heart and leading on life's pilgrims towards ever-increasing vistas of grandeur.

Both revelation and independent research exist: there is individual progress, including spiritual, intellectual and psychological discovery; and there are also revealings in the sense of unveilings, and these are all either initiations or inspirations. Initiation is a short method of attaining light and evolutionary development, and therefore is it so difficult. But it is sublime.

The result of the higher grades of initiation, when successfully achieved, is that the divine or spiritual parts of the initiant are temporarily identified with his own individual egoic character or mind — his ego. This really takes place first in the fifth initiation, characterized as that is by the special attributes of man's mānasic nature, the mānasaputra within him. High adepts who have passed at least the fifth and probably the sixth initiation know and feel and realize the constant and living presence within themselves of the god within; and in different countries, in moments of internal ecstasy, they address this inner divinity by name. Some have called it Father, others call it Father-Fire, Father-Flame, Father-Spirit, or Father in Heaven; but always Father, because the spirit within us is the ultimate essence and origin and therefore the source of our being.

Consider what immense dignity and grandeur this fact gives to human life. It means that every human being is a feeble expression of a deific entity, and that he can become self-consciously at one with this inner god — which is his inmost self — in proportion as he becomes, by *willing it,* incorporated in such an identity.

The adept, for instance, who has achieved at least once this supernal union, thereby achieves a communion thereafter virtually at will. The lower sort of adepts, who nevertheless have attained somewhat of this grade, feel or sense this, their inmost being, as some other, but yet mysteriously identic; and in moments of danger or stress of any kind, by an effort of the will they rise into communion, and therefore union, with the inner divinity, calling upon it and drawing from it power. The higher grade of adepts sense or feel the unity perfectly, no longer as an exteriorization, as it were, of the individual's self, but as the individual's inmost Self.

This is the inner Buddha or Christ within the man. The identic experi-

531

ence may be had by any high adept, and in a smaller degree by any normal human being. It is a wonderful thought to feel that we have this perennial and inexhaustible source of spiritual and intellectual light and strength within us, unto which we may appeal, upon which we may draw, if only we rise unto it. This likewise in a sense is the essence of the avatāra-doctrine in its anupapādaka-aspect. This is the real thing to be achieved in initiation.

The way of growth is not a difficult way. It is called 'a steep and thorny path,' but is so only to the selfish, acquisitive, passional lower man. The way of the spirit is the way of light, of peace, of hope; it is the way to the sun. It is a glorious feeling that we hold our destiny in our hands, being of divine origin, and that at the heart of each one of us lives a god, and that we can climb the mystic ladder of life higher and higher, forever extending the range of our consciousness and the sphere of our activities from a planet to a solar system, and from a solar system to a galaxy, and from a galaxy to a universe, and from a universe to other combinations of universes, increasing ever endlessly in expanding consciousness, power, wisdom and love.

When moments of trial or difficulty come upon us and we turn inwards and rise along that mystic inner ladder, that flaming column of splendor within us, we become transfigured then for the time being; and if we can achieve this union, all that we do will be perfectly done, and we shall be virtually infallible in our judgment.

I have often felt that if I did nothing else for the rest of my days on earth but teach this doctrine in its many forms — turning it, fashioning it, so as to appeal to different minds — I would be doing more than if I taught details of occult philosophy for the same length of time, choosing many different manners of doing so. It is the basic doctrine of esoteric theosophy; the fundamental identity of the human being in his spirit with the spiritual hierarch of the universe.

XI

Death and the
Circulations of the Cosmos - I

THE ONENESS OF ALL LIFE

The spiritual Ego of man moves in Eternity like a pendulum between the hours of life and death. But if these hours marking the periods of terrestrial and spiritual life are limited in their duration, and if the very number of such stages in Eternity between sleep and awakening, illusion and reality, has its beginning and its end, on the other hand the spiritual "Pilgrim" is eternal. Therefore are the hours of his *post-mortem* life — when, disembodied he stands face to face with truth and not the mirages of his transitory earthly existences during the period of that pilgrimage which we call "the cycle of rebirths" — the only reality in our conception. Such intervals, their limitation notwithstanding, do not prevent the Ego, while ever perfecting itself, to be following undeviatingly, though gradually and slowly, the path to its last transformation, when that Ego having reached its goal becomes the divine ALL.

— H. P. B. in *Lucifer*, January 1889, p. 414

THERE IS PROBABLY no subject in the modern world about which so little of value is known and which nevertheless is held so deeply in feeling and thought as that of death. However much we may try to ignore the unpleasant fact of the dissolution of the body, and however much the habit of mockery at things unknown may sway the mind, everyone is interested in, speculates upon, and yearns to know more about death.

The teachings of the esoteric philosophy with respect to that phase of universal life called death are simple to grasp in general outline, though difficult in their more recondite aspects. The principal theme of all the great Mystery schools of antiquity, and of the ceremonials which reflected in dramatic form these inner teachings, was the 'adventures' which the human entity enters upon when the physical body is cast aside. The strongest emphasis was upon the fact that death and sleep are fundamentally the same, not different except in degree; that sleep is an imperfect death and death is a perfect sleep. This is the main key to all the teachings on death; because if we understand what happens during sleep, we will have the Ariadne's thread to a relative comprehension of what takes place at, during, and after, dying.

This is the path of study and training by which neophytes become finally able to remain fully self-conscious while the body is in sleep; and the adept or high chela, through the same training pushed to a still greater length, is able to remain fully aware and active on inner planes after the body dies. The man who has thus made himself more or less fully acquainted with the functions and characteristics of his own nature can, during his lifetime, travel self-consciously out of his body to other parts of the earth and, with increased power, even to other planets. But greater than this is the power to visit self-consciously the inner worlds which environ us, and to bring back a relatively complete recollection of the experiences and knowledge so gained. Indeed, all initiation reposes upon this very fact.

Death is not the opposite of Life, but actually is one of the modes of living — a modification of consciousness, a change from one phase of living to others in subservience to karmic destiny. It were impossible for any entity to live for an instant if he were not dying at the same time: as Paul phrases it, "I die daily." Every man 'dies' when he sleeps; likewise, because our bodies are in a state of constant change, their atoms are in a continuous process of renewal which is nothing but a kind of dying, and which so far as the atoms are concerned is not a relative but a complete death *for them*. Even while imbodied we are living in the midst of innumerable tiny deaths. As Heraclitus used to say, *panta rhei*, "all things stream along," in an unceasing state of flux.

Now this incessant movement of change, or of dyings and rebirths — whether these cycles be in time periods of a fraction of a second or be reckoned in millions of years — is, in the last analysis, governed by and expressive of the majestic heartbeat of the cosmic life, of which every entity or being is but a life-atom, highly or less evolved.

It was precisely this general picture of the incomprehensibly vast interacting and interblending revolvings of the armies of beings which was in the minds of ancient initiate-philosophers, as for instance those of India, when they turned with infinite yearning of soul towards the nirvana, in order to gain the aeon-long bliss of the jīvanmukta and surcease from the intricate cyclings on the wheel of life, as the Buddha phrased it.

We likewise can apply the above to our own lives since we are all involved in these whirling cycles of the evolutionary movements of the cosmic life, and thus our incarnations and dyings are but ringing the changes of our karmic destiny. Hence we see that neither the Christian nor the scientific view of death is true because both misconstrue the taking up and dropping of bodies as events standing alone, instead of being episodes which we as actors play in the uninterrupted evolutionary progress of our souls.

Death is but a change, a falling into the 'great sleep,' to be inevitably followed not only by a reincarnation or reproduction of oneself upon earth in a future punarjanman,° but likewise by intermediate karmic reproductions of oneself in the small in all the different mansions of life which compose the outer and inner realms of the twelvefold universe. It is these whirlings or revolvings of the monad through space and time which are alluded to in the Buddhist writings as samsāra,† and in the Qabbālāh as the gilgūlīm, and again by the mystical Greeks of certain philosophical schools as the kuklos kosmou, 'cycling of (or through) kosmos' — all of them expressing in different ways the monad's ceaseless peregrinations throughout the cosmic manvantara in and through all the houses of life. While this has particular reference to the human monad, it applies also to all other monads. For as I have so often stated, the monad which begins in any one cosmic manvantara as an unself-conscious god-spark ends as a full-blown self-conscious god with respect to that particular period of manvantaric time, because it has learned through its evolutionary livings and dyings, its imbodiments and metempsychoses therein, all the lessons that that cosmic manvantara enables it to experience.

The death of a man, then, is but a journeying through the spaces of Space, as the monad follows the circulations of the solar system on and through the seven sacred planets and the sun, after which it returns along the same pathways to earth to assume a new human body.

It were quite wrong to imagine that the monad itself is imbodied here on earth, and that after death it is disimbodied. In the first place, the monad is perennially on its own high plane and works through sheaths

---

° A Sanskrit compound: punar, again; janman, birth.

† A Sanskrit compound formed of the prefix sam, with, and sāra, from the verbal root sri, meaning 'to flow along' — a word which when used theosophically implies the modification of consciousness that the excarnate being undergoes by 'flowing along' the rivers of lives, otherwise the circulations of the solar system. These rivers of lives are in constant motion in and on all planes of the visible and invisible worlds. To illustrate: every life-atom, of whatever class, in the solar universe must enter and leave the sun at least once with every beating of the solar heart, and there is one such beat with every cycle of sunspots.

FOUNTAIN-SOURCE OF OCCULTISM

of consciousness. Consequently, during its post-mortem peregrinations on the inner planes, it is reclothed in every sphere of life that it visits with a sheath or 'body' strictly correspondential to the forces and substances of the different planes of the cosmos through which it passes, both on its ascent and on its descent. On the higher planes of our universe the very ethereal vehicles — kośas in Sanskrit — that it assumes and works through are to us arūpa, formless, only because they are so unlike the gross matter of our physical bodies that they are like sheaths of dazzling light. All things are relative; so that while we speak of these highly ethereal or indeed spiritual spheres and their inhabitants as being arūpa, other entities living in and on divine planes superior to them would regard these lofty beings as clothed in rūpas or forms.

The spiritual tragedy of the West has been the loss of the consciousness of the oneness of cosmic life with all manifested existence. Due to centuries of religious miseducation, and later to erroneous scientific teaching, man today looks upon himself almost instinctively as being something different from the universe. It was Descartes, the seventeenth-century French philosopher, who was instrumental in bringing about this loss of awareness in man's soul of his spiritual identity with the universe, for his philosophical doctrine was based on a supposititious difference between spirit and matter; and this, aided by the loss of spirituality in the teachings and life of the Christian Church, has adversely affected all subsequent philosophy and science in the West. Fortunately, the greatest exponents of modern scientific theory are once more returning, however unconsciously, to the archaic teachings that the soul of man is a spark of the anima mundi, and that force and matter are but two aspects of the same underlying Reality.

THE CAUSAL ASPECTS OF DEATH

ALTOGETHER TOO MUCH emphasis has been placed upon the various bodies or sheaths in man's constitution. These after all are merely temporary vehicles thrown around himself by the inner man who is a monad, a flaming ray from the solar divinity, a ray which descends through all the spheres of cosmic life-consciousness until it reaches this physical plane where it manifests through the substances, mainly of the heart and brain, of imbodied man. Conversely, death and its phases consist in a laying aside of sheath after sheath of consciousness in which the ray had enmeshed itself.

If a man wishes to know his post-mortem destiny, it is necessary to follow the peregrinations of the monadic consciousness per se, for death is primarily a change of consciousness, an enlargement of its sphere of action. He must begin by studying his true self which is his inner individual essence, following in thought this ray continually upwards and inwards along the different foci or consciousness-centers of his constitution.

Cyclical action in nature is but one of the modes by which cosmic karma expresses itself. To give just one illustration: the process of death in man is identic with that of the life-atoms of his physico-astral constitution. When a life-atom 'dies,' which means that its extremely brief imbodied life term is ended, it passes by efflux out of the physical into the astral body, and there with equal rapidity undergoes certain transformations before the jīva or monad of that life-atom ascends through the superior element-principles of man's constitution. Then, after a period of recuperative rest, such a life-atom descends again through the element-principles of man's inner constitution, down into his linga-śarīra and thence into the physical vehicle where anew, for its short life term, it helps to build the human body.

Following the same general character of peregrinating efflux, assimilation and rest in the devachan, and the succeeding influx into the astral light and the earth sphere, the human monads pursue their own courses. What the life-atom is to man's physical body, from one viewpoint and on strictly analogical lines, the human spiritual life-atom or human monad is to the earth globe. This likewise applies to all other entities. Herein lies the secret of the true nature of death, which is thus seen to be only another phase of the marvelously intricate webwork of the functions of universal Life.

The life of man on earth is but a stage in the journeying of an ever-unfolding conscious ego, the reimbodying ego, through the physical sphere, and death but the continuance of this journey out of this sphere of earth-being into another one. Physical death is in a very large part brought about by the fact that the unfolding field of human consciousness spreads beyond the capacity of the body to contain it, which, feeling the strains thus put upon it, gradually glides into senescence, finally to be cast aside as a worn-out garment. A short time before the end occurs, the inner principles of the lower quaternary begin to separate on their own planes, and the body makes automatic response to this incipient separation, thus bringing about the physical decline of old age. This point is of great importance, for it shows that physical death does not cause the dissolution of the bonds of the lower element-principles; on the contrary, the body dies *because* these lower invisible forces, substances, and energies — collectively speaking, the inner and causal life of the quaternary man — have already begun to separate, and the physical body, as time passes, naturally and inevitably follows suit.

The immortal part of man is obviously incomparably more compelling in power and pervading influence in causal realms than is the merely human ego; and hence there is a constant pull upwards to the superior spheres wherein the higher triad of man is native. This mighty spiritual-intellectual attraction acting on the higher part of the *intermediate* nature of the human constitution, combined with the wear and tear on the physico-astral compound during earth life, are the two main contributing causes of physical death. Death, therefore, is caused primarily from within, and only secondarily from without, and involves an attraction of the reimbodying ego upwards to spiritual-divine spheres, and the progressive decay of the astral-vital-physical vehicle.

It should be clear that it is not a *lack* of vitality which brings about physical death, or indeed its twin brother sleep, but rather a superabundance of prānic activity. As W. Q. Judge stated, it is this excess of prānic force which through the years so weakens the organs by the stress and strain put upon them by the vital flow of which they are the carriers, that their cohesion and molecular and even atomic power to perform their respective 'duties' or functions are finally destroyed.

540

It has been frequently said that every individual has a certain limited store of vitality, and that when this has been exhausted, the man must die. What is meant is that the vital-astral-physical organism as a composite entity not only has a certain power of *resistance* to the streams of prānic life pouring through it, but likewise has its own cohesive power arising in the prānas of the individual molecules and atoms which in their aggregate make the body. In other words, when the prānic energies of the entire constitution wear the body out so that it can no longer function smoothly, it begins to weaken, perhaps becomes diseased. It might be added that this applies likewise to every organ of the body; so that if an excessive strain is put upon any one, it is this organ which weakens first, and in extreme cases may throw the remaining organs into such disarray that disease or even death may ensue.

Closely connected with this subject is the matter of the 'lives' or life-atoms of which every part of our constitution is built. At one time they may be builders or preservers and, at another time, because of undue stress or of some other disintegrative influence, these same life-atoms may become destroyers. But extremes are always dangerous: if, for instance, a group of life-atoms is forcibly compelled to change their atomic and therefore natural and healthy mode of procedure, they then and there — either immediately or progressively — become destroyers instead of builders or preservers. Indeed, the matter of death being caused by an excess of vitality, and likewise a man's falling to sleep, rests upon the fact that the life-atoms of the body have reached a point where their resistance vanishes, or decreases as in sleep. Hence it is that the life-atoms function at one moment as builders or preservers, and at another as destroyers — even regenerators in a sense.

Death, in the vast majority of cases, is preceded by a certain time spent in the withdrawal of the monadic individuality or rather of the reimbodying ego, which takes place coincidentally with the separation of the seven-principled being that man is.° The reimbodying ego obeys so strongly the attraction inwards to the unspeakable bliss of the inner worlds that the golden cord of life connecting it with the lower triad is snapped. This is followed by immediate unconsciousness; for nature is very merciful in these things, being guided by quasi-infinite wisdom.

°The separative action precedes physical death by a varying number of months or even years, depending upon the individual, and is thus a preparation for its forthcoming existence in what is for it the next succeeding sphere of effects — the devachan.

Old age is therefore merely the physical resultant of the preparatory withdrawal of the reimbodying ego from self-conscious participation in the affairs of earth life. With a great deal of truth it may be compared to the period — extending for months or even years — preceding the birth of a child, during which time the returning ego has been undergoing quasi-conscious preparation for its 'death' in the devachan and its descent through the intermediate lower realms into the state appropriate for its imbodiment on this plane. The characteristic conditions of what is known as second childhood represent *one* of the several natural ways of passing out of this earth life. There is nothing harmful about it; the life is simply ebbing away, while a 'birth' is in preparation in the invisible realms.

The cause of senescence or senility in our present fifth root-race is that the buddhi and the ātman are but foreshadowed in their powers as the individual passes beyond middle age, and thus old age is not yet enlightened and strengthened by these higher principles. Similarly, in the fourth root-race, when kāma and kāma-manas were unfolding, the mānasaputric or higher mānasic element was only feebly manifesting as a distant radiance. Therefore the average Atlantean, although living on the whole much longer physically than we now do, had an intense and exceedingly vigorous and passional physical life up to middle age, and after a certain period there followed a quick drop in power succeeded by a long and lingering old age.

Towards the end of the seventh root-race of this round we shall have learned to live, at least partially so, in every one of our seven element-principles or monads, so that then, as death approaches, there will be continuous increase not only in spiritual and intellectual faculty, but likewise in psychical attributes. In other words, there will be no 'old' people, because the individual humans will grow steadily grander, stronger and more efficient in every part of their being — until an extremely short period preceding 'death,' which then will be an instantaneous sinking into unconsciousness, a sudden sleep-trance, followed by the dropping of the physical integument.

THE PROCESS OF DISIMBODIMENT

When a man is suffering a mortal pain his kinsmen surround him and, offering him affection, say: "Do you know me? Do you know me?" So long as his speech does not merge into his mind (manas), his mind into the life (prāna), the life into the fire (tejas), the fire into the Supreme Divinity — so long he knows.

Now when his speech is merged into the mind, the mind into the life, the life into the fire, the fire into the Supreme Divinity — then he knows not.

That which is his minuteness (ani), that is one's own essence, that is all, that is truth (satya), that is Ātman. That thou art, O Śvetaketu.
— *Chhāndogya-Upanishad*, VI, 15, 1–3

ANYONE WHO HAS studied the writings of H.P.B. will realize that all the different parts of the human constitution are represented in the ākāśic aura permeating and surrounding the human body, and that each one of these parts has its own vibrational rate, its own color and, indeed, its own fundamental musical note. During life this ākāśic aura — which is the most physical efflux of the auric egg — presents a really marvelous play of color, varying from instant to instant according to the play of thought or of emotion; it is by this means that the trained seer is able to tell from a single glance just what condition of mind or of emotion the man is in, and what his evolutionary status on the ladder of life. This fact has been seized upon by half-baked mystics, and has been so exaggerated and overworked that one hesitates to dwell upon it even briefly.

It is with reference to this ākāśic aura that the phrases 'the golden cord' or 'the silver thread' of life apply. As death approaches, which implies a withdrawal of the vital essence from the incarnated human being, this ākāśic aura is co-ordinately indrawn, and thus becomes steadily less strong in action; and at the moment of complete death, which means the severing of the vital aura from the physical body, this ākāśic aura is reduced to a single cord or thread which finally breaks. Now this cord is of one or another color; sometimes it looks golden, sometimes silver or bluish in tint, sometimes brownish or red or green, and again at other times of a dirty muddy tint — the color depending in each case upon the last thoughts fleeting through the mind of the dying man. Often also the seer observes the cord as parti-colored — golden in its highest parts, verging into indigo-blue with an occasional flash of green, or at times it is shot with red, and the lowest part may be silver or violet.

In all cases the various prānas are involved, because they are the vital field in which the elements of man's constitution work and express themselves. Indeed, this cord is composed of the substance of several of the prānas which progressively leave the tissues and finally the vital organs of the body. When thus deprived of its psycho-vital-magnetic prānic life, the body thereupon is 'dead,' very much as the light bulb, when the electric current is switched off, glows for a short instant and then is dark.

The exact time of the snapping of the cord-filament is not the last breath, nor again even the last beat of the heart, although both of these do mark the moment of apparent death, which is the same as saying the moment of the vanishing of the larger part of the vital cord. For, as long as the panorama of the past life's experiences is passing through the brain, which occurs in all cases of death, there still remains a slender strand of the filament. Only when the panorama finally becomes blank unconsciousness does this last feebly glowing strand disappear — and this is the complete death of the body. *Rigor mortis* begins instantly then, this being an automatic auric reaction expressing itself as a temporary immobility or 'stiffness' of the prānas latent in the corpse which linger on in a vegetative condition before they fade away.

There is a curious connection between the snapping of the vital cord at death, and the first entrance of the vital influx into the foetus. Just as the breaking of the last strand of the cord means the beginning of complete death, so the first movement of the child in the womb means the first moment of true entrance into the unborn body of the monadic egoic ray from within-above. Then, when the child is born, its first breath is a more or less automatic astral-physical reaction to stimulus from within combined with stimulus from without.

The process of death is complicated. Roughly, the heart 'dies' first, and the brain is the last organ to be quitted by the vital cord. Yet, even after the heart stops, there remains a glowing point therein connected with the active ākāśa still functioning in the brain and producing the panorama of the past life — this glowing point in the heart vanishing an instant before the last thread of the vital filament disappears. As a general rule the withdrawal of the auric essence begins at the lower extremities and gradually proceeds upwards to the heart, where it pauses briefly and then ascends along the spinal cord into the brain.

However, it would be erroneous to suppose that all the prāṇas of the incarnated man, considered as an aggregate, leave by way of the brain only. Every orifice of the body during the process of dying becomes a vent or organ of expulsion for the corresponding prāṇa which during life works in and out through such orifice. The generative passages, the anus and the navel, emit certain lower parts of the human vital aura; while the heart, as said, finds its avenue of egress through the spinal cord to the brain. That portion of the imbodied astral, which is the carrier of the intermediate higher effluxes of the ego, leaves the physical vehicle in what would seem to be a cloud of vapor, passing out mainly through the mouth and nostrils. Another portion of the vitality leaves through the ears and eyes. The part of the astral man which, while imbodied, has been the organ of the spiritual and nobler intellectual elements of the constitution, exits the body through what is known in ancient Hindu writings as the brahmarandhra, which is generally described as an aperture or mystical opening in the top of the head in the vicinity of the pineal gland. Thus do the prāṇas of the body and of the liṅga-śarīra abandon their grip on the molecules and atoms of the physical body, and, leaving these with their own especial prāṇas, withdraw into the auric egg of the departing entity.

When we speak of the astral man, we refer specifically to the liṅga-śarīra and its withdrawal from the body of the dying man; in fact, once that death has taken place, the liṅga-śarīra hovers around and over the corpse, although linked to it by innumerable tenuous threads of astral prāṇic substance — what one might call electric or magnetic stuff. Actually, as pointed out, *every* orifice of the body exudes its own appropriate part of the astral man as a cloud of vapor; and, likewise, every molecule and atom of the body of the dying man gives up its own portion of the general prāṇas, which wrench themselves free from such molecular and atomic bonds, thus bringing to pass the 'explosion' or outburst of light or radiation which occurs at the moment of death.°

°Physical vital electricity, however ethereal and tenuous to our perceptions, is nevertheless quite substantial; and, indeed, the prāṇas of our physical plane, and almost equally so of our astral plane, are substances relatively material when compared with the prāṇas of the higher parts of the human constitution.

It may be of interest to append here a few remarks on the various methods of disposing of the body after death. The practices of mummification or of embalming, as these have been followed by different ancient peoples, and even in our own time by those who wish to keep the body from decay as long as they can, are not good, for the reason that they are an attempt to prevent the transmigration of the life-atoms.

These practices originated in the degenerate times of Atlantis when devachans were short and reimbodiments occurred in fairly rapid succession because of the widespread lack of spirituality among the peoples which then inhabited the earth. The sorcerers and magicians of that period, for unholy reasons of their own, tried to interfere with nature's purifying processes, by embalming and mummifying their dead; they hoped that by the time the ego was next incarnated these mummified bodies would still be intact. Sometimes when this actually happened the mummified cadavers were burned, in order then to free the life-atoms so that these might return to the new body of the reincarnated ego.

Now the embalming and mummification of the body was in part futile, because it had no effect whatsoever on any life-atoms superior to or more ethereal than the lowest astral and physical ones. But the attempt was also in part successful, for the grossest and most physicalized classes of the life-atoms, which otherwise would have pursued the most material circulations of transmigration, were kept from such circulations.

Therefore, when the entity returned to reincarnation after a few thousand years, it received these life-atoms in almost the identic condition to what they previously had been so far as the stamp of experience on them was concerned. These particular life-atoms were thus retarded in their own natural evolutionary journey. It is enough to say that the practice is without moral justification.

As just said, mummification originated in an act of Atlantean black magic — an attempt to thwart nature's all-wise and just processes. Likewise did it arise out of a very typical Atlantean view of the great importance of the material universe and of material life. The custom persisted through the ages long after its meaning was forgotten, and was continued by many Atlanto-Aryan peoples such as the Peruvians, the Egyptians, and others. (The Egyptians and Peruvians, however, were not true Atlanteans, but belonged to some of the carry-over Atlantean stocks living with the new peoples of the Aryan root-race.) It was a part of the heavy Atlantean karma still remaining in our fifth root-race, and expressing itself in material guise.

Far better was the custom of the earliest Aryans to give the bodies of their dead to the cleansing flame, thus freeing the life-atoms as soon as possible and allowing the splendor within to wing its way into the inner worlds without even the shadow of an attraction earthwards, which a dead body does provide. Dust to dust, souls to sun, and spirit to parent star — was the creed of our Aryan forefathers.

Cremation helps the astral body to disintegrate sooner than is the case when the physical body is allowed to decay in the grave, because both the astral body and the cadaver are very intimately conjoined physically and magnetically. In fact they disintegrate almost atom for atom (the only exception being that the skeleton due to its heavy mineral chemical composition may outlast even the astral 'skeleton' of the linga-śarīra). As long as the body is decaying in its coffin, the linga-śarīra hovers around it; and just so long is the kāma-rūpa to a certain extent psychomagnetically drawn to the neighborhood of the grave.

Fire is an electrical phenomenon, a manifestation of prānic electricity. Its influence is usually disruptive, but it is also the great constructive builder of the universe, and that is why some of the ancients worshiped it. Physical fire can dissolve nothing beyond its own range of action; it disintegrates the physical molecules and breaks up the cohesion of the chemical atoms and thus sets them free. Cremation, therefore, has no effect whatsoever on the life-atoms, except to hasten the process of chemical dissociation of atom from atom; instead of the slow 'burning' through the years by oxidation, cremation is a quick method of bringing about the same thing.

When a man is truly dead, there is absolutely nothing in him that is in the remotest sense cognizant of what is taking place when the body is cremated — except possibly a vague and pleasant sense of being liberated. This feeling arises because the consuming of the body by fire, and consequently of the linga-śarīra, frees the kāma-rūpa quickly; and in the case of average men, the kāma-rūpa rises into the higher regions of the kāma-loka out of the astral dregs thereof.

Once that the golden cord of life is snapped, there is nothing physical on earth that can disturb the passing of the soul. Nevertheless, about thirty-six hours at least should ensue between the last breath and the disposal of the physical shell. Preferably, funeral services should be short, simple, and with deference to the love that the deceased evoked in the hearts of others.

Among people who fear death, who expect to go to 'heaven' and yet shrink from that beatific experience with every atom of their being, there seems to be a paradoxical instinct to regard this very natural occurrence as a time of woe and desolation. In truth, there is more need for mourning over the birth of a little child than there is for the passing of one who has gone into supernal happiness.

THE PANORAMIC VISION

At the last moment, the whole life is reflected in our memory and emerges from all the forgotten nooks and corners picture after picture, one event after the other. The dying brain dislodges memory with a strong supreme impulse, and memory restores faithfully every impression entrusted to it during the period of the brain's activity. That impression and thought which was the strongest naturally becomes the most vivid and survives so to say all the rest which now vanish and disappear for ever, to reappear but in Deva Chan. No man dies insane or unconscious — as some physiologists assert. Even a *madman*, or one in a fit of *delirium tremens* will have his instant of perfect lucidity at the moment of death, though unable to say so to those present. The man may often appear dead. Yet from the last pulsation, from and between the last throbbing of his heart and the moment when the last spark of animal heat leaves the body — the *brain thinks* and the *Ego* lives over in those few brief seconds his whole life over again. Speak in whispers, ye, who assist at a death-bed and find yourselves in the solemn presence of Death. Especially have you to keep quiet just after Death has laid her clammy hand upon the body. Speak in whispers, I say, lest you disturb the quiet ripple of thought, and hinder the busy work of the Past casting on its reflection upon the Veil of the Future.

— *The Mahatma Letters*, pp. 170–1

THE PANORAMIC REVIEW usually begins when all the bodily activities and functions have ceased, sometimes indeed before the last heartbeat, and, as a rule, continues after the heart has stopped and the last breath has been expired. It is impossible to state how long this takes, because the length of the review varies so tremendously with the individual. In the case of those of high spirituality, the whole process is completed within a few hours; in that of others, it may be up to twelve hours, possibly longer. Probably six hours on the average is required for this last visioning of the māyā of the life just lived. But in all instances the panoramic vision occurs because the brain is suffused with the fleeting scintillations still reaching it from the feathery tendrils of the cord of life, which grows progressively thinner and thinner as the hours pass.

Such a panorama occurs even when a man dies suddenly as the result of some terrible accident, as for instance when the brain is blown to pieces or when the body is burned alive. In these cases, the panorama takes place in the higher parts of the astral brain, which, although it is seriously affected, especially in its more material parts, nevertheless endures as a cohering organ somewhat longer than does the physical brain.

In extreme old age the panorama begins in a vague and tentative manner some days or possibly weeks before physical death, and this is really the cause of the dazed condition that very old people frequently fall into shortly before they die.

Every incident, fact, event, thought, and emotion of a man's life is recorded in the different parts of his being: the emotional events in the kāma-mānasic part; the mental in the mānasic aspect of his constitution; and the spiritual in the buddhi-mānasic, etc.; while the linga-śarīra and the physical body are themselves permanently marked and often noticeably changed by the experiences undergone throughout the incarnation.

The panorama occurs in all its wondrous detail — no thought or point of action being omitted — because it is the result of instinctive action by the human monad, which, almost unconsciously to itself, dislodges from every secret recess of its inner records, imprinted as these are on its own vital substance, all the details of the life just past. Due to the spiritual forces at work, which are strictly harmonic and karmic, consciousness automatically functions in opening up the panorama by beginning with the first incident that memory has recorded in the life last past, and thereafter proceeds in stately pageantry of imagery until the last thought is reached, the last emotion felt, the last intuition had — and then comes unconsciousness, complete, sudden, and infinitely merciful. This is true death.

Now such a panorama cannot possibly take place in its fullness during the normal lifetime of the man, because his consciousness is so distracted by the manifold events in which he is living, that there is no opportunity for this. What we call memory is merely the ability to read more or less accurately the mental and physiological impressions stamped upon our auric egg, which impressions are carried by the auric flow to the body where they enter the texture of the physical brain and nervous system, and by reaction often make themselves felt as memories of the past.

It is a most marvelous thing that the human consciousness through its body and its various organs not only records with amazing accuracy every mental and emotional event that occurs from day to day, but even photographs on the registers of the inner being an incomprehensibly immense number of sense- and brain- and nerve-impressions of which the everyday consciousness is scarcely aware at all. Yet during the vision every single one of these incidents passes swiftly before the watching eye of the inner man, just preceding his passing from this plane.

Those around the dying often hear them muttering faintly of the events of early childhood, but not understanding this have supposed that it is a vision of heaven, or something of the kind. It is merely the mouth repeating what the brain sees — memories passing in review; and back, behind, stands the seeing Self and judges the past life, and its judgment is infallibly true. It sees the record of things done or undone, the thoughts had, the emotions followed, the temptations conquered or succumbed to; and when the end of the panorama is reached, it sees the justice of it all. In view of its vision of past karma it knows what is coming in the next life.°

There is a similar panoramic visioning of the past life, but in less vivid and complete degree, at what is called the second death in the kāma-loka. But this is not all, for there is a third recurrence of such a panorama before rebirth, i.e. just before the human monad leaves its devachanic dreaming and becomes again unself-conscious preceding reimbodiment in the human womb. The completeness and accuracy in detail in each case depend upon the type of the ego, for there is no ironclad

---

°To make a practice of reviewing the incidents of the day when one is preparing for sleep, is exceedingly important. Its effect is that of accustoming the mind to consider one's life as a field of action involving responsibility in conduct, giving one the opportunity to draw lessons therefrom. It likewise has the effect on the mind of initiating a habit of panoramic visioning, thus making the self-conscious realization of the events passing before the mind's eye at the moment of death far easier, quicker, and more complete. This habit has also the highly beneficial result of shortening the second panoramic review preceding the second death.

Such ethical or moral examination of the day's events is one of the best possible aids in inducing wisdom in meeting life's problems, and bringing about through reflection, even if more or less unconsciously performed, a spirit of kindliness and understanding for others. A great deal of unnecessary friction and trouble in the world arises out of the mechanical way in which we live in our minds, without adequate self-examination, with little or no analysis of our daily actions and of the thoughts and emotions which bring these actions about. Of course I do not here refer to unwholesome or morbid introspection, but rather to the careful, honest practice of reviewing impartially and critically, as an observer, one's thoughts and deeds. It is a great help in strengthening our moral intuitions.

rule which applies to everyone. There are variations of quality and intensity in all these visionings, depending upon the degree of evolution attained by the human ego.

In the case of individuals of unusual spiritual status, the panorama preceding death (and equally the one which takes place before leaving devachan) often contains glimpses into the second or third preceding lives and possibly into a more distant period in the human ego's past. The ability to see panoramically into the near or distant past of the human ego is proportionate to the degree of spirituality that has been unfolded: the more spiritual the ego, the greater is the power to look into the past; and, indeed, in high chelas or mahatmas this ability becomes active even during imbodied life. Just how far into the remote past the mahatma can delve — if he should want to — depends not only upon his evolved ability, but upon his *will* to do so; for most of them dislike peering into their former lives.°

Even the average man at rare intervals has glimpses not only into a past life or lives, but likewise prophetically into the future. However, he is so slightly trained to recognize these visions for what they actually are — records stamped in the fabric of his own auric egg or on the astral light — that he usually looks upon them as mere dreaming or phantasy. Since he is not evolved enough either to understand what he might see or to discriminate with any degree of accuracy between imagination and the actual auric records, it is downright dangerous for him to attempt to see into the past or future. At the same time it is not to be overlooked that sometimes in disease, or in a trance often brought about by disease, the sufferer may have distorted visions or pictures of the records in the astral light or in his auric egg, but in these cases, being so different from the true panorama occurring at death, the visioning is confused and distorted, and sometimes of so horrible a character as to leave the unfortunate sufferer in a cold sweat of helpless terror.

Those unfortunate people who want to see their past lives simply do not know what they are asking for. Could they do so and realize what the records would include, along with the obvious good that they had done, the likelihood is that they would do everything in their power utterly to erase the pictures from their memory. What normal man would like to look back into all the weak, heartless and ignoble thoughts and deeds

---

°Cf. *The Mahatma Letters*, p. 145.

recorded by him on nature's picture gallery during lives lived long ago?[*]

Also many people have periods of reminiscence when there seems to be an inflow of the events of early childhood, which memories later subside. This has nothing whatsoever to do with the situation which occurs at death, nor even in seeing one's past lives, but happens simply because the nervous system and brain are at the time in vibrational harmony with the records in one's auric egg, and the brain thus automatically registers these vague and transitory pictures of memory, enabling one to live for a while in the returned consciousness of former years. These cases are fairly common. Commenting upon the subject of memory at the moment of death, H.P.B. says in one of her articles:[†]

The fact is that the human brain is simply the canal between two planes — the psycho-spiritual and the material — through which every abstract and metaphysical idea filters from the Manasic down to the lower human consciousness. Therefore, the ideas about the infinite and the absolute are not, nor can they be, within *our* brain capacities. They can be faithfully mirrored only by our Spiritual consciousness, thence to be more or less faintly projected on to the tables of our perceptions on this plane. Thus while the records of even important events are often obliterated from our memory, not the most trifling action of our lives can disappear from the "Soul's" memory, because it is no MEMORY for it, but an ever present reality on the plane which lies outside our conceptions of space and time. . . . while physical memory in a healthy living man is often obscured, one fact crowding out another weaker one, at the moment of the great change that man calls death — that which we call "memory" seems to return to us in all its vigour and freshness.

May this not be due as just said, simply to the fact that, for a few seconds at least, our two memories (or rather the two states, the highest and the lowest state, of consciousness) blend together, thus forming one, and that the dying being finds himself on a plane wherein there is neither past nor future, but all is one present? Memory, as we all know, is strongest with regard to its early associations, then when the future man is only a child, and more of a soul than of a body; and if memory is a part of our Soul, then, as Thackeray has somewhere said, it must be of necessity eternal.

---

[*]Such a stage of remembrance of the details of our past incarnations, so far as the normal man is concerned, will not take place until our earth is inhabited by a race of far more gloriously evolved beings than we are; and this is very fortunate. The exceptions to this rule, as said, are the masters and some of the high chelas, not those who may lay claim to this so-called faculty or power.

[†]"Memory in the Dying," *Lucifer*, Oct. 1889, pp. 128–9.

These wonderful processes of the consciousness whereby the man sees the entirety of the life just ended, and realizes the utter justice of all that he has suffered or enjoyed, are in no sense an effort of the will of the reimbodying ego, but are automatic procedures of the functioning of its own substance. The soul-consciousness of the ego, watching this life-review, is for the time being entirely oblivious of everything else except this panoramic vision. The ego receives an indelible impression which remains with it throughout the devachanic interlude and aids in guiding it to the proper environment for its next physical rebirth.

To recapitulate: every human being who is 'average' — neither highly spiritual and far advanced, nor extremely gross and materialistic — has three panoramic visions: the first, just preceding complete death of the physical body; the second, just prior to and at the time of the second death in the higher kāma-lokic planes, meaning the dropping of the kāma-rūpa and the beginning of the entrance into the devachan; the third, after leaving the devachan and before the subsequent unconsciousness begins immediately preceding entrance of the egoic ray into the womb. This third panoramic vision likewise has something of a prophetic quality about it, for the human ego, thus preparing for the gestation preceding the birth into the physical body, not only sees its past but also has glimpses into the future, and recognizes the justice and the karmic need of the kind of physical environment and body it is entering into.

Now those human beings who are exceedingly gross and materialistic have no devachan, and consequently no true second death, and therefore practically no second panoramic vision; hence they are almost immediately attracted to reincarnation on earth again. They have the first panoramic vision, an adumbration of the second, but no third vision preceding rebirth. Others, such as lost souls and sorcerers of low grade have in every case the panoramic vision at death, always accordant with their psycho-intellectual power, but they can have no devachan. In the cases of congenital idiots and infants who die, these have no panoramic vision whatsoever because they have nothing in the life on earth just closed self-consciously to recollect or to review, the mānasic faculty being either 'dormant,' or not yet awakened within them.

Of course, those highly spiritual beings who have not yet learned to live self-consciously after death, have all three panoramic visions.

THE PRĀNAS OR VITAL ESSENCES

This life (prāna) is born from Ātman.

As in the case of a person there is this shadow extended, so it is in this case. By the action of the mind it comes into this body.

As an overlord commands his overseers, saying: "Superintend such and such villages," even so this life (prāna) controls the other life-breaths one by one.

The out-breath (apāna) is in the organs of excretion and generation. The life-breath (prāna) as such establishes itself in the eye and ear, together with the mouth and nose. While in the middle is the equalizing breath (samāna), for it is this that equalizes whatever has been offered as food. From this arise the seven flames.

In the heart, truly, is the self (ātman). Here there are those hundred and one arteries. To each one of these belong a hundred smaller arteries. To each of these belong seventy-two thousand branching arteries. Within them moves the diffused breath (vyāna).

Now, rising upward through one of these [arteries], the up-breath (udāna) leads in consequence of good work to the good world; in consequence of evil, to the evil world; in consequence of both, to the world of men.

The sun (Āditya), verily, rises externally as life; for it is that which helps the life-breath in the eye. The divinity which is in the earth supports a person's out-breath (apāna). What is between, namely space (ākāśa), is the equalizing breath (samāna). The wind (vāyu) is the diffused breath (vyāna).

Heat (tejas), verily, is the up-breath (udāna). Therefore one whose heat has ceased goes to rebirth, with his senses sunk in mind (manas).

Whatever is one's thinking, therewith he enters into life (prāna). His life joined with his heat, together with the self (ātman), leads to whatever world has been fashioned [in thought].

— Praśna-Upanishad, III, 3–10 (based on R. E. Hume's translation)

THE FUNCTION AND THE character of the prānas in the human body are reckoned as ten and even twelve in esotericism, yet they also are spoken of as being seven, for the same reasons that the planetary chain is usually stated as consisting of seven globes instead of the full number twelve. However, we use the term prāna as a generalizing word to signify the aggregate of psycho-vital-astral fluids which the prānas really are. We may otherwise call them the vital essences.

555

Even in mediaeval Europe — which of course drew its ideas from ancient Greek and Roman writings — pretty much the same conception of the human body, as being an entity infilled with vital spirits and with humors, prevailed until a relatively recent time, when these were rejected by medical science, which laughed at the superstitions of our forefathers. Nevertheless, these vital spirits and humors corresponded, however imperfectly, to the prānic fluids of ancient Hindu teaching — considered to be both ethereal essences and physical humors. From early mediaeval times up to the recent present, medicine consistently taught that normal physical health in the human body was maintained when these vital spirits and humors were operating in equilibrium, and that disease and even death were products of their malfunctioning. The archaic ages were unanimous in their agreement on these points.

Exoteric Hindu writings usually give their number as five: (1) Prāna,° 'a breathing forth,' and hence the vital essence which controls the respiration, particularly the outbreathing, the inbreathing or reflex action of the lungs is considered to be an automatic adjustment of the function. Its organ or seat is the lungs. (2) Vyāna, 'a breathing around or apart,' the vital psycho-astral-physical fluid governing the circulations, whether of the blood or the nerves, and therefore its organs are the veins and arteries on the one hand, and the nerves as the higher aspects of the general circulatory function on the other hand. (3) Samāna, 'a breathing together or around,' the breath or essence which has to do with controlling the digestive function as well as the assimilation and distribution of fluids; its organs are the stomach, the bowels, etc. (4) Apāna, 'a breathing down or away,' signifying a throwing off, governing the organs of excretion. (5) Udāna, 'a breathing upwards or above,' the vital essence which causes upward circulatory movement. Its locus is in the navel with corresponding sympathetic loci in the heart and the spinal column; it controls the movement of the vital essence from the lower organs upwards into the skull.

There are two higher 'prānas': the organ of one is located in the heart and the other in the head. Likewise, there are five other secret 'prānas,' which pertain not so much to the body as to the circulatory 'breathings' or movements of ātmic spirit and buddhi-manas in and throughout the human constitution.

° A Sanskrit compound: *pra*, forth; *an*, to breathe, this verbal root being found in the terms for all the prānas.

All the different prānas of the ākāśic vital stream really make up the completely imbodied man, because they are the vital fields, or what are sometimes spoken of as the nervous fluids, in and through which the finer spiritual, intellectual, and psychical essences work and manifest themselves. When all the prānas are properly balanced, and no one or more of them is either over-stimulated or sub-active, then the man is healthy throughout his entire constitution. This is why any attempt to meddle with these prānic currents — by yoga or psychic practice — brings about a change in the human constitution, which practice when conducted through ignorant experimentation, as is almost always the case, will invariably result in disease and very likely in subsequent death, or else in psychical and mental disturbance.

The various prānas are not merely vital winds, as the term is commonly translated, but *are streams or flows of psycho-astral substance which work in the body as substantial energies.* They are all formed of excessively minute particles or atomic units or entities, which indeed are the same as the life-atoms.

In the last analysis, a man's body is built out of these prānic streams of atomic particles. Furthermore, all the prānas which manifest themselves in the human body are the psycho-astral-physical expression of corresponding and causative currents of vitality in the auric egg. Indeed, they are the vital energic form which the auric egg takes on the physical plane; and the auras, which these prānas exude, producing something like a vapor or mist around the body, are their psychomagnetic atmosphere. In other words, the prānas are the vehicle of expression for all the higher attributes and qualities of the human constitution.

The prānas find their respective fields of action in the auric egg, from which they manifest in the physical body, which is the most material concretion of the grosser aspects of the auric egg. Corresponding to the various physical organs, including the different nervous ganglia or plexuses, there are equivalently active centers or foci or ganglia in the auric egg; and indeed, these latter are the originants or auric causes which produce their effects as corresponding centers or organs in the physical body.

Thus it is that the physical body receives the seven or ten prānas from the auric egg which, in its turn, receives them from the monadic centers in the human constitution — ranging from the ātman down to the physical body. Due to the unceasing activity of the forces or energies at work in man, these forces flow forth from the different monadic foci of his constitution as streams of vitality, i.e. currents of life-atoms, into the various layers of the auric egg. These streams of vital force actually compose the auric egg, with its compounded vital fluids and their characteristic auric qualities or swabhāvas; and thence from the various layers of the auric egg these prānic auras are reflected into the different organs or centers or chakras of the physical body.

Thus, then, the complete man during incarnation, when viewed as an objective entity, presents a most marvelous picture of interacting and continuously coruscating streams of prānic vitality, which in the higher ranges are like currents of flowing light, and in their lower ranges are like streams of quasi-material vitality.° What we call magnetism and electricity, each being the alter ego of the other, are but prānic or vital psychomagnetic flows of life. In the manifested cosmos, they are two aspects of the vital activity of our solar hierarch, interblending and combining with the vital magnetism and electricity of our planetary chain, and again with the magnetism and electricity of our globe earth — these cosmic forces representing in the solar system what the different prānas are in the human constitution.

Hence, man on earth, and equivalently other beings on other planets, is surrounded not only by all the prānas of the solar system and of the planetary chains, but likewise by the twelve cosmic magnetisms or electricities flowing into the solar system from the zodiacal constellations which surround it. Bearing this in mind, and remembering which planets are ruled by which houses of the zodiac — modern Occidental astrologers incorrectly say that the planets rule the signs — the student may correlate the swabhāvas of the different prānas of man not only to the swabhāvas of the planets but likewise to the prānic swabhāvas of the zodiacal houses or constellations.

During the lifetime of a man, all these prānas are more or less at work in his constitution. (In one sense, the only difference between a mahatma and an average man is that the mahatma centers his consciousness in his higher prānas, leaving the other prānas to do their quasi-automatic labors in the lower parts of the constitution.) That is why man during

---

°Frequent mention has been made in theosophical literature of the 'nervous fluids' of the physical body. The fact is there are as many nervous fluids in man's physical frame as there are prānas, these being but another name for the seven or ten prānas working in and through the nervous system. It is the prānas which cooperate in producing the general flow of nervous energy or force or nervous vitality.

incarnation is like a pillar of dazzling light, of which the top portion seems to vanish into the colorless glory of infinity, while the intermediate and lower parts grow progressively more concrete and more pronounced in color until, when the body is reached, the prānas become gross and heavy and furnish the combined swabhāva of the imbodied animal monad.

When a man dies, these prānas are successively indrawn by regular stages from the bottom upwards until the human ego undergoes the second death in the kāma-loka, sinks into its dreaming or swapna condition, and enters the devachan in the bosom of the spiritual monad. The prānas, which have been able to rise thus far, then re-enter the monads that originally gave them birth when the ego had previously descended from its devachan into incarnation. This is what is meant by the statement that the prānas return to their respective sources in nature.

Finally, it may be said that even the loftiest activities of the human being, such as consciousness, intellection, intuition, etc., are merely different ways of describing the swabhāvas of the divine and spiritual prānic forces pouring forth from the monads in the human constitution which are on its higher planes. The significance of this is that all of nature is but imbodied life, otherwise imbodied consciousness, thought, intelligence. It is the highest which produce the lower; so that the vital flows or fluids on the manifested planes, and therefore in and through the physical body, are but the expression of the higher vitality manifesting itself on the lower and lowest planes.

PHYSICAL DEATH – AN ELECTROMAGNETIC PHENOMENON

When the Self (ātman), having fallen into a state of weakness, enters into unconsciousness, as it were, then the life-currents (prānas) gather around it. Seizing wholly these shining elements, it then enters the heart. When the Spirit of the eye moves away in a circle, it loses knowledge of form.

"He becomes one, he does not see," they say. "He becomes one, he does not smell," they say. "He becomes one, he does not taste," they say. "He becomes one, he does not speak," they say. "He becomes one, he does not hear," they say. "He becomes one, he does not think," they say. "He becomes one, he does not touch," they say. "He becomes one, he does not know," they say. Then the entrance of the heart becomes luminous. By way of this radiance, the Self takes its exit, either from the eye, or from the head, or from other parts of the body. When it departs, the life (prāna) departs after it; when the life departs, all the vital airs depart. It becomes endowed with perception; it enters into that perception; knowledge and deeds, and the realization of the past, unite together and pervade it.

— *Brihadāranyaka-Upanishad*, IV, 4, 1–2

THERE IS NO ESSENTIAL difference between the death of a sun and that of a man or of the smallest atom. The details are different, that is all. The death of a sun produces an instantaneous vanishing of the sun's body of light, which is grosser than the light of the spiritual realms, but nevertheless light; and light is energy, and energy is matter. Similarly, a man's body, or the body of an atom, in fact all physical matter, is but compacted light. As the sun is a divine being, it clothes itself with an appropriate vehicle of pure ethereal light, not gross or concreted light such as our bodies are. Consequently, when the divine flame of the sun is withdrawn (which is what death is), its component atoms are dispersed in the winking of an eye, and this dispersion causes a glory, a spread of light, throughout enormous realms of space.

In the case of man, when the divine flame is withdrawn, which occurs also like a flash of lightning, the body, being too gross and heavy to fall instantly apart and vanish, still coheres as a corpse until the chemical work of the atoms among themselves brings about physical dissolution.

Our bodies are radiating light constantly, light of many colors, beautiful at times, repulsive at others. A human being in a passion of anger or hatred, for instance, sends forth light from his whole physical being in a stream which is coarse, red, fiery, and hateful to see, and by reaction produces feelings of hate in others whom this evil light touches. Contrariwise, a man whose heart is filled with impersonal love, radiates this constantly, especially in those moments when he is acting under the urge of compassion — even his physical body then sends forth streams of light of indescriptible beauty, of opalescent glory. This is the secret of the nimbus or aureole said to surround the heads of saints. Every human being has such a nimbus. Light, however, is not the only thing that emanates from the body; odors likewise do so. Some animals are more sensitive to the light-emanations, while others are more sensitive to the odors.

During one's lifetime, every emotion is accompanied by similar radiations of light, each of its own quality and kind, yet all expressing themselves by reaction through the aura of the physical body; and this is why the adept, watching a man under emotional or mental or even spiritual stress, is able to ascertain just what movement of consciousness is thus affecting the aura.

Man is a dynamo of energies. Everything he does, every thought he has, every emotion he feels, produces a corresponding effect throughout his entire constitution. At death, the rupturing of the cord of life is the result of the action of energy — energy suddenly loosed, which must produce its effect. Because of this, death cannot happen without causing an explosion of light-atoms which flow forth from every pore of his physical body. This explosion of light when the body blazes for an instant in glory — invisible to ordinary eyesight — is not something unique, for the same is true in greater or less degree of every entity, from suns and stars to animals and plants. It is but a larger exemplification of the process that occurs in radioactive disintegration of certain chemical elements, such as uranium, thorium, and radium. This dissociation of the atoms results from what we may perhaps graphically describe as the death of the respective atomic and subatomic particles.

It is a most interesting fact that every motion, whether on the macrocosmic or on the microcosmic scale, is accompanied by an emission of light; and light is an electromagnetic phenomenon expressing itself as a radiation. In fact, any moving entity, any movement anywhere, such as

561

the raising of our arm, the waving of a tree branch in the wind, the spark brought forth by the striking of steel on flint, or the whirling of the electron, invariably produces a flash, or conglomerate of tiny flashes, all of an electromagnetic character.

From the standpoint of causes, all these movements are produced by the electromagnetic vitality of innumerable hosts of lives and of living beings which are everywhere around us; for magnetism and electricity are but manifestations of the vitality of the solar system as well as of our earth, uniting in a fascinating web with all the interacting forces of the individual vitalities of the entities contained in these macrocosmic bodies. But this is not all: the very thought expressed as will — such as that which brings about the movement of the arm — sets into vital-electric activity the particles of the brain, molecular, atomic and astral; and each such tiny motion of the atoms of the brain answering the thought-command emits its particular flash of radiation.

Coming then to the point, the radiations or explosions of light, which enwrap the physical body at the moment of death, are brought about by the sudden withdrawal or ruptured connections of the various prānas from the molecules and atoms which compose the body. Such outburst of light lasts but a few fugitive instants. The body thereafter is an 'inanimate' corpse, although of course every one of its molecules and atoms contains its own swābhāvic prānas.

Finally, the intensity and volume of the light that exudes from the body at death vary in degree and in quality with the character of the dying man. When death takes place suddenly and with the body in full strength and maturity of years, the explosion of light is correspondingly intense and voluminous and probably of very brief duration; whereas in the case of a man's dying of old age, or passing out quietly in his sleep, or after a long illness, the outburst of luminous radiation is correspondingly less intense and less in volume because more protracted in time.

The concept of science with regard to electricity and magnetism and light and sound and heat, as being different octaves of radiation, closely approaches the esoteric philosophy, in the sense that all these forms of radiation are but various aspects of a fundamental and all-inclusive substratum of vitality expressing itself in different degrees of intensity. One of these days thought and consciousness will be recognized as belonging to the same vital scale of radiation, although belonging in their origin to higher planes of the universe than the physical.

KĀMA-LOKA AND THE SECOND DEATH

... for one who has no inner perception and faith, there is no immortality possible. In order to live in the world to come a conscious life, one has to believe first of all in that life during one's terrestrial existence. On these two aphorisms of the Secret Science all the philosophy about the *post-mortem* consciousness and the immortality of the soul is built. The Ego receives always according to its desserts. After the dissolution of the body, there commences for it either a period of full clear consciousness, a state of chaotic dreams, or an utterly dreamless sleep indistinguishable from annihilation; and these are the three states of consciousness. Our physiologists find the cause of dreams and visions in an unconscious preparation for them during the waking hours; why cannot the same be admitted for the *post-mortem* dreams? I repeat it, *death is sleep.* After death begins, before the spiritual eyes of the soul, a performance according to a programme learnt and very often composed unconsciously by ourselves: the practical carrying out of *correct* beliefs or of illusions which have been created by ourselves. A Methodist, will be Methodist, a Mussulman, a Mussulman, of course, just for a time — in a perfect fool's paradise of each man's creation and making. These are the *post-mortem* fruits of the tree of life. Naturally, our belief or unbelief in the fact of conscious immortality is unable to influence the unconditioned reality of the fact itself, once that it exists; but the belief or unbelief in that immortality, as the continuation or annihilation of separate entities, cannot fail to give colour to that fact in its application to each of these entities.   — H. P. B. in *Lucifer,* January 1889, p. 413

IN ORDER TO GRASP the teachings of occultism regarding the after-death states, it is important to keep in mind that man is composed of several element-principles forming the fields of action of the auric egg, in which the various consciousness centers function. All these element-principles with their appurtenant monads are intimately interrelated, and each is derived from its superior monad as a ray. We have then, first, a divine monadic essence, unconditionally immortal, of vast spiritual, intellectual and even physical powers, and of cosmic range of action and consciousness; second, a divine-spiritual monad, its ray or offspring, of purely spiritual nature and function; third, a spiritual-intellectual monad or higher ego; fourth, a human ego which in its turn is a ray of the preceding monadic center; fifth, the model-body, the field of the so-called astral monad; sixth, a physical body built around and partly from this astral body; and seventh and last, the vital essence or life, that is to say, the vital force or energy which runs through and unites all these element-principles. This life energy itself is progressively less ethereal as it descends through the lower parts of the constitution, and is composed in its turn, as are the other element-principles, of monadic units: vital corpuscles, so to say, entities of infinitesimal magnitude known as life-atoms.

In the last analysis man's constitution is twelvefold, consisting of the seven manifest and the five unmanifest units of far superior character; and the seven manifest may again be subdivided into an upper spiritual triad and a lower quaternary. When using the tenfold manner of division we should keep in mind the other two units, one of which is the superdivine link with the divinity of the universe, and the other is the polar link uniting the entity with the lower parts of the universe, thus making the twelve.

We must not suppose that the twelvefold division of the human constitution is to be preferred over either the seven- or tenfold. H.P.B. concentrated more on the septenary because it is easier to teach and understand. The main point is that all the element-principles are enclosed by and contained within the auric egg which has its original focus or source in the very highest of the twelve portions of the constitution; and in a sense the auric egg, because of its perpetuity, really is the objective sūtrātman or thread-self.

Now the ranges of consciousness of the different parts of the human constitution when divided into twelve, are easily enough understood. The unmanifest five we may call typically universal or kosmic, at least the higher units thereof, for their range of action extends far beyond our own galaxy or home-universe. The reach of the divine monad, which is essentially the ātmic monad with its buddhic vehicle, is the galaxy; the range of the spiritual monad, the buddhi-manas, is the solar system; while the field of action of the reimbodying ego is the planetary chain; and finally, the range of the astral monad or lower quaternary, as we may collectively describe it, is a single globe of a chain, our globe D for instance.

In this connection, we must make a distinction, even if it be not a real difference, between the reimbodying ego which has its range over the planetary chain, and its ray, the reincarnating ego, which applies to an imbodied human being in his physical vehicle on this globe D.

Man is indeed a compound of many substances, matters, forces and energies — each working in its own appropriate portion of the auric egg as an integral part of an ever-continuous stream of consciousness. Physical death brings about the temporary dissolution of the lower four-and-one-half principles of this composite entity.

When the constitution of man separates in the kāma-loka at the second death, all that has been noble and of a spiritual character in the past life — the beautiful aspirations and ideals, the grand memories that the higher soul retains in the fabric of its substance — is withdrawn into the highest triad, which is the immortal monadic essence of our constitution. The aggregate of these indrawn elements is properly viewed as the human monad, which rests as an embryo in the spiritual monad of the higher triad until the next rebirth on this earth.

Contrariwise, the lower part of the man that was attracts to itself the lowest part of the human ego, all the passional, emotional, and purely selfish portions; and these dissipate into their different grades of life-atoms, of which in fact they are composed. These life-atoms then pursue their transmigrations through the various kingdoms of nature. When the physical body dies and disintegrates, its life-atoms return to the elements of the earth, air, water, fire, and the ether, which originally gave them to the body. Then, at a later date in the kāma-loka of the astral light, each one of the life-atoms composing the intermediate sheaths of the excarnate being passes to its respective sphere of the cosmos. The saying, "earth to earth, water to water, air to air, fire to fire," etc., refers to the life-atoms of the different portions of man's constitution.

The same rule prevails for the monads in man, each of which seeks its own realm or sphere: the human monad enters its devachan; the spiritual monad undertakes its peregrinations through the spheres; and, at the instant of death, the divine ray bound into the human constitution is released from the human compound and flashes home more quickly than thought to its parent star, to the sphere of the divine monad, our inmost and our highest.°

°There are a large number of mysteries connected with the after-death states of the human entity. For example, it has been asked at what point in the different stages of the monad's 'descent' or reimbodiment does the ray from the divine monad make contact with the constitution of the man-to-be then in building? First of all,

Now the kāma-loka is that portion only of the astral light which is immediately contiguous to and which completely surrounds and penetrates our earth globe. In its grossest parts, it is a truly semimaterial plane although, because we cannot invariably see it or sense it, we call it invisible and 'subjective.' While the kāma-loka is divisible into different degrees of ethereality, it has no regions which we would call either beautiful or holy. It is the abode of the shades, that aspect of the astral world where, to use an early Christian expression, things which are rejected pass out in the draft. It contains the reliquiae, the astral-vital remains of beings who were. As for the astral light, this not only includes the kāma-loka, but likewise ranges 'upwards' in quality of ethereality, gradually becoming spiritual. In a certain sense the astral light in its fullness is the auric egg of the earth, while in another sense it occupies for the earth the analogical position that the model-body does for man. The astral light itself is but the vehicle of the anima mundi, the 'soul of our world.' In other words, we may speak of the anima mundi as being the soul of the astral light (which latter in its lowest parts is the linga-śarīra of the earth), and of the kāma-loka as the grossest dregs or most material part of the astral light.

The kāma-loka, in so far as its position in space goes, may be said to extend somewhat beyond the sphere of our moon in one direction, and to touch the earth's center in the other direction. When, however, we look upon the kāma-loka as a series of states or conditions of matter occupied by entities temporarily in it, because attracted to their own corresponding kāma-lokic quality, then we can say that the kāma-loka, considered as a sevenfold aggregate, is intermediate between the devachan and avīchi. However, neither devachan nor avīchi are places, but are *states of consciousness* which beings experience. Of course an entity in any state of consciousness must have position likewise.

Although the devachan and the avīchi are conditions or states *only,*

---

it varies with the individual; but speaking more generally, I would be inclined to say that, as far as I have understood this difficult point of teaching, the moment of reconnection of the divine ray with the spiritual monad takes place at the instant when the spiritual monad, having reached the acme of its post-mortem peregrinations, turns as it were preparatory to its pilgrimage downwards once more into the spheres of matter. Yet while this seems undoubtedly true, it must not be supposed that the constitution thus in process of rebuilding is wholly under the influence of the ray divine; if this were so, it would be the constitution of a god.

the kāma-loka is dual in character, being both a series of planes in the astral light immediately surrounding and within the earth, as well as qualities or states of matter fitting these planes to be the temporary abodes of the entities traversing them. What is said of the kāma-loka of our earth applies in principle to the kāma-lokas of the other globes of our chain — and indeed of any chain in the solar system — because each globe has its own astral light.

THE FOUR STATES OF CONSCIOUSNESS

THERE ARE FOUR BASIC qualities of consciousness into which a man can enter both in life and after death. In Sanskrit these are called jāgrat, swapna, sushupti, and turīya,° and every one of the seven states or conditions in which human consciousness can find itself contains its own relative jāgrat, swapna, sushupti, and turīya. These four types of consciousness can be allocated each to its proper locus in the human constitution, so that while the ordinary brain-mind consciousness of man usually is in the jāgrat state, another part may be in the swapna, another in the sushupti, while the highest part of his consciousness, the buddhi within him, is perennially in the turīya quality.

This accounts for the manifold differences in consciousness existing between man and man, and the moods in which people at various times may be, one man being distinctly in the physical jāgrat condition, whereas another, even though in the jāgrat quality, may seem to be in the dreaming-sleeping state of swapna, and a third may be almost oblivious of outside events and therefore temporarily be in the sushupti quality of the jāgrat, and so forth.

Let us take an average individual: he is in the normal waking state while on earth, yet he has intimations of something nobler and finer in him than the jāgrat quality shows. This is the higher manas or mānasaputra within him, expressing itself in this sphere of consciousness in the swapna quality because, although its power is already fully manifested on its own plane, it can but weakly express itself in such average man. Again, the buddhi within him, although fully functional on its own plane, nevertheless, because of the man's imperfections, only occasionally can reach him with a brilliant ray from itself, and this usually vaguely and more or less in the sushupti quality. Finally, the Buddha or Christ within him is functional on its own lofty spiritual plane, but cannot impress its fullness of consciousness on the mind of the ordinary individual, and thus *to him* his inner Buddha is of the turīya quality of consciousness.

°*Jāgrat*, the normal waking state; *swapna*, the dreaming-sleeping state; *sushupti*, the condition of profound and dreamless sleep; *turīya*, literally 'fourth,' the highest of all.

568

Also, at any time throughout a man's life, there are those very mystical and wonderful and all too infrequent 'revelations' or intuitions, which come into his consciousness like spiritual-intellectual illuminations. These momentary flashes of inspiration may occur even after true senescence has begun, and may still continue, if the man has lived a decent life, until there commences — only a short time preceding death — the 'ascending' of the higher portions of the man's constitution, announcing its preliminary breakup which is completed when the body is cast aside.

Now then, the particular part of man experiencing these various qualities of consciousness is the human ego, which is obviously self-conscious in the jāgrat quality of physical existence. Thus at the onset of both sleep and death the consciousness passes from the jāgrat into unconsciousness: the human ego first has a temporary condition of swapna or sleeping-dreaming, and then, quickly or slowly, according to the constitution, begins the 'unconscious' condition of the sushupti — unconscious from our standpoint only because we have not yet become accustomed to live *self-consciously* in our higher qualities.

Now these changings of consciousness from the jāgrat to the swapna and then to the sushupti do not take place with high adepts and those still greater, because they have learned to live in the loftier ranges of their consciousness. Therefore, when the adept or mahatma dies he can at will transfer his full self-consciousness to any quality or condition he pleases, and shortly thereafter take reimbodiment, or in rare instances lapse into a brief devachan, or even, in the cases of great adepts, into a temporary nirvana.

Exactly the same observations apply to the adept in the case of sleep. He can allow his body and brain-mind to pass into full unself-consciousness and thus repair their exhausted tissues, the while his self-conscious ego is fully functional on inner planes. But the ordinary man has not learned to do this, because his whole consciousness is centered in this plane, so that when he falls asleep his state of consciousness is according to what his imperfectly developed inner life permits, to wit: first a dreaming-sleeping consciousness, sinking into unconsciousness, then perhaps slipping back into the swapna or sleeping-dreaming condition, and so forth until he awakens. Likewise, the ordinary man after death lapses into the devachan, which is a state of spiritual swapna — a dreaming-sleeping condition of the human egoic consciousness, but on a spiritual plane where only things of great beauty and longings of a highly intellectual or of a spiritual

569

character pass like fleeting 'realities' before the vision of the devachanī.

This explains why the coarser, more materialistic man has very little devachan or perhaps none at all, because during his life on earth all his self-consciousness has been so heavily tied to matter and the sense-world around him that he has built up no inner life of aspiring thoughts calling for a quasi-dreaming consciousness after death. If a man desire to remain self-conscious while asleep or, equivalently, after death, he must have previously learned to live in his higher manas and buddhi. Thus centering his consciousness during his lifetime, he becomes thoroughly at home in these higher principles and remains therein when the body is recuperating itself in sleep, or is cast off at death.

After death the human ego-consciousness of the average man cannot remain or become self-conscious in the higher qualities of his constitution. Therefore the part that drops into unconsciousness is the ordinary brain-mind consciousness of daily life. It remains in this state except for the brief intervals in the kāma-loka when there is a more or less hazy reawakening and then a sinking into unconsciousness again, and then perhaps another reawakening, all dreamlike and shadowy, until the second death in the kāma-loka, at which time the human ego enters the dreaming of the devachan, where it remains more or less continuously until the impetus for the next reincarnation is felt.

No man is conscious of what is happening around him after *real* death;° and any claims that such is the fact are either frauds, or misinterpretations in cases of trance which are wrongly taken for death. Once actual death has occurred, unconsciousness supervenes in every instance, and the man

---

°Even violent death, whether by suicide or accident, is followed by instantaneous unconsciousness. Of course there is an enormous difference between the one who meets with accidental death and the one who takes his life because he is afraid to face the world, or no longer cares to do so. The victim of an accident after a while finds himself dreaming vague dreams until the state of devachan is entered. But the one who commits self-murder, because he is too weak to continue to do his duty as a man, does so by his own deliberate choice in a moment of intense emotional stress, and karma will exact retribution for that act. But let us not forget that it is thus the individual learns, for karmic retribution is not 'punishment,' but simply a reaction of nature. If I put my hand into the flame, my hand will be burned. Is this nature's fault? Just so with the suicide: he receives what he has done to himself; that is, he cuts short his life before his reservoir of vitality was expended, and he must therefore remain in a quasi-physical world so that he may there exhaust the quasi-physical vitality which still existed in his astral body at death. After that he has the kāma-loka to face.

is absolutely not aware of what happens around his deathbed, contrary to what has been occasionally reported by 'returning' kama-rūpas manifesting as 'spirits' through mediums. If a man is in trance, however, the links of consciousness with the physical brain may well be still sufficiently alert to enable the 'consciousness' vaguely to sense what is taking place around the sickbed. But once the golden cord of life is finally broken and death has definitely occurred, no such awareness of what is going on is at all possible because all links with the percipient brain, or even the linga-śarīra, have been snapped.

In one of the oldest Upanishads, the *Brihadāranyaka* (IV, v, 13), the sage Yājñavalkya says to his consort Maitreyī: "Having passed on, there is no sañjñā" — that is, no collected active self-conscious thinking. Now it is this faculty of self-conscious reflective thought which the entity in the kama-loka does not have, for the manas is non-functional then, being in its stupor of unconsciousness; and even in those fugitive moments when the kāma-lokic entity has a shadowy adumbration of self-consciousness, this comes merely because the auric egg of the entity automatically repeats, so to speak, what it was accustomed to do or to think during life.

Hence the kāma-lokic 'consciousness' ranges all the way from temporary obliteration of self-consciousness, through all intermediate degrees of unconsciousness, to the astral low-type self-consciousness that elementaries and lost souls have. The average man when in the kāma-loka is either in unconsciousness or in a state of figure-flitting dreaming. The purer the man, the deeper the unconsciousness.

Those strongly attached to things of earth and their material appetites and passions have quite an awakening in the kāma-loka, and there is a good deal of suffering about it, because they are in a sort of nightmare; although even here nature is kind, as the nightmare is dreamy, rather vague. The truly spiritual man, on the contrary, has scarcely any consciousness at all of passing through the kāma-loka, and speeds through it like a train through a tunnel, totally unaware of anything that is evil or unpleasant. Among average men, those with materialistic bias may have a hazy feeling that they are in a bad dream, while others of a more spiritual character may just have a dreamy notion that such conditions exist, but they do not experience them. In any case, the kāma-loka is not long, except for evil men and sorcerers. These indeed suffer sometimes terribly — not a physical suffering as we understand it, but a horrible nightmarish dream which keeps repeating itself with variations. They

571

have brought this upon themselves by their constant broodings, and the astral recorder inside, so to speak, having been wound up, now must run down.

On the other hand, in the case of those adepts and initiates who are not of the highest but yet belong to a class above even spiritual men, there is a certain suffering after death because of their awakened inner senses and vision, the suffering arising from an awareness of the horrors in the kāma-loka that are passing around them. But even here it does not last long, perhaps only a few moments or hours; and it may be slight or intense according to the inner awakening. As a matter of fact, initiates and chelas, even when imbodied, almost at will can sense (or close off their vision of) the astral light or the kāma-loka thereof.

Of course those who are still higher are not at all affected by the astral light, because they are fully acquainted with all its aspects even before they die and, shutting off all the avenues of impression, shoot through it like a star.

The suffering after death that H.P.B. alludes to in one or two passages is very much the same as that which the neophyte during initiation must go through. He must learn at first hand, by personal experience, all the facts of the underworld, as well as of the upper world; and to the neophyte who has to enter the kāma-loka with his eyes open and every faculty alert, the suffering is at times almost insupportable, because of the horror and misery and filth that he senses around him. But initiation has to be faced, in order to *know*. Once known, one becomes master of the situation, and thereafter is no longer so keenly affected.

Another point that I may comment upon is the *average* length of time during which the human entity, after death, is unconscious before regaining at least a shadowy self-consciousness in the kāma-loka. Each single case is unique. Highly spiritual men come to no self-consciousness of any kind in the kāma-loka except for a brief interval in connection with the second panoramic visioning at the second death just before entering the devachan. On the other hand, human beings of a grossly animal or material character range all the way from those destined to become elementaries to those who have sufficient spirituality in them to give them a short devachan before reincarnation.

Any such partial 'awakening' in the kāma-loka is invariably dependent upon the life just ended. The thoughts that a man has at the moment of death, which foreshadow the type of his after-death states, are but the almost automatic functioning of his consciousness showing what character of man he is; for his last thoughts will be of the general type of those most common to him and most cherished by him.

The length of time between physical death and the second death is again almost wholly dependent upon the nature of the excarnate human entity.[21] Here we have the same rules applying: the truly spiritual man will have an extremely short sojourn in the kāma-loka, perhaps passing through it without pause, and his second death will come soon; the average human being will have a much longer stay; while the man of strong material instincts and feelings will have a still longer period in the kāma-loka. Some remain for scores of years, possibly even a hundred or two, before having the second death and the subsequent short devachan. All those in whom the spiritual nature exercises no attraction 'upwards' — and this would include congenital idiots, and also infants who suffer premature death — will obviously have no true second death, which is really a new birth into higher conditions of consciousness.

In the very exceptional case of an elementary or lost soul — or any human being whose life has been so utterly animalistic and woven into matter that his consciousness is enchained thereto — there is an 'awakening' for a greater or less length of time to a self-conscious or quasi-self-conscious realization that he is dead, no longer a physically imbodied man.° But in no instance does such consciousness last until reincarnation occurs, because unconsciousness mercifully comes upon him before he assumes a new physical body.

In normal cases, once the man dies, unconsciousness, sweet and beautiful and infinitely compassionate, descends upon him like an enveloping veil of ākāśic protection; and then, with the exception of the few fugitive moments of dreaming consciousness in the kāma-loka, the devachanī begins the sequence of blissful spiritual mentation, which is not so different from the type of consciousness an individual has when he has pleasant dreams. We may call it 'self-consciousness' if we wish, for that is what it is in a sense; but it is the swapna state of self-consciousness, and not the jāgrat state of the imbodied human being.

° Cf. *The Mahatma Letters*, p. 128.

ANCIENT AND MODERN SPIRITUALISM CONTRASTED

MEDIUMSHIP IS NOT a gift; it is a fatal misfortune. There is nothing known so destructive of spiritual advancement. It dislocates the principles of the inner constitution, increasingly separating the refining influences of the higher self from the lower; so that the mediums' course of destiny is usually from bad to worse; and they are very fortunate indeed if they do not end in black magic. The medium is a helpless instrument under the sway of psychic forces, and is usually unconscious of what he or she does and of what takes place — a subject of any passing elemental or stream of psychic energy in the astral light, as well as passively subject to any well-directed and concentrated human will.

The mediator, on the other hand, is a fully self-conscious, highly developed intermediary between a spiritual-intellectual power and men. The post is self-chosen, one of high honor yet filled with dangers of its own, and almost always involves self-sacrifice. Furthermore, the mediator is a copy in human life of what certain ones of the higher gods are in the divine realms. They give themselves, that others toiling behind them may be helped. There is the same spiritual and ethical parallel between a mediator and a medium as there is between a white magician and a black one — between a son of the sun and a child of the moon.

In this connection, we should remember that H.P.B. came to the Western world with instructions to work in and among the particular body of men which would be most likely to respond to the teachings which she was directed to give. These were then the spiritists, who were in some respects among the brightest-minded people of the time, more or less awakened to the possibility of there being in the boundless universe something besides dead, soulless, material existences. She went into their ranks, championed in the public press such truth as she found there. She tried to lead them on to understanding that there was indeed a spiritual world, but that it was far above the astral world; that their summerland was a vague and distorted intuition of the devachan; and that the supposed 'returning spirits' were but the astral simulacra of human beings — decaying psycho-astral entities utterly unfit to commerce with.

574

They would not listen to her. Phenomenalism was then rampant. A tipping table, a rapping on the wall or on the table, were to them evidences of the immortality of those who had passed on. The philosophy that she brought they would not accept. So she founded the Theosophical Society as the vehicle to carry into the minds and hearts of men the message of the ancient wisdom-religion. For years the bitterest foes that H.P.B. had were the spiritists. They never could forgive her for leaving their ranks and going about her work. They called it treachery, not understanding the motives and reason for her action.

The attitude of genuine occultism towards the subject of so-called spiritism and the alleged intercourse with excarnate entities is unequivocally stated in certain Tibetan letters and manuscripts quoted by H.P.B. in her article "Tibetan Teachings."° According to her, the views expressed in the following extracts are those of the Venerable Chohan-Lama, who was "the chief of the Archive-registrars" of the libraries which contain manuscripts on esoteric teachings belonging to the Dalai and Tashi Lamas:

". . . we maintain that there is no possibility of an entirely pure 'self' remaining in the terrestrial atmosphere after his liberation from the physical body, in his own personality, in which he moved upon earth. Only three exceptions are made to this rule:

"The holy motive prompting a Bodhisatwa, a Sravaka, or Rahat to help to the same bliss those who remain behind him, the living; in which case he will stop to instruct them either from within or without; or, secondly, those who, however pure, harmless and comparatively free from sin during their lives, have been so engrossed with some particular idea in connection with one of the human mâyâs as to pass away amidst that all-absorbing thought; and, thirdly, persons in whom an intense and holy love, such as that of a mother for her orphaned children, creates or generates an indomitable will fed by that boundless love to tarry with and among the living in their inner selves.

"The periods allotted for these exceptional cases vary. In the first case, owing to the knowledge acquired in his condition of Anuttara Samyak Sambodhi — the most holy and enlightened heart — the Bodhisatwa has no fixed limit. Accustomed to remain for hours and days in his astral form during life, he has power after death to create around him his own conditions, calculated to check the natural tendency of the other principles to rejoin their respective elements, and can descend or even remain on earth for centuries and millenniums. In the second case, the period will last until the all-powerful magnetic attraction of the subject

---

° *Lucifer*, September and October 1894, pp. 15, 98–101.

of the thought — intensely concentrated at the moment of death — becomes weakened and gradually fades out. In the third, the attraction is broken either by the death or the moral unworthiness of the loved ones. It cannot in either case last more than a lifetime.

"In all other cases of apparitions or communications by whatever mode, the 'spirit' will prove a wicked 'bhûta' or 'ro-lang' at best — the soulless shell of an 'elementary.'. . .

"For we deprecate unqualifiedly and absolutely all ignorant intercourse with the Ro-lang. For what are they who return? What kind of creatures are they who can communicate at will objectively or by physical manifestation? They are impure, grossly sinful souls, 'a-tsa-ras'; suicides; and such as have come to premature deaths by accident and must linger in the earth's atmosphere until the full expiration of their natural term of life. . . .

"Now the beings included in the second and third classes — suicides and victims of accident — have not completed their natural term of life; and, as a consequence, though not of necessity mischievous, are earth-bound. The prematurely expelled soul is in an unnatural state; the original impulse under which the being was evolved and cast into the earth-life has not expended itself — the necessary cycle has not been completed, but must nevertheless be fulfilled.

"Yet, though earth-bound, these unfortunate beings, victims whether voluntary or involuntary, are only suspended, as it were, in the earth's magnetic attraction. They are not, like the first class, attracted to the living from a savage thirst to feed on their vitality. Their only impulse — and a blind one, since they are generally in a dazed or stunned condition — is, to get into the whirl of rebirth as soon as possible. Their state is that we call a false Bar-do — the period between two incarnations. According to the karma of the being — which is affected by his age and merits in the last birth — this interval will be longer or shorter.

"Nothing but some overpoweringly intense attraction, such as a holy love for some dear one in great peril, can draw them with their consent to the living; but by the mesmeric power of a Ba-po, a necromancer — the word is used advisedly, since the necromantic spell is Dzu-tul, or what you term a mesmeric attraction — can force them into our presence. This evocation, however, is totally condemned by those who hold to the Good Doctrine; for the soul thus evoked is made to suffer exceedingly, even though it is not itself but only its image that has been torn or stripped from itself to become the apparition; owing to its premature separation by violence from the body, the 'jang-khog' — animal soul — is yet heavily loaded with material particles — there has not been a natural disintegration of the coarser from the finer molecules — and the necromancer, in compelling this separation artificially, makes it, we might almost say, to suffer as one of us might if he were flayed alive.

"Thus, to evoke the first class — the grossly sinful souls — is dangerous for

576

the living; to compel the apparition of the second and third classes is cruel beyond expression to the dead.

"In the case of one who died a natural death totally different conditions exist; the soul is almost, and in the case of great purity, entirely beyond the necromancer's reach; hence beyond that of a circle of evokers, or spiritualists, who, unconsciously to themselves, practise a veritable necromancer's Sang-nyag, or magnetic incantation. . . .

"At all events it has neither will nor power at that time to give any thought to the living. But after its period of latency is over, and the new self enters in full consciousness the blessed region of Devachan — when all earthly mists have been dispersed, and the scenes and relations of the past life come clearly before its spiritual sight — then it may, and does occasionally, when espying all it loved, and that loved it upon earth, draw up to it for communion and by the sole attraction of love, the spirits of the living, who, when returned to their normal condition, imagine that it has descended to them.

"Therefore we differ radically from the western Ro-lang-pa — spiritualists — as to what they see or communicate with in their circles and through their unconscious necromancy. We say it is but the physical dregs, or spiritless remains of the late being; that which has been exuded, cast off and left behind when its finer particles passed onward into the great Beyond.

"In it linger some fragments of memory and intellect. It certainly was once a part of the being, and so possesses that modicum of interest; but it is not the being in reality and truth. Formed of matter, however etherealized, it must sooner or later be drawn away into vortices where the conditions for its atomic disintegration exist. . . .

"Such is the teaching. None can overshadow mortals but the elect, the 'Accomplished,' the 'Byang-tsiub,' or the 'Bodhisatwas' alone — they who have penetrated the great secret of life and death — as they are able to prolong, at will, their stay on earth after 'dying.' Rendered into the vulgar phraseology, such overshadowing is to 'be born again and again' for the benefit of mankind."

One sees from all this the folly of believing that the excarnate being can communicate with those he left behind, either through mediums or otherwise. Nevertheless, connection is possible in the case of 'earthbound' entities, such as elementaries, when conditions are appropriate for this very dangerous and spiritually and mentally unwholesome procedure.

Spiritism has been known by mankind for millions of years. Ever since the middle point of the fourth root-race, commerce with departed shades and its connection with so-called psychical powers in man, have always attracted certain types. But throughout all ancient times and in the Orient today, communication with the bhūtas has invariably been considered unclean, wrong, morally infectious. This very word bhūta, meaning 'has been,' is a curiously descriptive and apt term. On the other hand, the 'spiritualism' that H.P.B. taught was the doctrine of the cosmic spirit: *spiritualism* as contrasted with *materialism*.

True spiritualism has naught to do with necromancy, for the spiritualism of antiquity was the teaching that the world is one vast living organic entity, composed of cosmic spirits, and that every human being is in his inmost such a cosmic spirit, and has the duty and ineffable privilege of entering into communion with the spiritual realms through his own inner god. It was held also that every human being should become a mediator — one standing as the link between the divine and the lower kingdoms; and further, that every self-conscious entity is great precisely in proportion as he becomes a mediator between the divine sun and human beings.

That, in brief, was the spiritualism of H.P.Blavatsky, the spiritualism of the ancients, the wisdom-religion of mankind, taught by the theodidaktoi — the 'god-taught' — of the countries around the Mediterranean Sea about the time of the birth of Jesus the Avatāra, and also in the temples of Egypt and Persia and Babylonia. In India it was called the brahma-vidyā or, in a more esoteric sense, the gupta-vidyā, the theosophy taught also by the Druids, by the ancient Americans and Scandinavians — taught the world over.

THE NATURE OF THE KĀMA-RŪPA

THE KĀMA-RŪPA, which becomes the vehicle for the unconscious or quasi-conscious entity in the kāma-loka, is actually forming constantly during the life of the individual; in other words, it is in a continual state of modification or change, these changes beginning when the incarnated entity as a child first feels itself conscious of mental and emotional affections, attractions, etc. However, after the death of the physical body there is no further change or growth of the kāma-rūpic form, it remaining mor or less static, all modifications being of the nature of disintegration or slow decay. It is really that portion of the human constitution which is the kāma-mānasic-astral seat or focus of the passional, emotional, lower mental and psychic attributes; and these as an aggregate comprise all the lower skandhas of the human constitution, usually enumerated as five.[22]

This group of skandhas works through and has its focus in the lower portions of the auric egg, which lower layers must not be confused with the linga-śarīra or model-body. During life the constantly changing kāma-rūpa has its seat in the linga-śarīra, or uses it as a vehicle; and the linga-śarīra, instantly responding to the various emotional and passional movements in the kāma-rūpa, in its turn communicates these as impulses to the physical body, which then responds in corresponding action.

Now it is the human ego which works through the kāma-rūpa during incarnation, exactly as the kāma-rūpa works through the linga-śarīra, and this last again through the body. In fact, it is correct enough to say that the personal man, which is the reflection and usually distorted radiance of the reincarnating ego or human monad, is this kāma-rūpa itself; because, being a collection of skandhas, the kāma-rūpa is the expression of the merely personal qualities of the human ego.

Hence after death and after a certain time has been passed in the kāma-loka, this collection of skandhic attributes still continuing as the kāma-rūpa holds enchained by its attractions the reincarnating ego, the personal man being unconscious. This condition lasts until the event of the second death, which simply means that the moment has arrived when the reincarnating ego has succeeded in breaking each and every link of sympathetic or psychomagnetic attraction which unites it with the kāma-rūpa of the personal man that was.

The second death, therefore, is an astral reproduction of what took place at physical death; for just as at physical death the body is cast off with the linga-śarīra and the gross animal prānas, so at the second death the human ego, having snapped its links of psychomagnetic attraction with the kāma-rūpa, casts it off and enters into the devachanic condition, carrying with it all the spiritual yearnings or sympathies or memories which the personal man during earth life had stored in the web of consciousness.

This is the second death; when the last spiritual thought or image has been drawn upwards into the reincarnating ego, and there remains nothing more to keep it attached to the kāma-rūpa, the latter then is dropped as a kāma-rūpic corpse or shell. Henceforth the kāma-rūpa begins to disintegrate: rapidly in the case of men whose lives have been of spiritual type, less so in the case of ordinary men, and still less quickly with those who were strongly attracted to things of matter. This is the reason why *after* the second death the kāma-rūpa is called an astral shell. Moreover, if the shell is still more or less impregnated with the automatic passional impulses of a grossly materialistic or bad man, it is even an elementary of a sort; but the *true* elementary is the kāma-rūpa of a desperately evil man or of a sorcerer who cannot rise into the devachan.

For a certain period of brief duration, which depends in every instance upon the individual, kāma-rūpas retain a wavering, shadowy kind of quasi-animal consciousness because of the fact that they imbody mānasic life-atoms of low type whose thought-impulses and emotional activity have not yet run down, much as a machine will keep running for a while after the power is turned off. As these low-grade mānasic life-atoms leave the kāma-rūpa, it disintegrates and thereafter is as the shell of an egg from which the contents have been removed. Such kāma-rūpic shells are no longer even elementaries of a feeble type, but are completely emptied of consciousness and gradually dissipate as does a cloud. Some kāma-rūpas disintegrate in a few months; those of average humanity may take eight, ten, fifteen, possibly twenty years; while those of extremely materialistic or bad men, but who still had some spiritual good in them, may endure for several scores of years.

Now the term elementaries generally signifies two things: (a) the phantoms or spooks or astral eidola, i.e. the kāma-rūpas of all excarnate persons whose habitation is the kāma-loka; and (b) what H. P. B. calls the "disembodied souls of the depraved,"° that is, the depraved souls of those who after they die have a long and difficult time in the kāma-loka before their upper triad or collective monad can free itself for its devachanic rest.

An especial application of the word elementaries is made again in the case of lost souls on the one hand, and inveterate sorcerers on the other, neither of which have any second death and consequently no devachan. These elementaries are really disimbodied humans whose habitat is the astral light and who, though deprived of the body and also of the spiritual monad, can find neither unconsciousness nor devachan, but remain in the astral light until reimbodiment on earth, which takes place usually in a short time. Such lost souls and confirmed sorcerers reimbody themselves in bodies of continually decreasing efficiency; and if their condition of being 'lost souls' is so far complete that the human kingdom no longer attracts them they will, in their desperate hunger for physical imbodiment, turn to animal wombs and even, in the worst cases, attach themselves to plants.

It is to be noted in these last instances of completely lost souls that they are really astral monads, each one detached from its spiritual monad; they are properly called elementaries because they are thrown back to a condition of 'elementary' evolution and therefore return to the kingdoms through which they had previously passed as 'elemental souls.' However, they do not take imbodiment in these lower kingdoms as the *monads* of such animals or plants. The process is rather that of the lost soul or elementary coalescing astrally, psychically, and magnetically, with the auric egg of either the beast or the plant — and thus they are in a true but unconscious sense 'haunters' or 'dwellers' of these animal or plant entities. Hence it would be wrong to suppose that this or that animal is not an ordinary one with its own seven principles; but where such an event does occur, the animal or plant is afflicted by the coalescing with it of the astral life-atoms belonging to the elementary.

All elementaries of whatever kind are, generally speaking, reliquiae or remnants of what once had been imbodied human beings on earth. Sooner or later they are caught by the swirling currents of efflux carrying them into the Cloaca Maxima of our globe, these degraded astral monads

---

° *Theosophical Glossary*, p. 112.

being finally swept out of the earth's atmosphere into the Pit, the Planet of Death.

To consider the subject from a somewhat different angle: when a man dies, he is still a human being, except that he has cast off his physical body, the linga-śarīra, and the gross astral prānic vitality. This therefore leaves him a complete human in the sense that all the higher qualities remain in the kāma-rūpa; he is a four-principled entity, the ātman, buddhi, manas and kāma-manas being still conjoined. The human qualities and attributes are asleep, as it were, in the kāma-rūpa in the kāma-loka, and therefore are unconscious — a blessed provision of nature!

When the second death takes place the triune monad, the ātman-buddhi-manas, releases itself from all its *lower* kāma-mānasic substances and energies. These perishable elements remain in the kāma-rūpic shell and gradually fade out like the radiance in the sky after sunset; the energies producing this fading radiance gradually vanish 'upward' and, being belated life-atoms, become attached like sleeping seeds or tanhic elementals to the auric egg of the human ego which now has entered its devachan. It is these sleeping seeds of lower attributes and qualities, i.e. dormant skandhas which, preceding the next incarnation, will spring into action and take initial parts in forming the astral body-to-be.

At the separation of the triadic monad from the kāma-rūpa, all the most spiritual and highly intellectual attributes are withdrawn as a still more brilliant radiance into the reincarnating ego; and it is this spiritual aroma, the truly human being, which becomes the devachanī sleeping in the bosom of the reincarnating ego, the human monad. Distinguish here the human monad from its ray the human ego.

Thus, after physical death, the seven-principled man has become four-principled, consisting of the two duads, ātma-buddhi, and manas with the spiritual parts of kāma. Now when the four-principled man enters at the second death into the devachan, these two duads coalesce into the upper triad of ātma-buddhi and the higher part of manas, because of the dropping of the lower kāma-mānasic attributes.

As to the divine ray, at the instant of true death it flashes home to its parent star. While it is our inmost essence, it is only the most advanced of the human race who are cognizant of the dwelling within themselves of this supernal glory; and the greater in spiritual and intellectual power the imbodied man is, the more fully does the influence of the divine ray manifest itself in his life.

Average men today are only occasionally illumined by flashes of intuition that there abides Something within them which is higher than intellect, incomparably more glorious than emotion or feeling, and which is the "light that lighteth every man that cometh into the world" — the Light of Eternity. Such rare moments of inner illumination are the efflux from the spiritual monad within. Then, there are the noblest of the sons of men who, by a sudden wondrous and mystical transformation of their consciousness, experience as a reality that living Presence within them which transcends both time and space.

XII

Death and the
Circulations of the Cosmos - II

NATURE AND CHARACTERISTICS OF THE DEVACHAN

Why should it be supposed that *devachan* is a monotonous condition only because some one moment of earthly sensation is indefinitely perpetuated — stretched, so to say, throughout aeons? It is not, it *cannot* be so. . . .

Then — how can you think that "but one moment of earthly sensation *only* is selected for perpetuation?" Very true, that "moment" lasts from the first to last; but then it lasts but as the key-note of the whole harmony, a definite tone of appreciable pitch, around which cluster and develop in progressive variations of melody and as endless variations on a theme, all the aspirations, desires, hopes, dreams, which, in connection with that particular "moment" had ever crossed the *dreamer's* brain during his lifetime, without having ever found their realization on earth, and which he now finds fully realized in all their vividness in devachan, without ever suspecting that all that blissful reality is but the progeny begotten by his own fancy, the effects of the mental causes produced by himself. That particular one *moment* which will be most intense and uppermost in the thoughts of his dying brain at the time of dissolution will of course regulate all the other "moments." — *The Mahatma Letters*, pp. 191–2

ONE OF NATURE'S LAWS is that an entity cannot continue the same forever; for it is by exchanging the imperfect for the ever more perfect that we grow; and death is just such a change. The child must die in order to become a man, and the man must die frequently in order to become a god. There are many wonderful things around us of which we are cognizant all the time, and yet they are so commonplace that we do not draw the necessary deductions from them. Except the seed die, the plant cannot come into being. Except the man die, he cannot experience those post-mortem conditions of thought and consciousness which belong to his inner being, to the celestial spirit which he is in his essence.

Death is the most familiar thing in nature, yet it is the most feared because the least understood. We have all entered life by the gateway of birth, and because it is behind us we do not fear birth. But we look with apprehension toward that day when we shall go through the solemn change of death and be free.

After death we are going to be exactly as we have made ourselves during life. If we have lived a decent life, we shall be a decent entity after death; and if we have lived like a beast, we are then going to be a beastly entity, and will have to take what is coming to us. We are neither going to be saved from the consequences of our past life, nor are we going to be eternally damned. There is no heaven, there is no hell, in the old theological sense. But there are post-mortem states of many kinds, almost infinitely numerous; and because of nature's harmonious procedures no human being could ever die and be drawn to a condition or place in which he is unfitted to be. No miracles will be wrought for us at our death. No unnatural things, whether good or bad, are going to happen to us; nothing can occur outside of the unerring laws of the universe. A man goes to the particular lokas or talas in the interior worlds which during his life on earth he has fitted himself temporarily to inhabit. He makes for himself his own post-mortem destiny: good, bad, or indifferent.

When the second death supervenes, there is release from bondage for the intermediate nature of man, and the spirit-soul returns to its native realms, with the intermediate nature resting within it while undergoing a process of spiritual recuperation, of assimilation and mental digesting of the lessons learned in the life just lived. As the physical body rebuilds its energies during sleep, so the intermediate nature of man likewise has its own 'sleep' or devachan after each incarnation. Because the states of the consciousness of excarnate entities are many and various, the devachan may be considered as a hierarchical 'ladder' running downwards from the most spiritual to the least spiritual states, and imperceptibly merging into the highest or most ethereal realms of the kāma-loka.

Death is a *casting off* of limitations and fetters, a dropping of body after body, each one being more ethereal than the last. The more spiritual portion of the reincarnating ego frees itself of the ethereal bodies of man's inner constitution and, entering into its divine parent, the heart of the monadic essence, pursues its peregrinations through the sacred planets, finally passing the portals of the sun into realms and spheres of unspeakable glory.

As to the divine spark itself, it really is always free, even during life, except for its connection with the various vehicles through which it works. It is the central illuminating fire at the very core of man's spiritual essence, and simply sends its splendor down through enshrouding veil after veil until the tip of that descending ray touches the physical brain, giving it light and life.

The devachan, as a series of states of consciousness, is not in any sense a loka, or particular world or sphere. It is in the same category as the still sublimer states of consciousness called nirvana, and in the opposite direction as the avīchi, which is also a series of conditions of consciousness of the beings therein. We can imagine a ladder or continuity of states of consciousness of which every rung is one such; and we can divide this ladder into three distinct parts. The highest is the nirvana, which, since there are many types of nirvanīs, we may divide into seven or even twelve rungs or conditions. The second part we may call the devachan, in its turn divisible into its series of states of consciousness.[23] Underneath this last come the seven or twelve conditions of consciousness of avīchi.

These three parts of the all-inclusive ladder of consciousnesses blend into each other, so that the lowest condition of the nirvana merges into the highest of the devachan; and, similarly, the lowest devachanic state passes insensibly into the highest condition of consciousness in the kāma-loka; and again the lowest of the kāma-lokic states of consciousness blends into the highest of the avīchi. Now the inclusion of the kāma-loka with the states of consciousness of the series should not be misunderstood to mean that it is not also a series of lokas.° I am speaking here of the *beings* in the kāma-loka, whose states of consciousness, as a class, form the link between the avīchi-conditions and the superior consciousnesses in the devachan into which the kāma-lokic entities pass when their consciousness is no longer held in the kāma-loka.

Devachan is a period of spiritual and loftily intellectual flowering of immaterial energies which could find no adequate self-expression during life. These energies produce their effect on the fabric of character of the dreaming entity which experiences and thus assimilates and digests them. In fact, these spiritual and intellectual expansions of consciousness mold and modify the character of the excarnate ego even more than does

---

°The kāma-loka is, in fact, a series of sub-lokas, and forms part of the kāma-dhātu. The three dhātus in the rising scale, the kāma-dhātu, the rūpa-dhātu, and the arūpa-dhātu, are really a Buddhist way of naming the series of worlds or spheres, visible and invisible, which in the Brahmanical philosophies are called lokas. However, the devachan, being wholly a series of states of consciousness, is not in any sense a loka or dhātu, or a series of actual worlds or spheres. Were there no entities or beings in the devachanic condition of consciousness, there would obviously be no devachan.

the life on earth. In these respects the latter, therefore, can be viewed as a 'world of causes,' while the devachan is a 'world of effects.'

The devachanic condition for the average human being who has lived a creditably aspiring and moral life, is one of inexpressible spiritual and mental beauty and peace. Every high aspiration and unfulfilled desire to do good find their opportunity for expression in his consciousness, so that his devachan is filled with a glorification of all the noblest that he had hoped to do on earth — involving almost infinite variations on the fundamental thought-themes as the creative faculties of the ego work upon them.

Is there progress for the ego in devachan? It depends upon the meaning we attach to the word. If we think of it as a process of gradual assimilation and digestion of all that the entity has experienced and gathered into its consciousness during life on earth, then it can be said that there is 'progress' in the devachanic states.° But if by progress is meant the evolving of faculty and its use, and that the devachan is a sphere of originating spiritual causes which impel the entity then or later to further evolution, then there is none.

The reason why some spheres have been called spheres of causes, and others spheres of effects, is because of the difference between actions of will and thought inaugurated by a sevenfold entity, such as a fully incarnated man, and the dreaming state of a devachani which is but a threefold being — consisting of the upper duad plus the aroma or spiritual flowering, mentally and psychically speaking, of the man that was. It takes a complete septenary entity to become a real *causer* of effects in his own world which, in so far as the entity is concerned, is the sphere of causes. The same rule applies to beings of any and all planes, and to any locality, visible or invisible, in the cosmos. Wherever a septenary or duodenary entity acts or lives, that sphere for him is his world of causes, and when his term of imbodiment is over, his rest period becomes his world of effects.

It is clear that the human consciousness, having the range of a sevenfold

---

°In a very general sense, the devachanic ego may be said to 'evolve,' for though in a state of utter repose, there is an uninterrupted movement of the dreaming consciousness and, consequently, a movement of the particles of the enfolding ākāśic vehicle — the devachanic veil or garment — really those portions of the auric egg of the reimbodying ego which find their appropriate function in thus clothing the devachanically dreaming ego.

constitution, is thereby working in a wider sphere than when it is restricted to the dreaming illusion of the human monad asleep in its devachan. In other words, when living on earth — although we are in the māyā of incarnated existence — we have the chance of coming in touch with our spiritual and mānasic creative self. As septenary entities we can, if we so will, throw off the māyā and function in any part of our constitution as a *causing*, intellectually awakened, complete being. On the other hand, the devachanī is a threefold entity only; and whereas most of the devachanic experiences are māyāvi, to the dreaming ego they are perfect illusions and therefore have the appearance of reality, so that he revels in the notion that he is achieving wonderful results.

In fact, the devachanic dreams are incomparably more real than anything that our imperfect physical senses can report to us, because the human ego experiencing them is living in the realms of pure thought and spiritual consciousness, where relatively nothing dims the dreaming cognition of the fulfillment of its noblest ideals and aspirations. From this it follows that the devachan is not an objective sphere, but is in each and every case an *individual* condition of consciousness, always exactly correspondential to the dominating flow of the man's consciousness during his imbodied life.

Thus, the reimbodying ego in the devachan will follow in its consciousness those particular trains of *spiritual* and *intellectual* thought and feeling which were most dominant but had the least chance of fulfillment in the life just ended. But as the devachanic states are conditions of rest and bliss without the slightest possibility of suffering or misery, all the 'dreams' of the ego are of the loftiest and most ecstatically beautiful kind possible to the innate energies of the then active consciousness.

One of the greatest illusions held by the majority of mankind today is the notion that when those whom we love die, we have lost contact with them; and even many who believe that they will meet their loved ones again in a future life on earth, labor under the same illusion. Now it is most emphatically not true that the *spirit* can ever return after death in order to communicate with the living in any manner whatsoever. Outside of the positive cruelty both to the deceased and to the ones left behind, and quite outside of the extraordinarily materialistic atmosphere of this idea, it should be apparent that a disimbodied spirit cannot at any time nor in any circumstance 'descend' to earth. For after death, and after the various processes of casting off the prānic sheaths in the kāma-loka, the human ego rises into its devachanic repose, and thereafter it is unapproachable by anything *save what is of its own character or lofty spiritual type.* It is in just this last phrase that lies the reason why we need never think that we lose all spiritual communion with those whom we have loved; for the higher parts of our being can at any moment by means of vibrational sympathy conjoin its vibrations with those of the devachanī, and thus temporarily become at one with it. As H.P.B. writes in *The Key to Theosophy* (p. 150):

> We are with those whom we have lost in material form, and far, far nearer to them now, than when they were alive. And it is not only in the fancy of the *Devachanee,* as some may imagine, but in reality. For pure divine love is not merely the blossom of a human heart, but has its roots in eternity.

I may add that if indeed there be a truly spiritual love, there need not ever be any striving to commune with the one who has passed on, for such impersonal love will quite automatically rise to the devachanī, and will give the inner conviction to the one on earth that the link is not broken.

The devachanī is protected by nature's own laws. Nothing of earth can reach it, for the ākāśic veil which the devachanic entity has woven around itself, like the cocoon of the yet unborn butterfly, shields it against the intrusion of anything whatsoever beneath its own heights of consciousness. It is spiritual love only which can rise to inner communion with those who have preceded us; no love which has aught of the personal or selfish in it can ever reach the devachanic states. However, it is my earnest belief that it is incomparably better not even to attempt to enter into communion with the devachanī, because the love of very few of us is of so pure and holy a character as to be fit, or even able, to ascend to that high level of impersonality.

The devachanī is under the guardianship of spiritual entities, nature's own masters, and no human, however high his degree, would ever intrude; and, indeed, the higher the degree the less would be the impulse to trespass upon the holy mystery of the devachan.

592

LENGTH OF THE DEVACHANIC PERIOD

There are no clocks, no timepieces in devachan, . . . though the whole Cosmos is a gigantic chronometer in one sense. Nor do we, mortals, — *ici bas même* — take much, if any, cognizance of *time* during periods of happiness and bliss, and find them ever too short; a fact that does not in the least prevent us from enjoying that happiness all the same — when it does come. Have you ever given a thought to this little possibility that, perhaps, it is because their cup of bliss is full to its brim, that the "devachanee" loses "all sense of the lapse of time"; and that it is something that those who land in *Avitchi* do not, though as much as the *devachanee*, the *Avitchee* has no cognizance of time — i.e., of our earthly calculations of periods of time? I may also remind you in this connection that *time is something created entirely by ourselves;* . . . Finite similes are unfit to express the abstract and the infinite; nor can the objective ever mirror the subjective. To realize the bliss in *devachan*, or the woes in *Avitchi*, you have to assimilate them — as we do. — *The Mahatma Letters*, pp. 193–4

THERE IS A LAW IN occultism, based entirely on the operations of nature, that the human entity does not normally reincarnate under one hundred times the number of years lived on earth. The average life span at the present time is said to be some fifteen years, but this is only a statistical average, and there are of course millions of people who live to be much older than that, and their devachanic period will thus be correspondingly longer. Yet every ego's devachan is individual to itself, both as regards character and time-length. Some human beings are in the devachan far longer than 1500 years, whereas others of strongly materialistic bent and attributes have a devachan of possibly only a few hundred years.°

°Certain human beings have made so small a link with their spiritual nature that when death comes nothing has been built up in the life just past to bring the devachanic state into existence. As a result, they sink into a state of utter unconsciousness, in which they remain until the next incarnation which comes very quickly.

Several instances of almost immediate reimbodiment have been reported which, if genuine, would represent those rare and extraordinary cases of apparently normal human beings who, for one karmic reason or another, reincarnate possibly within a year or two after death. Compared with the great multitude of average individuals

It may seem to be a waste of time to spend so many years in the devachan; but, as a matter of fact, there are hundreds of thousands of human beings around us who are in a semi-devachanic state, so full of daydreamings that we speak of them as being impractical, dreamy, visionary, etc. The cause of this condition lies in the desire of the sleeping seeds of character to return to earth, a desire awaking prematurely in the devachan as seeds of impulse, of thought and of passion, thereby shortening the devachanic term before it has reached its full karmic end. Faint dreams of the glory that was experienced thus remain with the reincarnating ego; and to the degree to which the brain-mind consciousness is affected by these memories, is the entity still in devachan. This condition is not good, for such men are not fully awake and their partial devachanic state prevents the reincarnating ego from being alert to its opportunities to grow and expand while on earth. We should shake off the tendency to dream our life away, by being spiritually and mentally active, and being so with a will, and by aspiring to be ever nobler. The mere study of books, while valuable in its way, will not do it. It is the spiritual nature which should be cultivated under all conditions, even in the intricate affairs of human existence.

There are likewise individuals living on earth, although vastly fewer in number, who are really in one of the higher states of avīchi — who are, as it were, haunted by continuously recurring 'dreams' of misery and horror. And, by contrast, there are sublime human beings who even while in the body are in one or more of the lower planes of the nirvana; but these are very rare.

The ordinary man, could he escape the devachan by some work of magic, would probably return to earth a semi-idiot, because his intermediate nature would be so tired and his energy so depleted, that he would be very much like one who has gone without sleep for so long that he is in a condition of physical exhaustion and mental stupor. Nevertheless, every neophyte whose spiritual yearning is to give himself to the grand labors of the Hierarchy of Compassion, is helped in every way possible to evolve quickly, so that his devachan becomes less and less with each

who undergo both kāma-loka as well as devachan between incarnations, they are very few in number. Such are by no means evil or wicked, but are what one might call passive or neutral, spiritually, and, because during life they had not as yet awakened to that characteristically spiritual life which produces the devachanic experience, they pass a short time in the kāma-loka and then incarnate again.

incarnation; and finally he reaches the point where the devachan is not really necessary — except for brief periods. Yet even the most advanced must have at least a temporary surcease and oblivion for psychological and mental recuperation; the time comes when the inner constitution can stand no more strain.°

Devachan is strictly the mathematical resultant of one's spiritual state at the moment of death. The more spiritual the man, up to a certain point, the longer his devachan; the more materialistic he is, the shorter it is. There is a way, however, by which the devachan can indeed be greatly shortened: the way of dedication, of renunciation of the self in the cause of the Buddhas of Compassion. The choice is ours — if we are evolved enough to exercise that choice with the strength of will to make it effectual. Even the making of that choice will shorten the devachanic period.[24]

Another reason why the devachanic periods are so long to us is that man is an imbodied ray from the spiritual monad, which monad must have its full time for the purposes of the post-mortem peregrinations; and these can take place only when its link through the egoic ray with earth (or with other worlds or globes) has been broken, thus freeing it for adventures in other spheres. These reincarnations of ours are very, very far from being the 'whole show' — and we should note here that the periods of both manifestation and rest of a globe of a planetary chain are of equal duration. The key to this mystery lies in the fact that the human ego is a monad or spiritual being in its own spheres where its larger destiny is, and contacts these lower realms of matter only on the occasions

---

°The question has been asked whether a spiritual teacher who is in devachan can enter directly into an adult body, or whether he must first be born in the normal way, and only then make the transfer. When a Messenger enters into devachan, it is usually a very short experience for such a Servant of the Law, and he must leave that state of rest before he can take up his work again on earth. Practically never does a Messenger leave devachan and incarnate immediately in an adult body.

Moreover, it is quite possible for one to enter into devachan and yet not pass through the valley of death as ordinary human beings do. The physical body is gone, it is true; but there is a way by which certain high chelas are helped to get their devachanic rest and still retain enough of the form of the individuality, and of the personality that was, to enter into living adult bodies. Also, there are cases in which neither nirvana nor the devachanic state is experienced, but only a very brief period of blank unconsciousness; and this is made use of to enable a Messenger to recuperate before taking up his duties anew.

of incarnation by a projection of an egoic ray which makes the 'man' we know.°

It is quite understandable that active normal human beings almost instinctively resent the idea of passing nearly one hundred times as long in the sleeping-dreaming devachanic state as in the self-conscious cognition and activity of imbodied life. Yet the devachanī is not 'lazing' its time away, because the releasing of the human monad from the bonds of earth life gives it — the real man — the time and opportunity to perform its most needed and inevitable peregrinations of destiny.

The life of the earth-man, being but a phase of the human monad's manvantaric existence, is not a standard of comparison; nor is it the most important basis from which the human monad's peregrinations take their beginning. The exact reverse is the case, for the human monad's ray, which produces the earth-man, is but the occasional projection of consciousness from the human monad, whose sphere of activity is not only our planetary chain, but also, because of its link with the spiritual monad, the solar system. Hence its ray's repetitive imbodiments on earth are but phases of the cycle of peregrination, its far larger span of life being in and on the invisible globes of our chain.

Nature in the long run makes no great mistakes, and the time spent in the devachan is in each case equated by nature's invariable laws to the needs and spiritual and intellectual health and stability of the evolving ego. Hence it is philosophically inaccurate to regard as overlong or unnecessary the length of time passed by the ego in devachan. Such lengthy time periods are absolutely required by the human monad, not only for its peregrinations, but for the assimilation of the devachanic entity's past experiences as an imbodied man.

For the devachanī there is no realization of the passing of time as

---

°As an evolving soul, man is more advanced than the earth on which he lives and, therefore, more than the spirit of the earth does he have dreams of beauty, yearnings of selflessness, wonderful intuitions of spiritual and intellectual grandeur which no human life is long enough to bring to fulfillment. Consequently he requires a proportionately longer time of rest to digest and assimilate them; whereas a globe is not so far evolved as is a human monad, but is almost equilibrated on the line between the higher and the lower worlds of matter, making the duration of its imbodiment and disimbodiment of virtually equal length. Or when we speak of manvantara and pralaya, we have in mind the life periods of visible and physical things in which the scales are balanced; in our solar system, for instance, in its manvantara and pralaya, day equals night.

the earth-man experiences it. To us here, our sense of time is very strong, because of the continuous succession of events which in our consciousness mark off and produce our conception of time periods, such as our days and nights and the seasons, as well as the phases of human thought and feeling in which the consciousness of the projected ray is sunken and bound psychologically. But in the devachan all these things vanish as exterior impacts upon us. It is very much like what happens to a man who has a deep sleep; whether he is in the strongly dreaming consciousness of the swapna, or in the dreamless sleep of the sushupti, he has no sense whatsoever of the passage of exterior time, so that when he awakens he is scarcely able to say whether he has slept two or eight hours. Even more so is it with the devachanī. For him, time is no more, except in the dreaming sense of the succession of images of thought and blissful imaginings which infill his consciousness. In the higher and highest realms of the devachan even the unutterably beautiful visionings fade into something loftier still, which to our imbodied human consciousness is 'unconsciousness' — or the true sushupti.

Of course, in the far distant future, when the human race shall have evolved so high spiritually and intellectually that it will have passed beyond the need of the devachan, these rest periods will no longer occur. The monad will probably simply step from one then ethereal earth-body into another with scarcely a break in self-consciousness.

We have already mentioned the four general states in which the human consciousness can be. First, jāgrat, the waking consciousness; then swapna, the sleep with dreams; and the reason we do not remember our dreams better is because they are often too ethereal and too intense for the brain to hold the record thereof after we awake. It is not because they are too faint. Again, when a man sleeps and is utterly unconscious, this condition is sushupti. It is a consciousness so keen, so spiritual, with reaches so vast, that the poor limited brain — its physical substance as well as the astral substance of the brain-mind — cannot hold or record it.

The fourth and highest state which we as humans can attain is turīya-samādhi, and this is virtually the consciousness of the divine within us. If the sushupti state is so powerful that our brain cannot recall it, a thousand times more may this be said of the turīya condition. It is somewhat like our feeble brain trying to cognize the consciousness of the hierarch of our solar universe. All these states of consciousness can be, and in extremely rare cases are, experienced by men even when imbodied on earth.

Now when a man dies, he passes from the jāgrat into the swapna so far as his astral body is concerned. His human soul is unconscious in sushupti; but the spirit within him, which has gone to its parent source until recalled to earth again, is in turīya-samādhi. In future ages when we shall be demigods on earth, adumbrations of this divine consciousness will be familiar to all of us. We then shall understand because we shall know. Even today, where is the man who cannot have some inkling of the sublime? Every normal human being, if he so train himself, can raise his consciousness, his real self, and center it in the higher part of his being; and then, when he speaks, his word is truth and carries conviction.

DEVACHAN AND THE GLOBES OF THE PLANETARY CHAIN

He would say: "Verily as far as extends this Ākāśa, so far is the ākāśa within the heart. Within this ākāśa are contained both heaven and earth, both fire (*agni*) and air (*vāyu*), both sun and moon, both lightning and the stars, as well as whatever here is and is not — all *this* world is contained in that (ākāśa)."

He would say: "That does not become decrepit with old age, nor with death is it slain. That is truly the abode of Brahman (*Brahmapura*) — in it are contained all wishes. It is the Self (*ātman*), free from evil, ageless, deathless, sorrowless, hungerless, thirstless, whose desire is truth, whose resolve is truth."   — *Chhāndogya-Upanishad*, VIII, i, 3, 5

EVERY ONE OF THE seven manifest globes of our planetary chain has its own characteristic kāma-loka or astral atmosphere surrounding it. When the imbodied beings of a life-wave on a globe die, the accumulated attractions brought about by imbodiment have to be cast off in the kāma-loka of that globe. Obviously the lower the globe in the planetary chain, the grosser and coarser is its kāma-loka; and the higher it is, the more ethereal is its astral world.

Hence, when a human being dies, he has his second death in the earth's kāma-loka, i.e. in the earth's aura, during which process the human monad, rapidly or slowly according to the individual, drops first the grossest, and finally the least gross life-atoms and the corresponding attractions which keep it in the astral kāma-loka. The culmination of this purgatorial cleansing or gestation° is the second death, which means that the human monad

---

°The term gestation is used in modern theosophical writings to indicate a period of preparation, during which the entity is undergoing a series of modifications in order to enter into the next karmic condition — whether into another world or sphere, or into a change of consciousness, or both. Thus, gestation can signify either the casting off by the excarnate entity of the sheaths and life-atoms of the grosser types which hold it to the material spheres, this process being a rising from matter-realms into spiritual realms; or it can mean the reverse process: changes of modes of consciousness and the assumption of sheaths of grosser type preparing it to become an imbodied entity in material spheres. For the excarnate human entity, there are two main gestation periods: a) preparatory to its entrance into devachan, i.e. preceding the second death; and b) after leaving devachan, in order to prepare for its new life as an imbodied ego on earth.

has arrived at the point of casting off the last vestiges of its astral clothing, or what remains of its kāma-rūpa. From this moment it begins to glide into the devachanic condition.

As the radiance, which is the efflux from the reimbodying ego, ascends towards its Father in Heaven, the spiritual monad, it passes through different spheres of being in the interior worlds. In each of these it pauses for a varying period of time, in order to shed the life-atoms which are native to that sphere and are of too substantial a character to be gathered into this radiance, so that it may journey farther to still loftier and more spiritual spheres.

This passage of the peregrinating monad up the ascending arc of our planetary chain continues until globe G is reached. (Similarly, the monad passes through globes A, B, and C on the descending arc on its return to a new incarnation on our earth globe.) In each globe it has at least one imbodiment before it goes on: a birth, a maturity, a death. The superior globes on the ascending arc are very much higher than our globe D, both in spiritual status and in the types of entities living there, so that the very beasts on globes F and G, and almost so on globe E, are far higher than men are on this earth.°

Some human entities do not *fully* enter into their devachanic state until they have left globe G. Others slip into the devachan after the temporary sojourn on globe E or possibly globe F, while still others enter their devachan more or less completely even before reaching globe E. These several kinds of entrances into the devachan exemplify different grades in perfection of the gestation period undergone by the disincarnate entities. Thus individual cases vary greatly, but for the large majority of human beings the devachanic sleep begins after the second death in the earth's kāma-loka, as the monad enters the sphere of the next globe; and this sleep grows steadily deeper and more ecstatic, until finally the entity has become utterly oblivious of anything except its devachanic dreams.

With regard to the character of the imbodiments which the peregrinating monad undergoes on globes E, F, and G of the ascending arc, and

---

°Our human hierarchy finds both its heavens and hells in the globes of the earth chain. The only true hells are the material globes of a chain, whether it be in the higher or lower cosmic planes. For instance, our earth would be a 'hell' for families of monads which are passing through their phases of experience in the higher globes of our chain.

those that the monad returning to incarnation has to make on the three manifest globes of the descending arc, A, B, C, the question may well be asked: are these imbodiments those of different egos that the spiritual monad has emanated from itself, or are they actually imbodiments, however temporary, of the human monad?°

Now it will be impossible to grasp the true teaching in this connection if our ideas are too heavily crystallized around the notion that there is but one monad within the human constitution, when in fact it is built up of several monads in different degrees of evolutionary unfolding. We are here dealing with the subtle and flowing nature of consciousness: with the monad as a center of consciousness, rather than as a being 'occupying space' much as this apple occupies space on the desk before me.

When the human monad begins its devachan in the kāma-loka of earth, it falls asleep in the bosom of the spiritual monad, and is carried thus in its parent monad up through the globes of the ascending arc before it finally leaves our chain to make its peregrinations through the different planetary chains on the outer round. In order to do this, it obviously must pass *through* these globes, for each is a station on its outward peregrination, and it can omit none. Just as a traveler on a train is unaware of the stations passed through at night while he is asleep, but will be conscious when awake that he speeds by some stations and stops at others, just so on the various globes through which the spiritual monad passes, the human monad resting within it will either have a relative awakening — although always very slight — or none at all, every case depending upon its karma.

But we should not press the analogy too far. What actually happens is that those monadic qualities of consciousness, which will become relatively fully awake on the different globes when the general life-wave reaches them — these qualities (and not the full consciousness of the devachanic monad) are temporarily aroused into an illusory consciousness when such globes are passed through. These extrusions of qualities of consciousness are projected like thought-rays, and take temporary imbodiments on these globes which awaken them by their attractive pull. Such imbodiment is, of course, very imperfect and in a sense illusory, for the

___

°There are imbodiments of many kinds. 'Imbodiment' does not always mean an encasement of human flesh; there are also fiery, airy, watery, ethereal, as well as spiritual encasements; and the term of such imbodiments may be very short or very long, according to the individual's karma.

reason that the life-wave to which we belong is at present on earth and not on these higher globes.

Even in ordinary life we can find an illustration of the same partial functioning of consciousness; for it is not uncommon for a man to perform his duties or to be involved in his thoughts, and yet at the same time find his attention attracted to some other event or object; and, in a more or less evanescent fashion, a thought-ray is projected from his otherwise occupied mind, encompasses the event and very soon is again withdrawn into the man's consciousness. Or a man who is half-asleep is for the time living in two aspects of his consciousness: partly in the jāgrat condition, partly in the swapna; and he is vaguely conscious of being in both states.

Nothing that has been said should be misconstrued to mean that the devachanic bliss of the *main* part of the consciousness of the human monad is disturbed or interrupted. It is only a thought-ray, so to speak, which is attracted forth by this or that globe and, after such evanescent projection, is indrawn again into the devachanic consciousness. All the after-death states are really *functions of consciousness*.

During the time when the human ego is sleeping within its parent monad, as the latter passes through the ascending arc of the planetary chain, the cognizing intelligence of the average human entity does not perceive or feel what is going on around it to any appreciable degree. Hence, there can be no bringing back of the fruitage of experiences on the other globes of the chain. The human monad as a whole is virtually unconscious of the fleeting imbodiments of a portion of its consciousness on the globes passed through. It is almost an automatic occurrence so far as the human monad is concerned; and when I speak of the human monad, I am referring to the lower part of the reincarnating ego.

From this rule of unconscious experiences on the other globes we should except the sixth rounders, and also, in degrees depending upon the respective individuals, those who are on their way to becoming fifth and sixth rounders. This exception applies likewise to those who succeed in passing the gateway of initiation; for, if one can do that, he will be a living jīvanmukta, though for the time existing as a man. During the course of these initiations, the inner self of the initiant not only will wing its way to the other globes of our planetary chain, where he will gain firsthand experience by living there for the time being and by actually being a part of these globes, but he will also go out to the other planets and to the sun along the magnetic pathways of the universe.

In studying these teachings we should constantly endeavor to keep the processes of our thought and consciousness fluid, thus avoiding the danger of mental crystallization, or the perilous self-satisfaction of believing that there is 'not very much more to learn.' This feeling arises in the astral-material brain-mind, which dearly loves to pigeonhole facts — although, admittedly, having one's ideas in order is very necessary. The attempt to keep the mind fluid, while often making us uncomfortable, puts the brain-mind in its proper place and makes it a flexible servant instead of a rigid taskmaster.

NIRVANA

No Entity, whether angelic or human, can reach the state of Nirvana, or of absolute purity, except through aeons of suffering and the *knowledge* of EVIL as well as of good, as otherwise the latter remains incomprehensible.
— *The Secret Doctrine*, II, 81

THERE ARE CERTAIN analogies between nirvana and devachan: both are states of the consciousnesses which experience them, and neither is a locality or a place. If we look upon the manifold conditions in which consciousnesses may find themselves as a sort of hierarchical series, then we may say that the highest portions of the devachan blend into the lowest grades of the nirvana. The main difference between them can be stated in a few words: the devachan is more or less an illusion, whereas nirvana, being closer to the fundamental reality of cosmic life, is relatively Real and thus by just so much no truly māyāvi series of conditions.

When a monad has freed itself from its sheaths of consciousness, it becomes monadically conscious, i.e. fully self-conscious with its own inherent or native consciousness, and then, because it is in its essence a divine-spiritual entity, it is in a nirvana. All the enshrouding veils or garments have been 'blown out' or discarded, leaving the essential spiritual fire unveiled and free — a jīvanmukta, a freed monad.

Now it is only the most highly evolved monads which are jīvanmuktas or full-blown divinities; and any monad which has not reached this state of moksha or mukti is more or less clothed with the sheaths of thought and feeling produced from the substance of its auric egg. As human beings, we are enveloped by the veil of our human selfhood; in other words, we are not yet jīvanmuktas, not yet living in the sublime consciousness of our monadic essence and therefore can have only fugitive intuitions of nirvana. The sole exceptions are those grand human beings like the buddhas or the bodhisattvas, who have evolved so far along the evolutionary pathway that at times they can rise up into the purely spiritual parts of their constitution and therein — at least temporarily — enjoy one or another of the nirvanic degrees of self-conscious being.

There are different grades of nirvana; there is one so high that it blends imperceptibly with the condition of the cosmic hierarch of our universe, while the lower states of nirvana are quite frequently attained by very mystically inclined men who have undergone spiritual training.° They usually cannot remain in the nirvanic state for long. Yet this ability shows a high degree of evolutionary advancement, for even the inferior stages of nirvana are exceedingly lofty. Entering nirvana means leaving all interest in the world of men and the passing out of human into divine existence.

We humans have our blissful post-mortem rest periods in one or another of the grades of the devachanic scale of consciousness; yet, however much superior the devachanī's consciousness may be to that of the imbodied human, it is nevertheless a māyāvi state, because the devachanic consciousness is not essentially monadic. Indeed, the heavy māyā of our merely human state of consciousness still exists when we die and enter the devachan; but even while we are incarnated, our ātma-buddhi and higher mānasic parts are in nirvana when we consider the consciousness that these parts of our constitution enjoy on their own respective planes. Thus it is that even an imbodied man of highly evolved character can, at least temporarily, enter into the nirvana by raising and placing his percipient consciousness in the Buddha-like and Christ-like parts of his being.

When we remember that the universe is divisible into a virtually endless series of interlocking and interacting hierarchies from the divine down to the physical plane, we see that entities, who belong to and therefore live in hierarchical systems far higher than our own, will have devachans and nirvanas incomparably superior to our devachanic and nirvanic systems. What to us is nirvana would be to beings living on a higher scale merely a sort of devachan. Thus the scale of values rises steadily along the major hierarchical scheme of the universe, so that when we shall leave in the course of the macrocosmic ages our own hierarchy and enter into a higher one, we shall then have devachans and nirvanas incomparably more glorious than ours now are.

Nevertheless, for us human beings, and for all others like us who are inhabitants of our hierarchical system of the universe, the nirvana that

---

°To train the consciousness to enter into the nirvanic state is abnormal in the present period. In fact, the consciousness attained by intense spiritual training, after which one becomes a nirvanī, goes far beyond that of the seventh root-race on globe D in this fourth round. Actually, the consciousness of a nirvanī is similar to that which will be characteristic of the latter part of the sixth *round*.

lies before us is in very truth, to us, and to them, the Reality. This is
so because when we shall have attained this nirvana, we shall then have
reached the summit of our hierarchical system and be living in its ātma-
buddhic ranges of consciousness.

It is a fundamental teaching in Mahāyāna Buddhism[25] that the realization of nirvana° can never be attained by the mere intellect as such,
because the intellect of man dissects and analyzes things, and establishes
something it can take hold of; it then sees that "something" as if coming
into existential being and vanishing. But nirvana cannot be conceived
of as having any tangible form; it neither comes into existence nor ceases
to exist. To attain nirvana — which is, according to Mahāyāna phraseology,
a state of emptiness (Śūnyatā) inherent in the very nature of things and
also a state of self-realization obtained through the exercise of supreme
wisdom — there must take place a 'revulsion' within the deepest recesses
of consciousness, within the higher manas, itself a treasure house in which
are stored the ākāśic records of man's entire intellectual and spiritual
experiences.

The Mahāyānist considers the notions of being and non-being as one
of the greatest impediments to the realization of nirvana, and stresses
the fact that when nirvana is attained and the 'revulsion' has taken place,
the condition then achieved is utterly devoid of all predicates, of all pairs
of opposites. So long as dualism is adhered to, so long as nirvana is
intellectually considered as essentially the opposite of samsāra (the cycle
of births and deaths) or as the annihilation of the world of senses, there
is no true nirvana. The latter is beyond and above all relativity, blending
in itself the conceptions of being and non-being, and transcending both.

The nirvana of man has its direct analogical application to that of
a planetary chain when, at the end of its manvantara, it goes out of
manifested existence into its pralaya, which merely means that its higher
element-principles — or those of any of its globes — enter into the appropriate nirvanic condition. So at the death of human beings, the mānasic
portions enter into the māyāvi states of the devachan, while the still higher
or highest parts of the human constitution are at the same time evolving

---

°The term nirvana (nibbana in Pali) is met with very frequently in the scriptures
of the Hīnayāna Buddhism, but less often in the Mahāyāna schools where the idea
of nirvanic conditions or states is usually expressed by cognate terms such as prajñā,
sambodhi, dharmakāya, tathātā, pratyātmajñāna, and others, all of which have their
own specific significance.

and acting on their own planes; however, in their own highest consciousness-portions, so to speak, they are in their nirvana — having conscious experience in the unveiled Reality of the hierarchy to which each such monad belongs.

Thus the human or mānasic part is in its devachan; the spiritual ego is pursuing its peregrinations on the outer round through the sacred chains; but the highest portion or monadic essence of the spiritual monad is, as always, in nirvana. Even a man imbodied on earth has the highest portions of his constitution, the ātmic essence of his being, in a nirvanic state. Hence our consciousness during incarnation on earth, however real it may seem to us to be, is actually heavily illusory when contrasted with the unveiled and intensely active consciousness of the nirvana.

SLEEP AND DEATH ARE BROTHERS

... if we admit the existence of a higher or permanent *Ego* in us — which Ego must not be confused with what we call the "Higher Self," we can comprehend that what we often regard as dreams, generally accepted as idle fancies, are, in truth, stray pages torn out from the life and experiences of the *inner* man, and the dim recollection of which at the moment of awakening becomes more or less distorted by our physical memory. The latter catches mechanically a few impressions of the thoughts, facts witnessed, and deeds performed by the *inner* man during its hours of complete freedom. For our *Ego* lives its own separate life within its prison of clay whenever it becomes free from the trammels of matter, *i.e.*, during the sleep of the physical man. This Ego it is which is the actor, the real man, the true human self. But the physical man cannot feel or be conscious during dreams; for the personality, the outer man, with its brain and thinking apparatus, are paralyzed more or less completely.

— *Transactions of the Blavatsky Lodge*, p. 50

SLEEP AND DEATH ARE brothers, according to the old Greek proverb. However, they are not merely brothers, born of the same fabric of human consciousness, but are in all verity one, identical. Death is a perfect sleep, with its interim awakenings of a kind, such as in the devachan, and a full human awakening in the succeeding reincarnation. Sleep is an imperfect fulfillment of death, nature's prophecy of the future death. Nightly we sleep, and therefore nightly we partially die. Indeed, one may go still farther and say that sleep and death and all the various processes and realizations of initiation are but different phases or operations of consciousness, varied forms of the same fundamental thing. Sleep is largely an automatic functioning of the human consciousness; death is the same, but in immensely greater degree, and is a necessary habit of the consciousness in order that it may gain for the psychological part of the constitution a resting and an assimilation of experience.

Initiation is a kind of temporary 'death' of all the lower man, a 'sleep' of the lower psychological nature, and a magical awakening to an intense awareness of the higher psychological part upon which is then radiating the inner light of the man's monadic consciousness. Thus it is that initiation comprises both sleep and death and uses these functions of consciousness in order to free the 'inner man' for the marvelous experience on inner planes that initiation brings about.

Anyone who has stood at the bedside of one who is dying must have been strongly impressed with the extraordinary similitude between the coming of death and going to sleep. The sole distinction between death and sleep is one of degree. Precisely as in death, the consciousness during sleep becomes, following upon a brief period of complete unconsciousness, the seat or active focus of forms of inner mental activity which we call dreams.

In sleep, the psychological or personal part of man is non-manifesting through the physical brain; in point of fact, it is this absence, this temporary disjunction of the intermediate nature which is the efficient cause of sleep. The body sleeps because the personal man is no longer there. When we go to sleep at night, we slip into a state of complete unconsciousness only because we have not yet learned during the daytime to become self-conscious in the higher parts of us.

As a rule, the physical body is guarded during sleep by an ākāśic veil — a condensation of the substance of the auric egg itself, naturally thrown forth from the body as it sinks into repose — which usually prevents hurt. This is well exemplified in the case of sleepwalkers. There are other contributing agencies likewise, one of which is seen in the interesting fact that most animate beings do not touch with intent to injure a body which is quiescent. And even 'inanimate' nature is so constructed that there seems to be a corresponding response in it of peace and quiet. Still other factors are involved here, but the main one is the veil or wall of ākāśa surrounding the sleeping body which, however, is effective only in proportion as the life is pure.

The vital thread of life and consciousness still vibrates in even the physical brain of a man during sleep, producing dreams, some that delight him and others that harass and perplex him. The thread of radiance remains unbroken, so that the ego, which has left the lower mind and the body behind and is soaring out into the spaces, is able to return along this luminous thread linking the monad to the astral-vital brain of the sleeping body. When a man dies, it is exactly like falling into a very deep sleep, utter, sweet unconsciousness, except that the vital cord is snapped and then, instantaneously, like the sounding of a soft golden note, the soul is free.

What happens to a man during sleep is an adumbration of what will happen to him at death. The personal ego goes into oblivion and its consciousness is withdrawn into the spiritual part where it rests and has temporary peace. During sleep, certain parts of man's inner constitution wing their way into the spaces of the solar system. The migration of course is very short; sometimes like a lightning flash, where one has slept only a few moments. But time to pure consciousness does not exist; time pertains to material existence. Some men go to the moon when they sleep, some to their parent planet, others to the sun. And another part of the constitution flashes forth and back to its parent star. Certain other men visit the elemental world, go to the center of our own globe, for instance.

During sleep and after death, each individual goes to those places which he has earned for himself by his thought and his aspirations, or lack of them; in other words, it is all a matter of synchronous vibration — a man goes to his natural home, whether high or low. The cause of such peregrinations inheres fundamentally in the psychomagnetic attractions to these different localities in the solar systems, which are 'stations' along the devious routes of the circulations of the cosmos; and since the consciousness is accustomed to these routes through long ages of habit, each of the various parts of the human constitution follows its own particular direction in these circulations.

There is not only a close analogy, but an identity — both of process and of fact — between the dreams had during sleep and those of the after-death state. Dreams depend upon two main factors: (a) the mechanism of the psychic consciousness, and (b) the two kinds of forces impinging upon this mechanism, which control the direction and guide the operations of the psychic consciousness of the dreamer. Of these forces, the first kind is the solar, lunar, and planetary influences under which an individual is born; and the second is the automatic reaction to the events and experiences that had occurred during the waking state.

The astrological influences under which an individual is born are the conjoined action of all the solar, lunar, and planetary powers in the solar system; but in every case certain powers predominate because of their swabhāva — this swabhāva coalescing with the man's own swabhāva because of identity of origin; and it is this identity of origin or of powers which causes these forces or influences to act most strongly upon him.

Therefore, while all human beings have dreams which are more or less alike, everyone has dreams of his or her own characteristically unique type.

To phrase the matter in other words, every man is more particularly the offspring or under the influence of one of the twelve logoic forces of the solar system. Now as each such solar logos finds its own especial focus of action in one of the twelve sacred planets, we see how the planetary as well as the solar influences come into play in the psychic consciousness of the sleeping man. Also, as all human beings have a 'lunar body,' i.e. a 'lunar layer' in their auric egg, the moon likewise plays upon the mind of the sleeper; indeed, in most cases the lunar influences are by far the most powerful upon the sleeping man.

When asked what dreams were, H.P.B. answered that it depended upon the meaning attached to the term:

> You may "dream," or, as we say, sleep visions, awake or asleep. If the Astral Light is collected in a cup or metal vessel by will-power, and the eyes fixed on some point in it with a strong will to see, a waking vision or "dream" is the result, if the person is at all sensitive. The reflections in the Astral Light are seen better with closed eyes, and, in sleep, still more distinctly. From a lucid state, vision becomes translucid; from normal organic consciousness it rises to a transcendental state of consciousness. . . .
>
> There are many kinds of dreams, as we all know. Leaving the "digestion dream" aside, there are brain dreams and memory dreams, mechanical and conscious visions. Dreams of warning and premonition require the active co-operation of the inner Ego. They are also often due to the conscious or unconscious co-operation of the brains of two living persons, or of their two Egos. . . .
>
> [That which dreams is] generally the physical brain of the personal Ego, the seat of memory, radiating and throwing off sparks like the dying embers of a fire. The memory of the Sleeper is like an Aeolian seven-stringed harp; and his state of mind may be compared to the wind that sweeps over the chords.°

The nature of a man's dreams is determined almost wholly — yet by no means entirely — by his waking life. The little child, for example, has no positive dreams of any kind; its experiences are still too trifling. Its mind, even its brain, are not yet set or fully formed; nevertheless on occasion it will have frightening dreams, but these are usually caused

---

° *Transactions of the Blavatsky Lodge*, pp. 58–9.

by automatic psychologic reactions in the child's sleeping brain to some disturbance that it has experienced when awake.

Most of us have dreams which are neither very delightful nor very terrifying, but which often are mixed — inchoate and confused. The reason is obvious, for our dreams are but reflections of our waking hours. Sometimes our mind is bent to the things of the spirit and the ways of beauty and harmony, and at other times gives way to thoughts of a completely opposite character, which at night (or after death in the kāma-loka) return to us in our dreams.

It is *thought* that makes all dreams. The evil man, one who is so selfish, and whose imagination and feelings are so restricted and imprisoned that a kindly impulse seldom if ever enters his consciousness, feels the unfailing reaction: when he dreams, which is frequently, he is in an emotional and mental hell. His thoughts haunt his brain like avenging ghosts, and afflict his dreaming consciousness. Contrariwise, the man who yearns to help his fellows, is impersonal, of lofty thinking, very rarely has evil dreams; if he dreams at all, he has dreams that the gods might envy.

The above equally applies not only to the dreams of the devachanī but also to those of the kāma-rūpa in the kāma-loka. The cause is the same: mental deposits or thought impulses arising during the life of a man, and so affecting his mental structure that they automatically begin to act upon his consciousness. Thus thought and feeling not only make character throughout the evolving ages, but likewise bring happiness and peace or the nightmares of the kāma-loka.

Dreams of any kind are the earth-side of a man's character coming into pictorial action again in the mind, and therefore are 'effects' and not 'causes'; and this is why the devachan is called the sphere of effects and our earth-existence, wherein originate the causative life-impulses, the sphere of causes.° This does not mean that earth-life is the *only* sphere of causes; the statement refers only to incarnated human beings, and the effects produced after death by their thoughts and feelings and actions while imbodied. Thus, neither in the devachan nor when a man is dreaming at night does he originate any positive or inventive courses of action, although it is occasionally true that the dreams of a man, by reaction on the mind, may consciously or unconsciously somewhat influence the thoughts of the waking man.

°Cf. *The Mahatma Letters*, pp. 47–8.

There is a certain danger, however, in putting too much importance upon the matter of dreams and their interpretations. *Occasionally* dreams are prophetic, but to a large extent they 'come true' because they are the foreshadowings of the automatic working of consciousness, i.e. of what the consciousness itself, because of its biases and tendencies, will bring to pass in the future. Therefore, it could very plausibly be argued that if an observer of a dreaming man were quasi-omniscient, he would be able to discern in all the dreams of the man what his future would be. But it is obvious that there are very few such perfect soothsayers or dream-interpreters!

Truly prophetic dreams do not occur in the devachan, but can do so during sleep because they arise in the stored knowledge of the reincarnating ego, which latter attempts to impress the sleeping brain with a 'radiation' of prophetic foresight. This does happen upon very rare occasions, but one should examine such dreams very suspiciously and not automatically look upon them as guides in life. In general, it is far better to ignore one's dreams, for very few people indeed are sufficiently awakened inwardly to know whether a dream is of a prophetic character or one which is merely an ordinary psychic reaction of the usually erratic and confused brain-mind.°

If a man can — and will — study his consciousness during the day as well as the reactions upon his percipient mind to the various impacts of the daily events, he will have a master key to knowing precisely what will happen to him, as a center of consciousness, both during sleep and after death. If he desire to know how he will feel or what he will cognize at the moment of death, let him grip his consciousness with his will and study the actual processes of his falling asleep — if he can! No man, however, at that precise instant knows that he is lapsing into sleep. For a time he seems to himself to be thinking, and the more intensely he

---

°Many dreams, again, while not truly prophetic, nevertheless can tell the one who studies his own mental and vital processes something at least, and possibly much, of what his character is. Very often the body, or the passions and feelings, react upon the sleeping brain producing pictures therein, and the one who knows how to read these dreams from careful self-examination, without morbidity, may get useful warnings or reminders that his life and emotions are not just what they should be.

But, as said, it is far wiser to forget dreams of all kinds, unless they be of such immensely vivid character, and so impress us when we are awake, that we have the intuition that we had better hold such dreams in mind.

thinks the farther is sleep from him — and then he is off, he is asleep! Instant unconsciousness supervenes at the critical juncture, and it may or may not be succeeded by dreams.

Death is identical with this process of falling asleep. It matters not at all how we die: whether by age, by disease, or by violence. The instant of death always brings for a period the unutterable peace of perfect unconsciousness, which is like gliding into a beginning, a foretaste as it were, of the devachanic bliss, just as the careful observer will find to be his experience when falling to sleep.

Finally, I venture to call attention once more to the point that the mind will automatically go on functioning along the exact lines of thought which one had preceding either sleep or death. Hence the extreme importance of having one's mind in order and peaceful before going to sleep — or before dying; to refuse entrance to any thoughts of dislike, hatred or evil. As the great Pythagoras taught in the verses attributed to him by his disciple Lysis, which form a part of the so-called *Golden Verses of Pythagoras:*[26]

> Admit not sleep to thy drooping eyes,
> Ere thou hast well reviewed each one of the day's deeds.
> In what was I remiss? What did I do? What duty was not fulfilled?

THROUGH THE PORTALS OF DEATH

EVERY MONAD IN THE vast ranges of time descends through all the kingdoms on the passive side of nature, gathering experience in each; pausing in the mineral kingdom, it rises therefrom along the ascending arc towards the source from which it originally came. On this arc of ascent it evolves forth ever more largely the self-conscious attributes and qualities which, from an originally unself-conscious monad, make it become a self-conscious monadic god when it reaches its final goal.

In connection with the after-death existence of the ten main monadic classes or life-waves, the following diagram shows the path they travel during their rounds of the globes of a planetary chain.

We see that the three highest kingdoms, or three dhyāni-chohanic classes, are both the origin and the goal of the other seven. The diagram likewise shows a descent on the left side, a balancing at the bottom in the mineral kingdom, and a subsequent rise through the next three higher kingdoms, which again send their peregrinating monads upwards to the dhyāni-chohanic kingdoms.° Now not only the animals, but the plants, minerals and the three elemental kingdoms as well, are formed entirely of these respective classes of monads in different degrees of development. All these monads are evolving beings, both as classes and as individuals, unfolding from within dormant powers, capacities, attributes, functions, and the consequent organs which express these qualities during imbodied existence. The difference between a beast and a man, or a man and a plant, is not one of origin or of destiny, but solely one of evolutionary growth or unfolding.

Evolution as viewed in the esoteric philosophy most emphatically does not mean the Darwinistic hypothesis (nor any modified form thereof), that is, the slow mechanical accumulation through the ages of small

---

°All the various classes or kingdoms given in this diagram are called by H.P.B. "families," or sometimes "humanities" — not meaning that they are all human egos or human kingdoms, but humanities in the sense that in the future the entities in the kingdoms below man will *become* human; or, viewed from another standpoint, those beings now superior to our kingdom were human in some past cosmic manvantara.

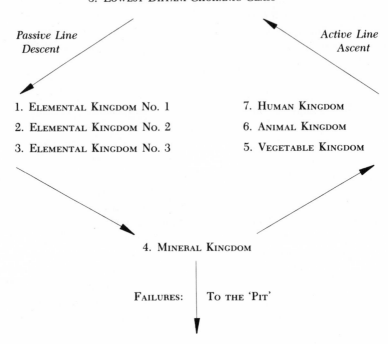

10. HIGHEST DHYĀNI-CHOHANIC CLASS

9. INTERMEDIATE DHYĀNI-CHOHANIC CLASS

8. LOWEST DHYĀNI-CHOHANIC CLASS

Passive Line
Descent

Active Line
Ascent

1. ELEMENTAL KINGDOM No. 1

2. ELEMENTAL KINGDOM No. 2

3. ELEMENTAL KINGDOM No. 3

7. HUMAN KINGDOM

6. ANIMAL KINGDOM

5. VEGETABLE KINGDOM

4. MINERAL KINGDOM

FAILURES: To THE 'PIT'

increments of any kind. It is just the contrary: the slow unfoldings from within in serial progressive stages of ever larger *outflowings* of inner power and inner substance.

For example, the monad of an animal, during its sojourn in the animal kingdom, expresses itself as such only because the unwrapping of this particular monad has reached that stage; and the monad of a man expresses itself in the human kingdom because the unfolding from within the monad has reached self-conscious egoity. Never does the *body* of a beast evolve into a human *body*. When the monads now manifesting in the animal kingdom have had their full measure of experience there, their bodies, although slowly refining and progressing in various evolutionary specializations, will simply die out or be dropped, and the monads thus freed from the beast 'Circle of Necessity' thereafter seek human bodies. These bodies will be of the very lowest grade because they have not as yet sufficiently developed from within themselves the powers and characteristics enabling them to function in more truly human vehicles.

That which reincarnates in the animals is a ray from the spiritual monad expressing itself in the realms of matter as the animal monad. As the animals have no awakened mind, no mānasaputric power of abstract thought, such as we have, they have evolved as yet no true ego which would allow them to have a devachan. For this reason the beasts as well as the plants, the minerals, and the three kingdoms of the elementals, reimbody almost immediately after the death of their physical bodies.

In the beasts, such reincarnation takes place after a time period which varies from a few days to possibly a year, for there are enormous differences among animals, as for instance between the faithful dog and the earthworm. The lower in development, the sooner the reimbodiment. When animals die, they have no post-mortem consciousness of any kind, except perhaps that a dog or a horse or a cat which has been a close companion of some human being may have a short and very shadowy kind of astral consciousness after the shock of death is ended; but even then, reimbodiment takes place very quickly.

The plants have even less of consciousness than have the animals; and consequently when a plant dies, it has its 'astral' liberated, so to speak, for a few moments or days in the kāma-loka, and then the monad reimbodies itself at the first possible opportunity. In this connection, the changing of the seasons, bringing seeding time, then months of rest, followed by the bursting of the seeds into bud and blossom in the spring and summer, must enter into the picture. In certain cases the plant monads remain in crystallized inactivity, like icicles, as it were, until the season of growth for their kind comes again.

As the minerals have even less 'consciousness' than the plants have — for the plants indeed have a vague kind of sensitivity in consciousness — the death and the reimbodiment of a mineral monad are to us humans with our notions of time periods practically simultaneous. In fact, what we

617

call chemical combinations are almost invariably the instances of mineral monads 'dying' and 'reimbodying.' Exactly the same thing may be said of the smaller entities in the mineral kingdom such as the atoms and the electrons.

Needless to say, the entities below the human kingdom have no devachan and make no peregrinations through the inner realms — other than unconscious flashings to and fro — because they are so closely joined to the worlds of matter that they cannot vacate them long enough to bring about the mystical and wondrous peregrinations that the spiritual monads have. In fact, devachan belongs almost exclusively to the human kingdom, because only human egos have evolved forth from the monad within them sufficient spiritual fire and high intellectual faculty to make the devachanic state a part of their Cycle of Necessity. Of course, the individual monads in the kingdoms higher than the human have passed beyond the need of the 'dreaming' of the devachan, and their rest periods are one or more of the various stages of nirvana.

Now every monad has its own individuality, which is its essential swabhāva, so that not only do the dhyāni-chohans show forth individuality (in far vaster degree than men do), but likewise every one of the animals and plants, minerals and elementals, has its own swabhāva. Hence no animal is identical with any other animal, no plant with any other plant, no mineral monad with any other mineral monad, and no elemental with any other elemental. It is this intrinsic marvel of characteristic individuality which distinguishes not only kingdom from kingdom, but likewise monad from monad.

In theosophic writings mention is sometimes made of group-souls, referring to the monads of the kingdoms below the human. This is a graphic term if used with care, and *if* we understand its meaning correctly: that these monads are so slightly in possession of an evolved mānasic power or individuality that, while they are indeed monadic individuals, they nevertheless are more closely alike than peas in a pod. Because of their lack of an evolved ego, they are incomparably more unionized with each other than are human beings, and hence they group together like drops of water in the ocean.

Also, and this is an even deeper reason, the hierarchical or class swabhāva of each of these lower kingdoms works in and through its respective individuals more sweepingly and in a more unitary sense than does the Silent Watcher of the human hierarchy. Just here is a most

618

interesting paradox: the kingdoms higher than the human are more faithful to the sweeping swabhāva of their respective Silent Watchers or king-souls than we are in the human kingdom; in this respect the kingdoms on the arc of ascent very curiously resemble the kingdoms on the arc of descent. On the other hand, there is this difference: the individuals of the kingdoms of the ascending arc are becoming with every important time period more fully self-conscious divine or spiritual egos, and thus their subservience to their hierarch is a gladly willing one; whereas the individuals of the kingdoms of the downward arc are blindly and unconsciously submissive to their respective kingdom-hierarchs because they have not sufficient egoity to become intellectual rebels as men so often are. This shows how the monad evolves from unself-consciousness into what is often assertive self-consciousness and, as it slowly ascends in evolution, the monad now become man changes his 'rebellious' self-consciousness into divine and buddha-like self-forgetful subservience to the divine will of the Silent Watcher of our hierarchy.

After the death of any entity on earth, the different 'lives' or life-atoms which compose its constitution sooner or later are liberated, and then immediately are drawn to their first and strongest focus of attraction. In the case of a man, the life-atoms of his body as it decays, or as they fly apart when it is cremated, peregrinate, each one, instantly to the man, animal, plant or stone to which it feels psychomagnetically drawn, has a brief imbodiment in such focus, and then follows the next attraction which at the moment is dominant; and so on through the ages.

The life-atoms of the other and higher parts of man's constitution follow exactly similar courses, each on its own plane. For example, the astral life-atoms forming parts of the linga-śarīra are drawn to men, to beasts or to plants, and so forth; the mānasic life-atoms are attracted to living men and help to feed or build their so-called 'mental bodies.' Similarly, the life-atoms of an animal body after its death find their respective ways to the kingdoms of nature to which they are most strongly drawn; and so likewise with the plants, etc.

It is also true that the life-atoms which aided in forming a man's brain will, after his death, probably be attracted to some other imbodied being of a higher type than would, let us say, the life-atoms which belonged to one of his bones. As a matter of fact, there is a good deal of deep and highly occult teaching connected with the transmigrations of the life-atoms; but it would require a bulky volume even to give an outline of it.

The often beautiful and fascinating world which surrounds us, but which at the same time has so many aspects of a horrible and repellent character, is built of the life-atoms of beings who both live and have lived, including, of course, the life-atoms which belong, because of their primary origin, to the imbodied beings which make up the various kingdoms. Thus a particular life-atom might be attracted to a venomous serpent because of the swabhāva inherent in itself, and also because of the 'accidental' swabhāva impressed upon it by the being from whom it last migrated. Another life-atom may be attracted to form the body of some lovely flower, or it may go to the water, a stone, an animal or a man.

To a certain extent the psychic and instinctual and astral parts of the animals are formed of life-atoms which are drawn from the human kingdom, and this shows how marvelously nature interblends in all its functions.° The animal is gradually helped by this psychic and astral and other contact with the human kingdom, just as we ourselves are aided by the life-atoms or 'lives' entering our constitution from the dhyāni-chohanic classes.

I might add that man's cast-off astral molds — the historic pictures made by him in the astral light which remain fixed for aeons and aeons — furnish the molds into which the evolving beings of the lower kingdoms enter in due course of evolution. The animals, for instance, slowly special-ize in their body-formations and try to approach the human form; it is these astral human molds which the beast bodies more or less perfectly reproduce. Thus the ape-like forms — certainly not apes — which the human bodies had in the third round, and which left their molds in the astral light, will be used in producing the body forms which the evolving animal monads will occupy in the next planetary chain manvantara, at which time the present animals will be the embryonic humans on that chain. Thus every kingdom 'blazes the way' for the one which follows it.

°Elementaries of human beings who have so greatly degenerated from the human norm that they are on the downward path, not infrequently — before they are caught in a current of efflux which carries them to the Pit — are so avid and hungry for physical life, that these wretched astral beings are drawn into the wombs of animals and become beasts corresponding to the innate vileness of the elementaries themselves. Indeed, some elementaries in the astral light are so far disintegrated that they cannot even enter an animal womb, but become attached to evil individuals of the plant world.

THE PROCESS OF REIMBODIMENT

> The "souls" of the departed pass through many other stages of existence after leaving this Earth-body, just as they were in many others anterior to their birth as men and women here. The exact truth about this mystery is known only to the highest adepts; but it may be said even by the lowest of the neophytes that each of us controls his future rebirths, making each next succeeding one better or worse according to his present efforts and desserts. — H.P.B. in *The Theosophist,* February 1881, p. 103

CONTINUANCE BY repetitive existences of the reimbodying monad, in various vehicles or rūpas, is the essence of the doctrine of rebirth.

Before the time of actual physical reincarnation on this earth-globe, the psycho-spiritual energies which had attracted the ego to the bosom of the spiritual monad during its post-mortem peregrinations reach a point when they become relatively exhausted; coincidently new attractions to the lower spheres begin to come into operation, impelling the ego back to earth. As the reimbodying ego works its ray 'downwards,' irresistibly drawn by the reawakening of memories of a previous incarnation, it is gradually pulled psychomagnetically to the planes wherein it had lived before, and finally enters the most physical part of the planetary chain of earth — actually the atomic world of globe D, including its inter-atomic and intra-atomic 'ethers.' With its gradual descent from the spiritual realms, the lower portions of its auric egg begin to stir. Simultaneously, the consciousness of the ego begins to sink from dreaming into unconsciousness, and the gestation period preceding rebirth begins. This is the time when the auric egg, acting automatically and instinctively under the driving urge of the awakening karma, gradually forms within itself the vague outlines of the astral form, which latter slowly drifts to the family or the woman to which the karmic psychomagnetic attraction is strongest.

In this connection, the following passage from the E.S. *Instructions* (III) issued by H.P.B. will be of value:

Now the Linga Sarîra remains with the Physical Body, and fades out along with it. An astral entity then has to be created, a new Linga Sarîra provided, to become the bearer of all the past Tanhas and future Karma. How is this accomplished? The mediumistic Spook, the "departed angel," fades out and vanishes also in its turn° as an entity or full image of the Personality that was, and leaves in the Kâmalôkic world of effects only the record of its misdeeds and sinful thoughts and acts, known in the phraseology of Occultists as Tanhic or human Elementals. Entering into the composition of the Astral Form of the new body, into which the Ego, upon its quitting the Dêvâchânic state, is to enter according to Karmic decree, the Elementals form that new astral entity which is born within the Auric Envelope, and of which it is often said "bad Karma waits at the threshold of Dêvâchân, with its army of Skandhas." For no sooner is the Dêvâchânic state of reward ended, than the Ego is indissolubly united with (or rather follows in the track of) the new Astral Form. Both are Karmically propelled towards the family or woman from whom is to be born the *animal child* chosen by Karma to become the vehicle of the Ego which has just awakened from the Dêvâchânic state. Then the *new* Astral Form, composed partly of the pure Âkâsic Essence of the Auric Egg, and partly of the terrestrial elements of the punishable sins and misdeeds of the last Personality, is drawn into the woman. Once there, Nature models the foetus of flesh around the Astral, out of the growing materials of the male seed in the female soil. Thus grows out of the essence of a decayed seed the fruit or eidolon of the dead seed, the physical fruit producing in its turn within itself another and other seeds for future plants.

The tanhic elementals may be otherwise described as the emotional and mental thought-deposits, as Patañjali did; and these remain after the second death — and before the ego's entering the devachan — stamped upon the various kinds of life-atoms which had functioned on all the lower planes of man's constitution. Some of these tanhic elementals or life-atoms peregrinate, and finally are psychomagnetically attracted back to the reincarnating ego during its process of bringing forth a new astral form preceding rebirth. Others belong to the monadic substances of the auric egg, and consequently remain therein in a latent condition, to awaken only when the devachanī leaves the devachan. Then these dormant tanhic

---

°This is accomplished in more or less time, according to the degree in which the Personality (whose dregs it now is) was spiritual or material. If spirituality prevailed, then the *Larva*, or spook, will fade out very soon; but if the Personality was very materialistic, the Kâma Rûpa may last centuries and — in some, though very exceptional cases — even survive with the help of some of its scattered Skandhas, which are all transformed in time into Elementals. See the *Key to Theosophy*, pp. 141 *et seq.*, in which work it was impossible to go into details, but where the Skandhas are spoken of as the germs of Karmic effects. — H.P.B.

elementals, in combination with the other life-atoms which had been peregrinating, combine in building up the new astral form that H. P. B. speaks of; and it is largely these two classes of tanhic life-atoms or elementals which compose the skandhas° of the man in his coming incarnation. And these skandhas are the various groups of mental, emotional, psychovital and physical characteristics which, when all collected together, make the new personality through which the higher man or egoic individuality works. They slowly begin to recombine and fall into their appropriate functions and places during the gestation period, continuing such 'fixation' in the womb, and finally after birth maturing as the entity grows to adulthood.[27]

Now the formation of the astral man takes place within the auric egg of the ex-devachanī. From the moment when the ego leaves the devachanic condition, the astral form becomes steadily more complete or definite as the gestating entity approaches the entrance into the womb. The ray from the reincarnating ego enters first the aura and later the womb of the mother-to-be by means of the growing astral form, which takes its rise in and from the most appropriate life-center or life-atom latent in the auric egg of the incoming entity.

The term astral form is descriptive not so much of an actual body (as we think of it in our physical world), as it is of an ethereal agglomerate of life-atoms in the auric egg which is at first but vaguely shadowed, yet gradually assumes more or less a definite human outline, and usually one of extremely small size. However, we should not concentrate our attention so much upon size and shape as upon forces and energies in the auric egg more or less aggregated into a focus of activity.

The entity thus preceding rebirth is attracted to the family to which its karma draws or impels it; and if the appropriate physiological activities take place at the right moment, then conception occurs and the growth of the embryo proceeds.

As the radiance or ray of the reincarnating ego reaches this plane, it gradually entangles itself in physical substance, and establishes thereby its link with the human reproductive cell. That link is made because of electromagnetic, or rather psychomagnetic, affinity between the reimbodying ray and the living germ cell. Every germ cell is a compact of inner forces and substances ranging from the divine to the physical, and

---

°A Sanskrit word meaning bundles or aggregates.

therefore is the 'precipitation' onto our plane of a psycho-ethereal radiation. In other words, it is an imbodiment of a ray-point that, originating in the invisible worlds and contacting physical matter by affinity, thus arouses a molecular aggregate of living substance into becoming a reproductive cell.

This molecular aggregate is the first or preliminary deposit or appearance on the physical plane of the action of the ray-point. We see that the germinal or reproductive cells are not 'created' by the parent's body, but appear in and work through it from the imbodying egoic force or entity 'outside' — the parent being the host or transmitter. The vital germ cell, whether of man or of woman, is originally an integral part of the model-body, which is an electromagnetic body of astral substance belonging to the plane just above the physical; and around this astral form the physical body is built cell for cell, bone for bone, and feature for feature.

When the life-atom as the chosen ray-point is invigorated by the descending energies of the reincarnating ray, it enters by psychomagnetic attraction into the father's astral body, and is in due course deposited into his appropriate physical organ as an astral precipitate. It thus becomes physicalized as a germ cell. In the mother this process of astral precipitation is the same in general outline, the precipitation being from the identic ray in both cases: in fact, each parent contains in his or her appropriate organ life-atoms belonging to and used by the reincarnating ego in past lives.

The female parent is the vehicle of what may be called the vegetative or passive side of the ray-point, and the male parent the vehicle for the positive or active side. The ray-point seems to split into two, later to reunite by the coalescence of the positive and negative sides after the fertilizing of the germinal cell. We are here dealing with subtle astral forces which obey their own laws and which are not hindered in their action by the heavy physical world in which our bodies live.

To restate the above in somewhat different language: the more material part of the new astral form is drawn first into the woman's aura and then into the womb wherein it produces the living ovum and finds its suitable milieu; coincidently the inner and more mānasic portion of the astral form, which is the more ethereal part of the tip of the ray from the reincarnating ego, flashes to the male parent and produces in its appropriate physiological seat the positive life-germ. The father sows the seed, the mother receives it, fosters it, and brings it forth.

The human egos awaiting incarnation are exceedingly numerous, so that there may be scores of entities which could become children of any one couple, yet there is always one whose attraction is strongest to the mother-to-be at any specific physiological moment, and it is *this* astral form which becomes the child. Many are the cases where the astral form, thus 'rayed' in two directions, so to speak, finds its progress into physical birth stopped because the man and the woman are either celibate or prefer no children, or for some other reason.° In such cases, the astral form under karmic urge and natural law tries again. Should the first environment prove a failure, the reincarnating ego may find itself drawn to another couple because of karmic relationships in other lives.

The reincarnating ego has in a sense very little choice in the matter, if by this we mean a deliberate selecting of one's future family. Such a choice as we understand it is almost non-existent, because the reincarnating ego has but just left the devachan and is sunken into the relative unconsciousness of the gestation period preceding rebirth, and thus is in no condition to choose with self-conscious intent. It is karma, which throughout controls these things; and karma in the abstract is infallible in its action.

Every human being is surrounded by his own emotional and passional as well as psychovital atmosphere, which is really a portion of the lower layers of his auric egg. Now this atmosphere is alive and, vibrating with varying intensities, has its own psycho-auric individuality or vibrational frequency. It becomes obvious therefore that the ray-point, which likewise possesses its own frequency, is drawn more or less on the line of magnetic attraction to the atmosphere of the parent or parents whose vibrational frequency is most sympathetic to its own and with whom its karmic affinities are strongest. To round out the picture, I might add that both hate and intense psychic dislike — each of which is a kind of inverted love — sometimes produce strong psycho-auric attractions, thus explaining the pathetic situation of parent and child who repel each other.

When the astral form has definite union with the human ovum, it

---

°I might point out that once conception has taken place and the embryo begins its growth, any attempt whatsoever to stop its development or to destroy it is plain murder. In the teaching of the esoteric philosophy, it is considered as being only a little less bad than the murder of an adult human—little less only because such destruction or abortion takes place before the self-consciousness of the victim has had a chance to come into flower.

begins to grow as the foetus. The lower or grosser portions of the astral form become the linga-śarīra of the child, in combination with the two general classes of tanhic elementals; whereas its higher portions, the vehicles of the 'ray' from the reincarnating ego (as the embryo and later as the child grows), become the intermediate parts of the constitution of the man.

We must always keep in mind the important part played by the auric egg of the reincarnating ego in all the various steps preceding rebirth. The astral form begins its first growth within the reimbodying auric egg, gestates within it and continues to be 'fed' by its essences throughout the prenatal processes, and in time brings about the stages of birth, infancy, childhood and adulthood; for, in fact, the auric egg is really the true manifested man considered as being the vital auric prānas flowing forth from the various foci of the reincarnating monad.

When the ray-point of the reimbodying ego, itself a ray from the spiritual monad, reaches its own intermediate sphere, it descends no farther into matter. But its psychomagnetic ray, having stronger affinities for the material worlds, descends still farther, awakening into activity the life-atoms in each one of the planes between that of the reimbodying ego and the astral-physical matter of our earth.

Just here we see that the 'life' or characteristic of each part of the composite human constitution remains on its own plane, but extrudes its excess of life from itself into the next lower one, until finally the physical plane is reached, wherein the tip of the ray, collecting unto itself life-atoms of this plane, builds or forms the physical germinal cell. It would be quite wrong to suppose that the reimbodying ego itself is *in* the germinal cell or on a plane only slightly less physical than ours. The process is an exact analogy of what occurs in the building of the globes of a planetary chain, where the passage of the excess of life takes place along and around the ranges of substance from cosmic plane to cosmic plane.

INNER AND OUTER ROUNDS

> It is on the Seven zones of *post mortem* ascent, in the Hermetic writings,
> that the "mortal" leaves, on each, one of his "Souls" (or Principles); until
> arrived on the plane above all zones he remains as the great Formless Serpent
> of absolute wisdom — or the Deity itself.
>
> *— The Secret Doctrine*, I, 411

As THE UNIVERSE is an organic entity, every part responds spiritually and intellectually, magnetically and physically, to every other part, the outward 'skin' of nature which we sense being but the garment of vast inner worlds and spheres. Therefore, the entire solar system is in very truth a plenum or pleroma, as the ancient Gnostics taught. In other words, the solar system is 'solid,' in the sense of being filled full with substances and forces in many grades and phases of activity, all interacting and interblending and thus composing a living entity — an immense cosmic body through which there works the fully self-conscious, partially self-conscious, and merely conscious, life and vitality of the governing cosmic divinity or hierarch.

This cosmic plenum or pleroma is actually the auric egg of the universe, everything that the universe is and contains, and all its substantial essences are the various and different layers of the cosmic auric egg. We have an exact analogy in man's auric egg, which is the *real* individual as it manifests itself during manvantara. When the manvantara of a universe or the incarnation of a man comes to its end, then the breakup of the lower portions of the constitution of the auric egg takes place, the life-atoms fall apart, and the higher principles collect themselves together, while coincidently the auric egg folds itself inwards surrounding the spiritual individuality as its sheath.

This explains why the outer forms of a universe — the lower layers of the auric egg — vanish out of manifestation, and what was once the locus of a universe is then filled with so-called interstellar ether. The auric egg, enshrouding all the higher principles of the former universe, is winging its way through the spaces, following the galactic circulations, while these higher principles are undergoing their nirvana.

627

The same process on a smaller scale takes place when a man dies. While it is true that every one of man's principles is ultimately derived, as from a focus, from one of the planetary chains of the solar system, these rays from the different planetary rectors which together compose the constitution of a man are not to be looked upon as being outside of his auric egg, but rather as being aggregated within it. For example, it would be utterly wrong to suppose that his buddhi is located on the planet Mercury, his higher manas on Venus, and his kāma on Mars, etc. The point is that although these planetary rectors or guardians are the spiritually and psychomagnetically sympathetic overseers or protectors of man's principles, nevertheless these principles are in and of his constitution, and in their aggregate pour forth the various streams of the vital essences which actually make and *are* the auric egg itself.

It is through the pleroma, whether in our planetary chain or in the entire solar system, that the spiritual monad of man during its peregrinations after death follows the circulations of the cosmos. These circulations are not merely poetic metaphors; they are as real in the inner economic working of the visible and invisible worlds of the universe, as are the nerves and blood vessels in the human body. Just as these provide the channels for the transmission of intellectual, psychical and nervous impulses and directions, as well as of the vital fluid or blood, so in analogous fashion the circulations of the cosmos — or kosmos — provide the pathways followed by the ascending and descending rivers of lives, composed as they are of the never-ending stream of entities of all classes peregrinating throughout the universal structure.

The framework of the universe is suffused with permeations of this vital essence. For the universe, whether solar or galactic, is an organism and therefore is alive in all its parts, infused with vitality and inherent intelligence and consciousness from its highest plane or principle to its lowest, everything within it being thus bathed in the vital essence as well as permeated with the cosmic intelligence.

Now the two main kinds of circulations followed by the various classes of monads, both as life-waves and as individuals, are referred to as the inner and the outer rounds. The inner rounds are made (a) collectively by the life-waves passing from globe to globe around a planetary chain; and (b) individually, in identic manner, by the ego or human monad after the death of the physical body. Likewise the outer rounds are made (a) collectively, after immense intervals of time, by the monadic classes or life-waves passing from planetary chain to planetary chain, and (b) individually, also in identic manner, by the spiritual monad of man.

We see therefore that the inner and outer rounds are analogically alike, yet differ in that the monad of a man in its post-mortem journey, while perforce following the same peregrinations that the monad pursues during the course of the outer rounds, does so in incomparably smaller periods of time, and merely stops temporarily in the various planetary 'stations.'

Hence, the phrase outer rounds can refer to two different things: first, to the grand or major outer round comprising the whole period of a solar manvantara, during which the spiritual monad makes a stay in each planetary chain; and second, to its post-mortem journey which takes it likewise to each of the seven planetary chains, but in this case its sojourn in any individual chain lasts only a relatively short time, and its various emissions of rays belonging to each one of the respective planets is likewise brief and temporary. We may call this the minor outer round.

To recapitulate: the outer rounds deal with the passage of the spiritual monad over the solar system, from planetary chain to planetary chain, and this seven times, these seven planetary chains being the seven sacred planets of the ancients; and the inner rounds refer to the long manvantaric sojourn of a monad in any one of these planetary chains during which the monad undergoes its aeons-long journeys on and in and through the seven (or twelve) globes of that chain.

Those particular monads of the human constitution which are especially involved in one or another of these rounds are the following: the earth-man, otherwise the human-animal monad; the human monad per se, the focus of all the genuinely human attributes; the spiritual monad, the source of all the truly spiritual or buddha-like qualities in man; and the divine monad or inner god which is the ātman in its buddhic veil. After death each of these different parts rises to the sphere to which it is attracted; in other words, each rises as high as it can. The divine monad, having a range over the entire galaxy, our home-universe, flashes from star to star and from solar system to solar system. As the spiritual monad is not strong enough to do this, it ranges over the solar system from planet to planet and to the heart of Father Sun; while the human monad, or the reincarnating ego, ranges over the entire twelve globes of our planetary chain.

Now when the earth-man dies, the human-animal monad then and there sinks into complete unconsciousness, almost instantly being ingathered into the human monad per se; the human monad, in its turn, after undergoing the second death in the kāma-loka, is ingathered into the spiritual monad and therein has its long devachanic dreaming, the devachan coming into full power at different times depending upon the karma of the individual. The merely earth-ego, which is you, is I, can ascend no higher than its little devachan, that is, it can go no farther than its native habitat which is the earth; beyond this, the human ego loses consciousness and is carried within the reincarnating ego as the latter goes its round of the globes.

We should remember that what is now our monadic parent was in far past manvantaras a human being, a child of *its* own spiritual parent, and that our present spiritual monad was a reincarnating ego, sleeping in the bosom of its then parent during the intervals between lives on material spheres. Similarly, when our present reincarnating ego shall have evolved forth from itself enough of its own inner spiritual powers and energies to enable it in its turn to become a monadic essence, it too will follow the outer rounds as its present parent monad now does. There is no break in this hierarchic chain.

Thus it is that we, children of this earth, have before us the sublime destiny of becoming gods, and of having the entire galaxy as our field of consciousness. When this happens, each one of us will be a sun in that galaxy.

The spiritual monad — carrying within itself the human monad, which in turn has the human-animal monad within it, somewhat after the manner of thought-deposits or tanhic seeds which will produce the future man in his next earth life — rises more or less rapidly through the globes of our planetary chain until it reaches the highest globe thereof, and is then ready to spread its wings. Leaving the topmost globe, it begins its peregrinations which involve the temporary sojourn in each and every one of the seven sacred planets, in regular serial order, according to the predetermined pathways which closely adhere to the lines of cosmic forces — the circulations of the cosmos. It is to be noted, however, that the order as popularly given by the ancients, to wit, Saturn, Jupiter, Mars, Sun, Venus, Mercury, Moon, is not that followed by the peregrinating monad.

The purpose of the passing of the monad after death through the various planetary chains is to allow it to free itself on each chain of the integument or vehicle which 'belongs' to the vital essence of that planetary chain. In this way the monad strips off from itself, one after the other, the seven coatings with which it had enwrapped itself during its previous return to reincarnation on earth, and is then ready to enter into its native spiritual home. When the return journey towards our earth chain begins, the monad passes through all these same seven planetary chains, but in reverse order, and in each planet it clothes itself anew in the life-atoms that had formed the coatings it had previously cast off.

Simply put, on its journey of 'ascent' towards spiritual freedom, it unclothes itself; and on its 'descent' or journey back it picks up again its former life-atoms, and thus is ready and able to work out the karmic consequences that were held over in abeyance when death came upon the man in his last earth-life.

INTERPLANETARY PEREGRINATIONS

> The Planetary origin of the Monad (Soul) and of its faculties was taught by the Gnostics. On its way to the Earth, as on its way back from the Earth, each soul born in, and from, the "Boundless Light," had to pass through the seven planetary regions both ways. — *The Secret Doctrine*, I, 577

IN ANCIENT RELIGION and philosophy a great deal of occult truth was stated under the catchwords the seven sacred planets; nevertheless, similar teachings were frequently referred to under the collateral phrase the seven heavens. These two aspects of the underlying doctrine, while closely parallel, were not quite identic; for the seven sacred planets pertained to the post-mortem destiny of the peregrinating monads, whereas the seven heavens pointed to the rest period in devachan of the seven main classes of monads.

The sacred heavens, often enumerated as ten and even eleven, when the teaching concerned the men of globe D, really had reference to the higher globes of our own planetary chain. The idea was that after death man ascended through a number of these heavens and descended through others, finally to take imbodiment on earth again. However, as every one of the globes of our chain is under the direct overseeing or governance of one of the seven planetary rectors, we see how closely connected the teaching regarding the sacred planets is with that of the seven heavens; and just here is a very open hint with regard to the outer rounds or the peregrination of the spiritual monad after death to and through the seven sacred planetary chains. No monad whatsoever is on its own in its journeyings, because it can follow only those certain channels of karmically vital intercommunication existing among the celestial bodies of the solar system.

As the hosts of life-atoms in a man's constitution not only belong to and thus compose it in its manifested appearances, but likewise are, each one, pilgrims or learning entities, so the multitudes of monads in the solar system belong to and form part of it, and yet at the same time are individual pilgrims in it. Indeed, just as the different classes of life-atoms in the human being are collected by psychomagnetic attraction in masses to form this or that organ, either in his inner constitution or in his physical body, so are the various classes of monads in the solar system drawn together to form the planetary chains which, in a very occult sense, are the 'organs' of the solar system — all these organs being comprised within the encircling and bounding sphere of the sun's auric egg.

Furthermore, all the planes or spheres of the solar system, and their variously related subplanes and subworlds, are interlinked by innumerable points of communication, centers through which the forces and substances of one plane or sphere pass into the next succeeding one. These are the laya-centers. Every celestial globe — and indeed every atom — is in its central core of essence such a laya-center or point of individual intercommunion, which is the individual entity's pathway of communication with the next higher or lower inner plane or world.

Through these laya-centers, whether it be of a solar or planetary globe, a human being, or an atom, the lowest or densest matter of a particular plane or world can pass downwards into the next lower plane, and manifest itself there as its most ethereal forces — which forces are equivalent to highly ethereal matter. Or, taking our own plane as an illustration, our most ethereal force or substance can pass upwards through these laya-centers into the next superior plane, where it becomes at one with the very densest substance of that cosmic plane.

Upon reflection, we see that these circulations can be envisaged in two ways: first, those taking place between plane and plane, or world and world, which we might call 'upwards' and 'downwards' or 'vertical'; and second, those lines of intercommunication existing on and working in and through any one plane, which we might think of as 'horizontal' circulations.

Thus is the passage from plane to plane or world to world accomplished, not after death alone, but even during imbodied life. The monad, on reaching the next planet after it has left our earth chain, produces from itself during its passage in and through such planetary chain a ray or egoic radiance, which is a psychomental 'soul' of temporary existence taking imbodiment there in a vehicle of spiritual, ethereal, astral or physical type, depending upon which one of the globes of the chain is entered. In reality, this ray is an effusion of the auric egg of the peregrinating monad, drawn from the bosom of the monad by the psychomagnetic attraction of the chain it is briefly entering; and it is this efflux of radiation, which is a body of its own kind, that enables it to clothe itself with appropriate life-atoms furnished by the chain, thus bringing about the brief imbodiment.

This ray, which is in a sense native to the planetary chain on which it manifests, passes through its various cyclical periods of monadic activity until it reaches the end of its life-term on that chain. Then, just as had previously happened on earth, it is withdrawn in its turn into the bosom of the monad, where it rests in its devachan, if any. And the higher principles pendant from the fundamental monad are released anew from this chain to proceed to still another planetary chain, to which they are carried by the psychomagnetic karmic attractions of their own substance as they follow the cosmic pathways laid down for them in the circulations of the cosmos.

These entrances into the various chains after the monad leaves our earth chain are, with but few exceptions, of extremely short duration, because during the present minor solar manvantara the monad has its main karmic destiny on our planetary chain. When such destiny is for the time being ended, it will proceed to the next planetary chain to which it will be attached through karma for another minor solar manvantara.

In this manner does the monad act through and on each of the seven sacred planetary chains: it passes through each of them in serial order until it finally reaches the solar chain wherein it makes its round through the solar globes. When the spiritual monad comes to the end of its peregrinations, it begins its return journey, drawn into the psychomagnetic line of attraction which impels it along the circulations of the cosmos back to the planetary chain of earth, through each of the seven sacred planetary chains, but in inverse order to that in which it had ascended. When at length it enters our planetary chain, it begins its descent through globes A, B, and C until it once more reaches our globe D. By this time the human monad, otherwise called the reincarnating ego, having nearly ended its devachan, now prepares for its new incarnation.

The reimbodying ego evolved forth in this earth's planetary chain is native to this chain, because it is the appropriate vehicle through which the spiritual monad can express itself in this particular variety of matters and energies of the cosmos. When our earth chain shall have ended its manvantaric course, and its family of spiritual monads goes to the next planetary chain, the reimbodying ego native to that succeeding chain will then become dominant in influence on the spiritual monad, while the reimbodying ego native to our present chain will be recessive, i.e. in its manvantaric nirvana.

So wonderfully are these spiritual and psychical processes adjusted by nature's laws, and so naturally do they all work together, that almost invariably, when the reimbodying ego is about to end its devachanic sleep, the spiritual monad has reached that part of its peregrinations which brings it to the highest globe of the earth chain. Consequently, an ego having its devachanic rest period, whether long or short, has no difficulty in following its reawakening attractions earthwards, because the spiritual monad is more or less strongly influenced by the spiritual condition or quality of the reimbodying ego which has been resting in its bosom. So it is that the peregrinations of the spiritual monad on the outer round are to a large extent controlled as regards the duration of its pilgrimage.°

We have thus far described the outer round as it concerns an individual spiritual monad. Exactly the same pilgrimage is made by the life-waves or monadic classes when the ending of our planetary chain manvantara frees them for *their* outer round. As far as the inner rounds are concerned, these too, as said, are made not only by the different life-waves from globe to globe of our planetary chain, but likewise by the individual monads after the physical body dies.

We have stated that the range of the human-animal monad is our globe earth, and that of the human monad or reincarnating ego is limited to our planetary chain so far as reaches of experience go; and, further, that the fields of action of the spiritual monad are our solar system, particularly the seven sacred planets and our earth as well as four other 'secret' planetary chains, while the ranges of the divine monad are the galaxy or our home-universe. From this it should be clear that the human-animal monad is 'released' from our globe when the body dies; and that our spiritual monad is 'released' from our planetary chain — and I am here speaking of the outer rounds of *individual* monads — when it has reached and left the highest globe of our planetary chain preparatory to winging its way to the next chain.

No monad or consciousness-center, precisely because it is a force or energy of spirit-essence, is ever at rest during the long term of the cosmic manvantara. Withdrawal of one ray of the monad from physical incarnation affects that monad not at all. It simply means that the ray is ingathered

---

°Cf. *The Esoteric Tradition*, ch. xxx, where the subject is treated in fuller detail.

into the substance or being of the monad, and remains there in its devachan or nirvana, as the case may be.

The monad is a spiritual living being, always in movement of its own kind and class; and this movement is not only continuous but, when we trace it sufficiently far back, is of the very substance of the cosmic intelligence. Throughout the life of a man as well as during his after-death experiences, the monad is always fully self-conscious in its own lofty realm. When the individual's post-mortem existence begins, the monad passes from sphere to sphere of the solar system, 'going the rounds' anew on its ceaseless peregrinations during the solar mahāmanvantara. It passes through these spheres not merely because it is native to all of them and is therefore drawn to them by its own spiritual and psychomagnetic attractions and impulses, but likewise because it itself wills spiritually to do so; for free will is a godlike thing and is an inherent and inseparable attribute of the monad.

An important point here is that, after the death of the man, the spiritual monad makes its outer rounds in and through the solar system in exactly the same manner in which a life-atom — although of course on its own much lower plane of action — makes its 'rounds' and peregrinations in and through the various layers of the man's auric egg while he is alive.°
Once more we see the really wonderful analogical workings of all parts of nature: what happens in the macrocosmic spheres or planes is copied in the microcosmic worlds.

°See "Transmigration of the Life Atoms," by H.P.B. in *The Theosophist*, August 1883.

RETURN JOURNEY OF THE REIMBODYING EGO

From *Gods* to *men*, from Worlds to atoms, from a star to a rush-light, from the Sun to the vital heat of the meanest organic being — the world of Form and Existence is an immense chain, whose links are all connected. The law of Analogy is the first key to the world-problem, and these links have to be studied co-ordinately in their occult relations to each other.
— *The Secret Doctrine*, I, 604

THE JOURNEYINGS OF the spiritual monad through the spheres of the solar system are due to several causes, one of the most important being expressed in the old proverb, "like attracts like." It is because of this that the higher spheres attract the higher part of man's nature which itself feels a corresponding inner urge toward them. Thus the monad rises steadily higher, there being with each step upwards an ever-stronger attraction to still more spiritual, more consciousness-like, worlds or spheres. On these journeyings the monad passes through and stays a while on and in each such world. No outside power either impels or compels the monad to this evolutionary course; it is but its innate attractions which, becoming active after death, are evoked forth from the fabric of its own essence by the man's spiritual and intellectual activity during earth life.

When the attractions and compelling inner aspirations which had previously caused this rising of the monad through the spheres have for the time exhausted their energies, the monad turns back and retraces its steps. The latent seeds of thought and feeling that imagination, spiritual yearnings and lofty intellectual aspirations had stored in the monad in former lives, because of their very origination in material spheres, now begin to pull the monad downwards, until the reimbodying ego finds its opportunity to project its own incarnating ray, or human ego, into the karmically appropriate human seed-germ.

Every cosmic plane or world as well as every planet provides its own suitable vehicles for the self-expression of the hosts of entitative monads journeying upwards or downwards along the circulations of the cosmos; and consequently no such vehicle or body can leave the sphere or planet to which it belongs. Death means the casting off and birth the reassuming of bodies. All such vehicles are built of life-atoms, most of which for any individual are its own psycho-spiritual offspring, the monad thus enwrapping itself in its own emanations which form its sheaths or transmitters for the purposes of self-expression.

We see here again that while the auric egg is in a certain sense the man himself, it also is the combined effluvia pouring forth from all the different monads which the human constitution, or that of any other living being, contains. In other words, all the life-atoms on every plane of the human constitution go to build the auric egg, and circulate in and through it continuously, leaving it at different times for their own individual peregrinations but returning to it ultimately. It must not be forgotten, however, that the auric egg likewise is constantly the host for other smaller armies of peregrinating life-atoms which enter and leave it as guests — these life-atoms coming from surrounding nature, and more particularly from other entities, whether they be higher than man, or lower, such as the beasts, plants, minerals or elementals.

Thus there is a constant circulation of vital essences in and through our constitution, this providing the karmic field of action in and on which we inaugurate causes and are acted upon from 'outside.' So likewise is the intercommunication and interflow of vitality maintained between solar system and solar system, and between galaxy and galaxy — the different solar systems intercommunicating not merely electrically and magnetically, but also psychically and intellectually and spiritually, by means of the rivers of streaming life-atoms passing in and out of their various auric eggs.

All the multitudes of *native* life-atoms on the different planes of the human constitution are karmically and forever most intimately related to the spiritual monad, their original parent. When returning to earth at the end of its long pilgrimage, the monad attracts back to itself these same life-atoms which it had previously cast off, and with their help forms for itself new sheaths; so that one might almost say that the reimbodying ego 'resurrects' the old bodies — intellectual, psychical, astral, and physical — which it had had in its last earth life. This is the esoteric basis of the teaching of the Christian Church regarding the "resurrection of the body."°

°If we were to say, however, that the new man is identic with the man of the last life, we should be emphasizing the old heresy that there is an unchanging human

Finally, on its interplanetary round, the spiritual monad reaches the spiritual-magnetic 'atmosphere' of our earth chain. At this point the human ego, hitherto asleep in the bosom of the spiritual monad, begins to feel, in response to the influences of the psychomagnetic atmosphere of our chain, a resurgent inrolling — at first extremely faint and diffuse — of old memories, former attractions and instincts, due to the awakening of tanhic elementals of the most spiritual type which had lain dormant during the devachan. Unconsciously impelled by these ancient recollections resurging ethereally into its consciousness, it seeks to renew the contacts of its former spheres, and is attracted by this chain somewhat as a man living long in a foreign country yearns to return home, and feels his heart beat with a stronger pulse when he sees the old familiar sights.

Vague and fleeting memories of scenes of previous earth lives that the indrawn reimbodying ego knew before, begin to pass in panorama across its field of consciousness; and these pull it steadily down towards the spheres it once inhabited. These impulses grow ever stronger as the monad 'sinks,' until finally it is ready and prepared for its new rebirth on our globe earth.

Since the return of the reimbodying or human ego towards incarnation takes place through the various planes of our planetary chain, each plane of increasing materiality, there is a natural 'descent' or continuous encasement or imbodying of the human ego through the globes of the descending arc. On each of these globes there is a transitory sojourn for the purpose of re-collecting the appropriate life-atoms which had been cast off by the monad during its former transits through the planes of

---

'soul' which remains forever and ever the same. But the soul is in constant process of change; and it is obvious that a being which changes continuously throughout eternity cannot remain identic for even an instant. Otherwise the infant would be identic with the man it finally grows to be.

Each incarnation produces from the karmic deposits of character a new man who is composite of what was brought over from the last incarnation, *plus* the new increments of faculty and attribute brought into function by its devachanic assimilation of the experiences of the monad's last life. The character of the new man also contains qualities, however imperfectly developed they may be, which were not fully functioning in previous lives; and yet this new man has to bear the karmic responsibility of the former man.

It was upon just this doctrine of a constantly changing and evolving focus of consciousness that the Buddha-Gautama based his rejection of the theory of an unchanging and ever-perduring 'soul' which remained more or less the same ego forever.

639

the globes. These life-atoms in their turn had been continuously peregrinating in the ages of this interim.

The life-atoms which the human ego reincorporates into its constitution at these stages of its return earthwards are actually waiting on the globes of the descending arc, because these life-atoms belong to the planes traversed by the ego in its descent and likewise *are* the planes on which the ego had dropped them on its previous ascent. It is after this manner that the man coming into physical birth rebuilds for himself a constitution of seven element-principles which are virtually identical with those of his preceding earth life. It is this that makes the reincarnating ego become in all respects practically the same man he was before, but improved, refined, because of the experiences of assimilation undergone in the higher globes; and, last but not least, because of its spiritual digestion of the experiences of the preceding earth life. Again, it is preparing to reap the harvest that it itself last sowed, attracted by the psychomagnetic interactions between the fields of life and the human monad's own character.

Perhaps the most important aspect of this teaching is what might be called the progenitive or creative activity of the fundamental or spiritual monad in pouring forth from itself as the ages pass its multitudes of consciousness-centers, which for them is the beginning — in the cosmic manvantara in which they appear — of the long, long evolutionary pilgrimage fitting them in space and time to pass from the earliest stage of unself-conscious god-sparks into the full-blown consciousness of gods.

In fact, it is thus that the galaxies in the abysses of endless space originally sprang into being, for every such child-monad is destined to evolve forth into a universe, which is but one cosmic milestone, so to speak, on its eternity-long wanderings. First an unself-conscious god-spark; then, after many revolvings throughout the lower kingdoms of nature, its inner faculties and powers manifest themselves in the human stage, the spark becoming a man, later on a divinity; and a glorious sun with its attendant family of planets, its own trailing and now partly grown monads; then a galaxy; and then a cluster of galaxies — and where may we place a limiting end to the fundamental monad's unending growth? There is never an ending, nor, indeed, was there ever a beginning.

Let us always remember that man is essentially one with the universe, that its destiny is his destiny, that he is held strictly accountable for all that he is, and for all that he does; that his will is supreme over all the energies of the physical universe, and that he carves his own pathway into the future. When man realizes all this, truly *knows* it, then indeed he will begin to think and act like a god, because he will be using the godlike powers locked up within himself.

The main lack in the world today is a sense of moral values. Men are ethically and spiritually ignorant; they have lost the knowledge of the inner vision. The old book of the Hebrews said: "Where there is no vision, the people perish." The man who has music in his soul senses that he is reflecting the cosmic symphony, the symmetrical and harmonious relationship existing everywhere, and that therefore he is morally responsible that this harmony not be broken. The way to peace, the way to knowledge, to wisdom, and to harmony, is in following universal laws. We then become a master of life. Such is the pathway.

The spirit-soul of man, the heart of the heart of him, is essentially one with Infinitude. Being co-extensive with boundless Space, born of its essence, life of its life, consciousness of its consciousness, it is timeless and deathless, for neither time nor death have sway over Infinitude.

Notes

NOTES

1. (p. 12) In regard to normal vision, W. Q. Judge in his Preface to Patañjali's *Yoga Aphorisms* speaks of the mind issuing through the eye and adopting the form and the qualities of the object seen. On its return, it reflects the information acquired to the soul. This is the ancient explanation, which was also propounded by Plato, among others. The theory was that a force issues from the eye which we may call the 'visual ray,' this force or ray being a projection of the consciousness or the mind; that normally its rate of projection or travel is very high, which rate actually can be increased by the will or by thought; that the ray or force darts forth from the eye, meets the object concerning which knowledge is desired, and returns accompanied with light; and when this combination re-enters the eyeball, the message that it carries is transmitted to the brain and thence into the receiving mind or consciousness.

Now when a study of a very distant object, such as a star or a planet, is required, this visual ray, which is ākāśic in essence, leaves the eye and darts with the speed of thought to the object, and all its conditions of travel and return, of impressions and of reception, are governed by the known laws of optics as well as by other laws at present unknown. It is not at all the mind which projects a tentacle of itself; though curiously enough this notion, wrong as it is, is an intuition of what the organ of vision was in earliest humanity. Then it was not an eye, but was actually more like a tentacle, and received its sensory impressions by touch; and through innumerable millions of instances of this kind of sensory experience the eye was gradually evolved, increasing in power and delicacy of function, until actual physical contact was no longer required.

(As a matter of fact, practically all the senses that we now have originated in a similar way; and the student of biology can gain many hints of how they began in the first, second and early third root-races from studying some of the strange sense-apparatuses of the lower beings.)

It is precisely this visual ray leaving the eye — which ray in normal function is of electromagnetic character — that also carries with it the man's magnetic atmosphere when the will is behind and propelling the personal auric magnetism; and it is also thus that in the cases of psychologization, commonly called hypnotism, a subject is held and fascinated so frequently by the eye. Allusion here to the question of hypnotism is not an approval of the practice, but an explanation of it and of the danger one incurs in allowing oneself to be subjected to another's will. Looking a person straight in the eye is always admired, and justly so, because it signifies a certain amount of character and poise; perhaps in this there is an unconscious understanding of the battle of magnetisms, friendly or unfriendly, as the case may be.

2. (p. 95) See the *Vajrachchhedikā-Sūtra* ('Diamond Cutter'), one of the most valued and widely studied religio-philosophical writings in Buddhist literature:

By this wisdom shall enlightened disciples be enabled to bring into subjection every inordinate desire! Every species of life, whether hatched from an egg, or formed in a womb, or evolved from spawn, or produced by metamorphosis, with or without form, possessing mental faculties or devoid of them, or both devoid and not devoid, or neither devoid nor not devoid — from these changeful conditions of being, I entreat you to seek release (*mieh-tu*), in the transcendental concept of Nirvana. Thus, you shall be released from an immeasurable, innumerable, and illimitable world of sentient life; but in reality, there is no world of sentient life to be released from, or sentient beings to be delivered from it. And why, Subhūti? Because should there exist in the minds of Bodhisattva-Mahāsattvas such arbitrary concepts of phenomena as an entity, a being, a living self, or a personal ego, they would be unworthy of being called Bodhisattva-Mahāsattvas. . . . Wherefore the conclusion is this — that all things possessed of personal or individual characteristics, all arbitrary conceptions and all conditioning factors, are as a dream, a phantom, a bubble, a shadow, as the evanescent dew, as the lightning flash; and they ought to be regarded as such.

— Sections 3 and 32

This Sūtra is read extensively throughout China, Japan, Tibet, and other Buddhist countries, and stands as high in popular estimation as do the *Saddharma-Pundarīka* ('Lotus of the law of Reality') and the famous *Shau-Leng-Yan-Ching* (or *Śūrangama-Sūtra*). The Diamond Cutter Sūtra was written originally in Sanskrit, but there is no definite knowledge as to its authorship or the date of its composition. The Sūtra forms the Ninth Section of the encyclopedic *Mahāprajñāpāramitā* in six hundred fasciculi.

In the process of time it was translated into Tibetan, Chinese, Mongolian, and Manchu, the Chinese title for it being *Chin-kang-ching*. The Chinese translation ascribed to Kumārajīva (a native of Kashmir, who labored in China in the interests of Buddhism during the later part of the fourth and the beginning of the fifth century A.D., and whose profound scholarship and spiritual attainment caused him to be known as one of the 'four suns' — *chatur-sūryas* — of Buddhism) has been the basis for European translations of this Sūtra, such as those of William Gemmel and the Rev. S. Beal. Unfortunately, neither these nor the translation of Max Müller give an adequate idea of the underlying subtleties of Buddhist thought and the esoteric meaning of various technical terms, to which Western scholars have lost the keys.

From the text itself it is fairly obvious that the Sūtra was intended especially for those who had already "entered the Path which leads to Nirvana," and who were striving to "attain the plane of Buddhic enlightenment." Besides imbodying a great deal of teaching concerning the practice of the pāramitās, the *Vajrachchhedikā-Sūtra* has as its main object the elucidation of the doctrine that all objective things, phenomena and ideas, are unreal and illusory, being merely a manifestation of one's own mind; and that even the highest concepts of the Dharma, the Tathāgata, and even deliverance itself, are mind-made and therefore 'empty' in the technical sense of this word, because human understanding is not yet liberated, and has not yet become at one with the Buddha within. It teaches a way of life in the light of the profoundly metaphysical doctrine that the only true essence is the *essence of mind* — what theosophy terms buddhi — behind which there is hidden an ultimate principle of which mind itself is only an aspect.

Some translators, ignorant of the methods of esoteric training and teaching, have asserted that the 'leaves' of the original Sanskrit text of the Sūtra must have become displaced at some time or other in the past, as the text is very much confused, and the logical development of the theme cannot be easily traced. In this connection, it is interesting to note and thereby to support the views of some Chinese scholars that the so-called 'logical confusion' can be far better explained by bearing in mind the ancient method of teaching, which consists in first presenting the central teaching, the main outline of the doctrine, and only then filling in the background and the details as thoughts may occur, and with a superb indifference to the vaunted brain-mind methods of 'logical sequence.'

There is a special interest attached to the Chinese term *mieh-tu* in the passage quoted above. It stands for deliverance or release; for while *mieh* has the meaning of disappearance or evanishment, and therefore could easily be misconstrued by Orientalists to signify annihilation, as has been done in the case of the term nirvana, the word *tu* means 'to cross over in safety' and therefore is related to the term *pāramitā*. The Chinese Buddhist appears therefore better prepared to refute, by the very structure of his technical term for deliverance, the erroneous conception regarding nirvana prevalent for so long among Orientalists.

3. (p. 97) The following selections will illustrate the thought.
From the *Īśvara-Gītā,* which forms a portion of the *Kūrma-Purāna:*

All is born from us, verily here (all) is dissolved,
The māyā-former, bound by māyā, makes manifold forms.   — ii, 6

I produce the whole (universe), I continually destroy the universe,
I am possessed of illusion-creating power, yet myself illusory, a divinity united
   with time.   — iii, 22

I am indeed the Destroyer, the Evolver, the Maintainer.
Māyā verily is my power, māyā the world-deluder.
Verily mine is the supreme power, which is knowledge, thus is it sung,
And I cause that māyā to vanish — I who am in the heart of yogins.
                                                                    — iv, 17–18

Of those snares māyā verily is the cause, it is said;
Mūlaprakriti (Root-substance) — the Unmanifest (*Avyakta*), that power exists in
   me.   — vii, 30

From the *Svetāśvatara-Upanishad:*

Sacred poetry, sacrifices, ceremonies, ordinances, past, future, and what is de-
clared by the Vedas —
All this the illusion-maker projects out of That, and in it by illusion all else
is confined.
One should know that Nature is Illusion, and the Mighty Lord — the Illusion-
Producer.
This entire world is pervaded with entities which are parts of Him.
                                                                    — iv, 9–10

From the *Rig-Veda:*

He matches in form every form; that is his form to be seen. Indra goes in many forms by his magic power (*māyā*); for ten hundred bay steeds are yoked for him.   — vi, 47, 18

From the *Bhagavad-Gītā:*

Although (I am) unborn, of imperishable selfhood, although (I am) lord of all beings, yet while abiding in my own natural state, I take birth through the illusion of self (or: I take birth by my own power — *ātmamāyayā*).   — iv, 6

The Lord of all beings, O Arjuna, stands in the region of the heart, turning all beings (which are as though) mounted on the engine (of the universe) by (his) *māyā* (mystic power).   — xviii, 61

For this my divine *māyā*, of the nature of the qualities (*gunas*), is difficult to transcend. It is they who betake themselves to me, who surmount this *māyā*.
                                                                           — vii, 14

4. (p. 98) The eighteen ways of describing the concept of 'emptiness' are:°

(1) *Adhyātmā-śūnyatā* — emptiness of the inner things, by which are meant the six vijñānas or consciousnesses, our psychological activities being thus looked upon as devoid of any permanency.

(2) *Bahirdhā-śūnyatā* — emptiness of the outer things, by which are meant objects of the six consciousnesses, which objects are said to be empty because our visioning mind does not understand the reality behind them.

(3) *Adhyātmā-bahirdhā-śūnyatā* — emptiness of the inner-and-outer things, meaning that even the distinction in the concepts of inner and outer has no reality in itself and can be reversed at any time; this relativity is called emptiness.

(4) *Śūnyatā-śūnyatā* — emptiness of emptiness. The very *idea* of emptiness has no reality either, nor is it objectively attainable.

(5) *Mahā-śūnyatā* — great emptiness, which has reference to the unreality of space considered as a container of objects with extension and location, and points to the esoteric significance of Space as the conscious and substantial totality of all that Is.

(6) *Paramārtha-śunyatā* — emptiness of the ultimate truth. By ultimate truth is meant the true *be-ness* of things, the state in which they truly

---

°Cf. *Essays in Zen Buddhism* (Third Series) by D.T.Suzuki, pp. 128, 222–8.

are, apart from any temporary subjective form assumed by them. This state of the thing per se cannot be described in any manner whatsoever, as it precludes all attributes or qualities, although it *Is;* hence it is said to be from the human standpoint empty.

(7) *Samskrita-śūnyatā* — emptiness of composite things that have come into existence owing to causative conditions.

(8) *Asamskrita-śūnyatā* — emptiness of things which are not subject to causation (such as Space itself). The first of these two again postulates the fact that all things, outer and inner, are empty, unreal. The asamskrita exist in the mind only because they are contrasted with the samskrita. The unreality of the latter establishes the emptiness of the former.

(9) *Atyanta-śūnyatā* — ultimate emptiness, emphasizing the unconditional unreality of all objective things, beyond any possible qualification or causative dependence, and signifying that even the first veil of māyā, spiritual as it is to us humans and long in duration, is nevertheless māyāvi, because as a veil it is not the eternal essence from which it springs.

(10) *Anavarāgra-śūnyatā* — emptiness of primordial beginning. When it is said that existence is beginningless, the mind clings to the idea of beginninglessness as something existing per se; therefore, in order to do away with this mental limitation, its emptiness is emphasized.

(11) *Anavakāra-śūnyatā* — emptiness of dispersion or differentiation, having particular bearing upon the composite nature of all objective things, whether visible or invisible, whether physical or mental.

(12) *Prakrita-śūnyatā* — emptiness of primary or absolute nature, pointing to the fact that in no being or thing is there anything that could be termed an entirely independent, solitary, self-originating primary or absolute nature per se.

(13) *Svalakshana-śūnyatā* — emptiness of self-appearance; lakshana is the intelligible or understandable aspect of any individual entity, inseparably related to its primary nature. Fire, for instance, is intelligible through its heat; water through its fluidity, etc. By the emptiness of these 'self-aspects' or 'self-characteristics' is meant that any specific object has no permanent and irreducible characteristics to be considered as its own.

(14) *Sarvadharmasya-śūnyatā* — emptiness of all objects of sense and of thought, emptiness of the entire objective universe. All characterizations are impermanent, relative and phenomenal. Even our human idea of Reality, as being eternal, blissful, self-originating, self-governing, and devoid of any defilement, is in itself a limitation, and therefore is not Reality.

(15) *Anupalambha-śūnyatā* — emptiness of non-comprehension or of unattainability. This implies that although Reality cannot be an object of relative thought, objectively comprehensible, and cannot therefore be said to be 'attainable,' yet it can be lived and directly realized through prajñā.

(16) *Abhāva-śūnyatā* — emptiness of non-being.

(17) *Swabhāva-śūnyatā* — emptiness of self-nature.

(18) *Abhāva-swabhāva-śūnyatā* — emptiness of the non-being of self-nature. These three terms point to the emptiness of such ideas as being and non-being, and the further emptiness of their contrast with each other. For Reality lies beyond this distinction, and is independent of it.

5. (p. 101) For those especially interested in the different schools of Hindu philosophy, the following may be helpful. There are actually six schools or darśanas, a Sanskrit word literally meaning vision. These are the Nyāya founded by Gotama; the Vaiśeshika founded by Kanāda; the Sānkhya of Kapila; the Yoga of Patañjali; and the Less and the Greater Vedānta founded by Vyāsa. Of the Greater Vedānta the most widely diffused school is the Adwaita, due to the teaching of Śankarāchārya. All of them contain truth in no small degree; but again each is but a single branch of the all-unifying master school which, whether recognized or not, is the esoteric philosophy.

These six great systems are logically reducible to three pairs: (a) the Nyāya and Vaiśeshika, which one may call the Atomistic school, corresponding with the Ārambha; (b) the Sānkhya and Yoga, which deal with emanational evolution combined with practice in aspiration and self-training, corresponding with the Parināma; (c) the Less and the Greater Vedānta, which may be called the Idealistic school, corresponding with the Vivarta.

6. (p. 117) Questions frequently arise concerning the differences among the various kinds of manvantaras and pralayas mentioned in Sanskrit literature, to wit: (1) Prākritika pralaya; (2) Saurya pralaya; (3) Bhaumika pralaya; (4) Paurusha pralaya; (5) Nitya pralaya. The same terms can be used equally well for the respective manvantaras.

The Prākritika pralaya is the dissolution of the universal solar system, which means the passing out of manifested existence into inner planes of all the various prakritis or worlds or planes of the cosmos — our solar universe. It is what Christians would probably call the 'end of the world.'

The Saurya pralaya has reference to the sun or Sūrya (Saurya being the adjective of this word). It means the death of our own solar chain and the dissolution of our solar system, but does not mean the pralaya of our *universal* solar system.

The Bhaumika pralaya means the death of Bhūmi, our earth. It is the dissolution of our earth planetary chain, when it has ended its life period.

Paurusha pralaya (from Purusha, meaning man) is a term of rare use, and simply signifies the death of a human being.

Nitya pralaya means that continuous breaking up or dissolution which goes on all around us and may be described as the incessant change which takes place uninterruptedly. Change is death of any being or entity which immediately thereupon passes into some karmically succeeding change of state or condition. Thus the revolving seasons of the year bring periodic and never-ending changes; the atoms in any living body, as well as its molecules and cells, are undergoing unceasing and continuous change. All these phenomena of life are grouped under the one term Nitya.

7. (p. 130) I might mention that in my *Fundamentals of the Esoteric Philosophy* (p. 459), the phrase "that revolve around the sun" should read, if we wish to be precise, "that revolve around the Rāja sun."

8. (p. 138) For the benefit of those readers to whom the phrase "Dweller on the Threshold" is new, the following explanation from my *Occult Glossary* may be helpful:

A literary invention of the English mystic and novelist Sir Bulwer-Lytton, found in his romance *Zanoni*. The term has obtained wide currency and usage in theosophical circles. In occultism the word "Dweller," or some exactly equivalent phrase or expression, has been known and used during long ages past. It refers to several things, but more particularly has an application to what H. P. Blavatsky calls "certain maleficent astral Doubles of defunct persons." This is exact. But there is another meaning of this phrase still more mystical and still more difficult to explain which refers to the imbodied karmic consequences or results of the man's past, haunting the thresholds which the initiant or initiate must pass before he can advance or progress into a higher degree of initiation. These dwellers, in the significance of the word just last referred to are, as it were, the imbodied quasi-human astral haunting parts of the constitution thrown off in past incarnations by the man who now has to face them and overcome them — very real and living beings, parts of the "new" man's haunting past. The initiant must face these old "selves" of himself and conquer or — fail, which failure may mean either insanity or death. They are verily ghosts of the dead men that the present man formerly was, now arising to dog his footsteps, and hence are very truly called "Dwellers on the Threshold." In a specific sense they may be truly called the kāma-rūpas of the man's past incarnations arising out of the records in the astral light left there by the "old" man of the "new" man who now is.

9. (p. 152) It may be of interest to quote two passages from H.P.B.'s E.S. *Instructions*, II:

. . . when the planets of the solar system are named or symbolized . . . it must not be supposed that the planetary bodies themselves are referred to, except as types on a purely physical plane of the septenary nature of the psychic and spiritual worlds. A material planet can correspond only to a material something. Thus when Mercury is said to correspond to the right eye it does not mean that the objective planet has any influence on the right optic organ, but that both stand rather as corresponding mystically through Buddhi. Man derives his Spiritual Soul (Buddhi) from the essence of the Mânasa Putra, the Sons of Wisdom, who are the Divine Beings (or Angels) ruling and presiding over the planet Mercury.

In the same way Venus, Manas and the left eye are set down as correspondences. Exoterically there is, in reality, no such association of physical eyes and physical planets; but esoterically there is; for the right eye is the "Eye of Wisdom," *i.e.*, it corresponds magnetically with that occult centre in the brain which we call the "Third Eye"; while the left corresponds with the intellectual brain, or those cells which are the organ on the physical plane of the thinking faculty. The Kabalistic triangle of Kether, Chocmah and Binah shows this. Chocmah and Binah, or Wisdom and Intelligence, the Father and the Mother, or, again, the Father and Son, are on the same plane and react mutually on one another.

When the individual consciousness is turned inward a conjunction of Manas and Buddhi takes place. In the spiritually regenerated man this conjunction is permanent, the Higher Manas clinging to Buddhi beyond the threshold of Devachan, and the soul, or rather the Spirit, which should not be confounded with Âtmâ (the Super-Spirit) is then said to have the "Single Eye." Esoterically, in other words, the "Third Eye" is active. Now Mercury is called Hermes, and Venus, Aphrodite, and thus their conjunction in man on the psycho-physical plane gives him the name of the Hermaphrodite, or Androgyne. The absolutely Spiritual Man is, however, entirely disconnected from sex. . . .

In the same way the right and left nostrils, into which is breathed the "Breath of Lives" (*Genesis*, ii, 7), are here said to correspond with the Sun and Moon, as Brahmâ-Prajâpati and Vach, or Osiris and Isis, are the parents of the natural life. This Quaternary, *viz.*, the two eyes and two nostrils, Mercury and Venus, Sun and Moon, constitutes the Kabalistic Guardian-Angels of the Four Corners of the Earth. It is the same in the Eastern esoteric philosophy, which, however, adds that the Sun is not a planet, but the central star of our system, and the Moon a dead planet, from which all the principles are gone, both being substitutes, the one for an invisible inter-Mercurial planet, and the other for a planet which seems to have now altogether disappeared from view. These are the Four Mahârâjahs of the *Secret Doctrine* [I, 122], the "Four Holy Ones" connected with Karma and Humanity, Kosmos and Man, in all their aspects. They are: the Sun, or its substitute Michael; Moon, or substitute Gabriel; Mercury, Raphael; and Venus, Uriel. It need hardly be said here again that the planetary bodies themselves, being only physical symbols, are not often referred to in the Esoteric System, but, as a rule, their cosmic, psychic, physical and spiritual forces are symbolized under these names. In short, it is the seven physical planets which are the lower Sephiroth of the Kabbala and our *triple* physical Sun whose reflection only we see, which is symbolized, or rather personified, by the Upper Triad, or Sephirothal Crown.

10. (p. 162) This is a truly profound and remarkable treatise, dealing with yugas and time periods of various lengths, divisions of time into infinitesimals, cycles of sun, moon and planets as well as with eclipses. In the opening verses it is stated that Sūrya, the sun, through his solar representative, communicated to Asuramaya "the science upon which time is founded, the grand system of the planets" (I, 5), and that this occurred at the end of the krita or satya yuga (I, 46–7). If we reckon back from the present day, we have already run through some 5000 years of the kali yuga, 864,000 of the dwāpara, and 1,296,000 of the tretā which followed the satya yuga. This would mean that the *Sūrya-Siddhānta* is over two million years old. As H.P.B. says in her *Secret Doctrine* (II, 49–50), the knowledge contained in this work was transmitted to this

654

great Atlantean astronomer during the closing epoch of the fourth and the beginnings of the fifth root-race.

We should not think, however, that the sun came down from heaven and dictated these very words, but rather that the solar glory illuminated the brain of this adept. In other words, in paying homage to Sūrya, Asuramaya was raising his inner nature to the solar ray of which he was an incarnation, and thereupon was inspired and taught by his own solar divinity some of the secrets of the universe.

11. (p. 208) Cf. *Isis Unveiled,* II, 605–6, where H.P.B. says:

The Hermetic philosophers taught, as we have seen, that the disappearance from sight of a flame does not imply its actual extinction. It has only passed from the visible to the invisible world, and may be perceived by the inner sense of vision, which is adapted to the things of that other and more real universe. The same rule applies to sound. As the physical ear discerns the vibrations of the atmosphere up to a certain point, not yet definitely fixed, but varying with the individual, so the adept whose interior hearing has been developed, can take the sound at this vanishing-point, and hear its vibrations in the astral light indefinitely. He needs no wires, helices, or sounding-boards; his will-power is all-sufficient. Hearing with the spirit, time and distance offer no impediments, and so he may converse with another adept at the antipodes with as great ease as though they were in the same room.

12. (p. 230) The following extract from the *Vishnu Purāna* (I, ii, 27–40) is here appended:

In the same manner as fragrance affects the mind from its proximity merely, and not from any immediate operation upon mind itself, so the Supreme influenced the elements of creation. Purushottama is both the agitator and the thing to be agitated; being present in the essence of matter, both when it is contracted and expanded. . . .

Then from that equilibrium of the qualities (Pradhána), presided over by soul, proceeds the unequal development of those qualities (constituting the principle Mahat or Intellect) at the time of creation. The Chief principle then invests that Great principle, Intellect; and it becomes threefold, as affected by the quality of goodness, foulness, or darkness, and invested by the Chief principle (matter), as seed is by its skin. From the great principle (Mahat) Intellect, threefold Egotism, (Ahamkára), denominated Vaikárika, 'pure'; Taijasa, 'passionate'; and

Bhútádi, 'rudimental,' is produced; the origin of the (subtile) elements, and of the organs of sense; invested, in consequence of its three qualities, by Intellect, as Intellect is by the Chief principle. Elementary Egotism, then becoming productive, as the rudiment of sound, produced from it Ether, of which sound is the characteristic, investing it with its rudiment of sound. Ether, becoming productive, engendered the rudiment of touch; whence originated strong wind, the property of which is touch; and Ether, with the rudiment of sound, enveloped the rudiment of touch. Then wind, becoming productive, produced the rudiment of form (colour); whence light (or fire) proceeded, of which, form (colour) is the attribute; and the rudiment of touch enveloped the wind with the rudiment of colour. Light, becoming productive, produced the rudiment of taste; whence proceed all juices in which flavour resides; and the rudiment of colour invested the juices with the rudiment of taste. The waters, becoming productive, engendered the rudiment of smell; whence an aggregate (earth) originates, of which smell is the property. In each several element resides its peculiar rudiment; thence the property of tanmátratá (type or rudiment) is ascribed to these elements. . . .

Then, ether, air, light, water, and earth, severally united with the properties of sound and the rest, existed as distinguishable according to their qualities, as soothing, terrific, or stupefying; but, possessing various energies and being unconnected, they could not, without combination, create living beings, not having blended with each other. Having combined, therefore, with one another, they assumed, through their mutual association, the character of one mass of entire unity; and, from the direction of spirit, with the acquiescence of the indiscrete Principle, Intellect and the rest, to the gross elements inclusive, formed an egg, which gradually expanded like a bubble of water. . . . In that egg, O Brahman, were the continents and seas and mountains, the planets and divisions of the universe, the gods, the demons, and mankind. And this egg was externally invested by seven natural envelopes; or by water, air, fire, ether, and Ahamkára, the origin of the elements, each tenfold the extent of that which it invested; next came the principle of Intelligence; and, finally, the whole was surrounded by the indiscrete Principle: resembling, thus, the cocoa-nut, filled interiorly with pulp, and exteriorly covered by husk and rind.

13. (p. 303) In this connection, the following passage from a little-known ancient work, *The Introduction of Alcinoüs, to the Doctrines of Plato* (14), may be of interest:°

The Sun is the leader of all, showing and illuminating all things. But the

---

°Cf. *The Works of Plato*, Vol. VI, translated by George Burges.

Moon is seen in the second rank, on account of her power; and the other planets proportionally, each according to its own share. Now the Moon makes the measure of a month, after it has completely gone through its own revolution, and overtaken the Sun in such (a time); but the Sun in that of a year. For after it has gone round the circle of the Zodiac, it completes the seasons of the year; while the rest make use singly of their own periodical revolutions, which are beheld, not by ordinary persons, but by the properly instructed. Now from all these revolutions the perfect number and time is completed, when all the planets, after arriving at the same point, obtain such an arrangement, that a straight line being conceived to be let fall from the non-wandering sphere to the earth in the manner of a perpendicular, the centres of all are seen upon that line. There being then seven spheres in the wandering sphere, the deity made seven visible bodies out of a substance, for the most part fire-like, and fitted them to the spheres, formed out of the circle of the different and the wandering. And he placed the Moon in the first circle after the Earth; and the Sun he arranged for the second circle, and Lucifer and the so-called sacred star of Hermes into the circle, which moves with a velocity equal to the Sun, but at a distance from it; and above the rest, (each) in its own sphere, the slowest of them lying under the sphere of the non-wandering, which some call by the name of the star of Saturn; and that, which is the next after it in slowness, by the name of Jupiter, under which is that of Mars. But in the eighth the power, which is above, is thrown around them all. And all these are living intellectual beings, and gods, and of a spherical form.

14. (p. 311) Even the famous Church Father Origen speaks of the Holy Spirit as being feminine, when saying:

Παιδίσκη δὲ κυρίας τοῦ ἁγίου Πνεύματος ἡ ψυχή.

The soul is handmaiden to her mistress, the Holy Spirit.

Another illustration is found in the now lost *Gospel of the Hebrews,* ° probably one of the first ever written by Christian hands, extracts from which have survived in the writings of Origen and Jerome. This particular passage is quoted by Origen and runs as follows:

Ἄρτι ἔλαβε μέ ἡ μήτηρ μοῦ τὸ ἅγιον πνεῦμα, ἐν μιᾷ τῶν τριχῶν μοῦ, καὶ ἀνήνεγκε μὲ εἰς τὸ ὄρος τὸ μέγα θαβώρ.

Straightway my mother the Holy Spirit took me in one of my hairs and bore me to the great mountain Thabor. — *Homily xv*, on Jeremiah and on John

---

°Cf. *The Lost and Hostile Gospels* by Rev. S. Baring-Gould, London, 1874, pp. 130–1.

Similarly Jerome, another Church Father, wrote (*Micheas*, vii, 6):

Modo tulit me mater mea Spiritus Sanctus in uno capillorum meorum.
Then my mother the Holy Spirit took me in one of my hairs.

15. (p. 314) The Greek text for the quotation from Plutarch is as follows:

Ἶσις ἐγώ εἰμι πᾶν τὸ γεγονὸς καὶ ὂν καὶ ἐσόμενον καὶ τὸν ἐμὸν πέπλον οὐδεὶς πῶ θνητὸς ἀπεκάλυψεν.

And for the additional phrase reported by Proclus:

Ὃν ἐγω καρπὸν ἔτεκον ἥλιος ἐγένετο

16. (p. 318) In Cory's *Ancient Fragments* (p. 264, 2nd ed., London, 1832), we find the following three selections from the "Chaldaean Oracles of Zoroaster":

Ἑπτὰ γὰρ ἐξώγκωσε πατὴρ στερεώματα κόσμων
Τὸν οὐρανὸν κυρτῷ σχήματι περικλεῖσας

For the Father caused to swell seven cosmic firmaments,
And enclosed the heaven within a convex form.

Ζώων καὶ πλανωμένων ὑφέστηκεν ἑπτάδα
He elevated a septenary of roaming animals.

Τὸ ἄτακτον αὐτῶν εὐτάκτοις ἀνακρέμασας ζώναις
Suspending their disorder in well-ordered belts.

To the ancients, 'animal' applies to the stellar, solar, and planetary bodies — in the sense of living things with a physical body, but nevertheless being animate or ensouled.

17. (p. 406) It is with a great deal of reluctance that I touch upon any medical question. For example, the modern method of animal experimentation, vivisection, claims that the knowledge so gained, with its supposed resulting benefits, justifies the means employed. A strange doctrine — for it is not possible that such knowledge can ever be of permanent benefit to mankind. Inhuman, cruel, and selfish acts do but blind the doers thereof, and shut the doors of both mind and heart to the acquirement

of truth. On the other hand, as a philosophical proposition it is quite true that even out of the offenses of men, the universe being so balanced in harmony and love, good ultimately will result. But the offender must pay his debt to the uttermost farthing.

One of the many things that have grown up concurrently with vivisection is the use of blood transfusion. Such ideas are all Atlantean in type. There is in this practice the possibility of transferring the latent seeds of disease from man to man, not to mention the psychic aspect. The Mosaic teaching is right: "In the blood is the life." For what is blood? It is actually condensed vitality, and therefore is the original carrier of disease as well as of health.

In regard to vaccines and serums it is claimed that by their use many diseases have been virtually wiped out, or at least brought under control. However, statistics show that new and strange diseases have appeared, and that these act virulently. Any method of treatment which has to do with injecting into the blood stream the secretions coming from some other diseased body is unwholesome: probably in the long run producing a larger number of mysterious diseases than the cases which the practice might possibly benefit.

This is not to condemn present-day physicians as a body. There are many splendid men passing lives of impersonal devotion in medical research, unselfishly working to better the condition of mankind physically. That fact is unquestionable; and of course it is understandable that they turn in any direction where they see the possibility of some new opening of discovery, where they see some better means of attacking a disease in its own center.

The physicians of the distant future will heal in a very different way. They will understand the virtues of simples and how certain juices of plants and mineral extracts can be used; and these will be much less harmful when injected than are those extracts taken from the bodies of unfortunate beasts. We hear a great deal about the successes of this latter method, but very little about the failures.

18. (p. 521) Every Orientalist knows that after the passing of the Buddha there gradually arose a number of schools which after one or two centuries became grouped under two main heads of philosophical thought: the Hīnayāna and the Mahāyāna. The different Mahāyāna schools

of northern Buddhism are all highly philosophic, but the mystical element predominates. In the Hīnayāna system of southern Asia, the technical philosophical element is dominant, but to those who know how to read its writings the rather closely veiled mystical thought and even esoteric wisdom in them become apparent enough. It has been stated by the greatest of the Mahāyāna teachers that the Hīnayāna represents the 'eye doctrine' of the Lord Buddha, whereas the Mahāyāna system and its writings comprise the esoteric teachings originally given by the Buddha to his arhats and later elaborated by them and their descendants, and hence these teachings are called his 'heart doctrine' — mystically signifying the hid essence of the Buddha's inner thought.

Both these schools, however, have more or less crystallized into formalisms. Certain branches of the Mahāyāna school have become largely intermixed with tāntrika ideas and symbols, and the followers of two or three of these sects actually teach to a certain extent the magic of the 'left hand.' Thus if we desire to gain a clear picture of the fullness of the Buddha's teaching, in so far as it has reached our own times, we should conjoin the mystical esotericism of the original Mahāyāna with the teaching of the Hīnayāna, the former elucidating the latter.

There were a number of really great men who initially built up the structure of the Mahāyāna system considered as a whole; they were high initiates who gave out as much of the genuinely esoteric Buddhism as they could in the times in which they taught, or as they were allowed to do by the Mahāchohan whose representatives for this special work they were. Two such were Nāgārjuna and Āryasangha, generally looked upon today by adherents of the Mahāyāna as having been bodhisattvas.

Nāgārjuna was the founder of the Mādhyamika school — meaning the Middle Way; whereas Āryasangha, the one who was a direct disciple of Gautama the Buddha himself, was the founder of the original or primitive Yogāchāra school. Now both these schools as they now exist contain a large amount of tāntrika teaching, and therefore have greatly degenerated. The student may be interested to read what H. P. B. says in her *Theosophical Glossary* under the head, "Āryasangha."

The Sanskrit terms Mahāyāna and Hīnayāna mean, respectively, great vehicle or path, and defective vehicle or path, *yāna* having the double significance of vehicle, and way or manner of going. *Mahā* means great; but the idea in the word *hīna*, defective, is not that of error but of a partial explanation only. This is precisely what the Mahāyānists say: that the Hīnayāna system is true as far as it goes, but that it is defective or imperfect because incomplete. In one way of looking at the matter, one may say that the Hīnayāna is the exoteric or incomplete teaching of the Buddha Gautama, while the inner or secret meaning of the Mahāyāna is the full or complete teaching that the Buddha gave to his arhats and chosen disciples.

So large a part of H.P.B.'s writings contains frequent allusions to them, especially to the Mahāyāna, that it has not been uncommon for many to imagine that theosophy is a kind of esoteric Buddhism only, instead of being the ancient cosmic wisdom of the gods, of which the teachings of Gautama the Buddha are but an interpretation. I might add that, while H.P.B. was a formal Buddhist herself for reasons of her own, she was *not* in her teachings a Buddhist in the *sectarian* sense of the word.

19. (p. 521) Many of the greatest figures in ancient Hindu mythology and history are stated to have been 'born' in either the Sūrya-vanśa or the Chandra-vanśa, meaning respectively 'solar race' and 'lunar race.' Now these 'races' are two family lineages, the Sūrya-vanśa being a line of kshattriyas originally springing from Ikshwāku, son of the Manu Vaivaswata, who was son of Vivaswat the sun; and the other line, the Chandra-vanśa, originally claiming descent from the moon, itself descended from the Rishi Atri. The great epic figure Rāma was born in the Sūrya-vanśa; and Krishna as well as the Buddha Gautama were born in the Chandra-vanśa.

The only point of importance in this somewhat sectarian mythological system is that these two 'races' really represent two different schools of archaic esotericism. The teaching which characterized the solar race was conservative, enfolding the wisdom of past ages and applying this without any noteworthy modifications to the conditions of the current period; whereas that of the Chandra-vanśa was rather a carving out of 'newer' methods, in addition to the holding of the wisdom of ancient times. The moon in this connection is not the moon of sorcery and black magic, but is a reference to the mystical fact that every neophyte, in his progress along his path, must cultivate and raise the 'lunar element' in himself to become at one with the inner god; in other words, to evolve the human monad into becoming its own divine monad.

20. (p. 529) In the *Vishnu-Purāna* the reference to Śambhala is as follows:

When the practices taught by the Vedas and the institutes of law shall nearly have ceased, and the close of the Kali age shall be nigh, a portion of that divine being who exists, of his own spiritual nature, in the character of Brahma, and who is the beginning and the end, and who comprehends all things, shall descend upon earth: he will be born in the family of Vishnuyaśas, — an eminent Brahman of Sambhala village, — as Kalki, endowed with the eight superhuman faculties. By his irresistible might he will destroy all the Mlechchhas and thieves, and all whose minds are devoted to iniquity. He will, then, reestablish righteousness upon earth; and the minds of those who live at the end of the Kali age shall be awakened, and shall be as pellucid as crystal. The men who are, thus, changed by virtue of that peculiar time shall be as the seeds of human beings, and shall give birth to a race who shall follow the laws of the Krita age (or age of purity). As it is said: "When the sun and moon, and (the lunar asterism) Tishya, and the planet Jupiter are in one mansion, the Krita age shall return."

— Book IV, Ch. xxiv, pp. 228–9 (H. H. Wilson's translation)

21. (p. 573) The after-death states of the excarnate entity are known in Tibet and its borderlands under the generalizing term of bardo — a word meaning 'between two,' around which imagination has woven many and various fabrics of imagery, all more or less patterned after esoteric facts. However, if we were to take these now quite exoteric teachings literally, and as being those of the archaic school, we would be seriously misled. Yet, they do have inherent mystical significance when properly understood.

In *The Mahatma Letters* (pp. 105–6) we find the following:

"Bardo" is the period between death and rebirth — and may last from a few years to a kalpa. It is divided into three sub-periods (1) when the *Ego* delivered of its mortal coil enters into *Kama-Loka* (the abode of Elementaries); (2) when it enters into its "Gestation State"; (3) when it is reborn in the *Rupa-Loka* of Deva-Chan. Sub-period (1) may last from a few minutes to a *number* of years — the phrase "a few years" becoming puzzling and utterly worthless without a more complete explanation; Sub-period (2) is "very long"; as you say, longer sometimes than you may even imagine, yet proportionate to the *Ego's* spiritual stamina; Sub-period (3) lasts in proportion to the good KARMA, after which the *monad* is again reincarnated.

Bardo therefore has the general significance of both the time period and the various states of consciousness undergone by the peregrinating monad between death and its next reincarnation. The three states of the general bardo are: the Chikhai-bardo, which is both the time period and the state of consciousness of the excarnate being from the moment of death until it definitely enters the devachan; the Chönyid-bardo, which is both the devachanic time period of such an entity and the various changings and ringings of the states of consciousness that the devachanī experiences; and the Sidpai-bardo, which is both the time period and the different adventures in consciousness of the entity from the moment it definitely has left the devachan until it actually finds itself a growing embryo in a human womb. It is thus evident that these three divisions of the bardo are merely the Tibetan manner of describing the after-death states.

There is a certain similitude between the Tibetan conception of the bardo, and the Days of Commemoration of the deceased in the Greek Orthodox Church, where ceremonies are held on the third, seventh, and fortieth, and even on other days, after a man's death. These Days are but a purely exoteric reflection of a one-time esoteric teaching concerning the different stages or stations through which the excarnate entity passes during the course of its post-mortem peregrinations. Actually these stages are individually and serially reached after the lapse of years, even of centuries, which time periods the Greek Orthodox Church, remembering nothing of the esoteric keys but still holding to the exoteric statement, has reduced to earth days in its ritual.

The reader will find some interesting material on the bardo in Dr. W.Y. Evans-Wentz' scholarly books on Tibetan teachings, religious literature and philosophical schools, particularly in his *Tibetan Yoga and Secret Doctrines*.

22. (p. 579) H.P.B. uses the term kāma-rūpa in the two senses in which I here employ it: one, for the imbodied personal man, and two, for the astral entity of the man after death, whether before or after the second death in kāma-loka. However, I believe that W.Q. Judge in one place strongly objects to any other use of the word kāma-rūpa than for the personal astral man after death, which usage is perfectly correct; nevertheless, when we go into a deeper philosophical analysis, we see that

we can logically speak of the kāma-rūpa even during the man's lifetime. I can only suppose that this emphasis by Judge was an attempt to make the teaching in those earlier times of the Theosophical Society as simple as possible.

It stands to reason that for a well-defined rūpa to exist after the death of the body, it must have been shaped or brought into being during the lifetime. The kāma-rūpa, the 'vehicle' between the higher manas and the physical man, is one of the most fluidic, changeable and plastic parts of our constitution, for it undergoes modification with every passing mood, indeed with every passing thought. But as each man has his own swabhāva, all these minor changes in the kāma-rūpa, whether sudden or gradual, do not affect its essential characteristics either of form or of substance. For example, a man's face has a distinct cast or set, including features and color and expression, and yet quick as lightning his face can change quite marvelously, as every actor knows; but these passing changes, while certainly marked, do not alter the fundamental type.

We men are kāma-rūpas of our manifesting seven principles. All of us have a desire-principle, kāma, and a mental principle, manas, and our emotions born of kāma; and these attributes make the personal man. When we die and cast off the body, there remains a kāma-rūpa with all the higher principles still attached; and when those higher principles slough off the kāma-rūpa, then there is only the empty kāma-rūpic shell. But while imbodied on this earth we are living kāma-rūpas, sevenfold entities. This last is the case of the sun; the former, the cast-off shell, is the case of the moon, the decaying kāma-rūpa of the moon that was.

Now if we make our kāma-rūpa while alive the vehicle of the god within us, that kāma-rūpa becomes the carrier, and we become a bodhi-sattva, a Buddha or Christ on this plane. Actually, all men together are what we might call kāma-rūpas of the body corporate of mankind, the *true* human race being the spiritual monads of these thousands of millions of men and women.

Just so any group of suns is analogous to an aggregation of the 'atoms' forming the kāma-rūpa of our own immense Brahmānda, the egg of Brahmā. Each sun in this solar aggregate is a cosmic atom, and therefore a manifestation of power derivative from fohat or cosmic Eros — using Eros not in the abstract sense of divine life, but in its lower sense of kāma or cosmic desire, this latter corresponding somewhat to the Latin Cupido.

The suns therefore, as cosmic 'atoms,' represent in their totality a kāma-rūpa of the vaster imbodied cosmos, i.e. the mental, passional, energic side of the universe, manifesting in those balls of terrific power we call the stars. Or we may call them sons of fohat.

23. (p. 589) The several degrees of consciousness of the "blessed region" of the devachan are variously described in Oriental philosophical schools, notably in Buddhistic writings under the term sukhāvatī, meaning 'happy condition.' Although the exoteric descriptions are flowery and quasi-imaginary, they do point to a central core of esoteric truth, that the devachan is rightly divisible into many different states of consciousness.

In this connection, the reader is referred to *The Mahatma Letters* (pp. 99–100):

The Deva-Chan, or land of "Sukhavati," is *allegorically* described by our Lord Buddha himself. What he said may be found in the *Shan-Mun-yi-Tung*. Says Tathâgata: —

"Many thousand myriads of systems of worlds beyond this (ours) there is a region of Bliss called *Sukhavati.* . . . This region is encircled with *seven* rows of railings, *seven* rows of vast curtains, *seven* rows of waving trees; this holy abode of Arahats is governed by the Tathâgatas (Dhyan Chohans) and is possessed by the Bodhisatwas. It hath *seven* precious lakes, in the midst of which flow crystaline waters having *'seven and one'* properties, or distinctive qualities (the 7 principles emanating from the ONE). This, O, Sariputra is the 'Deva Chan.' Its divine Udambara flower casts a root *in the shadow of every earth,* and blossoms for all those who reach it. Those born in the blessed region are truly felicitous, there are no more griefs or sorrows *in that cycle* for them. . . . Myriads of Spirits (Lha) resort there for rest and then *return to their own regions.*° Again, O Sariputra, in that land of joy many who are born in it are *Avaivartyas* . . ."†

24. (p. 595) From an unsigned article in *The Theosophist,* July 1884, p. 242:

Now those, who have studied the occult teachings concerning *Devachan* and our after-states, will remember that between two incarnations there is a considerable period of subjective existence. The greater the number of such *Devachanic* periods, the greater is the number of years over which this evolution is extended.

°Those who have not ended their earth rings. — K.H.
†Literally, those who will never return — the seventh round men, etc. — K.H.

The chief aim of the occultist is therefore to so control himself as to be able to control his future states, and thereby gradually shorten the duration of his *Devachanic* states between his two incarnations. In his progress, there comes a time when, between one physical death and his next re-birth, there is no *Devachan* but a kind of spiritual sleep, the shock of death, having, so to say, stunned him into a state of unconsciousness from which he gradually recovers to find himself reborn, to continue his purpose. The period of this sleep may vary from twenty-five to two hundred years, depending upon the degree of his advancement. But even this period may be said to be a waste of time, and hence all his exertions are directed to shorten its duration so as to gradually come to a point when the passage from one state of existence into another is almost imperceptible. This is his last incarnation, as it were, for the shock of death no more stuns him.

25. (p. 606) According to *The Lankāvatāra Sūtra*, one of nine principal Mahāyāna texts, nirvana is defined as the "unveiled vision of the suchness of Reality as it is," to somewhat paraphrase the original Sanskrit, *nirvānam iti yathābhūtārthasthāna-darśanam.* The unfortunate misunderstanding of Orientalists, to the effect that nirvana means annihilation, need not have arisen at all had they considered with an open mind the following passages:

Further, Mahāmati, those who, afraid of sufferings arising from the discrimination of birth-and-death, seek for Nirvana, do not know that birth-and-death and Nirvana are not to be separated the one from the other; and, seeing that all things subject to discrimination have no reality, imagine that Nirvana consists in the future annihilation of the senses and their fields. They are not aware, Mahāmati, of the fact that Nirvana is the Ālayavijñāna where a revulsion takes place by self-realisation. Therefore, Mahāmati, those who are stupid talk of the trinity of vehicles and not of the state of Mind-only where there are no images. Therefore, Mahāmati, those who do not understand the teachings of the Tathagatas of the past, present, and future, concerning the external world, which is of Mind itself, cling to the notion that there is a world outside what is seen of the Mind and, Mahāmati, go on rolling themselves along the wheel of birth-and-death.   — Ch. II, xviii, p. 55 (D.T.Suzuki's translation)

When the self-nature and the habit-energy of all the Vijñānas, including the Ālaya, Manas, and Manovijñāna, from which issues the habit-energy of wrong speculations — when all these go through a revulsion, I and all the Buddhas declare that there is Nirvana, and the way and the self-nature of this Nirvana is emptiness, which is the state of reality.

Further, Mahāmati, Nirvana is the realm of self-realisation attained by noble wisdom, which is free from the discrimination of eternality and annihilation, existence and non-existence. How is it not eternality? Because it has cast off the discrimination of individuality and generality, it is not eternality. How about its not being annihilation? It is because all the wise men of the past, present, and future have attained realisation. Therefore, it is not annihilation.

— Ch. II, xxxviii, pp. 86–7 (op. cit.)

26. (p. 614) The reader is referred to the "Examinations of the Golden Verses"° by Fabre d'Olivet (1768–1825), distinguished French linguist and philosopher, who states:

The ancients had the habit of comparing with gold all that they deemed without defects and pre-eminently beautiful: thus, by the *Golden Age* they understood, the age of virtues and of happiness; and by the *Golden Verses*, the verses wherein was concealed the most pure doctrine. They constantly attributed these Verses to Pythagoras, not that they believed that this philosopher had himself composed them, but because they knew that his disciple, whose work they were, had revealed the exact doctrine of his master and had based them all upon maxims issued from his mouth. This disciple, commendable through his learning, and especially through his devotion to the precepts of Pythagoras, was called Lysis. After the death of this philosopher and while his enemies, momentarily triumphant, had raised at Crotona and at Metaponte that terrible persecution which cost the lives of so great a number of Pythagoreans, crushed beneath the *débris* of their burned school, or constrained to die of hunger in the temple of the Muses, Lysis, happily escaped from these disasters, retired into Greece, where, wishing to spread the sect of Pythagoras, to whose principles calumnies had been attached, he felt it necessary to set up a sort of formulary which would contain the basis of morals and the principal rules of conduct given by this celebrated man. . . . These verses . . . contain the sentiments of Pythagoras and are all that remain to us, really authentic, concerning one of the greatest men of antiquity.

Hierocles, who has transmitted them to us with a long and masterly Commentary, assures us that they do not contain, as one might believe, the sentiment of one in particular, but the doctrine of all the sacred corps of Pythagoreans and the voice of all the assemblies. He adds that there existed a law which prescribed that each one, every morning upon rising and every evening upon retiring, should read these verses as the oracles of the Pythagorean school. One

---

°Cf. Nayán Louise Redfield's English version (1917) of *The Golden Verses of Pythagoras*, translated into French by Fabre d'Olivet.

sees, in reality, by many passages from Cicero, Horace, Seneca, and other writers worthy of belief, that this law was still vigorously executed in their time. We know by the testimony of Galen in his treatise on *The Understanding and the Cure of the Maladies of the Soul,* that he himself read every day, morning and evening, the Verses of Pythagoras; and that, after having read them, he recited them by heart. . . .

If his [Lysis'] name has not been attached to this work, it is because at the epoch when he wrote it, the ancient custom still existed of considering things and not individuals: it was with the doctrine of Pythagoras that one was concerned, and not with the talent of Lysis which had made it known. The disciples of a great man had no other name than his. All their works were attributed to him. This is an observation sufficiently important to make and which explains how Vyasa in India, Hermes in Egypt, Orpheus in Greece, have been the supposed authors of such a multitude of books that the lives of many men would not even suffice to read them.

The Greek text of the quoted verse is as follows:

Μήδ' ὕπνον μαλακοῖσιν ἐπ' ὄμμασι προσδέξασθαι,
Πρὶν τῶν ἡμερινῶν ἔργων τρὶς ἕκαστον ἐπελθεῖν.
Πῆ παρέβην; τί δ' ἔρεξα; τί μοι δέον οὐκ ἐτελέσθη;

27. (p. 623) In exoteric Buddhism, skandhas (literally 'bundles' or 'aggregates') are five in number: form (rūpa), sensation or sense-perception (vedanā), self-conscious intellection (sañjñā), mental propensities (samskāra), and consciousness (vijñāna). The first skandha represents the material world or the materiality of things, while the remaining four belong to the astral monad and the mind. The second one appertains to the perception of objects of sense; the third to that which is elaborated by the mind; the fourth refers to what might be termed the formative principle of the mind, creating mental molds vitalized by its own energies; and the fifth represents egoic mentation. Buddhist philosophical analysis has thrown these various characteristics and attributes into the five categories enumerated above.

Thus the skandhas are the various groups of personal attributes or characteristics which make one human personality different from another; and it is through these groups of psychological and psycho-emotional-astral attributes or characteristics that the higher man or ego, i.e. the egoic individuality, works.

Appendices

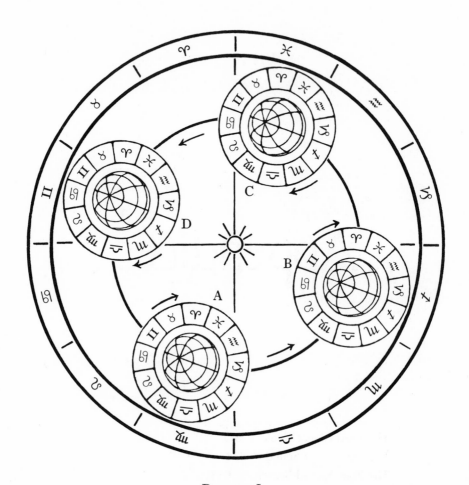

DIAGRAM I

THE PRECESSIONAL CYCLE

As to the occult teachings regarding the precessional motions, the following two diagrams may clarify the real causes why the pole of the earth, owing to the clockwise rotation of the signs of the zodiac around an axis, makes a complete revolution around the pole of the ecliptic during the zodiacal year of 25,920 terrestrial years.

In Diagram I let the plane of the paper indicate the plane of the ecliptic (the plane of the earth's orbit around the sun); the large circle shows this orbit, and the central point of it is the sun. The four small circles, each containing the signs of the zodiac in their proper serial order, represent four positions of the earth in its orbit around the sun. The earth globe is represented with its usual conventional meridians and parallels, showing in perspective the inclination of the earth's axis towards the plane of the ecliptic, which inclination or obliquity is at the present time (1936) equal to $23°26'51''$ (mean value). The direction of the earth's motion around the sun is indicated by arrows placed along the orbit; and the direction of rotation of the *signs* is shown by arrows placed along the circumference of the signs.

Now then, let it be stated first, that the auric egg of the solar system contains within itself the orbits of all the known planets, or rather planetary chains, as well as of other invisible planetary chains which belong to our own solar system. Next, consider the position of the pole of the ecliptic as remaining virtually stationary for immense ages of time; it has, indeed, minute but cumulative movements of its own, but of these modern astronomy knows almost nothing. Let us concentrate our attention for the time being on our earth.

The auric egg of the earth globe is of course the real earth globe; and our physical rocky globe is merely its lowest or most physically material or concrete deposit. The auric egg of the earth globe is a spheroid, or rather ovoid, whose axis or poles and equator coincide with and are inseparable from the poles and equator of our physical globe. Not only are the terrestrial poles identic with the poles of the earth globe's auric egg, but precisely because the auric egg is inclined to the plane of the

DIAGRAM II

ecliptic, the poles of our rocky globe are inclined identically, its various movements slavishly reflecting the movements of the earth globe's auric egg. In other words, the physical globe follows everything, both in movements, inclination, and in inversion, that the auric egg of the earth globe does.

The *signs* of the zodiac have their real positions in 'realms' or 'kingdoms' or 'segments' of the auric egg of the earth globe, as shown by the small circles of the diagram. The auric spheroid or ovoid containing the signs rotates clockwise to the extent of only 50 seconds of arc in round numbers during one annual revolution of the earth around our sun, and of course this small part-rotation, of only 50" of arc, makes little change in the direction in which the earth's poles point during one year. Therefore, the four positions of the earth in Diagram I show the same orientation of the *signs,* an orientation which has changed only to the extent of about 50" of arc within one year, and cannot be easily represented on a rough drawing.

Position A indicates the place on the ecliptic at the time of the vernal equinox when the sun, as viewed from the earth, stands in the first point of the sign Aries — this first point being at present projected approximately against the eleventh degree of the constellation of Pisces; position B shows the place and the time of the summer solstice, when the sun stands in the first point of the sign of Cancer, and is projected against the eleventh degree of the constellation of Gemini; position C shows conditions prevailing at the autumnal equinox; and position D indicates those prevailing at the winter solstice.

But this small change of 50" of arc is cumulative, obviously, and amounts to one degree of arc in some seventy-two years, or to 90° of arc in 6,480 years. Hence — turning now to Diagram II — whereas at one time in the past the first point of the *sign* of Aries (position A) coincided with the first point of the constellation of Aries at the vernal equinox, 6,480 (2,160 x 3) years later the same first point of the *sign* of Aries coincided with the first point of the constellation of Capricorn at the vernal equinox also (position B), owing to the rotatory motion of the ovoid of the earth globe in the opposite direction to the natural sequence of the constellations of the celestial zodiac. In another 6,480 years, the sign of Aries will have coincided with the constellation of Libra (position C); and in yet another 6,480 years, with the constellation of Cancer (position D); and the great zodiacal year is finally closed with a fourth period of 6,480 years which will bring the spheroid or ovoid of the earth globe back to its original position with regard to the constellations. Thus, one complete circuit of the zodiac is made — one complete zodiacal or precessional year has elapsed.

THE POTENCY OF SOUND

In the Tibetan Buddhist mantra, *Om Mani Padme Hum,* Om, the Jewel in the Lotus, the lotus flower is the human being, the soul, likewise the entire constitution of man; more accurately, his auric egg with its different layers of substance combined each with the others, like the closed petals of the lotus flower. The jewel within the lotus is the diamond heart, the vajradhara, as the initiate of ancient days was called — a mystical term signifying the expression in action of the inner god, the divine radiance or flame, sparkling, glorifying, and vivifying the one through whom it shines.

It is small wonder that Tibetans of all classes, whether quasi-initiates or merely the vast rank and file of the populace, have cherished this invocation and recite it with the spiritual longing arising in the aspiring soul. It is a way of saying, just as H.P.B. phrases it, "I am in Thee, and Thou art in me." When intoned with an understanding of what it represents, and with a yearning of the heart and mind always toward union with the divine within, it has a strong effect in purifying one's channels of thought and keeping one's aspirations constantly alive.

As to the pronunciation and significance of this mystic syllable OM आेम् or AUM आ॒ेम् : either way of writing this word in European characters is correct, and the meaning is practically identic. The pronunciation, however, is not the same. OM is pronounced O-M, but AUM is A-U-M, the two vowels being sounded distinctly, and the M in both cases sounded vibrating within the skull. The sectarian, modern Brahmanical devotee will say that AUM is emblematic of the three persons of the Hindu triad, Brahmā, Vishnu, and Śiva; but this is a lame attempt to explain in what we may call ecclesiastic fashion something more profound. A-U-M — spelling and pronunciation and sound — is the higher form of the word, and is perhaps the more effective when one knows how properly to sound it; OM is the simpler of the two, and in the beginning equally effective.

The vowel O, or the fluid diphthong A-U, combined with the sounding of the M within the skull, have a particularly strong effect upon the human aura; and when the aspiration is high, and the heart lifted with reverence and love, and the mind itself is allied with the sun, the influence of the 'sounding of the word' can be very great. It stills, calms, and refines the entire sphere of the auric egg, so that the differing vibrational periods in separate portions of the auric egg are reduced to one harmony. Then the inflow from the god within is easy; and, at such times, a man may receive the very inspiration of divinity.

The Jews also had a word of somewhat similar character, used by their initiates in much the same way, and this was 'Āmēn — the common Amen.

More important than the correct pronunciation is the *sounding* of the word. That verily can work magic if rightly done: its correct pronunciation combined with the proper reverberating resonant sounding made by one who understands, works magically. It is the physical sound of this sacred word which is used in the art of practical magic solely for the purpose of tranquillizing the atoms, as far as it is possible for that sound to do this. As I have said, when uttered by one who knows how to do it and who understands the meaning of the act, its power is very great; it tranquillizes and soothes the entire auric envelope, and makes much easier the passage of the soaring soul up towards the spirit and back to the human consciousness.

Let us remember this, however, that it is not the senseless repetition of words that will do anybody any good. The pattering of prayers would be of equal value. The singing of hymns and the chanting of chants and the muttering of mantras are in themselves all useless. What is important is to *know,* and knowing to do.

To one who knows, sound is perhaps the most important factor in cosmic workings. As H.P.B. has written in her *Secret Doctrine* (I, 464), the *"magic* of the ancient priests consisted, in those days, in addressing *their gods in their own language. . . .* sound being *the most potent and effectual magic agent, and the first of the keys which opens the door of communication between Mortals and the Immortals."* Verily it is so. We must learn to talk the language of the gods before we can confabulate with them; learn to control the elemental beings before we have mastery over them. We must learn to reach the hearts of our fellow humans before we can ever help them. And this speaking the language that is understood is, above everything else, through the instrumentality of sound, the great magic agent in the universe. For everything that is, great and small, visible and invisible, sings a song of life, and this is its vital keynote; and if one can strike that keynote, he has mastery over it.

But let us beware of black magic, and touch not the individuality or destiny of any other than ourself. The magic potency of sound is widely known. Political orators, the orators in the churches, sway the hearts and minds of multitudes, and do it not necessarily by words, though greatly by words at times, but by sound and intonation.

Those who teach the Law, the Dharma, however, use the wisdom and knowledge that have been placed in their hands as a sacred trust. It is by sound more than by words that the messages of truth and wisdom are carried into our consciousness through the crevices and crannies of the armor of personal selfhood built around the soul.

I might add that the members of the Brotherhood are continuously acting as a Guardian Wall shielding, protecting, mankind from dangers of cosmic and terrestrial character. The method used by these Great Ones is to 'sing' these dangers away from us, through the ākāśa — by *sound*. Now please do not misinterpret these words and picture a row of the Great Teachers standing there, clad in white garments, and opening their mouths and yelling and bellowing and squawking and squealing, as we human beings sometimes do and speak of it as singing! The singing may be utterly soundless to our ears, but it is a song, a song of which the mystics spoke, charming the evil away — charming means here to sing, to chant, to 'sound' it away.

Now what are these dangers? Let us not think for a moment that they are only material. No; they are of many kinds: spiritual, intellectual, psychical, astral, physical. They are cosmic dangers reaching our earth from outside, from other planets of the solar system, and from dead planets, our moon in particular, and the so-called Eighth Sphere or Planet of Death. Indeed, there are in constant movement along the circulations of the solar system, rivers of lives having as much right to be as we have; but inimical to us in our present evolutionary state, or dangerous at least, and which, if they could enter our earth's atmosphere and impinge upon us, would wipe out the human race overnight. Not a single human being would be left alive upon the earth when morning came.

We humans are pilgrims; we are not forever and unto eternity chained to our globe, nor linked to our planetary chain. We are transients here, although our sojourn is of an exceedingly long time period when judged by human standards. Consequently, there are dangers arising even in this planetary chain, and therefore in globe D of it, which could be highly inimical to man's well-being were they allowed to impinge upon us without a shield or barrier of some sort. These are the terrestrial hazards, and they are of many kinds and on all planes.

Incidentally, one of the greatest of these that we human beings are facing in our own era is the psychical crazes which are sweeping over the world, distracting our minds and diverting us from the thoughts of spirit, of spirituality. This is a psychical danger, which is fraught with tremendous perils *because* it can mislead human souls.

But let us remember always that we are protected by song, by sound, albeit the most powerful sounds are those which are inaudible to us. The sounds which the human ear can take in, on account of its present imperfections, are but a small part of the octaves of vibration. The greater by far is the inaudible sound. The Music of the Spheres, for instance, is so immense that our ears cannot take it in. Every smallest atom sings its keynote of life as it lives. It is thus by sound, inaudible to us, that it grows; it is thus by sound, inaudible to us because of its magnitude, that the planets and the suns follow their pathways of destiny, and weave their web of being and so grow to grander things.

Sound is a form of radiation. Radiation is but a form of sound. It was no vain way of speaking, when some of the ancient European peoples told us that their ancient magicians sang the storms away, sang diseases away, sang men into health and sanity, sang men into goodness and wisdom.

THE FOUR SACRED SEASONS

THERE ARE FOUR PERIODS of the year which, from the standpoint of the initiation ceremonies, are considered to be particularly holy: the Winter Solstice, the Spring Equinox, the Summer Solstice, and the Autumnal Equinox.

Each year at the time of the Winter Solstice one of the greatest phases of the ancient Initiatory Cycle has always taken place. There is at the time of the Spring Equinox, or at and during the Eastertide, an initiation which in one sense is more holy and sublime even than that of the Winter Solstice. There is another Initiation Cycle at the time of the Summer Solstice, which is the loftiest in one sense of all four; and the fourth is at the time of the Autumnal Equinox, and to this I will merely point by allusion, for of all the four it is the most sublime.

It may be as well to point out that these four so-called Sacred Seasons are in direct, and therefore necessarily intimate, connection with the four Mahārājas mentioned by H.P.B. in *The Secret Doctrine* as guarding the 'four quarters of Space.' Now the year, in its cycling turn or wheeling, mystically to the mind passes through the four different 'quarters of Space,' and when the four points of the year, which are the four Sacred Seasons, reach these 'four quarters of Space' occult powers and forces are at these times framed for corresponding consequences to ensue upon those who are ready.

The Winter Solstice is the mystic birth of the individuality, of the inner Buddha. In some countries it is called the Initiation into the Sun. In the Mediterranean countries at about the time of the beginning of the Christian Era it was called the birth of the Christ.

A certain conjunction of two of the planets, Mercury and Venus, with the Moon and the Earth, allows the passage along the mystic circulations of the Solar System of great spiritual forces having their native home in the Sun; and the human aspirant undertaking this course of the initiatory trials, either fails, or rises from his trance clothed with the Mystery Sun literally, enfolded as in a glory with the splendor of the inner Buddha, the inner god. In some cases this clothing of glory remains for many days. Usually, however, it is but a passing phase. But he who has passed through this most holy event in human mystical history ever afterwards lives and works among men as one who has in actual truth met his own inner god face to face, and is therefore called a Buddha or a Christ.

These statements please accept as literal truths, and not as metaphorical expressions. Each human being is a child of the Sun, a Son of the Sun; and this most holy of initiations is simply the allying of oneself with the god of the Sun, and for the time being the aspirant becomes omniscient because his consciousness is then universal.

Thereafter in the same or likely in a future year, at the time of the Spring Equinox, the aspirant enters individual spiritual activity, and dies to the world of men. In the Summer Initiation Cycle, the initiation is one which pertains to him as an individual worker in the ranks of the Guardians; and if he pass that Trial successfully, he is assigned his duty in the world of men.

At the time of the Autumnal Equinox the aspirant breaks the link with material existence entirely and is indrawn and withdrawn to his Parent Star.

The holiest of these four periods of initiation, *so far as chelas are concerned,* is that of the Winter Solstice; for on that occasion the man becomes the 'risen Christ' — the birth of the Christ out of the man, and this is the mystical birth. At the time of the Spring Equinox the aspirant takes up his duties, no longer in the world of men but in the world of the cosmic spirits belonging to our solar system, and more particularly belonging to our planet, Earth. At the time of the Summer Solstice he is assigned his duties as a Savior and Helper of men; and at the time of the Autumnal Equinox — he 'passes.'

When one of these sacred Initiatory Cycles opens, the proper astronomical conditions must prevail. The moon should be new so that the Initiant, winging his way through planes and spheres does so during the fourteen days of the waxing moon. It is at the time of a total solar eclipse, when such coincides with the time of one or the other of the solstices or equinoxes, that the greater of the Initiations take place. The ideal condition is thought to prevail when the initiation chamber is within the path of the moon's shadow as it passes over the earth.

679

H.P.B.

THERE IS STILL another aspect of the Avatāra doctrine which explains the psychological wonder that H.P.B. was, and I will now give in substance part of an address delivered at Visingsö, Sweden, in 1931, to commemorate the one hundredth anniversary of her birth:°

Does any Theosophist imagine for a moment that H.P.B. came to the Occidental world by chance, outside of Nature's laws and rigid concatenation of cause and effect which produce everything in due order? H.P.B. came in obedience to a law, one of Nature's laws, because it was time for her to come, one of the series of Teachers who come at certain stated periods throughout the ages, one Teacher after the other, and always when the time is right and ripe, and never by chance. H.P.B. was one of the links in what the ancient Greek Initiates called the living Chain of Hermes, the Golden Chain, in connection with the passing on of mystic and esoteric light and truth. One of this serial succession of Teachers, she came in the rhythmical order of the laws which control our planet. She came indeed at the beginning of one Messianic Cycle of two thousand one hundred and sixty years and at the end of the preceding cycle of the same term. She was the Messenger for her age, that is, for the age to come.

In a certain very true but little known sense, she was an Avatāra — an Avatāra of a certain type or kind, for there are different kinds of Avatāras. Every Teacher who comes to teach man comprises not only his or her body and an unusually received psychological apparatus, but is likewise at times infilled with the holy fire of a greater Soul, and therefore is *de facto* an Avatāra of a kind. Just as Jesus was an Avatāra of one kind for his age, so was she, our beloved H.P.B., an Avatāra of another kind for her age. Roughly speaking, some two thousand one hundred and sixty years before her birth, Jesus inaugurated for Europe the particular Messianic Cycle which, as its centuries followed one the other, plunged European countries into the darkness of the Middle Ages. Today, more or less 2,160 years afterwards, a new cycle opened when she was born, a rising cycle which should bring light, peace, knowledge, wisdom, to men.

°Cf. *The Theosophical Path*, December 1931.

A mighty power came into the world and worked and wrought, and the weaving of the web which she wrought has played a great part in producing the better conditions we find among us today. H.P.B. was of course a woman in body, but invigorating and inflaming this body with its brain-mind was the inner divine Sun, the inner Buddha, the living Christ within. But between this divine fire and the receptive and mystically-trained and educated brain of the woman, there was a psychological apparatus, commonly spoken of in Western parlance as the 'human soul,' which in the case of her — for she was an Initiate of the Order of the Buddhas of Compassion and Peace — could at times step aside and allow the entrance into the vacancy thus left of a 'human soul' loftier by far than even hers. It was this Buddhic Splendor which thus infilled the vacancy that she so gladly left for use, which in large part was responsible for the works of wonder that H.P.B. wrought.

You may remember that in her writings she often makes a distinction between what she calls H.P.B. and H. P. Blavatsky. H. P. Blavatsky was the woman, the chela, the aspiring, learning, splendid, noble, courageous chela. But H.P.B. was the Master's mind speaking through her: body and spirit, one entity, then the intermediate psychological apparatus, commonly called the 'soul,' temporarily removable at will. In fact, when H.P.B. was sent as the Messenger, that psychological apparatus in large part remained behind. This fact accounts for the so-called contrarieties and contradictions of her character that the people who attempted to write about her saw — and saw very plainly, because they could not help seeing — but which they did not understand, and by which they oft mis-judged her and misunderstood her. At times she was strong and virile, so that, as her friends said, it seemed verily as if man incarnate were manifesting through her — not any one man, but Man. There was a divine flame within her that occasionally seized her brain as it were — and then she spoke like a pythoness, like a prophetess, like an oracle at Delphi. And similarly so at other times, when she was infilled, as the Avatāra, with the holy flame of one of the Great Ones, then there was *H.P.B.*, *the Teacher*, the Sage, the Seer, the Teacher of great natural scientific truths which modern science today is but beginning to show to be true, the Teacher of a great hope for mankind, the giver of a Vision to men, the framer and former of a new Philosophy-Religion-Science for men. There is a psychological wonder, a mystery, in H.P.B., for H.P.B. *was* a mystery. Thus was she an Avatāra of her kind.

MESSENGERS FROM THE LODGE — THE INSIGNIA MAJESTATIS

> Ever since H. P. B. made the statement that "no Master of Wisdom would himself appear or send anyone to Europe or America . . . until the year 1975," speculation has been rife as to what type of teacher or messenger would then appear, and would he or would he not work among the formal theosophical organizations then in existence during the closing decades of this century.
>
> We reproduce hereunder the major portion of G. de Purucker's interpretation of H. P. B.'s statement, as given by him to his esoteric students in the 1930s.   — ED.

IT IS NOT INFREQUENTLY stated that the stream of inspiration from the Lodge of the Great Teachers ceased with the passing of H. P. Blavatsky, and that there will be no recurrence of the flow of that stream of inspiration and light until the Teacher comes whom she spoke of as coming about the beginning of the last quarter of the century. That idea is entirely erroneous.

All of you are doubtless familiar with the following passage from H. P. B.'s "First Preliminary Memorandum" issued by her in 1888 to the members of the E.S.:

> Let every member know, moreover, that the time for such priceless acquisition is limited. The writer of the present is old; her life is well-nigh worn out, and she may be summoned "home" any day and almost any hour. And if her place is even filled up, perchance by another worthier and more learned than herself, still *there remain but a few years* to the last hour of the term — namely, till December the 31st, 1899. Those who will not have profited by the opportunity (given to the world in every last quarter of a century), those who will not have reached a certain point of psychic and spiritual development, or that point from which begins the cycle of adeptship, by that day — those will advance no further than the knowledge already acquired. No Master of Wisdom from the East will himself appear or send anyone to Europe or America after that period, and the sluggards will have to renounce every chance of advancement in their present incarnation — until the year 1975. Such is the Law, for we are in *Kali-Yuga* — the

Black Age — and the restrictions in this cycle, the first 5,000 years of which will expire in 1897, are great and almost insuperable.

As a few words of help, I would like to point out that H.P.B. was writing at a critical time in the history of the T.S.; and furthermore was writing to what she called her Esotericists. She pointed out very clearly that she was soon to pass away. She gave a hint so broad that few have noticed it, so wide that it has escaped observation, so deep that nobody has felt it, to the effect that *someone would take her place*. She called attention to the obvious fact that those who, belonging to the E.S., did not reach a certain stage of inner development, of understanding; in other words, as she phrased it, who did not put their feet on the pathway leading to Adeptship, would be sluggards and would have to wait and bide their time, not merely some eighty-five or ninety years ahead, or whatever the number of years may be from the time when she wrote to, let us say, 1980; but they would have to bide their time perhaps until the next life.

No *Master of Wisdom* came before H.P.B. came, nor while she was alive, nor has come since her passing; and it is in the highest degree improbable that any Master of Wisdom will come openly until the next great epoch of spiritual rejuvenation — and the great epoch I have in mind will not come so soon as 1975. Messengers, however, will come regularly, as long as the 'link is unbroken.' But, as H.P.B. points out, none was 'sent' to Europe or America either while she was alive or after she passed on. And why should such come? As she herself points out in substance: someone will follow me in all likelihood.° For you, your time for learning from me these precious truths is *now*.

Writing to her then Esotericists, was she writing to people of the future, who would be esotericists twenty or thirty or forty or fifty or more years after she passed away: "If you do not take your chances now when I write — I a sick and dying woman soon to pass away — you will not learn from me"? Certainly not!

No Master of Wisdom will come himself or send anybody to Europe and America as H.P.B. was sent. Once in a century is enough in order to do propaganda in that way. Once the link is established, and the connections made between the Great Lodge and the outside world, the

---

° ". . . due to her being sent out alone into the world to gradually prepare the way for others." — K. H. in *The Mahatma Letters*, p. 203.

inner esoteric life begins to flow and the teaching is given for those who prove themselves ready to receive it — who come and knock at the door of the Temple.

The Messengers do not come and advertise themselves in the newspapers. They come quietly and in the silence, not with flashes and blaring of trumpets. Their message is to the hearts of men, to those who are ready *at any time;* for none is neglected. The Masters of Wisdom and Compassion are always ready and always waiting and always working. The door is never shut against those whose feet are on the pathway. The Great Ones work among men continuously, uninterruptedly; and have done so for ages. Anyone whose feet are on the path, who shows even the smallest glimmer of the Buddhic Splendor, is watched, guided, helped; and if he succeeds, he finally is openly received into the Brotherhood.

The Masters are working in the silence constantly; and the supposition that their work, the Theosophical Society in the world, and the E.S. which their Messenger H.P.B. founded, were to be left without guidance and light is a monstrous perversion of the truth.

Nor will it be a Master of Wisdom who will be that particular one of the Messengers to appear or to be at work (not necessarily to 'appear') during the last quarter of the century.

Yet, lest my words be misunderstood, I call upon you to bear witness in the records to what I am now going to tell you. Do not be too ready to receive anyone who may come with mere claims. Be not too ready to reject anyone who may be able to teach you. Do not fasten your minds upon a certain particular kind of Teacher or Messenger; for the high probability is that you will guess wrongly. Be awake; be alert; be earnest; be devoted; be loyal and steady; be compassionate; be forgiving; be loving; cultivate the virtues. Then, when the new effort of the end of this century begins, you will be good material to work with if you are still alive, and you will know whither to turn.

For I tell you now, and I warn you, that there will in all probability be conflicting claims. Even my present words will be quoted. Be awake, be prepared; cultivate the inner vision, the inner light.

Nor will the work of this particular Messenger — who in all probability will not be greater than those who have already come, but whose work will be a particularly precarious and difficult one, and who will merit all your devotion and help — necessarily begin in the month of January, 1975. Remember that he may not begin his work exactly on the New

Year of 1975, or on the esoteric New Year. He may begin a little before or a little after, or much before or much after. But his work will be during the last quarter of this century.

So far as that Messenger to come is concerned, there is a danger in building up too idealistic and too lofty a conception of who and what that Messenger will be — for his work will be greatly impeded, hindered, if there be among Theosophists of those days at the time of his coming an expectation, a conception, a notion, an idea, that an incarnate divinity has come to walk upon the earth and teach men. You will find that he will be — those of you who may be still alive — a quiet, simple, kindly, devoted, individual, who will be of course fully prepared and fitted for the work that he will have to do. Nor is it probable that he will be greater or farther advanced than are the Messengers who have already come.

I have no right to tell you anything that I am not sure of, but I think that Brother Judge was perfectly right when he suggested that it is very likely that H.P.B. herself will be the new Messenger who will come back at the end of this century. I think that it will be H.P.B., or rather the spirit-soul who in her last imbodiment was known as H.P.B.

In 1889, William Q. Judge, who was at that time secretary to H.P.B., wrote as follows:

If we succeed in carrying the T.S. well along into the twentieth century, there is a very great possibility that we can transmit it pure and undogmatic to such successors as will, after our death, keep it in being until the next twenty-five year cycle. At that time another messenger will come. In my opinion he will be the same being as now directs our efforts. In such an event there would be ready for his further work a Society that might be fit for greater things than our present T.S. is, and if so, all our efforts now will be crowned with success. If, on the contrary, the members fail now, great will be the responsibility upon every one of us then. In view of this, it is expected that the Section shall strive to become the *life* and *core* of the Theosophical movement, so that it may carry the spirit and genius of the movement through the seventy-five years which will begin at about the year 1900. If this shall be accomplished, then in 1975 there will be an instrument ready at hand for the returning Messenger to use during the last twenty-five years, instead of having to *construct* it anew amid jars and discords such as have surrounded H.P.B. for fifteen years. Now in the *Key to Theosophy* she plainly states that the strength and power of this ideal Section will not rest so much in the technical occult knowledge of the members

685

as in the spiritual development, coupled with good common-sense, which they shall have attained. . . .

Let everyone, then, who reads this listen to the call. A mental sacrifice is demanded, an abandonment of self, a complete renunciation, an entire devotion to this cause. Altruism must be made the line of our lives, for by that alone can the end in view be reached. We are not associated in this Section for our own individual profit, nor for the glory of H.P.B., nor for the making of new mysteries or dogmas, but only that men and races of men after us may become brothers such as we should be.   — *Suggestions and Aids*

The important thing about it will be that he will come at a cyclical period and will be greatly helped by the beginning of that cyclical period, a very short period but a very important one in each century; and therefore did H. P. Blavatsky, and therefore does every Messenger preceding him, point to that period as an important one. Cultivate within your own selves love, and you will understand the love that he will give you. Cultivate within your own hearts forgiveness, and you will then understand the forgiveness that will flow forth from him to you. Be truthful and you will recognize truthfulness when you hear it; and you will recognize his truthfulness when he comes.

In real Esotericism no appointing such as is often supposed is ever made in the ordinary way, by paper and ink, or by print, or by ribbons and seals and notarial certifications, and what not. That method is childish. Such documents can be destroyed or forged, laid aside or lost. The method is too uncertain altogether — too uncertain. The Successor is known by his life, by his teachings, and by the way in which his predecessor treated him. There may be, in addition to all this, a declaration, written or spoken, or there may not be such, but the written or spoken declaration would add not one feather's weight of importance to the reality.

A strange and curious situation; and some of you may say that it is a very parlous situation: "How are we to know?" The situation is usually deliberately left as I have told you. Think about the matter. Suppose that a Mahātman came to you with a legally drawn document with an imposing red or blue seal, and with a blue or black ribbon sealed upon the paper, the legend on the paper saying, or having words, something like this: "To all whom it may concern: Be it known that I, Mahā-Chohan of Śambhala, hereby certify that —— is my fully authorized agent to do such and such work in the Theosophical Society, and to be successor of so-and-so in the E.S." What would you think? Your first instinct would be one of amusement, perhaps. The second would be one of suspicion.

On the other hand, consider a man who comes among you, or who has been among you: he is quiet, unobtrusive, kindly, perhaps through the years you watch him; you see that he does no harm, that he is studious, that he is gentle, that he is forgiving; that he *lives* the life as far as you know; that he is faithful to duty, and that he carries out all the rules and regulations of the station of life in which his karma puts him. You hear him speak. You may or may not be impressed by what he says, but you are impressed at least with the feeling that he is an honest man. Then when the time comes, you suddenly realize that things are in safe hands; that there is strength in this man, strength of judgment, strength of will, that there are wisdom, knowledge, spiritual power. In other words, you are keenly conscious that the insignia of reality and of authority *are in the man himself.* Which of the two would you then choose to follow: the man who comes bringing a paper, or the man whom you know?

Remember also that the Servants of the Lodge come quietly and go quietly. They work quietly and they live quietly. Whatever they do, however public it may be, on however grand a scale, on however small or apparently insignificant a scale, it may be, in which they work, whatever they do carries a mark of power and ability.

I am writing in this way with great deliberation, because the time is coming in the future when you may have to make your choice — and mark you, I don't say that you will *have to.* It may be that events will follow some other path. But in emphasizing my words thus, I want to awaken intuition in your minds. I want to acquaint you with how things are conducted in the Esoteric Life, as far as I can do so.

Did H.P.B. bring anything except herself? No; she herself was her own proof. If H.P.B. had appeared in the world with a formally witnessed and attested document certifying her status as a Messenger of the Lodge, would she in any wise have been greater than she was? Would her position as a Messenger from the Lodge thereby have been 'proved'? The answer is an obvious No. H.P.B. proved what she was by what was in her.

There is in the exterior world, and outside the Great Lodge, this succession of Teachers, following each other in serial order — called in Sanskrit the *Guru-pāramparya*, i.e. the *Guruparamparā* — each one authorized to teach, each one capable of teaching, and each one therefore teaching. But will the succession continue, or will it be — even if temporarily — broken? If the call of your hearts is strong enough, and if the appeal of your minds is sincere enough, the line of succession will continue, and will endure, if these conditions prevail, throughout the ages of the future. Should it [not] happen, then make the call anew. If the call is strong enough and sincere enough, it will be answered.

No Teacher has ever passed on what Mystics and Occultists call the Living Word and Knowledge — in other words, the authority in the line of succession of teachings and Teachers, which line of succession always prevails in every truly occult School — by merely formal documents. The Successor is his own proof; and once you know the real man, nothing that is written against him or for him thereafter will cause you to change your mind. The man himself carries in himself the proofs of his high authority and lofty mission. It is a matter solely of merit and of spiritual standing of one called forth by the heart-cry of those who are hungry for truth and spiritual leadership.

NĀRADA°

Narada is here, there, and everywhere; and yet, none of the Purânas gives the true characteristics of this great enemy of physical procreation. Whatever those characteristics may be in Hindu Esotericism, Narada — who is called in Cis-Himalayan Occultism *Pesh-Hun*, the "Messenger," or the Greek *Angelos* — is the sole confidant and the executor of the universal decrees of Karma and *Adi-Budh:* a kind of active and ever incarnating logos, who leads and guides human affairs from the beginning to the end of the Kalpa.

"Pesh-Hun" is a general not a special Hindu possession. He is the mysterious guiding intelligent power, which gives the impulse to, and regulates the impetus of cycles, Kalpas and universal events. He is Karma's visible adjuster on a general scale; the *inspirer* and the leader of the greatest heroes of this Manvantara. In the exoteric works he is referred to by some very uncomplimentary names; such as "Kali-Kâraka," *strife-maker,* "Kapi-vaktra," *monkey-faced,* and even "Pisuna," the spy, though elsewhere he is called Deva-Brahmâ. — *The Secret Doctrine,* II, 48

NĀRADA AS THE Hindus call him, Pesh-Hun as the Tibetans call him, is in the world. That agent of destiny, whom Christians I suppose would call the agent of the vengeance of the Lord, is abroad in every land. His karmic work is proceeding: reaping in order that future crops may be sown. Terrible agent of what the Christians would call divine vengeance, and yet Nārada or Pesh-Hun is man's greatest friend for the men who will recognize him. His work is not that of fate, it is that of destiny, which man himself weaves. If he is a disturber of man's ways in order that the mandates of divine justice shall be carried out, he is also the bringer of peace, and the restorer of harmony. To use a beautiful Jewish phrase, it is, ultimately speaking, Nārada or Pesh-Hun who "will wipe away all tears."

H.P.B. speaks of Nārada, as the Hindus call him, or Pesh-Hun as she calls his name from Atlantean times (he is known by other names in other

---

°An address given by G. de Purucker on March 22, 1942, at Point Loma, California, but not included previously in any of his published works.

ages and lands), but she says very little about him indeed for the simple reason that his functions in nature are so difficult to explain to a world which is utterly unaccustomed to the spiritual and intellectual teachings of theosophy, that she just pointed to certain facts and left the matter there.

Who is Nārada, who is this Pesh-Hun? In the first place he is a Rishi. He is also a Prajāpati. Prajāpati means a parent of offspring; it does not say what kind of offsprings, maybe mind-born children, it may be children born of the body, for Prajāpati means either or both. He is also a Manu when his functions concerning the human races alone are involved. He is a Dhyān-Chohan or what the Christians would call an Archangel. Of course this reference does not mean much today because the Christians themselves hardly know what they mean by the term. But I am giving a few names in different systems of thought. In Greek and Latin mythology he would be a god or perhaps one of the highest of the Daimones, cosmic spirits. Put it this way: Nārada is a Dhyān-Chohan, also Prajāpati because of certain functions he performs, also a Rishi or great spiritual teacher because of certain functions he performs. Also a Manu because of the intimate connection with the destinies of the human race. That is why these three names are used, each name being appropriate to different sections of his activity. He is a Dhyān-Chohan of the highest or the next to the highest class. I am not now referring merely to the three great classes of Dhyān-Chohans higher than the humans. I am referring to classes in a different category. Every possibility of Dhyān-Chohanic type considered, Nārada belongs to the next to the highest type.

What are the functions of Nārada? Typically those of carrying out karmic destiny. There you have a key to all his activities. What the Lipikas have written down, Nārada as an individual agent or as an individuality, as an Archangel, sees are carried out. He is the agent of karmic destiny. The consequence is that, just because destiny to us humans is often so unpleasant due to our own faults and failings in the past, Nārada has been given very uncomplimentary titles by those who have seen his work in the world and in the world of men and who do not like it. When they do like it, when it is something that humans like, he is given very complimentary titles: the Benefactor, the Kindly Helper, the Warrior for Mankind, the bringer about of all the good things in destiny. But when as an impartial, impersonal agent of karmic destiny he brings about trouble on the human race, then he is given very uncomplimentary names, as for instance he is called Kali-Kāra, the Strife-Producer, because in the course of human destiny it is his work to bring about war and peace.

Now can you see why H.P.B. has side-stepped this very function, duty, character of Nārada? It is a ticklish thing because in the Occident we do not want to believe that the world is conducted by cosmic and spiritual laws, nor do we want to believe that the horrible things that happen to us are infallibly and inevitably our own self-earned destiny. We prefer: it is *his* fault. That is the way we pass the buck, and yet show me anything that happens to you as far as you can see that is not the result of your own action. There is the law.

So the functions of Nārada are to act as the agent of karma. How does he do this? Being a Dhyāni-Chohan he cannot come amongst us and work as a human being does, because he belongs to a much higher kingdom, among the very highest of the three Dhyān-Chohanic kingdoms. He is an impersonal, impartial agent of destiny. His duty is to see that the world is protected, that karmic law, destiny, be carried out irrespective of consequences; for it is the only way to re-establish law, order, equilibrium, justice, and ultimate wisdom and peace. Otherwise there would be Nature piling up a vast accumulation of unexpended karma which sometime or in time might flood the human race and utterly destroy it. No wonder H.P.B. side-stepped this question.

How does Nārada therefore work? Sometimes he overshadows men of the proper psychological, spiritual, intellectual, and even physical temperament and works through them. These men then are called by H.P.B. Men of Destiny. They may not in themselves be even good men, which is another reason why Nārada is often spoken of in uncomplimentary terms; but they may be good men, these Men of Destiny. But they are used as instruments and tools to carry out, to bring to pass, certain things that are lying in the womb of time and must come out, and there must be a guiding spiritual power to see that the performing of these events shall take place without the complete wrecking of mankind. This is Nārada's work: a protector of mankind and also an avenger.

The Occidental for centuries has been trained in a religious and philosophical system which is since early medieval times so utterly contrary to the facts of Nature that we have lost touch with how the world is ruled and governed. It is governed by spiritual and highly intellectual powers. For instance our own globe is, globe D of our chain. Not a thing takes place by chance, by hap, by hazard or by fortuity. Everything that takes place on this globe or in the solar system or in the sun or in the galaxy takes place according to law; and it takes place according to law because the agents of law, the agents of karma, are there to hold it firm, to prevent as it were the earthquake or the tidal wave or the cyclone, from going crazy and destroying indiscriminately. Do you see what I am trying to say? Destiny is held firmly in the hands of the gods; or as the early Christians phrased it in their own phrasing, a phrasing which has lost sense today, the world is ruled by God Almighty through the hierarchy of angels, which is the theosophical teaching taught in the Christian form. These Angels carry out the decrees of destiny, and we have remnants in Christian teaching today of this old Theosophy of early Christianity, as for instance when they speak of the Angel of Death or the Angel of Destiny or the Angel of Disease — or turning to the New Testament, the Four Angels of the Apocalypse. You might ask what are they now? War, disease or pestilence, starvation, and death: you remember the Spanish writer, Ibáñez, wrote a famous book *The Four Horsemen of the Apocalypse.*

Now it is Nārada who is in charge of these karmic productions of destiny. No wonder he is called Kali-Kāra, the Strife-Producer. He does not produce it out of nothing, out of a diabolic wish to injure mankind. He is simply the agent of karmic destiny bringing about, for instance, the breaking up of old crystallized conditions which are becoming a spiritual opiate for mankind, or stopping things that are threatening to injure mankind. You see, a teaching like this also could be dangerous if it fell into the minds of irresponsible or weak men who would twist it to personal and selfish uses. Such men have no conception of the profundities and intricacies of theosophic truths, which are the archaic wisdom-religion of mankind.

Once more let me ask what or who is Nārada? Nārada is not only the agent of karmic destiny but is mankind's savior, the bringer about of man's evolutionary progress, the bringer about of change tending upwards to nobler things, and likewise paradoxically enough the bringer about or restorer of spiritual and intellectual stability. Because there can be no stability when an accumulated reservoir of karma is waiting and threatening to burst the dam and cause devastation, destruction indiscriminately.

Take into your minds some of the consequences of these thoughts. They will make you charitable, less inclined to hate and misjudge other human beings. Take Napoleon for instance, or Julius Caesar or Alexander — three men who if you judge them in the balance of ordinary human justice are three evildoers because they were all upsetters, all destroyers of convention and of established things. But the world lived through them, and yet who were they? Average men, each one with a peculiar cast, psychological and other, which Nārada could work through to bring about the karmic changes. In other words Nārada is a kind of Śiva, destroyer and regenerator, but his destructions are always beneficial, he is always on the side of liberty, absolute justice to all irrespective of anything, and on the side of progress. If there is one thing that Nārada abhors, it is cruelty, cruelty of any kind, cruelty to friend or cruelty to foe. You immediately put yourself under the watchful eye of Nārada if you indulge in anything that is subhuman.

In passing, let me say that my reference to Alexander, Julius Caesar, and Napoleon, is not because I think these three men are patterns of human conduct, for I do not, very much to the contrary. But they are notable historical instances of men of destiny, who were used almost as pawns precisely because of their weaknesses and distorted strength to bring about noble things despite these men themselves.

It is a peculiar thing that if you will study the history of mankind you will find that the great plays of Nārada, the great activities of Nārada, are always accompanied by or followed very closely by a great manifestation of moral and religious life. The greatest religions are always established at the time of the greatest human turnovers. Nārada's work both of them. Nārada prepares the ground, guides the loosening of karmic destiny, and as it were beckons with his hand to the gods of teaching to come in along the pathway he opens.

Some may wonder if Nārada is the same as the Silent Watcher. No, the Silent Watcher is above all. We may perhaps at least figuratively say that Nārada is the Śiva-aspect of the Silent Watcher. Nārada is a kind of Logos for this globe throughout the entire kalpa. And what is the function of the Logoi, greater or smaller, higher or lower? Each one to guide all its children into the future of glorious achievement.

Let me point out another aspect. Suppose there were a great religion in the world which had lost the original inspiration, the theosophic inspiration of its Master, of its Founder, and it had become ecclesiastical and theological instead of continuing to be living and vital, a mighty and spiritually controlling power in the life of its followers. Suppose this religion — one of the noblest motors of human thought and conduct — had become mere formalism and rites, and there were even disputes whether the teaching of the Founder was really meant to be taken as we have received it. What does Nārada do? Nārada breaks that shell, releases the imprisoned spirit once again. Of course there is lots of trouble. Men on religious points are almost fanatic; you break up their crystallized beliefs, they can even become almost demons at times. But Nārada has a bigger work in view than the merely conventional feelings of numbers of these coryphaei and their millions of followers. Nārada in such instance works to release and restore to its pristine power and influence the imprisoned and perhaps forgotten spirit of the Founder. It may be done quickly in a crash, in a disaster. Or it may be done through years and years and years of slow expansion and breaking of the old shell. Nārada works in various ways always according to destiny and always in the kindest way that he can work, because he is a regenerator and a builder. That is the most important. Here you have an example. Religion had become a danger in a case like that. It had become a drug. People were going to sleep. The souls of men were so somnolent, so negative, as dominant factors in human life, that men actually were no longer truly ensouled by their souls. They were little more than bodies, blindly following merely conventional practices. But Nārada re-ensouls these men. Their souls awaken. They begin to think and to question. They want the spirit. They burst the shell; overthrow the forms. And we have a great religious revival or regeneration in a case like that.

But of course it is a painful process. The coryphaei don't like it. Millions of their followers don't like it. Their quiet, comfortable, smug beliefs are overthrown. They don't know that they are exchanging old soiled clothing for the garments of life, of spirit, exchanging the body for the spirit. They have not realized it yet. It is only after Time, the magic agent, has softened the woes of adversity, of the bursting shell, and has brought even those who are hurt to see and to say: "Why, it is the very best thing to happen. Now we understand the Master's teaching. Now religion has become a vital moving thing in my heart. It guides my life. It is something to believe in and to live by." Do you see? The work of Nārada! But during that time, what did Nārada do? He was a Kali-Kāra, Strife-Producer, he had to break the shell.

And that is the work of the Logos too, whichever Logos you mean, the Logos of our globe or of our chain or of the solar system. But mark you, distinguish between the work of Nārada and evil men. Evil men

694

may be used by Nārada for karmic purposes, and that is done constantly, just as Nārada will use good men. And be careful lest you set yourselves up as judges. But the distinction between the work of a bad man who is not guided by Nārada and Nārada's work is this: that the bad man is always working for himself, egoistic selfishness, the root of all evil; whereas the work of Nārada, no matter what the channel, is always for the world, even though his human instruments imagine they are working for their own ends. We may not always see it but it is there. For instance, when Nārada smashes a great organization by regenerating it, the bursting of the shell and the tortures suffered by those involved is torture for them, and they think it is hell. But actually it is not, it is a salvation, and they grow to know it after a while; but the process is to them a hell. So we have to be very, very careful in judgment, very charitable and understanding.

Nārada's functions therefore are so essentially spiritual and intellectual as well as psychic, that a preliminary study of the wisdom-religion is almost essential to prepare people to receive understandingly just who Nārada is and what his functions in the world are. The main point to grasp first is that our universe is governed by law and by order emanating from intelligent and spiritual sources, and consequently that everything that happens in that universe is within that sway of law and under the sway of that order, and in consequence there is no chance, which is to theosophists a word utterly devoid of all substantial meaning; and therefore that whatever happens has been caused — karma. The first thing this teaches us is to stop sitting in the judgment seat upon other men. It teaches us to stop arrogating to ourselves the all-capacity to condemn others. Judge not that ye be not judged. But keep it in mind that Nārada so works, call him an Angel of Destiny, an Archangel of Destiny, or a Dhyān-Chohan whose work in the world is just that, guiding mankind and the other kingdoms too, guiding mankind's steps through tribulation and suffering from their own folly, towards freedom and wisdom and love, with his immensely strong hand of the friend, upwards and onwards through suffering and pain, through joy and peace, through war and disturbance, through attainment and progress, upwards and onwards forever.

ERRATA

Page

ii   complete titles for:
     Golden Precepts of Esotericism
     The Dialogues of G. de Purucker

189   ¶ 3 line 4, last word: buddha- *should be* bodhi —

236n   *after* Bk. III *insert* Vol. I, p. 426, Thomas Taylor, London, 1820

313n   ¶ 2 line 7: *insert* [Merope] *after* Sterope

319n   line 4: Volcanus *should be* Vulcanus

360   ¶ 2 line 2: *insert* . *after* evolution

466   *add* Our Spiritual Home / 529

510   ¶ 3 line 4: sunken *should be* sunk

570n   line 4 from bottom: was *should be* is

579   ¶ 1 line 7: mor *should be* more

589   ¶ 2 last line: avichi *should be* avīchi

590   ¶ 4 line 4: devachani *should be* devachanī

633   ¶ 2 line 6: core of essence *should be* core or essence

657   line 3 from bottom, 5th Greek word: ὅρος *should be* ὄρος

658   lines 5 and 6, *replace with:*
     [Ἶσις] ἐγώ εἰμι πᾶν τὸ γεγονὸς καὶ ὂν καὶ ἐσόμενον
     καὶ τὸν ἐμὸν πέπλον οὐδείς πω θνητὸς ἀπεκάλυψεν.
     line 8, 2nd Greek word: ἐγω *should be* ἐγὼ

661   Note 19. End of first paragraph *insert* * *and add footnote* as follows:
     *Most authorities state that Buddha Gautama was of solar
     lineage.

666   line 5: *delete* , *after* death

702   (index): Bhūrloka-pātāla *should precede* Bhūtas

703   (index): after Boar *insert* Bodhi 189

Index

INDEX

Ab Soo, the Abyss 70–1
Abel, habēl, brother of Cain 105
Abortion 625
Absolute, The 89–90, 99
Absolutum (liberation) 89
Abyss 70. *See* Boundless, the
Accidental death 549–50, 570, 576
Adam and Eve, rib explained 287
Adam Kadmon (Heavenly Man) 207
Adept(s) 3, 14, 16, 76, 531,
    561, 572. *See* Brotherhood,
    Mahatmas, Śambhala
  answer 'right call' 7
  can modify pupil's karma 24–5
  death and sleep of 569
  Gautama and 521, 529
  higher loka-tala and 265
  Mahāchohan, chief of 470 ff.
  māyāvi-rūpas of 440, 442–3
  powers of 428–9
  travel circulations of cosmos 155
  trials of 55
  use nādīs 462
Adhishthāna 50
Ādi-buddha 44, 490, 507
  dhyāni-buddhas rays of 490
  First Logos 474, 490, 507
  in dharmakāya state 474
Ādi-buddhi 44, 49, 229, 437
Ādi-tattwa 229, 233, 238, 247
Aditi 118–19, 187
Ādityas 134, 187
Adwaita-Vedānta 87, 89, 95, 651
Aeneid, Virgil, quoted 305
Aeons of Simon, the Gnostic 194–5
Aether 229–30. *See* Ākāśa
  ether, lowest aspect of 116

Aether (con.)
  pradhāna 437
  primordial 72, 196–7
  swābhāvic 224
Age, Golden, of Saturn 168
Age of Brahmā 159
Agni or Agnīya chakra 461
Agnishwātta pitris 284–5, 480–3
  dhyāni-chohans 480, 482
  kumāras and 287, 482
  mānasaputras and 481–3
  seven classes 481
  three higher classes 287
Aham asmi Parabrahman 62
Ain ('Eyn) Sōph 70
Air element (vāyu-tattwa) 229–30,
    232, 238
  sylphs of 234
  touch and 240
Aisthêton of Plato 194
Ājñā or Ājñākhya chakra 461–2
Ākāśa 76–7, 238, 240–1, 315, 437
  aether 116
  Alaya, highest part 98, 437
  anima mundi and 77, 116, 437
  auric egg and 427
  brain wrapped in veil of 389
  fifth tattwa 77, 229, 233
  hearing and 240
Ākāśic
  aura 543–5
  veil protects the sleeping 609
  veil surrounds devachanī 592
Alaya 59, 98
  Amitābha 508
  Second Logos 98, 183, 437
Ālaya-vijñāna 98

Auric Egg(s) (con.)
626–8, 638
memory stamped on 550–1
monads and 145–6, 427–8,
431–2, 557–8
of gods 381
of nirmānakāya 526
on all planes 146, 427–8
organs and 428, 557
panoramic vision and 550–1
physical dregs of 146, 428,
442, 557
planetary 146–7
pores of, and protection 431
prānas and 427–31, 545, 557
principles and 427, 564
senses and 429–30
size of 146, 429, 431
sun's 135, 137, 146–7, 427, 430
sūtrātman and 446, 564
tanhic elementals in 622
universal 433–8, 627
Aurora (ae) 158, 305–7, 336
Authority, final test of viii
Automata 504
Autumnal Equinox 678–9. See Initiation
Avalokiteśvara 490–1, 507–9
Avatāra(s) 484–501, 680
among gods, beasts 499
anupapādaka 487–91, 531–2
buddhas and 484, 486, 489–90,
495–6
come cyclically 486, 490, 495
dhyāni-buddhas and 487–8, 490
Docetists and 485
force of, and mahatmas 523
Gautama and 484, 494, 496, 523
initiation of a divinity 499
Jesus an 484, 488, 495–501, 680
Krishna an 303, 488, 493
man's inner god and 489–90
minor 493–4
no karma of, explained 484
of Mahā-Śiva, Mahā-Vishnu 492–4
Rāja sun ultimate source of 492

Avatāra(s) (con.)
Śankarāchārya an 484, 495
upapādaka- 485, 487–91
Āveśa 42, 502–4
Avīchi 566
fate of Brothers of Shadow 456
kāma-loka between, and devachan 566
no cognizance of time in 593
some still on earth in 594
state, not a location 566, 589
twelve stages of 589
Avidyā 47
Axis, earth's 142, 346–7, 671

Babylonia 70, 162, 493
Bacteria 403
Banquet or *Symposium* of Plato 287
Banyan, the ever-living human
469–71, 473. See Silent Watcher
Bardo 576, 662–3
Barhishads 285, 480, 483. See Lunar
Pitris
Baring-Gould, Rev. S. 657
Barker, A. Trevor viii
Basilides 193
Bath Qōl 185
Battle between light and dark 5, 9
Beal, Samuel 67–8
Beel-Zebub 408
Bees, source of instinct in 213
Betrayal of teachings 31
Bhagavad-Gītā 97, 173, 385,
489, 649
Bhaumika Pralaya. See Pralaya
Bhön 510
Bhūman 76
Bhūtas 578
Bhūtātman 434–5
Bhūrloka-pātāla 257, 259–63,
265, 267
Bhuvarloka 258–9, 267. See Lokas
Birth. See Manvantara, Reimbodiment
Process
man's, like cosmos 111, 115, 383

Globe(s), Globe-chain (con.)
-śishtas 371–2
tattwas and globes 247
zodiac and 140–5, 322–4
Globes A, B, C 351–5
Globes A–G (or Z) 352, 600
diagrams 141, 196, 247, 259, 323
Globe D. See Earth
after human life-wave leaves 351
before obscuration 366
dhyāni-bodhisattva of 522
human śishtas on 371, 513
length of time on 361–2
mankind buddhi-manas of 450
most evolved loka-tala on 264
on seventh cosmic plane 245
planetary spirit of 368
prānas of man and 558
several 'humanities' on 363
Globe E 600
beasts on 352, 600
human life-wave and 351
loka influence stronger on 258, 264
Globes F and G 352, 600
Gnomes of earth 234
Gnosis 5
Gnostic Aeons 194–5
Gnostic school(s) 5, 71, 193,
195, 627
God
inner 55, 212–13, 383, 435, 452
our fate not dictated by 411, 421
personal 90, 379, 438
within, essence of Reality 105
God(s) 203, 236, 379–82, 415,
468, 692. See Angels,
Dhyāni-chohans, Monads
are monadic essences 384–5, 432
ascend to highest cosmic plane 254
avatāras among 499
causes of cycles, existence 150
celestial bodies and 302
classes (a) and (b) 380
descent into underworld 499

God(s) (con.)
dhyāni-chohans are 386
emanate monads 432
every sun a 87, 149
'failures' 380
four highest monadic classes 477
have unfolded seven principles 278
highest, subject to universal karma
414
keep universe in balance 416
light is vitality of 180
man an embodied 75, 87, 423
man a thought of 35
man shall become 203
no extracosmic 172
once god-sparks 225, 640
overshadow monads 150, 212
powers of nature 150, 380
Ring-pass-not confines 254
self-sacrifice of highest 150
Silent Watchers among 470
sun an invisible 294–6
training school among 468
Golden Age 168
Golden Chain 6, 7, 215, 474, 680
*Golden Verses of Pythagoras,
The* 667–8
Good 412
and evil 421–4
Gospel(s)
Apocryphal 499
of John on Logoi 182
of the Hebrews 657
Gotama, founder Nyāya school 651
Grand Architect, Third Logos 183
Gravitation 136, 190–1
Great Breath, the 65, 84, 114
'Great Heresy,' the 113
'Great Sacrifice' 467, 469
Greece, Mysteries of 3–5, 57, 174, 498.
See Initiation
Greek(s) 71–2, 150, 229–30,
344, 690
kuklos kosmou 537
mystics and Pleroma 65, 130

NDEX

INDEX

Inner Rounds (con.)
627–31, 635
devachan and upward arc 600
imbodiments on other globes
600–2, 639
reincarnating ego travels 630
Inner space 77
Insanity 10
Instinct 12, 213
Intellect 254, 606
Intelligence behind mechanism 171
Intuition(s) 12, 38, 69
higher dimensions 80
seventh sense 241–2
Inversion of poles 141, 346–7
Invisible worlds 223–4
Invocation, Tibetan 207–8
Involution 103, 123, 354, 360
Iron Age 168. See Kali Yuga
"Is the sun merely a cooling
mass?" 298, 300
Isis 309–11, 313–15, 658
Isis Unveiled 6, 114, 510, 515
quoted 309, 655
Island universe a cell 92
Īśvara-Gītā 648
Īśwara, cosmic 435
Italy 163–4
Ivory Door, Gate 305–6

Jāgrat (waking state) 568, 597
Janarloka. See Lokas and Talas
Jannaeus 495
Jeans, Sir James 83
Jerome in Micheas 658
Jesus 495–501
avatāra 484, 488, 494–9, 680
Buddha intermediary for 484,
496, 522
Christ in 497–8
crucifixion 498
Father and, are one 88
sacrifice of, explained 416

Jews, 'Āmēn of and AUM 674–5
Jīva(s) 154, 274, 388, 439
electricity, magnetism 153–4
spring from elements 225
Jīvanmukta(s) 44, 52, 89–90, 211–12,
225, 274, 391
buddhas, bodhisattvas are 604
must have nirvanic rest 268
Jīvānu (life-atom) 274–5
Jñāna-yoga 40–1, 460
Job, Book of 185
Jods of Pythagorean Tetraktys 208
John, Gospel of 182
Jordan River, mystical 43
Judge, William Q. 338, 540
quoted 20, 25, 41, 55,
398, 405–6
"Answers to Correspondence" 41, 55
Circular (1890) 21
Ocean of Theosophy, The 338
Path, The, magazine 405–6
Preface to Yoga Aphorisms 645
"Subsidiary Papers" (1894) 22–3
"Suggestions and Aids" 20–1,
398, 685–6
Juno, 'inspired by' 511
Jupiter 135, 151, 333–5
conditions on 334
infant sun 334
Mars and 326–7
'men' of, compared 200, 333–4
Rāja sun behind 135, 335
Saturn and 327, 334
sunspots and 302
Justifying oneself 32–3

Kāla-chakra 164
Kalahansa 179
Kali-Kāra 691–2
Kali yuga 163–8
death of Krishna began 163, 303
5000 years of, ended 163, 683
law of the Lodge and 682–3
of human being 164, 167

717

Life-atom(s) (con.)
cremation, embalming and 546
dhyāni-chohan, god at core 117,
391, 479
disease and 403–4
dropped in kāma-loka 599
enchain man 395
from cosmic space 448–9
gathered by comet 123
human, and animal 417, 620
jīvānu, called 274–5
manifestation of a jīva 388, 539
man was a 384, 394
monad of 175, 390, 448, 637–8
of skeleton endure longer 547
on all planes 388–9, 400, 638
paramānus 274–5, 388
reimbody innumerable times 399
same as last life 388–9, 394–5,
400, 404, 638
seven grades of 396
seven principles and 250–1
soul of atom 388
spiritual, human monad 539
stamped by man 399–400
swabhāva of 198
unevolved, are elementals 233
waiting on descending arc 639–40
Life-wave(s) 350–60. See Inner and
Outer Rounds, Kingdoms
beginning, root-Manu 374
circulate globes 144, 321, 350–68,
370, 615
circulate planets 156, 321,
628–9, 632–6
diagrams 259, 616
families of monads 361, 615–16
fifth and sixth rounders 365,
371, 512–16
form globes 248
gather on highest globe 364, 513
highest become śishtas 369–70
human 351, 362, 365, 450, 479
'humanity' higher than globes 367
in first, second rounds 248, 353–5

Life-wave(s) (con.)
interglobal nirvana 350, 361–3
interplanetary nirvana 363–4
leaving, seed-Manu 374
like human embryo 356–7
monads of, various origins 450
next, on earth described 363
nirvana of, devachan of globes 366
obscuration and 361–3, 366, 370
pass through lokas and talas 144
ten families of 512
time of, on globes 361–2
trailers (stragglers) 365–6, 512
Light. See Daivīprakriti
bodies of 300, 381, 560–1
'cold' 120, 122
darkness and 9, 179
death and explosion of 545, 561–2
deformed by atmosphere 206
emotion, thought radiate 561
invisible 179–80
is energy-matter 560
of the logos 191
vitality of a god 180
Light of Asia, The 106
Lightning 191
Lilith 319
Linga-śarīra 116, 400, 435,
445, 545, 547. See Astral Body
astral double of lunar pitris 284
elementals and 445
emanation of auric egg 439, 621
exudes physical 383
fades out with physical 621
hovers around corpse 547
kāma-rūpa has its seat in 579
of earth is astral light 218, 445
prānas of, abandon grip at death 545
Lipika(s) 216–19
Lives, former, remembering 552–3
Livings and dyings 537
Lodge of great teachers 682–8
Logoic forces, twelve 459, 611
Logos, Logoi 93, 182–8. See Triad,
Trimurti, Trinity

Man (con.)
446, 507–9
dhyāni-chohan, inner god 290
dhyāni-chohan lower grade 386
diagrams 229, 435
divine monad, inner god 212
elementals once were 232,
235–7, 394
evolutionary history of 289,
334, 391
five dhyāni-buddhas in 507–8
four lower monads builders 213–15
four states of consciousness
568–73, 597–8
heredity 394–7, 401
imbodied god 75, 87, 423
kali yuga of individual 164–5, 167
karma and 410–20
'know thyself' 14, 62
led into temptation 419–20
lives in kāma-manas 42, 202, 419
lokas and talas of 257, 266
lunar pitris and 284–9, 480, 483
māyā, subject to 14, 16, 95, 97
more advanced than globe 596
new body, same atoms 388–9, 394,
400, 404, 638
organs of, and auric egg 428, 557
parent star 200, 312, 565,
582, 610
Paurusha pralaya of 652
personality reincarnates 400
planets influence 151, 610–11
principles of 201, 427–8,
434–5, 445
radiates colors, odors 560–1
ray of solar divinity 539
reborn in different race 404
reincarnating mānasaputra 482
rising above karma 413–14
seven ātmans in 201
Silent Watcher of 392,
446, 470–3
solar pitris in higher parts 480
Sons of the Sun 314, 480, 482

Man (con.)
spiritual monad in 420, 629
stamps life-atoms 399–400
sun and, compared 154, 300–1, 393
sūtrātman and 433, 446–8, 564
swabhāva of 198, 201–3
thought of a god 35
three divisions of 275–6
three higher monads in 524–5
to become suns 88, 113, 293,
393, 471
trailokya and 254
travels planets to sun 156, 316
trikāya and 254, 474–6
twelvefold 564
unevolved dhyāni-chohan 479
unexpressed buddha 519
universe and, one 223
vital-astral monad of 271,
383, 453
will be a Silent Watcher 203
will be dhyāni-chohans 107, 356,
470, 479
will mānasaputrize animals 285
will of, rooted in buddhi-manas 12
Manas 181, 435, 439–40
buddhi- 42, 202
buddhi-, of earth 450
fifth principle, fifth round 514
higher- 205, 508
life-atoms of 400
non-functional in kāma-loka 571
Venus, left eye and 653
Mānasa-dhyānis 284, 289
Mānasaputras (Sons of Mind)
agnishwāttas and 481–3
awaken men's minds 285, 440, 481–2
bodhisattva or 525
in man 446, 481
man shall be, to animals 285
man taught by 100
seven classes 481
Mānasic 9, 12, 338, 435
knot of personality 15
Manifestation 67, 180

Monad(s) (con.)
  no rest in cosmic manvantara 635
  not embodied 537–8
  passage into higher kingdom 617
  passes through all kingdoms
    357, 615
  planetary chains and 633–6
  principles and 281, 443–5
  rays of 199, 388, 454,
    600–3, 633–4
  repeatedly enter sun 303
  seven in man 282
  sevenfold 444
  solar 117
  spiritual, after death 453,
    563–5, 629–30
  spiritual, in man 271, 383,
    420, 435, 453, 563–4
  spiritual, of Gautama 527
  sūtrātman of each 446–7
  swabhāva of 198–9, 202, 618
  tenfold division 279, 615–20
  theos and 211–12
  threefold grouping of 284
  twelve classes 150, 224–5,
    277, 477–83
  twelvefold in man 564
  unevolved, explained 449
  unmanifest, five 564
  vital-astral 271, 383, 453
  work through sheaths 537–8
  wraps itself in own emanations 638
  younger, elementals 225
Monadic centers 522, 557–8
Monadic eggs, spheres 371–2
Monadic elements enter nirvana 607
Monadic envelope 435
Monadic essence 60, 390,
  432–8, 607
  evolution and 60, 289–90, 293
  gods are 384, 432
  of man 86, 289, 384–5
  rays of, explained 385–6
Monadic foci 448–9
Monadic ray 435, 454, 544

Monadic sparks 212–13
Monas monadum, Paramātman
  271, 310, 433, 435, 437
Mongolians on fohat 189
Monotheistic, Occidentals are 379
Moon(s) 340–45
  beasts on, now men 356
  black magic and 344
  Brotherhood protects man from 676
  -cycles 306
  Dweller on Threshold 138,
    320, 341–2
  earth will become a 357
  globe-corpses 138, 340, 342
  H.P.B. re 340–1, 345, 654
  kāma-rūpa 138, 341–2
  seven globes of 246
  some go to, in sleep 610
  stands for secret planet 151,
    319–20, 324
  twelvefold Dweller 320, 341
  waxing 344, 679
Moon Chain 340, 343, 359, 515
'Moon struck,' epileptics 408
Mother love 575
Mother school 3, 4
Mother-substance (pradhāna) 294, 330
Motion accompanied by light 561–2
Mount Meru or Sumeru 530
Movement 121–2, 150, 536, 561
  apsides, axis, etc. 140–2
  never ceases 215
  planetary, explained 141, 336
  sun's 137, 141
Moving Stones 503–4
Mritānda, Mārttānda 126, 147
Mukti, Moksha 47, 89, 604
Mūlādhāra chakra 460–1
Mūlaprakriti 72, 86, 89–93,
  173, 212, 437
Mummification and embalming 546
Mummu Tiamatu (Boundless) 70
Mundane Egg 176
Music 208
  of Spheres 34, 203, 677

Sacred Planet(s) (con.)
logoic forces and 322, 611
man travels the 156, 316, 390
Mars, Jupiter compared 326
minor Eggs of Brahmā 147
monad leaves life-atoms on 630-1
monadic embodiments on 633-6
moon stands for secret 151,
319, 320, 324
movements of 141, 336
Neptune, Uranus, Pluto 129, 324
order of, in peregrinations 630
organs of sun 302, 306, 633
rectors of 318-19, 322,
628, 632
reimbodying ego native to
each 634-5
rule re age, advancement of 327
seven or twelve 129, 319
seven senses, states of
consciousness 240
"Seven Sons of Light" 317
spiritual monad peregrinates
607, 628-9, 632-6
sun stands for secret (Vulcan)
151, 319-20, 324
Swayambhūva 373
transmitters to earth 320-2
visited during initiation 536
Sacred Seasons, Four 678-9. See
Autumn, Spring, Summer, Winter
Saddharma-Pundarīka 646
Sahasrāra chakra 461-2
Śākyamuni, see Buddha Gautama
Salamanders, fire elementals 234
Samāna (prāna) 556
Śambhala 529-32
Gautama and 486, 528
initiations take place 486
Vishnu-Purāna on 662
Sambhogakāya 474-6
Gautama and 527
rūpa-dhātu and 254, 475
Sambodhi 606
Sambuddhi 50

Samothrace, Mysteries of 57
Samsāra (Circulations of Cosmos) 537
Sandhyās (rest periods) 160, 165
Sañjñā 571
Śankarāchārya
Adwaita-Vedānta 87, 651
avatāra 484, 488
Buddha intermediary for 484, 522
Jesus lived 500 years after 495
Sānkhya school 229, 651
Śāriputra (a sage) 48
Śatarūpā (hundred-formed) 186
Sattva 242-3
Saturn
earth and 330
influenced fourth race 151
more ethereal than Jupiter 327, 334
mūlādhāra chakra under 460
rings explained 144
Satya 50
Satya yuga (Golden Age) 164-5, 168
Satyaloka. See Lokas and Talas
Saurya Manvantara 117, 651. See
Manvantara
Saurya Pralaya 652. See Pralaya
Scandinavia(ns) 5, 70, 578
School(s)
exoteric, of thought 100
occult, on every continent 4
of Buddhism 95, 659-61
of Hindu philosophy 100-2, 651
Science, Scientific
māyā of 94-5
medical, scoffs at humors 556
of chakras 460
view of death 537
Second Birth 50
Second childhood 542
'Second Coming' of Christ 488-9
Kalki avatāra 493
Second Death
devachan after 580, 599-600
frees reincarnating ego 579-80, 588
kāma-rūpa cast off 554, 580,
582, 599-600

Second Death (con.)
    occurs in kāma-loka 551, 599
    panoramic review before 551, 554
    parallels physical death 580
    time between death and 572–3
Second Logos. *See* Logos
Secrecy, oath of 4, 72
Secret Doctrine, The quoted throughout
'Sects of deniers' (healers) 407
Sedimentation, this round 161
Seed(s)
    cosmic, and nebula 120
    human 400–2
    of sixth race, subrace 165
Seed-Manu(s) 112, 370, 374–5
Self
    advancement 518
    conquest 16
    defense 32–3
    forgetfulness 18, 33, 409
    judges past life 551
    justification 32
    sacrifice of Divinity 150
Self-Existent 71
Selfhood, abandoning lower 18–19
Selfishness 14, 405, 409, 458
Selflessness 36
Senility, Senescence 542
Senses 78, 238–43, 429, 645
Separateness 113, 385–6
Sephiroth 216
Septenary Principle in Esotericism,"
    "The 374–5
Seven embryonic humanities 287–8
Seven Eternities 178
Seven heavens (sacred planets) 632
Seven principles 49, 266, 443–5
Seven, ten, twelvefold
    schemes 277, 279
Seventh, culmination of cycle 262–3
Seventh initiation. *See* Initiation
Seventh rounders, none yet 515–16
Shaberon 510
Shades, necromancer compels 576–7
Shadowy Arc. *See* Descending Arc

Sheaths of consciousness 272, 388,
    445, 537–8
Shau-Leng-Yan-Chin 646
Siddhārtha. *See* Buddha Gautama
    name defined 9
Siddhis 9. *See* Powers, Senses
Sight 240, 645–6
Signs of Zodiac 139–45
    all, in man 151
    diagrams of 141, 323, 670, 672
Śīla 44, 45
Silent Watcher(s). *See*
        Wondrous Being
    an Absolute 89–90
    atomic 470
    becoming at-one with 62
    global 24, 62, 467–73, 506
    have unfolded ten principles 278
    Hierarchy of Compassion and
        468–9, 510
    human 392, 446, 470–2
    Mahā-guru 506
    man will become 203, 471–2
    Nārada, Śiva aspect of 693
    planetary 62, 469–70, 472, 510
    solar 469, 471–2
    supreme teacher of globe 24
    universal 382, 469
    virtually infinite number 469–70
Simon, Gnostic school of 193–5, 217
Simulacra (shades) 574, 576–7.
        See Kāma-rūpa
Śishtas (seeds) 287, 369–75
    fifth rounders and 371, 513
    globe- 371–2
    globe D, awakened by lunar
        pitris 287
    on Mars 332
    ready in second round 353
    root- 371–2
Sitter, Willem de 81
Śiva 183. *See* Triad
    avatāras of 492–4
    'eye of' 106, 411
    Nārada and 693

Sixth dimension 80
Sixth rounder(s) 365, 371, 512–16
  become śishtas 371, 513
  Gautama a 512–13, 515
Skandhas. *See* Reimbodiment Process
  five lower 579, 668
  germs of karmic effects 622
  tanhic elementals 623
Sleep 22, 39, 308
  adepts, neophytes during 536, 569
  ākāśic veil protects during 609
  death and, compared 535–7, 541,
    569, 608–14
  dreams and 610–14
  four states of consciousness 568–73
  go whither attracted in 610
  initiation, and death 608–9
  reviewing day prior to 551,
    614, 667–8
  thread of life unbroken 609
  time sense lost in 597
Sleepwalkers, protection of 609
Smell 240. *See* Senses
Socrates, daimon of 13
Solar Chain 437
  dhyāni-buddha of 294–5
  every globe of, an entity 295
  globe D of 294, 296
  monads circulate 634
Solar comet 126–7, 132, 325
Solar devas 284
Solar eclipse and initiation 679
Solar heart 303
Solar Lhas 345, 349, 480
Solar logoic forces 459, 461, 611
Solar Manvantara. *See* Manvantara
Solar monads 117
Solar pitris. *See* Agnishwātta pitris
Solar System(s) 226, 294, 382, 447. *See*
  Circulations of Cosmos, Planets,
  Sacred Planets, Sun, Sunspots
  billions of, inhabited 382
  birth of 115–128
  Brahmānda 66, 97, 225, 311
  captures of 129, 324–5

Solar System(s) (con.)
  circulations of 153–6, 299–304,
    316, 390, 536–7
  comet stage of 126–7, 132, 325
  Egg of Brahmā and 66, 130,
    225, 471
  galactic system of 132
  lokas, talas and 267–9
  manvantara of 115, 117, 159–61,
    235, 313, 634, 651
  movements of 140–2
  nebular stage of 119–20, 127
  Night of Brahmā 117, 159–61
  planetary chains organs of 154, 302,
    306, 633
  planetary reimbodiments 131,
    134, 160
  pralaya of 115–17, 159–61,
    313, 652
  rivers of lives in 149–50, 154,
    303, 628
  seven, ten, twelve planes 130
  Silent Watcher of 469, 471–2
  'solid' 627
  twelvefold chain 129, 186
  universal solar system 118–24,
    130–1, 324
  Uranus 129, 324
  vast substantial body 304, 627
Soma (Hindu god, moon) 343
Soma drink 345
Son(s)
  of the Sun 314, 480, 482
  Third Logos 183
Sorcery, Sorcerers 10, 554, 580–1
Soul(s) 432–5, 454
  constantly changing 385
  diagrams 229, 435
  incoming, and parents 397
  leaves body via brahmarandhra 462
  -memory 553
  psychomental, veil of monad 271
Soulless men 452
Sound(s) 204–6
  'Āmēn, AUM, OM 674–5

Sound(s) (con.)
color, number and 206
magic potency of 676–7
mankind protected by 676
Music of the Spheres 34, 203, 677
Second Logos 184–5
seven 186
stars have their 205–6
South pole 305–6
Space(s) 65–9, 74–8, 81–4, 102, 116,
118, 195, 270. *See* Boundless,
Śūnyatā
all, alive 75–6
boundless 80–1, 90, 113,
118, 214
cosmic bodies are their 74–5
every point of, a monad 270
filled with monads 91
fullness of 65–78, 91,
270, 387
inward and outward 74–8
life-atoms from cosmic 448–9
manifested, has dimensions 79–80
Parabrahman and 85–6, 91
seven, ten, twelvefold 74
substantial entity 157
śūnyatā aspect of 65, 67–8
time and, inseparable 81, 157
Spaces of Space 74, 78
Spain 163–4
'Sparks of Eternity' 68, 187
Sparrow that falleth 19
Spatium and ākāśa 77
Spectroscope unreliable 206
Spectrum 206, 208
Spheres
crystalline 147–8
Music of the 34, 203, 677
Spinal column 462
Spirit 172–3, 210, 229,
389, 435
body, soul and 275, 283
death is birth of 178–80
manifestation dream of 96
matter is condensed 210

Spiritual
balance of material and 422
development, and psychic 8–9
home of mankind 529–30
love and departed 592
will 11, 22
Spiritual ego 96, 435, 535, 607, 609
Spiritual monad 96, 527
after death 453, 565, 600,
621, 629–30
Father in Heaven 600
in man 271, 383, 420, 435,
453, 563, 629
native life-atoms forever
related to 638
of Gautama became dharmakāya 527
parent of reimbodying
ego 626, 634–6
peregrinations of 595, 621,
630, 633–8
ranges solar system 564,
628–9, 635
reincarnating ego 271, 419–20
tastes of Reality 96
Spiritual plasm 400–1
Spiritualism, Spiritism 574–8
Spirituality and ethereality 330
Spook 441, 443, 622
Spring Equinox 678–9
Śrāddha 45
Stanzas of Dzyan 157, 178
Star(s) 112, 149, 205,
209, 312, 392–3
astrological 312, 501
circulations among 156
of Bethlehem 500–1
parent 200, 565, 582, 610
"Star-Angel-Worship" 322
Statues, animated 503–4
Stellar clusters 127
Sthūla-śarīra 383, 435,
437, 444
dregs of auric egg 146, 428, 442
sevenfold 367–8
Stoicheia of Plato 228